COLLEGE Writing Skills WITH READINGS

FIFTH CANADIAN EDITION

John Langan

Atlantic Community College

Sharon Winstanley

Seneca College

McGraw-Hill Ryerson

Toronto   Montréal   Boston   Burr Ridge, IL   Dubuque, IA   Madison, WI   New York
San Francisco   St. Louis   Bangkok   Bogotá   Caracas   Kuala Lumpur   Lisbon   London
Madrid   Mexico City   Milan   New Delhi   Santiago   Seoul   Singapore   Sydney   Taipei

The McGraw·Hill Companies

McGraw-Hill Ryerson

College Writing Skills with Readings
Fifth Canadian Edition

Copyright © 2008, 2005, 2003, 2000, 1996 by McGraw-Hill Ryerson Limited, a Subsidiary of The McGraw-Hill Companies. All rights reserved. No part of this publication may be reproduced or transmitted in any form or by any means, or stored in a data base or retrieval system, without the prior written permission of McGraw-Hill Ryerson Limited, or in the case of photocopying or other reprographic copying, a license from The Canadian Copyright Licensing Agency (Access Copyright). For an Access Copyright licence, visit www.accesscopyright.ca or call toll free to 1-800-893-5777.

ISBN-13: 978-0-07-097266-7
ISBN-10: 0-07-097266-4

1 2 3 4 5 6 7 8 9 10   TCP   0 9 8

Printed and bound in Canada.

Care has been taken to trace ownership of copyright material contained in this text; however, the publisher will welcome any information that enables them to rectify any reference or credit for subsequent editions.

Editorial Director: Joanna Cotton
Publisher: Nicole Lukach
Sponsoring Editor: Lisa Rahn
Marketing Manager: Michele Peach
Developmental Editors: Liz Radojkovic, Sara Braithwaite
Editorial Associate: Marina Seguin
Supervising Editor: Joanne Limebeer
Copy Editor: Evan Turner
Senior Production Coordinator: Paula Brown
Cover Design: Michelle Losier, Fine Lines
Cover Image: © Brand X Pictures/Jupiter Images
Interior Design: Michelle Losier, Fine Lines
Page Layout: Bookman Typesetting Co. Inc.
Printer: Transcontinental Printing Group

Library and Archives Canada Cataloguing in Publication Data
Langan, John, 1942–
    College writing skills with readings / John Langan, Sharon Winstanley. — 5th Canadian ed.

Includes index.
ISBN 978-0-07-097266-7

    1. English language—Rhetoric.   2. English language—Grammar.   3. College readers.
    I. Winstanley, Sharon   II. Title.

PE1408.L27 2008   808'.0427   C2008-900985-1

Table of Contents

Part 2   PATTERNS OF ESSAY DEVELOPMENT

Readings Listed by Rhetorical Mode

Definition

Division and Classification

Argumentation

Note: Some selections are cross-referenced because they illustrate more than one rhetorical mode.

Preface

Publication of this Fifth Canadian Edition of *College Writing Skills with Readings* is a happy and significant event. Four well-received editions have encouraged us to continue with the successful and time-tested **four bases of writing** approach to help students master both the five-paragraph and the longer essay. With this edition, we continue to tailor our text to the learning needs of Canadian post-secondary students; we place new emphasis on understanding voice and viewpoint in writing, and we strengthen our commitment to the importance of effective and correct research as the keystone of students' educational development.

The Four Bases of Writing—Unity, Support, Coherence, and Sentence Skills

The central learning framework for essay writing of *College Writing Skills with Readings* is the four bases of writing—unity, support, coherence, and sentence skills. These are presented on the inside front cover, as well as integrated and reinforced throughout the text. Why highlight the four bases on the inside front cover? To remind students of these important principles and to provide a handy reference that will help guide them through the process of essay writing.

Base 1: Unity

- Clearly stated thesis in the introductory paragraph
- All supporting paragraphs on target in backing up the thesis

Base 2: Support

- Three (or more) separate supporting points for the thesis
- *Specific* evidence for each supporting point
- *Plenty* of specific evidence for each supporting point

Base 3: Coherence

- Clear method of organization
- Transitions and other connective devices
- Effective introduction, conclusion, and title

Base 4: Sentence Skills

- Grammatical errors removed through editing and proofreading
- Effective words and varied sentences employed
- Well-chosen words and varied sentences employed
- Correct manuscript form

How This Book is Organized

Part 1: Essay Writing focuses first on the writing process itself, then on the four bases of writing. **Part 2: Patterns of Essay Development** shows the four bases of effective writing as they apply to different rhetorical modes. **Part 3: Special Skills and Research** guides students through summary writing, through conducting effective research, and finally through writing a research paper. Extensive examples of MLA and APA citation, as well as a full research essay in the MLA style are included.

Part 4: Sentence Skills, which serves as a concise and easy-to-use handbook, focuses specifically on the fourth base of the writing process.

Part 5: Readings provides a variety of engaging, mainly contemporary readings that represent each of the rhetorical modes presented in Part 2. Accompanying each reading are questions and activities that reinforce and enhance, for students, the four bases of writing.

What's New in the Fifth Canadian Edition?

The Fifth Canadian Edition of *College Writing Skills with Readings* has been refined and revised very carefully to speak to the specific requirements of Canadian post-secondary students today. In response to extensive reviewer feedback, the following are the highlights of what is new in this edition.

Significant new additions to this edition include:

- Point of view and pedagogy on choices regarding its use are introduced in the first chapter; these concerns are re-addressed throughout the text. This added pedagogy appears notably in Part 2, where concise yet thorough coverage of the impact of choices in voicing is presented within the pedagogy for each rhetorical mode. Thus, students' awareness of, and sensitivity to aspects of the relationship of viewpoint to content, purpose, and audience are significantly enhanced.
- Research and its importance are given more emphasis and more coverage throughout this edition, beginning on the first page, continuing through Part 2, making up most of Part 3, and featured in assignments in Part 5. Research is considered to be an essential skill, and this edition treats it as such. To this end, Chapters 18 and 19 allow students to shadow a fellow student as she works through the processes of conducting research and writing a research essay.
- Pedagogy on purpose, audience, voice, and tone as these relate to content-choices has been added to nearly every chapter in Parts 1, 2, 3, and 5.
- Plagiarism coverage has been expanded and includes examples, and now appears in Chapter 18.
- More individual and group activities than ever appear in this edition, in Parts 1, 2, and 3.
- Chapter 17, "Learning Skills and Essay Exams," from the Fourth Canadian Edition, now appears on the Online Learning Centre.
- Chapter 19, "Writing a Review," from the Fourth Canadian Edition, now appears on the Online Learning Centre.

Part 1: Essay Writing

- New "Computer Writing Tip" boxes appear throughout Part 1, including variant information for PC and Mac users.
- New content and new exercises on drafting and writing effective thesis statements have been added, beginning with Chapter 2.
- New content on purpose and audience has been added to pedagogy and activities connected to prewriting in Chapter 2.
- Increased emphasis is placed on maturity of tone and word-choice for post-secondary students in writing tasks.
- In keeping with this emphasis on less subjective writing, this edition stresses and maintains the importance of gaining experience and expertise with writing in the third-person voice.
- Revised and new exemplars appear, presenting third-person voice.
- A new introduction to the writing process opens Chapter 2.
- New exemplars sometimes demonstrate the use of research, and always present more mature subject-matter and fresh, relevant content.
- Many new activities and exercises have been added, including group prewriting activities in Chapter 2, paragraph editing exercises in Chapter 5, and exercises based on revising from first-person to third-person viewpoint.

Part 2: Patterns of Essay Development

- A new section "Point of View" (as introduced in Part 1) appears in the pedagogy of each chapter for each rhetorical mode.
- "Writing a Thesis Statement" boxes, introduced in the previous edition, have been revised and expanded to include examples for each rhetorical mode.
- New and revised exemplars and pedagogy appear in many chapters, reflecting distinctly Canadian interests and demonstrating use of third-person viewpoint.
- New pedagogy on logic in cause/effect essays appears in Chapter 12.

Part 3: Special Skills and Research

- Chapter 18, "Research Skills," has been significantly revised to help students follow research as a process similar to the writing process.
- Chapter 18 offers a new introduction to the research process.
- New and updated coverage of plagiarism is presented, relative to today's student.
- New exercises on avoiding plagiarism have been added to Chapter 18.
- New guidelines for assessing and preparing for various research assignments have been added.
- The steps for effective research have been amplified and made more specific to facilitate students' understanding and use.
- New material on planning research and a time-planning chart have been added to Chapter 18.
- "Research Tip" boxes are new to Chapters 18 and 19; these give concise information on keyword searches, primary and secondary sources, and other research-related topics.

- Chapter 19 has augmented its MLA and APA research guidelines and examples, and has newly added content on in-text citation.
- Chapter 19 now offers extensive listings of MLA and APA citations of print and online resources.

Part 5: Readings

Eight new readings appear in this edition, so that half of the selections are fresh; they range from the contemporary to the classical in prose style. All readings, and especially the new selections, represent striking uses of the rhetorical modes to reinforce and extend the book's pedagogy. Part 5 again includes new writing assignments; these extend this new edition's points of emphasis by requiring third-person voice and, frequently, research.

Supplements and Services

An extensive selection of Canadian supplements and services is available to complement *College Writing Skills with Readings*, Fifth Canadian Edition.

Instructor Resources

Instructor's Manual

The **Instructor's Manual** contains a wealth of teaching resources, including hints and tips for approaching the course, a model syllabus, and supplementary activities and tests. The Instructor's Manual is available for download in the passcode-protected Instructor's Centre of the Online Learning Centre (www.mcgrawhill.ca/olc/langan).

Online Learning Centre

The **Online Learning Centre** for *College Writing Skills with Readings*, Fifth Canadian Edition (www.mcgrawhill.ca/olc/langan), features learning and study tools as well as a passcode-protected Instructor's Centre with downloadable supplements, including the complete Instructor's Manual and Microsoft® PowerPoint® slides.

iLearning Sales Specialist

Your **Integrated Learning Sales Specialist** is a McGraw-Hill Ryerson representative who has the experience, product knowledge, training, and support to help you assess and integrate any of the products, technology, and services listed below into your course for optimum teaching and learning performance. Whether helping your students to improve their grades or putting your entire course online, your *i*Learning Sales Specialist is there to help you do it. Contact your *i*Learning Sales Specialist today to learn how to maximize all of McGraw-Hill Ryerson's resources.

iServices Program

At McGraw-Hill Ryerson, we take great pride in developing high-quality learning resources while working hard to provide you with the tools necessary to utilize them. We want to help bring your teaching to life, and we do this by integrating technology, events, conferences, training, and other services. We call it *i*Services. For more information, visit www.mcgrawhill.ca/olc/iservices/.

Course Management

Visit www.mhhe.com/pageout to create a Web page for your course, using our resources. **PageOut**™ is the McGraw-Hill Ryerson Web site development centre. This Web page-generation software is free to adopters and is designed to help faculty create an online course, complete with assignments, quizzes, links to relevant Web sites, and more—all in a matter of minutes.

In addition, content cartridges are available for the course management systems **WebCT** and **Blackboard**. These platforms provide instructors with user-friendly, flexible teaching tools. Please contact your local McGraw-Hill Ryerson *i*Learning Sales Specialist for details.

Student Resources

Online Learning Centre

The **Online Learning Centre** for *College Writing Skills with Readings*, Fifth Canadian Edition (www.mcgrawhill.ca/olc/langan) offers students such benefits as:

- Study quizzes
- Weblinks
- Interactive exercises such as essay activities
- A *Globe and Mail* news feed
- Coverage of learning skills and writing essay exams
- Coverage of writing review material

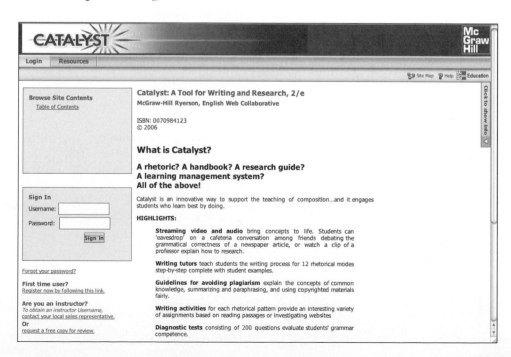

Also, whenever the icon above appears in the body of the text, please go to the Online Learning Centre (www.mcgrawhill.ca/olc/langan) for further information, material, or activities pertaining to that particular topic or chapter.

Acknowledgments

As with each edition, I am grateful for the continuing enthusiasm, support, and assistance of the editors at McGraw-Hill Ryerson. Each editor's dedication to excellence is an inspiration, and each one's expertise has taught me invaluable lessons. They are "the voices at the other end of the line" who console and reassure me, and offer fresh perspectives on familiar tasks. I would like to thank Lisa Rahn, Humanities Sponsoring Editor, for her energy and special help with this edition, and Joanne Limebeer, Supervising Editor, and Christine Gilbert as well. I would especially wish to thank Liz Radojkovic, Developmental Editor; her astuteness, support, and good humour have been delightful to experience. Finally, my thanks go to Evan Turner for her care and concern with editing the copy.

My thanks always go to my students at Seneca@York. They inspire me, delight me, amuse me, and make me happy to teach them.

Finally, I would like to thank the reviewers who provided helpful ideas and feedback for the Fifth Canadian Edition:

Sue Adams, Sheridan College
Brent Cotton, Georgian College
Jill Hornick, George Brown College
Lina Lens, Seneca College
Anne MacKenzie-Rivers, George Brown College
Jane Ann McLachlan, Conestoga College
Jennifer Mei, Centennial College
Jean Mills, Conestoga College
Kathleen Moran, Conestoga College
Margo Novak, George Brown College
Paula Pedwell, Georgian College
Brad Reed, George Brown College
Nancy Rishor, Fleming College
Rhonda Sandberg, George Brown College
Jill A. Singleton-Jackson, University of Windsor
Angela Woollam, Algonquin College in the Ottawa Valley

SHARON WINSTANLEY
SENECA COLLEGE

Permissions

CHAPTER 1

An Introduction to Writing

LEARNING OUTCOMES

After reading this chapter and working through its activities, you will

- identify writing as a skill you can learn, work on, and master;
- use writing as a way of discovering your thoughts;
- determine purpose and audience each time you begin a writing task;
- recognize research as an essential component of writing;
- identify immediate and longer-term benefits of writing effective essays;
- learn to write an effective paragraph;
- understand and identify the structural elements of the typical academic essay.

The questions and experiences of Canadian post-secondary students shape this book. Those students, like you, wished to be prepared for the writing tasks to come. Those students generally enjoyed writing stories, website text, and e-mails: they asked how to maintain that enjoyment while writing more structured forms. They asked for tested methods that would help them express and arrange their ideas more clearly; they asked how to undertake and manage research; and often they asked how essay writing would relate to their future careers.

Beginning with the sections that follow, you will find answers to those questions. Here are the main concepts reinforced throughout this book.

- Writing is a skill, and confusion decreases as writers learn to follow specific methods and practices.
- Writing is a process of discovering, arranging, and revising thoughts, and a clear expression of ideas results from understanding and following this process.
- Writing that communicates its meaning effectively clearly focuses on the document's purpose and audience.
- Writing that delivers solid, specific content, supported and strengthened by appropriate research, is key to academic and workplace success.
- Writing the traditional essay, whose main point is logically supported, is the best preparation for effective, appropriate communication in most media.

College Writing Skills with Readings, fifth Canadian edition, offers concrete, practical help with post-secondary writing tasks. The writing process is broken down into a series of logical, easy-to-follow steps, beginning with prewriting and concluding with revising final drafts. For the student in twenty-first-century Canada, writing and communicating information effectively are essential skills in a technology-based society.

Part 1 begins with a look at the act of writing itself and with some basic concepts to help students approach writing with greater confidence and motivation.

WRITING IS A SKILL

Students who ordinarily enjoy writing in casual, spontaneous situations for audiences of friends and family may feel some hesitation in their first English or Communications classes. The enjoyable aspects of writing—the spontaneity, the "safe audiences," and the lack of any required structure—seem to have disappeared. In fact, these students, along with those who are reluctant writers, may feel a little uncertain about new writing assignments, new audiences, and new standards for marking.

Instead of uncertainty, why not adopt a positive, yet realistic attitude toward writing? All students—those who enjoy this activity, as well as those less confident of their skills—should realize that virtually everyone has the ability to express him- or herself clearly in formats appropriate to various situations. By learning and practising tested approaches to generating and structuring content, and by grasping the relationship of writing structures to reading audiences, students discover new aspects of, and approaches to writing. As they gain proficiency in the various parts of the writing process, uncertainty gives way to the reassuring sense of following an established and workable set of steps.

A realistic, positive attitude about writing begins with the idea that **writing is a skill**. All skills are acquired and mastered in stages. Like learning to conduct research, drive, or design websites, learning to write is a step-by-step process. Writing requires willingness, patience, and determination to learn and work through those steps.

Good writing is the result of completing tasks or meeting challenges. It is not a gift or a single flash of inspiration. The calm clear thinking required for clear writing is a challenge to most people. Finding words and phrases that transfer ideas to paper can be demanding. Deciding what is worth keeping out of an hour's worth of writing is difficult. Discovering that an apparently simple topic has become complex is frustrating. **Writing well is work.** But learning any skill requires work—and the reward is achievement.

If you have the desire to learn, the patience to review and revise your work, and the determination to write well, this book will give you the extensive practice needed to develop and hone your writing skills.

WRITING IS A PROCESS OF DISCOVERY

Writing is a discovery process—a series of stages. Good writing is never a simple one-draft trip to a flawless final draft.

As it proceeds through the different stages, it may loop and zigzag in many directions as the writer finds new ideas and connections between thoughts and associated feelings and mental images. Most people have only a vague sense of what they have to say about any subject until they begin forming their ideas into words. Forming one idea into words leads to other ideas. Discovery leads to focus. You will learn where your focus will be as you allow yourself to follow your thoughts and then put those thoughts into words. The illustrations below demonstrate the writing process:

Seldom the case:

Starting point ————————————————→ Finished paper

Usually the case:

Starting point ⟿————————→ Finished paper

Now, follow the discovery process of Julian Lopez, author of the paragraph and the essay in this chapter. His assignment was to write about how people use technology today. Julian did not know where to begin, so he started writing about the items of technology he relied on and used most. He used his cell phone constantly, so he filled a screen with details about how convenient his phone was, how he played games with it and took pictures with it. One single detail, though—playing games on screens—led Julian to think about playing video games with his friends on his computer, taking online tests for fun, and listening to music downloads. He switched directions; he decided that he and his friends used their computers for entertainment when they got together. One apparent "detour" in Julian's writing journey led to an interesting focus—people in their early twenties socializing around their computers.

As he chased this line of thought, Julian started thinking that his essay's main idea might be how he and his friends enjoyed online gaming. This triggered memories of his friends challenging each other on *Star Wars* trivia and looking for the answers on their favourite sites. Then, he recalled another evening when the same group of friends started out watching a DVD and ended up pursuing a number of different activities online. Julian changed direction a second time, finding that he had a lot to say about the IQ tests and online trivia and personality tests he and his friends enjoyed and about how one person would suddenly remember some song he wanted to find and listen to. Julian was not really sure of where he was going, but he kept typing, getting more ideas down. He had "opened the tap" in his mind, and although he was uncertain of how to fit gaming, tests, and MP3s into a finished paper, he just kept writing, knowing that eventually his ideas would come together.

Writing is usually a continuing discovery; as you write, you find new avenues of thought, change direction, or even go backwards. When beginning to write, be relaxed and open enough to let these things happen. You are discovering what you want to say and the shape and direction of your paper.

EFFECTIVE WRITING SUITS ITS PURPOSE AND AUDIENCE

When you talk, chances are you do not speak to everyone the same way. For example, you are not likely to speak to your manager at work in the same way that you chat with a young child. Instead, you adjust what you say and probably the type of words you use as well as the tone in which you speak to suit both your **purpose** and **audience**.

The same holds true for writing, where you *write intentionally for others*. Writing to communicate to another person—an audience—means *relating information in a way that reaches your reader most successfully*. Learning to tailor your writing—your content, your word-choices, your voice or viewpoint, and your tone—to best suit your purpose and audience will make you a competent and effective academic and professional writer.

Purpose and audience, as well as voice or viewpoint and tone are explained further throughout Parts 1 and 2.

WRITING REQUIRES RESEARCH

Research is an essential component of both post-secondary and career writing assignments. Reading audiences, beginning with instructors, expect students to explore, understand, and work with carefully selected information from reliable authorities in their areas of study. The purposes of class assignments generally involve demonstrating the acquisition of expanded knowledge in areas relevant to subject or course material, and showing competence in integrating new information within an assignment's parameters or structure.

Your first and second semesters bring the challenge of learning how to conduct effective research and discovering your library's resources. This is followed, in various subjects, by learning the forms of research assignment each subject utilizes. Next, you will learn and practise integrating and documenting several types of research information for assignments for nearly every subject on your timetable.

Academic writing assignments, including most in this book, do not involve only personal responses to a topic. You will usually find it necessary to refer to sources of information other than your own experience. Determining as clearly as possible the purpose and audience for each writing task or assignment will help you decide on the depth and type of information needed. Like writing, research is a learnable skill, and mastering the methods involved in discovering and retrieving information pays lifelong benefits, not the least of which are career success and personal enrichment. Because of the importance of research, two chapters of this book, Chapters 18 and 19, take you step-by-step through the process of conducting, integrating, and documenting research, giving you a solid set of guidelines to follow.

WRITING THE FIVE-PARAGRAPH ESSAY BRINGS BENEFITS

Now you know some facts about writing in general. But before you move on to an overview of the essay as a specific form, consider the **benefits of writing the five-paragraph essay**—benefits that may surprise and motivate you.

Mastering the demands of the essay's structure and content gives you the foundation for all academic writing assignments. Whether you are in the classroom, in the lab, in an online course, or on co-op, you will be assigned a variety of writing formats: reports, analyses, business or technical documents, website text, broadcast copy, and research papers. These writing formats contain differing numbers of body paragraphs, but the essay structure, which begins with a main idea and follows through with clear proof and support, is the core of almost all of them.

As you look ahead, and to other media, essay writing readies you for the requirements of electronic communication. During your career, you may write online as often as on paper. Stating a point and backing it up concisely are the essentials of time-efficient e-mail correspondence and website content.

Essay writing will also strengthen other essential communication skills: reading and speaking. In this "age of information," you will be evaluated on how well you absorb, use, and transmit information. Learning to manage and position ideas in essays makes you a more acute reader; your judgment improves with awareness of how other writers handle ideas and proof. Structuring and creating essay content will make you a better speaker too. You will be prepared to develop and present ideas orally, using the elements and structure of an effective essay: an interesting opening, a solid and coherent body, and a reassuring conclusion.

Most important, essay writing makes you a stronger thinker. Writing a clearly reasoned five-paragraph essay requires mental discipline and close attention to a logical progression of ideas. Each time you meet the challenge of creating an essay with a guiding thesis statement and supporting paragraphs, your ability to express, order, and defend ideas grows stronger. To sum up, essay writing trains you to think clearly, and that ability is of value in every phase of your life.

Now, consider an overview of the essay and its components, beginning with four steps that will help you construct organized, coherent essays.

AN OVERVIEW OF THE ESSAY

Although the writing process may be unpredictable, there are four steps that break essay writing into clear and manageable tasks. These steps guide you to work on one thing and one goal at a time. You may go back and forth between these steps as you work; the important things are to keep writing and to refer often to the goals in each step.

Four Steps for Effective Essay Writing

1 Discover your point, and advance a clear thesis statement.

2 Support your thesis with specific evidence.

3 Organize and connect your specific evidence.

4 Revise, edit, and proofread your essay.

Part 1 of this book explains each step in detail and provides many practical materials to help you absorb and master each one. First, though, consider the two essential elements of an essay: point and support.

POINT AND SUPPORT

The five-paragraph essay is a writing format with a purpose. That is, it makes a point and then defends, explains, illustrates, or proves that point.

Making a Point in Speech and in Print: Your Audiences

People make points all the time in ordinary conversation, for all sorts of reasons. You might say, "C++ is really hard," "There aren't enough good videos on the *MuchMusic* stations," or "Students should work for a while before going to college." Your listeners will not usually push you to justify your assertions. They may know you and already know your reasoning, or they may not want to challenge you. As well, conversations generally move quickly from subject to subject, so people do not usually expect a long explanation.

Print is different from everyday speech. Readers of your printed words do not always know you. They cannot see or feel the context for your ideas. Your readers may not agree with you, and you are not there with them to break into your text and clarify what you mean. Moreover, reading requires two things of your readers—time and concentration. Readers do not like wasting time and energy; they want to know what you are writing about and why you are writing. To communicate effectively with readers, to reward their patience, *you must make your point clearly and back it up thoroughly with specific reasons or illustrative details.*

Visualize your reading audience as reasonable people, curious about what you have to say. If you pay them the respect of thinking through your point so that you support it clearly and logically, your readers will be ready to accept what you say.

Point and Support in a Paragraph

Paragraphs that stand alone and body paragraphs in an essay support a point with details. The main difference between the two is the depth of coverage given to supporting evidence. An independent paragraph usually backs up its point with a variety of supporting details; a body paragraph in an essay explores one supporting point of the essay's thesis in some depth. Like Julian Lopez, author of the paragraph on the social use of computers (page 7), you may begin by working on paragraphs intended as independent pieces of writing.

In a paragraph, every sentence serves a purpose. The first is **the topic sentence**; it **states the point of the paragraph**. The point is the specific topic and your viewpoint on it. When you write your point in a topic sentence, you give a compressed version of your whole paragraph.

> **A topic sentence does at least one of the following:**
> - States the writer's intention for the paragraph that follows
> - Suggests the writer's viewpoint or judgment on the subject
> - Previews the focus and limits for supporting details
> - Guides the reader into the paragraph's content

Notice the key phrase, "an ingenious new use for computers," in the topic sentence of Julian's paragraph. This key phrase expresses both the topic (*new use for computers*) and the writer's attitude or viewpoint on that subject (*ingenious*). Julian's intention is clear; he is writing about some new aspects of his subject, and the phrase, "use for computers," is general, yet definite enough to suggest and cover all supporting details in his paragraph.

Following from the topic sentence, each sentence in a paragraph explains and clarifies the topic sentence.

> **Sentences in the paragraph body do one or more of the following:**
> - Make the point clearer with examples
> - Prove the truth of the topic sentence with explanations
> - Recount one extended example or narrative to demonstrate the point
> - Clarify or expand on the point with comparisons to similar ideas or situations
> - Give logical consequences resulting from the point

The support in sentences in the body of the paragraph is specific. As you read Julian's paragraph, you see what he means by "an ingenious new use for computers." You share the ideas he discovered while remembering how he and his friends spend some typical evenings: entertaining themselves individually and together with movies, games, and online quizzes. The supporting details expand the general idea in the topic sentence into specific facts. These specifics—the details, examples, and explanations—reinforce the paragraph's point and make it clearer. **The paragraph's meaning is unified because each piece of support relates back to the single point of the topic sentence.** Whether you use facts, word-pictures, quoted opinions, statistics, or personal anecdotes as supporting details, you communicate your meaning with specific ideas directly connected to your point.

Now, read Julian Lopez's paragraph on socializing with computers:

Socializing Computers

People in their early twenties, the "iGeneration," have an ingenious new use for computers. They now use them as a hub for group socializing. One of the first discoveries people make about the "social computer" is how helpful it can be with decision making and reaching compromises when friends are choosing entertainment. If a group decides to watch a *Halloween* marathon, and several people become bored with the movies, then different entertainment options are only a few mouse-clicks away. Online cartoons or an hour or two of gaming with Everquest or Halo may suit everyone. Boredom and arguments are less likely, and people agree on compromises when they can control their choices. Another appealing aspect of the computer as social companion is its ability to interact with guests. The current generation enjoys feedback from its technology, and online tests and quizzes provide all sorts of insights and information. People challenge each other with personality and IQ tests, trivia quizzes, and the phenomenon of purity tests, available on subjects from personal hygiene to YouTube content statistics. Ultimately, the most interesting reason why today's young people socialize with their computers reflects just how much they have become like their computers. Both they and their machines comfortably do several things at once. Groups of friends multitask together; they can download entertainment for later in the evening while listening to music files and chatting online. They can send or receive instant messages and check the Internet for information on another window. Everyone in the room enjoys the same overall experience, while each person pursues a specific interest. Computers may have created a new kind of socializing—individually and in groups at the same time.

You should now see what Julian's **supporting evidence** has done. The specific details catch your attention and each detail brings his point into clearer focus. By showing you the experiences that led to his point, he gives you a basis for understanding his views.

Structuring Support in a Paragraph

During the writing process, supporting details usually come to you in random order. You then have two tasks: first, to decide which details best explain your point, and, second, to place those details in an order that demonstrates your point most clearly. Making an outline is the best way to work out an effective order for your paragraph's details and explanations.

Julian Lopez's supporting evidence is clear and easy to follow because he has arranged it in a logical pattern. He offers three reasons why his generation uses computers as a focus for socializing; **each reason** (supporting detail) **is a subtopic**. A subtopic is a smaller division of the topic, an aspect of the proof. Julian follows each subtopic with examples or short explanations that are even more specific.

Your subject itself, allied with your purpose in writing, could suggest an order for your subtopics. For example, if your subject is a particular event, and your purpose is to explain why that event occurred, you may put the causes of the event in the order in which they occurred. Your reading audience's needs may also help determine an order for your support; decide which subtopic and details would be most relevant to your readers' interests or requirements, and thus most important to them, and place the most important or relevant suptopic first or last. For more information on organizing supporting material, see pages 71–74.

• • • • Activity 1: Individual Work

You have learned why the paragraph on socializing with computers supports its point effectively. Now, make a copy of the paragraph outline pattern on page 10. Fill in the outline by taking Julian Lopez's paragraph apart and filling in the Topic

Sentence, Subtopic, and Subtopic Support lines on the outline with appropriate material from his paragraph.

Activity 2: Group Work

1. Create your group's topic by writing your version of the following phrase:

   " *(Some leisure activity)* *is* *(enjoyable, boring, healthy . . .)* ."

2. Come up with reasons why each person might hold this view. Have someone list the reasons.
3. Decide which reasons your group finds strongest. Make a new list for those.
4. Under each reason (subtopic/supporting detail), jot down a few specific examples that make the subtopic-reason easy to understand.
5. Copy the outline pattern on page 10 onto paper of your own. Now, make an outline as a group, consisting of your point, your supporting subtopics, and the examples or situations that illustrate your subtopics.

Compare your group's outline with those of the other groups in the class.

Outlining a Paragraph

Students sometimes avoid making outlines, or they make quick outlines *after* writing paragraphs or essays. Outlining takes work, but it makes writing a good paper much easier. Rather than avoiding outlining, use it to map your thoughts and keep your intentions for your paragraph clear.

A good time to make an outline is after you have jotted down some ideas. Pause so that you see your ideas with a fresh mind. Remember that outlines tend to change as you work on them, so try not to judge yourself harshly while you work.

Computer *Writing Tip*

Try creating template files for your paragraph and essay outline documents.

For Macs
- In Word, under "File," open the *Project Gallery* option.
- On bottom right of the *Blank Documents* screen, there is an option "Create," followed by a selector that offers either "Document" or "Template."
- Choose "Template."
- A new Word document will appear onscreen, named "Template."
- Type in a paragraph or essay outline diagram as it appears in this book.
- Save the template as "paragraph outline" or "essay outline."
- The template will be saved as a ".dot" document, and will be saved in your Word application under the *My Templates* option in the *Project Gallery* index screen.

For PCs
- In Word, create your outline document.
- Under "File," use "Save as…."
- From the "Save as…" menu, choose "Template."
- Save the template as "paragraph outline" or "essay outline."
- The template will be saved as a ".dot" document.
- You will want to save a copy of each outline template to the disk or USB key that you take to college with you.

There are many ways to start an outline, but the following method works if you allow yourself the time to go through it a step at a time.

1. Copy the outline pattern that follows. Write it by hand, leaving spaces to fill in, or create a template or blank document that you can copy and paste for repeated use.

Point

Topic Sentence: _____

Support

    Subtopic 1: _____

        Suptopic Support (examples, explanations)

        a.

        b.

        c.

    Subtopic 2: _____

        Subtopic Support

        a.

        b.

        c.

    Subtopic 3: _____

        Subtopic Support

        a.

        b.

        c.

Concluding Sentence: _____

Note: You should adjust this outline to suit your supporting evidence. Your paragraph may have two subtopics and four examples for each or some variation on this pattern. Be sure, though, that each subtopic and support unit is roughly the same length.

2. Before you begin your outline, take a clean piece of paper, or open a new document onscreen. Ask yourself two questions: What is my point, and why do I believe my point is true? Write out your point in one sentence. (Be prepared to change the sentence if you find your point changing.) Now, list any words or phrases that bring to mind facts, examples, or situations that back up your point.

3. Look at your prewriting as well as at the page or screen document where you just noted your point and reasons. If some reasons seem more important to your readers than others, put your reasons (subtopics) in order of importance or in an order that seems appropriate to your purpose and reading audience.

4. You are ready to start your outline. Don't worry if you change or eliminate examples or think of a new way to explain a detail. The point of outlining is to see and shape your thoughts; you can always rearrange parts of your outline. A messy outline is usually a good outline.

A Note about Paragraph Length

You know that proving your point in writing requires more words than you might use in conversation, but after reading the preceding section of this book, you may wonder: How long should a paragraph be?

Paragraph length depends on three main considerations:

- The purpose of the paragraph
- The reading audience's needs
- The medium and format in which the paragraph appears

Paragraphs range from one sentence to several pages in length; the student paragraph you read contains fifteen sentences. Short paragraphs in newspapers give easy-to-manage information quickly to a wide variety of readers. Article paragraphs are broken into short pieces so their appearance does not intimidate readers. Websites entertain and inform in a competitive electronic environment. Web-based paragraphs may appear brief to attract readers, but in fact, they use "three-dimensional support"—hypertext links to material on other parts of the same page or other sites. Stories and novels imitate life in entertaining ways, with fascinating characters and plots. Paragraphs may be only a single line of dialogue or may run to twenty sentences of intense action or vivid description.

Essays, reports, textbooks, non-fiction books, and career writing formats inform readers. These formats are generally printed so that readers can consider, judge, and sometimes act on their content. Paragraph length depends on making a point and supporting it with logical and sufficient explanation. This is the type of writing that you are practising now, and this is why "print-bite" paragraphs are rarely found in college writing. Instead of asking how long your paragraph should be, ask yourself: Does my paragraph make my point clear?

STRUCTURE OF THE FIVE-PARAGRAPH ESSAY

The Paragraph as Model for the Essay

Writing a well-structured paragraph is the best preparation for essay writing. The key structural elements and development of a paragraph mimic the structure and development of a five-paragraph essay. For example, the topic sentence in a paragraph becomes the thesis statement in an essay. The functions of the topic sentence and the thesis statement are basically the same: they present the main point to be pursued. Moreover, the body of a paragraph is essentially a smaller version of the body paragraphs of an essay. In an essay, the paragraph's subtopics develop into the essay's supporting points, each with its own paragraph. And finally, the concluding sentence in the paragraph expands into the essay's concluding paragraph.

Point and Support in an Essay

Like the paragraph, the essay, which consists of an introductory paragraph, two or more supporting paragraphs, and a concluding paragraph, supports and develops one point. The essay's main point or central idea is called a **thesis statement**. It appears in the introductory paragraph; specific points that support the thesis appear in the paragraphs that make up the body of the essay. Each body paragraph develops a single supporting point, so an essay's internal paragraphs treat evidence for the essay's thesis point more fully than would be possible in a single paragraph.

A Model Essay

The following model will help you clearly understand the form of an essay. Julian Lopez, who wrote the paragraph about socializing with computers, later decided to develop his subject more fully. Here is the essay that resulted:

Socializing Computers

INTRODUCTORY
PARAGRAPH

If curious scientists peered through the windows of college or university residences or apartments in Bowmanville, Moosejaw, or Abbotsford to find out what young people do in their leisure time, what would they see? Chances are, they would see a group, eighteen to twenty-five, amusing themselves in front of a computer screen. Their parents' generation may enjoy a solitary and monogamous relationship with their computers, but these "iGeneration" friends, who grew up with computers, are exploring new ways of interacting with their technology. Today's youth has an ingenious new use for the computer, as the hub for group entertainment, social interaction, and group multitasking.   1

FIRST SUPPORTING
PARAGRAPH

One asset the "social computer" brings to a gathering is its helpfulness when groups are choosing entertainment. The computer helps people make decisions and reach compromises easily and quickly. Suppose a group of five friends decides to watch a *Halloween* marathon on DVD. What happens when, an hour into the first movie, three out of five people get bored? No need for bad   2 tempers or arguments because any number of entertainment options is only a few mouse-clicks away. Four out of five may be happy to watch online cartoons or TV show episodes on YouTube, or everyone could just as happily enjoy an hour or two of gaming with Everquest or Halo. Friends can play or watch in twos or as a group, but any choice starts conversations and friendly competitions. People reach quick decisions and compromises when they control their choices and have lots to choose from.

SECOND SUPPORTING PARAGRAPH

Another reason why the computer is an indispensable guest at social evenings is its ability, once it is happily online, to challenge and interact with others. As such, it seems made for a generation that enjoys testing itself and expects quick feedback. The Internet is ready to serve individuals and groups with personality and IQ tests, trivia sites, quizzes, and the phenomenon of purity tests, available on subjects as wide-ranging as personal hygiene and *Star Wars* obsessions. Instead of gossiping, friends can see who knows more about the original cast of *DeGrassi Junior High* or torment each other with facts about quantum physics. Quizzes encourage interaction between people and the computer and between the people themselves. Friends challenge themselves, compare their results amongst themselves, and learn more about one another as part of an evening's fun.

3

THIRD SUPPORTING PARAGRAPH

Ultimately, though, the most interesting reason why computers are such regularly invited guests reflects the effect they have had on their owners' minds. Computers and young people are both multitaskers; they comfortably do several things at one time. While listening to the latest K-OS or Billy Talent MP3s, people set up their evening's music downloads, check their favourite sites or message boards, print movie or sports schedules, and chat with friends on Instant Messenger. Other groups play games as they chat with players on the other side of the world and compare scores on yet another site. Such social multitasking allows everyone in the room to be sharing the same overall experience while individuals or pairs of people pursue particular interests of their own.

4

CONCLUDING PARAGRAPH

Younger generations and computers have adapted well to each other; they are now constant companions. Computers offer control and the choice of passive entertainment or active participation, while allowing their users to exercise both these options at once. The computer and its human friends work well together, and when it's time to play, the "social computer" is ready for any occasion. Perhaps humans and technology will live "happily ever after."

5

The Academic Essay: Purpose, Voice, and Tone

"Socializing Computers" is a good example of a five-paragraph essay. The word essay, from the French *essai*, means "a try," or "an attempt." The essay, far from being a stuffy or outdated writing vehicle, is a versatile and efficient format. Essays flexibly accommodate personal expressions of feeling, detailed comparisons, and complex, carefully researched arguments. The word *essai* itself reveals the essay's one consistent characteristic: purposefulness; the attempt to reach a goal with readers. In the academic essay, that purposefulness appears in the thesis statement, the essay's point. While precise purposes vary by assignment and subject-area, overall academic essays argue, explore, explain, or analyze some idea or viewpoint. In this respect, as well as in voice and tone, these essays differ fundamentally from the type of personal, exploratory, subjective writing that students often practise in high school. Within the spectrum of essay types, the academic essay is a distinct, structured writing pattern, with its emphasis on the quality of its content.

The content of the academic essay focuses wholly on pursuing and clarifying the writer's point, rather than on revealing the writer's personality. Julian Lopez does not appear as an active presence in his essay; he does not write using the first-person pronoun "I"; instead, he writes in the "invisible" third-person point of view or voice, leaving the reader able to concentrate on his clear points and careful, lucid supporting details. Voice in writing is the writer's presence, his or her point of view, and often indicates where the writer chooses to place his or her emphasis as related to subject. Writing in the first-person voice, writing as "I," emphatically and often intrusively connects the writer to the essay's content, shifting the reader's attention away from the material. While such a subjective, personal voice may suit diaries, blogs, or eye-witness reports, it is generally inappropriate for academic essays, where the reader's focus is intended to be on the quality of point and support. Practice with the third-person writing voice helps develop a sense of which subjects, which audiences, and which writing tasks will benefit from each voice.

As writers choose a voice, they consciously or unconsciously adopt a tone. Tone is created by a combination of word-choice and idea selection, as it is in speech. Academic essays ideally display a thoughtful, considered tone, showing that the writer cares enough for his or her readers to have chosen words and details that suit the subject material, the essay's purpose, and the reader's general background and educational level. Julian's essay is lighthearted, but not jokey or juvenile; he informs readers in a clear, even tone. Academic writing ideally is neither unduly serious nor pompous; rather it seeks to speak to readers in a direct, level tone aimed at facilitating understanding of the material.

As the essay's aim is clarity of understanding by its audience, a sound, functional structure is key. And as with all good design, a standard essay's form follows function to create an audience-focused writing format. The reader finds the essay's purpose or goal efficiently placed in its opening paragraph, signalling and suggesting that a structured pattern of supporting information will follow. Now see how "Socializing Computers" makes effective use of standard five-paragraph essay structure, with its one-paragraph introduction, three-paragraph body, and one-paragraph conclusion. The functions of these paragraphs are described and illustrated below.

Introductory Paragraph

In your introductory paragraph, your reader sees your subject and your relationship to that subject. Your first few sentences attract the reader's attention, giving context or background for the main idea you will develop. Then, you advance the central idea, or thesis, that will be explored in the essay. **The *thesis* contains your subject and viewpoint and often includes a plan of development—the major points that will support the thesis.** These supporting points should be listed in the order in which they will appear in the essay. In some cases, the plan of development is presented in a sentence separate from the thesis; in other cases, it is suggested in general terms.

Activity

1. In "Socializing Computers," which sentences attract the reader's interest by offering background information?
   a. First sentence
   b. First two sentences
   c. First three sentences

2. What is the writer's thesis? Explain his thesis in your own words. In which sentence in the introductory paragraph is the essay's thesis presented?

3. Does the thesis contain a plan of development? If so, explain how the writer will present his supporting points.

4. What are the three supporting points for the thesis?

5. Who do you believe could be the reading audience, or audiences, for this essay? Why?

6. What voice (point of view) has the writer chosen? How do you know this?

Body: Supporting Paragraphs

Most essays have three supporting points, developed at length over three separate paragraphs. (Some essays will have two supporting points, others four or more.) For the purposes of this book, your goal will be three supporting points (unless your instructor indicates otherwise). **Each of the supporting paragraphs should begin with a *topic sentence* that guides your choice of details and states the point to be explained in that paragraph.** As well, each supporting paragraph examines one of the thesis statement's main points, and in its "proof" or supporting details, each paragraph advances and develops its part of the entire essay.

Activity

1. What is the topic sentence for the first supporting paragraph of the essay?

   _____

   _____

2. The first topic sentence is then supported by the following details (*fill in the missing words*):
   a. *Helps people make decisions and reach compromises* _____

   b. _____

   c. _____

d. _____

e. _____

f. _____

3. What is the topic sentence for the second supporting paragraph of the essay?

_____

_____

4. The second topic sentence is then supported by the following examples:
    a. *Current generation enjoys testing itself and feedback*_____

    b. *Internet offers individuals and groups tests and quizzes*_____

    c. _____

    d. _____

5. What is the topic sentence for the third supporting paragraph of the essay?

_____

_____

6. The third topic sentence is then supported by the following details:
    a. _____

    b. _____

    c. *People play online games while chatting online with other players and comparing scores on other sites*_____

Concluding Paragraph

The concluding paragraph summarizes the essay by briefly restating the thesis, and at times, the main supporting points of the essay. In addition, you should present a more general or "outward looking" concluding thought about the subject of the essay.

• • • • **Activity**

1. Which two sentences in the concluding paragraph restate the thesis and supporting points of the essay?
    a. First and second   b. Second and third   c. Third and fourth

2. Which sentence contains the concluding thought of the essay?
    a. First   b. Second   c. Fourth

Diagram of an Essay

The following diagram shows you at a glance the different parts of a standard academic essay, also known as a **one-three-one essay**. This diagram will serve as a helpful guide when you are writing or evaluating essays.

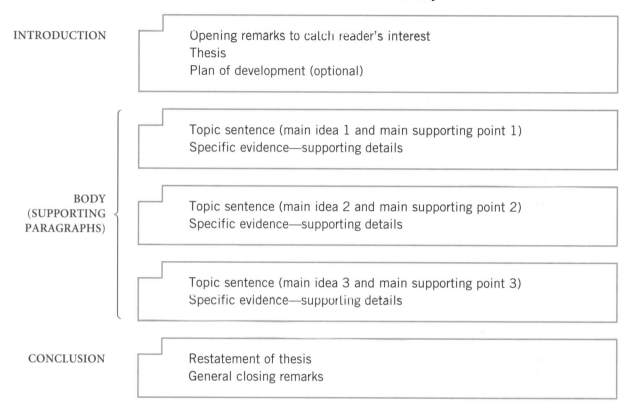

Title of the Essay

INTRODUCTION

Opening remarks to catch reader's interest
Thesis
Plan of development (optional)

BODY
(SUPPORTING
PARAGRAPHS)

Topic sentence (main idea 1 and main supporting point 1)
Specific evidence—supporting details

Topic sentence (main idea 2 and main supporting point 2)
Specific evidence—supporting details

Topic sentence (main idea 3 and main supporting point 3)
Specific evidence—supporting details

CONCLUSION

Restatement of thesis
General closing remarks

You now have an overview of the five-paragraph essay. In the next chapter, you will learn just how to go about writing an effective essay.

A Note about Standard English and Communication

In the section above, the ideas of *purpose* and *tone* are discussed. Earlier in this chapter, the relevance of the *medium* (page, computer screen) and *format* (essay, e-mail, phone/PDA message) in which a piece of writing appears is covered. All three concepts—purpose, tone, and medium—become very important when the issue of Standard English versus "IMspeak" or "Chatspeak" arises.

Today, with tiny cell phone or PDA screens, with small rectangular chatroom or messenger dialogue boxes, a new subcategory of English colloquial usage has appeared. Every student reading these words knows what *CUL8R, LOL,* and so on mean. But not everyone knows why these "sound/letter codes" are not suitable for writing essays or e-mails in academic or professional environments.

"IMspeak" developed because the screens and dialogue boxes of the media involved are small, and therefore unsuitable for the full words and sentences of Standard English. Moreover, text messages and chats are usually communications between close friends, where misunderstandings are rare and informality is the rule. Your professor or instructor, on the other hand, is not your close friend. You do not speak to him or her the same way you speak to friends; therefore, why risk misunderstanding and possible offence by writing to him or her in an inappropriate tone and "language"? A "language," code, or slang meant for a cell phone text message is never appropriate for general printed text in an academic or professional context. Codes and slang are "pseudo languages" devised by small groups to exclude other groups; their purpose is not clear communication; instead, their purpose is to confuse outsiders. If your purpose, when writing an essay or other course assignment, or an e-mail to a professor, is to be understood by your audience, then why use a code or slang? In terms of media-appropriateness, any page, e-mail window, or computer screen is certainly large enough for Standard English and correct grammar.

Whether essays or assignments appear in hard copy or on a computer screen as part of an online course, they are written in Standard English. The first audience for such writing is obviously an instructor. Additional audiences may be other students in revising groups or online course discussion groups. The overall purpose is always the same: maximum understanding by the largest audience. Only Standard English guarantees this.

ACTIVITIES

Activity 1

Julian Lopez's essay indicates that people tend to adapt technology to suit their needs, and sometimes technology develops to create new uses for a single item. Consider, for example, the cell phone: originally just a portable wireless phone, the cell phone now functions as MP3 player, camera, television, satellite radio player, and more.

Option 1: Group or Class Activity
In groups, list at least four of the best or most satisfying uses for cell phones or one other developing item of technology such as the USB key—give each type of use a suitable heading. In the case of cell phones, try headings such as Security, Entertainment, Information, and so on. Under each heading, list as many details or examples related to that heading as possible. Discuss common and interesting preferences and experiences, and prioritize the list items in terms of usefulness or enjoyment.

Option 2: Individual Activity
Which item of personal technology or application/piece of software do you find most useful and vital to your everyday life, and why?

For fifteen minutes, freewrite on your topic choice making note of specific ways in which this item benefits you in various aspects of your life. Based on your freewriting, create an outline for a paragraph similar to Julian Lopez's example paragraph on page 7, following the paragraph outline pattern on page 10.

● ● ● ● **Activity 2**

Developing Audience Awareness

Use the brainstorming technique and the topic for Activity 1, Option 1 above. Choose a piece of technology, then decide on and list some headings that best characterize its main assets or benefits.

- Now, assume you will outline and write a paragraph for an audience of your acquaintances or peers. Revise, if needed, the headings you have noted; for each heading, list as many supporting details or examples as possible to clarify and explain your chosen benefits.
- Next, imagine you will outline and write a paragraph for an audience made up of your instructors on the same topic—the benefits and advantages of this same technological item. Revise your headings to suit this group of people, and list appropriate supporting details and examples for your headings.

How much, and why did you revise your headings for the second audience? How did your supporting details and examples change, and why? Write a brief explanation, in the third-person voice, for your revisions and changes, based on varying your audience.

Your instructor may choose to have individual students outline and write a paragraph in the third-person voice for one of these audiences.

College Writing Skills will help you learn, practise, and apply the thinking and writing skills necessary to communicate effectively. The ability to express yourself clearly and logically can open doors of opportunity for you, both in school and in your career. If you decide that you want such language power, this book will help you reach that goal.

CHECKLIST OF LEARNING OUTCOMES FOR CHAPTER 1

To ensure that you have understood and met the learning outcomes for this chapter, answer the following questions:

- ✓ What does the concept of writing as a "learnable skill" mean to you?
- ✓ How can writing help you to discover your thoughts?
- ✓ In what ways do people adjust their speech for different purposes and audiences? How could this apply to your writing assignments?
- ✓ Explain why research is essential for academic assignments. Why is research referred to as a "process"?

- ✓ What benefits will you gain from essay writing during your post-secondary years? How will essay writing skills help you during your career?
- ✓ What are the components of an effective paragraph, and what is the function of each?
- ✓ Describe the structure of an essay. What are its main parts?

CHAPTER 2

The Writing Process

LEARNING OUTCOMES

After reading this chapter and working through its activities, you will

- follow the sequence of steps in writing an effective essay;
- be ready to work effectively during the stages of the writing process;
- be prepared to use prewriting strategies to generate ideas;
- create a solid and useful outline;
- write increasingly effective and clear drafts of an essay;
- know how to approach revising and editing.

Chapter 1 introduced you to three concepts that will help you each time you face a writing task: that writing is a learnable skill, a process that proceeds in stages, and is most effective when based on knowledge of purpose and audience. You became aware of the importance of research for all your academic subjects, and learned that conducting research, like writing, is a learnable skill. You also explored fundamentals of paragraph and essay structure. This chapter turns your attention to learning and practising techniques to sharpen and expand skills you will use during the discovery, ordering, drafting, and revising stages of the writing process.

Chapter 3 will focus on writing an effective thesis and supporting it specifically and adequately. Chapter 4 will deepen your understanding of organizing and connecting your support, and of writing better introductions and conclusions. Finally, revising and editing your essay drafts is covered in Chapter 5.

While this process does not usually proceed in a completely straightforward way, there are general stages *every writer* works through in each writing situation, and this knowledge will prepare you to learn special skills for each stage. Once you are conscious of which stage in the process you are working on, you are able to focus on using specific strategies to guide and assist you in that stage. Writing is less intimidating because you can separate it into clear tasks. Furthermore, you will be following a map tested by other writers.

With your awareness of the writing process, you will be ready to apply what you have learned to the sequence of steps for creating effective essays:

> ### *Four Steps for Effective Essay Writing*
>
> 1 Discover your point, and advance a clear thesis statement.
> 2 Support your thesis with specific evidence.
> 3 Organize and connect your specific evidence.
> 4 Revise, edit, and proofread your essay.

These steps will guide and direct you every time you begin writing an essay. This sequential approach will also support you when you come to write memos, reports, editorials, or evaluations. Each step uses different parts of your mind, different ways of thinking, and beginning with this chapter, you will learn techniques to help you with each one. The chapters that follow cover each step in detail. With practice, you will relax and do the type of clear thinking that each step requires.

THE WRITING PROCESS

The writing process often begins not with writing, but with staring blankly at the page or screen. If that sounds familiar, and if you have felt intimidated by writing tasks, you may never have learned a technique to start writing. Although writing is a learnable skill, students often enter college or university with behaviours and feelings related to writing that keep them from learning and mastering that skill. In this chapter you will learn how and why the writing process works; you need only learn and practise following through on each stage consistently. Each time you follow this method, you will reduce your anxiety and your desire to avoid writing, and replace those feelings with the knowledge that you have a sensible, effective procedure to follow.

The Psychology of Tackling a Writing Task

Do you ever sit down to work on an essay, then get right up again and do something else? If, instead of writing or typing, you clean your room or check a chatline, you are procrastinating, having a normal response to a challenge. Avoidance behaviours like procrastination do not mean you are lazy; instead, these may mean that you feel unprepared or uncertain. What you are trying to avoid is not actually writing, but facing the blank, edgy feeling of not knowing where to begin or what to write.

Not knowing where or how to begin the writing process leads to several possible scenarios. First, you may feel your mind is utterly blank, and suspect that sensation, a so-called "mental block," means your mind is empty—that you have nothing to say. Actually, your mind is offering an anxiety-driven sensation of blankness while, in fact, it is racing; churning with ideas and connections. The anxiety blocks the calmer, more logical parts of your mind from finding an appropriate starting point in the writing process. To relieve or sidestep their anxiety, some students try for inspiration by visualizing their goal, the finished essay. Visualizing that final product with little or no idea of how to achieve it creates frustration, not inspiration. The goal is too many steps away; try visualizing a full page of freewriting instead. Writing is a multi-stage process that uses different parts of the brain for different tasks, so envisioning the end product too far in advance is attempting to trick your mind. Finally, other students use a "combination approach" to handling writing anxiety: they combine avoidance with trying to write a finished essay in one frantic, last-minute draft. Writing well is work, not magic. Good writing is never the result of these desperate efforts; the work involved in creating solid, polished essays cannot be cheated.

Instead of avoiding writing, succumbing to phantom blankness, visualizing the wrong thing, or trying to write an "all-at-once" essay, begin the writing process at the beginning, and focus on one stage of the process at a time.

Here are three essential tips as you begin.

1 Leave enough time to do a good job. This is key: to work through the writing process effectively takes a minimum of three days.

2 If you are unclear about any part of your assignment, speak to or e-mail your instructor. Writing instructors appreciate your concern and are willing to help.

3 If language or sentence-structure problems are major concerns, and make you delay starting writing assignments, ask your instructor about language or writing skills assistance available from your college. As you begin working on these issues, you will find expressing yourself less intimidating.

Each time you begin a writing task, review the box below to settle your mind on the fact that you will work on only one stage at a time.

The Stages of the Writing Process

1 The Discovery Stage: Prewriting
You generate raw material, finding out what you have to say. You use the creative, spontaneous parts of your mind as you explore your thoughts. You may refine your focus on your topic as you work through two phases of prewriting, as this chapter demonstrates.

2 The Organizing Stage: Outlining
Now is the time to use the ordering parts of your mind. You give the ideas from your prewriting a structured shape by creating an outline. You form your essay's skeleton, and begin to see its full shape, and how it reveals your thoughts about your topic.

3 The Drafting Stage: Writing Drafts
As you draft, you first put your outline into full sentence form. You concentrate on your content, on expressing your ideas and support as clearly as possible. You do not yet worry about sentence structure or grammar; focus on your content. Be prepared to write at least two drafts.

4 The Revising Stage: Polishing Ideas and Sentences
In the final stage, you have two tasks: revising your content and proofreading your writing. This stage is crucial to writing effectively for your purpose and audience; leave yourself enough time to do your ideas justice.

With the first stage, always "begin at the beginning." Choose one type of prewriting strategy, and start writing about your topic. Do not worry about choosing a "right" or "wrong" strategy to start with. Once you start writing, you will have material to work with, and that is where every writer begins…with raw material.

In the following pages, you will learn about the general stages of essay writing, which correspond to the steps on page 21, and you will explore tested strategies to help you with blocks and problems—skills you can practise in writing situations for the rest of your life.

STAGE 1: PREWRITING—FOUR TECHNIQUES

Prewriting describes the first stages of writing, the creative "discovery" period. During prewriting, you should free your mind to discover the directions in which your ideas flow most freely. This is not a time to use "ordering" or "correcting" functions.

To help you open up your mind and imagination, there are certain techniques, sometimes referred to as "brainstorming," which can help. The following section describes four techniques that will encourage you to think about and develop a topic and get words on paper: (1) freewriting, (2) questioning, (3) making a list, and (4) diagramming. Each prewriting technique can be used for different purposes: to free the mind so it can generate ideas or to organize and refine material that is generated. Prewriting techniques may also be used in combination with each other, as you will see in the following sections.

Technique 1: Freewriting

Freewriting means jotting down, in rough sentences or phrases, everything that comes to mind about a possible topic. Write non-stop for ten minutes or more. Explore any idea by putting down whatever pops into your head. If you get stuck for words, repeat yourself until more words come.

When you freewrite, your only goal is to generate raw material to work on. Every writing task is easier when you have *something* to work from rather than the dreaded blank screen or page. **Focus only on discovering what you want to say** about a subject. Your initial ideas and impressions will often become clearer after you have put them on paper, and they may lead to other ideas and impressions or even another possible focus. That's fine. If your freewriting tells you that you have unexpected thoughts, go with them. Revise those new ideas *later* to take advantage of your discoveries. Through continued practice in freewriting, you will develop the habit of thinking as you write.

Now, put away the eraser or liquid paper, resist the urge to hit "delete," and start freewriting. Forget about spelling, grammar, and punctuation; let the inventive part of your mind run free. You have no audience, no censor to worry about; there are no mistakes in freewriting.

Freewriting: A Student Model

During general freewriting, two possibilities usually emerge: your focus simply appears as the thing you are writing most about, or, like Julian Lopez, you consciously decide on one idea that "sparks a connection" for you. Many writers use freewriting in two stages: to generate ideas about some broad topic and then to explore a single focus, their specific topic.

Freewriting to Generate Ideas

Julian Lopez's essay "Socializing Computers" on pages 12–13 was written in response to an assigned general topic about people and technology. Julian started freewriting about the pieces of personal technology he owned. Here is his freewriting:

> Well, my cell phone is one piece of technology I use all the time. I can hardly remember what it was like not to have one—yes, I do remember—I had to look for pay phones all the time, and lots of times they were dirty or they didn't work, or I didn't have a quarter or a phone card. My phone keeps me connected to my parents and my friends, and I really enjoy owning it. I play games on it when I'm sitting on the bus. Okay, that reminds me—gaming. I love gaming, mostly first-person shooter games, not RPGs so much. So I guess my computer's just as important to me as my phone—I play a lot online and chat with other gamers, too, while I'm doing it. Last night, John, Lisa, and a bunch of people were playing Halo 3 and comparing our scores on a new site from Korea. Marco came late and wanted to download a bunch of music, so we ended up talking about The Stills' new songs and burning mix CDs. This Friday, we're having a *Lord of the Rings* festival. We're doing it at my place because I have a new wide-screen monitor. My friends and I will probably continue our IQ challenge, too. We seem to end up most weekends doing stuff with our computers now that I think of it.

Focused Freewriting

When Julian read over his first freewriting notes, he commented, "I have a few potential topics here, I think. But what point can I make that I can explain in an essay? What do I have the most information about? I think my purpose is to explain how my friends and I use our computers when we get together; I have a lot of ideas and I think what we do is pretty common." Because his purpose was to explain his peers' use of computers, Julian decided his general audience was people who used computers for work or to pursue personal interests online, and who used computers alone. This one distinguishing point, and Julian's wish to explain how he and his friends were different in this respect, suggested a more focused audience: readers mainly in his parents' (and possibly his instructors') generation. These people would know about his general subject, but would not be so familiar with more all-purpose uses of computers; therefore, they could be interested in some new ideas. Julian then did some focused freewriting to work out reasons why he believed he and his friends used their computers in a new way.

> Young people today use their computers differently than their parents do. My friends and I spend a lot of evenings sitting around our computers rather than watching TV. For one thing, if we decide to rent a DVD, and some people don't like it, it's easy to do something else. And we don't argue as much because somebody's going to come up with another choice like watching online

cartoons or gaming. Lisa and Nelson are RPG fanatics, and they love digging up new character ideas from sites. Plus, we're pretty competitive generally, so we have these big online test competitions—we've tried hundreds of IQ and personality tests, and purity tests always get people either embarrassed or laughing. The computer lets us download and listen to music while we're playing, chatting, or looking stuff up, too. If we can't afford to go out, we use our computers to entertain us—we each have our favourite things we do on the computer, but sometimes it's good to do those things together.

Tips and Comments

Julian's freewriting drafts contain errors in grammar and punctuation. They are shown uncorrected to make three points:

- Freewriting is *for you;* you are the audience and no one is checking "over your shoulder."
- The whole point of freewriting is to go with the flow of your ideas; keep writing, and don't stop as you discover what's in your mind.
- Correcting problems is a mental process different from exploring; "shifting mental gears" can slow or stop the discovery stage of the writing process. If worrying about your sentences is slowing you down, write your ideas in point form.

Activity 1: Individual Work

To get some practice freewriting, take a sheet of paper, and do some general freewriting about the everyday annoyances in your life. See how much material you can accumulate in ten minutes. And remember not to worry about "mistakes." You are just thinking on paper.

Choose the three annoyances about which you wrote the most. Write each as a heading on a new page or document, leaving space after the individual headings. Look for details about each potential topic in your freewriting, and come up with other details if possible.

Find an overall focus by asking yourself questions such as what do these annoyances have in common, and why are these items more annoying than others? Make up a possible title based on the focus you discover.

Activity 2: Group Work

Find a partner. Individually, each of you should freewrite for ten minutes about your ideal day. Now, exchange papers with each other.

Reviewing your partner's paper, look for the strongest ideas or those with the most details. Make brief notes of those ideas and their supporting details. Orally present your partner's "ideal day" to him or her. When you have both presented to each other, evaluate how well your presentation reflected your partner's original ideas. What would each of you change, and why?

Technique 2: Questioning

Questioning can reveal thoughts to you in a different way from freewriting. If you are a methodical individual who thrives on order and structure, questioning may offer you a comfortable method to work with. Freewriting goes around the order-ing parts of your mind; the structured approach of questioning is a set framework of inquiry. This framework gives a sense of direction and works for those who find an unstructured approach intimidating or too "loose." Questioning is particu-larly effective in writing situations where you have some knowledge of your sub-ject, whether gained through experience or research. This approach can help you through a temporary blank period. Ask yourself as many questions as you can think of about your subject; your answers will be a series of different "takes" or focuses on it. Such questions include *Why? When? Where? Who?* and *How?*

To begin, divide your page or screen into two columns: "Questions" and "Answers," as you see below. Leave enough space in the "Answers" column so that you can return to a particular response if more details come to you later. Next, ask yourself these preliminary questions: "What is my subject?" "What is my purpose?", and "Who is my audience?" For the moment, rough answers to the purpose and audience questions are enough; you may adjust these as you work on your questioning. Then, write your answers as reference points for the rest of your question-and-answer series. If one question stops you, just go on to another.

Here are some questions that Tina, a student writer, might ask while develop-ing an essay on the disadvantages of seeing movies in theatres:

Questioning: A Student Model

Questions	*Answers*
What is my subject?	I do not like seeing movies in theatres.
What is my purpose?	To explain why I dislike going to movie theatres—to justify myself?
Who is my audience?	People my age? Other movie fans who like or dislike going to the theatre?
Why don't I like to go to the theatre?	Just too many problems involved.
When is going to the movies a problem?	Could be any time—when movie is popular the theatre is too crowded, when traffic is bad the trip is a drag.
Where are problems with movie-going?	On the highway, in the parking lot, at the concession stand, in the theatre itself.
Who creates the problems?	I do by wanting to eat too much. The patrons do by creating disturbances. The theatre owners do by not having enough parking space and showing too many commercials.
How can I deal with the problem?	I can stay home and watch movies on DVD or cable TV.

Tips and Comments

Asking questions can be an effective way of getting you to think about a topic from a number of different angles. The questions can really help you generate details about a topic.

Questioning as Second-Stage Prewriting

If you have done some general freewriting, but still are not sure of a focus for your paper, try questioning, using your freewriting as a reference. If you feel that you "almost have a focus," but are uncertain, look for key words or phrases in your freewriting. A key word or phrase may be one you have returned to or one that seems particularly connected to your topic. Use that word or phrase in your series of questions. Questioning can lead to a surer sense of purpose, or to revising your purpose. For example, if you find more details accumulating under a "why" question than under a "how" question, your overall purpose could be to show causes of something or to persuade readers, rather than to explain something to them. As well, questioning may reveal more about audience focus. If points explain too much or too little for an anticipated audience, or information in answers is inconsistent with your presumed audience's needs, this is the ideal time to either change your audience focus or to work further on your prewriting if your audience is predetermined by your assignment.

- Questioning may reveal your main supporting points clearly as answers to one or more questions.
- Questioning can yield answers that may be rich sources of *connected* details— potential topics—making some of your organizing and outlining a little easier.
- Questioning can show you directions for paragraphs within an essay; if you have many answers to *Why*, you may want to explore the causes of a subject.

Activity 1: Individual Work

To get some practice with the questioning process, write down a series of questions about a good or bad experience that you have had recently. See how many details you can accumulate in your answers in ten minutes. Again, remember not to be concerned about "mistakes" because you are just thinking on paper.

Now, examine the answers to your questions about good or bad experiences. You are looking for a potential direction or focus, based on the questions that yielded the most responses.

Choosing the question that generated the most answers, answer these three questions: *What is my subject and my viewpoint on my subject?*, *What would be my purpose in writing about my subject?*, and *Who would be my audience?*

For example, assume you asked yourself questions about the good experience of learning to ride horses, and the most fruitful question was *Why?*. Your subject is learning to ride; your viewpoint on it is that it is a valuable and/or healthful experience. Your purposes in writing about learning to ride could be *to inform and persuade* in general, and more specifically, to show and explain to readers why riding is such and excellent activity. Your audiences would likely be your peers and instructor, and people who do not already ride horses.

• • • • Activity 2: Group Work

In groups of four, work individually to create five questions about your favourite pastime. Each person will need two sheets of paper. On your first sheet of paper, list as many answers as possible for your five questions. This is the sheet you will exchange with someone else in your group.

Now, before exchanging papers, choose the question that resulted in the most answers. Take your second piece of paper, and look over the most productive question and its answers. Note possible responses to these questions: *What is the subject and a possible viewpoint on it?*, *What is my purpose or purposes?*, and *Who could be the audience(s)?* Hold onto this second sheet of paper. Do not exchange it. Trade only your first sheet of paper with another person in your group.

One student, Kristina, came up with five questions about playing pool. Her questions included, "Why did I start playing pool in the first place?", "Why is pool considered an odd choice of game for women?", and "What benefits have I derived from playing pool?" She traded her questions and answers with Zunaira. Zunaira saw that the "odd choice of game for women" question elicited the most answers. Zunaira then worked on deciding what Kristina's subject and viewpoint might be, and what her purpose and audience might be. Kristina did the same with Zunaira's question and answers.

Finally, return each sheet of paper to its owner and compare your partner's views with your own. For all the papers in your group, which might make the best essay and why?

Technique 3: List Making

List making is simply noting, in point form, ideas and details that relate to your subject. Just write, as separate points, as many ideas as you can about your subject. Avoid making sentences out of your points, and never worry about repeating yourself; your mind may be trying out a variation on some idea. Listing is an everyday informal behaviour that comes naturally to most people. Lists have more shape than freewriting, but less structure than questioning, so list making appeals to a variety of writers.

One risk associated with listing is that because it is basically an ordering activity, you could be tempted to organize your ideas prematurely. If this happens, keep adding new items. If you are listing as a first stage of prewriting, resist the urge to order. Use listing for its value as an informal, clean-looking way to record ideas on the page or screen.

After Julian did his freewriting about socializing around the computer, he made up the following list of details to help him see his ideas more clearly.

List Making: A Student Model

- My generation uses computers together, not always alone
- We're all used to computers, so we do lots of different activities
- Doing "group blogs"
- Downloading TV shows to our iPods
- TV isn't interactive; computers can be
- Watching movies together

- Having movie marathons
- Easy to change what we're doing
- Downloading music while we watch movies
- Making mix-CDs
- Gaming—consoles vs. online
- RPGs and combat games
- One-person games or playing in groups
- Chatting with gamers
- Online tests and quizzes
- Competitions with tests
- Being alone and together doing stuff

Tips and Comments

One detail led to another as Julian expanded his list. Slowly more details emerged, some of which he would use in developing his essay. By the time he finished his list, he was ready to start grouping his points under trial topic headings.

List making works as a first or second stage of prewriting. As a first stage, listing is a quick, easy method you are already familiar with from making everyday "to-do" lists.

List Making as Second-Stage Prewriting

List making is an excellent organizing method to use for the second stage of prewriting. Take advantage of listing as a simple way to sort your ideas into a cleaner format. With a second-stage list, you can sort your points and details into a hierarchy that is closer to the way these things will appear in your first draft.

- List making after freewriting can stimulate you to think of more points and details.
- List making after freewriting or questioning displays your thoughts in a simple, uncluttered form, so you can proceed to evaluate them.
- List making is an excellent method of organizing; number your points and ideas before outlining, or sort out points and their related supporting details from your list.
- List making is useful for writers who like to connect ideas graphically with lines and circles.

 Computer *Writing Tip*

Try making a second-stage list that you can sort and modify on the computer. You can move items around easily and copy, cut, and paste phrases into different positions. You can keep your screen clean and tidy as you work, making the ordering process less confusing. As well as numbering points, you may try bolding main points and grouping related ideas beneath them in plain text. Additionally, you can save any ideas about which you are uncertain at the bottom of the screen or in a separate document.

Remember though, people are more likely to overlook errors when editing or revising any onscreen work. Especially when you are drafting and revising, you may achieve better results if you print copies of your documents. Work on the hard copy, then transfer the changes to a copy of the most recent version of your document. Begin the habit of saving each stage of an essay's progress, clearly identifying each version.

Activity 1: Individual Work

To practise list making, list a series of realistic goals, major or minor, that you would like to accomplish within the next year. Your goals can involve personal, academic, and career matters.

Now, imagine you are listing your goals for your best friend to read—revise your list to reflect any changes. Next, revise your list to suit your instructor as your reading audience. Finally, adjust your list for a complete stranger, someone sitting next to you on a bus, to read. What changes did you make, and why, in each case?

Activity 2: Group Work

With a group of students, do some second-stage list making. Using the lists of goals you created individually, try making a list of "Major Goals" and "Minor Goals" or a list broken into categories such as "Academic Goals" and "Personal Goals."

Consult with the members of your group about which items belong on your lists and how you will order the items within your lists. Will you go from most to least important or vice versa? Will you order your items according to when you hope to achieve your goals? Your group may wish to try some lists ordered by one method and some by another.

Technique 4: Clustering

Clustering, also known as "diagramming" or "mapping," is another strategy for generating ideas. People who enjoy thinking in a visual or graphic way can use lines, boxes, arrows, and circles to show relationships among the ideas and details that occur to them.

State your subject in a few words in the centre of a blank sheet of paper. Then, as ideas and details come to you, put them in boxes or circles around the subject. As you find connections or relationships between ideas and groups of ideas, draw lines to connect them to each other and to the subject. When you cluster to generate ideas, keep creating "word bubbles" and connecting them to each other. You will need to allow some time after completing your first stage to decide which ideas are more important than others. Clustering, like freewriting, is non-hierarchical; it shows relationships rather than the order of importance of items.

There is no right or wrong way of clustering; it is a way to think on paper about how various ideas and details relate to one another. On the following page is an example of clustering that Tina, the student writing about the disadvantages of movie-going, might have produced to develop her ideas *after* freewriting.

Clustering: A Student Model

When you wish to use clustering to organize your first-stage prewriting, it becomes necessary to show the specific relationships between items in your diagram. Decide on a method for doing so. You may work vertically on the page, placing your main idea at the top and extending your supporting-point bubbles below it, followed by detail-bubbles beneath each. You could also, as Tina has done, work from the centre of the page outward, showing your levels of structure in different colours or degrees of boldness. In this case, the main-idea and supporting-point bubbles are in bold, and the relationship of details to supporting points is clearly visible.

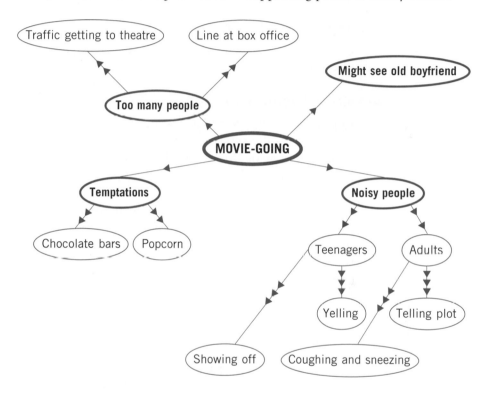

Tips and Comments

Clustering is especially useful for the visually minded writer, for both the first and second stages of prewriting. As a primary method of generating ideas, clustering frees you from the linearity of the page or screen.

- Clustering allows writers to get started with few clear ideas about their subject; first-stage clustering is an excellent exploratory technique.
- Clustering prevents "sentence block." You note points and details in words and phrases.
- Clustering instantly shows connections between your ideas as you use lines and arrows to link one thing with another.

The only limitation of clustering is that your page can sometimes become too messy to follow. Avoid this by starting a clean second page where you can distinguish between possible supporting points and details. Refer back to the diagram of clustering for techniques to help you clarify levels of support and connections.

Clustering as Second-Stage Prewriting

The pictorial aspect of clustering makes it useful for the second stage of prewriting. When you are trying to discern between main points and details, and show how these fit together, a cluster diagram with visual ordering cues will help you to see the overall shape and content of an essay.

- Second-stage clustering can reveal a paragraph's focus and the levels of details within, as Tina's "noisy people" set of clusters shows.
- Second-stage clustering can prepare you for outlining and drafting if you show different levels of links between points and details.

Activity 1: Individual Work

Use clustering to organize the list of year-ahead goals that you created for the previous activities (page 30).

Activity 2: Group Work

In groups of four, do some "second-stage clustering." Assume that the first-stage clustering on the subject of "the value of a post-secondary education" has been done; it has yielded some first-level areas of focus such as "job skills," "personal growth," "jobs available," and "networking contacts."

Begin your clustering diagram with the words "value of post-secondary education" in the centre of the page, and add first-level connection bubbles with the phrases listed above and any others that occur to your group. Now, look back to the clustering diagram on page 31, and, as a group, add as many second-level and third-level detail bubbles (based on the first-level areas of focus) as your group can create, using different colours for the second and third levels and added arrows on the second- and third-level connecting lines.

A Final Note on the First Stage of the Writing Process

Prewriting is the "no rules" first stage of the writing process. Following rules or worrying about spelling or sentence structure actually works against the "idea generating" way of using your mind. No matter which technique you prefer, there is only one guideline: go with what works for you. Any technique that gets your ideas flowing is good.

Occasionally, you may use several techniques at once. For example, you may ask yourself questions while writing a list, or you may cluster and sort through a list at the same time. When one technique is not working, simply stop and try another. The writing process is not a straightforward path, and each journey may begin differently.

STAGE 2: WRITING AN OUTLINE

Stage 2 of the writing process involves **outlining**. Generally, you will create an outline from your prewriting, followed by a first draft; this is the sequence this book demonstrates. Outlining, and sometimes re-outlining, is needed to untangle and clarify your prewriting. True, some writers write a trial draft *before* outlining. If you have worked successfully this way, continue to do so; this is actually an extra stage of prewriting. The sorting and decision-making step of outlining is still needed.

Preparing a correctly structured, detailed outline is an essential step in writing. The quality of your outline can determine the success or failure of your essay. Essays are highly organized forms of writing. They communicate effectively only when their content is logically arranged and sufficiently detailed. Therefore, an effective essay does not result from patching together random pieces of prewriting into a final draft. Essays written without good outlines are as ramshackle as buildings constructed without blueprints.

- **Creating a formal outline requires three thought processes:** sorting, ordering, and evaluating. You will think about the point you wish to make about your topic as you compose your thesis. You will consider and evaluate the supporting evidence (subtopics or supporting points and details) for that thesis. The quality and the arrangement of your raw material are what add up to a solid essay.
- **Sorting, ordering, and evaluating** are organizational skills that develop your ability to think clearly and logically. Outlining lets you work on the bare bones of your essay. You will see both your ideas and the connections between them.
- **A good outline** allows you to relax and write your first draft without worrying about what you will say next. You have your "blueprint" at hand.

You have seen both a paragraph outline diagram (page 10) and a diagram of an essay's general shape (page 17) in Chapter 1. The full essay outline pattern simply expands the paragraph model to accommodate the thesis statement and support structure for each body paragraph in the essay. On page 36, you will see a complete essay outline diagram.

Drafting a Thesis

Writing an effective thesis statement takes some practice. The following tips may help with the process of discovering and refining a thesis from prewriting notes.

First, what is a thesis statement? It is, among other things, a statement of an essay's subject and the writer's viewpoint on that subject. By the conclusion of your prewriting, you will know what your subject is; therefore, you are now looking for an appropriate way to state your viewpoint—a word or phrase that relates solidly to the ideas in your prewriting.

Next, if you worked through the Activities on pages 27 and 28, either individually or in a group, you have already explored one method of drafting a thesis from prewriting. You decided, based on responses from questioning, what your subject, viewpoint, purpose, and audience were. Following this process will yield a trial thesis statement in most cases.

After writing a trial thesis statement (simply your subject and viewpoint), follow the same pattern that you did with the questioning type of prewriting. Come up with as many question words (*who, what, when, where, why*) and question phrases (*What are the benefits/disadvantages of…?, What is different/special/unique about…?*) as you can.

To create thesis questions, write down your subject word or phrase and your viewpoint word or phrase. For instance, assume your subject is "credit cards for students," and the viewpoint or attitude emerging from your prewriting is that credit cards for students have some good points. Begin by combining your subject and your viewpoint with question words: *What is good about credit cards for students?, For whom are student credit cards a good thing?, When are credit cards for students a good idea?, Why are credit cards for students a good idea?* Depending on the content of your prewriting, any of these thesis questions could yield a good essay. You may also wish to try question phrases; for example, *What are the benefits of credit cards for students?*

Julian Lopez, author of "Socializing Computers," had a trial thesis statement: "Young people today have an ingenious new use for computers." His subject is the phrase, *young people using computers*. His viewpoint is expressed by the key word *ingenious*. While working on drafting his thesis, he turned his trial thesis into the following questions: *What is the ingenious use young people have for their computers?, Why is this new use for computers so ingenious?,* and *Where did young people's ingenious new way of using computers come from?*

Activity 1

Read Julian's essay (pages 12–13) again. What do you believe his final, "true" thesis question was? Why, based on the essay?

Activity 2

Following is a list of subjects and viewpoints. Select three of each, and compose a trial thesis statement for each one. Now create three thesis questions for each of the trial thesis statements. You will have nine thesis questions in all.

Which thesis question(s) would make the best essay? Why?

Subjects	Viewpoints
Laptops in class	Useful
Combining diplomas and degrees	Annoying
Learning another language	Important
Facebook	Silly
Cooking for one's self	Clever
Large families	Essential

The Transition from Prewriting to Outlining

With your prewriting done, you already have most of your content. There are some informal "sorting out" techniques you can use to bridge the gap between rough notes, lists, or clusters and a finished outline.

1. Begin by writing a statement of your point, a "trial thesis statement." Write your focused version of your topic and your viewpoint on it. Don't worry about

writing a polished thesis statement. (The next chapter will give you extensive practice in creating one.) You can always go back and change it later.

2. Turn your trial thesis statement into a question. Follow the instructions in the section above.

3. Now, ask yourself your "thesis question" as you look over your freewriting for ideas that answer the question.

   Asking a thesis question helps you discover the best supporting reasons for the point stated in your thesis. The best reasons are usually those for which your mind supplies lots of examples or details, or those you feel most strongly about. Don't worry if one of those reasons started out as a detail. If your thesis question changes while you are looking for answers, try that new version of the question.

4. Choose the three best answers to your thesis question, and write your trial thesis. List your three answers below it in point form.

5. Think about an appropriate order for your answers/reasons. Is one idea more important than another? Is the order in which your points occurred in time important? After deciding on an order, list the points again, leaving space after each to fill in details. Revise your trial thesis if necessary.

6. Now you have the basics of your outline; work on supplying, in point form, the details and examples that explain your reasons most clearly. Chapters 3 and 4 will give you extensive practice in discovering and selecting supporting points and adequate details.

Computer *Writing Tip*

Many writers prefer to work on outlines on the computer. Here are some tips to make outlining easier and more productive:

- Create an outline template of your own by copying the outline diagram in this chapter into a new document. Save this as "Outline." In Word, you can save this as a template, rather than a document.
- Every time you reach the outlining stage of an essay assignment, copy and paste the "Outline" template into a new document. Save this with an appropriate name.
- Working onscreen allows you to easily add, delete, and move material around on your outline. Deletions do not clutter the screen, and you can save ideas at the foot of your document.

Activity

Create an essay outline that could serve as a guide if you were to write an essay on your goals for the coming year.

Essay Outline Diagram

Photocopy this outline pattern, or create your own computer template. (See the "Computer Writing Tip" above.)

Opening Paragraph: Thesis Statement
    Supporting Points
    1.
    2.
    3.

Body Paragraph: Supporting Point #1
    Supporting Details & Examples
    1.
    2.
    3.

Body Paragraph: Supporting Point #2
    Supporting Details & Examples
    1.
    2.
    3.

Body Paragraph: Supporting Point #3
    Supporting Details & Examples
    1.
    2.
    3.

Concluding Paragraph: Conclusion

STAGE 3: WRITING DRAFTS

Developing a First Draft from an Outline

Here are tips to help make writing a first draft easier and more effective. The two chapters that follow offer further information about essay construction, but with a completed outline at hand, you are ready to turn that outline into sentences and paragraphs. Try to write in a relaxed frame of mind; a first draft is the beginning of your essay's final form, not a finished product. Keep your outline open onscreen beside your draft document, or to the side on your desk if you prefer to write by hand. But do not be rigidly shackled to your outline as you proceed—the essential thing is just to keep shaping your ideas as you write your draft.

- Write your thesis or main point at the top of your document, to help keep you focused.
- If additional thoughts and details come to you, put them in your draft and note them on your outline.
- If one of your points or details no longer works for you, and you feel blocked as you try to replace that material, just leave a blank space and add a comment like, "Do later," and then keep going to finish your draft.
- Do not worry about spelling, punctuation, or grammar; you will correct these things in a later draft as you revise.
- Stay focused on the goal of stating your thesis clearly and pursuing its supporting points with plenty of specific details.

In your first draft, concentrate on the general shape of your essay, not on fine details. Revising, the next stage of the writing process, is the time for polishing your ideas, words, and sentences.

Writing a First Draft: A Student Model

Here is Julian Lopez's first draft:

Today's generation uses computers differently than their parents' generation does. The "iGeneration," who grew up with computers, have found an ingenious new use for their favourite technology. 1

If some friends want to watch a *Halloween* double-bill on DVD, chances are a few may not enjoy it. Bad tempers or arguments are less common when people socialize with a computer because many entertainment options are only a few mouse-clicks away. People can choose online cartoons at The Cartoon Network, TV show episodes on YouTube or an hour or two of gaming with Everquest or Halo. Friends can play or watch in twos or as a group. Making choices starts conversations and friendly competitions. People like to control their choices and have lots to choose from. 2

Another reason why the computer appears at social evenings is its ability, when online, to challenge and interact with others. My generation enjoys testing itself and expects quick feedback. The Internet is full of IQ tests, quizzes, and even purity tests, on personal hygiene and movie trivia; these are mostly interactive. Friends like to compete over silly things like the names of the original cast of *DeGrassi Junior High* or even over facts about quantum physics. People interact with the computer as well as with each other. They can compare their results amongst themselves and learn more about one another as part of an evening's fun. 3

The most interesting thing about "social computers" is how much their owners are like them. Computers and young people multitask, doing several things at one time. We listen to MP3s while getting ready to download a whole 4 evening's music. [Be specific.] Sometimes, friends check their favourite sites or message boards, print pages, and chat, all together, all at the same time. Or people play games as they chat with players online and compare scores on other sites. Multitasking this way means everyone shares an overall experience while individuals or pairs of people pursue their own interests.

The computer and its human companions play well together. Perhaps this generation has discovered how humans and technology can live "happily ever after."   5

Comment

After Julian finished the first draft, he was able to put it aside until the next day. You will benefit as well if you can allow some time between finishing a draft and starting to revise.

Review Julian's first draft as you work on the activity that follows.

• • • • • Activity

1. **The Introductory Paragraph**
   Julian's first paragraph is very brief. He knows he can develop his opening further in a later draft. Which sentence contains his thesis statement? What is the purpose of his other sentence?

2. **The Body Paragraphs**
   a. One of Julian's paragraphs lacks a topic sentence. This is something he can return to and fix later. Which paragraph's opening sentence is not a topic sentence? Why?
   b. Later in his essay, Julian cannot think of details to add to clarify an example, so he makes a note to himself to "be specific." Which subtopic in which paragraph needs more attention, and why?
   c. Julian uses the third-person point of view because he wants his essay to focus on his ideas. In this first draft, there are some sentences in which the first-person point of view is used. In which sentences is there a shift in pronoun point of view? How could these sentences be revised?

3. **The Concluding Paragraph**
   Julian's conclusion is very brief because he will expand it later. What could he add to make it more complete?

STAGE 4: REVISING

Revising is as essential to the writing process as prewriting, outlining, and writing the first draft. Revising means literally "re-seeing." It means that you rewrite a paper, building upon what has already been done in order to make it stronger. Some professional writers say, "writing *is* revising." In other words, writing a first draft simply produces raw material, and the work of revising, restructuring, and restating is what creates a good piece of writing. Another writer sees revising this way: "It's like cleaning house—getting rid of all the junk and putting things in the right order."

Too many students think that a first draft *is* the paper. They start to become writers when they realize that revising a rough draft three or four times is often the heart of writing.

General Revising Tips

- First, set your first draft aside for a while. Then, come back to it with a fresh, more objective point of view.
- Second, work from typed or printed text. You'll be able to see your work more impartially than if you were just looking at your own familiar handwriting.
- Next, read your draft aloud. Hearing how your writing sounds will help you spot problems with meaning and style.
- Finally, as you do all these things, add your thoughts and changes above the lines or in the margins of your paper. Your written comments can serve as a guide when you work on the next draft. When you revise on the computer, create a "Notes" section at the end of your document for your comments.

Computer *Writing Tip*

Revising works best on the computer. When you are revising drafts of an essay, try the following:

- Save your first draft as "Draft #1." Now, copy and paste this draft into a new document. Save this document as "Draft #2," and so on.
- When you start revising "Draft #2," change the colour of your text for your revising work. To do so in Word, find the capital A with a bar beneath it on the toolbars. Simply click on the inverted triangle to the right of the A, and choose a colour. Using two colours makes your changes instantly visible. Follow the same procedure with each successive draft.
- Each time you revise a draft, print a copy to which you can refer and on which you can make manual changes as these occur to you.

Revising is not a "one-shot" activity. Here, its basic goals and activities are introduced. Chapter 6 will give you specific instruction and practice in revision. When you revise or "re-see" your essay draft, you are not examining one aspect of your writing, but three: your *content*, your *sentences*, and finally, your *language*—grammar, punctuation, and spelling. Never try to revise all three levels of your writing at once. Instead, leave yourself enough time to give your ideas and language the attention they deserve.

Revising Content

When revising the content of your essay, ask the following questions related to the specific bases for effective essay writing:

1 Is my essay **unified**?

- Do I have a thesis that is clearly stated or implied in the introductory paragraph of my essay?
- Do all of my supporting paragraphs relate directly to my thesis?

2 Is my essay **supported**?

- Are there three separate supporting points for the thesis?
- Do I have plenty of specific evidence for each of the three supporting points?

3 Is my essay **organized** and **coherent**?

- Do I have an interesting introduction, a solid conclusion, and an accurate title?
- Do I have a clear method of organizing my essay?
- Do I use transitions and other connecting words?

Chapters 3 and 4 will give you practice in achieving **unity**, **support**, and **coherence** in your writing.

As you revise the essay's content, consider again purpose and audience. When you read through your first draft, is your purpose still the same? Is it clear, and suggested by the thesis statement? Review the content with regard to your intended audience: are the points and support relevant to that audience? Are there any special terms that your audience would need explained?

Revising Sentences

The fourth base for effective essay writing is effective sentence skills. Refer to the pages listed as you ask yourself the following questions:

1 Do I use parallel structure to balance my words and ideas? (pages 93–94)

2 Do I have a consistent point of view? (pages 94–96)

3 Do I use specific words? (pages 96–98)

4 Do I use active verbs? (pages 99–100)

5 Do I use words effectively by avoiding wordiness? (pages 100–101)

6 Do I vary my sentences? (pages 101–107)

Chapter 5 will give you further practice in achieving **effective sentence skills**.

Editing

After you have revised your essay for content and style, you are ready to edit for errors in grammar, punctuation, and spelling. Students often find it hard to edit an essay carefully. They have put so much work into their writing (or so little) that it is almost painful for them to look at it one more time. Remember that eliminating sentence-level mistakes will improve an average essay and help ensure a strong mark on a good essay. Further, as you get into the habit of checking your essays, you will also get into the habit of using the sentence skills consistently. They are an integral part of clear and effective writing.

Chapter 5 and the handbook of sentence skills in Part 4 (pages 323–454) will serve as guides while you are editing your essay for mistakes in **grammar**, **punctuation**, and **spelling**.

PRACTICE IN PREWRITING, OUTLINING, AND REVISING

You now have a good overview of the writing process, from prewriting to first draft, to revising and editing. To reinforce the information about the writing process that you have learned in this chapter, you can now work through the following activities:

1   Prewriting

• • • **Review Activity**

Below are examples of how the four prewriting techniques discussed in this chapter could be used to develop material for the topic "Problems of Combining Work and College or University."

1. Identify each technique by writing F (for freewriting), Q (for questioning), L (for list making), or C (for clustering) in the answer space.

2. Some of these examples demonstrate a second stage of prewriting. Which examples do so, and why?

_____ Never enough time
Miss parties with people in my program
Had to study (only two free hours a night)
Gave up activities with friends
No time to rewrite essays
Can't stay at school to play video games or talk
Friends don't call me to go out any more
Sunday no longer relaxing day—have to study
Missing sleep I need
Marks aren't as good as they could be
Can't just watch TV weeknights
Really need the money
Tired when I sit down to study at nine o'clock

_____ <u>What</u> are some of the problems of combining work and college?

Schoolwork suffers because I don't have enough time to study, rewrite essays, or do enough research. I've had to give up things I enjoy, like sleep and ball hockey. I don't have any time for RTV parties because I have to go to work as soon as my last class is over.

<u>How</u> have these problems changed my life?

My marks are not as good as they were when I wasn't working. Some of my friends have stopped calling me. My relationship with a girl I liked fell apart because I couldn't spend time with her. I miss TV.

<u>What</u> do I do in a typical day?

I get up at 7 to make an 8 a.m. class. I have classes till 1:30 two days, and those days, I drive to Sobeys where I work till 8. I drive home, shower, and by then it's around 9. So I only have a couple of hours those days to study—work on media assignments, read textbooks, write essays. The other two days, I finish classes at 5 and work till 9, so schoolwork's a write-off. I work all day Friday, and I just don't do schoolwork Friday night.

<u>Why</u> do I keep up this schedule?

I can't pay tuition or buy books without working, and I need a diploma and airtime practice to try to get into radio. If I can make this work, I'll be doing what I've always wanted to do.

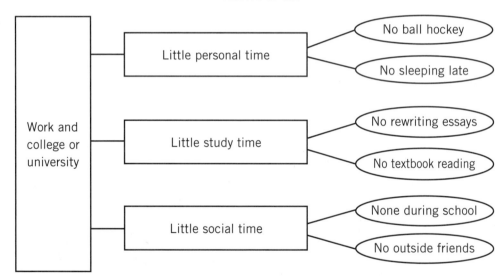

It's hard working and going to school at the same time. I never realized how much I'd have to give up. I won't be quitting my job because I need every dollar just to stay in my program. And the people at Sobeys are pretty good. I've had to give up a lot more than I thought. We used to play ball hockey and touch football every Sunday. It was fun and we'd go for drinks afterwards. Sundays are now just catch-up time for assignments for my courses, and I don't know how I'll handle an internship when that comes up. I have to catch up because I don't get home until 8 some days and nearly 10 other days, and I work all day Friday and Saturday. So even two nights a week, I can't get to school work until after 9 p.m. I've been up since before 7 a.m. Sometimes I write an English essay in half an hour and don't even read it over. I feel that I'm missing out on a lot in college. The other day, people I like were sitting outside listening to music and talking after class. I would have given anything to stay and not to have to go to work. I almost called in sick. I used to get invited to parties. I don't much anymore. My friends know I never make it, so nobody bothers. I can't sleep late on weekends or watch TV during the week.

2 Outlining

● ● ● ● **Review Activity 1**

One key to effective outlining is the ability to distinguish between the **major ideas** and **details** that fit under those ideas. In each of the three lists below, major and supporting items are mixed together. Put the items into logical order by filling in the outline that follows each list.

1. **Thesis:** My high school had three problem areas.

Involved with drugs	a. _____
Leaky ceilings	(1) _____
Students	(2) _____
Unwilling to help after class	b. _____
Formed cliques	(1) _____
Teachers	(2) _____
Buildings	c. _____
Poorly equipped gym	(1) _____
Much too strict	(2) _____

2. **Thesis:** Working as a dishwasher in a restaurant was my worst job.

Ten-hour shifts	a. _____
Heat in kitchen	(1) _____
Working conditions	(2) _____
Minimum wage	b. _____
Hours changed every week	(1) _____
No bonus for overtime	(2) _____
Hours	c. _____
Pay	(1) _____
Noisy work area	(2) _____

3. **Thesis:** Joining an aerobics class has many benefits.

Make new friends	a. _____
Reduce mental stress	(1) _____
Social benefits	(2) _____
Strengthens heart	b. _____
Improves self-image	(1) _____
Mental benefits	(2) _____

Tones muscles   c. _____

Meet interesting instructors   (1) _____

Physical benefits   (2) _____

• • • • Review Activity 2

Read the essay below, and outline it in the spaces provided. Write out the thesis and topic sentences. Then, summarize, in a few words, the supporting material that fits under each topic sentence. One item is summarized for you as an example.

Losing Touch

Steve, a typical Canadian, stays home on workdays. He turns on his computer in order to hook up with the office, and he sends and receives work during the day by e-mail and fax. Evenings, he listens to his iPod, slides a DVD into his computer's player, or spends time online. On many days, Steve doesn't talk to any other human beings, and he doesn't see any people except those on a screen. Steve is imaginary, but his lifestyle is very common. More and more, the inventions of modern technology seem to be cutting us off from contact with our fellow human beings.

Thesis: _____

_____

The world of business is one area in which technology is isolating us. Many people now work alone at home. With access to a large central computer, employees such as secretaries, insurance agents, and accountants do their jobs at terminals in their own homes. They no longer actually have to see the people they're dealing with. In addition, employees are often paid in an impersonal way. Workers' salaries are automatically credited to their bank accounts, eliminating the need for paycheques. Fewer people stand in line with their co-workers to receive their pay or cash their cheques. Finally, personal banking is now a detached process. Customers interact with machines or pay bills online rather than contacting people to deposit or withdraw money from their accounts. Even some bank loans are approved or rejected, not in an interview with a loan officer, but through a display on a bank's website.

First topic sentence: _____

_____

Support: 1. *Many people now work alone at home.* _____

          2. _____

          3. _____

             a. _____

             b. _____

Another area that technology is changing is entertainment. Music, for instance, was once a group experience. People listened to music in concert halls or at small social gatherings. For many people now, however, music is a solitary experience. Walking along the street or sitting in their living rooms, they wear headphones to build a wall of music around them. Movie entertainment is changing, too. Movies used to be social events. Now, fewer people are going out to see a movie. Many more choose to wait for a film to appear on DVD or cable television or download it online. Instead of being involved with the laughter, applause, or hisses of the audience, viewers watch movies in the isolation of their own living rooms.

Second topic sentence: _____

_____

Support: 1. _____

           2. _____

Education is the third important area in which technology is separating us from others. From elementary schools to colleges and universities, students spend more and more time sitting by themselves in front of computers. The computers give them feedback, while teachers spend more time checking how applications work and less time interacting with their classes. A similar problem occurs in homes. As families buy multiple computers, increasing numbers of students practise their math and reading skills with software programs instead of with their friends, brothers and sisters, and parents. Last, alienation is occurring as a result of CDs, DVDs and online information. People buy CDs and DVDs or go online to learn about subjects such as cooking, real estate investment, speaking, and speed-reading. They then practise their skills at home rather than taking group classes in which rich human interaction can occur.

Third topic sentence: _____

_____

Support: 1. _____

           2. _____

           3. _____

Technology, then, seems to be driving human beings apart. Soon, people may no longer need to communicate with other human beings in order to do their work, entertain themselves, or pursue an education. Technology will be the co-worker and companion of the future.

3   Revising

• • • • **Review Activity**

Below is the second supporting paragraph from the personal essay "Problems of Combining Work and College or University" that is featured in the prewriting activity. The paragraph is shown in four different stages of development: (1) the first full draft, (2) the revised second draft, (3) the edited next-to-final draft, and (4) the final draft. The four stages appear in scrambled order. Write the number 1 in the answer blank for the first full draft, and number the remaining stages in sequence.

_____ I have also given up some personal pleasures in my life. On sundays for example I used to play street hockey or football, now I use the entire day to study. Good old-fashioned sleep is another lost pleasure for me now. I never get as much as I like because their just isn't time. Finally I miss having the chance to just sit in front of the TV, on weeknights. In order to watch the whole line-up of movies and sports that I used to watch regularly. These sound like small pleasures, but you realize how important they are when you have to give them up.

_____ I've had to give up pleasures in my life. I use to spend sundays playing games, now I have to study. I'm the sort of person who needs a lot of sleep, but I don't have the time for that either. Sleeping nine or ten hours a night wouldn't be unusual for me. Pyschologists say that each individual need a different amount of sleep, some people need as little as five hours, some need as much as nine or ten. So I'm not unusual in that. But Ive given up that pleasure too. And I can't watch the TV shows I use to enjoy. This is another personal pleasure Ive lost because of doing work and school. These may seem like small things, but you realize how good they are when you give them up.

_____ Besides missing the social side of college life, I've also had to give up some of my special personal pleasures. I used to spend Sunday afternoons, for example, playing street hockey or touch football depending on the season. Now, I use Sunday as a catch-up day for my studies. Another pleasure I've lost is sleeping late on days off and weekends. I once loved mornings when I could check the clock, bury my head in the pillow, and drift off for another hour. These days, I'm forced to crawl out of bed the minute the alarm lets out its piercing ring. Finally, I no longer have the chance to just sit watching the movies and sports shows that I enjoy. A leisurely night of playing Full Auto 2 or renting a Jet Li movie is a pleasure of the past for me now.

_____ Besides missing the social side of college life, I've also had to give up some of my special personal pleasures. I used to spend sunday afternoons, for example playing street hockey or touch football, depending on the season. Now I use the day as a catch-up day for my studies. Another pleasure I've lost is sleeping late on days off and weekends. I once loved mornings when I could check the clock, then burying my head in the pillow, and you drift off to sleep for another hour. These days I'm forced to get out of bed the minute the alarm lets out it's ring. Finally I no longer have the chance to just sit watching the movies and also programs with sports that I enjoy. A leisurely night of playing Full Auto 2 or renting a Jet Li movie is a pleasure of the past for me now.

Final Questions

- Which errors in some of the drafts are the most distracting to the reader?

_____

- Which sample paragraph conveys its meaning most clearly? Why?

_____

_____

_____

CHECKLIST OF LEARNING OUTCOMES FOR CHAPTER 2

To ensure that you have understood and met the learning outcomes for this chapter, answer the following questions:

✓ What steps are involved in creating an effective essay?

✓ What are the main stages in the writing process? Which of these stages do you feel you need to work on most? Why?

✓ What are the four prewriting techniques? Which techniques might suit which types of thinkers?

✓ Why is outlining essential? What are the four parts of a formal outline?

✓ What is the main focus in writing a first draft, and why?

✓ Explain the statement, "Writing is revising."

CHAPTER 3

Thesis and Support Development: The First and Second Steps in Essay Writing

Chapter 2 introduced you to the stages of the writing process. Working on any writing task stage by stage will make you a more effective writer. As you practise taking one stage at a time, you will begin to follow this pattern automatically whenever you have a writing assignment, and you will develop your own variations on the techniques involved.

This chapter returns to the steps that lead to effective essay writing. It focuses on the first two steps in writing a solid essay: **advancing a thesis** and **supporting it with specific evidence**. You will learn how to narrow a subject, write a strong thesis statement, and then defend your thesis statement with specific and adequate details.

STEP 1: BEGIN WITH A POINT OR THESIS

Understanding Thesis Statements

In Chapter 1, you learned that effective essays are based upon a **thesis statement** or main point that a writer wishes to express. This central idea is usually presented in an essay's introductory paragraph.

A good thesis statement does two things at least. First, it tells readers an essay's *topic*. Second, it presents the writer's attitude, opinion, idea, or *viewpoint* about that topic. By showing what aspects of a topic will be pursued, it, therefore, controls the content of an essay. Consider the following thesis statement:

Owning a pet has several important benefits.

In this thesis statement, the topic is *owning a pet*; the writer's main point or viewpoint is that owning a pet *has several important benefits*. Readers know immediately that the essay to follow will discuss only these benefits and why they are important.

Activity

For each thesis statement below, single-underline the topic and double-underline the viewpoint that the writer wishes to express about the topic.

Examples   Hiphop culture is artistically important for three main reasons.

The Internet has led to new kinds of frustration in everyday life.

1. The college cafeteria would be greatly improved if several changes were made.

2. Celebrities often make poor role models because of the way they dress, talk, and behave.

3. My first night as a security guard turned out to be one of the most frightening experiences of my life.

4. Canada's one-tier health care system is superior to the U.S. system in terms of cost, equity, and efficiency.

5. Reality shows have changed network television in three ways.

6. Stress in the fast-food workplace has led to serious physical, psychological, and emotional problems for employees.

7. Canadian advertisers target young people to market fashion, personal electronics, and beer.

8. Living in downtown Thunder Bay has certain advantages over living in the suburbs.

9. Before moving away from home, every person should have mastered certain key life skills.

10. Independently owned stores are preferable to chain stores for a variety of reasons.

Writing a Good Thesis Statement I

Now that you see how thesis statements work, you can prepare to write your own. Occasionally, you may be assigned an "essay-size topic," but more often you will be given a general subject or asked to choose a topic for your essay. In these writing situations, try the techniques that follow.

First, follow your interests. Perhaps the truest writing rules are, "Write about what interests you," and "Write about what you know." When you write with interest and understanding about your topic, your energy flows through to your words, and your confidence helps you to relax and concentrate on expressing your ideas.

Second, do some research. You may be asked to write on subjects about which you have little experience or knowledge. Before working out a reasonable topic for such assignments, you should carry out some research to find and explore your area of interest. The chapter "Research Skills" on pages 268–291 will show you how to find relevant, appropriate information.

Third, to write a good thesis, regardless of the topic, you must find an "angle," a limited aspect of your subject that is neither too broad nor too narrow. Suppose, for example, that an instructor asks you to write an essay about the Internet. A subject like the Internet is just too large to cover in a five-hundred word essay. What you need to do, then, is limit your subject, as the box below demonstrates. Narrow it down until you have a thesis that you can deal with specifically in five hundred words or so. In the box that follows are (1) several general subjects, (2) limited versions of those general subjects (or topics), and (3) thesis statements about the limited subjects.

General Subject	Limited Subject/Topic	Thesis (Limited Subject/Topic + One Viewpoint on It)
The Internet	E-mail	E-mail is a great way to stay in touch with friends.
Family	Older sister	My older sister helped me overcome my shyness.
Television	Cable stations	Cable stations offer more interesting kinds of programs than network TV.
College	Studying post-secondary English	Studying post-secondary English is very different from taking high school English.
Sports	Players' salaries	High players' salaries are bad for the game, anger the fans, and distort the values children are developing.

Activity 1

Sometimes a subject must go through several stages before it is narrow enough to write about. What follows are four lists reflecting several stages that writers went through in moving from a general subject to a narrow thesis statement. Number the stages in each list from 1 to 5, with 1 indicating the most general stage and 5 marking the thesis.

List 1

_____ Teachers

_____ Education

_____ Math teacher

_____ My high school math teacher was peculiar sometimes.

_____ High school math teacher

List 2

_____ Bicycles

_____ Dangers of bike riding

_____ Recreation

_____ Recreational vehicles

_____ Bike riding in the city is a dangerous activity.

List 3	*List 4*
_____ Retail companies	_____ Camping
_____ Supermarket	_____ First camping trip
_____ Dealing with customers	_____ Summer vacation
_____ Working in a supermarket	_____ First camping trips can be disastrous experiences.
_____ Student workers must learn how to handle unpleasant supermarket customers.	_____ Vacations

● ● ● ● **Activity 2**

Write *TN* in the space next to the two statements that are *too narrow* to be developed in an essay. Write *TB* in the space next to the two statements that are *too broad* to be covered in an essay. Then, in the spaces provided, revise each too-narrow statement and each too-broad statement to make them each an effective thesis statement.

_____   1. The way Western society treats elderly people is unbelievable.

_____

_____   2. Up to 70 per cent of teenage marriages end in divorce.

_____

_____   3. Action must be taken against drugs.

_____

_____   4. I failed my microbiology course.

_____

Writing a Good Thesis Statement II

The thesis statement, for a brief essay, should express your point clearly in a single sentence. However, this is not as easy as it seems, and there are some common mistakes that may undermine your chances of writing an effective essay. One mistake is to simply announce a topic rather than present a viewpoint on it. A second mistake is to write a thesis that is too broad, and a third is to write a thesis that is too narrow. A fourth error is to write a thesis containing more than one idea.

Here are some guidelines for avoiding such mistakes and writing good thesis statements:

1   Write statements with a viewpoint, not announcements.

The subject of this essay will be soccer fans.
We will discuss closings of Vancouver high schools.
Video-gaming is the concern of this essay.

In this first group, the sentences are not thesis statements but simply announcements of a topic. Each sentence is also redundant. In other words, readers do not need to be told, "The subject is . . . ." Most important, sentences such as "The subject of this essay will be skateboarding" do not make any point about their subject. The following sentences, based on those above, represent effective thesis statements.

Soccer fans are the most loyal sports fans of all.
The possible closing of some Vancouver high schools is cause for concern.
Players develop some useful skills from time spent on video-gaming.

2   Avoid broad, general statements.

Disease has shaped human history.
Insects are fascinating creatures.
Since the beginning of time, men and women have been very different.

In the above examples, each statement is too broad to be supported adequately in a five-hundred word essay. Thesis statements that begin with phrases like, "All over the world . . ." or "People everywhere . . ." belong to this category. The following sentences, based on the topics above, represent effective thesis statements.

Plane travel has made local diseases global problems.
Strength, organization, and communication make ants one of nature's most successful insects.
Men and women are often treated very differently in entry-level positions.

3   Avoid statements of fact that require no support.

There are no speed bumps in the west end of Kitchener.
Since 2007, Wolfville, Nova Scotia, no longer hosts the Atlantic Theatre Festival.
Students bring phones to classes.

In this third group, there is no room in any of the three statements for support to be given. For instance, "There are no speed bumps in the west end of Kitchener" is a simple fact that does not present a viewpoint or require any support. Such a statement is sometimes called a "dead-end" statement. Remember, a thesis statement must be broad enough to require support in an essay. The following sentences, based on those above, represent successful thesis statements.

Speed bumps should be installed in the west end of Kitchener for several reasons.
Wolfville, Nova Scotia's Atlantic Theatre Festival finally closed down for a number of reasons.
Students' phones are unnecessary distractions during classes.

4   Make sure statements develop only one idea.

One of the most serious problems affecting young people today is bullying, and it is time more kids learned the value of helping others.
Studying with others has several benefits, but it also has drawbacks and can be difficult to schedule.
The "baby boom" generation has had many advantages, but it also faces many problems.

In this fourth group, each statement contains more than one idea. For instance, "One of the most serious problems affecting young people today is bullying, and it is time more kids learned the value of helping people" clearly has two separate ideas ("One of the most serious problems affecting young people today is bullying" and "it is time more kids learned the value of helping others"). Remember, the point of an essay is to communicate a *single* main idea to readers. The following sentences, based on each of the examples above, represent more effective thesis statements.

One of the most serious problems affecting young people today is bullying.
Studying with others has several benefits.
The "baby boom" generation has enjoyed many advantages.

Activity 1

Write *A* beside the statement in each pair that is an *announcement* rather than a thesis statement. Write *OK* beside the statement that is a clear, limited point that could be developed in an essay.

_____   1. a. This essay will discuss the people you meet in exercise class.

_____   b. The kinds of workout clothes worn in most aerobics classes identify "jocks," "strugglers," and "shopping fanatics."

_____   2. a. Step-parents may make mistakes in the process of trying to win the respect and affection of their stepchildren.

_____   b. My thesis in this essay is relationships between step-parents and stepchildren.

Activity 2

Write *TN* beside the statement in each pair that is *too narrow* to be developed in an essay. Write *OK* beside the statement that is a clear, limited point.

_____   1. a. I had squash, tomatoes, and corn in my garden last summer.

_____   b. Vegetable gardening can be a frustrating hobby.

_____   2. a. The main road into our town is lined with fast-food outlets.

_____   b. For several reasons, the number of fast-food chain outlets should not be allowed to dominate main roads.

Activity 3

Write *TB* beside the statement in each pair that is *too broad* to be developed in an essay. Write *OK* beside the statement that is a clear, limited point.

_____   1. a. In many ways, sports are an important part of Canadian life.

_____   b. Widespread gambling in some Canadian cities has changed people's lives for the worse.

_____   2. a. Toy ads on television teach children to be greedy, competitive, and snobbish.

_____   b. Advertising has bad effects on all of society.

Activity 4

Write *2* beside the statement in each pair that contains *more than one idea*. Write *OK* beside the statement that is a clear, limited point.

_____   1. a. Working with old people changes stereotyped ideas about the elderly.

_____   b. My life has moved in new directions since the rewarding job I had working with older people last summer.

_____   2. a. Some of the most entertaining ads on television today are those on the cable shopping stations.

_____   b. Although ads on cable shopping stations are often misleading, they can still be very entertaining.

STEP 2: SUPPORT THE THESIS WITH SPECIFIC EVIDENCE

The Importance of Supporting Points

The first essential step in writing a successful essay is to formulate a clearly stated thesis. The second basic step is to defend or explain the thesis with supporting points and details.

To begin, write down a brief version of your thesis, and then jot down the three points that will support that thesis.

A brief outline looks simple, but developing one often requires careful thinking. Once you have determined the supporting points, you will be in an excellent position to prepare a formal outline and write an effective essay.

Activities in this section will give you practice in the crucial skill of supporting your essay.

Activity

Complete the brief outlines that follow by adding a third logical supporting point (*c*) that will parallel the two already provided (*a* and *b*).

1. The first day on a new job can be nerve-wracking.
   a. Meeting new people
   b. Finding your way around a new place

   c. _____

2. The resource centre in McLellan Hall is the worst place to study.
   a. Uncomfortable chairs and tables
   b. Little privacy

   c. _____

3. College and university students should live at home.
   a. Stay in touch with family
   b. Avoid distractions of residence or apartment life

   c. _____

The Relationship of Thesis to Supporting Points

Thesis statements make points that writers support or prove in different ways. Supporting points are often called the "reasons why" a thesis is true. In the Activity above, this is the case, whether it concerns the "reasons why" a "first day on a new job" is "nerve-wracking," the "resource centre" is the "worst place to study," or "college and university students should live at home."

Another way to discover effective support for a thesis is to analyze the type of support the thesis requires. Do this by turning your trial thesis into a thesis question and examining the types of answers you provide. In the previous chapter, you were introduced to the "thesis question" (pages 25–28). A thesis question may begin with the interrogative or question word(s), "What is . . . ?" as in the following example:

Trial Thesis: The main characteristics of a good friend never vary.

Thesis Question: *What are* the main characteristics of a good friend?

Trial Answers to Thesis Question: The main characteristics of a good friend are *honesty, kindness . . .*

Form of Support: "Honesty" and "kindness" are synonymous with "characteristics" here.
(a) The writer of this thesis may look for *examples* of "honesty" and "kindness" in certain individuals' behaviour as specific details to expand on his support.
(b) Alternatively, the writer could *define* in detail what "honesty" and "kindness" mean in those supporting points' paragraphs (perhaps including some examples in his or her definitions).

Many thesis questions begin with the interrogative word "Why?", as is the case below:

Trial Thesis: The rise in the value of the Canadian dollar may cause problems.

Thesis Question: *Why* will the rise in value of the Canadian dollar cause problems?

Trial Answers to Thesis Question: The rise in value in the Canadian dollar will cause problems *because costs of manufacturing products for export will rise, because Canada will no longer be a bargain for American tourists, and . . .*

Form of Support: Asking a "Why?" thesis question will result in a list of *causes* or *effects* of the situation that is the thesis subject, as above.

Note: This writer could also have composed a "What?" thesis question here: i.e., "*What* problems will the rise in the Canadian dollar cause?"

The trial answers then, will be, as in the first example above, a list of nouns that are the problems (synonyms): *high-priced export products, loss of tourist dollars, . . .*

Sometimes a "Why?" thesis question will be best answered by *descriptions of places or items.* Example 2 in the Activity above demonstrates this. An example follows:

Trial Thesis: Cuts in provincial funding have led to deteriorating conditions in schools.

Thesis Question: *What kind of deteriorating conditions* have cuts in provincial funding led to in schools?

Trial Answers to Thesis Question: Deteriorating conditions such as *peeling paint in classrooms, dirty washrooms with flooded floors, and . . .*

Form of Support: Here, to prove the point that funding cuts have caused schools to become run down, *examples* with vivid *description* are good choices for effective support: they show readers why the writer's thesis is valid.

Note: This writer could also have decided on a thesis question using the interrogative word "How?": "*How* have cuts in provincial funding led to deteriorating conditions in schools?"

The trial answers will be *causes* of the conditions, if the thesis question begins with the word "How?"; for example, *no funding for building maintenance, layoffs of janitorial staff, . . .*

When you work on generating support for your trial thesis or on a brief three-point outline, try a variety of thesis questions first. Compare the types of trial answers you receive, then try some second-stage listing or brainstorming (pages 29–30) to find out which set of trial answers generates the most details for you. Remember, there is no one "correct" interrogative word—trying thesis questions will show you where your viewpoint and ideas lie.

The value of the thesis question method of finding supporting points is that it exposes the type of logic that underlies your supporting points. This method also eliminates the likelihood of repeated or unrelated supporting points.

The Importance of *Specific* Details

Just as a thesis must be developed with three (or more) supporting points, those supporting points must be developed with specific details. Specific details have two key values. First of all, details excite the reader's interest. They make writing a pleasure to read. Second, details serve to explain a writer's points. They give the evidence needed for us to understand the general ideas.

Too often, body paragraphs in essays contain vague generalities rather than specific supporting details. Here is what one of the paragraphs in "Socializing Computers" would have looked like if the writer had not used specific details to explain his main point.

> Ultimately, though, the most interesting reason why computers are such regularly invited guests reflects the effect they have had on their owners' minds. Computers and young people are both multitaskers; they do several things at one time. While listening to MP3s, people set up their evening's music downloads, surf the Web, print screens, and chat. Others play games while they chat and compare scores on sites. Such social multitasking allows everyone in the room to be sharing the same overall experience while individuals or pairs of people pursue particular interests of their own.

Compare the paragraph above with the fourth paragraph in Julian Lopez's finished essay on page 13. The effective paragraph in the finished essay provides details that clarify the point that young people are comfortable doing many specific activities at once. Julian *specifies* which MP3s these people might be listening to; he *specifies* which online activities they are enjoying as they multitask together. These specific details and examples bring Julian's ideas to life. They enable the reading audience to visualize such an evening more clearly. Reading audiences are hooked by specifics; they do not enjoy guessing what writers mean.

Activity

Write *S* in front of the selections below that provide specific evidence to support the opening point. Write *X* in front of the selections that follow the opening point with vague, general, wordy sentences.

_____   1. Building a wooden deck can be an enjoyable project only if you take certain precautions.

> Get a building permit before you start. If you don't have one, you may have to tear down everything you've built when the local building inspector learns of your project. Also, purchase pressure-treated lumber for any posts that will be set into the ground. Ordinary wood, not treated with preservatives, will eventually rot from contact with soil and moisture.

_____   2. Software piracy is a huge blow to the income of software developers.

> They are losing millions due to theft. Anyone with an Internet connection and basic Googling skills can pirate software from the Internet. Now this software, often called "Warez," has improved over the years. But yesterday's P2P music sharing and today's Bit Torrents piracy offer the same temptation, getting something for nothing. It is probable that two out of three people have pirated software on their personal computers and do not think of it as theft.

_____   3. Some things are worse when they're "improved."

> A good cheesecake, for one thing, is perfect. It doesn't need pineapple, cherries, blueberries, or whipped cream smeared all over it. Plain old blue jeans, the ones with five pockets and copper rivets, are perfect too. Manufacturers only made them worse when they made them "low rise" or made them baggy-fitting and plastered logos and designers' names all over them.

_____   4. Pets can be more trouble than children.

> Dogs, unlike children, cannot be completely housebroken. If overexcited or nervous, they are prone to accidents. Unlike children, dogs can never grow up enough to take care of themselves when their owners go away, or take themselves to the vet for a checkup. Parents may stop worrying about their grown children, but they will always have to hire pet-sitters and walkers for their dogs.

The Importance of *Adequate* Details

Readers cannot "see what you see" in your mind, so your words must do the work of showing your thoughts clearly. This is where providing *enough* specifics becomes important. Finding details and examples to explain and clarify a supporting point shows your readers what you "see" that makes that point true for you.

A common and serious problem in students' writing is inadequate development. You must provide enough specific details to fully support the point in a body paragraph. You could not, for example, include a paragraph about a friend's unreliability and provide only a one- or two-sentence example. Without additional support, your paragraph would be underdeveloped, and readers would not "see" why your friend was unreliable.

Students may try to disguise unsupported paragraphs through repetition and generalities. Do not fall into this "wordiness trap." Be prepared to do the hard work needed to ensure that each paragraph has solid support.

Activity 1

Both of the following body paragraphs were written on the same topic, and both have clear opening points. Which one is adequately developed? Which one uses mostly vague, general, wordy sentences to conceal the fact that it lacks specific details?

Turn Back Time? No Thanks

Most men wouldn't want to be teenage boys again, mainly because no one would want to worry about talking to teenage girls. If they are honest, men in their twenties still remember how nerve-wracking it was to call a girl and ask her out. Just the act of dialing a girl's phone number was enough to start a teenage boy's heart racing, make the hand holding the receiver clammy with sweat, and make his face turn bright red. Next, there were the terrors about how his voice would sound if he actually got around to speaking. Would he sound like some casual deep-voiced deejay or squeak like a squirrel? Then, there were questions he tortured himself with: Would she be at home? If she was, would she want to talk? And if she did talk, what was there to say? Most men who admit to these worries remember a date or two that sometimes resulted from one of these calls. They still squirm as they recall staring straight ahead and silent at an empty movie screen, clutching a popcorn box, waiting for the film to start. These men are probably still wondering why those girls ever went out with them in the first place.

Terror and the Teenage Male

Most men wouldn't want to be teenagers again—first of all, because they wouldn't want to worry about talking to teenage girls. Calling up a girl to ask her out was something they completely dreaded. They felt like they didn't know what words to express or how to express them. Every time they got on the phone, they would have all kinds of nervous symptoms. They worried a great deal about how they would sound and had a lot of doubts about the girl's reaction. And when they occasionally managed to call up a girl to go out, the evening turned out to be a disaster. Too unsure of themselves to act in a confident way, they couldn't think of anything to say and just kept quiet. Looking back on these memories, most men feel like they made fools of themselves. Agonizing over their attempts at relationships with the opposite sex made adolescence a very uncomfortable time.

The first paragraph offers a series of detailed examples of the author's memories of nerve-wracking experiences, as a teenager, with girls. The second paragraph, on the other hand, is underdeveloped. For instance, it makes only the general observation, "Every time they got on the phone, they would have all kinds of nervous symptoms," while the first paragraph specifies, "Just the act of dialing a girl's phone number was enough to start a teenage boy's heart racing, make the hand holding the receiver clammy with sweat . . . ." The second paragraph makes the general statement, "They worried a great deal about how they would sound," whereas in the first paragraph, the author wonders if his voice will "sound like some casual deep-voiced deejay or squeak like a squirrel." In the second paragraph, there is also no specific description of an evening that turned into a disaster. In summary, the second paragraph lacks the full, detailed support needed to develop its opening point convincingly.

Activity 2

Take a few minutes to write a paragraph in the third-person point of view (like those above) supporting the point, "Managing time is a student's biggest problem." Afterward, form small groups, and read your paragraphs aloud. The best received paragraphs are almost sure to be those with plenty of specific details.

Note that when writing in the "invisible" third-person point of view, close attention to specific details is even more essential.

PRACTICE IN ADVANCING AND SUPPORTING A THESIS

You now know the two most important steps in competent essay writing: (1) advancing a point, or thesis, and (2) supporting that thesis. The purpose of this section is to expand and strengthen your understanding of these two basic steps. You will first work through a series of activities on *developing* a thesis. These include:

1 Identifying the parts of an essay

2 Evaluating thesis statements

3 Completing thesis statements

4 Writing thesis statements

You will then sharpen your understanding of how to *support* a thesis effectively by working through the following activities:

5 Providing specific evidence

6 Identifying adequate supporting evidence

7 Adding details to complete an essay

1   Identifying the Parts of an Essay

• • • • **Review Activity 1**

Each group below contains one topic, one thesis statement, and two supporting sentences. In the space provided, label each item as follows:

> **T—topic**
>
> **TH—thesis statement**
>
> **S—supporting sentence**

Group 1

_____ a. TV forces politicians to focus more on appearance than substance.

_____ b. Television is having an increasingly strong impact on the way Canadian elections are conducted.

_____ c. The time and expense involved in creating commercials for parties and leaders might be better used in serving the public.

_____ d. Television

Group 2

_____ a. Canadian colleges are more affordable than most universities.

_____ b. There are several advantages to attending a college rather than a university.

_____ c. Colleges

_____ d. Canadian colleges typically offer more career-oriented programs and more internship opportunities than do universities.

Group 3

_____ a. Medicine

_____ b. Antibiotics have enabled doctors to control many diseases that were once fatal.

_____ c. Organ transplants have prolonged the lives of thousands of people.

_____ d. Advances in modern medicine have had great success in helping people.

Group 4

_____ a. Reading

_____ b. There are steps parents can take to encourage their children to enjoy reading.

_____ c. The adults' own behaviour can influence children to become readers.

_____ d. Parents can make sure the physical environment of the home encourages reading.

Review Activity 2

The essay below, "Blogs: Creating Communities," has no indentations between paragraphs. Read this essay carefully, and then <u>double-underline</u> the thesis and <u>single-underline</u> the topic sentence for each of the three supporting paragraphs and the first sentence of the conclusion. Write the numbers of those sentences in the spaces provided at the end.

Blogs: Creating Communities

[1]Blogs are changing the way individuals and groups communicate with each other. [2]Personal blogs with text, video, and sound files, are interactive views of people's lives. [3]News blogs instantly update global viewers about important events and people's reactions to them. [4]Corporate and institutional blogs are focuses of social and consumer interest. [5]With all these types of blogs, viewers are able to select those that suit their purposes and interests. [6]First and most popular are personal blogs. [7]Casual, curious viewers with social interests visit these. [8]As viewers and posters, they visit friends' or families' blogs, or snoop into the sites of unknown bloggers, just to share others' lives. [9]But LiveJournal, Blogspot, and Facebook are more than just online diaries, they are new ways of using interactivity. [10]One Dutch student in a Vancouver college's graphic design program stays in daily contact with family via their blog, and continues to work for the family's advertising agency with discussions and image proposals. [11]Others use personal blogs as artistic outlets and ways to make professional connections, such as the Humber College animation graduate whose videos caught the attention of Nelvana Studios and resulted in a career. [12]Personal blogs may attract mostly the curious, but they offer opportunities to learn and understand others, and their uses are still developing. [13]Next in popularity and viewership are news and media blogs, which attract serious and habitual visitors and contributors. [14]Worldwide, these surpass network and cable news services in instant delivery of world events news. [15]Devoted news followers become keen judges of source reliability; they check information by comparing CNN with Metafilter or check Ryerson University's "Review of Journalism" blog. [16]As news blog readers sift through many sites, they gain a wider view of events. [17]During Hurricane Katrina, New Orleans bloggers offered more accurate and faster information than did television or cable reporting. [18]Similarly, cell phone photographs of the 2005 London bombings and messages uploaded to news blogs reached families and interested viewers much faster than traditional media could have. [19]Newsblog viewers, who return to preferred sources to follow through on reportage and offer opinions, participate in events and coverage in a new way. [20]Last, and least familiar to most people, are institutional or organizational blogs, maintained by libraries, political parties, educational institutions, and corporations. Users and viewers consult these and post their ideas for personal, educational, or career purposes. [21]Creating, consulting, and posting to these blogs is based on specific needs, and is done for definite purposes. [22]Public Relations firm Hill and Knowlton's blogs provide information and receive input on new media use for corporations. [23]Employees

use institutional blogs to set up, staff, and promote conferences, and involve participants in presentation content and feedback. [24]College and university administrators set up blogs to present policy proposals and ideas for discussion and consultation among faculty and students. [25]Special-interest groups like the Sikh Students of Canada maintain blogs to create and strengthen communities as well. [26]Likewise, fundraising groups like WorldVision use blogs to raise awareness and involve people as active participants. [27]Viewers and contributors to institutional blogs are motivated by special interests or career concerns. [28]They interact purposefully and engage with varied communities of like-minded people. [29]Today, blogs number in the millions and are more than an Internet fad. [30]They are interactive windows into all the worlds within one world, places where people see each other, share themselves, learn about each other and events, and create connections and communities.

Thesis statement in "Blogs: Creating Communities": _____

Topic sentence of first supporting paragraph: _____

Topic sentence of second supporting paragraph: _____

Topic sentence of third supporting paragraph: _____

First sentence of the conclusion: _____

2   Evaluating Thesis Statements

Review Activity 1

Write *A* beside the statement in each pair that is *an announcement* rather than a thesis statement. Write *OK* beside the statement that is a clear, limited point that could be developed in an essay.

_____ 1. a. This essay will discuss personal electronics popular with students.

_____   b. The personal electronics that students enjoy most are cell phones, PDAs, and MP3 players.

_____ 2. a. Winnipeg made several errors in city planning in its downtown area.

_____   b. The thesis of this essay concerns Winnipeg's downtown development.

_____ 3. a. A period of loneliness can teach people to use their creativity, sort out their values, and feel empathy for others.

_____   b. Loneliness is the subject of this paper.

Review Activity 2

Write *TN* beside the statement in each pair that is *too narrow* to be developed in an essay. Write *OK* beside the statement that is a clear, limited point.

_____ 1. a. There are now more single-parent households in Vancouver than ever before.

_____   b. Organization is the key to being a successful single parent.

_____ 2. a. First jobs have a way of training people out of bad work habits.

_____   b. Because I was late for work yesterday, I lost an hour's pay and was called in to see the supervisor.

_____ 3. a. Legalized gambling has been financially beneficial to Ontario cities and towns.

_____   b. Gambling is now an ordinary entertainment option for many people.

Review Activity 3

Write *TB* beside the statement in each pair that is *too broad* to be developed in an essay. Write *OK* beside the statement that is a clear, limited point.

_____ 1. a. Modern life makes people suspicious and unfriendly.

_____   b. One frightening experience on a street at night made me a more cautious person in several ways.

_____ 2. a. Learning new skills can be difficult and frustrating.

_____   b. Learning to write takes work, patience, and a sense of humour.

_____ 3. a. College is a challenge.

_____   b. Just getting through first semester teaches several lessons that are not taught in the classroom.

Review Activity 4

Write *2* beside the statement in each pair that contains *more than one idea*. Write *OK* beside the statement that is a clear, limited point.

_____ 1. a. Rappers like Kanye West and Lupe Fiasco are taking rap music in new directions.

_____   b. Even though rappers like Kanye West and Lupe Fiasco are changing rap music, most of the popular artists portray tired stereotypes.

_____ 2. a. My roommate and I are compatible in most ways, but we still have conflicts most of the time.

_____   b. My roommate has his own unique system for studying, doing assignments, and cleaning.

_____ 3. a. Cycling to school is a great alternative to taking the bus, even if inhaling exhaust is a problem.

_____   b. Cycling to school beats taking the bus, keeps students in shape, and relaxes them on the ride home.

3 Completing Thesis Statements

Review Activity

Complete the following thesis statements by adding a third supporting point that will parallel the two already provided. Parallel structure means that items or phrases in a list follow the same grammatical pattern. You might first want to check the section on parallel structure (pages 93–94) to make sure you understand parallel form.

1. Being a successful vegetarian is difficult because cooking meals takes more effort, menu choices in restaurants are limited, and _____ .

2. A good salesperson needs to like people, to be aggressive, and _____ .

3. Rather than blame themselves for failing courses, students blame the instructor, their advisors, and even _____ .

4. Anyone who buys an old house and is planning to fix it up should be prepared to put in a lot of time, hard work, and _____ .

5. Older cars may use too much gas, have worn tires, and _____ .

6. Second semesters in college or university can be more challenging than first semesters because of heavier workloads, more difficult courses, and

    _____ .

7. Living together as a couple while still in school is often a mistake because both partners are trying to finish their education, the couple may have trouble handling their money, and _____ .

8. Some restaurant patrons seem to leave their honesty, their cleanliness, and their _____ at home.

4 | Writing Thesis Statements

• • • • Review Activity 1

The following activity will give you practice in writing an effective essay thesis—one that is neither too broad nor too narrow. It will also help you understand the logical relationship between a thesis and its topic sentences.

For each item below, write an appropriate thesis statement.

1. Thesis: _____
    a. Soccer, and sports fans in general, hang some interesting items from their rearview mirrors.
    b. Sentimental drivers, on the other hand, have a completely different set of ornaments for their mirrors.
    c. Last, the serious motorist is the person who will display only absolutely necessary items up front.

2. Thesis: _____
    a. Attending a college offers the chance to prepare for a career or further educational demands.
    b. If the college is nearby, there are no room-and-board costs.

    c. The course credits that are accumulated can be transferred to most universities.

3. Thesis: _____

    a. First, avoid the snack aisle of the supermarket.
    b. Then, limit the number of snacks per day.
    c. Finally, bag up and hide snacks in a container at the back of a cupboard.

4. Thesis: _____

    a. The first pattern a student may notice is repeatedly worrying about one concern.
    b. "Free-floating anxiety," or worry that just will not go away, is also a concern.
    c. Avoidance behaviours, though, are the most frequent reason why students seek counselling.

The following two activities will give you practice in distinguishing general from limited subjects while writing a thesis.

Review Activity 2

Look carefully at the six general and six limited subjects below. Then, write a thesis for four of the limited subjects.

Hint: To create a thesis, ask yourself, "What point do I want to make about _____?"

General Subject	*Limited Subject*
1. Apartment	1. Sharing an apartment with a roommate
2. Self-improvement	2. Behaviour toward others
3. Eating out	3. Fast-food restaurants
4. Automobiles	4. Bad driving habits
5. Health	5. Regular exercise
6. The Internet	6. Chatrooms

Review Activity 3: Group Work

Below is a list of six general subjects. Form groups of four, and as a group, choose four of the subjects; write a limited version of each; and then produce a thesis statement for each. Compare your limited subjects and thesis statements with other groups.

General Subject	*Limited Subject*
1. Pets	_____
2. Television	_____
3. Work	_____
4. Post-secondary education	_____
5. Vacations	_____
6. Cooking	_____

5 Providing Specific Evidence

• • • • Review Activity

Provide three details that logically support each of the following points. Your details can be drawn from your own experience, or they can be invented. State your details briefly in several words rather than in complete sentences.

Example   Learning to cook every day for themselves is a challenge for students living on their own.

1. *Shopping takes time and energy.*

2. *Cooking nutritious meals takes work.*

3. *Tempting and expensive to order out.*

1. The evening was a disaster.

_____

_____

_____

2. Cell phones are essential to personal safety.

_____

_____

_____

3. Independence has several challenges.

_____

_____

_____

4. There are several ways in which students can earn extra cash.

_____

_____

_____

6 Identifying Adequate Supporting Evidence

• • • • Review Activity

The following body paragraphs were taken from student essays. Two of the paragraphs provide sufficient details to support their topic sentences convincingly. Write *AD* for *adequate development* beside those paragraphs. Three paragraphs use vague, wordy, general, or irrelevant sentences instead of real supporting details. Write *U* for *underdeveloped* beside those paragraphs.

_____ 1. Another consideration in adopting a dog is the cost. Initial fees for shots and a licence might add up to $80. Annual visits to the vet for heartworm pills, rabies or distemper shots, and general checkups could cost $100 or more. Then, there is the cost of food. A 10 kilogram bag of dry food costs at least $20. A large dog can eat that much in a couple of weeks.

_____ 2. People can be cruel to pets simply by being thoughtless. They don't think about a pet's needs or simply ignore those needs. It never occurs to them that their pet can be experiencing a great deal of discomfort as a result of their failure to be sensitive. The cruelty is a result of the basic lack of attention and concern—qualities that should be there but aren't.

_____ 3. Prime-time programming on Canadian television would benefit from some major changes. Some shows should be eliminated completely. In fact, all the boring "made in Canada" shows that no one watches should be cancelled. Commercials, Canadian or American, should be changed so people could watch them without wanting to channel-surf or turn off the TV. Expand good, popular programs so that viewers stay loyal to Canadian programming and interests. The ideal Canadian prime-time lineup would be a big improvement over what is now available on the three major networks.

_____ 4. A friend's rudeness is much more damaging than a stranger's. When a friend says sharply, "I don't have time to talk to you just now," people feel hurt instead of angry. When a friend shows up late for lunch or a shopping trip, with no good reason, it is easy to feel taken for granted. Worst, though, is when a friend pretends to be listening, but his or her wandering eyes show a lack of attention. Then, anyone feels betrayed. Friends, after all, are supposed to make up for the thoughtless cruelties of strangers.

_____ 5. Sitting in the cockpit of a real plane, one of the school's Cessnas, after weeks of sitting in model cockpits and flight simulators, is an exciting experience. Students feel momentarily confident because everything is familiar; all the controls are exactly where they were in "rehearsals." The familiarity soon joins forces with excitement, though, when the instructor begins to take them step-by-step through the pre-flight checks. The repetition of the pattern of words "fuel gauge" and "altimeter" works like a soothing charm—everything will be fine. It is only when the student aviator knows that the instructor's next words will be, "Start it up," that he or she feels a flutter of nervous anticipation. The instructor's voice is confident and normal. The student's stomach tightens. And he or she reaches for the starter, ready to fly . . . or just taxi down the runway.

7 Adding Details to Complete an Essay

• • • • **Review Activity**

In the following essay, specific details are needed to explain the ideas in the supporting paragraphs. Using the spaces provided, add a sentence or two of clear, convincing details for each supporting idea.

Life Without Computers

INTRODUCTION

INTRODUCTION

When computers break down, they have a way of throwing their owners into states of confusion. How will they get their e-mail? How will they do their paperwork? How will they check up on their favourite episodes of *Heroes* or *The Y & R* on YouTube? How will they play all those MP3s they haven't put on the iPod yet? After an hour or so of panic, most people go into a state of grieving, as if they have lost a friend. They morosely look up a technician, suffer through estimates of repair time and cost, and feel generally glum and at a loss for what to do. Then, as if a cloud is lifting, they find that their release from keyboard and screen bondage is a stroke of good luck. They discover "real life" again, pursuing neglected personal interests, catching up with postponed chores, and spending time with other people.

FIRST SUPPORTING PARAGRAPH

First of all, with no computer or Internet to retreat to, the temporarily computer-deprived person finds hours to rediscover personal interests. The stack of books on the bedside table looks inviting again.

_____

_____

_____

Then, the computer-free person rediscovers hobbies and crafts projects abandoned months ago.

_____

_____

_____

In addition, instead of procrastinating with completing that overdue report, the guilt-ridden person starts making notes by hand.

_____

_____

_____

SECOND SUPPORTING PARAGRAPH

Second, each person who has ever suffered computer-loss realizes the same thing: all that household work did not go away, it is just waiting to be tackled.

_____

_____

_____

They check out those pages of to-do lists.

_____

_____

_____

And organizing closets, drawers, and CD and DVD collections suddenly looks like an idea whose time has come.

_____

_____

_____

THIRD SUPPORTING PARAGRAPH

    Finally, and probably most important, life without a computer leads to rediscovering other people. Instead of lurking at a desk in the cool glow of a screen, the tech-free person starts spending time with others in the house.

_____

_____

_____

Moreover, simple social pastimes like board games and cards start to be fun again.

_____

_____

_____

Because there is no itch to check the inbox, and no distracting websites to view, the urge to actually go out and see friends suddenly seems appealing.

_____

_____

_____

CONCLUSION

    Once the computer is successfully repaired and returned home, people may not be ready or able to severely limit their use of it. But they do have a better sense of how much of their time it can take over. They may become more selective about the time they spend with their computers, choosing to keep up with "real life" activities, obligations, and human companions. By doing so, they will have learned valuable lessons about balancing living and technology.

CHECKLIST OF LEARNING OUTCOMES FOR CHAPTER 3

To ensure that you have understood and met the learning outcomes for this chapter, answer the following questions:

✓ Why must writers narrow a general subject before writing a workable thesis?

✓ What are the four most common errors encountered in writing thesis statements?

✓ Why does a brief outline help you see if your main points truly support your thesis?

✓ What two characteristics must supporting details have in order to be effective, and why?

CHAPTER 4

Coherence and Structure:
The Third Step in Essay Writing

L E A R N I N G   O U T C O M E S

After reading this chapter and working through its activities, you will

- write essays that are coherent at three levels;
- choose an effective pattern of organization for your support;
- use various techniques to achieve coherence;
- connect the paragraphs within an essay;

- use a variety of transitions to signal your intentions and create connections between your sentences;
- write engaging and appropriate introductory paragraphs for your essays;
- write effective conclusions for your essays.

Chapter 3 demonstrated the first two steps in writing an effective essay: advancing a thesis and supporting it with specific evidence. This chapter deals with the third step for writing effective essays: **organizing and connecting your specific evidence**. You will learn how to organize your essay's content, and you will practise techniques to connect the supporting information. You'll also see how to start an essay with a suitable introductory paragraph and how to finish it with a well-rounded concluding paragraph. In short, you will learn how to create a **coherent** essay that flows smoothly from beginning to end.

STEP 3: ORGANIZE AND CONNECT THE SPECIFIC EVIDENCE

Achieving Coherence

Coherence, the third base for an effective essay, is the product of conscious choices you make in the drafting and revising stages of the writing process. Coherence means literally "sticking together." Coherent writing shows your reading audience the sequence of and connections between your ideas.

To achieve coherence, you must make conscious choices at two stages of writing your essay. First, as you outline and draft, *organize* your entire essay according to an order appropriate to your subject and purpose. Second, as you write and revise, *connect* paragraphs and sentences with appropriate methods of transition.

The boxed summary below provides techniques for achieving coherence at the essay level, paragraph level, and sentence level.

---

1. **Creating Coherence at the Essay Level**
   - Write an effective thesis statement with clear, logically derived supporting points.
   - Indicate the order for the supporting points of your thesis, and sustain that order through your topic sentences and body paragraphs.
2. **Creating Coherence at the Paragraph Level**
   - Write topic sentences that refer clearly to the thesis point covered by that paragraph.
   - Write topic sentences that cover all details and examples found in each body paragraph.
   - Reinforce, with transitional phrases or structures, the order established in your thesis in each body paragraph's topic sentence.
   - Use transitions in each body paragraph's topic sentence that connect the reader to the ending of the previous paragraph.
   - Use transitional phrases or structures in each body paragraph's closing sentence that connect that paragraph with the one that follows.
   - Use concluding or summarizing phrases to signal your concluding paragraph.
3. **Creating Coherence at the Sentence Level**
   - Within each paragraph of your essay, use transitional phrases or devices to show relationships between sentences and to mark changes of direction, meaning, or emphasis.

A well-organized essay whose ideas flow logically and relate clearly to each other meets the three bases of **unity**, **support**, and **coherence**. This chapter will emphasize coherence as it shows you how to organize and connect supporting details by the use of (1) common methods of organization, and (2) transitions, transitional sentences, and other transitional structures.

Common Methods of Organization

Knowing how to write an effective thesis statement gives you a good start on achieving coherence at the essay level. Your thesis and supporting points guide readers' expectations about what will be found in your body paragraphs.

Achieving coherence at both the essay and paragraph levels first involves choosing an appropriate *order* for your supporting points and details. When you order your points in a way that follows logically from the point your thesis makes, you *organize* your support in a way that reassures your readers that your paragraphs follow in a reasonable sequence.

Time order and **emphatic order** are two common methods used to organize an essay and its supporting points and details. (You will learn more specific methods of development in Part 2 of this book.)

Time or **chronological order** simply means that paragraphs are ordered and details are listed as they occur in time. *First* this is done; *next* this; *then* this; *after* that, this; and so on. Here is a four-point outline of an essay in this book in which time order is used. Note that the thesis in this brief outline lists its supporting points in time order and that the topic-sentence points follow this order.

Thesis: However, for success in exercise, you should follow a simple plan consisting of arranging the time, making preparations, and warming up properly.

> 1. To begin with, set aside a regular hour for exercise.
> 2. Next, prepare for your exercise session.
> 3. Finally, do a series of warm-up activities.

Which words and phrases in the topic sentences above indicate that the writer will use time order?

Here is one supporting paragraph from the essay:

> Next, prepare for your exercise session. You do this, first, by not eating or drinking anything for an hour before the session. Why risk an upset stomach? Then, dress comfortably in something that allows you to move freely. Because you'll be in your own home, there's no need to invest in a high-fashion outfit. A loose T-shirt and shorts are good. A bathing suit is great in summer, and, in winter, a set of long underwear is warm and comfortable. If your hair tends to flop in your eyes, pin it back or wear a headband or scarf. After dressing, prepare the exercise area. Turn off the phone and lock the door to prevent interruptions. Shove the coffee table out of the way so that you won't bruise yourself on it. Finally, get out the simple materials you'll need to exercise on.

Note: To use time order effectively, list your details in time sequence in your outline and draft. Then, see where transitions ("signal words") could be used to clarify or emphasize the order or your details.

Which five words in the sentences in the paragraph above help to show the time order or sequence?

Emphatic order is sometimes described as "saving the best till last." It is a way to put emphasis on the most interesting or important detail by placing it in the last part of a paragraph or in the final supporting paragraph of an essay. (When all the details seem equal in importance, the writer should use an order that seems logical or appropriate to the content.) Final positions are the most emphatic because the reader is most likely to remember the last thing read. *Finally, last of all,* and *most important* are typical words or phrases showing emphasis. Here is a brief outline of an essay in this book that uses emphatic order:

Thesis: Celebrities lead very stressful lives.

> 1. For one thing, celebrities don't have the privacy an ordinary person does.
> 2. In addition, celebrities are under constant pressure.
> 3. Most important, celebrities must deal with the stress of being in constant danger.

Which words or phrases in the topic sentences above help to show emphatic order and achieve coherence at the essay level?

Here is the third supporting paragraph from the essay:

> Most important, celebrities must deal with the stress of being in constant danger. The friendly grabs, hugs, and kisses of enthusiastic fans can quickly turn into uncontrolled assaults on a celebrity's hair, clothes, and car. Photographers must bear some responsibility for hounding celebrities such as Britney Spears and Lindsay Lohan. Whether or not their actions add to the behaviour and substance abuse problems is unclear but they cause stress. And celebrity can lead to deranged and even lethal attacks. The near-fatal stabbing of the late George Harrison in his home and the murder of John Lennon came about because two unbalanced people developed obsessions with the two Beatles. Famous people must live with the fact that they are always fair game— and never out of season.

Which words in the paragraph above are used to mark the most emphatic or most important detail?

Note: Some essays combine time order and emphatic order—mainly because their subject matter suits the combination.

● ● ● ● ● Activity

A Read the essay titled "Accessing a Challenge" in Chapter 8. Which method of organization or combination of methods has the writer chosen? Why, based on the subject of the essay, might the writer have chosen this method or combination of methods? How does the writer indicate the method of organization?

B Read the essay titled "Movie Night in the Bush" in Chapter 10. Which method of organization or combination of methods has the writer chosen? Why, based on the subject of the essay, might the writer have chosen this method or combination of methods? How does the writer indicate the method of organization?

TRANSITIONS AND TRANSITIONAL SENTENCES

1 Transitions

Transitions have two functions:

1. Transitions signal the direction of a writer's thought.
2. Transitions are links or "bridges" between paragraphs, sentences, and thoughts. They are like the road signs that guide travellers.

Transitions are not "ornaments" or additional words to be plugged in mechanically at certain points in an essay. Transitional words, phrases, and sentences form essential parts of an essay's coherent and logical movement from one idea to the next. Writers often know the direction in which they are proceeding, but the reading audience may not; transitions are essential to a reader's clear understanding of an essay.

Sentence-Level Transitions

To achieve coherence *within* paragraphs, at the sentence level, use transitions to guide readers through the logical pattern behind your arrangement of examples, details, and sentences. Transitions *show* readers what you mean more accurately.

In the box below are some common transitions, grouped according to the kind of signal they give to readers. Note that certain words provide more than one kind of signal.

Addition signals: one, first of all, second, the third reason, also, next, another, and, in addition, moreover, furthermore, finally, last of all

Time signals: first, then, next, after, as, before, while, meanwhile, soon, now, during, finally

Space signals: next to, across, on the opposite side, to the left, to the right, above, below, near(by)

Change-of-direction signals: but, however, yet, in contrast, although, otherwise, still, on the contrary, on the other hand

Illustration signals: for example, for instance, specifically, as an illustration, once, such as

Conclusion signals: therefore, consequently, thus, then, as a result, in summary, to conclude, last of all, finally

---

Activity

1. To sharpen your awareness of sentence-level transitions, underline the three *addition* signals in the following selection:

> Traditional advice about making more time for difficult courses by choosing so-called easy ones does not usually work. Hallway gossip is full of such legendary courses with nearly no assignments, group tests, and dozing professors. One way to see if one of these courses exists is to ask those students in the hall exactly which subject got them an A after 20 percent attendance. See how vague their answers will be. Chances are that this course has suddenly disappeared from the calendar. Also, inquire around the same hallway to see which professors lecture from the same notes each semester and give the same tests. Just as suddenly no one will remember the name of any professor who actually does anything that predictable. Another time-tested strategy for picking easy courses is to check the college or university calendar for the telltale course titles that signal a quick trip through a painless subject—courses like "The History of Nutrition" or "Disco and Society." Now, follow up by reading the course outlines for those easy-sounding subjects . . . three essays each, a report or two, and some research assignments. So much for traditional advice; just give in, register for what's required, and do the work.

2. Underline the four *time* signals in the following selection:

> After you've snagged the job of TV sports reporter, you have to begin working on the details of your image. First, invest in two or three truly loud sports jackets. Look for gigantic plaid patterns in odd colour combinations like purple and green or orange and blue; your role model is Don Cherry. These should become familiar enough to viewers that they will associate that crazy jacket with that dynamic sportscaster. Next, try to cultivate a distinctive voice that will be just annoying enough to be memorable. A nasal whine or a gravelly growl will do it. Be sure to speak only in tough, punchy sentences that seem to be punctuated with imaginary exclamation points. Finally, you must share lots of pompous, obnoxious opinions with your viewers. Your tone of voice must convey the hidden message, "I dare anyone to disagree with me." If the home teams lose, call them bums. If players strike, talk sarcastically about the good old days. If a sports franchise leaves town, say, "Good riddance."

3. Underline the three *space* signals in the following selection:

> The vegetable bin of the refrigerator contained an assortment of weird-looking items. Next to a shrivelled, white-coated lemon was a pair of oranges covered with blue fuzz. To the right of the oranges was a bunch of carrots that had begun to sprout points, spikes, knobs, and tendrils. The carrots drooped limply over a bundle of celery. Near the carrots was a net bag of onions; each onion had sent curling shoots through the net until the whole thing resembled a mass of green spaghetti. The most horrible item, though, was a head of lettuce that had turned into a pool of brown goo. It had seeped out of its bag and coated the bottom of the bin with a sticky, evil-smelling liquid.

4. Underline the two *change-of-direction* signals in the following selection:

> Taking small children on vacation sounds like a wonderful experience for the entire family. But vacations can be scary or emotionally overwhelming times for children. When children are taken away from their usual routine and brought to an unfamiliar place, they can become very frightened. That strange bed in the motel room or the unusual noises in Grandma's spare bedroom may cause nightmares. On vacations, too, children usually clamour to do as many things in one day as they can and to stay up past their usual bedtime. And, since it is vacation time, parents may decide to give in to the children's demands. A parental attitude like this, however, can lead to problems. After a sixteen-hour day of touring the amusement park, eating in a restaurant, and seeing a movie, children can experience sensory and emotional overload. They become cranky, unhappy, or even rebellious and angry.

5. Underline the two *illustration* signals in the following selection:

> Supermarkets also use psychology to encourage people to buy. For example, in most supermarkets, the milk and the bread are either at opposite ends of the store or located far away from the first aisle. Even if a shopper stops at the market only for staples like these, he or she must

pass hundreds of items in order to reach them. The odds are that instead of leaving with just a litre of milk, the shopper leaves with additional purchases as well. Special displays, such as a pyramid of canned green beans in an aisle or a large end display of cartons of paper towels, also increase sales. Because people assume that these items are a good buy, they may pick them up. However, they may not even be on sale! Store managers know that the customer is automatically attracted to a display like this, and they will use it to move an overstocked product.

6. Underline the two *conclusion* signals in the following selection:

To sum up, because data storage formats have evolved so significantly, maintaining a clean hard drive is easier than ever. Twenty years ago, computer users—worried about power outage-related file losses—saved 50 to 200 KB of data on flimsy five-inch diskettes. These certainly helped unclog those little 186K hard drives, but they were fragile and prone to damage caused by handling or exposure to extreme temperatures. Increasing use of computers in the early 1990s led to improvements, notably the 3.5-inch hard-case disk. Often requiring the addition of a new drive on home PCs, they were durable and stored nearly ten times more data than a five-inch diskette. As all disks record information magnetically, however, their content could still be erased by contact with magnets. The smaller disks still degraded or the information simply disappeared after unpredictable lengths of time. By the end of the decade, the heavily cased Zip drive delivered over one gigabyte of storage to accommodate larger image and text files, again for the price of a new drive. Its reign was cut short by the entry of CD technology into the file-storage race; CD and DVD slots and writers became common on new computers. Unfortunately, readable-only CDs "seal" their contents and do not allow re-entry, and while writable CDs can be erased and reused, both versions are easily scratched. Finally, the "key" to safe, portable data appeared. The tiny USB key, with up to 10 MB capacity, can hold as much as many computers' hard drives. "Keys" require only standard USB ports, no formatting, and easily store huge MP3, image, video, and text files. So, now that the hard drive is clean, and the computer is running quickly, just do not lose the keys.

2   Transitional Sentences

Paragraph-Level Transitions

To achieve coherence *between* the paragraphs in your essay, use transitional material at the "entrance" and "exit" points of each paragraph.

Following are the specific uses for transitions and transitional sentences at the paragraph level, as indicated in the box on page 72:

- Topic sentence transitions: signal and reinforce time sequence, emphatic order, or another order **or** link the paragraph topic with the preceding paragraph's topic
- Concluding sentence transitions: link to the following paragraph's topic **or** suggest a conclusion

● ● ● ● **Activity**

Below is a brief sentence outline of an essay. The second and third topic sentences serve as transitional, or linking, sentences. Each reminds us of the point in the preceding paragraph while announcing the point to be developed in the current paragraph. In the spaces provided, add the words needed to complete the second and third topic sentences. If possible, try to write a concluding sentence that leads into the paragraph that follows.

THESIS   The most important values parents can teach are the importance of family support, hard work, and a good education.

FIRST SUPPORTING PARAGRAPH

> First, good parents show that family members should stick together, especially in times of trouble . . .

SECOND SUPPORTING PARAGRAPH

> In addition to teaching about the importance of _____
>
> _____ ,
>
> parents should emphasize the value of _____
>
> _____ . . . .

THIRD SUPPORTING PARAGRAPH

> Along with the value of _____
>
> _____ ,
>
> parents must stress the importance of _____
>
> _____ . . . .

3   Other Transitional Structures

In addition to transitions and transitional sentences, there are three other kinds of connecting words and phrases that help tie together the specific evidence in an essay: repeated words, pronouns, and synonyms. Each will be discussed in turn.

Repeated Words

Many of us have been taught not to repeat ourselves in writing. However, repeating *key* words helps tie together the flow of thought in an essay. Below, repeated words remind readers of the selection's central idea.

One reason for studying <u>psychology</u> is to help parents deal with children. Perhaps a young daughter refuses to go to bed when parents want her to and bursts into tears at the least mention of "lights out." A little knowledge of <u>psychology</u> comes in handy. Offer her a choice of staying up until 7:30 p.m. with her parents or going upstairs and playing until 8:00 p.m. Since she gets to make the choice, she does not feel so powerless and will not resist. <u>Psychology</u> is also useful in rewarding a child for a job well done. Instead of telling a ten-year-old son what a good boy he is when he makes his own bed, tell him how neat it looks, how pleasing it is, and how proud of him you are for doing it by himself. The <u>psychology</u> books all say that being a good boy is much harder to live up to than doing one job well.

Pronouns

Pronouns (*he, she, it, you, they*) are another way to connect ideas. Also, using pronouns in place of other words can help you avoid needless repetition. (Note, however, that pronouns should be used with care to avoid the problems described on pages 95–96.) Here is a selection that makes good use of pronouns:

> Another way for people to economize at an amusement park is to bring <u>their</u> own food. If <u>they</u> pack a nourishing, well-balanced lunch of cold chicken, carrot sticks, and fruit, <u>they</u> will avoid having to pay high prices for hamburgers and hot dogs. They won't eat as many calories. Also, instead of filling up on soft drinks, <u>they</u> should bring a thermos of iced tea. Iced tea is more refreshing than pop, and <u>it</u> is a great deal cheaper. Every dollar that is not spent at a refreshment stand is <u>one</u> that can be spent on another ride.

Synonyms

Using synonyms (words alike in meaning) can also help move the reader clearly from one thought to the next. In addition, the use of synonyms increases variety and interest by avoiding needless repetition. To strengthen your vocabulary and widen your knowledge of synonyms, you may use either a thesaurus or the "thesaurus" function under "tools" on your word-processing program. A print thesaurus and the thesaurus tool in Word both supply you with lists of *alternate words or phrases* for any word you look up. Alternate words or phrases or synonyms are not exact substitute-words, though. Neither type of thesaurus can understand the shadings of meaning a synonym presents. Only you know the exact meaning you intend. Always have a dictionary at hand when you use either type of thesaurus; check the meaning of any word presented to you as a synonym.

Note the synonyms for *method* in the following selection:

> There are several methods of fundraising that work well with small organizations. One <u>technique</u> is to hold an auction, with everyone either contributing an item from home or obtaining a donation from a sympathetic local merchant. Because all the merchandise, including the services of the auctioneer, has been donated, the entire proceeds can be placed in the organization's treasury. A second fundraising <u>procedure</u> is a car wash. Club members and their children get together on a Saturday and wash all the cars in the neighbourhood for a few dollars apiece. A final, time-tested <u>way</u> to raise money is to hold a bake sale, with each family contributing homemade cookies, brownies, layer cakes, or cupcakes. Sold by the piece or by the box, these baked goods will satisfyingly fill both the stomach and the pocketbook.

• • • • • **Activity**

Read the selection below, and then answer the questions about it that follow.

[1]Merrill writes of one winter day in an Alberta childhood during the Depression, and life today seems luxurious by comparison. [2]In his home, there was only a wood-burning cookstove in the kitchen to warm the entire house. [3]Waking first in the morning cold, his father braved the bitter chill to relight the iron range for the day. [4]Children put off rising as long as possible, and did not dress in their bedrooms. [5]Because there was no indoor plumbing, the family washed their hands and faces in bedroom water basins; this was difficult because the water froze overnight. [6]Even in the kitchen, with the stove lit for a time, the children could see their breath as they shivered into their school clothes. [7]Their one-room school did not offer much relief from the cold either. [8]Students wore fingerless woollen mitts, which left their fingers free but covered their palms and wrists. [9]Even with these, they occasionally suffered chilblains, something nearly unknown today. [10]The throbbing swellings on their hands made writing a painful process. [11]Like most families, they spent late afternoons and evenings in the warm kitchen; the rest of the house was unbearably frigid. [12]The only comforts at the end of the day were the hot water bottles and bricks heated in the oven that warmed the family's bitterly cold bedclothes for a short time.

1. How many times is the key word *cold* repeated? _____

2. Write the words in sentence 3 that are used as a synonym for *cookstove:*

   _____; write the words in sentence 10 that are used as a synonym

   for *chilblains:* _____; write the word in sentence 11 that is used as

   a synonym for *cold:* _____.

INTRODUCTIONS, CONCLUSIONS, AND TITLES

So far, this chapter has discussed ways to organize and connect the supporting paragraphs and sentences of an essay. A well-organized and coherent essay, however, also needs a strong introductory paragraph, an effective concluding paragraph, and a good title.

Introductory Paragraph

A good introduction welcomes readers, makes them comfortable with your subject, states your thesis, and leads on to your first body paragraph. Below is a list of the functions of a well-written introductory paragraph.

1 It attracts the readers' interest, encouraging them to continue reading the essay.

2 It supplies any background information that may be needed to understand the essay.

3 It presents a thesis statement. This clear, direct statement of the main idea of the essay usually appears near the end of the introductory paragraph.

4 It indicates a plan of development. In this plan of development, the major supporting points for the thesis are listed in the order in which they will be presented. In some cases, the thesis and plan of development appear in the same sentence. (However, writers sometimes choose to omit the plan of development, relying instead on a general phrase that suggests the support and pattern of development for the essay.)

Common Methods of Introduction

As you think about how to open your essay, take into account three considerations: your purpose, your audience, and your essay's general tone. If your purpose is to explain the seriousness of some issue, and you are uncertain of your audience's understanding of its gravity or relation to their concerns, you will likely avoid a general opening and proceed immediately to establish this issue's relevance to readers. Should you be writing about a subject about which your audience knows little, always open with enough background context information to help them understand your essay's content. Alternatively, if your subject suits a light approach, you could take a humorous tone and begin with an amusing anecdote or question.

Here are some common methods of introduction. Use any one method, or a combination of methods, as appropriate, to introduce your subject in an interesting way to the reader.

1 *Begin with a somewhat general statement of your topic, and narrow it down to your thesis statement.* General statements ease the reader into your thesis statement by first introducing the topic. However, avoid sweeping statements like "the world these days," or "humanity's problems"; no writer could handle such huge concepts. In the example below, the writer talks generally about diets and then narrows down to comments on a specific diet.

> Bookstore shelves today are crammed with dozens of different diet books. The Canadian public seems willing to try any sort of diet, especially the ones that promise instant, miraculous results. As well, authors are more than willing to invent new fad diets to cash in on this craze. Unfortunately, some of these fad diets are ineffective or even unsafe. One of the worst fad diets is the "Zone Diet." It is expensive, doesn't achieve the results it claims, and is a sure route to poor nutrition.

2 *Supply background information or context.* Much of your future career writing and some assignments will cover subject matter unfamiliar to general readers. Therefore, this introductory approach is relevant and useful. Whenever you write about a subject that is not considered "general knowledge" or "common interest," use this method. If you must explain an accounting method, analyze some technical process, or evaluate a software's operation, always give enough background information to make your thesis and support clear and understandable to your audience.

MP3 is a three-character code seen everywhere today—even phones have MP3 players. But what is an MP3? It is simply a compressed file containing audio data: music, speech, or sound effects. Sounds are compressed from earlier, larger WAV files for quick downloading. MP3 compression matches twelve bytes of a WAV with only a single byte in MP3 format; it removes sounds people's ears cannot usually hear. MP3s are an important part of the downsizing of media since they offer good audio quality, they are divisible into cuts or sections, and they are very portable—just like cell phones.

3 *Start with an idea or situation that is the opposite of the one you will develop.* This approach works because your readers will be surprised, and then intrigued, by the contrast between the opening idea and the thesis that follows it.

Technology is the enemy of art. The keyboard and mouse are no substitutes for the artist's hand and eye. Screens are not galleries. Or, so traditionalists would say. But what about displaying the artist's work, or getting feedback on it? Here, the emergence of online art communities has been a blessing for anyone looking to share their craft and garner critique from fellow artists. PHP Scripting has created user-friendly interfaces containing easy-to-upload personal galleries, comment features and message boards. One popular example of this type of free-for-all art community is www.deviantart.com. Millions of users submit art pieces every minute for show and/or critique. With its wide range of categories including digital art, photography, analog painting, and more, artists are bound to find similar creators in their genre to inspire them and commune with.

4 *Explain the importance of your topic to the reader.* If you can convince your readers that the subject applies to them, or is something they should know more about, they will want to keep reading.

Diseases like scarlet fever and whooping cough used to kill more young children than any other illness. Today, however, child mortality due to disease has been almost completely eliminated by medical science. Instead, car accidents are the number one killer of children. Most of the children fatally injured in car accidents were not protected by car seats, belts, or restraints of any kind. Several steps must be taken to reduce the serious dangers car accidents pose to children.

5 *Use an incident or brief story.* Stories are naturally interesting. They appeal to a reader's curiosity. In your introduction, an anecdote will grab the reader's attention right away. The story should be brief and should be related to your main idea. The incident in the story can be something that happened to you or something you have heard or read about. Students who must write reports for courses in Business and Human Services disciplines find anecdotal introductions useful.

On a Friday morning in a large Canadian mall, a woman buys two sweatshirts, jeans, a doormat, baby sleepers, and a leather backpack. Her bill comes to $650.00. She pays cheerfully with a platinum credit card, smiling at the clerk who sports several piercings and a headset. Not a single customer or clerk notices her. Why should they? Well, she is sixty-seven years of age, and except for the baby pajamas, she is shopping for herself at an apparently youth-oriented store. Consumer groups used to be fairly predictable. In stores like The Gap, Old Navy, or Roots, where this woman just shopped, demographics should be even more predictable. However, in the new millennium, consumer patterns are changing rapidly, and retailers must understand and respond to new age groups, new buying habits, and new merchandise mixes.

6 *Ask one or more questions.* You may simply want the reader to think about possible answers, or you may plan to answer the questions yourself later in the paper.

What is love? How do we know that we are really in love? When we meet that special person, how can we tell that our feelings are genuine and not merely infatuation? If they are genuine, will these feelings last? Love, as we all know, is difficult to define. Yet most people agree that true and lasting love involves far more than mere physical attraction. Love involves mutual respect, the desire to give rather than take, and the feeling of being wholly at ease.

7 *Use a quotation.* A quotation can be something you have read in a book or article. It can also be something that you have heard: a popular saying or proverb ("Never give advice to a friend"), a current or recent advertising slogan ("I am Canadian"), or a favourite expression used by friends or family. Using a quotation in your introductory paragraph lets you add someone else's voice to your own.

"To figure something out, you've got to be confused." So said K-OS, the dean of Canadian hip-hop artists. The story behind the growth of Canadian hip hop began with some confusing blends of rap and rock. Although Devon and Maestro Fresh Wes were successes in the early 1990s, what broke the music through to mainstream audiences of the time was the unlikely mix of Frankie Fudge's rap breaks on Celine Dion's hit single "Unison." For Canadian rappers, figuring out how to reach their audiences would mean negotiating with various media groups, developing their own music association, and waiting until 2001 for urban music stations to be licensed.

Activity 1

The box below summarizes the seven common methods of introduction. Read the introductions that follow it, and, in the space provided, write the letter of the method of introduction used in each case.

A. General to narrow	E. Incident or story
B. Background information	F. Question(s)
C. Starting with an opposite	G. Quotation
D. Stating importance of topic	

_____   1. The ad, in full colour on a glossy magazine page, shows a beautiful kitchen with gleaming counters. In the foreground, on one of the counters, stands a shiny new food processor. Usually, a feminine hand is touching it lovingly. Around the main picture are other, smaller shots. They show mounds of perfectly sliced onion rings, thin rounds of juicy tomatoes, heaps of matchstick-sized potatoes, and piles of golden, evenly grated cheese. The ad copy tells how wonderful, how easy food preparation will be with a processor. Don't believe it. My processor turned out to be expensive, difficult to operate, and very limited in its use.

_____   2. People say, "You can often tell a book by its cover," and when it comes to certain paperbacks, this is true. When people browse in the drugstore or supermarket and see a paperback featuring an attractive young woman in a low-cut dress, fleeing from a handsome dark figure in a shadowy castle, they know exactly what they're getting. Every romance novel has the same elements: an innocent heroine, an exotic setting, and a cruel but fascinating hero.

_____   3. Canadians in the new millennium have become incredibly lazy. Instead of cooking a simple, nourishing meal, they pop a frozen dinner into the microwave. Instead of studying daily newspapers, they scan online versions or the capsule summaries on network news. Worst of all, instead of walking even a few blocks to the local convenience store, they jump into cars. This dependence on the automobile, even for short trips, has taken away a valuable experience—walking. If people drove less and walked more, they would save money, become healthier, and discover fascinating things about their surroundings.

Activity 2

In groups or on your own, write introductory paragraphs on any three of the following topics, using a *different* method for each. Be sure your method suits your subject.

1. Computer viruses
2. Daycare problems
3. Student newspapers
4. First-semester challenges
5. Online courses
6. The best things in life . . .

Concluding Paragraph

The concluding paragraph is your chance to remind the reader of your thesis and bring the essay to a satisfactory end.

As you begin to write a final paragraph, consider, once again, your purpose, your essay's content, your audience, and also the impression or effect you would like to leave with readers. Do you want readers to smile, to think seriously, or to take some action?

Whichever concluding method you choose, remind readers of where they began—your thesis statement. They will recognize this return to the beginning as a signal of completion and will appreciate your effort to close the essay in a satisfying way.

Common Methods of Conclusion

Any one of the methods below, or a combination of methods, may be used to conclude your essay.

1 *End with a summary and final thought.* In other words, restate the thesis and supporting points without using the wording you used before. Instead, reinforce how you arrived at your thesis. This should be followed by a final comment that "rounds off" and broadens the scope of the essay. This combination of a summary and a final thought is the most common method of concluding an essay. Here is an example:

> Catalogue shopping at home, then, has several advantages. Such shopping is convenient, saves consumers money, and saves time. It is not surprising that growing numbers of devoted catalogue shoppers are welcoming those full-colour mail brochures that offer everything from turnip seeds to televisions.

2 *Include a thought-provoking question or short series of questions.* A question grabs the reader's attention. It is a direct appeal to your reader to think further about what you have written. It may involve (1) why the subject of your essay is important; (2) what might happen in the future; (3) what should be done about this subject; or (4) which choice should be made. In any case, be sure that the question is closely related to your thesis. Here is an example:

> What, then, happens now in the twenty-first century when most of the population will be over sixty years old? Retirement policies may change dramatically, with the age-sixty-five testimonial dinner and gold watch postponed for five or ten years. Television is already changing as the Metamucil generation replaces the Pepsi generation. Glamorous grey-haired models sell everything from prescription medicine to banking plans. New soap operas and situation comedies will reveal the secrets of the "sunset years." It will be a different world indeed when the young find themselves outnumbered.

3 *End with a prediction or recommendation to act.* Like questions, predictions and recommendations also involve your readers. Recommendations to take some action are also useful for many types of business writing, including cover letters for résumés. A *prediction* states what may happen in the future:

> If people stopped to think before acquiring pets, there would be fewer instances of cruelty to animals. Many times, it is the people who adopt pets without considering the expense and responsibility involved who mistreat and

neglect their animals. Pets are living creatures. They do not deserve to be treated as carelessly as one would treat a stuffed toy.

A *recommendation* suggests some action that should be taken about a situation or problem:

> Stereotypes such as the helpless homemaker, harried female executive, and dotty grandma are insulting enough to begin with. In magazine ads or television commercials, they become even more insulting. Such hackneyed caricatures of women are not just the objects of derisive humour; these stereotypes now pitch a range of products to an unsuspecting public. Consumers should boycott companies whose advertising continues to use such stereotypes.

Activity

In the space provided, note whether each concluding paragraph ends with a summary and final thought (write *S* in the space), a prediction or recommendation (write *P/R*), or a question (write *Q*).

_____ 1. Disappointments are unwelcome but regular visitors to everyone's life. People can feel depressed about them, or they can try to escape from them. The best thing, though, is to accept a disappointment and then try to use it somehow. Step over the unwelcome visitor and then get on with life.

_____ 2. Holidays, it is clear, are often not the fulfilling experiences they are supposed to be. They can, in fact, be very stressful. But would we rather have a holiday-free calendar?

_____ 3. People's dreams of stardom, of seeing their names in lights and their pictures on the covers of magazines, are based on illusions. The celebrities whose lives are documented for all to see give up their private lives, endure constant pressure, and are never completely safe. The price of fame is too high, and never worth its cost.

Titles

A well-written title may take a variety of forms, depending, once again, on an essay's purpose, audience, and tone. Generally, titles seek to entice audiences to read what follows. Essays aimed at informing readers often display titles that are highly condensed summaries of their content. An essay whose audience is the writer's peer group would find a reference to common interests or a familiar phrase reworked to suit content intriguing. A humorous essay should have a title that fits its tone, suggesting that what follows will entertain its readers. Titles are always a few words or a brief phrase, not complete sentences. Most writers find it easier to compose a title *after* they have written their essay.

Do not underline the title or put quotation marks around it. You should, though, capitalize all but small connecting words in the title. Skip a space between the title and the first line of the text. (See "Manuscript Form," pages 386–387.)

Activity

Write an appropriate title for the paragraphs that follow.

1. When people see rock-concert audiences only on television or in newspaper photos, the audiences at these events may all seem to be excited teenagers. However, attending a few rock shows would show people that several kinds of ticket-buyers make up the crowd. At any concert, there are usually the typical fan, the out-of-place person, and the troublemaker.

   Title: _____

2. Are you sitting in a messy room right now? Are piles of papers or heaps of clothes tilting at weird angles and leaning on towers of magazines, boxes, and bags all around you? You are not alone, and you should not feel ashamed. Messes are just the natural overflow of our personalities. Messes say that we are too busy, too interesting to spend time cleaning, organizing, and turning into obsessive organizers. Most of all, a good mess is full of potential treasures. A mess is a safety zone, a sign of an active life, and a source of inspiration.

   Title: _____

PRACTICE IN ORGANIZING AND CONNECTING SPECIFIC EVIDENCE

You now know the third step in effective essay writing: organizing and connecting the specific evidence used to support the thesis. This closing section will expand and strengthen your understanding of the third step in writing. You will work through the following series of review activities:

1 Organizing through time or emphatic order

2 Identifying transitions and other transitional structures

3 Completing transitional sentences

4 Identifying introductions and conclusions

1   Organizing Through Time or Emphatic Order

Review Activity 1

Use **time order** to organize the scrambled lists of supporting ideas below. Write *1* beside the supporting idea that should come first in time, *2* beside the idea that logically follows, and *3* beside the idea that comes last in time.

1. *Thesis:*   Classic Disney movies frighten some children more than any other animated films.

   _____   Five-year-olds can be terrified by *The Little Mermaid* with its nasty octopus-witch threatening poor Ariel.

   _____   Although *Bambi* is a heart-warming story, the scene during which Bambi's mother is killed horrifies many children.

_____ The new version of *Fantasia* is considerably less frightening than the original.

2. ***Thesis***:   Applying for unemployment benefits is often a depressing, frustrating experience.

_____ People arrive at the office feeling downhearted, and the tangle of paperwork they face only adds to their misery.

_____ Long lineups are only the beginning; processing a claim is not straightforward.

_____ There are weeks to wait for that first cheque, even after a claim goes through.

Review Activity 2

Use **emphatic order**, or order of importance, to organize the following scrambled lists of supporting ideas. For each thesis, write *1* beside the supporting point that is perhaps less important or interesting than the other two, *2* beside the point that appears more important or interesting, and *3* beside the point that should be most emphasized.

1. ***Thesis***:   Part-time jobs can be valuable life experiences for students.

_____ Working with the public teaches young people how to get along with many kinds of people.

_____ Balancing work and school teaches lessons in time management.

_____ Paying for tuition, books, and possibly rent means that part-time work is a necessity for most students.

2. ***Thesis***:   Gift-giving brings out strange behaviour in people.

_____ "Regifters" are the worst of all.

_____ People who make gift bags out of dollar-store items are just cheap.

_____ Those who only ever buy gift certificates are even more thoughtless.

2 | Identifying Transitions and Other Transitional Structures

Review Activity

The following items use connecting words to help tie ideas together. The connecting words you are to identify are set off in italics. In the space, write *T* for *transition*, *RW* for *repeated word*, *S* for *synonym*, or *P* for *pronoun*.

_____ 1. Maurizio wears a puffy, quilted, down-filled jacket. In this *garment*, he resembles a stack of inflated inner tubes.

_____ 2. Plants like holly and mistletoe are pretty. *They* are also poisonous.

_____ 3. A strip of strong cloth can be used as an emergency fan-belt replacement. *In addition*, a roll of duct tape can be used to patch a leaky hose temporarily.

———————   4. I'm always losing my soft contact lenses, which resemble little circles of thick Saran Wrap. One day, I dropped both of *them* into a cup of hot tea.

———————   5. The moulded plastic chairs in the classrooms are hard and uncomfortable. When I sit in one of these *chairs*, I feel as if I were sitting in a bucket.

———————   6. One way to tell if your skin is ageing is to pinch a fold of skin on the back of your hand. If *it* doesn't smooth out quickly, your skin is losing its youthful tone.

3   Completing Transitional Sentences

• • • • Review Activity

Below is a brief sentence outline for an essay. The second and third topic sentences serve as transitional, or linking, sentences. Each reminds us of the point in the preceding paragraph and announces the point to be developed in the current paragraph. In the spaces provided, add the words needed to complete the second and third topic sentences.

THESIS   In order to set up a daycare centre in your home, you must make sure your house will conform to provincial and municipal regulations, obtain the necessary legal permits, and advertise your service in the right places.

FIRST SUPPORTING PARAGRAPH

> First of all, as a potential operator of a home daycare centre, you must make sure your house will conform to provincial and municipal regulations. . . .

SECOND SUPPORTING PARAGRAPH

> After making certain that ———————————————————————
>
> ————————————————————————————————————— ,
>
> you must obtain ——————————————————————————— .

THIRD SUPPORTING PARAGRAPH

> Finally, once you have the necessary ———————————————
>
> ————————————————————————————————————— ,
>
> you can begin to ——————————————————————————— .

4   Identifying Introductions and Conclusions

• • • • Review Activity

In the box below are seven common kinds of introductions and three common kinds of conclusions. After reading the three pairs of introductory and concluding paragraphs that follow, use the space provided to write the number of the kind of introduction and conclusion used in each case.

Introductions	*Conclusions*
1. General to narrow	1. Summary and final thought
2. Background information	2. Question(s)
3. Starting with an opposite	3. Prediction or recommendation
4. Stating importance of topic	
5. Incident or story	
6. Question(s)	
7. Quotation	

Pair 1

One March night at 2 a.m., I lay curled up, shivering and coughing in a sleeping bag outside the Air Canada Centre. No, I am not homeless, and I was not alone. I was lying on the cement with at least a few thousand other people in their late teens and early twenties. For the first seven or eight hours, I enjoyed myself, singing and sharing stories and food. But by two o'clock, my throat hurt and I was losing interest in the piece of paper that was my shortcut to stardom. At four o'clock in the morning, I packed up my bags, gave someone my number, and decided I was not going to be the next *Canadian Idol*. Becoming a professional singer has no shortcuts; it means more voice lessons, more auditions, and more experience.

Shows like *Canadian Idol* encourage people to dream of instant stardom. The reality of learning to be an entertainer is not a matter of a magic moment of discovery; it involves patience, work, and tough skin. No one applauds when I miss notes or lose at an audition; no one cares. People who are stars at their local karaoke place should think twice before they decide they are ready to be an "idol."

Pair 2

What would life be like if we could read each other's minds? Would communications be instantaneous and perfectly clear? These questions will never be answered unless mental telepathy becomes a fact of life. Until then, we will have to make do with less perfect means of communication. Letters, e-mail, telephone calls, and face-to-face conversations do have serious drawbacks.

Letters, e-mail, phone calls, or conversations cannot guarantee perfect communication. With all our sophisticated skills, we human beings often communicate less effectively than howling wolves or chattering monkeys. Even if we were able to read each other's minds, we'd probably still find some way to foul up the message.

Pair 3

Canada "is going to be a great country when they finish unpacking it," said an American journalist. That sounds like a smug, patronizing statement made by someone who believes their country is more highly evolved, doesn't it? If it is true that Canada is still developing as a nation, that may be a good thing as the world adjusts to the twenty-first century. Adaptable by nature, Canada provides military troops when necessary, but is renowned for its peacekeeping; and our national policy of multiculturalism has developed into a model that countries like the U.S. might envy. Our huge land mass may yet develop into one the greatest assets of an overcrowded world.

Although Canada has been the butt of American media humour because of its apparent polite neutrality and low news profile, our huge multicultural country may have simply been slumbering, getting ready to play a larger role in a new century. Canada's success in the future may rest on its very flexibility, its adaptable nature, and its nearly endless "room to grow."

CHECKLIST OF LEARNING OUTCOMES FOR CHAPTER 4

To ensure that you have understood and met the learning outcomes for this chapter, answer the following questions:

✓ What are the three levels at which an essay must be coherent? Why is coherence so important at each level?

✓ What are the two most common methods for organizing supporting material? What are two subjects that would suit each method?

✓ Which techniques are used to achieve coherence at the paragraph level?

✓ Where, in paragraphs, are transitional words and phrases essential? Why?

✓ How many types of transitions exist for achieving coherence at the sentence level? Explain how three of these work. Why do readers need sentence-level coherence?

✓ What are the seven common methods used for writing introductions? Which subjects would suit these methods?

✓ What are the three common methods used for writing conclusions? What is the purpose for each method?

CHAPTER 5

Revising, Editing, and Proofreading: The Fourth Step in Essay Writing

L E A R N I N G   O U T C O M E S

After reading this chapter and working through its activities, you will

- write sentences that show correct parallel structure;
- keep verb tenses consistent in your essays;
- maintain a consistent pronoun point of view in essays;
- use specific vocabulary to make your meaning clear to readers;
- use active verbs wherever possible;
- use concise wording to avoid "wordiness";
- vary your sentence structures when needed;
- revise and then edit and proofread for errors in grammar, punctuation, and spelling.

Chapters 3 and 4 of this book focused on the first three steps for effective essay writing: advancing a thesis, supporting it with specific evidence, and then organizing and connecting this evidence. These are essential to the content and structure of good essays. This chapter introduces you to the fourth step for writing an effective essay: **revising, editing, and proofreading**. Effective and correctly structured sentences help guarantee your reader's understanding of your point and support.

REVISING SENTENCES

The following strategies will help you to revise your sentences effectively.

- Use parallel structure.
- Use a consistent point of view.
- Use specific words.
- Use active verbs.
- Use concise words.
- Vary your sentences.

Use Parallel Structure

Words and phrases in a pair, a series, or a list should have parallel structure. By balancing the items in a pair or a series so that they have the same grammatical structure, you will make the sentence clearer and easier to read. Notice how the parallel sentences that follow read more smoothly than the non-parallel ones.

Non-parallel (Not Balanced)	*Parallel (Balanced)*
The stock clerk's job includes checking the inventory, initialling the orders, and *to call* the suppliers.	The stock clerk's job includes checking the inventory, initialling the orders, and calling the suppliers. (A balanced series of participles or *-ing* words: *checking, initialling, calling*)
The game-show contestant was told to be cheerful, charming, and *with enthusiasm.*	The game-show contestant was told to be cheerful, charming, and enthusiastic. (A balanced series of adjectives: *cheerful, charming, enthusiastic*)
The lab trainer demonstrates equipment and protection procedures; *hands-on instruction is not offered.*	The lab trainer demonstrates equipment and protection procedures; she does not offer hands-on instruction. (Balanced use of the active voice: *The lab trainer demonstrates . . . ; she does not offer . . .*)

Assembling balanced sentences is not a skill to worry about when writing your first draft. But when you rewrite, you should try to put matching words and ideas into matching structures. Errors in parallel structure often show up in lists of items within sentences.

• • • • Activity

Cross out and revise the unbalanced part of each of the following sentences.

break

Example   Chocolate makes Raj gain weight, lose his appetite, and ~~breaking~~ out in hives.

1. The novelty store sells hand buzzers, plastic fangs, and insects that are fake.

2. Many people share the same three great fears: being in high places, working with numbers, and speeches.

3. To decide on a career, students should think carefully about their interests, hobbies, and where their skills lie.

4. At the body shop, the car was sanded down to the bare metal, painted with primer, and red enamel was sprayed on.

5. In order to become a dancer, Irina is taking lessons, working in amateur shows, and auditioned for professional companies.

Parallel Structure in Thesis Statements

You will often write thesis statements containing a list or series of supporting points, so you should be prepared to revise your thesis so that it presents a grammatically parallel set of items. Whether your supporting points appear as three words or three phrases, be sure they match each other.

● ● ● Activity

Revise the following thesis statements so that each flows smoothly and lists its supporting points in parallel form.

1. E-mail is an asset to communication today because of its speed and convenience, online conferencing which lets people meet without travelling, and it allows for graphics and sounds to be attached.

2. Case studies in classes really bring lessons to life: students learn from real-life situations, really interesting, and make group work fun.

3. Working at each job in a kitchen brigade is a must for anyone who hopes to be a head chef responsible for daily preparation, being really good at basic sauces, and then working on menu design and budgets.

Use a Consistent Point of View

Consistent Verb Tenses

Do not shift verb tenses unnecessarily. Keep a consistent sense of time in your essay. (For information about verb tenses, refer to Chapter 25 of this book.) If you begin writing an essay in the present tense, do not shift suddenly to the past. If you begin in the past, do not shift, without reason, to the present. Notice the inconsistent verb tenses in the following example:

Kizzy *punched* down the risen yeast dough in the bowl. Then, she *dumps* it onto the floured worktable and *kneaded* it into a smooth, shiny ball.

The verbs must be consistently in the **present tense:**

Kizzy *punches* down the risen yeast dough in the bowl. Then, she *dumps* it onto the floured worktable and *kneads* it into a smooth, shiny ball.

Or the verbs must be consistently in the **past tense:**

Kizzy *punched* down the risen yeast dough in the bowl. Then, she *dumped* it onto the floured worktable and *kneaded* it into a smooth, shiny ball.

Computer *Writing Tip*

Try this simple tip to make revising your sentences easier.

- With your draft on the screen, pull down the *View* menu.
- Go to the *Toolbars* option and select the *Formatting* toolbar.
- On the *Formatting* menu, you will see a pencil-like icon with a colour bar beneath it. This is the *Highlighting* tool.
- This tool will mark items in your draft that you highlight with your mouse. Highlight a word with the mouse, then click on the *Highlighting* tool.

To check the verb tenses in your draft, begin by highlighting each verb. Then, go back, and make each highlighted verb consistent in tense.

● ● ● Activity

Make the verbs in each sentence consistent with the *first* verb used. Cross out the incorrect verb and write the correct form in the space at the left.

_____*ran*_____   ***Example***   Aunt Helen tried to kiss her little nephew, but he ~~runs~~ out of the room.

_____   1. An aggressive news photographer knocked a reporter to the ground as the stars arrive for the MuchMusic Video Awards.

_____   2. The winning wheelchair racer in the marathon slumped back in exhaustion and asks for some ice to soothe his blistered hands.

_____   3. "Martial arts movies are so incredible," said Sean. "They're more than just action; they showed real ethical values."

_____   4. The SUV swerved around the corner, went up on two wheels, and tips over on its side.

_____   5. When windstorms struck Vancouver's Stanley Park in 2006, many trees are severely damaged.

Consistent Pronouns: Consistent Voice

Do not shift your point of view or voice unnecessarily. Be consistent in your use of first-, second-, or third-person pronouns.

	Singular	*Plural*
First-person pronouns	I (my, mine, me)	we (our, us)
Second-person pronouns	you (your)	you (your)
Third-person pronouns	he (his, him)	they (their, them)
	she (her)	
	it (its)	

Note: Any person, place, or thing, as well as any indefinite pronoun such as *one, anyone, someone*, and so on (page 366), is a third-person pronoun.

For instance, if you start writing in the first person, *I*, do not jump suddenly to the second person, *you*. Or if you are writing in the third person, *they*, do not shift unexpectedly to *you*. Look at the examples.

Inconsistent	*Consistent*
One of the fringe benefits of my job is that **you** can use a company credit card for gas. (The writer begins with the first-person pronoun *my*, but then shifts to the second-person *you*.)	One of the fringe benefits of my job is that **I** can use a company credit card for gas.
Though **we** like most of **our** neighbours, there are a few **you** can't get along with. (Again, the writer begins with the first-person pronouns *we* and *our*, but then shifts to the second-person *you*.)	Though **we** like most of **our** neighbours, there are a few **we** can't get along with.

● ● ● ● **Activity**

Cross out inconsistent pronouns in the following sentences, and revise with the correct form of the pronoun above each crossed-out word.

Example   When I examined the used car, ~~you~~ *I* could see that one of the front fenders had been replaced.

1. Many people are ignorant of side effects that diets can have on your health.

2. It is expensive for us to take public transportation to work every day, but what choice do you have if you can't afford a car?

3. During the border crisis, each country refused to change their aggressive stance.

4. One of the things I love about my new apartment is that you can own a pet.

5. It's hard for us to keep taking student loans, but you can't afford tuition without them.

Use Specific Words 1

To be an effective writer, you must use specific rather than general words. Specific words create pictures in the reader's mind. They help capture interest and make your meaning clear.

● ● ● ● **Activity**

Revise the following sentences, changing the vague, indefinite words into sharp, specific ones.

Example   *Several of our appliances* broke down at the same time.

Our washer, refrigerator, and television broke down at the same time.

1. *Salty snacks* are my diet downfall.

   _____

   _____

2. I swept aside the *things* on my desk in order to spread out the road map.

   _____

   _____

3. Our neighbour's family room has *a lot of electronic equipment.*

   _____

   _____

4. *Several sections* of the newspaper were missing.

   _____

   _____

Use Specific Words 2

Again, changing vague, indefinite writing into lively, image-filled writing captures the reader's interest and makes your meaning clear. This is especially important in descriptive writing (see Chapter 9).

Compare the following sentences:

General

She walked down the street.
Animals came into the space.
The man signed the paper.

Specific

Anne wandered slowly along Rogers Lane.
Hungry lions padded silently into the sawdust-covered arena.
The biology teacher hastily scribbled his name on the course withdrawal slip.

The specific sentences create clear pictures in our minds. The details show us exactly what has happened. Here are four ways to make your sentences specific.

1 Use exact names.

   He sold his *bike.*
   Vince sold his *Honda.*

2 Use lively verbs.

   The flag *moved* in the breeze.
   The flag *fluttered* in the breeze.

3 Use adjectives before nouns.

   A man strained to lift the crate.
   A *heavyset, perspiring* man strained to lift the *heavy wooden* crate.

4 Use adjectives that relate to the senses—sight, hearing, taste, touch, smell.

That woman jogs three kilometres a day.
That *fragile-looking, grey-haired* woman jogs three kilometres a day. *(sight)*

A whistle told the crowd that there were two minutes left to play.
A *piercing* whistle told the *cheering* crowd that there were two minutes left to play. *(hearing)*

When he returned, all he found in the refrigerator was bread and milk.
When he returned, all he found in the refrigerator was *stale* bread and *sour* milk. *(taste)*

Neil stroked the kitten's fur until he felt its tiny claws on his hand.
Neil stroked the kitten's *velvety* fur until he felt its tiny, *needle-sharp* claws on his hand. *(touch)*

Sonia placed a sachet in her bureau drawer.
Sonia placed a *lilac-scented* sachet in her bureau drawer. *(smell)*

Activity

Using the methods described above, add specific details to the five sentences that follow.

Example   The person got off the bus.

The teenage boy bounded down the steps of the shiny yellow

school bus.

1. The car would not start.

_____

_____

2. The test was difficult.

_____

_____

3. The boy was tired.

_____

_____

4. My room needs cleaning.

_____

_____

5. A vehicle blocked traffic.

_____

_____

Use Active Verbs

When the subject of a sentence performs the action of the verb, the verb is in the *active voice*. When the subject of a sentence receives the action of a verb, the verb is in the *passive voice*.

The passive form of a verb consists of a form of the verb *to be (am, is, are, was, were)* and the past participle of the main verb (which is usually the same as its past tense form). In general, active verbs are more effective than passive ones. Active verbs give your writing a simpler and more vigorous style.

Passive	*Active*
The computer *was turned on* by Aaron.	Aaron *turned on* the computer.
The car's air conditioner *was fixed* by the mechanic.	The mechanic *fixed* the car's air conditioner.

Using the active voice communicates directly to readers—notice how much simpler the active-voice sentences above are to understand. Grammatically, these sentences are more straightforward.

Using the passive voice involves using a "by structure" to indicate a sentence's subject, or the agent or "doer." Because of this, passive voice places less emphasis on the subject; the subject, in fact, will not appear first in the sentence. The emphasis is on the object that receives the verb's action; here, the computer and the air conditioner.

Choosing a verb voice means considering where you wish emphasis to be placed for your reading audience. If your intention, as it should be, generally is to make your points clearly, active verbs are your choice. However, there are writing occasions when the passive voice is suitable:

- When you wish to emphasize the thing or person acted upon.

    Your behaviour will be reviewed by the disciplinary committee.

- When you wish to de-emphasize the subject of a sentence, or when the subject is not known.

    The hit-and-run driver was eventually stopped by police after a wild chase.

Activity

Revise the following sentences, changing verbs from the passive to the active voice and making any other word changes necessary.

Example   Fruits and vegetables <u>are painted</u> often by artists.

Artists often paint fruits and vegetables.

1. Many unhealthy foods are included in the typical Canadian diet.

2. The family picnic was invaded by hundreds of biting ants.

3. Antibiotics are used by doctors to treat many infections.

_____

4. The fatal traffic accident was caused by a drunk driver.

_____

Use Concise Words

Using more words than necessary to express a meaning—"wordiness"—is often a sign of lazy or careless writing. Your readers may resent the extra time and energy they must spend when you have not done the work needed to make your writing direct, clear, and concise.

Here are some examples of wordy sentences:

In this paper, I am planning to describe the hobby that I enjoy of collecting old comic books.
In Ben's opinion, he thinks that digital television will change and alter our lives in the future.
The officer apprehended the intoxicated operator of the vehicle.

Omitting needless words improves these sentences:

I enjoy collecting old comic books.
Ben thinks that digital television will change our lives.
The officer arrested the drunk driver.

Following is a list of some wordy expressions that could be reduced to single words.

Wordy Form	Short Form
at the present time	now
in the event that	if
in the near future	soon
due to the fact that	because
for the reason that	because
is able to	can
in every instance	always
in this day and age	today
during the time that	while
a large number of	many
big in size	big
red in colour	red
five in number	five
commute back and forth	commute
postponed until later	postponed

● ● ● ● **Activity**

Revise the following sentences, omitting needless words.

1. In conclusion, I would like to end my essay by summarizing each of the major points that were covered within my paper.

   _____

   _____

2. Controlling the quality and level of the television shows that children watch is a continuing challenge to parents that they must meet on a daily basis.

   _____

   _____

3. In general, I am the sort of person who tends to be shy, especially in large crowds or with strangers I don't know well.

   _____

   _____

4. Someone who is analyzing magazine advertising can find hidden messages that, once uncovered, are seen to be clever and persuasive.

   _____

   _____

Vary Your Sentences

One part of effective writing involves varying the kinds of sentences you write. If every sentence follows the same pattern, writing may become monotonous to read. While your main goal is always to write clear, straightforward sentences, you may occasionally wish to emphasize some idea within a sentence more than another idea.

Following are four ways to create variety and interest in your writing style.

1 Add a second complete thought (coordination).

2 Add a dependent thought (subordination).

3 Begin with a special opening word or phrase.

4 Place adjectives or verbs in a series.

Revise by Adding a Second Complete Thought

When you add a second complete thought to a simple sentence, the result is a *compound* sentence, which gives equal weight to two closely related ideas. The two complete statements in a compound sentence are usually connected by a comma plus a joining or coordinating word *(and, but, for, or, nor, so, yet)*. The technique of showing that ideas have equal importance is called *coordination*. Following are compound sentences, which each contain two ideas that the writer considers equal in importance.

> Sameer worked on the engine for three hours, but the car still wouldn't start.
> Bananas were on sale this week, so I bought a bunch for the children's lunches.
> We laced up our roller skates, and then we moved cautiously onto the rink.

Activity

Combine the following pairs of simple sentences to form compound sentences. Use a comma and a logical joining word *(and, but, for, so)* to connect each pair of statements.

Example   The weather was cold and windy.
Al brought a thick blanket to the football game.

The weather was cold and windy, so Al brought a thick blanket to

the football game.

1. My son can't eat peanut butter snacks or sandwiches.
   He is allergic to peanuts.

   _____

   _____

2. Diego tried to sleep.
   The thought of tomorrow's math exam kept him awake.

   _____

   _____

3. This coffee bar has its own bakery.
   It has takeout service as well.

   _____

   _____

4. The cardboard storage boxes were soggy.
   Rainwater had seeped into the basement during the storm.

   _____

   _____

Revise by Adding a Dependent Thought

When you add a dependent thought to a simple sentence, the result is a *complex* sentence. A complex sentence is used when you want to emphasize one idea over another. The dependent thought begins with one of the following subordinating words:

after	if, even if	when, whenever
although, though	in order that	where, wherever
as	since	whether
because	that, so that	which, whichever
before	unless	while
even though	until	who
how	what, whatever	whose

Look at the following complex sentence:

Although the exam room was very quiet, I still couldn't concentrate.

The idea that the writer wishes to emphasize here—*I still couldn't concentrate*—is expressed as a complete thought. The less important idea—*Although the exam room was very quiet*—is subordinate to the complete thought. The technique of giving one idea less emphasis than another is called subordination.

Following are other examples of complex sentences. In each case, the part starting with the dependent word is the less emphasized part of the sentence.

Even though I was tired, I stayed up to watch the horror movie.
Before I take a bath, I check for spiders in the tub.
When Ivy feels nervous, she pulls on her earlobe.

Activity

Use appropriate subordinating words to combine the following pairs of simple sentences and form new sentences that contain a dependent thought. Place a comma after a dependent statement when it starts the sentence.

Example   Rita bit into the hard taffy.
She broke a filling.

When Rita bit into the hard taffy, she broke a filling.
_____

1. I had forgotten to lock the front door.
I had to drive back to the house.

   _____

   _____

2. The bear turned over the rotten log.
Fat white grubs crawled in every direction.

   _____

   _____

3. Kevin had sent away for a set of tools.
He changed his mind about spending the money.

   _____

   _____

Revise by Beginning with a Special Opening Word or Phrase

Among the special opening words that can be used to start sentences are past participles of verbs (*-ed* words), present participles of verbs (*-ing* words), adverbs (*-ly* words), infinitive forms of verbs (*to* word groups), and prepositional phrases. Here are examples of all five kinds of openers:

Past participle (*-ed*) word):
Concerned about his son's fever, Paul called a doctor.

Present participle (*-ing* word):
Humming softly, Renata browsed through the rack of CDs.

Adverb (*-ly* word):
Hesitantly, Winston approached the instructor's desk.

Infinitive (*to* word group):
To protect her hair, Shastyn uses the lowest setting on her blow dryer.

Prepositional phrase:
During the exam, the exhaust fan hummed loudly. (For information about prepositional phrases, see pages 324–326.)

Activity

Combine each of the following pairs of simple sentences into one sentence by using the opener shown at the left and omitting repeated words. Use a comma to set off the opener from the rest of the sentence.

Example	*-ing* word	The pelican scooped small fish into its baggy bill. It dipped into the waves.

Dipping into the waves, the pelican scooped small fish

into its baggy bill.

-ly word   1. Amber signed the repair contract.
             She was reluctant.

_____

_____

to word group   2. The interns volunteered to work overtime.
                  They wanted to improve their chances of obtaining permanent positions.

_____

_____

prepositional
phrase   3. The accused murderer grinned at the witnesses.
         He did this during the trial.

_____

_____

-ed word   4. The vet's office was noisy and confusing.
              It was crowded with nervous pets.

_____

_____

-ing word   5. Aakash tried to find something worth watching.
               He flipped from channel to channel.

_____

_____

Revise by Placing Adjectives or Verbs in a Series

Some parts of a sentence may be placed in a series. Among these parts are adjectives and verbs. Here are examples of both in a series:

Adjectives

I gently applied a *sticky new* Band-Aid to the *deep, ragged* cut on my finger.

Verbs

The truck *bounced* off a guardrail, *sideswiped* a tree, and *plunged* down the embankment.

● ● ● ● Activity

Combine the simple sentences into one sentence by using adjectives or verbs in a series and by omitting repeated words. In most cases, use a comma between the adjectives or verbs in a series.

Example   Scott spun the basketball on one finger.
             He rolled it along his arms.
             He dribbled it between his legs.

             Scott spun the basketball on one finger, rolled it along his arms, and

             dribbled it between his legs.

1. The baby toddled across the rug.
   He picked up a button.
   He put the button in his mouth.

_____

_____

2. Water trickled out of the tap.
   The water was brown.
   The water was foul-tasting.
   The tap was rusty.
   The tap was metal.

_____

_____

3. By 6 a.m. I had read the textbook chapter.
I had taken notes on it.
I had studied the notes.
I had drunk eight cups of coffee.

_____

_____

Editing Activity 1: Individual Work

Following is a draft of a student's paragraph. Revise the paragraph's sentences where needed to demonstrate effective use of:

- Parallel structure
- Consistent verb tense
- Consistent pronoun point of view or voice
- Specific words
- Concise words
- Active verbs
- Varied sentence structure

Violence in video games has been around since the beginning of video game history. Space Invaders and Pac-Man were the first violent games, even though blood and gore were not parts of the action when you "killed" the "enemy." The game industry and graphics evolved, so video games have become more realistic to look at, faster to respond, and experiencing them is more of a thrill. But the more real the game looked, the more powerfully is presented the message of violence. At this point in time, a child can play a game where they chop up a body into pieces with a rusty sword. And to them that's pure entertainment. Grand Theft Auto is controversial for its brutality because it gave players freedom to do what they want; you are able to grab any weapon, shoot a huge selection of people in your town, and it lets you escape the police. Many offences around North America have been blamed on this game. The offences were serious. A boy in the United States was hooked on this game and became a very aggressive boy. He was arrested for a little offence that was not major and taken to the police station where two cops were shot by him and he stole their cars soon after that took place. More than a very large percent of teenage boys in America have played the game Grand Theft Auto and are more likely to commit a crime than those who have not played. There are many issues surrounding the fact that violent video games have a psychological effect on children and young people alike.

Editing Activity 2: Group Work

In a group of four, work as pairs to revise this draft of a student's paragraph where needed to demonstrate effective use of:

- Parallel structure
- Consistent verb tense
- Consistent pronoun point of view or voice
- Specific words

- Concise words
- Active verbs
- Varied sentence structure

When you and your partner have completed your revision, compare your revised version of the paragraph with that of the other pair in your group. How many changes did each pair make? Which revision seems preferable, and why?

> Mountain bikes for people who want to ride in competitions are technically advanced, made of durable new materials, disc brakes, and with advanced suspensions. Races and events are participated in by these riders as competitors, and due to this fact, riders are willing to go that extra mile to find the best bike. Their mountain bikes are not the typical Canadian Tire bike. They are made of high-end materials like carbon fibre, specially manipulated aluminum, and they are ten times stronger than street bikes. Many are half the weight of your typical bicycle. Many also have disc brakes. The disc brakes last longer than rim brakes. Stopping power is improved with disc brakes and the rotors do not get bent as much as rims did. The most advanced bike suspensions on the market have a mind of its own because of the fact that it changes to be more efficient, depending on the terrain. If you are riding on smooth terrain, the suspension locks out so the rider loses no power at the pedal from springing up and down. When the bike is being ridden on rough terrain, the suspension kicks in and you glide over tree roots, stumps, rocks, and whatever kind of thing may be in the way. These technological advances made it easier for competitors to ride in 24-hour races and keep up with the leader.

EDITING SENTENCES

After revising sentences in your essay so that they flow smoothly and clearly, you need to edit for mistakes in grammar, punctuation, spelling, mechanics, and usage. Even if an essay is otherwise well written, it will make an unfavourable impression on readers if it contains such mistakes. To edit an essay, check it against the agreed-upon rules or conventions of written English. Here are the most common of these conventions, followed by the pages in Part 4 of this book where these matters are covered:

1 Write complete sentences rather than fragments. (327–338)
2 Do not write run-ons. (339–348)
3 Use verb forms correctly. (349–354)
4 Make sure that subjects, verbs, and pronouns agree. (355–359)
5 Eliminate faulty modifiers. (382–385)
6 Use pronoun forms correctly. (365–369)
7 Use capital letters where needed. (388–393)
8 Use the following marks of punctuation correctly: apostrophe, quotation marks, comma, semicolon, colon, hyphen, dash, parentheses. (397–419)
9 Use correct manuscript form. (386–387)
10 Eliminate slang and clichés. (428–431)
11 Eliminate careless spelling errors. (420–427)

Both the list of sentence skills on the inside front cover of this book and the correction symbols on the inside back cover also include page references so that you can turn quickly to any skill you want to check.

Editing Hints

Here are hints that can help you edit the next-to-final draft of an essay for sentence-skills mistakes:

1 Have at hand two essential tools: a good dictionary and a grammar handbook. (You can use the one in this book on pages 323–454). Even if you use the spell checker and grammar checker on your word-processing program, you will still need to check spellings and uses of certain phrases.

2 Use a sheet of paper to cover your essay so that you can expose only one sentence at a time. It may help to read each sentence out loud. If it does not read clearly and smoothly, chances are something is wrong.

3 Pay special attention to the kinds of errors you tend to make. For example, if you tend to write run-ons or fragments, be especially on the lookout for those errors.

4 Try to work on a word-processed draft, where you will be able to see your writing more objectively than you can on a handwritten page. Use a pen with coloured ink so that your corrections will stand out.

5 Work on one item at a time. Check your spelling, each verb for subject/verb agreement, tense for use and consistency, pronoun reference and agreement, and so on. Finally, check each sentence for correct structure, and then go over punctuation carefully. Use Part 4 of the text and this chapter as references.

Activity 1: Individual Work

Using final drafts of one or two of your essays or paragraphs assigned thus far in the semester, choose two sentences from each that you think are effective. Explain why, in each case.

Now, look at all four sentences and judge them with the following criteria:

- Correctness of sentence structure
- Varied structure compared to sentences before and after
- Appropriateness to intended meaning

Activity 2: Group Work

Using one of the readings that you have been assigned from Part 5 of this book, have each member of the group choose three sentences that he or she finds especially effective.

After each person makes some notes about what aspect in each of their three sentences works so well, group members will compare sentence choices and reasons for their choices. What criteria did people use to decide? Which criterion did the group think was best, and why?

A Final Note on Editing

A series of editing tests appears on pages 442–454. You will probably find it most helpful to take these tests after reviewing the sentence skills in Part 4.

PROOFREADING

Proofreading means checking the final, edited draft of your work closely for typos and other careless errors. A helpful strategy is to read your essay backward, from the last sentence to the first. This prevents you from getting caught up in the flow of the essay and missing small mistakes.

Like editing, proofreading is a necessary skill. With practice, it should become "second nature" to you.

 Computer *Writing Tip*

While you may want to use your computer's spell check function at the proofreading stage (setting your application to Canadian spelling), be aware of the shortcomings of this tool:

- Spell check works by comparing the letters you have typed with similar patterns of letters in its word-list. It then offers you a list of alternative spellings and words. You need to use a dictionary to be sure which spelling is the correct one to choose.
- Spell check does not "know" what you mean by a word. It simply finds comparable patterns of letters. To a spell check tool, *Thank ewe four the complement* is as correct as *Thank you for the compliment.*
- Spell check cannot distinguish between the various forms of such commonly misspelled and misused words as *it's* and *its* or *there, their,* and *they're.* Keep a list of words you tend to misspell, and check those words in your dictionary every time you submit an assignment.

Similarly, you should use grammar-checking tools very cautiously. Like spell check, grammar check will pick up some simple errors, but you will still need to know which option to choose from the list of suggestions it offers. Furthermore, grammar checkers frequently ignore some errors or offer inappropriate substitutions.

PRACTICE IN REVISING SENTENCES

You now know the fourth step in effective writing: revising, editing, and proofreading sentences. This closing section will provide further practice in *revising* sentences, using a variety of methods to ensure that your sentences flow in a smooth, clear, and interesting way. You will work through the following series of review activities:

1 Using parallel structure

2 Using a consistent point of view

3 Using specific words

    4 Using active verbs

    5 Using concise words

    6 Varying your sentences

1   Using Parallel Structure

• • • • Review Activity

Cross out the unbalanced part of each sentence. In the space provided, revise the unbalanced part so that it matches the other item or items in the sentence.

Example   Cigarette smoking is expensive, disgusting, and ~~a health risk~~.

       unhealthy

1. A sale on electrical appliances, furniture for the home office, and stereo equipment begins this Friday.

    _____

2. To escape the stresses of everyday life, people rely upon watching television, reading books, and the kitchen.

    _____

3. The keys to improving grades are to take effective notes in class, to plan study time, and preparing carefully for exams.

    _____

4. Qualities that are important in friendship are a sense of humour, being kind, and dependability.

    _____

5. My three favourite jobs were veterinary assistant, gardener, and selling toys.

    _____

6. Housekeeping shortcuts will help you do a fast job of doing laundry, cleaning rooms, and food on the table.

    _____

7. Studying a little every day is more effective than to cram.

    _____

8. The speaker impressed the audience because of his clear, reasonable presentation with friendliness as well.

    _____

9. While waiting for the exam to start, small groups of nervous students glanced over their notes, drank coffee, and were whispering to each other.

    _____

10. A public service industry strike now would mean interruptions in food deliveries, a slowdown in the economy, and losing wages for workers.

---

2   Using a Consistent Point of View

● ● ● ● **Review Activity 1**

Change verbs, where needed, in the following selection so that they are consistently in the past tense. Cross out each incorrect verb, and write the correct form above it, as shown in the example. You will need to make ten corrections.

My uncle's shopping trip last Thursday was discouraging to him. First of all,

found
he had to drive around for fifteen minutes until he ~~finds~~ a parking space. There

was a half-price special on paper products at Dominion, and every spot is taken.

Then, when he finally got inside, many of the items on his list were not where

he expected. For example, the pickles he wanted are not on the same shelf as

all the other pickles. Instead, they were in a refrigerated case next to the bacon.

And the granola was not on the cereal shelves, but in the health food section.

Shopping, therefore, proceeds slowly. About halfway through his list, he knew

there would not be time to cook dinner and decides to pick up a barbecued

chicken. The chicken, he learned, was available at the end of the aisle he had

already passed. So he parks his shopping cart in an aisle, gets the chicken,

and came back. After adding half a dozen more items to his cart, he suddenly

realizes it contained someone else's food. So he retraced his steps, found his

own cart, transfers the groceries, and continued to shop. Later, when he began

loading items onto the checkout counter, he notices that the barbecued chicken

was missing. He must have left it in the other cart, certainly gone by now.

Feeling totally defeated, he returned to the deli counter and says to the clerk,

"Give me another chicken. I lost the first one." My uncle told me that when he

saw the look on the clerk's face, he felt as if he'd flunked Food Shopping.

> > > > **Review Activity 2**

Cross out inconsistent pronouns in the following sentences, and write the correct form of the pronoun above each crossed-out word.

Example   Many shoppers are staying away from the local music store because

they

~~you~~ can now download songs from the Internet.

1. These days people never seem to get the recognition they deserve, no matter how hard you work.

2. All you could hear was the maddening rattle of the furnace fan, even though I buried my face in the pillow.

3. When we answer the telephone at work, you are supposed to say the company name.

4. Each year I pay more money for my college tuition. Despite the cost, however, one must complete college in order to get a better, more meaningful job.

5. Matheus bought the used car from a local dealership. The car was so clean and shiny that you could not tell that the engine needed to be replaced.

6. I would like to go to a school where one can meet many people who are different from me.

7. When I first began to work as a server, I was surprised at how rude some customers were to you.

8. When you drive on the highway, I get disgusted at the amount of trash I see.

9. Students may not leave the exam room unless you have turned in the exam.

10. Nina wanted to just browse through the store, but in every department a salesperson came up and asked to help you.

3   Using Specific Words

> > > > **Review Activity 1**

Revise the following sentences, changing vague, indefinite words into sharp, specific ones.

1. When my relationship broke up, I felt *various emotions.*

_____

_____

2. The *food choices* in the cafeteria were unappetizing.

_____

_____

3. *Bugs* invaded our kitchen and pantry this summer.

_____

_____

4. All last week, *the weather was terrible.*

_____

_____

5. In the car accident, our teacher suffered *a number of injuries.*

_____

_____

Review Activity 2

Using the methods described on pages 96–98, add specific details to the sentences that follow.

1. The salesperson was obnoxious.

_____

_____

2. The child started to cry.

_____

_____

3. The game was exciting.

_____

_____

4. The lounge area was busy.

_____

_____

5. A passenger on the bus was acting strangely.

_____

_____

4 Using Active Verbs

Review Activity

Revise the following sentences, changing verbs from the passive to the active voice and making any other word changes necessary.

Example   Soccer is played by children all over the world.

Children all over the world play soccer.

1. The pizza restaurant was closed by the health inspector.

   _____

2. Huge stacks of donated books were sorted by the workers in the library.

   _____

3. My computer was infected by a virus.

   _____

4. Gasoline prices will not be increased by suppliers this winter.

   _____

5. High-powered lights were used by the crew during filming of the commercial.

   _____

5 Using Concise Words

Review Activity

Revise the following sentences, omitting needless words.

1. I finally made up my mind and decided to look for a new job.

   _____

   _____

2. Due to the fact that the printer was out of paper, Ayesha went to the store for the purpose of buying some.

   _____

   _____

3. Marika realized suddenly that her date had stood her up and was not going to show up.

   _____

   _____

4. Our teacher does not know at this point in time if she will return to our school next year.

   _____

   _____

5. The salesperson advised us not to buy the computer at this time because it was going to have a drop in price in the very near future.

   _____

   _____

6   Varying Your Sentences

● ● ● ● **Review Activity 1**

Combine each of the following groups of simple sentences into one longer sentence. Omit repeated words. Various combinations are often possible, so try to find a combination in each group that flows most smoothly and clearly.

1. Pavitra had repaired her broken watchband with a paper clip.
   The clip snapped.
   The watch slid off her wrist.

   _____

   _____

2. The physical therapist watched.
   Julie tried to stand on her weakened legs.
   They crumpled under her.

   _____

   _____

3. There were parking spaces on the street.
   Winston pulled into an expensive garage.
   He did not want to risk damage to his new car.

   _____

   _____

4. The truck was speeding.
   The truck was brown.
   The truck skidded on some ice.
   The truck almost hit a police officer.
   The police officer was startled.
   The police officer was young.

   _____

   _____

5. The rainstorm flooded our basement.
   The rainstorm was sudden.
   The rainstorm was terrible.
   It knocked shingles off the roof.
   It uprooted a young tree.

   _____

   _____

● ● ● ● ● **Review Activity 2**

Combine the sentences in the following paragraph to form four sentences. Omit repeated words. Try to find combinations in each case that flow as smoothly and clearly as possible.

> Lena and Miles wanted a vacation. They wanted a vacation that was nice. They wanted one that was quiet. They wanted one that was relaxing. They rented a small cottage on Shuswap Lake. Their first day there was very peaceful. The situation quickly changed. A large family moved into a nearby cottage. They played music at top volume. They raced around in a speedboat with a loud whining engine. Lena and Miles were no longer very relaxed. They packed up their things. They drove off. They returned to their quiet apartment.

_____

_____

_____

_____

_____

_____

_____

_____

_____

_____

CHECKLIST OF LEARNING OUTCOMES FOR CHAPTER 5

To ensure that you have understood and met the learning outcomes for this chapter, answer the following questions:

✓ What does "parallel structure" mean? Why is parallel structure relevant to writing clear thesis statements?

✓ How will you check your essays for consistent verb tenses?

✓ Why is it important to maintain a consistent pronoun point of view in essays?

✓ Why do readers prefer specific, rather than vague word choices?

✓ What is an active verb, and why are active verb forms preferable?

✓ How do readers benefit from concise wording in essays?

✓ What is the difference between a compound and complex sentence?

✓ How does revising differ from editing and proofreading?

CHAPTER 6

Four Bases for Revising Essays

L E A R N I N G   O U T C O M E S

After reading this chapter and working through its activities, you will

- understand the importance of each of the four bases for revising essays and their relationship to the four steps for effective essay writing;

- revise your own work with techniques for achieving the four bases.

Four Steps	Four Bases Defined
1 Discover your point, and advance a clear thesis statement. →	**Unity**: a single main idea pursued and supported by the points and details of the essay
2 Support your thesis with specific evidence. →	**Support**: specific details and examples to explain each supporting point
3 Organize and connect the specific evidence at essay, paragraph, and sentence levels. →	**Coherence**: clear organization and logical connections between paragraphs, supporting points, and sentences
4 Revise, edit, and proofread your essay. →	**Effective Sentence Skills**: sentence structure, grammar, spelling, and punctuation free of errors

This chapter focuses on the **four bases** defined above—*unity, support, coherence,* and *effective sentence skills*—and will show how they can be used to evaluate and revise an essay.

BASE 1: UNITY

* * * * **Activity**

The following personal student essays are based on the topic "Problems or Pleasures of My Teenage Years." Which one makes its point *more* clearly and effectively, and why?

Essay 1

Teenage Pranks

Looking back at some of the things I did as a teenager makes me break   1
out in a sweat. The purpose of each adventure was fun, but occasionally things
got out of hand. In my search for good times, I was involved in three notable
pranks, ranging from fairly harmless to fairly serious.

The first prank proved that good, clean fun does not have to be dull. As   2
a high school student, I was credited with making the world's largest dessert.
With several friends, I spent an entire year collecting boxes of Jell-O. Entering
our school's indoor pool one night, we turned the water temperature up as high
as it would go and poured in box after box of the strawberry powder. The next
morning, school officials arrived to find the pool filled with fifty thousand litres
of the quivering, rubbery stuff. No one was hurt by the prank, but we did suffer
through three days of massive cleanup.

Not all my pranks were harmless, and one involved risking my life. As soon   3
as I got my driver's licence, I wanted to join the "Flyers' Club." Membership
in this club was limited to those who could make their cars fly a distance of at
least three metres. The qualifying site was an old quarry field near Orillia where
friends and I had built a ramp made of dirt. I drove my battered Ford Pinto up
this ramp as fast as it would go. The Pinto flew three metres, but one of the
tires exploded when I landed. The car rolled on its side, and I luckily escaped
with only a bruised arm.

Risking my own life was bad enough, but there was another prank in   4
which other people could have been hurt, too. On this occasion, I accidentally
set a valley on fire. Two of my friends and I were sitting on a hill sharing a
few beers. It was a warm summer night, and there was absolutely nothing to
do. The idea came like a thunderclap. We collected a supply of large plastic
garbage bags, emergency highway flares, and the half tank of helium left over
from a science fair experiment. Then, we began to construct a fleet of UFOs.
Filling the bags with helium, we tied them closed with wire and suspended
several burning flares below each bag. Our UFOs leaped into the air like an
army of invading Martians. Rising and darting in the blackness, they convinced
even us. Our fun turned into horror, though, as we watched the balloons begin
to drop onto the wooded valley of expensive homes below. Soon, a brush
fire started and, quickly sobered, we hurried off to call the fire department
anonymously.

Every so often, I think back on the things that I did as a teenager. I   5
chuckle at the innocent pranks and feel lucky that I didn't harm myself or

others with the not-so-innocent ones. Those years were filled with wild times. Today, I'm older, wiser—and maybe just a little more boring.

Essay 2

Problems of My Adolescence

In the unreal worlds of movies and television, teenagers are care-free, smart, funny, wise-cracking, and self-assured. In fact, most of them are more "together" than adults. This, however, isn't how I recall my teenage years at all. As a teen, I suffered. Every day, I battled the terrible physical, family, and social troubles of adolescence.   1

For one thing, I had to deal with a demoralizing physical problem—acne. Some days, I would wake up in the morning with a red bump the size of a tail-light on my nose. Since I worried constantly about my appearance anyway, acne outbreaks could turn me into a crying, screaming maniac. Plastering on a layer of (at the time) orange-coloured Clearasil, which didn't fool anybody, I would slink into school, hoping that the boy I had a crush on would be absent that day. Within the last few years, however, treatments for acne have improved. Now, skin doctors prescribe special drugs that clear up pimples almost immediately. An acne attack could shatter whatever small amount of self-esteem I had managed to build up.   2

In addition to fighting acne, I felt compelled to fight my family. As a teenager, I needed to be independent. At that time, the most important thing in life was to be close to my friends and to try out new, more adult experiences. Unfortunately, my family seemed to get in the way. My little brother, for instance, turned into my enemy. We are close now, though. In fact, Eddie recently painted my new apartment for me. Eddie used to barge into my room, listen to my phone conversations, and read my secret letters. I would threaten to tie him up and leave him in a Dumpster. He would scream, my mother would yell, and all hell would break loose. My parents, too, were my enemies. They wouldn't let me stay out late, wear the clothes I wanted to wear, or hang around with the friends I liked. So I tried to get revenge on them by being miserable, sulky, and sarcastic at home.   3

Worst of all, I had to face the social traumas of being a teenager. Things that were supposed to be fun, like dates and dances, were actually horrible. On the few occasions when I had a real date, I agonized over everything—my hair, my weight, my pimples. After a date, I would come home, raid the kitchen, and drown my insecurities in a sea of junk food. Dances were also stressful events. My friends and I would pretend we were too cool to care or sneak a couple of beers just to get up the nerve to walk into the school gym. Now, I realize that half the kids in the gym were just as nervous as we were and that seventeen-year-olds are not smart to drink. They can't handle the consequences. At dances, I never relaxed. It was too important to look exactly right, to act really cool, and to pretend I was having fun.   4

I'm glad I'm not a teenager anymore. I wouldn't ever want to feel so unattractive, so confused, and so insecure again. I'll gladly accept the odd line on my face in exchange for a little peace of mind.   5

Understanding Unity

Essay 1 is more effective because it is completely unified. All the details in this essay are on target; they support and develop each of its three topic sentences.

Here is an outline of essay 1. This shows exactly why it is unified.

Thesis: In my search for good times, I was involved in three notable pranks, ranging from fairly harmless to fairly serious.

Supporting Point 1: First prank proved that fun does not have to be dull.

Supporting Details:
- spent a year collecting boxes of Jell-O
- heated up pool water and poured in jelly powder
- pool next morning was giant pool of jelly
- only penalty was three days of cleaning

Supporting Point 2: A more daring prank risked writer's life.

Supporting Details:
- wanted to join "Flyer's Club" when he got driver's licence
- members made their cars fly at least three metres
- they flew off a ramp in an old quarry
- the writer "flew," but a tire exploded on landing, rolling the car
- he only bruised his arm

Supporting Point 3: His final prank risked others' lives as well as his own.

Supporting Details:
- he accidentally set a valley on fire
- with friends, he was bored and drinking beer
- they collected big garbage bags, highway flares, and a partial tank of helium
- they inflated the bags, and suspended the flares beneath the bags
- the bags rose in the air
- the bags dropped down in a wooded suburb, starting a fire
- they called fire department anonymously

On the other hand, essay 2 contains some details irrelevant to its topic sentences. In the first supporting paragraph (paragraph 2), the sentences, "Within the last few years, however, treatments for acne have improved. Now, skin doctors prescribe special drugs that clear up pimples almost immediately," do not directly support the writer's topic sentence about dealing with the physical problem of acne. Such details should be left out in the interest of unity.

Revising for Unity

• • • • Activity

Go back to essay 2, and cross out the two sentences in the second supporting paragraph (paragraph 3) and the two sentences in the third supporting paragraph (paragraph 4) that are off target and do not help support their topic sentences.

The difference between these two essays illustrates the first important base or goal for revising your essay: **unity**. To achieve unity is to have all the details in your essay related to your thesis and three supporting topic sentences. Each time you think of something to put into your essay, ask yourself whether it relates to your thesis and supporting points. If it does not, leave it out.

Voice and Point of View in Writing

Both essay 1 and essay 2 are written in the first-person voice or point of view. The first essay is based on the writer's personal experiences and so his connection to those experiences and their outcomes is clear and relevant. Essays such as this, which make a clear point and support it with vivid details, but are written entirely from a subjective viewpoint, are often starting points for a semester's writing assignments. Moving from that first-person voice and purely personal handling of a subject, though, is one of the essential learning experiences of college writing and communication courses.

Essay 2, about a more generally experienced subject, could also be written in the third-person point of view. The essay's purpose could change from explaining one writer's experiences to a purpose related to offering a more objective look at teenage problems. The writer's presence, in a third-person-voice version of the essay, will not be so evident; there will be no "I" competing with the point and details to distract readers from the content. As well, supporting details themselves will differ to a degree: personal anecdotes will be replaced with generally accepted facts, or details derived from research.

Writing in the third-person point of view, where the subject and purpose are appropriate, results in a more objective, content-focused essay. Career writing tasks will most often require you to offer an analysis or explanation of something; in these instances, your focus and energy will be on providing your reading audiences with solid information in a concise and organized way, rather than emphasizing your connection to your content.

Point of View Revision Exercise

Following is an incomplete revised version of essay 2, in the third-person viewpoint. Complete the essay, maintaining the third-person voice, and remembering to keep supporting details relevant to each paragraph's topic.

The Teenage Reality Show

In the unreal worlds of television and movies, teenagers are smart, funny, wise-cracking, and self-assured. In fact, most of them are sharper and more self-confident than adults. This, however, is not what most teenagers experience or how they behave. Teenagers suffer. Each day they struggle with physical changes, family challenges, and social problems.

For one thing, teenagers have to endure physical changes just as their appearance becomes most important to them. When acne turns a teenager's face into an inflamed, angry mask of bumps, it can twist unsteady emotions into a storm of rage and self-hatred. One look in the mirror in the morning . . .

_____

_____

_____

_____

While teenagers agonize within themselves over physical changes, they turn their outer environments into battlefields. Parents are the first, but not the only adversaries in the teenage home wars for independence. A simple request, such as . . .

_____

_____

_____

_____

The major sources of suffering for most teens, though, are social traumas. The word "fun" can lose its meaning when it is applied to dates, parties, and dances. These are occasions when low self-esteem makes finding a partner or asking someone out pure misery. Dating is a particularly scary prospect . . .

_____

_____

_____

_____

A quick survey of people in their twenties and thirties would reveal that most would never revisit their teenage years. If they are honest, they would never want to feel that unattractive, confused, and miserably insecure again. That is reality—and those people who write those teen-based shows and movies are probably in their forties.

When you have completed the exercise, answer the following questions:

1. How does "The Teenage Reality Show" differ, compared to "Problems of My Adolescence," with the change in point of view?

2. Who would the potential reading audience be for the first-person version of essay 2? Would there be different potential audience for the third-person version of essay 2? Why, in your opinion?

3. How did your choice of supporting details for "The Teenage Reality Show" differ from those in "Problems of My Adolescence"?

4. Which version of essay 2 do you feel makes its point more effectively, and why?

Computer *Writing Tip*

Let the computer help you revise your drafts:

- You can move words, phrases, and sentences around with the *Copy* and *Paste* functions. Your draft stays clean so that you can concentrate on your content and not be distracted by strike-outs and scribbled words between lines or in the margins.
- You can easily insert new or different supporting details into existing lines of text, exactly where you wish them to be.
- You can save material, which you have removed, at the bottom of your document until you have completed your draft.
- Even if you accidentally delete some text, you can use the *Undo* function under the *Edit* option to retrieve material.
- Remember to save each draft separately. Use a system such as "Essay V 1," "Essay V 2," or any pattern that works for you. Be consistent in whichever system you use. Also, never overwrite an existing draft when revising. Copy your entire previous draft to a new document before you begin a new draft.
- Many students and instructors prefer to do at least one hard-copy edit. Often the eye will catch more errors and/or awkward sentences on a printed page than on a screen. Hard-copy editing is even more effective if you allow at least a day between writing and editing. Create a new version of your essay document, and add your changes.

BASE 2: SUPPORT

• • • • Activity

The following essays were written in the less personal third-person point of view. Both are unified. Which one communicates *more* clearly and effectively, and why?

Essay 1

Dealing with Disappointment

One way to look at life is as a series of disappointments. Life can certainly   1
appear that way because disappointment crops up in the life of everyone more often, it seems, than satisfaction. How disappointments are handled can have a great bearing on how life is viewed. People can react negatively by sulking or by blaming others, or they can react positively by trying to understand the reasons behind the disappointment.

Sulking is one way to deal with disappointment. This "Why does everything   2
always happen to me?" attitude is common because it is an easy attitude to adopt, but it is not very productive. Everyone has had the experience of meeting

people who specialize in feeling sorry for themselves. A sulky manner will often discourage others from wanting to lend support, and it prevents the sulker from making positive moves toward self-help. It becomes easier just to sit back and sulk. Unfortunately, feeling sorry for oneself does nothing to lessen the pain of disappointment. It may, in fact, increase the pain. It certainly does not make future disappointments easier to bear.

Blaming others is another negative and nonproductive way to cope with disappointment. This all-too-common response of pointing the finger at someone else doesn't help one's situation. This posture will lead only to anger, resentment, and, therefore, further unhappiness. Disappointment in another's performance does not necessarily indicate that the performer is at fault. Perhaps expectations were too high, or there could have been a misunderstanding as to what the performer actually intended to accomplish.   **3**

A positive way to handle disappointment is to try to understand the reasons behind the disappointment. An analysis of the causes for disappointment can have an excellent chance of producing desirable results. Often, understanding alone can help alleviate the pain of disappointment and can help prevent future disappointments. Also, it is wise to try to remember that what would be ideal is not necessarily what is reasonable to expect in any given situation. The ability to look disappointment squarely in the face and then go on from there is the first step on the road back.   **4**

Continuous handling of disappointment in a negative manner can lead to a negative view of life itself. Chances for personal happiness in such a state of being are understandably slim. Learning not to expect perfection in an imperfect world and keeping in mind those times when expectations were actually surpassed are positive steps toward allowing the joys of life to prevail.   **5**

Essay 2

Reactions to Disappointment

Gertrude Stein said that people have "to learn to do everything, even to die." In life, everyone may face and master many unavoidable adversities; one misery everyone experiences is disappointment. No one gets through life without experiencing many disappointments. Strangely, though, most people seem unprepared for disappointment and react to it in negative ways. They feel depressed or try to escape their troubles instead of using disappointment as an opportunity for growth.   **1**

One negative reaction to disappointment is depression. A woman trying to win a promotion, for example, works hard for over a year in her department. Halina is so sure she will get the promotion, in fact, that she has already picked out the car she will buy when her salary increase comes through. However, the boss names one of Halina's co-workers to the position. The fact that all the other department employees tell Halina that she is the one who really deserved the promotion doesn't help her deal with the crushing disappointment. Deeply depressed, Halina decides that all her goals are doomed to defeat. She loses her enthusiasm for her job and can barely force herself to show up every day. Halina tells herself that she is a failure and that doing a good job just isn't worth the work.   **2**

Another negative reaction to disappointment, and one that often follows   3
depression, is the desire to escape. Jamal fails to get into the college his
brother is attending—the college that was the focus of all his dreams—and
decides to escape his disappointment. Why worry about college at all?
Instead, he covers up his real feelings by giving up on his schoolwork and
getting completely involved with friends, parties, and "good times." When
Carla doesn't make the college basketball team—something she wanted very
badly—she refuses to play sports at all. She decides to hang around with a
new set of friends who get high every day; then she won't have to confront her
disappointment and learn to live with it.

The positive way to react to disappointment is to use it as a chance for   4
growth. This isn't easy, but it's the only useful way to deal with an inevitable
part of life. Halina, the woman who wasn't promoted, could have handled
her disappointment by looking at other options. If her boss doesn't recognize
talent and hard work, perhaps she could transfer to another department. Or
she could ask the boss how to improve her performance so that she would
be a sure candidate for the next promotion. Jamal, the fellow who didn't get
into the college of his choice, should look into other schools. Going to another
college may encourage him to be his own person, step out of his brother's
shadow, and realize that being turned down by one college isn't a final
judgment on his abilities or potential. Rather than escape into drugs, Carla
could improve her basketball skills for a year or pick up another sport—like
swimming or tennis—that would probably turn out to be more useful to her
as an adult.

Disappointments are unwelcome but regular visitors to everyone's life.   5
People can feel depressed about them, or they can try to escape from them.
The best thing, though, is to accept a disappointment and then try to use it
somehow. Step over the unwelcome visitor on the doorstep and get on with life.

Understanding Support

Here, essay 2 is more effective; it offers specific examples of how people deal with disappointment, so we can see for ourselves people's reactions to disappointment.

Essay 1, on the other hand, gives us no *specific* evidence. The writer tells us
about sulking, blaming others, and trying to understand the reasons behind a
disappointment but never shows us any of these responses in action. In an essay
like this one, we would want to see *examples* of how sulking and blaming others
are negative responses to disappointment and, similarly, how understanding the
reasons behind the disappointment is a positive response.

Revising for Support

Activity

Create an outline like that shown on page 120. Fill in the outline with the thesis,
supporting points, and details for essay 2.

Next, try filling in an outline for essay 1. Where will you need more specific
supporting details?

Now on a separate sheet of paper, revise one of the three supporting paragraphs in "Dealing with Disappointment" by providing specific supporting examples.

Examining these essays leads to the second base or goal for revising your essay: **support**. After realizing the importance of adequate and specific supporting details, one student revised an essay about being lost in the woods, the worst experience of her childhood. In the revised essay, instead of talking about "the terror of being separated from my parents," she wrote, "tears streamed down my cheeks as I pictured the faces I would never see again," and "I clutched the locket my parents had given me as if it were a lucky charm that could help me find my way back to the campsite." All writing should include such vivid details!

BASE 3: COHERENCE

● ● ● ● Activity

The following essays are based on the topic "Positive or Negative Effects of Television." Both are unified, and both are supported. Which one communicates *more* clearly and effectively, and why?

Essay 1

Harmful Effects of Watching Television

In a recent cartoon, one character said to another, "When you think of the awesome power of television to educate, aren't you glad it doesn't?" It's true that television has the power to educate and to entertain, but unfortunately, these benefits are outweighed by the harm it does to dedicated viewers. Television is harmful because it creates passivity, discourages communication, and presents a false picture of reality. 1

Television makes viewers passive. Children who have an electronic babysitter spend most of their waking hours in a semi-conscious state. Older viewers watch tennis matches and basketball games with none of the excitement of being in the stands. Even if children are watching *Backyardigan* or TVO's children's programs, they are being educated passively. The child actors are going on nature walks, building crafts projects, playing with animals, and participating in games, but the little viewers are simply watching. Older viewers watch guests discuss issues with Steve Paikin or George Stromboulopoulos, but no one will turn to the home viewers to ask their opinions. 2

Worst of all, TV presents a false picture of reality that leaves viewers frustrated because they don't have the beauty or wealth of characters on television. Viewers absorb the idea that everyone else in North America owns a lavish condo, suburban house, sleek car, and expensive wardrobe. Although some Canadian shows use less glamorous actors, Canadian music videos show performers and extras just as unrealistically as their U.S. counterparts. The material possessions on TV shows and "reality" shows contribute to the false image of reality. News anchors and reporters, with their perfect hair and 3 make-up, must fit television's standard of beauty. From their modest homes or cramped apartments, many viewers tune in daily to the upper-middle-class world that TV glorifies.

Television discourages communication. Families watching television do very little talking except for brief exchanges during commercials. If Uncle Bernie or the next-door neighbours drop in for a visit, the most comfortable activity for everyone may not be conversation, but watching *Corner Gas*. The family may not even be watching the same set; instead, in some households, all the family members head for their own rooms to watch their own sets. At dinner, plates are plopped on the coffee table in front of the set, and the meal is wolfed down during *Coronation Street* or syndicated reruns of *Friends*. During commercials, the only communication a family has all night may consist of questions like, "Do we have any popcorn?"   4

Television, like cigarettes, is harmful to our health. We are becoming isolated, passive, and frustrated. And, most frightening, the average viewer spends more time watching television than ever.   5

Essay 2

The Benefits of Television

We hear a lot about the negative effects of television on the viewer. Obviously, television can be harmful if it is watched constantly, to the exclusion of other activities. It would be just as harmful to listen to CDs all the time or to eat constantly. However, when television is watched in moderation, it is extremely valuable, as it provides relaxation, entertainment, and education.   1

First of all, watching television has the value of sheer relaxation. Watching TV can be soothing and restful after an eight-hour day of pressure, challenges, or concentration. After working hard all day, people look forward to a new episode of a favourite show or another showing of *The Sopranos* or a favourite movie on cable. This period of relaxation leaves viewers refreshed and ready to take on the world again. Watching TV also seems to reduce stress in some people. This benefit of television is just beginning to be recognized. One doctor, for example, advises his patients with high blood pressure to relax in the evening with a few hours of television.   2

In addition to being relaxing, television is entertaining. Along with the standard comedies, dramas, and game shows that provide enjoyment to viewers, television offers a variety of movies and sports events. Moreover, in most areas, viewers have cable or satellite TV programming. With this service, viewers can watch first-run movies, rock and classical music concerts, cooking shows, and specialized sports events, like international soccer and Grand Prix racing. Viewers can also buy or rent movies to show on their television sets with DVD players. Still another growing area of TV entertainment is video games. Discs are available for everything from electronic baseball to *Halo 3,* allowing the owner to have a video game arcade in the living room.   3

Most important, television is educational. Preschoolers learn reading skills, numbers, and social lessons from YTV, TVO shows, and *Mumble Bumble*.   4

Science shows for older children run on Canadian network and cable stations; they go on location to analyze everything from life in the Arctic to rocket launches. Many adults are hooked on the History Channel. Also, television widens our knowledge by covering important events and current news. Viewers watching CNN can see and hear international news events, natural disasters, and election results as they are happening. Finally, with newer connections and services, like on-demand TV programming, television allows any member of the family to access and learn from all the information resources on the Internet.

Perhaps because television is such a powerful force, we like to criticize it and search for its flaws. However, the benefits of television should not be ignored. We can use television to relax, to have fun, and to make ourselves smarter. This electronic wonder, then, is a servant, not a master.

5

Understanding Coherence

In this case, essay 2 is more effective because the material is clearly organized and logically connected. Using emphatic order, the writer develops three positive uses of television, ending with the most important use: television as an educational tool. The writer includes transitional words as signposts, making movement from one idea to the next easy to follow. Major transitions include *first of all*, *in addition*, and *most important*; transitions within paragraphs include such words as *moreover*, *still another*, *too*, *also*, and *finally*. This writer also uses a linking sentence ("In addition to being relaxing, television is entertaining") to tie the first and second supporting paragraphs together clearly.

Although essay 1 is unified and supported, the writer does not clearly organize and connect the material. The most important idea (signalled by the phrase, "Worst of all") is discussed in the second supporting paragraph instead of being saved for last. None of the supporting paragraphs organizes its details in a logical fashion. The first supporting paragraph discusses children, then older viewers, then younger viewers, and then jumps back to older people again. The third supporting paragraph, like the first, leaps from an opening idea (families talking only during commercials) to several intervening ideas and then back to the original idea (talking during commercials). In addition, essay 1 uses practically no transitional devices to guide the reader.

Revising for Coherence

Activity

On a separate sheet of paper, revise one of the three supporting paragraphs in "Harmful Effects of Watching Television" by providing a clear method of organizing the material and by including transitional words.

These two essays lead to the third base or goal for revising essays: **coherence**. To achieve coherence, all the paragraphs, supporting ideas, and sentences must be clearly organized and connected. As already mentioned, key techniques for achieving coherence in an essay include the use of time order or emphatic order, transitions, and other connecting words.

BASE 4: EFFECTIVE SENTENCE SKILLS

● ● ● ● **Activity**

Following are the opening paragraphs from two drafts of the same essay. Both are unified, supported, and organized, but which one communicates *more* clearly and effectively, and why?

Draft 1

"electric rock"

[1]Where would Rock & Roll be without electric guitars? [2]The answer: where Blues, Country, and folk music was in the 1940s. [3]Rock's ancestors were played on and accompanied by acoustic guitars, fragile hollow instruments. [4]Travelling Blues musicians usually played in noisy bars, so they attached microphones and amplifiers to their acoustics—what they got was mostly feedback. [5]What they really needed appeared in 1950. [6]The solid-body electric guitar. [7]Rock's tradmark instrument brought a whole new style of music, the ways for people to make new sounds, and new playing techniques.

[8]With the invention of the electric guitar by Les Paul and Leo Fender came Rock & Roll. [9]Young musicians like Chuck Berry and Elvis Presley could be heard over the crowds of teenagers they attract. [10]The new guitars were solid pieces of lightweight plastic; performers could swing them around easily and move while they played and sang. [11]The metal strings produce louder and sharper sounds, suited to the new musics raw emotions and fast beat. [12]When Tv brought Rock to audiences in the mid-1950s the electric guitar was a required accessory for young artists—as much a part of their look as their shiny pompadour hairdos.

Draft 2

Rock Plugs In

Where would Rock & Roll be without electric guitars? The answer: where Blues, Country, and folk music were in the 1940s. Rock's ancestors were played on and accompanied by acoustic guitars, fragile hollow instruments. Travelling Blues musicians usually played in noisy bars, so they attached microphones and amplifiers to their acoustics—what they got was mostly feedback. What they really needed appeared in 1950, the solid-body electric guitar. Rock's trademark instrument brought a whole new style of music, new sounds, and new playing techniques.

With the invention of the electric guitar by Les Paul and Leo Fender came Rock & Roll. Young musicians like Chuck Berry and Elvis Presley could be heard over the crowds of teenagers they attracted. The new guitars were solid pieces of lightweight plastic; performers could swing them around easily and move while they played and sang. The metal strings produced louder and sharper sounds, suited to the new music's raw emotions and fast beat. When

TV brought Rock to audiences in the mid-1950s, the electric guitar was a required accessory for young artists—as much a part of their look as their shiny pompadour hairdos.

Understanding Sentence Skills

Draft 2 is more effective because it incorporates effective sentence skills. Here are the sentence-skills mistakes in draft 1:

1 The title should not be set off in quotation marks.

2 The main words in the title should be capitalized.

3 The plural subject *Blues, Country, and folk music* in sentence 2 should have a plural verb: *was* should be *were.*

4 Word group 6 is a fragment; it can be corrected by attaching it to the previous sentence.

5 There is a lack of parallel structure in sentence 7. The *ways for people to make new sounds* in the thesis should be *new sounds.*

6 The word *tradmark* in sentence 7 is misspelled; it should be *trademark.*

7 The word *attract* in sentence 9 should be *attracted* to be consistent in tense with *could be heard,* the other verb in the sentence.

8 The word *musics* in sentence 11 should be a possessive form: *music's.*

9 The abbreviation *Tv* in sentence 12 must be two capitalized letters: *TV.*

10 The dependent clause in sentence 12—*When TV brought Rock to audiences in the mid-1950s*—requires a comma after it.

Revising for Effective Sentence Skills

 • • • **Activity**

Below are the final three paragraphs from draft 1. Edit the sentences in this draft to make the corrections needed. This activity highlights the fourth base or goal for revising essays: **effective sentence skills**. Achieving strong sentence skills depends on attention to sentence structure, grammar, spelling, and punctuation. You may want to refer to Part 4 for a review of these points.

Last Part of Draft 1

   [13]Just as the electric guitar helped create the sound and look of Rock, it also challenged musicians to create new sounds. [14]As early as the 1951 song "Rocket 88," musicians discovered that distortion wasn't necessarily a mistake. [15]Heavy Metal owe everything to this discovery. [16]British bands like the Stones first used fuzz tone when they complained about no "Satisfaction," and the wah wah pedal added something special to Psychedelic Rock, Cream, and the 70s scene. [17]Rocks sound boundaries expanded into the experimental zone.

   [18]By the late 60s and early 70s artists moved beyond toying with equipment; they started to push the limits of playing techniques. [19]Eric Clapton may have been and still may be the supreme artist, but Led Zeppelin had the

nerve to use a bow on their lead guitar. [20]Jimi Hendrix bent his guitar body to bend and change the notes he played, then he played with his guitar on his back finally he set it on fire. [21]But the ultimate testimony to Rock's new style and to the durability of the electric guitar is the image of the who's Pete Townshend smashing his Stratocaster against the stage. [22]He discovered that solid body guitars, just like Rock & Roll, are indestructible.

[23]So Mr. Paul's and Mr. Fender's invention, an instrument that can be moulded into any shape created a new form of music and changed the shape and style of how that music sounds. [24]No matter how many new computerized instruments are invented, the electric guitar still rules Rock.

PRACTICE IN APPLYING THE FOUR BASES

You are now familiar with the four bases for revising essays: *unity, support, coherence,* and *effective sentence skills.* In this section you will expand and strengthen your understanding of these four bases as you evaluate and revise essays for each of them.

1 Revising Essays for Unity

• • • Review Activity

The following essay contains sentences that either do not relate to the thesis of the essay or do not support the topic sentence of the paragraph in which they appear. Cross out the irrelevant sentences, and write the numbers of those sentences in the spaces provided.

Covering the Bases

[1]For the past three years, Samantha has played ball with the boys. [2]In fact, she plays first base with the York University Men's baseball team. [3]The team plays a long schedule and they are serious about the game. [4]In those respects, they are no different from other university baseball teams. [5]In one respect, the York Lions are different from every other team in their league in Canada—they are the first to have a female player. [6]As a fourth-year psychology student, Samantha has had chances to observe male behaviour at first hand. [7]Some players are tough to convince; others are still occasionally patronizing; fortunately, most just see her as a great first base-player.

1

[8]At Samantha's debut game, a couple of George Brown Huskies' players were not too ready for a mixed-gender team. [9]During the warm-up, no one commented or paid any special attention to Samantha, but the game itself was another thing. [10]A fielder sniped, "You mean you're on the starting line, with three guys still on the bench?" [11]Samantha let that one roll. [12]Another asked if she had custom equipment; her answer was not printable. [13]When she came up to bat, the Huskies pitcher called his outfielders to move in on her. [14]This amused Samantha, who also plays varsity hockey. [15]She works out daily at the

2

university's fitness centre, doing general cardio and specialized weight training. [16]That first game, she confounded the skeptics by hitting a line drive over the left fielder's head.

The number of the irrelevant sentence: _____

[17]Later that first season at another conference game, the Carleton team treated Samantha to some patronizing attitude. [18]The Ravens had watched her in batting practice, so they did not try anything as obvious as drawing their outfield in. [19]They could not have avoided hearing about her ability as a player. [20]Instead, they tried a more subtle approach, annoying her with fake concern. [21]For example, one Ravens' player on base during the first inning said to her, "Careful, Hon. When you have your foot on the bag, someone might step on it. I know it's not hockey, but it's a tough game." [22]Samantha takes most ribbing in good spirit; she laughs it off. [23]Anger management is just basic psychology. [24]Needless to say, this great all round athlete survived the first season without injury, either to her body or her self-esteem.

3

The number of the irrelevant sentence: _____

[25]Happily, most of the university ball teams just accept her, as her Lions' team-mates do. [26]They criticize, coach, and curse her out just as they do each other. [27]No one questions her batting average; it has been rising every year. [28]The York Lions are not amazed when she makes a solid hit or stretches for a wide throw. [29]She was in the top three in the Baseball Canada Senior Women's Invitational, and is looking forward to a career in sports psychology. [30]If she is taken out of a game for a pinch runner, she takes it in stride; nearly every player is taken out sometimes. [31]André Lachance, her manager on Baseball Canada's women's national team said, "She's a true leader and a gifted athlete, and she's bound to strengthen the Lions' lineup."

4

The number of the irrelevant sentence: _____

[32]Because of Samantha's education and intuitive reading of people, she feels that the defensive attitudes she encountered in her first year were simply normal human behaviour in an unfamiliar situation, not blatant sexism. [33]Once the other conference teams adjusted to her presence, she was "just one of the guys."

5

2   Revising Essays for Support

● ● ● ● Review Activity

The following first draft of an essay lacks supporting details at certain key points. Identify the spots where details are needed.

Formula for Happiness

[1]Everyone has his or her own formula for happiness. [2]As we go through life, we discover the activities that make us feel best. [3]I've already discovered three keys for my happiness. [4]I depend on karate, music, and self-hypnosis.

1

[5]Karate helps me feel good physically. [6]Before taking karate lessons, I was tired most of the time, my muscles felt like foam rubber, and I was twenty pounds overweight. [7]After three months of these lessons, I saw an improvement in my physical condition. [8]Also, my endurance has increased. [9]At the end of my workday, I used to drag myself home to eat and watch television all night. [10]Now, I have enough energy to play with my children, shop, or see a movie. [11]Karate has made me feel healthy, strong, and happy.

2

The spot where supporting details are needed occurs after sentence _____.

[12]Singing with a chorus has helped me achieve emotional well-being by expressing my feelings. [13]In situations where other people would reveal their feelings, I would remain quiet. [14]Since joining the chorus, however, I have an outlet for joy, anger, or sadness. [15]When I sing, I pour my emotions into the music and don't have to feel shy. [16]For this reason, I enjoy singing certain kinds of music the most since they demand real depth of feeling.

3

The first spot where supporting details are needed occurs after sentence _____.

The second spot occurs after sentence _____.

[17]Self-hypnosis gives me peace of mind. [18]This is a total relaxation technique that I learned several years ago. [19]Essentially, I breathe deeply and concentrate on relaxing all my muscles. [20]I then repeat a key suggestion to myself. [21]Through self-hypnosis, I have gained control over several bad habits that have long been haunting me. [22]I have also learned to reduce the stress that goes along with my clerical job. [23]Now, I can handle the boss's demands or unexpected work without feeling tense.

4

The first spot where supporting details are needed occurs after sentence _____.

The second spot occurs after sentence _____.

[24]In short, my physical, emotional, and mental well-being have been greatly increased through karate, music, and self-hypnosis. [25]These activities have become important elements in my formula for happiness.

5

3 Revising Essays for Coherence

● ● ● ● **Review Activity**

The essay that follows could be revised to improve its coherence. Answer the questions about coherence that come after the essay.

Noise Pollution

[1]Natural sounds—waves, wind, bird songs—are so soothing that companies sell CDs of them to anxious people seeking a relaxing atmosphere in their homes or cars. [2]One reason why "environmental sounds" are big business is the fact that ordinary citizens—especially city dwellers—are bombarded by noise pollution. [3]On the way to work, on the job, and on the way home, the typical urban resident must cope with a continuing barrage of unpleasant sounds.

1

⁴The noise level in an office can be unbearable. ⁵From nine to five, phones and fax machines ring, modems sound, computer keyboards chatter, intercoms buzz, and copy machines thump back and forth. ⁶Every time the receptionists can't find people, they resort to a nerve-shattering public address system. ⁷And because the managers worry about the employees' morale, they graciously provide the endless droning of canned music. ⁸This effectively eliminates any possibility of a moment of blessed silence.

⁹Travelling home from work provides no relief from the noisiness of the office. ¹⁰The ordinary sounds of blaring taxi horns and rumbling buses are occasionally punctuated by the ear-piercing screech of car brakes. ¹¹Taking a shortcut through the park will bring the weary worker face to face with chanting religious cults, freelance musicians, screaming children, and barking dogs. ¹²None of these sounds can compare with the large radios many park visitors carry. ¹³Each radio blasts out something different, from heavy metal to baseball, at decibel levels so strong that they make eardrums throb in pain. ¹⁴If there are birds singing or there is wind in the trees, the harried commuter will never hear them.

¹⁵Even a trip to work at 6 or 7 a.m. isn't quiet. ¹⁶No matter which route a worker takes, there is bound to be a noisy construction site somewhere along the way. ¹⁷Hard hats will shout from third-storey windows to warn their co-workers below before heaving debris out and sending it crashing to earth. ¹⁸Huge front-end loaders will crunch into these piles of rubble and back up, their warning signals letting out loud, jarring beeps. ¹⁹Air hammers begin an ear-splitting chorus of rat-a-tat-tat sounds guaranteed to shatter sanity as well as concrete. ²⁰Before reaching the office, the worker is already completely frazzled.

²¹Noise pollution is as dangerous as any other kind of pollution. ²²The endless pressure of noise probably triggers countless nervous breakdowns, vicious arguments, and bouts of depression. ²³And imagine the world problems we could solve, if only the noise stopped long enough to let us think.

1. What is the number of the sentence to which the transition word *Also* could be added in paragraph 2? _____

2. In the last sentence of paragraph 2, to what does the pronoun *This* refer?

_____

3. What is the number of the sentence to which the transition word *But* could be added in paragraph 3? _____

4. What is the number of the sentence to which the transition word *Then* could be added in paragraph 4? _____

5. What is the number of the sentence to which the transition word *Meanwhile* could be added in paragraph 4? _____

6. What word is used as a synonym for *debris* in paragraph 4? _____

7. How many times is the key word *sounds* repeated in the essay? ⎯⎯⎯⎯⎯

8. The time order of the three supporting paragraphs is confused. Which supporting paragraph should come first? ⎯⎯⎯⎯ Second? ⎯⎯⎯⎯ Third? ⎯⎯⎯⎯

4 Revising Essays for All Four Bases: Unity, Support, Coherence, and Effective Sentence Skills

Review Activity

In this activity, you will evaluate and revise an essay in terms of all four bases: unity, support, coherence, and effective sentence skills. Comments follow each supporting paragraph. Circle the letter of the *one* statement that applies in each case.

The Hazards of Being an Only Child

Many people who have grown up in multi-child families think that being an only child is the best of all possible worlds. They point to such benefits as the only child's annual new wardrobe and lack of competition for parental love. But single-child status isn't as good as people say it is. Instead of having everything they want, only children are sometimes denied certain basic human needs.   1

Only children lack companionship. An only child can have trouble making friends since he or she isn't used to being around other children. Often, the only child comes home to an empty house; both parents are working, and there are no brothers or sisters to play with or to talk to about the day. At dinner, the single child can't tell jokes, giggle, or throw food while the adults discuss boring adult subjects. An only child always has his or her own room but never has anyone to whisper to half the night when sleep doesn't come. Some only children thrive on this isolation and channel their energies into creative activities like writing or drawing. Because of this lack of companionship, an only child sometimes lacks the social ease and self-confidence that come from being part of a closely knit group of contemporaries.   2

a. Paragraph 2 contains an irrelevant sentence.
b. Paragraph 2 lacks supporting details at one key spot.
c. Paragraph 2 lacks transitional words.
d. Paragraph 2 contains one fragment and one run-on.

Second, only children lack privacy. An only child is automatically the centre of parental concern. There's never any doubt about which child tried to sneak in after midnight on a weekday and who will get the lecture the next morning. Also, whenever an only child gives in to a bad mood, runs into his or her room, and slams the door, the door will open thirty seconds later, revealing an anxious parent. Parents of only children sometimes don't even understand the child's need for privacy. For example, they may not understand why a teenager wants a lock on the door or a personal telephone. After all, the parents think, there are only three of us; there's no need for secrets.   3

a. Paragraph 3 contains an irrelevant sentence.
b. Paragraph 3 lacks supporting details at one key spot.
c. Paragraph 3 lacks transitional words.
d. Paragraph 3 contains one fragment and one run-on.

Most important, only children lack power. They get all the love; but if   4
something goes wrong, they also get all the punishment. When a bottle of
perfume is knocked to the floor or the television is left on all night, there's no
little sister or brother to blame it on. Moreover, an only child has no recourse
when asking for a privilege of some kind, such as permission to stay out late or
to take an overnight trip with friends. There are no other siblings to point to and
say, "You let them do it. Why won't you let me?" With no allies their own age,
only children are always outnumbered, two to one. An only child doesn't have a
chance of influencing any major family decisions either.

a. Paragraph 4 contains an irrelevant sentence.
b. Paragraph 4 lacks supporting details at one key spot.
c. Paragraph 4 lacks transitional words.
d. Paragraph 4 contains one fragment and one run-on.

Being an only child isn't as special as some people think. It's no fun being   5
without friends, without privacy, and without power in one's own home. Yet, the
child who can triumph over these hardships grows up self-reliant and strong.
Perhaps for this reason alone, the hazards are worth it.

CHECKLIST OF LEARNING OUTCOMES FOR CHAPTER 6

To ensure that you have understood and met the learning outcomes for this chapter, answer the following questions:

✓ How can you achieve unity in your essays?

✓ How can you make supporting evidence effective?

✓ What three items might you put on a checklist for achieving coherence in your essays?

✓ How do weak sentence skills interfere with the effectiveness of an essay?

CHAPTER 7

Introduction to Essay Development

L E A R N I N G   O U T C O M E S

After reading this chapter, you will

- identify the main patterns of development for essays;
- know why each pattern is used;
- relate the use of different patterns of essay development to college writing assignments;
- choose a pronoun point of view that is appropriate to your essay's subject and the nature of your writing assignment.

Patterns of Essay Development

Narration and **description** are basic to all writing. As we arrange ideas into any pattern, we create a narrative line: a certain thread for readers to follow. When we try to show readers how something looks, feels, or works, we are using description.

Exposition refers to different patterns or ways of presenting the supporting points in the body of the essay. Usually, the subject of the essay will determine which expository pattern, or combination of patterns, is most appropriate.

- **Essays that mainly offer examples** clarify each supporting point with examples to clearly illustrate that point's meaning and importance.
- **Essays that demonstrate or break down a process** instruct or show how something works or how some task is achieved.
- **Essays that show or analyze causes and effects** emphasize either the reasons for or the consequences of some situation or issue.
- **Essays that compare or contrast** two subjects or two aspects of one subject can either focus on one side at a time or make a point-by-point comparison.
- **Essays that mainly define** a subject explore various meanings of a concept.
- **Essays that classify** a subject offer different groupings or categories to help explain potentially complex issues.

Argumentation or **persuasion** naturally occurs in many well-supported essays as the thesis point is carefully explained and defended.

- Essays whose *main* goal is arguing a point use specific tactics either to gain support for a potentially contentious idea or defend a position about which there might be differences of opinion.
- Essays whose *main* goal is persuasion are intended to alter the thinking of the reading audience, or to move their emotions in the direction of the writer's position. Persuasion is meant to lead to action on the reader's part; or at least to some uncertainty about his or her position, an openness to change. Persuasion, unlike argumentation, will rarely openly challenge a reader; instead it will offer a series of appeals, based on knowledge of the audience.

The chapters in this section further explain each of these patterns of development. You will have the chance to explore how the different patterns can help to organize material for essays and other writing formats in many of your college subjects. Each pattern or method has its own internal logic and uses, and each offers special strategies for ordering and exploring different types of subject material.

Keep two important points in mind, as you practise "pure forms" of each pattern of development:

---

1. **Essays rarely use only one pattern of development.**
   You will practise writing essays that follow a single pattern for supporting your point. However, more often than not, you will consciously or unconsciously use additional or subordinate methods to explain your points. You will probably use at least an example or two, whether you write about a process or trace the causes of some problem. The essay "Altered States" (pages 168–169) uses *examples* as a main method, but the writer also uses the *cause and effect* pattern to explain the origins of altered states of mind.

2. **Essays generally involve presenting an argument.**
   No matter which pattern you choose for your subject, your essay will generally offer some form of argumentation or persuasion. The overall essay structure of opening with a thesis and then providing support constitutes an argument.
   The writer of "Everyday Common Scents" (page 158) does not merely *describe* a variety of ordinary smells; her descriptive details make an effective *argument* for the importance of paying attention to everyday pleasures. Another writer *contrasts* home-cooked meals with fast-food meals; the contrasts, based on taste, nutrition, and cost, form a *persuasive argument* for his thesis ("What's For Dinner?", pages 208–209). Your essays generally have the overriding purpose of persuading your reader that the argument or point you advance is valid.

How to Use Part 2: The Progression in Each Chapter

After each type of essay development is explained in the following chapters, student essays, illustrating that type, are presented and then followed by questions about the essays. The questions relate to unity, support, and coherence—the bases of effective writing and revising explained earlier in this book.

You are then asked to write your own essay. In most cases, the first assignment is fairly structured and provides a good deal of guidance for the writing process. The other assignments offer a wide and interesting choice of writing topics. In each case, the last or next-to-last assignment involves writing an essay with a specific purpose and for a specific audience. In two instances (cause and effect, and comparison and contrast), there are assignments requiring outside reading or research.

Important Considerations in Essay Development

Before you begin work on particular types of essays, always consider the following points basic to all writing tasks:

- The nature and length of the assignment
- Your understanding of your subject
- Your purpose and your reading audience
- Your point of view

Understanding the Nature and Length of an Assignment

Writing tasks and assignments in Canadian colleges and universities are highly varied. In English and Communications courses, you will sometimes write on a topic of your own choice or on some point you discover within a given topic. Other times, in both English and your program subjects, highly specific assigned topics will be given to you.

The writing formats assigned to you may include essays, summaries, reports, letters, case studies, and analyses. Essay structures, as set out in this book, will prepare you to manage information appropriately within various types of essays as well as in formats other than the essay.

Whatever the writing task, do not begin an assignment until you know exactly *what type* of paper the instructor has in mind. Is the assignment mainly a research summary of other people's ideas? Should it be based entirely on your own ideas? Or should it consist of a comparison of your ideas with those of other authorities?

If you are uncertain about the nature of an assignment, chances are that other students feel similar confusion. Never hesitate to ask an instructor about an assignment. This will benefit both you and the instructor.

Finally, find out *how long* the paper is expected to be. Most instructors indicate the approximate length desired in assignments. Knowing the expected length of a paper will help you decide how detailed your treatment of a subject should be and how much time to allot to it.

Knowing Your Subject

Whenever possible, try to write on a subject that interests you. You will find it easier to put more time and energy into your work. More importantly, try to write on a subject that you already know something about. If you have no direct experience with the subject, you may still have some indirect experience—knowledge gained from thinking, reading, or talking about the subject as well as from prewriting.

If you are asked to write on a topic about which you have no experience or knowledge, do whatever research is needed to gain background information you may need. "Research Skills" on pages 268–291 will show you how to find and use relevant information. Without direct or indirect experience, or the information you gain through research, your writing task will seem overwhelming and you may be unable to provide the specific evidence needed to develop your paper.

Knowing Your Purpose and Audience

The three most common purposes of essay writing are to inform, to persuade, and to entertain. Most of the writing in this book requires you to persuade. You will advance a thesis and then support it in a variety of ways. To some extent, you will also write essays that inform readers about a particular subject.

Your main audience will be your instructor, and sometimes, fellow students as well. Your instructor is really a symbol of the larger audience you should see yourself writing for—an educated, adult audience that expects you to present your ideas in a clear, direct, and organized way. If you can learn to persuade or inform such a general audience, you will have accomplished a great deal.

You will learn, with practice, to customize your essay's content, viewpoint, tone, and words for a given purpose and a given audience. This part of the book includes assignments that ask you to write with very specific purposes in mind and for very specific audiences.

Determining Your Point of View or Voice

When you write, you can take any one of three approaches or points of view: first person, second person, or third person. Each is a different "writing voice," and each creates a different response in your reader. By suggesting a certain level of involvement in your material, you set up a specific distance, or lack thereof, between you and your reader.

First-Person Approach

With the first-person approach—a strongly individualized point of view—you draw on your own experience and speak to your audience in your own voice, using pronouns like *I, me, mine, we, our,* and *us.* Speaking as *I,* you speak subjectively; your audience is very aware of your presence in your writing. Using *we,* you may suggest that you include your reader or that others share your views.

The first-person approach is most common in narrative essays based on personal experience. The *I* voice in first-person writing also suits writing tasks in which most of the evidence presented consists of personal observation; this is a forceful and strong voice when your main purpose is to present your personal connection to your material. For example, your connection to detailed information is often essential in such career writing tasks as evaluations and reports in health, social, and law enforcement services, and, for this reason, they are generally written in the first-person point of view. Often, though, the limitation of the first-person viewpoint is its subjectivity. It may be an intrusive voice if you wish to emphasize your information rather than your connection to it.

Here is a first-person supporting paragraph from an essay on balancing college and work:

> The first problem I faced when I decided to enter college in my late twenties was money. That problem had a lot of questions connected to it. How was I going to pay rent and bills, buy groceries, afford tuition fees and books, and just stay alive? My job as a data-entry clerk paid well enough to let me live pretty comfortably, but my position didn't exist as a part-time job. Because I felt I was going nowhere and that I needed to find a career with a future, I wanted to learn new skills and to be paid for using my mind as well as my typing ability. I read about provincial student loan programs, but I hated the idea of going into debt. The only solution to my first problem was a part-time job. But I was still afraid of two years of learning without that regular weekly paycheque.

We, as a point-of-view choice, may suit essays in which you hope for agreement from your reader. Writing as *we* allows you to "disappear" slightly as writer, to blur your presence; *we* implies, to some degree, a common viewpoint already held.

Second-Person Approach

With the second-person approach, the writer speaks directly to the reader, using the pronoun *you*. The second-person approach is considered appropriate for giving direct instructions and explanations to the reader. That is why *you* is used throughout this book.

Use the second-person approach only when writing a process essay. Otherwise, as a general rule, do not use the word *you* in essay writing.

In English, *you* is used in conversation as a "false third-person" pronoun. Students sometimes carry this habit into their writing: "Internet research seems easy at first; *you* simply type in a key word." Is this writer addressing "you the reader"? Probably not. Rather than "you the reader," the student likely means "people," "students," or some specific group. If you discover a "false third-person" *you*, decide whom you mean by *you*. Replace that *you* with a noun describing persons you mean. If these "false third people" occur frequently in your writing, you should review the rule about pronoun point of view on pages 95–96.

Third-Person Approach

The third-person approach is by far the most common point of view in academic and much business, technical, and career-related writing. Writing as the third person, the writer includes no direct references to the reader *(you)* or the self *(I, me)*. Third person gets its name from the stance it suggests—that of an outsider or "third person." It involves observing and reporting on matters of general rather than private importance. With this approach, you suggest some distance from your subject; you allow readers some "space" for responses; and you suggest that your information is derived less from direct experience than from observation, thinking, or reading.

Here is the paragraph on balancing work and college, recast in the third person. Note the third-person pronouns *their*, *them*, and *they*, and the nouns *students* and *people*. These replace the *I* of the previous example. Note also your changed response, as reader, to this new version of the paragraph.

> The first problem many students face when they decide to enter college as mature students is money. Money is a problem with a lot of questions connected to it. How will students, without full-time incomes, pay rent and bills, buy groceries, afford tuition fees and books, and just stay alive? Many students who return to their education have held jobs that paid well enough to let them live pretty comfortably, but many positions are not available as part-time jobs. People enter college because they feel their jobs are going nowhere, and they need to find a career with a future. They know they want to learn new skills and to be paid for using their minds. Provincial student loan programs are available, but the idea of going into debt may be unappealing. The only solution to such students' first problem may be a part-time job. But these students may still be afraid of two years of learning without that regular weekly paycheque.

CHECKLIST OF LEARNING OUTCOMES FOR CHAPTER 7

To ensure that you have understood and met the learning outcomes for this chapter, answer the following questions:

✓ What are the main patterns for developing the content of an essay, and where will you find each in this book?

✓ How do the expository methods of development differ from narration and description?

✓ Why is argumentation or persuasion consistently part of essay writing?

✓ If you are assigned an essay on the subject of "Attendance and Success," which pattern of development would you choose, and why? If your essay serves to show readers how to install a software package, which pattern would you choose, and why?

✓ Which of the three pronoun points of view is generally best suited to college writing assignments, and why?

CHAPTER 8

Narration

Children beg to hear a favourite story read again and again. Over dinner, people tell each other of their day. A restless class settles down when a teacher says, "Let me tell you about something strange that happened to me once." Our ancestors' myths, tales of great hunts and battles, of angry gods and foolish humans instructed as they entertained their audiences. Narratives and epic stories still teach humanity's lessons as they engross audiences. The popularity of the film franchises such as the *Harry Potter* and the *Indiana Jones* movies testifies to the power of narrative. Whatever our age, we never outgrow our hunger for stories.

Generally, **narration** presents the events and details of a story in the order in which they happened. Someone might say, "I was really embarrassed the day I took my driver's test," and then go on to develop that statement with a chronological account of the experience.

While narrative essays often relate personal experience, not all narrative is first-person or subjective. Case studies and reports, though not personal, require narrative skill for accurate recreation of events and their meanings. Indeed, every profession's writing tasks use narration to record and recreate events and experiences.

In this chapter, you will be asked to write a narrative essay that illustrates some point. To prepare for this task, first read the student essays that follow, and then work through the questions accompanying the essays. Both essays use narrative as their main method of developing their points.

Student Essays to Consider

Accessing a Challenge

During my third semester in Social Services, I was an intern at a provincial   **1**
government agency during their "Accessibility Awareness" campaign. The
purpose of the campaign was to make service workers more sensitive to the
problems faced by people with various physical challenges. Along with two
other students from Fanshawe, I was asked to "adopt a challenge" for a day,
doing all my work without one physical ability. Some of the workers, like me,
chose to use wheelchairs; others wore sound-blocking earplugs, hobbled around
on crutches, or wore eye masks.

Just sitting in the wheelchair was instructive. I had never considered before   **2**
how awkward it would be to use one. As soon as I sat down, my weight made
the chair begin to roll. Its wheels were not locked, and I fumbled clumsily to
correct that. Another awkward moment occurred when I realized I had no place
to put my feet. I fumbled some more to turn the metal footrest into place. I felt
psychologically awkward as well, as I took my first uneasy look at what was to
be my only source of mobility for several hours. I realized that for many people,
"adopting a wheelchair" is not a temporary experiment. That was a sobering
thought as I sank back into my seat.

Once I sat down, I had to learn how to cope with the wheelchair. I shifted   **3**
around, trying to find a comfortable position. I thought it might be restful,
even kind of nice, to be pushed around for a while. I glanced around to see
who would be pushing me and then realized I would have to navigate the
contraption by myself! My palms reddened and my wrist and forearm muscles
started to ache as I tugged at the heavy metal wheels. I realized as I veered this
way and that that steering and turning were not going to be easy tasks. Trying
to make a right-angle turn between aisles of office partitions, I steered straight
into a divider and knocked it over. I felt as though everyone was staring at me
and commenting on my clumsiness.

When I had to actually settle down to work, other problems cropped up,   **4**
one after another. If someone working in another cubicle called out a question
to me, I could not just stand up to see him or her. No matter how I strained
to raise myself with my arms, I could not see over the partition. I had to figure
out how to turn my wheels in the confined space of my cubicle and then wheel
down the aisle between work stations to find whoever asked me the question.
Also, those aisles were so narrow that there was no "passing lane" where people
could get by me. For instance, a visiting MPP had to squeeze embarrassingly
close to me just to move past my wheelchair. This made me feel like a nuisance
as well as an impostor and added to my sense of powerlessness. Thanks to a
provincial initiative, however, this whole building will soon have full wheelchair
accessibility with ramps and arm-level elevator buttons.

My wheelchair experiment was soon over. It's true that it made an   **5**
impression on me. I learned more from my internship than I ever expected
to, and I wouldn't dream of parking my car in a wheelchair space. At the
same time, I also realize how little I know about working with physically

challenged people. A few hours of "voluntary challenge" gave me only a hint of the challenges, both physical and emotional, that people with any physical limitation must overcome.

The Gift

"Only one more thing on my list," Marlena said contentedly to herself. Walking back from lunchtime errands, she paused at the holiday display in the museum's gift shop window. Atop a velvety navy blue pillow sat a lustrous silver pin. She imagined crossing that last item off her list, thinking she'd found the perfect thing for her mother. But her contentment faded as a salesperson lifted the pin away, making room for a glossy book on vintage Canadian motor boats and a toy sailboat. Sometimes, moments of satisfaction and the tidiest plans just seem meant to be disturbed. 1

"My grandson would love that little boat. His father is away sailing right now, you know, off the coast of Argentina." The voice, bright as a bird's chirp, seemed to carry a melody. Its owner was an older woman who had joined Marlena at the window. Dressed head to toe in shades of green, she looked like an elf. Everything about her was bright, except for the bluish foggy layer on her eyes. Surprised to find herself so interested, Marlena listened attentively to the woman's stories of her seagoing son and of her grandson's boat collection. 2

While she listened, one thought chased round and round in her mind: her boyfriend's obsession with wooden motorboats. He went to boat shows, wrote to online lists of old boat fans, and doodled endless plans for hulls and frames on his notepads. In fact, he'd priced the very book the clerk had placed in the window. But once Marlena was inside, questions nagged her. What about the Maple Leafs sweater she'd already bought and wrapped for him? If she bought the book and the sweater, her careful budget would be shot. Agonized with doubt, she entered the store and watched the older woman buy the toy boat. She envisioned her tidy mental list scarred with cross-out lines and stood arguing with herself about changing plans and spending more than she'd budgeted. Then, startled from her thoughts by a cheery "Goodbye," she nodded and smiled at the grandmother in green and glanced back at the window display with the book. 3

Finally, she walked purposefully to the cashier. "I'm afraid I'll have to ask you to take that book out of the window." Her brother Luciano would be the one to get the hockey sweater, she decided; in fact, he would get two presents this year. She pictured her younger brother's surprise at such generosity after months of quarrels. She saw her boyfriend's face as he unwrapped the motorboat book, and she smiled to herself. No longer was she bothered by visions of untidy lists and changes to her bank balance. 4

As she left the museum to return to work, Marlena spotted the green coat and hat ahead of her at the stoplights. She hoped the sailor's son would like his gift and enjoy his own voyages. Smiling again at no one in particular, she felt quite a different kind of contentment. Organization may be a gift, but sometimes an unexpected change is the best gift of all. 5

■ Questions

About Unity

1. Which essay lacks an opening thesis statement?

2. Which sentence in paragraph 4 of "Accessing a Challenge" should be omitted in the interest of paragraph unity?

3. Which sentence in paragraph 2 of "The Gift" should be omitted in the interest of paragraph unity?

About Support

4. Label as *sight*, *touch*, *hearing*, or *smell* all the sensory details in the following sentences taken from the essays.

   a. "My palms reddened and my wrist and forearm muscles started to ache as I tugged at the heavy metal wheels."
   b. "No matter how I strained to raise myself with my arms, I could not see over the partition."
   c. "Atop a velvety navy blue pillow sat a lustrous silver pin."
   d. "The voice, bright as a bird's chirp, seemed to carry a melody."

5. In a narrative, the main method of organization is time order. Which sentence in paragraph 3 of "The Gift" is placed out of order?

About Coherence

6. The first stage of the writer's experience in "Accessing a Challenge" might be called *sitting down in the wheelchair*. What are the other two stages of the experience?

7. List three time transitions used in the third paragraph of "The Gift."

About the Introduction

8. What methods of introduction are used in first paragraph of "The Gift"? Circle the appropriate letters.

   a. Broad, general statement narrowing to a thesis
   b. Idea that is the opposite of the one to be developed
   c. An incident

About the Method of Development

9. Which aspects of "Adopting a Challenge" and "The Gift" suggest to readers that these are not fictional stories? Narrative essays, by definition, have the purpose of recounting events, or telling stories, but they are essays nevertheless.

   What are the points of difference between the two narrative essays and short stories?

Developing a Narrative Essay

Purpose and Audience

The main purpose of a narrative essay is to tell a story. Colourful details and interesting events that build up to a point of some kind make narrative essays enjoyable for readers and writers alike.

At one time or another, you have probably listened to someone tell a rambling story that didn't seem to go anywhere. You might have impatiently wondered, "Where is this story going?" or "Is there a point here?" Keep these reactions, these questions in mind as you think about your own narrative essay. To satisfy your audience, your story must have a clear overall purpose and point.

Also, keep in mind that your story should deal with an event or a topic that will appeal to your audience. A group of young children, for example, would probably be bored by a narrative essay about your first job interview. They might, however, be very interested if you wrote about the time you were chased by three tiny terriers or stood up to a class bully.

As you plan your narrative essay, think about how many background details you will need to make your story "come alive" for your audience. If you are sure that your audience knows or shares aspects of the experience you will recount, then you may choose not to include too much background information. If, however, you know that readers will need some context to understand how or why your story occurred, then you should supply enough background to help them follow your narrative with understanding and pleasure.

In general, narrative essays that involve change, discovery, or human conflict—internal or external—are entertaining to readers of all ages.

Point of View in Narrative Essays

Narrative essays recount their authors' experiences. Because they are based on these experiences, as well as on the writer's thoughts and emotions, some narrative essays may be effectively written in the first-person point of view. Here, "Accessing a Challenge" is this type of first-person essay. Such essays show and emphasize the writer's close connection to his or her subject material. The connection is essential to the essay's point. The "I" in a first-person narrative essay is *not* the essay's subject, but the "host" presenting a meaningful truth to an invited audience in such a way that they experience it as clearly as possible. In their occasional use of first-person point of view, narrative essays are alone among the methods of essay development. For the purposes of academic writing, third-person voice is preferable for the other essay types covered in Part 2.

Other narrative essays, such as "The Gift," written in the third-person point of view, allow the reader to follow the writer through the storyline at a comfortable distance. Readers "watch" Marlena as they would a character in a story or movie. Third-person narrative essays do not insistently remind the reader of the writer's presence. Writing in the third-person voice, an author can place emphasis on any aspect of the essay that he or she feels best serves the thesis' point.

- What do you feel that the writer of "The Gift" wishes to emphasize? The look and feel of settings and objects? The events in the storyline? The characters' emotions?
- Why, based on the essay, do you make this choice?

While narrative essays have the form and feel of the story as their basis, their structure is not that of a fictional story. First, narrative essay writers do not simply relate their essays as if they were telling a chronologically structured story. They do not write, "First, I did this, and then I did this . . ." type of narrative, even when writing as "I." Writing a narrative essays means choosing events and situations that best support the writer's point. A writer of a fictional story may not reveal a clear point at all; the story's point may be in the characters' actions or feelings. But the writer of a narrative essay has a duty to select events and emotions that will immediately involve the reading audience in meaning of the story.

- How does Dorota, the author of "Adopting a Challenge" keep your attention on her point throughout the essay?
- Why do you believe she chose the events she did to support her point?
- If Dorota had written about her experience as a fictional short story, what would she have written? How would it differ from her essay?

In conclusion, the narrative essay writer uses his or her story to persuade the audience of the truth of the thesis "lesson." Doing so means making a choice of point of view or voice. The choice depends on the nature of the story events, and on how important the writer feels it is to display his or her connection with those events. Sometimes an essay is more effective if its focus is on the events, elements, and/or sequence of the story, *not* on the writer—to "show" readers what occurred and what it meant. This essay will be written in the third-person point of view. Other times, if the writer's complete involvement in the essay's events is essential to the point, the first-person voice is appropriate. Whichever point of view the writer selects, a good narrative essay will offer vivid details and active, precise verbs that "sell" the story's meaning to readers.

Prewriting: Stage 1

The first stage of prewriting for a narrative essay involves **discovering your story and its meaning.** Freewriting is a particularly helpful technique at this stage. (For more about freewriting, see pages 23–25.) As you consider the story you want to relate, many ideas will crowd into your head. Simply writing them down in free-form style will jog details you may have forgotten and help you decide what the main point of your story really is.

Dorota, the writer of "Accessing a Challenge," spent a half-hour freewriting before she wrote the first draft of her essay. Here is a section of her freewriting:

> My third semester was a co-op in a provincial social services office.
> I learned more there in one day in a wheelchair than I did in an ordinary
> week's work. A lot of companies object to spending money on making places
> accessible, not just for wheelchairs, but having computers set up for people
> with visual problems and things like that. Everyone should have the opportunity

to work. At my office, they had this "Accessiblity Awareness" campaign, and at first, I didn't take it too seriously. We were given a handout, and we had to sign up for a "challenge," like wearing an eye-mask or earplugs. I chose to try a wheelchair. For some reason, I thought it would be fun. No way. It was scary and a lot of physical work. I felt really clumsy trying to get it rolling, and my arms ached. Stopping or turning it was worse. And the aisles between office partitions are really narrow. I knocked over one partition . . .

Often the writer's point emerges from freewriting about some memory or feeling, and the writer usually discovers some **conflict** or **change**. The conflict or change may be within the writer, or it may be between the writer and some force in the outside world. In either case, the conflict or change is the catalyst that drives the narrator to act. When you discover the source of your main emotional response to the events in your narrative, you will have found the point you wish to illuminate for your readers.

Prewriting: Stage 2

Once you have discovered your story and its meaning, the next stage of prewriting for the narrative essay involves **organizing the events and details**. You will develop that story in chronological order—in time sequence—from what happened first, to what happened next, and so on.

One of the challenges in creating a successful narrative essay is making sure that all the material contributes to your point. You must decide which events, or aspects of the experience, contribute most directly to your main point or to the conflict of feelings you are recreating. Too many details, or unrelated details, "sidetrack" your reader and weaken your point. Too few details, or details not vividly described in lively words, will leave your narrative "hollow" and fail to create interest among your readers. Accuracy in choice and type of details is essential to good narrative writing.

As Dorota read over her freewriting, she decided that the main point of her narrative essay was her new realization of how difficult it would be to face a constant physical challenge. She had felt discomfort and embarrassment as she tried to work in the wheelchair. In order to support that central point, she needed details that demonstrated the frustrations she felt. She created a trial outline for the first draft of her essay:

Thesis Statement: An accessibility campaign showed me the hardship of spending the day in a wheelchair.

1. Sitting in the wheelchair
   a. Awkward because it rolled
   b. Awkward because the footrest was out of place
   c. Psychologically awkward

2. Moving the wheelchair
   a. I thought someone would push me
   b. It was hard to make the chair move and it hurt my hands
   c. Difficult to steer

3. Ways the wheelchair affected me
   a. Couldn't see
   b. I felt in the way
   c. I felt funny talking to people as they bent down over me

Writing a Thesis Statement
for a Narrative Essay

Narrative essays tend to be about conflict, change, or discovery. Each of these leads people to new states of awareness or alters their views of themselves or their lives in some way.

A narrative essay's thesis can be some general truth that the conflict or discovery reveals. The essay illustrates or illuminates how the writer came to understand the thesis—this general truth can be an easily understood truth that is quite personal, as in "The Gift." Whether the narrative essay's thesis is explained as an alteration or as a human truth, it is the point or "lesson" of the essay.

A thesis for a narrative essay focused on change might be similar to the following:

That turn in the road was a genuine turning point for Yonggi.

A thesis based on an easily understood human truth could be something like this:

The value of family is, and should be, an unforgettable lesson.

When you work on a thesis statement for a narrative essay, ask yourself, "What specific moment or event changed me?" or "What truth did I learn from that experience?" The moment or event will be your topic and what you learned or the new feelings resulting from that pivotal experience will be the viewpoint that shapes your thesis statement.

First Draft and Revision

Dorota based her first draft on her trial outline. Here it is:

My co-op job for Social Services involved taking on a physical challenge for an "Accessibility Awareness" campaign. Like a few other people I worked with, I chose a wheelchair. Others used earplugs or wore eye masks.   1

It surprised me that I felt nervous about sitting down in my wheelchair. I'm not sure why I felt scared about it. I guess I realized that most people who use wheelchairs don't do it by choice—they have to.   2

When I sat down, I thought that Paula, another co-op student, would push me around. We had talked about her doing that earlier. But she decided instead to "adopt" her own challenge, and she pretended to be blind. I saw her with an eye mask on, trying to fix herself a cup of coffee and knocking it off the table as she stirred it. So I had to figure out how to make the chair move by myself. It wasn't so easy. Pushing the wheels made my hands and arms sore. I also kept bumping into things. I felt really awkward. I even had trouble locking the wheels and finding the footrest.   3

I couldn't see anything above eye level when I sat in the chair. When I tried to get down to work, I could only see inside my cubicle. When somebody asked me a question, or asked me to hand them a file, I couldn't just stand up to see them or reach over with the papers. I kept trying to boost myself up with my arms, but I couldn't see over the top of the partition. So I had to wheel myself out into the aisle every time, and just turning the chair was hard to do. The aisle was too narrow for anyone to get by my chair. The new provincial initiative I was working on will make problems like that better by widening aisles and making office spaces large enough to turn chairs around in. It will be expensive, but it's a worthwhile thing. Another thing I disliked was how I felt when people talked to me. They had to lean down as though I were a kid, and I had to stare up at them as though I were too. One person I talked to who seemed to understand what I was experiencing was Phil Chung, who mentioned that his brother-in-law uses a wheelchair.

4

Dorota waited a day before starting to revise her draft. She focused on the goals for creating an effective narrative. She had her main point and supporting points in her outline, and she tried to use vivid language and related physical details to strengthen the explanation of *what* she had felt and *why*. Here are Dorota's notes:

- The second paragraph is kind of weak. Instead of saying, "I'm not sure why I felt scared," I should try to say specifically what was scary about the experience.
- The stuff about Paula doesn't really add to my <u>main</u> point. The story is about what I learned about Paula.
- Maybe I shouldn't talk so much about the new building plans. They're related to people with physical challenges, but putting them in doesn't really relate directly to the idea that my day in a wheelchair was frustrating.
- Eliminate the part about Phil Chung. It doesn't contribute to my feeling frustrated.
- The essay ends too abruptly. I need to wrap it up with some sort of conclusion.

Look at the final draft of her essay on pages 144–145 of this chapter, and answer the following questions about her revised narrative:

- What are the conflicts Dorota feels?
- What are the origins of these conflicts?
- To which events or physical occurrences are these strong feelings connected?
- In Dorota's revised essay, which aspects of her experience are most vividly recreated? How?
- Is Dorota's narrative most effective in the first-person point of view? Why or why not?

Writing a Narrative Essay

Writing Assignment 1

Write an essay telling about a specific experience in which a certain emotion predominated. Your task will be to discover two things: an experience that triggered this emotion and the "lesson" you wish to make into the point of your essay. The emotion might be any of the following:

Fear	Anger	Silliness
Pride	Nostalgia	Disgust
Jealousy	Relief	Loss
Sadness	Greed	Sympathy
Terror	Nervousness	Disappointment
Regret	Hate	Bitterness
Shock	Surprise	Envy
Love	Shyness	Loneliness
Embarrassment	Happiness	Frustration

Prewriting

1 Spend at least ten minutes freewriting about the experience you have chosen. Do not worry at this point about such matters as spelling or grammar or putting things in the right order; instead, just try to get down as many details as you can think of that seem related to the experience.

2 This preliminary writing will help you decide whether your topic is promising enough to continue working on. If it is not, choose another emotion. If it is, do three things:

(1) Write out your thesis in a single sentence, underlining the emotion you will focus on. For example:

"Driving in winter always makes me incredibly nervous."

(2) Think about just what creates the conflict—the source of tension—in your narrative. What details can you add that will create enough tension to "hook" readers and keep them interested?

(3) Make up a list of all the details involved in the experience. Then, arrange those details in chronological (time) order.

3 Using the list as a guide, prepare an outline showing the major events in your narrative and the supporting details for each stage. Write a first draft based on your outline.

Revising

Once you have a first draft, review the four bases for revising essays as you work on the second draft:

1 **Unity**: Do you state the thesis of your narrative in the introductory paragraph? Ask yourself if there are any parts of the essay that do not support the thesis and that should, therefore, be eliminated or rewritten.

2 **Support**: Do you have enough details? Careful detailing and occasional use of dialogue help make a situation come alive. Try to add more vivid, exact details that will help your readers experience the event as it actually happened.

3 **Coherence**: Use time signals such as *first, then, next, after, while, during,* and *finally* to help connect details as you move from the beginning, to the middle, to the end of your narrative.

4 **Effective sentence skills**: Refer to the checklist on the inside front cover to edit and proofread your next-to-final draft for sentence-skills mistakes.

Writing Assignment 2

Think of an experience in your life that supports one of the following statements. Then, using that statement as your thesis, write a narrative essay about that experience.

- "The chains of habit are too weak to be felt until they are too strong to be broken."—Samuel Johnson
- "Words in mouth, no load upon head."—Jamaican proverb
- "Everyone thinks of changing the world, but no one thinks of changing himself."—Leo Tolstoy
- "Don't grieve. Anything you lose comes round in another form."—Djalal ad-Din Rumi
- "You can close your eyes to reality, but not to memories."—Stanislaw Jerzy Lec
- "When you plant lettuce, if it does not grow well, you don't blame the lettuce."—Thich Nhat Hanh
- "Love is so holy, so confusing. It makes a man anxious, tormented."—Gao Xingjian
- "He who awaits much can expect little."—Gabriel Garcia Marquez
- "Stories can conquer fear, you know. They can make the heart bigger."—Ben Okri
- "Words were not given to a man to conceal his thoughts."—Jose Saramago
- "It is better to walk than curse the road."—Senegalese proverb
- "Silence is an argument carried out by other means."—Ernesto "Che" Guevara
- "All the things one has forgotten scream for help in dreams."—Elias Canetti
- "Anger is just a cowardly extension of sadness."—Alanis Morisette
- "Man needs his difficulties because they are necessary to enjoy success."—Abdul Kalam
- "There are some things you learn best in calm, and some in storm."—Willa Cather
- "We lie loudest when we lie to ourselves."—Eric Hoffer
- "A little learning is a dangerous thing."—Alexander Pope
- "Follow your heart and you perish."—Margaret Laurence

Before proceeding with your first draft, you may want to consider the following example of how one student tested whether his plan for his narrative essay was a good one.

- What statement have I chosen as my thesis?
  "The chains of habit are too weak to be felt until they are too strong to be broken."—Samuel Johnson
- Does the incident I have chosen include some kind of conflict, change, or discovery?
  Yes, I am going to write about the day my grade twelve math teacher told me I had no chance of passing his subject or most of my other subjects. The

conflict I felt was between the fantasy I had been living—believing I would pass somehow—and the reality of the habits I'd gotten into: skipping school half the time and wasting whole days sitting in coffee shops with my friends.

- Is the incident limited in time?
  Yes, I'm writing about a twenty-minute conversation.
- Does the incident evoke an emotional response in me?
  Yes, I was ashamed, frightened, and angry at myself.
- Does the incident support the statement I have chosen?
  Yes. I had picked up the "habits" of skipping school and wasting time, so I got used to fooling myself. I was so caught in those "chains" that I wasted a year of school.

Writing Assignment 3

In this narrative essay, you will write with a **specific purpose** and for a **specific audience**.

Imagine that you are in a town one hundred kilometres from home, that your car has broken down several kilometres from a gas station, and that you are carrying no money.

Option 1: A Personal Narrative You thought you were going to have a terrible time, but the friendly people who helped you turned your experience into a positive one. It was such a good day, in fact, that you don't want to forget what happened.

Write a narrative of the day's events in your diary so that you can read it ten years from now and remember exactly what happened. Begin with the moment you realized your car had broken down, and continue until you were safely back at home.

Option 2: An Accurate Objective Narrative Among the pleasant people who helped you was a police officer who arranged for a tow truck and for emergency repairs to your car. However, she must file a report, which will include your record of events.

Write a third-person narrative report from the point of view of the officer. Describe the situation and all the assistance provided. Consider carefully all details needed for an accurate record of the event.

Option 3: An Instructive Narrative Imagine that a friend or relative is an inexperienced and nervous driver. You wish to recreate your experience as a reassuring narrative.

Write a narrative that uses your experience as an instructive series of events to demonstrate that your reader can deal with and even learn from an accident. To discover and state your point clearly, try to visualize someone you know who is nervous about driving, and as you do so, consider the details that would be most reassuring to him or her.

■ Writing Assignment 4

Read the selection "Diogenes and Alexander" by Gilbert Highet on pages 506–510. In Highet's essay, Alexander the Great learns a significant lesson from a seemingly unlikely person, Diogenes. Note especially the careful descriptions of Diogenes, descriptions that appear to work against his credibility as an influence on someone like Alexander.

After considering Highet's selection, write a narrative essay about a situation in your life where you learned an important lesson from an unlikely person. Be sure to include sufficient and specific details, as Highet does, to point out why the individual who taught you the lesson was so unlikely to have done so. Consider also how the lesson you learned, as well as the person who taught you that lesson, changed you.

CHECKLIST OF LEARNING OUTCOMES FOR CHAPTER 8

To ensure that you have understood and met the learning outcomes for this chapter, answer the following questions upon completing any of its writing assignments:

✔ Does your essay's opening paragraph state or clearly imply its point about the emotion or experience you will focus on?

✔ Are your details arranged in time order, with transitional words and phrases to show relationships between paragraphs and events?

✔ Does each detail included in your narrative help to clarify the point in your thesis?

✔ Are your details vivid and accurate enough to recreate your experience for readers?

✔ Do you conclude by returning to your point in an interesting way in your final paragraph?

CHAPTER 9

Description

Descriptions are our attempts to "photograph with words." Camera lenses are mechanically accurate; our senses and minds record places, emotions, and people in complex ways. Our word-pictures must give readers clear, vivid versions of our subjects, using sharp, colourful, and specific details that speak to their senses. Some descriptive writing tries to evoke emotions caused by what is described; other descriptive tasks involve precise recreations of something observed.

Here is a sentence in which there is almost no appeal to the senses: "In the window was a fan." In contrast, here is a description rich in sense impressions: "The blades of the rusty window fan clattered and whirled as they blew out a stream of warm, soggy air." Sense impressions in this second example include sight *(rusty window fan, whirled)*, hearing *(clattered)*, and touch *(warm, soggy air)*. The vividness and sharpness provided by the sensory details give us a clear picture of the fan and enable us to share the writer's experience.

Description is essential for explaining our observations of the world. In fact, descriptive writing skills are needed constantly in academic assignments in which any event, procedure, technology, human behaviour pattern, or strategy must be carefully recreated in words. Similarly, career writing tasks require the consistent precision and detail selection associated with good descriptive writing.

In this chapter, you will be asked to describe a person, place, or thing, using words rich in sensory details. To prepare for this task, first read the student essays that follow, and then work through the questions that accompany the essays.

Student Essays to Consider

Family Portrait

Not many people see Beatrice DaSilva as a woman of mystery. She lives in   1
Hamilton, has been happily married to her husband, Lou, for forty-eight years,
and volunteers at the Royal Botanical Gardens. Now seventy, she spends five
months a year in her Fort Myers condominium. It was there in her cool grey
concrete storage room, while rummaging through moving cartons, that she
found the photo that opened up a window to her past—a past her daughters
knew so little about. That picture of my mother as a twenty-year-old woman and
the story behind it have fascinated me from the moment I first looked at it.

The young woman in the picture has a face that resembles my own in many   2
ways. Her face is a bit more oval than mine, but the softly waving brown hair
around it is identical. The small, straight nose is the same model I was born
with. My mother's mouth is closed, yet there is just the slightest hint of a smile
on her full lips. I know that if she had smiled, she would have shown the same
wide grin and downcurving "smile lines" that appear in my own snapshots.
The most haunting features in the photo, however, are my mother's eyes. They
are exact duplicates of my own large, dark brown ones. Her brows are plucked
into thin lines, which are like two pencil strokes added to highlight those fine,
luminous eyes.

More tempting clues to my mother's past lie in the clothing and jewellery   3
she chose to wear for her portrait. The blouse and skirt, although the photo was
taken fifty years ago, would not look out of place on a street today. The blouse
is made of heavy, eggshell-coloured satin and reflects the light in its folds and
hollows. It has a turned down cowl collar and smocking on the shoulders and
below the collar. The smocking (tiny rows of gathered material) looks hand-
done. The skirt, which covers my mother's calves, is straight and made of light
wool or flannel. My mother is wearing silver drop earrings. They are about two
inches long and roughly shield-shaped. On her left wrist is a matching bracelet.
My mother can't find this bracelet now, despite the fact that we spent hours
searching through the attic for it. On the third finger of her left hand is a ring
with a large, square-cut stone.

The story behind the picture is even more revealing about the young   4
woman it captures. Mom, who was earning twenty-five dollars a week as a
file clerk, decided to give her boyfriend (my father) a picture of herself. She
spent almost two weeks' salary on the skirt and blouse, which she bought at
a fancy department store downtown. She borrowed the earrings and bracelet
from her older sister, my aunt, Dorothy. The ring she wore was a present from
another young man she was dating at the time. Another chunk of her salary
went to pay the portrait photographer for soft colours in the hand-coloured
print. Just before giving the picture to my father, she scrawled at the lower left,
"Sincerely, Beatrice."

Beatrice, not yet Mom, was quite the mysterious young lady, it seems. She   5
carefully plotted that picture to make an impression on a young man she barely

knew. That "Mona Lisa" half-smile, the expensive, soft-textured blouse, and most of all, the ring to inspire a little jealousy; Beatrice left a trail of tempting hints and clues for Lou. Then she daintily hid her clues behind the shy and serious formal inscription. Her portrait reveals more today than it tried to suggest so long ago: the beginnings of love, and a connection to who I am today.

Everyday Common Scents

Smells go straight to the brain where they wake up memories and feelings. A whiff of some scent wanders idly up the nostrils, then races off to work in the mind's twisty passages. The mind is a busier place than anyone knows. People usually consider only the extremes of the scent scale: a wonderful perfume or a really evil stench. But it's the ordinary smells of everyday places that bring back fragile memories of long ago and forgotten feelings about the recent past.   1

Offices used to have distinct smells, for instance. Workplaces today just smell like whatever is whooshing through the ventilation system but not the places where yesterday's fathers went every day. Those pale green or grey offices of the 1940s and '50s with their dark wood moldings had a whole menu of smells. There were layers of aromas that surely seeped into the people who toiled there—tired cigarette smoke, prickly twinges of hot wiring, the carbon-y traces of typewriter and elevator oil, and the odd light waft of piney aftershave. This mixture filled the buses too every day, fifty years ago.   2

Elementary schools, on the other hand, probably still smell the way they always did. The chattering hallways are full of the warm familiar smell of kids' hair and breath, soft and kind to the nose as a pet's fur. In winter, the hot breath of school furnaces ripens half-sour aromas of damp boots, sodden snowsuits, and sweet blackening bananas hiding in lockers. All seasons bring hints of that mysterious, minty, poisonous-looking green sweeping powder, and for some reason, canned vegetable soup. These days, however, classrooms may be missing one traditional ingredient in the "school aroma" recipe: the flat, nose-choking dusty smell of chalk; it's been replaced by the solvent stink of whiteboard marker.   3

Take a trip to the corner convenience store. Inhaling brings back dreamy scents and memories—the soapy, powdery smells of baby-pink bubblegum squares, the heavy smell of chocolate, and even the strangely medicinal breath of the ice cream cooler. Adults' and children's noses alike twitch at the chemical hint of printer's ink from tied bundles of magazines and comics waiting to be shelved, but only the grown-ups remember the coarse stink of sulphur rising every May from flame-red tissue paper packs of firecrackers. Corner stores have always smelled like excitement and dreams to children, and to most adults, too, if they admit it.   4

So every day can be a feast for the mind and memory. The past and present jostle for attention right under our noses. Maybe it's time to wake up and smell the coffee, the dog, the classroom, and that fresh basket of clean laundry waiting on the stairs.   5

■ Questions

About Unity

1. In which supporting paragraph of "Everyday Common Scents" does the topic sentence appear at the paragraph's end rather than the beginning?

2. Which sentence in paragraph 2 of "Everyday Common Scents" should be eliminated in the interest of paragraph unity?

3. Which sentence from paragraph 3 of "Family Portrait" should be omitted in the interest of paragraph unity?

About Support

4. How many separate items of clothing and jewellery are described in paragraph 3 of "Family Portrait"?

5. Label as *sight, touch, hearing,* or *smell* all the sensory details in the following sentences taken from the two essays.
   a. "The chattering hallways are full of the warm familiar smell of kids' hair and breath, soft and kind to the nose as a pet's fur."
   b. "In winter, the hot breath of school furnaces ripens half-sour aromas of damp boots, sodden snowsuits, and sweet blackening bananas hiding in lockers."
   c. "The blouse is made of heavy, eggshell-coloured satin and reflects the light in its folds and hollows."

6. What are three details in paragraph 3 of "Everyday Common Scents" that reinforce the idea expressed in the topic sentence that school smells do not change?

About Coherence

7. Which method of organization does paragraph 2 of "Family Portrait" use?
   a. Time order
   b. Emphatic order

8. Which sentence in paragraph 2 of "Family Portrait" suggests the method of organization?

9. The last paragraph of "Everyday Common Scents" begins with a word that serves as which type of signal?
   a. Time
   b. Addition
   c. Contrast
   d. Illustration

About the Introduction

10. Which of the following best describes the introduction to "Everyday Common Scents"?

    a. Idea that is the opposite of the one to be developed
    b. Explanation of the importance of the topic

    c. Broad, general statement narrowing to a thesis
    d. Anecdote

Developing a Descriptive Essay

Purpose and Audience

The main purpose of a descriptive essay is to make your audience see, hear, taste, smell, or feel what you are writing about. Vivid details are the key to descriptive essays, enabling your audience to picture and experience what you describe.

When selecting your topic, consider how much your audience already knows about it. If your topic is a familiar one, you can assume your audience already understands the general idea. However, if you are presenting something new or unfamiliar to your readers—perhaps a description of one of your relatives or some place where you have lived—you must provide enough background information to create a "frame" for your word-picture.

Also, consider the dominant impression you want to convey to your audience. For instance, if you choose, as your topic, a park you used to visit as a child, decide if your objective is to make your audience see the park as a pleasant and familiar place or a run-down and depressing one. The dominant impression you choose will determine the kinds of supporting details and examples to include.

Point of View in Descriptive Essays

Descriptive essays focus exclusively on presenting vivid and accurate word-pictures of their subjects. Therefore, the writer's presence is always at least secondary, if not invisible. The writer's point of view is less defined, and should generally be less evident than it is with narrative writing because the purpose of descriptive writing is to convey the impression and details of something other than the writer. For this reason, in considering voice or pronoun point of view in descriptive writing, third-person voice is preferable.

An exception to this would be writing situations where your connection to your subject is essential to presenting an effective description of that subject, as it is in "Family Portrait." Informal or journalistic descriptive essays often follow this pattern; the writer begins with his or her relationship to a person, place, or object, then moves on to recreate and describe objects and situations as clearly as possible while minimizing the writer's presence. The writer's presence as "I" often risks distracting readers from the impact of the descriptive details. Notice how the writer of "Family Portrait" becomes less prominent in the third and fourth paragraphs of her essay, placing the emphasis on details in the photograph so that readers share her impressions and ideas.

Prewriting

When Luisa, the author of "Family Portrait," began considering a topic for her essay, she looked around her apartment for inspiration. She thought about describing her own bedroom. Then, she looked out her window, thinking of describing the view. That seemed more promising. She was jotting down details about the view when she glanced at the framed portrait of her mother on her desk. "I stopped and stared at it, as I often do, wondering again about this twenty-year-old girl who became my mother," she said. "While I sat there studying it, I realized that the best topic was right under my nose."

As she looked at the photograph, Luisa began to freewrite. This is what she wrote:

> Mom is twenty in the picture. She's wearing a beautiful skirt and blouse and jewellery she borrowed from Dorothy. Looks a lot like me—nose, eyes, mouth. She's shorter than I am but you really can't tell in the picture. Looks a lot like old photos I've seen of Grandma too—all the DaSilva women resemble each other. Earrings and bracelet are of silver and they match. Ring might be amber or topaz? We've laughed about "the other man" who gave it to her. Her brown hair is down loose on her shoulders. She's smiling a little. That doesn't really look like her—her usual smile is bigger and opens her mouth. Looking at the photo makes me a little sad even though I really like it. Makes me realize how much older she's getting and I wonder how long she'll be with us. It's funny to see a picture of your parent at a younger age than you are now—stirs up all kinds of weird feelings. Picture was taken at a studio in Hamilton to give to Dad. Signed "Sincerely, Beatrice." So serious! Hard to imagine them being so formal with each other.

Writing a Thesis Statement
for a Descriptive Essay

Descriptive essays need an organizing principle—a focus that shapes the writer's choice of details. This focus is called a dominant impression.

When you work on a thesis statement for a descriptive essay, ask yourself, "What do I feel (or think of) when I see (my topic) in my mind?" or "What words come to mind when I think about (my topic)?" Your point, in a descriptive essay, is the dominant impression you have of the person, place, or thing you will write about. Your thesis statement, then, should clearly express that dominant impression.

A thesis for a descriptive essay about a motorcycle trip could be something like this:

> The trip that was such a thrilling idea was, in reality, gruelling days of bone-chilling wind and stinging rain.

First Draft and Revision

As Luisa began preparing an outline, she thought of describing how the photograph *looked*. She thought her main points might be (1) what her mother's face looked like and (2) what she was wearing. But she was stuck for a third main point.

As she looked back at the picture, two other ideas struck her. One was her own emotional reaction to the photo—how it made her feel. The other was the story of the photo—how and why it was taken. Still unsure of which would be the third main point in her outline, she began to write. This is her first draft:

Family Portrait

I have a photograph of my mother that was taken fifty years ago, when she was only twenty. She sent it to me only recently, and I find it very interesting.   1

In the photo, I see a girl who looks a lot like I do, even though it's been a long time since I was twenty. Like most of the women in her family, including me, she's got the DaSilva family nose, waving brown hair, and large brown eyes. Her mouth is closed and she is smiling slightly. That isn't my mother's usual big grin that shows her teeth and her "smile lines."   2

In the photo, Mom is wearing a very pretty skirt and blouse. They look like something that would be fashionable today. The blouse is made of heavy satin. The satin falls in lines and hollows that reflect the light. It has a turned-down cowl collar and smocking on the shoulders and under the collar. Her skirt is below her knees and looks like it is made of light wool. She is wearing jewellery. Her silver earrings and bracelet match. She had borrowed them from her sister. Dorothy eventually gave them both to her, but the bracelet has disappeared. On her left hand is a ring with a big yellow stone.   3

When I look at this photo, I feel conflicting emotions. It gives me pleasure to see Mom as a pretty young woman. It makes me sad, too, to think how quickly time passes and realize how old she is getting. It amuses me to read the inscription to my father, her boyfriend at the time. She wrote, "Sincerely, Beatrice." It's hard for me to imagine Mom and Dad ever being so formal with each other.   4

Mom had the photograph taken at a studio near where she worked in Hamilton. She spent nearly two weeks' salary on the outfit she wore for it. And I think she wore the ring, which another boy had given her, to make Dad jealous. She must have really wanted to impress my father to go to all that trouble and expense.   5

Luisa's class was asked to exchange essay drafts with each other in preparation for revision. Her classmate, Hoi Yee, gave Luisa the following comments about her paper:

In your first paragraph, you don't say if this is the first time you've seen this picture of your mother. Also, "very interesting" is a kind of neutral reaction. What did you feel like?

What does the "DaSilva nose" look like? You should describe it. Also, is there one thing about her face that really stands out?

The stuff about her blouse is really good. I can picture the material. What colour is it, and what's smocking?

The 4th paragraph seems like it should come at the end. Your essay is about your mom, but suddenly you're talking about how you feel. Then, you go back to your mother's story in the conclusion. Try moving the part about how much work she put into having her picture taken (it's really good) into the main part of the essay. Then, put your feelings in your conclusion.

Making use of Hoi Yee's comments and her own reactions upon rereading her essay, Luisa wrote the final draft that appears on pages 157–158.

Writing a Descriptive Essay

Writing Assignment 1

Write an essay about a particular place that you can observe carefully or that you already know well. Choose a store you know well, a room you have lived in for some time, or a room in the college or university you attend.

Prewriting

1 **Point of View**: If you are describing a place with which you have a strong personal connection or about which you have strong emotions, then writing in the first-person point of view may be the appropriate choice. If, however, your main focus is on describing a particular location and creating a "word picture" in which you are the "photographer" rather than a participant, using the third-person approach will keep readers' attention on your subject.

2 **Dominant Impression**: Write a short single sentence in which you name the place or object you want to describe and the dominant impression you have about that place or object. The dominant impression is your organizing principle. Any details you include in later drafts should agree with or support this dominant impression. For now, don't worry if your sentence doesn't seem quite right as a thesis; you can refine it later. Here are some examples of such sentences:

The study area was noisy.	The restaurant was noisy.
The bus terminal was frightening.	The variety store was a wild jumble.

3 **Details**: Once you have written your sentence about the dominant impression, make a list of as many details as you can that support that general impression. Here, for example, is the list made by Darren, the writer of "Everyday Common Scents":

Office ventilation air	Caretakers and green sweeping powder
Old cigarette smoke	Old black bananas—smell too sweet
Overheated wiring smell	Chalk smell—sneezing?
Small machine oil—grandfather	Bubblegum—pink, powdery pieces
Hot school hallways	Freezers had a smell, odd
Wet boots—mildew smell?	Firecrackers—Mom remembers

Use as many sensory details as possible in describing a scene. Remember that it is through the richness of your sensory details that the reader will gain a picture of the scene.

4 **Organization and Outline**: When you are creating an outline, decide which method of organization is most appropriate for your subject. Use any of the following or one that is unique to your subject.

Physical order—Move from left to right, move from far to near, or follow some other consistent order.
Size—Begin with large features or objects and work down to smaller ones.
Importance—Move from least dominant or important to most dominant or important (or vice versa).

Using your outline, proceed to the first draft of your essay.

Revising

After you have completed the first draft of your essay, set it aside for a while. When you review the draft, try to do so as critically as you would if it were not your own work. Ask yourself these questions:

- Does my essay have a thesis that clearly states my dominant impression?
- Have I chosen an appropriate voice or pronoun point of view? Is my connection to what I am describing important enough to justify my presence in the essay?
- Have I provided rich, specific details that appeal to a variety of senses (sight, hearing, smell, taste, touch)? Do all of my details relate to my dominant impression?
- Is there any irrelevant material that should be eliminated or rewritten?
- Have I organized my essay in some logical manner—physical order, size, importance—or in some other way that is appropriate to my subject?
- Have I used transition words to help readers follow my train of thought and my organization?
- Do I have a concluding paragraph that provides a summary, a final thought, or both?

Continue to revise your essay until you can answer "yes" to each question. Then, be sure to check the next-to-final draft for the sentence skills listed on the inside front cover.

Writing Assignment 2

Write an essay about a family portrait. (The picture may be of an individual or a group.)

1 Decide how you will organize your essay. Your decision will depend on what seems appropriate for the photograph. Two possibilities are these:

- As in "Family Portrait," your first supporting paragraph might describe the subjects' faces; the second, their clothing and jewellery; and the third, the story behind the picture.
- Your first supporting paragraph might describe the people in the photograph (and how they look); the second, the relationships among the people (and what they are doing in the photo); and the third, the story behind the picture (time, place, occasion, other circumstances).

2 Make an outline for your essay, based on the organization you have chosen.

3 Use your outline to make a list of details that support each of your main points.

4 Use your outline and its list of details to write your first draft.

5 Refer to the guidelines for revising your descriptive essay provided on page 164.

Writing Assignment 3

For this descriptive essay, you will write with a **specific purpose** and for a **specific audience**.

You are writing an e-mail to designers working on a new building on your campus. Their firm has asked for input from students and faculty on how a classroom *should* be designed. Choose a type of classroom or lab where you would logically spend a fair amount of class time, and describe your ideal room layout, furniture, and equipment. Give your feedback in the third-person point of view so that the emphasis is on your details.

Writing Assignment 4

Read the selection "The Greatest Story Never Told" on pages 491–498. Then, write an essay describing a location that you find (or have found) strange, unpleasant, and disorienting. For the sailors in McKeown's essay, the Arctic was such a place. For most of us, less distant, more mundane places can feel unpleasant or simply unfamiliar.

In your introductory paragraph, explain where the place is and your connection with it. Explain what aspects of the location are unappealing, unpleasant, and/or otherwise strange, and why. Be sure to state in the thesis your dominant impression of this place. Use any order in your supporting paragraphs that you feel is appropriate. Generally, a spatial method of organization will be best, but you could also go from the least strange aspect of the location to its most unappealing aspect, based on your emotional responses to the place. Use vivid images and sensory details, as McKeown does in his selection, to show readers exactly why you feel as you do about your choice of location.

CHECKLIST OF LEARNING OUTCOMES FOR CHAPTER 9

To ensure that you have understood and met the learning outcomes for this chapter, answer the following questions upon completing any of its writing assignments:

- ✓ Is there a clear dominant impression of my subject in the thesis?

- ✓ Have I used vivid sensory details to illustrate each aspect of the dominant impression?

- ✓ Does the essay sustain one point of view and one clear method of organization?

- ✓ Does the final paragraph contain ideas that reinforce the dominant impression in the reader's mind?

CHAPTER 10

Examples

In our daily conversations, we often provide examples to explain statements we make. **Examples** in exposition give readers clear *pictures* of what your supporting points mean to you. Each time you illustrate your ideas with clear examples, you increase the likelihood that your audience will understand what you say and will see for themselves the truth of your statement.

Note the examples that follow the general statement below:

The first day of classes was frustrating.	My marketing class was cancelled. Then, I couldn't find the computer lab. The lines at the bookstore were so long that I went home without buying my textbooks.

Often, examples are the *reasons* for a particular point.

That washing machine is unreliable.	The water temperature can't be predicted; it stops in midcycle; and it sometimes shreds clothing.

Learning to provide specific, relevant examples in your writing also has distinct benefits for your future. Case studies, proposals, and many types of reports are extensively supported by examples that show a precedent, similar results, or illustrative material to help readers understand the main point.

In this chapter, you will be asked to provide a series of examples to support the thesis of your essay. First, read the student essays that follow, and then work through the questions that accompany the essays. Both essays use examples to develop their points.

Student Essays to Consider

Movie Night in the Bush

Today, neighbourhood movie theatres are only memories and multiplex cinemas sell fewer tickets than ever. People watch movies at home on DVDs or computers, or squint at tiny images on iPods or cell phones. Does anyone still relax with an audience in the dark in front of a huge screen, enjoying "a night at the movies"? Well, from May until October, as many as fifty thousand people do—in a "fiveplex" in a house on a tree-covered hillside in the tiny village of Kinmount, Ontario. If the element of surprise is half the battle in attracting people, the Highland Cinemas offer more surprises than most movie houses.

First, no one ever forgets just finding the cottage-country movie theatre for the first time. "It's just on the left as you drive out of town; you can't miss it," goes the standard answer to a visitor's question. Hidden among trees and bush, perched atop a hill just past a lumber store at the village limits, people can and do miss it all the time, as they zip along Highway 121. At first glance, Keith Stata's theatre looks like a two-storey wood-panelled house. Only its small marquee, partly hidden by leafy branches, suggests that this is not just an oversized cottage or country home. Kinmount's population is less than four hundred people, not enough to support a movie house of any kind. But those who climb Mr. Stata's winding driveway are in for unexpected treats.

Once visitors open the large glass double doors, they leave the bush behind to discover more surprises—a nest of well-equipped and fantastically decorated facilities. Since 1979, the owner has expanded from one basement 35 mm projection room to five air-conditioned theatres presenting a menu of current movies. The screening rooms range in size from eighty seats up to nearly three hundred, all with multi-channel sound systems, and several featuring raked-floor stadium seating. As soon as visitors enter any one of the theatres, they are surrounded by detailed décor—anything from Art Deco wall paintings to mannequins in 1970s garb to gilded cherubs and velvet curtains. In fact, the movie-going experience is so complete that people sometimes forget they are in the middle of the woods; that is, until the occasional bat swoops through.

The most surprising aspect of the movie capital of the Kawarthas is not the bat or the décor, though. It's what consumes every inch of the lobby: Canada's largest movie memorabilia museum. Walls are papered floor to ceiling with posters and lobby cards from Hollywood and Europe. Keith Stata particularly enjoys showing off his collection of film projectors to interested visitors; he bought them up as neighbourhood theatres folded, and now owns over four hundred, some from the early 1900s. Visitors occasionally bump into one of the 110 mannequins on display. Each is dressed in a movie costume. "Going to the movies used to be an event. That's what we've tried to recreate here," says Stata. And, judging from the thousands of ordinary filmgoers and obsessed movie buffs he attracts each year, he has succeeded.

Even though summer lineups mean fighting off mosquitoes and the occasional bear lured by the scent of popcorn, the Highland Cinemas are probably the most successful multiplex in Canada. As the owner says, in Kinmount, you remember not only the movie but the movie theatre!   5

Altered States

Most Canadians are not alcoholics. Most do not cruise seedy city streets looking to score crack cocaine or heroin. Relatively few try to con their doctors into prescribing unneeded mood-altering medications. And yet, many Canadians are travelling through life with their minds slightly out of kilter. In its attempt to cope with modern life, the human mind seems to have developed some defence strategies. Confronted with inventions like the television, the shopping mall, and the Internet, the mind will slip—all by itself—into an altered state.   1

Never in the history of humanity have people been expected to sit passively for hours, staring at moving pictures emanating from an electronic box. Since too much exposure to flickering images of "reality-show" contestants, detectives, and talk-show hosts can be dangerous to human sanity, the mind automatically goes into a TV-hypnosis state. The eyes see the sitcom or the dog food commercial, but the mind goes into a holding pattern. None of the televised images or sounds actually enters the brain. This is why, when questioned, people cannot remember commercials they have seen five seconds before or why the TV cops are chasing a certain suspect. In this hypnotic, trance-like state, the mind resembles an armoured armadillo. It rolls up in self-defence, letting the stream of televised information pass by harmlessly.   2

If a TV watcher arises from the couch and goes to a shopping mall, he or she will again cope by slipping into an altered state. In the mall, the mind is bombarded with the sights, smells, and sounds of dozens of stores, restaurants, and movie theatres competing for the mind's attention. There are hundreds of questions to be answered: Should I start with the upper or lower mall level? Which stores should I look in? Should I bother with the sweater sale at the Bay? Should I eat fried chicken or try the healthier-sounding pita wrap? Where is my car parked? To combat this mental overload, the mind goes into a state resembling the whiteout experienced by mountain climbers trapped in a blinding snowstorm. Suddenly, everything looks the same. The shopper is unsure where to go next and cannot remember what he or she came for in the first place. The mind enters this state deliberately, so the shopper has no choice but to leave. Some kids can be in a shopping mall for hours, but they are the exceptions to the rule.   3

No part of everyday life, however, so quickly triggers the mind's protective shutdown mode as that favourite pastime of the new millennium: cruising the Internet. A computer user sits down with the intention of briefly checking e-mail or looking up a fact for a research paper. But once tapped into the immense storehouse of information, entertainment, and seemingly intimate   4 personal connections that the Internet offers, the user loses all sense of time and priorities. Prospects flood the mind: Should I explore real estate prices in Vancouver? Subscribe to a mailing list? Chat with a lonely stranger in Kamloops? With a mind dazed with information overload, the user numbly hits one key after another, leaping from topic to topic, from distraction to distraction. Hours fly by as he or she sits hunched over the terminal, unable to account for the time that has passed.

Therefore, the next time you see TV viewers, shoppers, or Internet users   5
with eyes as glazed and empty as polished doorknobs, you'll know these people are in a protective altered state. Be gentle with them. They are merely trying to cope with the mind-numbing inventions of modern life.

■ Questions

About Unity

1. Which sentence in paragraph 3 of "Altered States" should be omitted in the interest of paragraph unity?

2. Which sentence in paragraph 2 of "Movie Night in the Bush" should be omitted in the interest of paragraph unity?

About Support

3. Which sentence in paragraph 4 of "Movie Night in the Bush" needs to be followed by more supporting details?

4. What three pieces of evidence does the writer of "Altered States" offer to support the statement that the Internet is an "immense storehouse of information, entertainment, and seemingly intimate personal connections"?

About Coherence

5. In paragraph 3 of "Movie Night in the Bush," which three time signals does the author begin sentences with?

6. Which sentence in "Altered States" indicates that the author has used emphatic order, saving his most important point for last?

About the Introduction and Conclusion

7. Which essay indicates, in its introduction, the essay's plan of development? Write the title of the essay and the opening words of the sentence that indicates the plan.

8. Which of the following best describes the concluding paragraph of "Altered States"?
   a. A prediction
   b. A summary with a recommendation
   c. A reference to the point made in the introduction
   d. Thought-provoking questions

Developing an Examples Essay

Purpose and Audience

The main purpose of an examples essay is to support your point by illustrating it with examples. If, for instance, you decide to write an essay that asserts that online chatrooms are dangerous for children, you might cite several examples of cases in which children were harmed by contacts made through chatting. At all times, your examples must connect clearly to your main point so that readers will see the truth of your assertion.

Keep in mind two factors related to your audience's needs when you write an examples essay. First, evaluate how much your audience may already know about your topic and whether you need to provide background information. Next, consider the kinds of examples that would be most appropriate for your audience. For a group already opposed to children chatting online, it may be sufficient to use some fairly common examples. However, if your audience is undecided about the dangers to children of chatrooms, you might need more specific, more persuasive examples.

Point of View in Examples Essays

Essays that support their point with examples focus on the quality, specific nature, and relevance of those examples. The writer's presence is not necessarily desirable; it may intrude on the reading audience's understanding of the exemplary support. Both student essays in this chapter are written in the third-person "invisible" voice for just this reason.

Notice, in comparing the prewriting samples shown for "Altered States" with the final draft, that the student writer revises his drafts to remove his "first person" presence from the essay. By doing so, he ensures that the reader's attention remains on the quality of support for his point, rather than on any personal connection to supporting details.

Prewriting

When Tony, the student author of "Altered States," was considering a topic for his examples essay, he looked around his apartment at his roommates for inspiration. He first considered examples of different types of people: jocks, brains, and spaceheads. Then, he thought about examples of rooms he had shared: the Slob Kingdom, the Neat Freak Room, and the Packrat's Place.

"But that evening I noticed how one roommate acted as he was cruising the Internet," Tony said. "He sat down to e-mail his brother, and three hours later he was still there, cruising from website to website. His eyes were glassy, and he seemed to be in another reality. It reminded me of how spaced out I get when I go to a mall. I began to think about how our minds have to adjust to challenges that our grandparents didn't know anything about. I added 'watching television' as the third category, and I had a pretty good idea of what my essay would be about."

Tony had his three examples but needed to do some more work in order to generate supporting details for each. He used diagramming to help inspire his thinking. His full diagram follows.

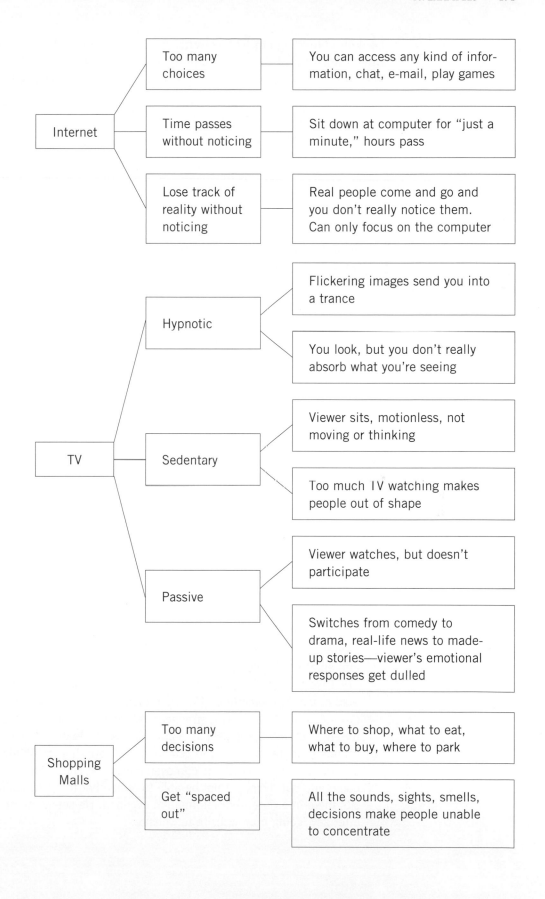

Looking at his diagram, Tony saw his thesis: People's minds go into an "altered state" when they watch TV, go to shopping malls, or use the Internet. He then turned his diagram information into an outline, which he used to produce his first draft.

Writing a Thesis Statement
for an Examples Essay

An examples essay, as the name suggests, uses examples to prove a point.

As you work on a thesis statement for an examples essay, ask yourself, "What do the examples I came up with in my prewriting add up to?" If you feel like you have a strong thesis, double-check to see if your examples truly say why it is so. If not, revise your thesis statement. There should be a clear and logical relationship between the point in your thesis and the examples that you will subsequently present.

A thesis for an examples essay could be something like this:

The HMCS *Scotian* recruitment ceremony, with its marching bands, spectacular stage lighting, and lines of highly decorated officers seemed more like a show than a military procedure.

Note also the thesis statement in "Movie Night in the Bush": "If the element of surprise is half the battle in attracting people, the Highland Cinemas offer more *surprises* than most movie houses." The writer's examples, she decided, added up to things that are surprising about the country movie house.

First Draft and Revision

Read the first draft of Tony's essay, below, and then answer the questions that follow by comparing his first draft to his revised draft on pages 168–169.

Altered States

Modern life makes demands on the human mind that no other period in history has made. As society becomes more and more complex, the mind has developed some defence mechanisms. Confronted with inventions like the Internet, television, and the shopping mall, the mind will slip—all by itself—into an altered state.

Take the Internet, for example. A computer user sits down to check his e-mail or look up something. But once tapped into the Internet, you lose all sense of time. You can chat with strangers, research any topic, play a game, or shop for any product. Some people begin to think of the online world and online friends as more real than the people in their own homes. While my roommate is absorbed in the Internet, he can even have brief conversations with people who come into our room, yet not be able to remember the conversations later. He sits there in a daze from information overload. He seems numb as he hits key after key, going from website to website.

Then there's TV. Our grandparents could not have imagined the idea of sitting passively for hours, staring at moving pictures emanating from a box. It's not a normal state of affairs, so the mind goes into something like a hypnotic trance. You see the sitcom or the dogfood commercial, but your mind goes into a holding pattern. You don't really absorb the pictures or sounds. Five minutes after I watch a show, I can't remember commercials I've seen or why the TV cops are chasing a certain suspect.

If the TV watcher arises from the couch and journeys into the real world, he often goes to the shopping mall. Here, the mind is bombarded with the sights, smells, and sounds of dozens of stores, restaurants, and movie theatres competing for its attention. Dazed shoppers begin to feel like mountain climbers trapped in a blinding snowstorm. Suddenly, everything looks the same. My father is the worst of all when it comes to shopping in an altered state. He comes back from the mall looking like he'd been through a war. After about fifteen minutes of shopping, he can't concentrate enough to know what he's looking for.

Internet surfers, TV viewers, and shoppers all have one thing in common. They're just trying to cope with the mind-numbing inventions of modern life. Hopefully some day we'll turn away from such inventions and return to a simpler and more healthy way of life.

- Where are the examples of inconsistent pronoun point of view that Tony corrected for his final draft?
- In which paragraphs did Tony expand his support? What details did he add to these paragraphs?
- Where did Tony remove a supporting detail that he considered too personal, too subjective to truly support his thesis? Was this change effective in your view?
- Where did Tony revise his essay substantially by reordering his support? Why did he do so?
- What change did he make to his final paragraph? Why?

Writing an Examples Essay

Writing Assignment 1

For this assignment, you will complete an unfinished essay by adding an appropriate third main example as well as supporting examples. Here is the incomplete essay:

Problems with My Apartment

When I was younger, I fantasized about how wonderful life would be when I moved into my own apartment. Now, I'm a bit older and wiser, and my fantasies have turned into nightmares. My apartment has given me nothing but headaches. From the day I signed the lease, I've had to deal with an uncooperative building owner, an incompetent caretaker, and _____.

First of all, the owner of the building has been uncooperative. _____

_____ .

I've had a problem, not only with the owner, but also with an incompetent caretaker. _____ .

_____ .

Perhaps the worst problem has been with _____ .

_____ .

Sometimes, my apartment seems like a small, friendly oasis surrounded by hostile enemies. I never know what side trouble is going to come from next: the owner, the caretaker, or _____ . Home may be where the heart is, but my head is thinking about moving out.

Note: If you do not have experience with an apartment, write instead about problems of living in a student residence or problems of living at home. Revise the introduction and conclusion to fit your topic.

Prewriting

1 In addition to thinking about three *main* examples to illustrate why your apartment (or residence or home) is a constant source of headaches, you should provide several *specific* examples and details to support each main point. You could begin by asking yourself the following questions:

- How has the owner or your family been uncooperative?
- In what ways have you been inconvenienced? How often?
- What has been your reaction?
- Who is the caretaker? Who does the cleaning at home?
- How has this person inconvenienced you?
- What is the worst example of incompetence?

2 Use the details and examples generated by your questioning to prepare an outline and then a first draft.

Revising

After you have completed the first draft of your essay, set it aside for a while. When you review it, try to do so as critically as you would if it were not your own work. Ask yourself these questions:

- Do I have a clearly stated thesis?
- Have I provided three distinct, relevant main examples to support my thesis?

- Have I provided enough specific examples and details to support each of the three main examples?
- Have I used transitions, including transitions between paragraphs, to help readers follow my train of thought?
- Do I have a concluding paragraph that provides a summary, a final thought, or both?

Continue to revise your essay until you can answer "yes" to each question. Then, be sure to check the next-to-final draft for the sentence skills listed on the inside front cover.

Writing Assignment 2

Write an examples essay that develops one of the following statements or a statement of your own. Write your essay using the third-person approach.

- If you look hard enough, you can see complete strangers being kind to one another.
- Supermarket tabloids use several techniques to lure consumers into buying them.
- Hockey is no longer Canadian nowadays.
- The best things in life are definitely not free.
- Living with a roommate teaches people honesty, tolerance, and consideration.
- There is more joy in simple pleasures than in life's great events.
- Looking for a job is a job in itself.
- Pets in Canada are treated like surrogate children.
- Technology is no longer our servant, but our master.
- Canadian culture is American culture with different spelling.

Be sure to choose examples that actually support your thesis. They should be relevant facts, statistics, personal experiences, or incidents you have heard or read about. Focus on why and how each example clarifies your supporting points, and your focus will naturally move toward the third-person approach.

Writing Assignment 3

In this examples essay, you will write with a **specific purpose** and for a **specific audience**.

Imagine that you have completed a year of college or university and have agreed to take part in your school's summer orientation program for incoming students. You will be meeting with a small group of new students to help them get ready for post-secondary life.

Prepare a brief presentation to the new students in which you make the point that they must be ready to take on more responsibility than they may have had to do in high school. Use clear examples to illustrate this point. You might want to focus on three of the following areas: instructors, class attendance, time management, class note-taking, textbook study, establishing regular times and places for study, and getting help when needed. You could also focus on just one area and then develop three main examples that pertain to that area.

■   Writing Assignment 4

Read the selection titled "Imagining Canada's 153rd Birthday" by Andrew Cohen on pages 533–536. Then write a third-person voice essay that supports its thesis with examples. Your essay will imagine your college or university in 2050. You may even want to write a dramatic opening paragraph, like Cohen's, taking readers to some location on your campus and showing them what it will be like in forty-plus years.

As you consider your thesis, try to imagine how education and courses, buildings, technology, and even students and professors could change in four decades. Then focus on your college or university and even on your program as you speculate on what is likely or unlikely to change where it is concerned. Your thesis will reflect your views about what could or should change by mid-century.

CHECKLIST OF LEARNING OUTCOMES FOR CHAPTER 10

To ensure that you have understood and met the learning outcomes for this chapter, answer the following questions upon completing any of its writing assignments:

✓ Are there distinct and relevant examples to support my thesis?

✓ Are there enough details and minor examples to make each main example clear?

✓ Does my conclusion reinforce what my examples have shown?

CHAPTER 11

Process

Every day we perform many activities that are processes—a series of steps carried out in a definite order. Many of these processes are familiar and automatic: for example, opening a word-processing program on the computer or starting the car. We are seldom aware of the sequence of steps that makes up such activities. In other cases, such as when a person asks us for directions to a particular place, when we try to follow the directions for installing a new piece of software on our computers, or when we are learning a new skill in one of our college courses, we become painfully conscious of the whole series of steps involved in the process of giving information or of learning something new.

Process writing involves becoming aware of the sequence of steps in a procedure and of the overall stages into which we group these steps. Process essays are, therefore, informative. They use *narrative* skills in creating a careful time sequence for ordering steps; they use *descriptive* skills in creating word pictures of objects, actions, and locations; and they often use *examples* to clarify instructions or the results of following those instructions.

In our jobs, we are asked to follow or to give instructions. We may also be asked to describe technical procedures or steps in a marketing campaign or some other project.

Whether the process writing related to these tasks involves *prescribing* (telling "how to" do something) or *describing* (showing how something is done), it should always establish the goal, analyze the steps in reaching that goal, and reiterate the value of following the process.

In this chapter, you will be asked to write a process essay—one that explains clearly how to do or make something. To prepare for this task, you should first read the student essays that follow, and then work through the questions that accompany the essays.

Student Essays to Consider

Successful Exercise

Regular exercise is something like the weather—people talk about it, but they tend not to do anything about it! Exercise classes on television, exercise programs on DVDs, as well as instructions in books, magazines, and pamphlets now make it easy to have a personal, low-cost exercise program without leaving home. However, for success in exercise, you should follow a simple plan consisting of arranging the time, making preparations, and following the sequence with care.   1

Everyone has an excuse: a heavy schedule at work or school, being rushed in the morning and exhausted at night, too many responsibilities. However, one solution is simply to get up half an hour earlier in the morning. Look at it this way: If you're already getting up too early, what's an extra half hour? Of course, that time could be cut to fifteen minutes earlier if you could lay out your clothes, set the breakfast table, fill the coffee maker, and gather your books and materials for the next day before you go to bed.   2

Next, prepare for your exercise session. To begin with, get yourself ready by not eating or drinking anything before exercising. Why risk an upset stomach? Then, dress comfortably in something that allows you to move freely. Since you'll be in your own home, there's no need to invest in a high-fashion outfit. A loose T-shirt and shorts are good. A bathing suit is great in summer, and, in winter, a set of long underwear is warm and comfortable. If your hair tends to flop in your eyes, pin it back or wear a headband or scarf. Prepare the exercise area, too. Turn off the phone and lock the door to prevent interruptions. Shove the coffee table out of the way, so you won't bruise yourself on it or other furniture. The last important task in preparing is to get out the simple materials you'll need to exercise on.   3

Finally, use common sense in getting started. Common sense isn't so common, as anyone who reads the newspaper and watches the world can tell you. You do not need to do each movement the full number of times at first, but you should *try* each one. After five or six sessions, you should be able to do each one the full number of times. Try to move in a smooth, rhythmic way; doing so will help prevent injuries and pulled muscles. Pretend you're a dancer, and make each move graceful, even if it's just climbing up off the floor. After the last exercise, give yourself five minutes to relax and cool off; you have earned it. Finally, put those sore muscles under a hot shower and get ready for a great day.   4

Establishing an exercise program isn't difficult, but it can't be achieved   5
by reading about it, talking about it, or watching models exercise on television.
To begin with, you're going to have to get up off that couch and do something
about it. Otherwise, as the expression goes, "If you don't use it, you'll lose it."

How Search Engines Work

Search engines are everyone's best online friend, but how well do users   1
know how their friends work? Why do searches sometimes yield nothing useful,
and other times produce pages of hits? A general look at how search engines
operate may help users to understand why searches go right and wrong, and
how to improve those quests for information.

To begin with, search engines do not simply passively log, then place   2
documents in a closed "library." They continuously use automated softwares
called spiders or bots that scan the Web and build up and revise their indexes.
As spiders or bots scan, they retrieve online documents, then analyze them
for possible relevance to the engine's requirements. Collected data from all
selected sites is added to an engine's index base. Searchers' queries send
commands to check every webpage in the index at that moment. For example,
a search for "hound dog" asks the engine to find any and all sites containing
the words "hound" and/or "dog." The sites judged as the best are then, in a
few seconds, returned to the user as hits or results, usually ranked in order of
priority from best to worst.

Now, how does the search engine rank those results? Once the search terms   3
are entered, the engine's software evaluates each document in the engine's
index. It judges relevance based on the position and frequency of occurrence
of the key words. For instance, if "hound" and/or "dog" appear in a site's title,
headers, and opening paragraphs, that site is given a priority position in the
results. If the words occur repeatedly within the site as well, it will be ranked
even higher. Website designers simplify indexing and searching by identifying
a site's key words with special html coding called meta tags. Spammers meta
tag misleading words to lure searchers to their sites. Search engine rankings
do not, however, guarantee relevance or consistency; a website for "Hound Dog
Drill Bits" would probably be quite highly rated, especially if the brand name
was used repeatedly, and yesterday's top-ranked site could be displaced or
disappear overnight as the busy spiders and bots refresh engines' indexes.

Ultimately, though, even though search engines are not perfect, they are   4
better friends when users try to speak their language by using advanced search
techniques. These include options for searching for groups of words, linking
words, and excluding words that could hinder the search. "Boolean operators"
are the logic-based terms AND, OR, NOT, and the "proximal locators" NEAR
and FOLLOWED BY. "Hound" AND "dog" tells the search engine to retrieve
only documents containing both terms; using OR specifies that at least one of
the terms must appear. NOT included in a word-string can eliminate irrelevant
sites; for example, someone looking up dog breeds might type in "hound AND
dog NOT elvis presley." NEAR used between search words tells the engine that
"hound" should be within a certain number of words of "dog," and "hound"
FOLLOWED BY "dog" means the words must appear in that order. Search

engines that allow users to search for phrases work this way, or require the phrase to be placed within quotation marks, "hound dog." Advanced searches allow users to speak a language that engines understand, so they generally yield more focused results.

Search engines are not the total answer for every researcher, but they are   5
instant-acting assets for curious minds. With just a little knowledge of how their engine friend works, searchers are more likely to find rewarding and relevant information. If not, it's because search engine technology has not quite reached the point where humans and computers can read each other's minds.

■ Questions

About Unity

1. Which supporting paragraph of "Successful Exercise" lacks a topic sentence? Write the paragraph number and a topic sentence that expresses its main point.

2. Which sentences from paragraph 4 of "Successful Exercise" should be omitted in the interest of paragraph unity?

3. Which sentence in paragraph 3 of "How Search Engines Work" should be omitted in the interest of paragraph unity?

About Support

4. Which sentence in paragraph 3 of "Successful Exercise" needs to be followed by more supporting details?

5. In "How Search Engines Work," how many examples are used in paragraphs 2, 3, and 4? Describe in a few words what each example is about.

About Coherence

6. Indicate the three time transition words used in paragraph 3 of "Successful Exercise."

7. In "How Search Engines Work," which time transition phrase is used in the topic sentence of paragraph 2? In the topic sentence of paragraph 3?

About the Introduction and Conclusion

8. Which best describes the introduction of "How Search Engines Work"?

   a. Broad, general statements narrowing to a thesis
   b. Explanation of the importance of the topic
   c. Anecdote
   d. Question

9. Which method of conclusion is used in "Successful Exercise"?

   a. Summary
   b. Thought-provoking question
   c. Prediction
   d. Recommendation

Developing a Process Essay

Purpose and Audience

The main purpose of a process essay is to explain the steps involved in a particular action, process, or event. Some process essays focus on giving readers actual instructions while others concentrate on showing how something happens or works. The type of essay you write depends on the specific topic and purpose you choose.

As you prepare to write your process essay, begin by asking yourself what you want your audience to know. If, for example, you want to explain how to make the ultimate chocolate chip cookie, your process essay would include directions telling your audience exactly what to do, which ingredients and equipment are required, and how to use them. On the other hand, if you want your audience to know the steps involved in digesting a chocolate chip cookie, you would, instead, detail the events that happen in the body as it turns food into energy. In this second instance, you would not be giving instructions or "prescribing" how to digest; you would be giving information or "describing" how digestion occurs.

Among the things that your audience should know are any problems that could occur at any stage in the process. Acknowledging possible setbacks and showing how to prevent or fix them, should these happen, is both reassuring and comforting to readers.

As with any other pattern of essay development, it is essential to consider how much your audience already knows about your topic. An audience unfamiliar with financial aid, for example, may need background information and some explanation of terms used in order to understand the process you have chosen to describe. If readers have never driven a car, then beginning the first body paragraph with "Put the car in gear . . ." will not help them. What does a non-driver need to know to start a car? Always write a process essay with your audience at the front of your mind. And always, before submitting it, read your essay aloud to someone who does not know how to do your process or does not already know how your process works. Make careful note of anything your listener does not understand and make the appropriate changes.

Also, be sure to follow a clear sequence in your essay, putting events or steps in an order that your audience can easily follow. Typically, steps in a process essay should be presented in time order. Therefore, transitions are essential to process essays; they reinforce the sequence of instructions or events and guide readers towards completion.

Point of View in Process Essays

Process essays, as noted in this chapter's introduction and shown in the two student examples, are of two types: prescriptive essays that instruct readers how to do something, and descriptive essays that explain how something works or happens.

Prescriptive essays generally address readers directly, so they speak to the reading audience as "you." For this reason, prescriptive process essays are unique among essay types in their use of second-person voice or point of view, as in "Successful Exercise." The writer advises readers, "prepare for your exercise session," and "use common sense." Take care with pronoun point of view consistency in writing a prescriptive process; do not allow "I" or "we" to slip in; your focus is entirely on showing your readers exactly how to do something.

Descriptive process essays, such as "How Search Engines Work," detail the operation of something or show the stages in an event. These essays do not address readers directly; they provide information. The writer is only a background presence, and does not intrude on his or her careful explanation of all information needed for readers to understand a sequence. Therefore, the third-person point of view is used, as in the second student essay.

Prewriting

Melissa, the author of "Successful Exercise," was thinking about possible topics for a process essay. The audience for the essay was to be other students in the class, so she wondered about topics they could relate to. She also considered her instructor's advice, "Write about a process that's fairly straightforward. Explaining something complex means writing a lot of background information for readers, just so they can follow the steps in the process—think of the poor student who tried to explain assembling a car engine." That tip was helpful because she first thought of explaining how to use the new version of Photoshop, and had no idea how much her fellow students knew about the program.

As her English professor continued talking, he repeated the phrase "step by step" several times, and that got Melissa thinking about anything she usually did in a step-by-step way. "Feeding the cats? No, not enough steps there, probably. Driving to school? Too many people would try that one. Well, what do I do regularly that other people perhaps don't do? What am I any good at?" Then it came to her—working out! "Well, I'm a fitness instructor, but I always exercise at home every morning. And I'm always telling customers who are beginners how to do it, anyway."

Melissa started by making a list of what she ordinarily tells her customers at the gym when they ask what they need to buy or do to exercise at home. Here is her list:

- Exercise at the same time every day—it'll become a habit
- Don't try movements that are too demanding for your fitness level
- Never eat or drink before working out
- Follow a plan, but follow it!
- Turn off the ringer on the phone and lock the door—the kids will manage
- Move the coffee tables and chairs out of the way
- Just try basic stretches and movements at first
- No jerky movements
- Don't do anything that hurts—start with gradual tries at a movement
- Give yourself cool-off time
- Making time isn't so hard—20 minutes is fine to start with
- Set your morning stuff up ahead of time
- Get up a little earlier or make time when you get home, but don't work out before bed
- Turn the heat up a bit—it's easier on your muscles
- Cut down on coffee and pop—drink more water and green tea
- Fancy workout clothes aren't necessary

- Buy some magazines, get a DVD, or go online for the right kind of exercises for you
- Don't work with weights, no matter how light, if you aren't trained

Before her next class, when her prewriting and a three-point list of the general stages for her process was due, Melissa worked on numbering the steps and pointers in her list. She wanted to put them into an order that made sense, then take out any that weren't really necessary:

~~Exercise at the same time every day—it'll become a habit~~
9 Don't try movements that are too demanding for your fitness level
5 Never eat or drink before working out
2 Follow a plan, but follow it!
7 Turn off the ringer on the phone and lock the door—the kids will manage
8 Move the coffee tables and chairs out of the way
11 Just try basic stretches and movements at first
~~No jerky movements~~ Maybe this is 12?
12 Don't do anything that hurts—start with gradual tries at a movement
13 Give yourself cool-off time
3 Making time isn't so hard—20 minutes is fine to start with
4 Set your morning stuff up ahead of time
2? Get up a little earlier or make time when you get home, but don't work out before bed
? Turn the heat up a bit—it's easier on your muscles
~~Cut down on coffee and pop—drink more water and green tea~~
6 Fancy workout clothes aren't necessary
1 Buy some magazines, get a DVD, or go online for the right kind of exercises for you
10? Don't work with weights, no matter how light, if you aren't trained

Melissa was still unsure about some items on her list, but thought she could at least group her steps and tips into three stages, to begin with. The stages she determined on were (1) Making time, (2) Preparing for each session, and (3) Getting started properly.

Writing a Thesis Statement
for a Process Essay

Process essays tell readers how to do something or how something happens. As such, they focus closely on two particular concepts: what their audience knows about the essay's topic, and how to supply just enough information so that the audience understands each step in the process.

A process essay's ideal thesis statement should present (1) a clear statement or definition of its subject, (2) the reason for, or purpose of the process, (3) an indication of the intended audience, and (4) the level of the knowledge needed for this audience to understand or complete the process. A brief description of the stages involved in the process may be included. Not every process essay's thesis will include all five of the elements above, but it must include the subject, intended audience, and reason or purpose.

A formula for writing a process-essay thesis statement could be a response to the following questions: *What?*, *To* or *for whom?*, and *Why?*

A thesis for a prescriptive, "how to" process essay could be something like this:

> Tired of takeout? Following these fairly easy steps will make the most helpless student a decent "survival cook."

A thesis for a descriptive process essay might be similar to the following:

> Learning how plant fertilizers work can make even a beginner's thumb "green" and increase the eco-friendliness of a home.

First Draft and Revision

With some preparation done, Melissa wrote her first draft:

People can come up with all kinds of reasons not to exercise regularly at home. Today, it's easy to keep up a fitness program. There are so many magazines, DVDs, and books full of tips and good information. To help you succeed at exercising every day, I've developed a basic plan for you to follow. 1

Most people say they have no extra time. They may go to the gym, but they say that between school and other responsibilities, there's no time left to do a daily workout at home. And it's really necessary to maintain stamina and overall fitness. Get up just a bit earlier, set up your coffee maker and all your morning stuff, and you'll be surprised how much you can get done before you leave for your first classes. But don't schedule exercise time before going to bed. 2

Next, you need to prepare for your exercise session. Don't eat or drink anything, even a cup of coffee, before you start, or you could get cramps or an upset stomach. Wear anything comfortable. Save the fancy workout clothes for the gym. Pull your hair back or put it in a ponytail—you don't want it in your eyes. No interruptions! Turn off the ringer on the phone and lock the door. Shove the coffee table out of the way and move the chairs so you don't hurt yourself when you move. Then get out the basic materials you'll need to exercise on. 3

Use common sense when you're starting out. Don't use weights if you're not trained to do so. Just try each of the basic movements you've chosen a few times at first. Don't keep going if an exercise or movement hurts. After several sessions, you should be able to do each exercise the full number of times. Move as smoothly as you can. Jerky motions will hurt muscles and joints. After you've finished, give yourself five minutes cool-off time. Now, take a hot shower and enjoy all that extra energy. 4

Now I've shown you how to get started on maintaining fitness at home. You just have to stop talking and do something about it. 5

When she finished her draft, Melissa put it aside for a few days. When she reread it after looking at her class notes, she was able to make some critical changes. Here are her comments:

> I think I've got the main ideas here, and my three stages, but it still needs more—and it's not too smooth, either. For instance, that first paragraph should probably at least say *what* my basic plan consists of. There's an "I" in there, too. That has to come out. Paragraph 2 seems all right, but I could be a little more specific about what to do ahead. And why did I mention not exercising at night, if this is about doing it in the morning? The third paragraph needs some more support, especially about what kind of clothes to wear; I just told people what not to wear. The last stage is almost right, but I didn't use any transitions, and I could explain how to move a bit more clearly. I need to make this less bumpy, and give it a better concluding wrap up, and take the "I" out, too.

With her self-critique in mind, Melissa revised her draft, producing the version of "Successful Exercise" that appears on pages 178–179.

Writing a Process Essay

Writing Assignment 1

Choose a topic from the list below to use as the basis for a "prescriptive" (or "how to") process essay.

- How to break a bad habit
- How to shop for a car (new or used), rent an apartment, or buy a house
- How to do a search on the Internet
- How to survive a Canadian winter
- How to find an internship (co-op position, summer job)
- How to manage your money while in college or university
- How to fall out of love
- How _____ became the successful person he or she is
- How to make hot and sour soup, oatmeal cookies, rotis, or some other dish
- How a cell phone (or other technological or mechanical item) works

Prewriting

1 Freewrite for ten minutes on the topic you have chosen. Don't worry about spelling, grammar, or organization. Concentrate mainly on the steps involved in the process. Then, ask yourself if there is enough material available to you to support a process essay. If so, keep following the steps below. If not, choose another topic, and freewrite about it for ten minutes.

2 Develop a single clear sentence that will serve as your thesis. Your thesis can either (a) state your opinion about this process ("Falling out of love is a hard skill to learn, but a skill that pays off in emotional health.") or (b) say it is important that your readers know about this process ("Knowing how to shop for a car can save you money, time, and future heartache.").

3 Develop your trial thesis statement. *What*, precisely, is your subject/process? *To*, or *for whom* is your process intended? *Why* should your audience follow or know about your process? What will be the reward, value, or outcome of this process for them?

4 Before you begin explaining your process, think again about your audience. Do they need some background information to follow the steps in your process? If you are explaining how to do something technical or some activity with its own vocabulary, do you need to provide definitions?

5 Make a list of all the steps that you are describing.

6 Number your items in time order; delete items that do not fit the list; add others you can think of.

7 Decide how the items on the list can be grouped into a minimum of three steps. For example, with a topic like "How to Grow Tomatoes," you might divide the process into (a) soil preparation, (b) planting, and (c) care.

8 Use your list to prepare an outline for your essay.

9 Consider which of the following concepts used to complete a process essay might be appropriate to your subject:

- Restating the steps and intended result of the process
- Confirming with the reader that the process is complete and/or successful
- Reassuring the reader of the value in following the steps and of the importance of the process
- Encouraging the reader to try your process
- Offering or repeating any necessary cautions, restrictions, or warnings needed at any stage of the process

Revising

Since the goal of all process writing is to show, using easy-to-follow steps, how to do something (or how something is done), the best way to "test" your draft is to have someone else read it.

Having completed your first rough draft, exchange essays with a fellow student, and ask yourselves these questions after reading:

1. Does the writer describe the steps in a clear, logical way? Is there any essential information missing?

2. Has the writer used transitions such as *first, next, also, then, after, now, during,* and *finally* to make the essay flow smoothly and to guide the reader carefully from one step to another?

3. Does the concluding paragraph provide a summary that restates the steps and intended result of the process, a final thought that encourages the reader to try the process, or any of the other recommended conclusion techniques for process essays?

4. Have any sentence-skills errors that you noticed in the essay while reading been noted for correction?

Continue to revise your essay until you can answer "yes" to each question. Then, be sure to proofread the next-to-final draft for the sentence skills listed on the inside front cover.

Writing Assignment 2

Everyone is an expert at something. Write a "descriptive" process essay on some skill that you can perform well. Write from the point of view that "This is how _____ *should* be done." Your skill need not be unusual. It can be anything from "creating a perfect meal" to "setting up a new sound system," "dealing with unpleasant customers," or "designing your first website." Write in the third-person voice.

1 If possible, perform the task and take notes on what you are doing as you go along. If that's not possible, as in "dealing with unpleasant customers," visualize a particular time you had to deal with such a customer. Make notes about what you did and where something did or could go wrong.

2 Look over your notes, and make a list of the steps you followed.

3 Decide how you can divide the items on your list into at least three steps. To guide you with this task, look at the following list of items for the process of "Dealing with an Unsatisfied Customer." Then, fill in the blanks on the trial outline that follows.

Dealing with an Unsatisfied Customer

This is how an unhappy customer should be dealt with so that other customers do not become involved and so that the customer feels that he or she has been treated fairly.

1. Introduce yourself courteously and ask for the customer's name.

2. Encourage the customer to step away from other people in the store so that he or she can explain the situation to you.

3. Use a calm and reassuring tone of voice, and suggest that you have lots of time to listen to the customer's problems.

4. Sit down with the customer, if possible, and find a notepad and pen to record the details of the situation.

5. Gently ask the customer to relate the details of the problem in the order in which the events occurred.

6. List these details and ask for clarification as you do so; never challenge the customer as he or she speaks to you.

7. If the customer is justified in any part of his or her complaint, and the product is unsatisfactory, make the adjustment calmly and quietly.

8. If the product is simply not what the customer wanted, and he or she has the receipt from its purchase, offer a refund or replacement, according to company policy.

9. If the customer has no receipt and is still displeased, state the company's policy for this situation, and offer to call your supervisor or manager to provide any additional assistance.

Step 1: Introduce yourself to the customer; treat him or her calmly and courteously

Items _____ through _____

Step 2: Carefully note all details of the customer's situation

Items _____ through _____

Step 3: Provide any adjustments you can, or ask for management assistance

Items _____ through _____

4 Prepare an outline with which to write the rough draft of your process essay.

5 Refer to the guidelines for revising your process essay provided on page 186.

Writing Assignment 3

Write a process essay that explains how a student in your program can prepare for a specific career in your area of study. This is a "descriptive" rather than "prescriptive" process essay and should be written in the third-person point of view. In your first paragraph, you will want to introduce readers to your program and to the types of career positions that it leads to. Your body paragraphs may describe courses, internships, labs, and any other specific learning methods that prepare students for this specific career.

Writing Assignment 4

In this process essay, you will write with a **specific purpose** and for a **specific audience**.

Imagine that your campus newsaper has asked you to write an article to help prepare first-semester students for the challenges of academic life.

Write an informal but helpful essay, drawing from your own experience, in which you summarize the steps involved in successfully meeting the challenges of a first semester.

Before starting this essay, you should read "Writing a Summary" on pages 257–267.

Writing Assignment 5

Read the selection titled "How to Make It in College, Now That You're Here" on pages 543–548. Then, write a process essay with the thesis, "Here are the tips that will help a student succeed in _____" (name a course in which you are now enrolled or one that you have taken in the past).

To get started, think of the advice you would like to have had *before* you took that particular course: What would you have wanted to know about the professor? The assignments? The exams? Policies about attendance, lateness, and so on? Pick three tips that you believe would be most helpful to other students, and discuss each one in a separate supporting paragraph. Model your introduction after the one in

"How to Make It in College" by telling your readers that, on the basis of your own experience, you are going to pass on the secrets for succeeding in this course.

Below are three sample topic sentences for "How to Succeed in Communications 101."

First topic sentence: First of all, a student who wants a good grade in Communications 101 should be prepared at every class meeting for a surprise quiz.

Second topic sentence: In addition, students should speak up during class discussion because Professor Knox adds "participation" into final grades.

Third topic sentence: Most important, students should start early on term essays and turn them in on time.

CHECKLIST OF LEARNING OUTCOMES FOR CHAPTER 11

To ensure that you have understood and met the learning outcomes for this chapter, answer the following questions upon completing any of its writing assignments:

✓ Does my opening paragraph state why the reading audience should follow the process?

✓ Have I supplied enough background information to make my process understandable to readers? Is there any special or technical vocabulary that should be explained?

✓ Have I mentioned any equipment or supplies that are needed as well as problems that might be encountered?

✓ Are the main stages and steps in exactly the right order to complete the process?

✓ Are there enough transitions to make the steps in the process clear?

✓ Is each step explained clearly enough with examples where appropriate?

✓ Have I finished with an effective and appropriate method of conclusion?

CHAPTER 12

Cause and Effect

Why did Stacey decide to move out of her parents' house? Why are action movies so popular? What are the consequences of a lack of exercise or too much pollution? **Cause-effect** essays often spring from questions like these. We frequently seek to understand the reasons or causes for things as well as the consequences or effects.

Cause-effect essays, therefore, involve analysis as we attempt to examine either causes or effects of some situation, event, or phenomenon. This process is not always easy, and for this reason, cause-effect essays need careful attention at the prewriting stage.

Your ability to carry out such analysis is, furthermore, often required in post-secondary writing tasks that involve explaining why a technical procedure happens or what its effects may be. Similarly, in career writing tasks, you may be required to explain why a product doesn't sell or what the effects are of either a technical process or business decision.

In this chapter, you will be asked to write an essay about causes or effects. To prepare for this task, first read the student essays that follow, and then work through the questions that accompany the essays.

Student Essays to Consider

New Country, New Person

The "foreign student" sitting quietly in a classroom is doing more than just taking careful notes or daydreaming. He or she is more likely worrying, planning, or just feeling really lonely. Living far away from home can be a new beginning, but it does have major consequences. Foreign students learn some life-changing lessons.   1

For most students, the first major consequence of moving is finding out what it's like to live away from their families and homes. No more of the comforts of home that it's so easy to take for granted: there is no mother cooking meals or tidying up, no sisters or brothers to talk to or tease, and no familiar room and belongings to return to after classes. Being a foreign student means living in a residence, a room, or an apartment. With no one to take care of them, students must learn basic survival skills fast, perhaps shopping for food and cooking for the first time. Figuring out new and often unfamiliar ingredients is difficult; so is constantly translating instructions and recipes. After preparing a dish that probably does not taste very good, cleaning up the mess is another new and tiring job. Paying bills, rent, and tuition fees means learning to handle money responsibly. Learning to live independently is a day-to-day challenge.   2

Students sometimes look up the new city where their college or university is located on "Mapquest," or buy a guidebook before leaving home. But when they arrive, they still find themselves in a completely new environment where they have to get around every day. If the student is lucky enough to have a car, he or she may have the time to just get lost a few times, see where streets lead, and find a way back home. Most are not so fortunate, so they must quickly learn about bus and subway routes, and even how much taxis cost. Learning to find their way to class is just the first step, though, because students immediately have to figure out how long trips to school will take so they can plan their time. These experiences use up time and energy that students would rather use for schoolwork or making friends, but they are valuable lessons in planning.   3

Finally, foreign students often feel lonely and isolated. They are lucky if family friends live in their new city, but usually they spend a lot of time alone. They sit alone on the bus, in class, and at meals. Most who live by themselves try to start meeting people and making friends as soon as possible, by joining student or faith-based groups, usually groups where others speak the same first language. Socializing takes a lot more courage and effort than seeing old friends at home did, but putting up with feeling unsure can be endured, if it means finding a new acquaintance or two. Otherwise, the foreign student is always just "the quiet one" in classes. New friends are so important; they help when students just need someone to talk to, or when they face problems with school or money. But most of all, making new friends means new experiences, and living a new life with others.   4

Leaving home and going to another country brings changes and experiences that cannot be compared to anything else in life. It is a new start, where students learn how to be independent, to navigate new places, manage their   5 time, and meet new people. It is difficult to manage without family and friends in another country, but "foreign students" learn how to live and also how to appreciate what they left behind.

Celebrity Stress

A fan who signed himself "Britney's Defender" wrote to her official site with a desperate plea. "Please give me some proof," he begged, "that Britney hasn't had plastic surgery." Luckily his question was ignored by the webmaster, but it's typical of the fact that everyone feels entitled to know everything about celebrities today. Stars and politicians lead stressful lives because no matter how glamorous or powerful they are, the Internet and the media generally take away their privacy, pressure them in public, and often endanger their safety.

For one thing, celebrities lack the privacy an ordinary person takes for granted. Every personal detail and thousands of lies about them are splashed over the front pages of the tabloids so that bored shoppers waiting in line at Safeway can read about "Avril and Deryck's Hidden Children" or "Ben Mulroney's Private Agony." Even a celebrity's family is hauled into the spotlight. Lindsay Lohan's drinking or some actor's sad uncle on welfare in Saskatoon end up as glaring headlines. Photographers hound celebrities at home, in restaurants, and even while they're driving, hoping for Paris Hilton to have another accident or for Avril Lavigne to lose her temper. When celebrities try to do the things that normal people do, like eat out or attend a basketball game, they risk being interrupted by thoughtless autograph seekers or harassed by aggressive fans.

In addition to losing their privacy, celebrities must cope with the constant pressure to look great and act properly. Their physical appearance is always under observation, and if they should suffer a major illness, like Michael J. Fox, the cameras will track them down, even on bad days. Famous women, especially, suffer from nasty media comments, drawing remarks like, "She's really put on weight" or "Has she ever gotten old." Unflattering pictures of celebrities are photographers' prizes to be sold to the highest bidder; this increases pressures on people in public to look good at all times. Famous people are also under pressure to act calm and collected under any circumstances. Because they are constantly observed, they have few opportunities to blow off steam or act a little crazy.

Most important, celebrities must deal with the stress of being in constant danger. The friendly grabs, hugs, and kisses of enthusiastic fans can quickly turn into uncontrolled assaults on a celebrity's hair, clothes, and car. Photographers must bear some responsibility for hounding the Britneys and Lindsays. Whether or not their actions add to the behaviour and substance-abuse problems is unclear, but they cause stress. And celebrity can lead to deranged and even lethal attacks. The near-fatal stabbing of the late George Harrison in his home and the murder of John Lennon came about because two unbalanced people developed obsessions with the two Beatles. Famous people must live with the fact that they are always fair game—and never out of season.

Some people dream of starring roles, huge power, and their picture on   5
the cover of magazines. But the cost is far too high. A famous person gives
up private life, feels pressure to look and act certain ways all the time, and is
never completely safe. An ordinary, mundane life is far safer and saner than a
life in the spotlight.

■ Questions

About Unity

1. Which supporting paragraph in "New Country, New Person" lacks a topic sentence?

2. Rewrite the thesis statement of "New Country, New Person" to include a plan of development.

About Support

3. In paragraph 4 of "Celebrity Stress," the author supports the idea that "celebrities must deal with the stress of being in constant danger" with which *two* of the following:
   a. Statistics
   b. An explanation
   c. A quotation by an expert
   d. Examples

4. In "New Country, New Person," how many examples are given to support the topic sentence of paragraph 2?

5. After which sentence in paragraph 2 of "New Country, New Person," should more supporting details be added?

About Coherence

6. Which topic sentence in "Celebrity Stress" functions as a linking sentence between paragraphs?

7. Paragraph 3 of "Celebrity Stress" includes two main transition words or phrases. Identify those words or phrases.

8. What are the two transition words or phrases in "New Country, New Person" that signal two major points of support for the thesis?

About the Conclusion

9. Which of the following methods is used in the conclusion of "New Country, New Person"?
   a. Summary and a final thought
   b. Thought-provoking question
   c. Recommendation

Developing a Cause or Effect Essay

Logic in Cause-Effect Essays

"Causes" or "effects" essays, at the prewriting stage, require an extra step in their preparation. These essays are *analytical*; they *break apart* some situation or event and *examine* either its logically sound causes or effects. Causes must be true causes, and effects must truly be effects. Therefore, performing a "logic check" on supporting points for a "causes" or "effects" thesis is necessary before drafting. Following are some criteria for a "logic check."

1 **"Time–sequence" logical errors**: a cause is not necessarily a cause because it happens before an effect. For example, if a dog crosses the road before your car stalls, it is not the cause of the stalling. Similarly, anything that simply happens after another event is not necessarily an effect. You must establish a logical causal connection between the prior, or causal and the following, or consequential events.

2 **Logical forms of causes and multiple causes**: There are three main types of causal relationships. A *necessary cause* is one that must be present for an effect to occur; for example, internal combustion is necessary for a gas engine to function. A *sufficient cause* is one that can produce an effect with no assistance; generally, there will be more than one sufficient cause of any situation or effect. An example here would be a car that will not start; a dead battery is enough to prevent its starting, so that is a sufficient cause, but an empty gas tank or faulty starter motor could produce the same effect, so they too are sufficient causes. Finally, a *contributory cause* is one that helps produce an effect but cannot do so by itself; for example, running a red light can help cause an accident, but other factors/causes must also be present as contributing causes: pedestrians and other cars. Sufficient and contributory causes are often analyzed in "causes" essays. Be certain that your supporting points and details reveal and examine enough logical causes for a situation.

3 **Chains of effects**: As you prewrite, consider that, for most situations, effects happen differently: some effects occur all at once, simultaneously. For an "effects" essay where this is the case, put your effects in order of importance. Other times, effects happen in a sequence; one effect may lead to another; these are logically sequential; therefore, they should be structured in chronological or time order, as they are in "New Country, New Person."

Purpose and Audience

The main purpose of a cause-effect essay is to explain the causes of a particular event or situation, the effects of an event or situation, or, more rarely, a combination of both.

The type of essay you write will depend on the topic you choose and the main point you wish to communicate. If, for example, your purpose is to explain why you chose your program of studies, your essay would focus on the *causes* for that decision. However, if your purpose is to tell your audience about the impact a special person has had on your life, your essay would focus mainly on the *effects* of knowing that person. Your audience will want to understand clearly, from your first paragraph, which of these options you are pursuing.

As with all essays, try to pick a topic that will appeal to your audience. An essay on the negative effects of steroids on professional athletes may be especially interesting to an audience of sports fans. On the other hand, this same topic might not be as appealing to people who are neutral about, or dislike sports. Also, consider, once again, whether your audience requires any background information on the topic. Finally, in addition to selecting a meaningful topic, be sure to make your main point clear so that your audience will readily understand the importance of the causes or effects you will explain.

Point of View in Cause-Effect Essays

Cause or effect essays are rooted in logic. Therefore, these essays, which *examine* logical relationships between ideas or events, are analytical by nature. Writing a cause or effect essay may require more preparation and skill from the writer than narrative or descriptive essays. The writer has to demonstrate his or her ability to give clear presentation of the factual material, focusing on presenting a logical sequence of supporting points and carefully explained details.

Ideally, therefore, cause or effect essays deflect attention away from the writer's "personal opinion" and presence; they are written in the third-person voice. The intrusion of "I" or narrative style can weaken readers' confidence in the truth of the essay's point and logical validity of specified causes or effects. First-person voice can make it seem that the writer is attempting to justify his or her own views rather than demonstrating the logical truth of the essay's point. For example, if a thesis stated, "I believe Canadian gun-control laws should be strengthened," then it could work as a narrative essay's argument, to be supported by incidents from the writer's experiences. But the first-person thesis actually limits the meaning of the sentence to the writer alone; it does not suggest an analytical examination of either causes or effects related to the statement. If, on the other hand, the thesis begins, "Canadian gun-control laws should be strengthened because . . .", then it has more definite impartial force. Third-person point of view does not limit itself simply to what the writer believes; instead, it hints here that causal support will be objective and logical. The purpose of a cause or effect essay is to convince readers with logic to accept the causes or effects as plausible.

Prewriting

Tony, the author of "New Country, New Person," was assigned a cause-effect essay. Because he had come to Toronto from Hong Kong a year ago, he thought about his reasons for doing so. He spent a few minutes doing some point-form brainstorming, thinking about *why* he had wanted to attend college so far from home:

- wanted to get out on my own—my whole family always in the same business
- I inherited a bit of money from my grandfather
- working in China doesn't appeal to me, and not enough opportunities in HK
- just seemed too easy, nothing was my own, and nothing new
- looking after myself is tough
- now I feel like a different person, not the "second son"

- my cousin went to university in Vancouver and is really doing well
- it was so hard at first though and sometimes I miss everybody
- I wish I'd listened to my father when he talked about handling my money

The next day, when he went back to his notes, he noticed that in his list of points, he was starting to include ideas that were *results,* or *consequences* of coming to college on his own in Canada, such as having to take care of himself and missing his family. He explained, "I started at George Brown when I'd only been in Canada for a month, so the first semester was really difficult. I didn't know anyone in Toronto, really, except for some friends of my uncle, and they lived in Markham, north of the city. I guess I was kind of spoiled at home and trying to live on my own made me grow up in a hurry. Now, I really hate the term 'foreign student'; it sounds like a sitcom character." Thinking more about the experiences that resulted from leaving Hong Kong, he started writing about the last year:

- Being independent is good, but it's a lot of work
- Had to figure out how to meet people
- I hated going back to my empty room every night
- The TTC is okay, but I was late to early classes a few times—had to time bus and subway trips
- People say HK is hard to get around in, but Toronto was worse at first—I got lost so many times
- Could talk to people in restaurants in Chinese but too expensive to eat out a lot
- I can't cook! I miss everything my mother made; I miss HK street food
- Bank machines are everywhere, and I spent so much at first
- Had to get a loan from my father—he wasn't happy
- I miss my brothers and Mei—there's nobody home here
- I was so shy when I joined that design club
- My spoken English wasn't as good as I thought it was
- Didn't recognize a lot of the food in supermarkets—Asian stores are fine, though
- Cleaning my room all the time is annoying, so is doing laundry
- I ate lunch by myself for so long
- Never had enough time for schoolwork the first semester
- Found a group of gamers I really like last winter
- I hate snow
- Never talked in classes at first, sat by myself

Taking a look at this list, Tony believed he had some ideas that might make an essay about the effects of coming to Canada to go to college. Now he needed to find three categories, groupings for the consequences of moving.

First, he tried:
1. Missing home
2. Living in a new city
3. Being lonely

Concerned that "missing home" and "being lonely" were too similar, he looked at his list again, and the word "independent" in the first item caught his eye. Sure, he missed home, but having to do everything for himself was really the first consequence of being on his own. Next, he noticed that he had items about finding his way around Toronto, and he remembered talking about getting lost and taking the wrong bus with other students. "Learning to get around" was probably more specifically a consequence than just "living" in a new city. So, he revised his groups:

1. Learning to be independent
2. Trying to get around in a new city
3. Being lonely and finding new friends

Now Tony decided he could try placing the list items in those three groups:

1 Being independent is good, but it's a lot of work
3 Had to figure out how to meet people
1 I hated going back to my empty room every night
2 The TTC is okay, but sometimes I was late to early classes—had to time bus and subway trips
2 People say HK is hard to get around in, but Toronto was worse at first—I got lost so many times
1? Could talk to people in restaurants in Chinese but too expensive to eat out a lot
1 I can't cook! I miss everything my mother made; I miss HK street food
? Bank machines are everywhere, and I spent so much at first
~~Had to get a loan from my father—he wasn't happy~~
2 I miss my brothers and Mei—there's nobody home here
3 I was so shy when I joined that design club
~~My spoken English wasn't as good as I thought it was~~
1 Didn't recognize a lot of the food in supermarkets—Asian stores are fine, though
1 Cleaning my room all the time is annoying, so is doing laundry
3 I ate lunch by myself for so long
2 Never had enough time for schoolwork the first semester
3 Found a group of gamers I really like last winter
~~I hate snow~~
3 Never talked in classes at first, sat by myself

With some idea of how he could support his three consequence-points, Tony wrote a trial thesis, "Foreign students learn life-changing lessons," then made an outline for his essay.

Writing a Thesis Statement
for a Cause or Effect Essay

Essays that deal with *causes* set out the reasons why some debatable or interesting situation exists. Their thesis statements usually contain a brief description of the effect, then provide an argument for the rightness of the causes offered. To be sure that such a thesis truly involves causes, test it by writing your topic and viewpoint, followed by *because*: for example, "Students from Japan would find Canadian college students lazy because . . . ."

Essays that discuss *effects* set out the results of a similarly debatable situation or circumstance. Their thesis statements reverse the procedure of those for *causes* essays by briefly describing or discussing the cause, then presenting an argument for the rightness of effects offered. To be sure that such a thesis truly supplies effects, test it by writing it this way: "Lower standards in high school caused these results: . . . ."

In either case, you will need to suggest or state directly whether your essay will deal with causes or effects.

First Draft and Revision

With his outline, Tony produced this as a first draft:

Coming to a new country to study, becoming a "foreign student," means more changes than I ever imagined. Moving away from home has had major consequences for me.   1

One result of coming to Canada was learning to be independent. I took all the comforts of home for granted. Now, I had to cook, clean up after myself, and worst of all, I had no one to talk to when I got home after classes. In fact, I hated going home sometimes, and facing my mess. Because I never learned to cook or shop for groceries, I was really confused in supermarkets. I had never seen a lot of the packages and products before, and I had no idea how to prepare most meats and vegetables. Downtown where my apartment is, there are Asian markets, and the food there is familiar, but I still had to learn how to cook it. Night after night, I made awful meals, then spent time cleaning up when I should have been doing homework. And I had real problems handling my money, too.   2

Before I left Hong Kong, I looked up Toronto on Mapquest, so I thought I could get around the area where my college is without too many problems. I did not count on using the TTC, though. At first, I sometimes took the wrong streetcar because I didn't think to get a transit map, so I was late to morning classes. I should have bought a street guide sooner than I did because I got lost once just trying to go to a convenience store. Finally, I had to actually sit down and plan how I was going to get to the college, time my trips, and work out how long it was going to take if I took different routes. Learning to plan just my trips to school was an important lesson—it helped me to start planning my time better.   3

But the biggest consequence of leaving home was loneliness. Friends of my uncle live in Markham, but I hardly ever saw them because the trip up there took nearly two hours by subway and bus. Most of the time, I was alone. E-mailing and chatting online with family and friends at home helped, but I knew I'd have to start meeting people. After a month of sitting by myself in classes and at lunch, I worked up the courage to join a design club at college, but for the first while I felt too shy to say much. What really helped was meeting a group of gamers; it was so easy to discuss the games we all play. By the end of first semester, I actually had two new friends.   4

Leaving home and moving across the world to another country is not like any other experience. It's a challenge and a chance to make a new start.   5

Having written only narrative and examples essays so far, Tony was uncertain about his first draft, so he made an appointment with his instructor. First, she mentioned that his draft contained good specific details about his experiences, but suggested that it seemed more like a narrative essay about how he felt when he first arrived in Canada. An "effects" essay, she said, should focus completely on demonstrating how his consequences followed from the "cause" of leaving home to study. It should be a bit less personal, not limited only to Tony's experience, but make its point by showing how specific consequences arise necessarily from his "cause." She suggested that, for this reason, this essay was the ideal occasion for him to work on writing in the third-person voice.

To clear up his thinking about the way he stated his supporting details, Tony started by revising his outline to start with his "cause." That way, when he rewrote his draft, he would be less tempted to use first-person point of view. Instead, he would look only at his outline to focus himself on its points and support. Here is his revised outline for his effects essay:

Cause: Leaving home to go to college

Thesis: Coming to another country to study has life-changing consequences

Effect # 1: Learning to be independent
Because of leaving home and family . . .
- No cooked meals, no clean room
- Missing belongings
- Missing family and friends to talk to
- Living in apartment or residence
- Having to cook and shop
- Handling money and budgeting

Effect # 2: Trying to get around in a new city (& manage time)
Because of living someplace new . . .
- Have to learn city streets quickly, getting lost
- Carry a map book all the time
- No car, so need to figure out transit system
- [This means] Hard to get to college on time
- Making "trial runs" to time streetcar & bus trips to college
- Learning to plan time

Effect # 3: Being alone and needing to meet new people
Because of knowing nearly no one . . .
- Sit alone in classes and at lunch
- No one to talk to in evening (same as Effect # 1?)
- [This means] Need to get to know people
- Use a lot of courage, time, & energy to find a group or club
- Have to find common interest with others
- Scared to talk to people at first
- Worrying too much about school & money problems if no friends

Tony now felt ready to tackle writing the third-person final version of "New Country, New Person," that appears on pages 191–192.

> ### *Synonyms for "Cause" and "Effect"*
>
> When writing "causes" or "effects" essays, students often stumble on avoiding repetition of their key words. Following are lists of some synonyms for each:
>
> Cause: reason why, factor (in), grounds (for), having roots (in), source, basis (of/for)
>
> Effect: result, consequence, outcome, offshoot, end product

Writing a Cause or Effect Essay

Writing Assignment 1

Choose one of the statements below, and begin by generating three briefly stated causes or effects for it. Be sure that you have three separate and distinct causes or effects.

1. Cuts in funding for education have had damaging effects on Canadian colleges and universities.
2. Many politicians and top executives are the offspring of first-generation Canadian families.
3. Garbage disposal problems in Canadian cities and towns have damaged the environment.
4. Career opportunities in computer programming are diminishing in this decade.

Prewriting

1 Examine the series of causes or effects you created, and formulate a thesis statement. The three causes or effects will function as your main points. Make sure that each of your main points is a *separate* and *distinct* point, not a restatement of one of the other points. Also, make sure that *causes* really cause or create the situation identified in your thesis statement and don't simply "come before" it and that *effects* actually result from the situation and don't just "occur after" that situation.

2 Prepare an outline for your essay. As you are doing so, decide whether you will support each of your main points with several examples or with one extended example.

3 Write a first draft with an introduction that attracts the reader's interest, gives some background information, and presents a thesis statement and plan of development that clearly indicates whether you are focusing on causes or effects.

Revising

After you have completed the first draft of the essay, set it aside for a while. When you reread what you have written, prepare for revising by asking yourself these questions:

- Does the essay have a clearly stated thesis?
- Have I backed up each main point with one extended example or several shorter examples? Do I have enough detailed support? Do I have a relatively equal amount of support for each main point?
- Have I performed a "logic check" on my causes or effects?
  (1) Have I made a "time-sequence" logical error?
  (2) Have I considered "multiple causes and chains of effects"?
- Have I used transition words to help readers follow sequence and causality in my train of thought?
- Does my concluding paragraph wrap up my essay and either strengthen my point or give it wider meaning?

Continue to revise your essay until you can answer "yes" to each question. Then, be sure to check the next-to-final draft for the sentence skills listed on the inside front cover.

Writing Assignment 2

If students from another country decided to visit your college or university, they would encounter some surprising customs and attitudes. You would have reasons to feel both proud and perhaps embarrassed by the situations the foreign students would encounter. Write a cause essay explaining your feelings about specific aspects of a Canadian post-secondary student's daily life. Give reasons for your feelings.

1 You will probably have an instant, gut reaction to the question, "Am I more proud of or embarrassed by my everyday academic and lifestyle habits?" Go with that reaction; you will find it easier to come up with supporting points for the thesis. Then, generate supporting points and details by making a list. Call it "Reasons I'm proud of Canadian post-secondary life" or "Reasons I'm embarrassed by Canadian post-secondary life." Don't worry about whether the reasons are important, silly, significant, or trivial. Just write down as many as possible.

2 Review your list and ask yourself if some of the items could be grouped into one category. For instance, a list of reasons to be proud of Canadian post-secondary life might include items such as, "We're up to date on technological career training" and "Students in most colleges are asked for input about their courses." These could be a category called "Advances in Canadian Colleges and Universities." That category, in turn, could serve as a main supporting point in your essay.

3 Having decided on three main supporting points, write an outline that includes those points, details, and examples (one extended example or several shorter ones). The ideas described in #2 above would be outlined like this:

Point: Canadian colleges and universities have made several important advances in recent years.

1. Technology is used to prepare students for careers
2. Academic programs are tuned in to career growth areas, like digital animation
3. Students are consulted about satisfaction with courses each year

4   Using your outline, write the first draft of your cause essay using third-person point of view.

5   Refer to the guidelines for revising your cause essay provided on pages 200–201.

■ Writing Assignment 3

In this essay, you will write with a **specific purpose** and for a **specific audience**.

Imagine that several friends of yours complain they are having a hard time learning anything in a class taught by Professor X. You volunteer to attend the class and see for yourself. You also get information from your friends about the course requirements.

Afterwards, you write a letter to Professor X, calling attention to what you see as causes of the learning problems that students are having in the class. To organize your essay letter, you might develop each of these causes in a separate supporting paragraph. In the second part of each supporting paragraph, you might suggest changes that Professor X could make to deal with each problem.

■ Writing Assignment 4

Write an essay that discusses the effects of one of the following:

- Plagiarizing material for an essay
- Not attending class
- Not preparing for class
- Arriving late to class

You may also, with your instructor's permission, select another topic related to a certain college or university experience.

This essay should present some support drawn from sources other than your own experience. For example, if you discuss the effects of plagiarizing, you may want to read the relevant sections of your student handbook. You may also talk to other students about their experiences, or you may do some online research by going to a search engine such as Google and trying out various key words. For information about quoting or paraphrasing material in your essay, refer to the "Research Skills" chapter in this book.

■ Writing Assignment 5

Read the selection titled "What is Poverty?" by Jo Goodwin Parker on pages 479–482. Consider Goodwin Parker's position that poverty may be near-impossible to rise above, that poverty entraps and imprisons the poor. Do you agree or do you see her attitude as defeatist or passive? What about the poor, the street people, or the unemployed in your area? Are they trapped or unwilling to try? What do the media say?

Do some online research about poverty, or street people, or unemployment where you live. What is your response to viewpoints of the media and politicians? As noted in Chapter 18, make careful research notes of your findings so that you are able to quote and paraphrase any relevant ideas correctly. Then, write a causes or effects essay presenting your viewpoint and findings on poverty or street people or unemployment in your city or town. Your thesis could be something like the following:

> The reasons why children of welfare families do not fare well in school are malnutrition, . . . (causes)

> Shelter closings in downtown Vancouver have driven street people to desperation; closings have made addicts more desperate, sick people more. . . (effects)

CHECKLIST OF LEARNING OUTCOMES FOR CHAPTER 12

To ensure that you have understood and met the learning outcomes for this chapter, answer the following questions upon completing any of its writing assignments:

✔ Does the thesis state a clear viewpoint and indicate whether the essay deals with causes or effects?

✔ Is each cause or effect truly a cause or effect? Does each clearly support the point of your thesis?

✔ Are your causes or effects presented in an effective order with appropriate transitions to reinforce meaning and to guide the reader?

✔ Are the supporting points adequately explained and clarified by specific details and examples?

✔ Does the conclusion offer reinforcement of the thesis point?

CHAPTER 13

Comparison and Contrast

Comparing and contrasting are everyday thought processes. When we *compare* two things, we show how they are similar; when we *contrast* two things, we show how they are different. We may compare or contrast two brand-name products, two television shows, two jobs, or two possible solutions to a problem we are having.

Comparison or **contrast** writing begins with this ordinary way of thinking about things. It presents items with some common basis for examination and then uses analysis to formulate several points of comparison or contrast. We use examples of similarities or differences to make the comparison or contrast clear to readers.

Comparison essays may inform readers of new material by showing the similarities between familiar ideas, people, or issues and unfamiliar or seemingly dissimilar concepts. Essays that contrast may sometimes persuade as the writer examines the differences between two subjects and makes judgments or decisions about them.

Comparison and contrast structures are used constantly in both academic and career writing tasks. You may compare one software package with another; you may contrast the accuracy of two accounting procedures; or your manager may need you to prepare a report comparing the work patterns of two employees.

In this chapter, you will be asked to write a comparison or contrast essay, using one of two methods of essay development for comparison or contrast writing. Each displays, in different ways, similarities and differences between things or ideas that reflect our natural thinking patterns.

To prepare for this task, first read about the two methods of development you can use in writing this type of essay. Then, read the student essays that follow, and work through the questions that accompany the essays.

Methods of Development

Comparing or contrasting two subjects requires you to do three things during the prewriting stage:

1 Decide on two ideas, people, or items that have a *valid basis for comparison or contrast*. For example, you could compare or contrast Windows XP with Macintosh OS X. Your basis for comparison or contrast would be *computer operating systems*. In this case, you can readily compare or contrast one system with the other. On the other hand, if you tried to compare or contrast Firefox with Macintosh OS X, there would be no valid basis for comparing or contrasting the two. You could, however, compare or contrast Firefox with Safari because both are Internet browsers with shared characteristics such as e-mail and web navigation.

2 Develop a viewpoint about what you are comparing. In other words, decide what point you wish to make, what you have learned as you focus on similarities or differences. For example, if you are listing points to compare a year you spent in university with the year you are now spending in college, you may find that there are good points about both experiences. Gradually, you may emerge with a thesis stating that both forms of education have value but in *different* ways.

3 Finally, you should choose one of two methods of development: the *one-side-at-a-time* method or the *point-by-point* method. Each of these methods is illustrated below.

One Side at a Time

The one-side-at-a-time structure may be used either for the supporting paragraphs or for the entire essay. Whether you choose this method for your body paragraphs or for an essay, the one-side-at-a-time method does what its name states: presents all the points for one side, followed by all the points for the other side.

Look at the following supporting paragraph from "Betting on My Future," one of the student essays that follows.

> Although I knew I could not work full-time and attend college, I did not know what life with a part-time paycheque would be like. A year ago, I ate in restaurants once or twice a week and went to movies and hockey games; fifty dollars never seemed like much to spend for an evening out. Because I worked downtown, I enjoyed dressing well, and I never worried about putting a two-hundred-dollar jacket on my credit card; after all, I could pay off my cards every month and still save enough for a vacation every year. I was proud of myself for

staying out of debt and for being able to live as well as my friends. However, I don't see those friends for a meal now since I eat a brown-bag dinner on my break at the store where I work. I barely cover my rent, bills, and groceries, so I have to work the maximum hours and do without many things. Furthermore, since I have to watch what I spend on groceries, I don't invite people over anymore. Jeans and T-shirts are now my fashion statement; I can't afford dry cleaning these days, and my credit cards are in my safety deposit box at the bank. Because I paid my tuition fees with my savings and vacation money, and because I am still not comfortable with debt, I have avoided provincial student loans. I no longer live the way my friends do, so maybe my pride and my lack of time have a price.

The first half of the paragraph explains fully one side of the contrast: the comfort of the student's life a year ago. The second half of the paragraph deals entirely with the other side: the financial constraints of the student's life today. The following outline of the paragraph illustrates the one-side-at-a-time method.

Outline (One Side at a Time)

Life with a full-time paycheque was easier than life today.

1. A year ago
   a. Restaurants, movies, hockey games
   b. Using credit cards
   c. Saving for vacations
   d. No debts

2. Today
   a. Take my lunches—have to pay rent and bills
   b. No credit card spending
   c. Savings used for tuition, no "cushion"
   d. Afraid of taking loan and carrying debt

Point by Point

Now, look at the supporting paragraph below, which is taken from the essay "What's For Dinner?"

Another area where the home-cooked meal shines is nutrition. Fast-food options are often full of empty calories and fat. A fast-food burger, if it is a Big Mac, contains 560 calories, of which 270 come from fat; the fat makes up 46 percent of the burger (calorie-count.com). Add fries, and it adds another 610 calories, with 261 of those coming from fat. A quarter-pound burger pan-broiled at home amounts to about 200 calories, and with sides of oven-roasted potatoes and steamed vegetables, will add up to the calorie-count of just the Big Mac alone, and a much lower proportion of fats. A KFC deep-fried, battered chicken breast contains about 500 calories, and more than half of those are fats. A Swiss Chalet chicken breast is a little better at 300 calories, but a chicken breast, with skin, floured, seasoned, and fried at home will add up to only 150 calories, with one-third of those coming from fats. Takeout burger or chicken meals are rarely balanced, either; generally takeout means no vegetables other than potatoes.

In this case, the paragraph contrasts the nutritional value of the same food cooked two different ways point by point. The following outline of the paragraph illustrates the point-by-point method.

Outline (Point by Point)

Another area where the home-cooked meal shines is nutrition.

1. Hamburgers
    a. Big Mac with fries
    b. Home-cooked burger with oven-roasted potatoes and vegetables

2. Chicken
    a. KFC or Swiss Chalet chicken breast
    b. Home-cooked, pan-fried chicken breast

Before you begin writing a comparison or contrast essay, decide whether you are going to use the one-side-at-a-time format or the point-by-point format. Use that format as you create the outline for your essay.

Student Essays to Consider

Betting on My Future

I never thought I was a gambler, but a year ago I took a big chance: I decided to start college at the age of thirty-two. I put my money, my time, and my abilities on the line. When I look at the contrasts between my life a year ago and my life now, I feel like I'm facing uncertainties that would make any gambler nervous. My payoff could be a solid career, but in contrast to my life a year ago, I now face changes in my income, my social life, and my self-confidence.

Although I knew I could not work full-time and attend college, I did not know what living on a part-time paycheque would be like. A year ago, I ate in restaurants once or twice a week and went to movies and hockey games; fifty dollars never seemed like much to spend for an evening out. Because I worked downtown, I enjoyed dressing well, and I never worried about putting a two-hundred-dollar jacket on my credit card; after all, I could pay off my cards every month and still save enough for a vacation every year. I was proud of myself for staying out of debt and for being able to live as well as my friends. However, I don't see those friends for a meal now since I eat a brown-bag dinner on my break at the store where I work. I barely cover my rent, bills, and groceries, so I have to work the maximum hours and do without many things. Furthermore, since I have to watch what I spend on groceries, I don't invite people over anymore. Jeans and T-shirts are now my fashion statement; I can't afford dry cleaning these days, and my credit cards are in my safety deposit box at the bank. Because I paid my tuition fees with my savings and vacation money, and because I am still not comfortable with debt, I have avoided provincial student

1

2

loans. I no longer live the way my friends do, so maybe my pride and my lack of time have a price.

Friends and hobbies used to fill my time. I saw my friends nearly every day after work; we went to movies and bought good seats for the major hockey games. On weekends, we partied, went skiing, and shopped for clothes and the latest sporting equipment. Three nights a week, I worked out at a fitness club, and I was quite proud of the shape I was in. My job as a data processing clerk had a regular schedule without much pressure and no paperwork to take home. A year ago, I never had to keep track of time; now, I juggle every minute to manage classes, assignments, job, and trying to keep it all organized. Every day, as soon as my last class is over, I run for the bus to get to work by 5:00 p.m. I can't stay around to chat and make friends with other students, and, except for Sundays, I can't stay at school to work in the computer labs or the library. I spend spare time between classes trying to read my textbooks, keep up with assignments, or print out work. During evenings, I work until 9:00 p.m., and after the trip home, I try to do an hour or two of homework before I fall asleep. Sometimes, I wonder which is my biggest challenge: budgeting money or time.

Looking back from today, I realize my biggest problem was boredom. I liked the company I worked for; I enjoyed the people I worked with, and being downtown was always exciting. Data processing seemed like a "job," not a career. I simply moved from one project to the next and waited for the next raise to come along. There was no push to do better and nearly no chance for promotion. No major worries meant no challenges. Now, though, I face a series of challenges every day. The technical courses are intense, and it takes effort and concentration to do well at new subjects like digital graphics. After being out of school for fifteen years, an even bigger challenge is writing; every essay assignment feels like a battle. Because of my age and my investment in college, I pressure myself to do well. My biggest challenge may come in two years, though, from competition I will face for a new career; a lot of that competition will be younger than I am.

If I look at my life today, contrasted with one year ago, I know that I miss my friends and my comfortable life. Still, although I may be exhausted, a little anxious about my future, and concerned about doing well in my courses, I feel I'm taking a "solid bet": on myself. And I never have time to be bored.

What's For Dinner?

Swiss Chalet, McDonald's, and Tim Hortons tempt hungry Canadians every day with billboards and TV commercials. Hot succulent chicken, fries and a roll, wholesome sandwiches with a doughnut on the side, or the Darth Vader of food, the Big Mac: they are all ready, right now, nearby. How can home cooking compete? Well, on the basis of taste and ease or preparation, nutritional value, and cost, the home-made meal wins every time.

Sometimes people are hungry and just do not feel like cooking. A burger, fried chicken, or pizza seem like tasty ideas—at first bite. Let those cool down for a few minutes, though, and the sliver-thin burger leaves a fatty scum in the mouth and the chicken batter tastes like fried socks. There are better-tasting alternatives that are quick and easy to prepare. In half an hour, even inexperienced cooks can sauté a chicken breast, chop, or burger, bake a potato, and make a salad. The meat will be juicy inside and crispy outside; the baked potato will be hot and ready for toppings, and the salad will taste cool and fresh. Each can be seasoned and cooked exactly to taste, not according to a corporate formula. If the palate craves Italian flavour, takeout pizza is not the only option; the crust is usually chewier than the box it came in. Anyone can buy a good crust at the supermarket and dress it up or down to taste with different cheeses, seasonings, and toppings in exactly the desired quantities. A comforting bowl of pasta is as easy as boiling water, then opening a jar of gourmet sauce or just applying oil, garlic, and parmesan cheese. Add raw vegetables and dip, and dinner is complete. Cooking a simple meal is easy and always tastes better than predictable takeout options.

Another area where the home-cooked meal shines is nutrition. Fast-food options are often full of empty calories and fat. A fast-food burger, if it is a Big Mac, contains 560 calories, of which 270 come from fat; the fat makes up 46 percent of the burger (calorie-count.com). Add fries, and it adds another 610 calories, with 261 of those coming from fat. A quarter-pound burger pan-broiled at home amounts to about 200 calories, and with sides of oven-roasted potatoes and steamed vegetables, will add up to the calorie-count of just the Big Mac alone, and a much lower proportion of fats. A KFC deep-fried, battered chicken breast contains about 500 calories, and more than half of those are fats. A Swiss Chalet chicken breast is a little better at 300 calories, but a chicken breast, with skin, floured, seasoned, and fried at home will add up to only 150 calories, with one-third of those coming from fats. Takeout burger or chicken meals are rarely balanced, either; generally takeout means no vegetables other than potatoes.   **3**

Finally, home cooking is always less expensive than takeout. Most ingredients for an ordinary dinner add up to about five dollars at the supermarket. In contrast, a quarter chicken takeout dinner for one costs at least eight or nine dollars. A chicken breast bought at the supermarket is at most two dollars, a potato thirty cents, and vegetables a dollar or two—the whole meal cooked at home costs about half of the takeout bill. Burgers and fries are cheaper forms of fast food, in general. But a quarter pound of ground beef is perhaps eighty cents at most; add the potato and vegetables, and the home-made burger meal tops out at about $2.50, compared to most burger-and-fries (no veggies) combos, which will be at least $4.00 or more. Even a fully loaded pizza made at home is better value than the delivery model. The supermarket crust, jar of sauce, mozzarella, and even pepperoni may total six or seven dollars, but in most places, a medium or large pizza will be over ten dollars, and there will be a delivery charge. Where economy is concerned, do-it-yourself meals are clear winners.   **4**

Stopping at a drive-through window or picking up the phone are tempting when hunger strikes. But the food never tastes as good as it looks in the menu pictures, and it's nearly never nutritionally balanced. And if the savings that result from cooking at home are not enough, consider the ritual of making a meal exactly to taste as a soothing end to a busy day.   **5**

■ Questions

About Unity

1. Which paragraph in "Betting on My Future" contains its topic sentence within the paragraph rather than at its beginning?

2. Which sentence in paragraph 4 of "Betting on My Future" should be omitted in the interest of paragraph unity?

3. In which paragraph in "What's For Dinner?" is the topic sentence at the end rather than at the beginning, where it generally belongs in student essays?

About Support

4. In paragraph 3 of "Betting on My Future," what three examples does the writer give to support his claim that he must budget every minute of his time?

5. Which sentence in paragraph 4 of "Betting on My Future" should be followed by supporting details?

6. Which sentence in paragraph 3 of "What's For Dinner?" should be followed by supporting details?

About Coherence

7. In paragraph 2 of "Betting on My Future," what "change of direction" signal does the author use to indicate he has finished discussing his life last year and is now going to discuss his life this year?

8. Write the words in the last section of paragraph 4 of "Betting on My Future" that indicate the writer has used emphatic order in organizing his supporting points.

About the Introduction and Conclusion

9. Which best describes the opening paragraph of "What's For Dinner"?
   a. Broad, general statement narrowing to a thesis
   b. Explanation of the importance of the topic
   c. Beginning with an opposite
   d. Question

10. The conclusion of "Betting on My Future" falls into which category?
    a. Some observations and a prediction
    b. Summary and final thought
    c. Question or series of questions

Developing a Comparison or Contrast Essay

Purpose and Audience

The main purpose of a comparison or contrast essay is to make a point by showing your audience that two distinct items are either similar or different. Whether you choose to compare or contrast two items depends on the specific point you want to convey to your audience. Suppose, for instance, the main point of your essay is that home-made hamburgers are superior to boxed burgers. To convince your audience of your claim, you might *contrast* the two items, pointing out those differences—price, taste, and nutrition—that make the home-made burger better. If, however, your main point is that Kingston's tap water is just as good as bottled water, you could *compare* the two, pointing out the similarities that support your point. Kingston's tap water and bottled water, for example, might be equally clean, fresh, and mineral-rich; a small amount of research would give you the facts you need. In both examples above, comparing or contrasting is used to convince readers of a larger main point.

Be sure to keep your audience in mind when planning your essay. If you are writing about Macs and PCs for computer studies or technology students, for example, you could assume your audience is familiar with the two systems and with specialized terminology. On the other hand, if your audience is made up of health care or broadcast students, you could not make such assumptions, and it would be up to you to provide background information and to define specialized terms. Thinking about your audience will help you determine the tone of your essay as well. Once again, if you are writing for an audience of programmers, it is appropriate to write in an objective, technical tone. However, if you are writing for a more general audience, you should assume a friendly, less formal tone.

Point of View in Comparison or Contrast Essays

Comparing or contrasting two ideas or things requires intensive work in the pre-writing stage in order to create a solid and clear pattern that exposes and explains similarities and/or differences. In the first few semesters at college or university, the first priority for students to focus on is discovering and setting up an effective comparison/contrast structure. Decisions relating to first- and third-person point of view or voice can depend on an instructor's preference at this stage; initially, the main issue with this pattern of development is developing skills required to provide a clear structure to compare and/or contrast two items, and to show in the thesis a point that emerges clearly from such comparing or contrasting.

As with most patterns of essay development, when writers select a point of view or voice for a comparison/contrast assignment, they should consider how essential their connection to their topic is to effectively making the essay's point. Does their presence as "I" contribute something necessary or will it intrude on the reader's understanding of their argument? The student essays in this chapter present examples of a first-person point of view, in "Betting on My Future," and of a third-person point of view, in "What's For Dinner?" These resulted from an assigned general topic requiring students to contrast two concepts relating to their everyday lives. Max, the author of "Betting on My Future," as noted in the "Prewriting" section following, developed his essay from personal experience. The strength of his thesis, pattern of contrast, and supporting details derive from his personal connections to his topic, so first-person voice is appropriate here. For many writing assignments, however, first-person comparisons and/or contrasts will not likely be the rule; focus and emphasis will fall on the quality of factual support. Sari, author of "What's For Dinner?", felt that any first-person presence in her essay would detract from the impartial support she wished to provide for her thesis.

Her essay's strength would be based on specific facts that would be as accurate as possible, so she did some quick online research about nutritional content in various foods, and then included her source within the essay. Otherwise, she felt her essay would seem more the product of her own opinions than of objective facts. This type of third-person, factually supported comparison or contrast essay is more characteristic of later academic or career writing tasks.

Prewriting

Both students featured in this chapter contrasted some aspects of their lives as students. Max, who wrote "Betting on My Future," had started college four months earlier at the age of thirty-two.

"The evening before, a friend came into the store where I work part-time," he said, "and asked why no one ever saw me any more. I tried to explain that if I weren't in classes, or at work, or doing assignments, I was probably asleep. As I said this, I realized how different my life was now from the way it used to be less than a year ago. So the contrasts between the two parts of my life were the clearest things in my mind."

To generate ideas for his paper, Max decided to try freewriting. He tried to write "an open letter" to his friends, explaining why he never had any free time these days. He asked himself, "Why has my life changed so much? What are the differences between my life before college and my life now? If life is so demanding now, why am I doing this?" Here is what Max wrote:

Dear friends,

I know none of you has heard from me for a while, so I thought I'd try to tell you why, and how different my life is, now that I'm back in school after nearly fifteen years. I know I never thought of myself as someone who took chances, but now I just hope the gamble is worth it. Right now, I'm betting everything on college: all my money, my time, and all my fears about what I can do. I'm so beat most of the time that I don't even pick up the phone, and I don't have the extra money to go out anyway. When Judy came into the store last night, I'd even forgotten how long it's been since we all went out to a movie or since I worked out. And do I miss those paycheques! Right now, between tuition and textbooks, I haven't got $10 left over this week. What I make part-time barely buys me groceries after the rent and the bills. I used to be bored at work. Now, I worry about failing or messing up on my courses—I hardly have time to eat, let alone panic. Going back to school is a bigger change than I'd thought it would be. I feel like an outsider with a lot of the students because I'm at least ten years older than they are, and I have to leave right after classes to get to work, so I haven't gotten to know people at college anyway. Younger students probably find me too serious, too, because I sit there in classes trying to take it all in. I can't afford not to because I've bet my whole future on trying to train for a career.

So, I guess I'm apologizing for dropping out of the life we all used to share. I just don't feel like I have much of a choice. There's so much riding on going back to school that I don't want to take chances.

Max

As Max looked over his letter, he saw that most of what he had written fell into three categories that he could use as the three points for comparison in his essay. He saw that his main feeling, or viewpoint, was that he felt the risk was worthwhile. Working from this view, and using these three points, he prepared this first outline for the essay:

Thesis: My life this year is so different from last year, and I hope the risks pay off.

1. Used to have enough money for a social life and hobbies; now, I'm scraping by.
   - Entertainment and clothes
   - Budgets and no extras
   - Debt and savings

2. Last year, I had time for people and for workouts; now, I'm always rushing.
   - Movies and free time vs no free time
   - Work vs school schedules
   - Have to use every minute now

3. I was bored at work; this year, everything is a challenge.
   - Nothing to try for at work
   - Courses are hard and I'm older than other students
   - It's all a competition now

Writing a Thesis Statement
for a Comparison or Contrast Essay

In academic, business, or technical writing, comparison and contrast is valuable because it offers readers a new way to see familiar concepts or things. Writing an effective thesis for an essay that is exclusively comparison or contrast, or a blend of the two, asks the writer to have a purpose for examining and interpreting the results of setting up likenesses and/or differences.

That purpose will usually emerge during prewriting. As you work on your comparison/contrast essay, ask yourself, "What did I learn from this?", "Why did I compare or contrast these?", or "What important or significant ideas emerged from putting these two ideas together?" Your point is what you learned.

A comparison or contrast thesis does not *announce* "A and B are very different," or "A and B have important similarities." Neither of these offers a point derived from the acts of comparing or contrasting. Instead, an effective comparison or contrast thesis offers readers what the writer discovered from setting one thing up against another—that "something new" is the writer's purpose. For example, "A and B's similarities are so pronounced that buyers could easily be fooled . . ."

Therefore, a formula for a comparison/contrast thesis might be *topic + intention to compare and/or contrast + suggestion or statement of outcome/discovery gained from comparing and/or contrasting.* In some cases, it may also be appropriate to mention the basis of comparison and/or contrast (see page 205).

An example of a comparison essay's thesis, following the formula above, would be:

The coverage of the student walk-out in the *Vancouver Sun* and the *Vancouver Province* was so similar that the reporters might have plagiarized from each other.

An example of a contrast essay's thesis, following the formula above would be:

The contrasts between the cooking styles of the two chefs are so pronounced that diners often do not recognize a dish they ordered previously.

First Draft and Revision

Working from his outline, Max wrote the following first draft of his essay:

Judy asked me last night why no one ever sees me anymore. I told her my life feels like "risky business" right now because I've spent all my money to go back to school, and everything in my life has changed this year. 1

Last year, my friends and I went to the movies nearly every week and ate in restaurants whenever we felt like it. Now, I can't even afford takeout. I had some savings put aside, but I used them for my tuition for college this year. We all used our charge cards for clothes and ski trips. Recently, though, I had to put my cards in the deposit box at the bank because I don't have enough income to pay the minimum on credit-card bills. Without a full-time paycheque, I'm afraid of debt, so I have to watch every penny this year. It all feels like such a gamble. 2

Workouts three times a week were a big part of my life last year and so was all the time I spent with my friends. Now, I barely have time to sleep. Classes, studying, printing my assignments during spare hours, and running for the bus to work eat up every minute of my days. I fall asleep trying to do homework at night when I get home from my part-time job. Even though I miss my friends, I don't have time to meet new people at college because I'm always in such a rush and because the other students seem so much younger and more carefree. 3

Now, I am never bored, but I am not sure I enjoy the pressure of my life these days. Work used to be dull but predictable; there were never any challenges or any chances for growth. That's why I decided to go to college—for the opportunity for a career. Every essay is a struggle for me and so are the courses like digital graphics; there are so many new things and so many things I remember that I used to find difficult and still do. There will be so much competition for jobs when I finish; that scares me too. And most of those people applying for jobs along with me will be so much younger. At least I feel like I'm trying to make something out of my life. 4

So, if all these things sound like challenges, they are. My life has changed completely from the way it was a year ago, and I keep trying to believe the costs in money, time, and energy are worth it. 5

Max put the first draft of his essay aside and took it to his English class the next day. His instructor asked Max and the other students to work in small groups, reading their drafts aloud and making revision suggestions to one another. Here are the notes Max made on the basis of his group's comments:

- I don't need to bring up Judy—I think I can explain my situation without that story.
- I'm not consistent about developing my paragraphs. I forgot to do a "one-side-at-a-time" or "point-by-point" comparison. I think I'll try a "one-side-at-a-time" technique. I'll describe in each paragraph what last year was like, then describe how different each aspect of this year is.
- I could use more support for some of my points, especially the points about where my money goes now and about how little time I have.
- I should clarify my point about why this "bet" in my life is worth it—say why what I'm doing feels right to me.

After making these observations about his first draft, Max proceeded to write the final version of "Betting on My Future," which appears on pages 207–208.

Writing a Comparison or Contrast Essay

■ Writing Assignment 1

Write an essay of comparison or contrast on one of the topics below:

- Two search engines
- Two bosses you've worked for
- Two groups or two genres of music you listen to
- Two possessions you prize
- Two fashion designers
- Two games, sports, or leisure activities
- Two magazines you read regularly
- Two forms of communication (e.g., phone calls and e-mail)
- Two ways of spending (e.g., cash and credit cards)

Prewriting

1 As you select your topic, keep in mind that you won't merely be *describing* the two things you're writing about; you will be *emphasizing* the ways they are different or alike.

2 Make two columns on a sheet of paper—one for each of the subjects you'll write about. In the left-hand column, jot down words or phrases that describe the first of the two. Write anything that comes into your head. Then, go back and write a corresponding word or phrase about the subject in the right-hand column. For example, here is Nazima's list of characteristics about two games she plays. She began brainstorming for words and phrases to describe Scrabble. She then wrote a corresponding list of characteristics for volleyball, which she added to complete her list.

Scrabble	*Volleyball*
Quiet	Noisy, talking and yelling
Involves words	Involves ball and a net
Played sitting down	Played standing up, jumping
Involves as few as 2 players	Involves 12 players
Can let mind wander when it's not your turn	Have to stay alert every minute
Mental concentration, not physical	Mental and physical concentration required
Part chance (what letters you get) Part strategy and skill	Mostly skill, strategy; little chance
Some see as boring, nerdy game	Seen as glamorous—stars get advertising contracts
Players' size doesn't matter	Being tall helps

3   Your list of characteristics will help you decide if the two things you are writing about are more alike (in which case you'll write an essay *comparing* them) or different (in which case you'll write an essay *contrasting* them.)

4   As you look over your lists, think about how the characteristics you've written down (and others that occur to you) could fit into three categories that can serve as your supporting points or "points of comparison or contrast."

5   Decide if you will design your essay with the *one-side-at-a-time* method of development or the *point-by-point* method of development. Be consistent in your use of one method or the other as you prepare an outline.

Nazima decided on three headings under which the two games could be contrasted, and she resolved to use the *point-by-point* method of development.

Fill in the blanks in her outline to indicate the supporting points, or points of contrast, between the two games.

Trial Thesis: Although they are two of my favourite activities, Scrabble and volleyball could hardly be more different.

Point: _____

- Scrabble requires a board and letter tiles
- Volleyball needs a ball and a net
- Scrabble can be played by two people
- Twelve people needed for a volleyball game
- Scrabble can be played anywhere there's room for two people to sit down
- Volleyball needs a large room and high ceilings or an outdoor playing area

Point: _____

- You have to concentrate mentally to play Scrabble
- You need mental and physical concentration to play volleyball
- It doesn't matter what size you are to play Scrabble

- It helps to be tall to play volleyball
- There's some chance involved in Scrabble
- Chance is not a big part of volleyball

Point: _____

- Scrabble players are seen as "eggheads" by the general public
- Star volleyball players are seen as glamorous by public
- Volleyball players get contracts to endorse athletic shoes
- Scrabble players don't endorse anything, even dictionaries
- Volleyball players are admired for the power of their spike
- Scrabble players are admired for the number of unusual two-letter words they know

6 Using your own outline, proceed to write the first draft of your essay.

Revising

As you review the first draft of your essay, ask yourself these questions:

- Have I made it clear in my thesis statement what two things I am writing about, my viewpoint about them, and whether I will compare or contrast them?
- Do my supporting points represent three ways in which I will compare or contrast my two subjects?
- Does each of my supporting paragraphs have a clear topic sentence?
- Have I consistently used either the *one-side-at-a-time* or the *point-by-point* method of development?
- Have I used transition words to help readers follow my train of thought?
- Have I rounded off my essay with a conclusion that confirms what my comparison or contrast has shown?

Continue to revise your essay until you can answer "yes" to each question. Then, be sure to check the next-to-final draft for the sentence skills listed on the inside front cover.

Writing Assignment 2

Write an essay that contrasts two attitudes on a controversial subject. You may want to contrast your views with those of someone else or contrast the way you felt about the subject in the past with the way you feel now. Essays that strongly contrast two views tend to be more dramatic and sound more forceful to readers.

This is an essay assignment in which writing in the third-person point of view is recommended.

Here are some subjects you might consider writing about:

- Women serving in combat positions in the Canadian Armed Forces
- Legal marriage status for gay couples
- Censorship of the Internet
- Tax-funded shelters for street people
- Cuts in education (or hospital/medical) funding
- "The right to die an assisted death"
- Canada's unemployment insurance system

1   In order to gather information about an attitude that contrasts with your own, you will need to do some research. Two approaches may help you to find useful material: going to the library to search through article indexes for recent Canadian and international news magazines (ask your instructor or library assistant if you need help) or doing an Internet search, using key words to find websites on these subjects. For help with using search engines, incorporating quotations, paraphrasing material from your sources, and correctly acknowledging your sources in your essay, refer to the "Research Skills" chapter on pages 268–291. Alternatively, you could interview friends and acquaintances whose attitude on the subject is different from yours.

2   As you examine your research and your own attitude about the issue, note the strongest points on both sides. From them, formulate your three main supporting points.

3   Decide whether it is more effective to contrast your attitude and the opposing one point by point within each paragraph or one side at a time

4   Write a thesis statement, and prepare an outline, which reflects the method of development you have chosen. Using your outline, write the first draft of your contrast essay.

5   Refer to the guidelines for revising your contrast essay provided on page 217.

Writing Assignment 3

In this comparison or contrast essay, you will write with a **specific purpose** and for a **specific audience**.

Option 1: Your niece or nephew is finishing high school soon and is thinking about getting a job instead of going to college or university. You would prefer to see him or her give college a try. Write him or her a letter in which you contrast the two courses of action. Use a one-side-at-a-time method in making your analysis.

Option 2: Write a letter to your boss in which you compare your abilities with those of the "ideal" candidate for a position to which you would like to be promoted. Use a point-by-point method to discuss each ideal requirement, and then describe how well you measure up to it. Use the requirements of a job you're relatively familiar with or a job you would really like to apply for some day.

Writing Assignment 4

Read the selection titled "Smash Thy Neighbor" on pages 469–473. Pay special attention to how the author compares and contrasts football and war in paragraphs 5–8 and compares football and the rest of society in paragraph 14. Notice how he makes the comparisons and contrasts in order to describe football more fully. Then, write an essay in which you use a comparison to fully describe three aspects of an activity, place, or person. You may use serious or humorous supporting details.

Following are some suggestions that you might consider for a thesis statement:

Thesis: In a few significant ways,

- going to college or university is like working at a career.
- meditation is like exercise.
- instructors should be like parents.

Feel free to use any other thesis that makes a comparison in order to fill out a description of an activity, person, or place. (Note that a comparison that points out similarities between things that are otherwise quite different, as in the above examples, is called an *analogy*.)

CHECKLIST OF LEARNING OUTCOMES FOR CHAPTER 13

To ensure that you have understood and met the learning outcomes for this chapter, answer the following questions upon completing any of its writing assignments:

✓ Have you chosen two subjects or two sides of one subject that can logically be compared or contrasted? Does a worthwhile point emerge from the process of comparing or contrasting the two parts of your thesis?

✓ Does your thesis statement state both subjects (or both sides of your subject), whether you will compare or contrast, and the point you will make based on that action?

✓ Have you consistently used the method of development (either the *point-by-point* or *one-side-at-a-time* method) most appropriate to your subject(s)?

✓ Have you used a valid basis for comparing or contrasting and presented an equal amount of supporting material for both sides or both subjects?

✓ Does the conclusion sum up the points made during the comparison or contrast and reinforce your thesis point?

CHAPTER 14

Definition

In talking with other people, we give informal definitions to explain just what we mean by a particular term. Suppose, for example, we say to a friend, "Bob is really an inconsiderate person." We might then explain what we mean by *inconsiderate* by saying, "He borrowed my accounting book 'overnight' but didn't return it for a week. And when I got it back, it was covered with coffee stains."

Definition essays continue this process of explaining and clarifying. In a written definition, we explain, in a more complete and formal way, our personal understanding of a term. Thus, definition writing makes use of skills from many methods of development: *Narration* creates the line and sequence for your explanation; *description* gives precision and specificity to details; *comparing* or *contrasting* ideas establishes what something is or is not; and *examples* illustrate different aspects of a word or phrase's meaning.

Today, knowing what new phrases mean is a daily necessity. We hear and read new terms constantly: *visioning*, or *imagineering*, for instance. Insurance policies and credit card agreements are filled with definitions. Accountants use terms like *statistical sampling inventory*; childcare workers speak of *attention deficits* in children; and technology creates its own vocabulary at a bewildering rate: consider *data integrity* and *ISP*.

Defining is a fundamental communications skill in most careers. Engineers define *stress* differently from psychologists; police and security officers need clear understandings of *reasonable grounds* for some action they take. Instructions and reports of every kind must make many terms and phrases clear to their readers.

In this chapter, you will be asked to write an essay in which you define and illustrate a term. To prepare for this task, first read the student essays that follow, and then work through the questions that accompany the essays.

Student Essays to Consider

Definition of a Baseball Fan

What is a baseball fan? The word *fan* is an abbreviation of *fanatic,* meaning "an insane or crazy person." In fact, baseball fans seem to define insanity because they not only behave insanely, they are insane about trivia, and they are insanely loyal. **1**

Baseball fans wear their official team T-shirts and warm-up jackets to the mall, the supermarket, the classroom, and even—if they can get away with it—to work. If the team offers a give-away item, the fans rush to the stadium to claim the hat or sports bag or water bottle that is being handed out that day. Soccer fans go similarly crazy when World Cup time comes around. Baseball fans just plain behave insanely. Even the fact that fans spend the most beautiful summer months sweating at Rogers Centre proves it. In addition, baseball fans decorate their cars and their houses with baseball-related items of every kind. To them, Jays vanity plates are only the beginning, and team bumper stickers don't belong only on car bumpers, but also on fireplace mantels and front doors. When they go to a game, which they do as often as possible, they also decorate their bodies. True baseball fans not only put on their team jackets and grab their pennants, but also paint their heads blue to look like bluejays or wear big foam "Blue Jayheads." At the game, these fans devote enormous energy to trying to get a "wave" going. **2**

Baseball fans are insanely fascinated by trivia. They talk about players as though Alex Rios and B.J. Ryan were close friends. Every day, they turn to the Jays' site and the sports page and study last night's statistics. They simply have to see who has extended his hitting streak and how many strike-outs the winning pitcher recorded. Their bookshelves are crammed with record books, magazines, team yearbooks, and baseball almanacs. They delight in remembering such significant facts as who the last left-handed third baseman was to hit into an inning-ending double play in the fifth game of the playoffs. Then, if you can't manage to get all that excited about such earth-shaking issues, they look at you as though *you* were the insane one. **3**

Last of all, baseball fans are insanely loyal to the team of their choice, often dangerously so. Should their beloved team lose three in a row, fans may begin to criticize their team. They still obsessively watch each game and spend the entire day afterwards reading and listening to the post-game commentary in newspapers, on TSN, and on sports radio. Further, this intense loyalty makes fans dangerous. To anyone who dares to say to a loyal fan that another team has better players or coaches or, God forbid, to anyone wandering near the home cheering section wearing the jacket of the opposing team, physical damage is a real possibility. While hockey players and fans hold the record for fights, incidents of violence on the baseball field have increased in recent years and are a matter of growing concern. **4**

From mid-October through March, baseball fans are like any other human   5
beings. They pay their taxes, take out the garbage, and complain about the high
cost of living. But when April comes, the TVs go on, the record books come off
the shelves, and the devotion returns. For the true baseball fan, another season
of insanity has begun.

Student Zombies

Schools divide people up into categories. From first grade on up, students   1
are labelled "advanced" or "deprived" or "remedial" or "antisocial." Students
pigeon-hole their fellow students, too; there's the "brain," the "jock," the
"dummy," and the "teacher's pet." In most cases, these narrow labels are
misleading and inaccurate. But there is one label for a certain type of college
student that is actually accurate in a frightening way—the "zombie."

Zombies are the living dead. Most people haven't known a lot of real   2
zombies personally, but they do know how zombies act. Horror movies have
provided guidance for us. The special effects in horror movies are much better
these days. Over the years, movies have shown that zombies stalk around
graveyards, their eyes glued open by Hollywood makeup artists, bumping like
cheap toy robots into living people. Zombie students in college do just about
the same thing. They stalk around campus, eyes glazed, staring off into space.
When they do manage to wander into a classroom, they sit down mechanically
and contemplate the ceiling. Zombie students rarely eat, dance, talk, laugh, or
toss Frisbees on college lawns. Instead, they vanish when class is dismissed
and return only when some mysterious zombie signal summons them back into
a classroom. The signal may not occur for weeks.

Zombies are controlled by some mysterious force. According to legend,   3
zombies are corpses that have been brought back to life to do the bidding of
some voodoo master. Student zombies, too, seem directed by a strange power.
They continue to attend school although they have no apparent desire to do so.
They show no interest in college-related activities like tests, marks, papers, and
projects. Yet, some inner force compels them to wander through the halls of
higher education.

An awful fate awaits all zombies unless something happens to break the   4
spell they're under. In the movies, zombies are often shot, stabbed, drowned, or
electrocuted, all to no avail. Finally, the hero or heroine realizes that a counter-
spell is needed. Once that spell is cast, with the appropriate props of chicken
feet, human hair, and bats' eyeballs, the zombie-corpse can return peacefully
to its coffin. The only hope for a student zombie to change is for him or her
to undergo a similarly traumatic experience. Sometimes the evil spell can be
broken by a grade transcript decorated with large red "Fs." At other times, a
professor will succeed through a private, intensive exorcism session. In other
cases, though, zombies blunder around for years until they are gently persuaded
by college administration to head for another institution. Then, they enrol in a
new college or get a job in the family business.

Every college student knows that it's not necessary to see *Shaun of the Dead*   5
or *Twenty-Eight Days* in order to see zombies in action—or non-action. Forget the
campus film series or the late-late show. Just sit in a classroom and wait. You

know who you're looking for—the students who walk in without books or papers of any kind and sit in the very last row of seats. The ones with MP3 players plugged into their ears don't count as zombies; that's a whole different category of "student." *Day of the Living Dead* is showing every day in a classroom near you.

■ Questions

About Unity

1. Which paragraph in "Definition of a Baseball Fan" has a topic sentence buried within the paragraph rather than at the paragraph's beginning?

2. Which sentence in paragraph 2 of "Definition of a Baseball Fan" should be omitted in the interest of paragraph unity?

3. Which sentence in paragraph 2 of "Student Zombies" should be omitted in the interest of paragraph unity?

4. Which sentence in the final paragraph of "Student Zombies" introduces a new topic and so should be eliminated?

About Support

5. Which essay develops its definitions through a series of comparisons?

6. Which sentence in paragraph 4 of "Definition of a Baseball Fan" should be followed by supporting details?

7. In the second paragraph of "Definition of a Baseball Fan," how many examples are given of fans' "insane" behaviour?

About Coherence

8. Which paragraph in "Definition of a Baseball Fan" begins with a transitional phrase?

9. Which sentence in paragraph 2 of "Student Zombies" begins with a change-of-direction transitional word?

About the Introduction

10. Which method of introduction is used in the opening paragraph of "Student Zombies"?

    a. Anecdote
    b. Opposite
    c. Quotation
    d. Broad, general statement narrowing to a thesis
    e. Questions

Developing a Definition Essay

Purpose and Audience

The main purpose of a definition essay is to explain your understanding of a key term or concept. Your secondary purpose is to persuade your audience that your definition is a legitimate one.

Keep in mind that a definition essay *does not* simply repeat a word's dictionary meaning. In fact, never begin a definition essay with, "According to the Oxford Dictionary . . . ." Instead, a definition essay conveys what a particular term means *to you*. For example, if you were to write about the term "patriotism," you might begin by presenting your definition of the word. You might say patriotism means wearing a red maple-leaf pin when you travel, putting out decorations on Canada Day, or supporting Canadian artists and companies. Perhaps you think patriotism is about becoming politically active and developing intelligent views on Canada's national and international policies. Whatever definition you choose, be sure to provide specific details and examples so that your audience can fully understand your meaning of the term.

As with other essay forms, consider your audience. If you are writing a highly personal definition of a concept like patriotism, an audience will expect a less formal essay. Additionally, an audience of politically minded people might require different examples from an audience of peers. If you choose to write a slightly more formal definition essay—one that takes a serious tone and deals with a technical or more abstract topic—be sure that you supply enough background information so that a general reader will understand and follow your supporting details.

Point of View in Definition Essays

Definition essays focus on making clear to readers as precisely as possible a writer's ideas about the meaning of some term, concept, or process. Therefore, at a post-secondary level, it is more appropriate for writers to place their emphasis on the topic being defined, on clarifying their ideas, rather than on their connection to the topic. In other words, writing in the third-person point of view or voice is preferable.

Although your definition or interpretation of the meaning of something will derive to some degree from your own experiences, it is not necessary to assert your presence as "I" in your definition or supporting evidence. Readers are aware that your definition essay delineates your view of something's meaning, they need not be reminded of, or distracted by your first-person presence. Although highly personal and effective informal first-person definition essays may inform and amuse readers, these tend to tell readers more about the writer than about the topic they define. As preparation for other academic and career writing tasks that clarify the meanings of technical or abstract terms, writing in the third-person, less intrusive voice is more effective. For this reason, both student essays in this chapter show focus and emphasis on the topic being defined, not on the writers themselves.

Prewriting

Cameron, the author of "Definition of a Baseball Fan," had ideas that he knew a lot about or at least had an interest in exploring. He was interested in sports, outdoor activities, and history, so he considered defining a snowboarder, a war-history buff, and a Blue Jays fan, among other things. He selected "A true Blue Jays fan" as the topic that interested him most, thinking it would lend itself well to a lighthearted essay that defined the sometimes loony fans of the Toronto baseball team. After some thought, Cameron decided to broaden his topic to include all baseball fans.

"I realized that, from what I'd seen on sports shows, trying to define the weirdness of Canadian baseball fans would make a better topic for my essay," he said.

As a person who likes to think in visual terms, Cameron decided to develop ideas and details about his topic by diagramming his thoughts:

Baseball fans

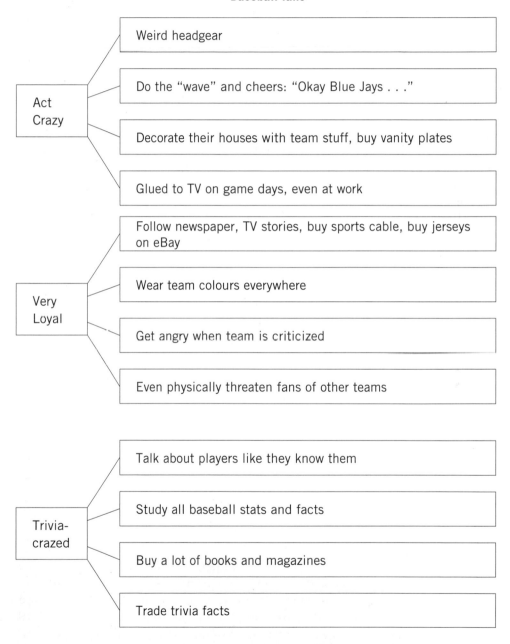

Cameron realized his diagram showed that he could characterize each of his three main topics as a kind of "insanity." He decided on a thesis that would indicate his essay's plan of development: "They act insanely, they are obsessed by trivia, and they are insanely loyal."

Writing a Thesis Statement
for a Definition Essay

The thesis statement for a definition essay identifies the subject (term being defined) and provides a brief, general statement of the writer's understanding of that term's meaning.

Effective thesis statements, depending on the subject, (1) place a term within a larger category of like things, or (2) specify a term's meaning by stating what it is and what it is not, or (3) explain the origin of the term.

An example of a definition thesis statement that places its subject (or term) within larger category of like things follows:

Anger is an intense emotion.

An example of a definition thesis statement that states what the subject is and what it is not:

A good friend is honest and caring, never harsh or smothering.

An example of a definition thesis statement that explains the origin of the term/subject:

Being consistently virtuous requires strength of character; in fact, the Latin root of the word "virtue," *virtus*, meant "strength."

Definition essay thesis statements may also suggest the writer's point of view by suggesting his or her reason for presenting a more detailed definition; i.e., ". . . baseball fans seem to define insanity because they are insanely loyal."

First Draft and Revision

With his thesis and a plan of development in mind, Cameron wrote the first draft of his essay:

Baseball fans are by definition crazy. They behave insanely, they are insane about trivia, and they are insanely loyal.

If their team gives away a freebie, the fans rush to the stadium to get the hat, or whatever. Baseball fans just plain behave insanely. Soccer fans go similarly crazy when World Cup time comes around. But baseball fans are even worse. Baseball fans sit sweating in order to watch their favourite game. In addition, baseball fans decorate their houses with baseball-related items of every kind. When they go to a game, which they do as often as possible, the true baseball fans make themselves look ridiculous by decorating themselves in weird, team-related ways. At the game, these fans do the "wave" more than they watch the game.

Baseball fans are insane about trivia. They talk about players as though their favourites were close friends. Every day, they turn to the sports page and study last night's statistics. Their bookshelves are crammed with record books, magazines, team yearbooks, and baseball almanacs. They remember every significant fact about the most obscure, forgotten game. They think everybody is as fascinated by all their trivial knowledge as they are.

Last of all, baseball fans are insanely loyal to the team of their choice. Baseball fans wear their team T-shirts and warm-up jackets everywhere, even to work. Of course, if they have to dress up in business clothes, they can't do that. Should their beloved team lose three in a row, their fans may begin to criticize their team. But these reactions only hide their broken hearts. They still obsessively watch each game and read all the newspaper stories about it. Their intense loyalty makes fans dangerous. To anyone who dares to say to a loyal fan that another team is better or, God forbid, to anyone wandering near the home cheering section wearing the jacket of the opposing team, physical damage is a real possibility. Incidents of violence in the baseball stadiums have increased in recent years and are a matter of growing concern.

Baseball fans really act like they're crazy. They behave insanely, are crazy about trivia, and they're too loyal!

The main weakness in Cameron's first draft was not providing enough specific details in his support. Aware of this, he left his first draft for a day and then returned to it to focus on the body paragraphs.

Reread his finished essay on pages 221–222. Then, compare it with Cameron's first draft above, and answer the following questions:

- Where, in paragraph 2, does he add more details? Which point needed more details?
- What is the supporting point for paragraph 3? How has Cameron clarified his point when revising his essay?
- In paragraph 4, Cameron decides that two ideas do not support that paragraph's topic. What are these ideas, and how does he revise this paragraph to support its point accurately?

Writing a Definition Essay

Writing Assignment 1

Choose one of the terms below as the subject of a definition essay. Each term refers to a certain kind of person.

Intellectual	Optimist	Spiritualist
Fashionista	Pessimist	Sophisticate
Artist	Team player	Musician
Good neighbour	Nerd	Procrastinator
Busybody	Gourmet	Loner
Athlete	Workaholic	Environmentalist

Prewriting

1 As you devise your opening paragraph, you may want to refer to the dictionary definition of the term. Depending on your term and on your dictionary, you may find an "essential definition," or you may find a range of meanings. If you find several meanings, be sure to use only one. *Don't* begin your essay with the overused line, "According to *Oxford*..."

2 Remember that the thesis of a definition essay is actually a more polished version of "what _____ means to me." The thesis presents what *you* think the term actually means, without using the words "I" or "me."

3 As you plan your supporting paragraphs, think of the different parts or qualities of your term. Here is the three-part division of the student essay about baseball fans, considered in this chapter:

"They behave insanely, they are insane about trivia, and they are insanely loyal."

4 Support each part of your division with either a series of examples or a single extended example. Examples may also "limit" your description by saying what some quality or type of person is *not*.

5 You may find outlining to be the most helpful strategy for creating your definition essay. As a guide, put your thesis and three main supporting points in the spaces below:

Thesis: _____

_____

_____

Support: 1. _____

          2. _____

          3. _____

Revising

Once you have completed the first draft of your essay, review it with these questions in mind:

- Does my thesis statement indicate how I define the term, and does it indicate my plan of development for the essay? Have I introduced my term with enough background to interest my reader?
- Does each of my supporting paragraphs have a clear topic?
- Have I supported each of my three topic sentences with one extended example or a series of examples? Does each clearly illustrate one aspect of my term?
- Have I rounded off my essay with an appropriate concluding paragraph?

Continue to revise your essay until you can answer "yes" to each question. Then, be sure to check the next-to-final draft for the sentence skills listed on the inside front cover.

Writing Assignment 2

In this essay, you will write with a **specific purpose** and for a **specific audience**.

Option 1: You work in a doctor's office and have been asked to write a brochure that will be placed in the patients' waiting room. The brochure is intended to tell patients what a healthy lifestyle is. Write a definition of a *healthy lifestyle* for your readers, using examples wherever appropriate. Your definition might focus on both mental and physical health and might include eating, sleeping, exercise, and recreational habits.

Alternatively, you might decide to take a playful point of view and write a brochure defining an *unhealthy lifestyle*.

Option 2: The students in the first year of your program will be hosts to some students from Quebec. The class is preparing a mini-dictionary of slang for the visitors. Your job is to write a paragraph in which you define the phrase *to gross out*.

In your introduction, consider including the non-slang definition of *gross*, which led to the slang usage. To find that definition, consult a dictionary. Your thesis statement should reflect your understanding of the slang usage of *to gross out*. The supporting paragraphs, in which you extend your definition, can involve illustrating an example of how the term is used or a circumstance in which the term is appropriate.

Alternatively, you may write about any other slang term. If necessary, first get the approval of your instructor.

■ Writing Assignment 3

Read the selection titled "Shame" on pages 459–462. Then, write an essay in which you define a term, as Dick Gregory does in "Shame," through narration. You can use one of the terms listed in Writing Assignment 1 or think of one of your own. In your introduction, fill in a brief background for your readers—when and where the experience happened. Your thesis should express the idea that because of this experience, you (or the person or people you are writing about) learned the meaning of the word _____ (fill in the term you have chosen). Break the narrative at logical points to create three supporting paragraphs. You might first want to look at the examples of narrative essays given on pages 144–145.

Alternatively, you might develop your definition with three experiences that seem to embody the word you have chosen. These could be experiences of your own, ones you know about, or ones you have read about. Develop each in a separate supporting paragraph.

CHECKLIST OF LEARNING OUTCOMES FOR CHAPTER 14

To ensure that you have understood and met the learning outcomes for this chapter, answer the following questions upon completing any of its writing assignments:

✔ Is the subject in an appropriate and limited category of subjects?

✔ Does your thesis and/or introductory paragraph locate your subject within its class and state how it is unique?

✔ Does the opening paragraph set the tone and degree of subjectivity or objectivity with which you defined your subject?

✔ Does each supporting point clearly expand on and illustrate your subject, and is the type of support chosen appropriate to your subject?

✔ Does the final paragraph summarize all meanings presented and suggest the significance of your particular definition?

CHAPTER 15

Division and Classification

We divide and classify every single day; we do so to make collections of items more manageable. We sort out everything from socks to documents, then place them into groups of like items, whether those "classification groups" are black ankle socks or document files. Dividing and classifying objects and ideas are attempts to organize our complex environment.

Dividing and **classifying** begin in infancy, as we sort and classify all the information we receive. As we move on, we constantly break down and manage large or complex subjects. Our textbooks break concepts into chapters and headings, and in many subject areas, we must divide a topic into manageable or appropriate categories for writing assignments.

Division and classification essays require you to choose a classifying principle that suits your audience and your purpose. For example, writing about contemporary music for fellow students might involve the classifying principle of *tastes* in music and the categories of *R&B, Punk,* and *Rap.* Writing about software for graphic design or animation for a computer animation course would require you to find a classifying principle and categories relevant to that course's content.

Division and classification activities will be part of much of your academic and career writing. Marketing students and professionals sort consumers into groups or categories to facilitate product development and sales decisions. Accounting students may have to sort out different procedures and programs suitable for businesses of various sizes.

In this chapter, you will be asked to write an essay in which you divide or classify a subject according to a single principle. To prepare for this task, first read the student essays that follow, and then work through the questions that accompany the essays.

Student Essays to Consider

Mall People

Just what goes into "having fun"? For many people, "fun" involves getting out of the house, seeing other people, having something interesting to look at, and enjoying a choice of activities, all at a reasonable price. Going out to dinner or to the movies may satisfy some of those desires, but often not all. An attractive alternative does exist in the form of the free-admission shopping mall. Teenagers, couples on dates, and the nuclear family can all be observed having a good time at the mall.   1

Teenagers are drawn to the malls to pass time with pals and be seen by other teens. The guys saunter by in ball caps, T-shirts, and baggy jeans, with headsets on at all times. The girls stumble along in high-heeled shoes and tank tops, with cell phones tucked in the pockets of their track pants or low-rise jeans. Travelling in a gang that resembles a wolf pack, the teenagers make the shopping mall their hunting ground. Mall managers have obviously made a decision to attract all the teenage activity. Their raised voices, loud laughter, and occasional shouted obscenities can be heard from as far as half a mall away. They come to "pick up chicks," to "meet guys," and just to "hang out."   2

Couples find fun of another sort at shopping malls. The young lovers are easy to spot because they walk hand in hand, stopping to sneak a quick kiss after every few steps. They pause at jewellery store windows so they can gaze at diamond engagement rings and gold wedding bands. Then, they wander into furniture departments in the large mall stores. Finally, they drift away, their arms wrapped around each other's waists.   3

Mom, Dad, little Jenny, and Fred, Jr., visit the mall on Friday and Saturday evenings for inexpensive recreation. Hearing the music of the antique carousel housed there, Jenny begs to ride her favourite pony, with its shining golden mane. Shouting, "I'm starving!" Fred, Jr., drags the family towards the food court, where he detects the seductive odour of pizza. Mom walks through a fabric store, running her hand over the soft velvet and slippery silk materials she finds. Meanwhile, Dad has wandered into an electronics store and is admiring the flat-screen TV he'd love to buy someday. The mall provides something special for every member of the family.   4

Sure, some people visit the mall in a brief, businesslike way, just to pick up a specific purchase or two. But many more are shopping for inexpensive recreation. The teenagers, the dating couples, and the nuclear families all find cheap entertainment at the mall.   5

The Beer Up Here

The other night, my six-year-old son turned to me and asked for a light beer. 1
My husband and I sat there for a moment, stunned, and then explained to him
that beer was only for grown-ups. I suddenly realized how many, and how often,
beer ads appear on television. To my little boy, it must seem that every Canadian
drinks beer after work, or after playing ball, or at every sort of social occasion.
Beer makers have pounded audiences with all kinds of campaigns to sell beer,
and there seems to be an ad to appeal to the self-image of every beer drinker.

One type of Canadian beer ad attracts people who think of themselves as 2
as grown-up kids. "Patrols" of fun-loving young men from one beer company
apparently show up at people's backyard barbeques to check beverage choices
and take part in recruiting sessions featuring attractive young women who
are checked for their "beer loyalty." Another set of ads that are a hit with the
underage set as well as with adult beer drinkers is the "I am Canadian" series
in which true Canadians identify themselves with their "national beverage."
These humorous ads suggest that beer is a necessary and even patriotic part of
a light-hearted approach to life.

A second kind of ad is not aimed at fun-loving kids of all ages but at 3
macho men—guys who think of themselves as "men's men," doing "guy
things" together. One particular campaign features men who see themselves
as victims of their nagging wives. Ads in this series show men howling with
laughter about how they've fooled their wives into thinking they're home doing
chores (by leaving dummy-stuffed pants lying under leaky sinks or broken
furnaces) while they're really out drinking. Other beer ads show fantasy macho
jobs like capping blazing oil-well fires and herding snowbound prairie cattle by
helicopter. Beer is a man's drink, the ads seem to say, and women are either
irrelevant or a nuisance to be gotten around.

European and European-sounding beers such as Amstel and Heineken 4
like to show handsome, wealthy-looking adults enjoying their money and
leisure time. A typical scene is such people enjoying an expensive hobby in a
luxurious location. Beer, these ads say, is an essential part of "the good life."
This type of ad appeals to people who want to see themselves as successful
and upper class.

To a little boy, it may seem that beer is necessary to every adult's life. 5
After all, people need it to make them feel young, to bond with friends, and to
celebrate financial success. At least, that's what advertisers tell him—and us.

■ Questions

About Unity

1. In which paragraph in "The Beer Up Here" is the topic sentence at the end
   rather than, more appropriately for student essays, at the beginning?

2. Which sentence in paragraph 2 of "Mall People" should be omitted in the
   interest of paragraph unity?

3. Which sentence in paragraph 2 of "The Beer Up Here" should be omitted in
   the interest of paragraph unity?

About Support

4. After which sentence in paragraph 3 of "Mall People" are more supporting details needed?

5. Which paragraph in "The Beer Up Here" lacks sufficient specific details?

6. Label as *sight, touch, hearing,* or *smell* all the sensory details in the following sentences taken from "Mall People."

   a. "Hearing the music of the antique carousel housed there, Jenny begs to ride her favourite pony, with its shining golden mane."
   b. "Shouting, 'I'm starving!' Fred, Jr., drags the family towards the food court, where he detects the seductive odour of pizza."
   c. "Mom walks through a fabric store, running her hand over the soft velvet and slippery silk materials she finds."

About Coherence

7. What are the time transition words used in the second supporting paragraph of "Mall People"?

8. Which topic sentence in "The Beer Up Here" functions as a linking sentence between paragraphs?

About the Introduction and Conclusion

9. What kind of introduction is used in "The Beer Up Here"?

   a. Broad, general statement narrowing to a thesis
   b. Idea that is the opposite of the one to be developed
   c. Quotation
   d. Anecdote
   e. Questions

10. What conclusion technique is used in "Mall People"?

   a. Summary
   b. Prediction or recommendation
   c. Question

Classification Prewriting Activity

This activity will sharpen your understanding of the classifying process. In each of the following groups, cross out the one item that does not belong with the other four. Also, indicate in the space provided the single principle of classification used for the four items. Note the examples:

Examples	Shirts	Sports
	a. Flannel	a. Swimming
	b. Cotton	b. Sailing
	c. ~~Tuxedo~~	c. ~~Basketball~~
	d. Denim	d. Water polo
	e. Silk	e. Scuba diving
	(Classifying principle: _material_)	(Classifying principle: _water sports_)

1. School subjects
   a. Algebra
   b. History
   c. Geometry
   d. Trigonometry
   e. Calculus

   (Classifying principle: _____)

2. Movies
   a. *The Kingdom*
   b. *Sunshine*
   c. *Bee Movie*
   d. *The Darjeeling Limited*
   e. *3:10 to Yuma*

   (Classifying principle: _____)

3. Clothing
   a. Sweatshirt
   b. Shorts
   c. T-shirt
   d. Evening gown
   e. Sweatpants

   (Classifying principle: _____)

4. Sources of information
   a. *Maclean's*
   b. *The Globe and Mail*
   c. *Canadian Geographic*
   d. *Chatelaine*
   e. *The Walrus*

   (Classifying principle: _____)

5. Famous buildings
   a. CN Tower
   b. Expo Stadium
   c. Saddledome
   d. Bell Centre
   e. Rogers Centre

   (Classifying principle: _____)

6. Fibres
   a. Wool
   b. Acrylic
   c. Cotton
   d. Silk
   e. Linen

   (Classifying principle: _____)

Developing a Division and Classification Essay

Purpose and Audience

The main purpose of a division and classification essay is to present your own unique way of dividing and classifying a particular topic. In order to write a successful essay, you will need to first choose a topic that lends itself to being divided and classified. Once you pick your topic, you will then have to come up with your own unique sorting system—one that your audience will be able to understand.

For example, if you choose clothing, there are a number of ways to sort this topic into categories. You could divide clothing by the function it serves: shirts and jackets (to cover the upper body), pants and skirts (for the lower body), and shoes and socks (for the feet). You could also divide clothes according to the materials they are made from: animal products, plant products, and synthetic materials. A more interesting and potentially humorous way to divide clothes is by fashion: clothes that are stylish, clothes that are going out of style, and clothes that are so unattractive that they never were in style. Notice that in all three of these cases, the broad topic of clothing has been divided into categories according to a particular classifying principle (function, materials, and fashion). When you divide your topic for your essay, be sure to figure out your own classifying principle, and make it clear to your readers.

Once you've selected your topic and figured out how to divide it, you will need to provide specific details so that your audience fully understands the categories you made. For the example about fashion above, you might classify skateboarding shorts as part of the "going out of style" category, while velour tracksuits might belong in the "clothes that are stylish" group, and Metallica T-shirts might fit in the "never stylish" group. As always, keep your audience in mind. An audience of fashion-conscious young people would probably have very different opinions about what is and isn't stylish than an audience of investment bankers. For that matter, an audience of style-obsessed, label-conscious "downtown people" would have much more interest in clothing and accessory styles than an audience of academic instructors.

Point of View in Division and Classification Essays

As an essay structure, division and classification is based on *analysis*, or breaking up a topic or concept into components or categories. The main focus of these essays, and their most notable characteristic for readers, is the way they present valid and interesting divisions of a topic into various classifications. Analytical writing, and often expository writing in general, is expected to be about more than just the writer's personal opinion or experience. To quote David Rayside's article, "Essay Writing: A Personal View," ". . . most essays are about some phenomenon that you are expected to reflect upon with ideas and evidence and logic that are not just about you."

The division and classification essay, which is the product of rigorous thought, and follows a definite and noticeable pattern of development, is an essay type where structure and quality of ideas predominate. Therefore, the less intrusive third-person point of view is ideal. A first-person "I" presence constantly referencing the writer's connection to the essay's ideas will distract readers. Notice in the student essay, "The Beer Up Here," that the writer uses the first-person point of view only in her introductory anecdote and final thoughts, not in the body-paragraphs of the essay.

Prewriting

Julia liked malls and liked to look at people; she thought her observations about "people at malls" would make a good topic for a division and classification essay. However, she did not immediately know how she wanted to group those people or what she wanted to say about them, so she began her prewriting by listing observations about mall shoppers. Here is what she came up with:

- Families with kids
- Lots of snacking
- Crowds around special displays—automobiles, kiddie rides
- Older people walking mall for exercise
- Groups of teenagers
- Women getting made up at makeup counter
- Dating couples
- Blind woman with guide dog
- Lots of people talking and laughing rather than shopping
- Interviewers stopping shoppers to fill out questionnaires
- Kids hanging out, meeting each other

As Julia reviewed her list, she concluded that the three largest groups of "mall people" were families with children, groups of teens, and dating couples. She decided to organize her essay around those three groups and created a trial outline that her essay would follow. Here is Julia's outline:

Thesis: The shopping mall offers inexpensive fun for several groups.

1. Teens
   a. Roam in packs
   b. Dress alike
   c. Meet new people

2. Dating couples
   a. Act romantic
   b. Window shop for future home
   c. Have lovers' quarrels

3. Families
   a. Kids' activities
   b. Cheap food
   c. Adults shop

Writing a Thesis Statement
for a Division and Classification Essay

The division and classification essay is built upon the particular divisions or categories of a given topic as well as the classifying principle for those divisions.

Your thesis statement should, then, present (1) your topic, (2) your classifying principle (or purpose for dividing the topic), and (3) your categories, if appropriate. You may also mention the point you make by dividing the subjects as you do.

Since the dividing principle and categories you choose to apply to your topic really represent your viewpoint, this kind of thesis statement is yet another variation of the "topic + viewpoint" formula.

An example of a division and classification thesis statement following this formula:

There are many different brands and models of cell phones, but, based on users' preferences, they all fall into three categories: the functional, the decorative, and the fully loaded.

First Draft and Revision

Julia's list making and outlining prepared her to write the first draft of her essay:

Malls aren't only places to go shopping. They also offer free or at least cheap fun and activities for lots of people. Teenagers, dating couples, and families all like to visit the mall.

1

Teenagers love to roam the mall in packs, like wolves. They, often dress   2
alike, depending on the latest fashion. They're noisy and sometimes rude,
and mall security sometimes kicks them out of the building. Then, they find
somewhere else to go, maybe one of the warehouse-sized amusement and
video-game arcades that are springing up everywhere. Those places are fun,
but they tend to be more expensive than just "hanging out" at the mall. Teens
are usually not as interested in shopping at the mall as they are in picking up
members of the opposite sex and seeing their friends.

Dating couples also enjoy wandering around the mall. They are easy to   3
spot because they walk along holding hands and sometimes kissing. They
stare at diamond rings and wedding bands and shop for furniture together.
Sometimes, they have spats, and one of them stamps off to sulk on a bench
for a while.

Little kids and their parents make up a big group of mall-goers. There   4
is something for every member of the family there. There are usually some
special displays that interest the kids, and Mom and Dad can always find
things they like to window shop for. Another plus for the family is that
there is inexpensive food, like burgers and pizza, available at the mall's
food court.

After completing her first draft, Julia put it aside. From previous experience, she
knew that she was a better critic of her own writing after she took a break from it.
The next morning, reading over her first draft, she noticed several places where it
could be improved. Here are the observations she put in her writing journal:

- My first paragraph does present a thesis (malls offer inexpensive entertainment), and it tells how I'm going to develop that thesis (by discussing
  three groups of people). But it isn't very interesting. I think I could do a
  better job of drawing readers in by describing what is fun about malls.
- Some of the details in the essay aren't necessary; they don't support my
  main idea. For instance, the points about teens being kicked out of the mall
  and about dating couples having fights don't have anything to do with the
  entertainment malls provide. I'll eliminate them.
- Some of my statements that do support the main idea need more support.
  For example, when I say there are "special displays that interest the kids" in
  paragraph 4, I should give an example of such a display. I should also back
  up the idea that many teens dress alike.

With those observations in mind, Julia returned to her essay and revised it,
producing the version that appears on page 231.

Writing a Division and Classification Essay

◼ Writing Assignment 1

What follows are an introduction and a thesis statement for a classification essay
on academic stress. Using a separate piece of paper, plan and write the supporting
paragraphs and a conclusion for the essay.

Post-Secondary Stress

Jack's heart pounds as he casts panicked looks around the classroom. He doesn't recognize the professor, he doesn't know any of the students, and he can't even figure out what the subject is. In front of him is a test. At the last minute, his roommate awakens him. It's only another anxiety dream. The very fact that dreams like Jack's are common suggests that college and university are stressful situations for young people. The causes of this stress can be academic, financial, and personal.

Prewriting

1 Freewrite for five minutes apiece on (1) *academic*, (2) *financial*, and (3) *personal* problems of college and university students.

2 Then, add to the material you have written by asking yourself these questions:

- What are some examples of academic problems that are stressful for students?
- What are some examples of financial problems that students must contend with?
- What are some examples of personal problems that create stress in students?

Write down quickly whatever answers occur to you. As with freewriting, do not worry at this stage about writing correct sentences. Instead, concentrate on getting down as much information as you can think of that supports each of the three points.

3 Go through all the material you have accumulated. Perhaps some of the details you have written down may help you think of even better details that would fit. If so, write down these additional details. Then, make decisions about the exact information that you will use in each supporting paragraph. Number the details according to the order in which you will present them.

4 Write out the first draft of your essay.

Revising

After you have completed the first draft of the essay (and ideally set it aside for a while), you should prepare yourself to rewrite by asking the following questions:

- Have I included relevant examples for each of the three divisions?
- Have I provided enough details to support each of the three divisions?
- Have I used transition words and sentences to help readers follow my train of thought?
- Does the concluding paragraph round off the essay by returning to the overall subject?

Continue to revise your essay until you can answer "yes" to each question. Then, be sure to check the next-to-final draft for the sentence skills listed on the inside front cover.

Writing Assignment 2

Choose one of the following as the subject for a division and classification essay.

Music	Attitudes toward exercise
Videos	Pet owners
TV shows	Junk food
Comic strips	Post-secondary courses
Vacations	Couples
Voice-mail messages	Shoppers
Breakfast foods	Video games
Pets	Parties
Sales clerks	Advertisements

1 For a division and classification essay, outlining is essential. The success of your outline and essay will depend on the division of your topic into three well-balanced parts. Begin by establishing a principle of classification. For example, the topic of "Hit Movies" could be divided in the following ways:

Divided by the principle of film categories: Action, comedy, romance

Divided by the principle of intended audience: Families, dating couples, teens

If you look back at the essay "Mall People," which appears earlier in this chapter, you will see that the topic is divided as follows:

Divided by the principle of groups of shoppers: Teens, dating couples, families

In the essay "The Beer Up Here," which also appears earlier in the chapter, the topic could be divided in these ways:

Divided by the principle of beer drinkers' self-images: Grown-up kids, men's men, upper-class wannabes

2 With your principle of classification, complete this outline, and answer the question that follows:

Topic: _____

Principle of classification: _____

Three-part division of topic: _____

a. _____

b. _____

c. _____

Have I used the same principle of classification for each of the three parts?

3 Before writing your first draft, you may want to freewrite on each of the three parts, make lists, or ask and answer questions to generate the supporting details you will need to develop your ideas. Write your essay in the third-person point of view.

4 When you have completed the first draft of your essay, refer to the guidelines for revising your division and classification essay provided on page 238.

Writing Assignment 3

In this division and classification essay, you will write with a **specific purpose** and for a **specific audience**.

Unsure about your career direction, you have gone to a vocational counselling service. To help you select the type of work for which you are best suited, a counsellor has asked you to write a detailed description of your "ideal job." You will present this description to three other people who are also seeking to make a career choice.

To describe your ideal job, divide "work life" into three or more elements, using one of the following principles of classification:

- Activities done on the job
- Skills used on the job
- Physical environment
- People you work with and under
- Effects of the job on society

In your essay, explain your ideals for each element. You may have more than three supporting paragraphs, if needed. Use specific details and examples where possible to illustrate your points.

Writing Assignment 4

Read the selection "The Plot Against People" by Russell Baker on pages 551–552. Baker divides and classifies ordinary objects according to an interesting principle. Now, writing in the third-person viewpoint, divide and classify an ordinary activity according to some appropriate, interesting, or funny principle. The activity could be one of the following:

- Grooming
- Using a cell phone
- Dancing
- Cleaning
- Studying

Think of a principle of classification for dividing the activity you choose. If you were considering grooming, you could imagine several principles of classification such as:

- Occasions for which people groom themselves
- Places where people groom themselves
- Reasons why people choose certain styles of grooming

Once you have an appropriate principle of classification, you will find it easy to divide your subject into three groups or divisions.

CHECKLIST OF LEARNING OUTCOMES FOR CHAPTER 15

To ensure that you have understood and met the learning outcomes for this chapter, answer the following questions upon completing any of its writing assignments:

✓ Do the divisions in your essay's subject follow a consistent principle of classification? Is this principle logically related to your purpose in writing about your subject? Does your dividing principle lead to interesting new thoughts about your subject?

✓ Does your thesis statement mention your subject, your principle of classification, and if appropriate, your categories or classifications?

✓ Do your category/classification paragraphs appear in an order that best supports your thesis?

✓ Is the number of supporting details for each category roughly balanced, and are all details adequately explained?

✓ Does your conclusion remind readers of your thesis and propose final thoughts about the subject's main divisions?

CHAPTER 16

Argumentation

We all know someone who enjoys a good argument. Such a person likes to challenge any sweeping statement we might make. When we say something like, "Ms. Lucci doesn't grade fairly," he or she comes back with, "Why do you say that? What are your reasons?"

Argumentation concerns our natural tendency to "ask why" of any point of view or opinion. No two minds perceive a person or situation in exactly the same way, so listeners or readers nearly always suspend agreement until they are satisfied with our "reasons why."

The student asking why we believe Ms. Lucci marks unfairly would listen carefully as we state our case, judging if we really do have solid evidence to support our point of view. We realize that saying, "Ms. Lucci just doesn't, that's all," sounds weak and unconvincing, so we try to come up with stronger evidence to back up our statement. Such a questioner may make us feel uncomfortable, but we may also feel grateful to him or her for helping us clarify our opinion.

Arguing a point in an essay requires you to do three things: (1) search for logical answers to why you hold an opinion, (2) examine and weigh the usefulness of the emotions associated with your opinion, and (3) present clear and credible information to support the viewpoint you are arguing.

The ability to present sound and compelling arguments is an important skill in everyday life. You can use argumentation to make a point in a discussion, persuade a friend to lend you money, or talk an employer into giving you a day off. Becoming skilled in clear, logical reasoning can also help you see through faulty arguments that others may make. You'll become a better critic of advertisements, newspaper articles, political speeches, and the other persuasive appeals you see and hear every day.

Argumentation is also crucially important for both academic- and career-related communication tasks. In a business course, you may be asked to defend a particular management style; in a technical program, you may be required to analyze and defend the use of a particular procedure. In the workplace, you may write proposals that request funding or new equipment, or you may create advertising copy to promote some product or service. The uses of good argumentation skills are endless.

In this chapter, you will be asked to write an essay in which you defend a position with a series of logical reasons. In a general way, you have already done this in the previous chapters of this section by making a point and supporting it. The difference is that argumentation advances a *controversial* point—one that at least some of your readers will not be inclined to accept. To prepare for the task of writing an argument essay, first read about five strategies you can use in advancing an argument. Then, read the student essays that follow, and work through the questions that accompany the essays.

Strategies for Argumentation

Because argumentation normally involves controversy, you have to work carefully to convince readers of the validity of your position. Here are five strategies you can use to persuade readers whose viewpoint may differ from yours.

1   Use Tactful, Courteous Language

In order to truly persuade readers to accept your viewpoint, it is important not to anger them by referring to them or their opinions in rude or belittling terms. Stay away from sweeping statements like, "Everybody knows that . . ." or "People with any intelligence agree that . . . ." Also, keep the focus on the issue you are discussing, *not on the people* involved in the debate. The third-person viewpoint is especially useful for maintaining the readers' focus on your ideas and for suggesting some objective distance between you and your subject. Don't write, "*My opponents* say that orphanages cost less than foster care." Instead, write, "*Supporters of orphanages* say they cost less than foster care." Terms like *my opponents* imply that the argument is between you and the "bad guys"—an attitude that puts more distance between you and anyone who disagrees with you. By contrast, an expression like *supporters of orphanages* suggests that those who don't agree are, nevertheless, reasonable people who are willing to consider differing opinions.

2   Point Out Common Ground

Another way to persuade readers to consider your opinion is to point out common ground or ideas that you share. Find points with which people on all sides of the argument can agree. You may be arguing in favour of longer access hours for the computer labs at your college. Before going into detail about your proposal, remind readers who could be opposed to increased hours that you and they share certain ideas such as enabling students with outside jobs to use the facilities and allowing more students to do better work. Readers will be more receptive to your idea once they have considered the ways in which you and they think alike.

3   Acknowledge Differing Viewpoints

Do not simply ignore points of view that conflict with yours. Acknowledging other viewpoints strengthens your position in several ways. First, it helps you spot flaws in the opposing position as well as in your own argument. Second, and equally important, it gives the impression that you are a reasonable person, willing to see all sides of an issue. Readers are more likely to consider your point of view if you indicate a willingness to consider theirs.

At what point in your essay should you acknowledge opposing arguments? The earlier the better—ideally, in the introduction. By quickly establishing that you recognize the other side's position, you get your readers "on board" with you, ready to hear what you have to say.

One effective technique is to cite the opposing viewpoint in your thesis statement. Do this by dividing your thesis into two parts. In the first part, you acknowledge the other side's point of view; in the second, state your opinion, suggesting that yours is the stronger viewpoint. Below, the opposing viewpoint is underlined once; the writer's own position is underlined twice:

> Although some students believe that studying another language is a waste of time, two years of second-language study should be required of all post-secondary graduates.

For another example of a thesis that acknowledges an opposing viewpoint, look at this thesis statement, taken from the student essay titled "Once Over Lightly: Local TV News" (pages 246–248):

> While local TV newscasts can provide a valuable community resource, too often such programs provide mere entertainment at the expense of solid news.

Another effective technique is to use one or two sentences (separate from the thesis) in the introduction to acknowledge the alternative position. To see this technique used, look at the introduction to "Teenagers and Jobs" (pages 245–246), noting the sentence, "Many people argue that working can be a valuable experience for the young."

A third technique is to use a paragraph within the body of your essay to summarize opposing opinions in greater detail. To do this successfully, you must spend time researching opposing arguments. A fair, well-developed summary of the other side's ideas will help convince readers that you have looked at the issue from all angles before deciding on your position. Imagine that you are writing an essay arguing that foreign ownership of Canadian businesses should be less limited. Begin by doing some library or Internet research to find information on both sides of the issue, paying special attention to materials that argue for your viewpoint. You could talk to local business owners or organizations that support Canadian ownership of businesses. You would then be in a good position to write a paragraph summarizing opposing viewpoints (Canadian business owners' fears of competition from U.S. companies, profit cuts caused by currency exchange, and so on).

Once you demonstrate your understanding of opposing views, you are in a stronger position to present your own views.

4   When Appropriate, Acknowledge the Merits of Differing Viewpoints

Sometimes an opposing argument contains a point whose validity you cannot deny. What should you do then? The strongest strategy is to admit that the point is a good one. You will lose credibility if you argue against something that clearly makes sense. Acknowledge the merit of one aspect of the other argument while making it clear that you still believe your argument. The author of "Teenagers and Jobs" (pages 245–246) takes this approach when discussing the negative effects on students of working more than fifteen hours per week. The sentence, "Many people argue that working can be a valuable experience for the young," admits that the other side has a valid point. But the author quickly follows this admission with a statement making her own viewpoint clear: "However, working more than fifteen hours a week is harmful to adolescents because it reduces their involvement with school, encourages a materialistic and expensive lifestyle, and increases the chance of having problems with drugs and alcohol."

5   Rebut Differing Viewpoints

Sometimes it may not be enough simply to acknowledge the other points of view and present your own argument. When you are dealing with an issue that your readers feel strongly about, you may need to *rebut* the opposing arguments. To rebut simply means to point out problems with an opposing view.

Imagine your essay states that your college or university should use money intended to build a campus fitness centre to upgrade the library instead. From reading the school paper, you know that supporters of the centre say it will help attract new students. You can rebut that point by citing a study conducted by management showing that most students choose a school because of affordable tuition and because of its academic and professional programs and facilities. You also emphasize that many students, already financially strapped, would have trouble paying charges to use the centre.

A rebuttal can take two forms, similar to the two methods of development used for comparison-contrast essays. You can first mention all the points raised by the other side and then present your counter-argument to each of those points, *or* you can present the first point raised by the opposition, rebut that point, then move on to the second opposing point, rebut that, and so on.

Student Essays to Consider

Teenagers and Jobs

"The lives of adolescents and adults are not as different as they used to   1
be. Students juggle jobs and school and leisure time in much the same way
their parents juggle careers and families; they make important choices—how
often they work, what classes they take, what they spend their money on—with
almost no adult input . . . if they make unwise choices, there are no safety

nets." So wrote Kate Fillion of Toronto high school students ("High School Undercover," *Toronto Life*, August 1990). Many people argue that working can be a valuable experience for the young. However, working more than fifteen hours a week is harmful to adolescents because it reduces their involvement with school, encourages a materialistic and expensive lifestyle, and increases the chance of having problems with drugs and alcohol.

Schoolwork and the benefits of extracurricular activities tend to go by the wayside when adolescents work long hours. As more and more teens have filled the numerous part-time jobs offered by fast-food restaurants and malls, teachers have faced increasing difficulties. They must keep the attention of tired pupils and give homework to students who simply don't have time to do it. In addition, educators have noticed less involvement in the extracurricular activities that many consider a healthy influence on young people. School bands and athletic teams are losing players to work, and sports events are poorly attended by working students. Those teenagers who try to do it all— homework, extracurricular activities, and work—may find themselves exhausted and prone to illness. A recent newspaper story, for example, described a girl who came down with mononucleosis as a result of aiming for good grades, playing on two school athletic teams, and working thirty hours a week.

Another drawback of too much work is that it may promote materialism and an unrealistic lifestyle. Some parents claim that working helps teach adolescents the value of a dollar. Undoubtedly, that can be true. It's also true that some teens work to help out with the family budget or to save for college or university. However, surveys have shown that the majority of working teens use their earnings to buy luxuries—video-game systems, MP3 players, clothing, and even cars. These young people, some of whom earn $1000 or more a month, don't worry about spending wisely; they can just about have it all. In many cases, experts point out, they are becoming accustomed to a lifestyle they won't be able to afford several years down the road when they no longer have parents paying for car insurance, food, lodging, and so on. At that point, they'll be hard-pressed to pay for necessities as well as luxuries.

Finally, teenagers who work a lot are more likely than others to get involved with alcohol and drugs. Teens who put in long hours may seek a quick release from stress, just like the adults who need to drink a couple of martinis after a hard day at work. Stress is probably greater in our society today than it has been at any time in the past. Also, teens who have money are more likely to get involved with drugs.

Teenagers can enjoy the benefits of work while avoiding its drawbacks by simply limiting their work hours during the school year. As is often the case, a moderate approach will be the most healthy and rewarding.

Once Over Lightly: Local TV News

Are local television newscasts a reliable source of news? Do they provide in-depth coverage and analysis of important local issues? Unfortunately, all too often they do not. While local TV newscasts can provide a valuable community resource, too often such programs provide mere entertainment instead of solid news. In their battle for high ratings, local programs emphasize news personalities at the expense of stories, visual appeal at the expense of actual news, and brevity at the expense of analysis.

Local TV newscasters are as much the subject of the news as are the stories they present. Nowhere is this more obvious than in weather reports. Weatherpersons spend valuable news time joking, drawing cartoons, chatting about weather fronts as "good guys" and "bad guys," and dispensing weather trivia such as statistics about relative humidity and record highs and lows for the date. Reporters, too, draw attention to themselves. Rather than just getting the story, reporters are shown jumping into or getting out of helicopters to get the story. When reporters interview crime victims or the residents of poor neighbourhoods, the camera angle typically includes them and their reaction as well as their subjects. When they report on a storm, they stand outside in the storm, their styled hair blowing, so viewers can admire how they "brave the elements." Then, there are the anchorpersons, who are chosen as much for their looks as their skills. They, too, dilute the news by putting their personalities centre stage.

2

Often the selection of stories and the way they are presented are based on visual impact rather than news value. If a story is not accompanied by an interesting film clip, it is not likely to be shown on the local news. The result is an over-emphasis on fires and car crashes and little attention to such important issues as the economy. A tractor-trailer spill on the highway slightly injures one person and inconveniences motorists for only an hour. However, because it provides dramatic pictures—the big truck on its side, its load spilled, emergency personnel running around, and lots of flashing lights—it is given greater emphasis in the local newscast than a rise in local taxes, which has a far more lasting effect on the viewer. "If it bleeds, it leads" is the unofficial motto of many local news programs. A story that includes pictures of death and destruction, no matter how meaningless, is preferable on the local news to a solid, important story without flashy visuals. The mania for visuals is so strong that local news programs will even slap irrelevant visuals on an otherwise strong story. A recent story on rising oil prices, for example, was accompanied by footage of a working oil well that drew attention away from the important economic information in the report.

3

On the average, about half a minute is devoted to a story. Clearly, stories that take less than half a minute are superficial. Even the longest stories, which can take up to several minutes, are not accompanied by meaningful analysis. Instead, the camera jumps from one location to another, and the newscaster simplifies and trivializes the issues. For instance, one recent "in-depth" story about the homeless consisted of a glamorous reporter talking to a homeless person and asking him what should be done about the problem. The poor man was in no condition to respond intelligently. The story then cut to an interview with a city bureaucrat who mechanically rambled on about the need for more government funding. Is raising taxes the answer to every social problem? There were also shots of homeless people sleeping in doorways and on top of heating vents, and there were interviews with people in the street, all of whom said something should be done about the terrible problem of homelessness. There was, in all of this, no real exploration of the issue and no proposed solution. It was also apparent that the homeless were just the issue of the week. After the week's coverage was over, the topic was not mentioned again.

4

Because of the emphasis on newscasters' personalities and the visual   5
impact of stories, and because of the short time span for stories, local news
shows provide little more than diversion. What viewers need instead is news
that has real significance. Rather than being amused and entertained, people
need to deal with complex issues and learn uncomfortable truths that will help
them become more responsible consumers and citizens.

■ Questions

About Unity

1. Which paragraph in "Once Over Lightly" is lacking a topic sentence? Write a topic sentence for the paragraph.

2. Which sentence in paragraph 4 of "Once Over Lightly" should be omitted in the interest of paragraph unity?

3. Which sentence in paragraph 4 of "Teenagers and Jobs" should be omitted in the interest of paragraph unity?

About Support

4. Which sentence in paragraph 4 of "Teenagers and Jobs" needs to be followed by more supporting details? Which sentence in paragraph 2 of "Once Over Lightly" needs to be followed by supporting details?

5. Which supporting paragraph in "Teenagers and Jobs" raises an opposing idea and then argues against that idea? What transition word is used to signal the author's change of direction?"

6. In the second paragraph of "Once Over Lightly," the topic sentence is supported by details about three types of newscasters. What are those three types?

About Coherence

7. Which two paragraphs of "Teenagers and Jobs" begin with an addition transition, and what are those words?

8. What are the change-of-direction and the illustration transitions in paragraph 3 of "Once Over Lightly"?

About the Introduction and Conclusion

9. Which two methods of introduction are used in "Teenagers and Jobs"?
   a. Broad, general statement narrowing to a thesis
   b. Idea that is the opposite of the one to be developed
   c. Quotation
   d. Anecdote
   e. Questions

10. Both essays end with the same type of conclusion. Which method do they use?
   a. Summary only
   b. Summary and recommendation
   c. Prediction

Argumentation Prewriting Activity

In outline form, provide brief supporting arguments, or reasons, for at least four of the eight statements that follow. Note the example. Make sure that you have at least three *separate* and *distinct* arguments for each statement.

> ***Example***   The recycling of newspapers, cans, and bottles should be mandatory.
> a. Towns sell recycled items rather than pay for dumping.
> b. Natural resources are protected.
> c. Respect for the environment is encouraged.

1 Couples should be required to live together for six months before marriage.

2 High schools should give birth control devices and information to students.

3 All instructors should be marked by their students.

4 Cultural diversity should be given less encouragement in Canada.

5 Gambling should not be legal in any province.

6 School does not prepare people for life.

7 All companies should be required to have daycare centres.

8 Canadian TV should not carry so much U.S. programming.

Developing an Argumentation Essay

Purpose and Audience

The main purpose of an argumentation essay is to convince your audience that your particular view or opinion on a *controversial* issue is correct. In addition, you may, at times, have a second purpose: to persuade your audience to take some sort of action.

In order to convince your audience in an argumentation essay, it is important to provide them with a clear main point and plenty of logical evidence to back it up. Say, for example, that you want to argue that public schools should require students to wear uniforms. In this case, you might do some research to gather as much evidence as possible to support your point. You may check to see, for instance, if uniforms are cheaper than the alternative. Perhaps you could find out if schools with uniforms have a lower incidence of violent behaviour than those without them or if students' academic performance improves when school uniforms are adopted. As you search for evidence, be sure that it clearly links to your topic and supports the main point you are trying to get across to your audience.

While consideration of your audience is important to all essay forms, it is absolutely critical to the success of your argumentation essay. Depending on the main point you choose, your audience may be firmly opposed to your view or somewhat supportive of it. As you begin planning your own argumentation essay, consider, then, what your audience already knows and how it feels about the main point of your argument. Using the example above, ask yourself what opinion your audience holds about school uniforms. What might their objections be to your argument? Why would people *not* support your main point? What, if anything, are the merits of the opposing point of view? In order to "get inside the head" of your opposition, you might even want to interview a few people you are sure will disagree with you. By becoming aware of the points of view your audience might have, you will know how to proceed in researching and presenting your rebuttal to their arguments. (For more information on how to deal with opposing views in your essay, see pages 244–245.) By directly addressing your opposition, you add credibility to your argument, give your audience confidence that you have explored alternative views, and increase the chances that others will be convinced of your main point.

Point of View in Argumentation Essays

Essays whose focus is persuading or arguing a point must be carefully tailored to their audiences. If not, audiences may abandon the effort of even reading an essay that is irrelevant, unsuited, or unrelated to their interests or background. The purpose of these essays is to convince readers of the rightness of some viewpoint, but that does not mean the writer appears directly to "lecture" readers. Such an approach, writing as "I," could put off readers for various reasons, many connected to consideration of audience.

First, an effective argument is supported with logic, rather than with what may appear to be merely subjective, personally derived reasons. Readers confronted with the argument, "I believe failing students hurts their chances of ever succeeding . . ." usually suspect the writer speaks from personal interest, if not an agenda. Instead, the same opinion, stated more neutrally as, "Failing students damages their self-esteem and desire to learn . . . ," suggests that the writer will reveal some impartial evidence to back up the points. Effective persuasive writers background their presence and rely on their ideas, writing as someone informed about the topic and willing to give a logical, well-detailed argument to back it up.

Moreover, readers do not feel "pressured," "crowded," or manipulated by the writer's presence in a well supported third-person essay; instead, they may be at least willing to entertain the views in the paper. Nowhere might reading audiences feel less inclined to trust or value the views expressed than in a first-person, completely subjective argumentation essay. If an essay's writer seems to derive thesis and support only from personal experience or opinions, then the basis for credibility (leaving aside persuasion of the audience) is extremely narrow. One person's experience does not make a thing true. Empathy might be possible for a few readers, but not much else.

Prewriting

Before choosing a topic for her essay, Anna, the writer of "Teenagers and Jobs," asked herself what controversial subject she was particularly well qualified to argue for or against. She wanted to select something she cared about, something she could "sink her teeth into." As a person who had been active in her high-school community—working on the newspaper, playing basketball, and singing in a chorus—Anna first thought about "student apathy." She had never understood students ignoring opportunities available to them in school. Then, she began to consider individual students she knew and their reasons for not getting more involved in school and extracurricular activities, and she changed her opinion. "I realized that 'apathy' was not really the problem," she explained. "Many of them worked so much that they literally didn't have time for school life."

After focusing her thesis on the idea of "teenagers and work," Anna made a list of what she perceived as the bad points of students working too much:

- No time for sports and other activities
- Students leave right after school—can't stay for clubs, practices
- Don't have time to attend games, other school functions
- Students sleep in class and skip homework
- Stress, extra money contribute to drug and alcohol use
- Teachers frustrated trying to teach tired students
- Ability to buy luxuries makes teens materialistic, unrealistic about lifestyle
- Some drop out of school to work full-time
- Students miss the fun of being young, developing talents and social abilities
- Students burn out, even get sick

Anna reviewed her list of points and identified three main points to develop in her essay.

Realizing that some other items she had listed were related ideas that could be useful as support for her main topics, she marked those with the number of the main idea they supported in parentheses.

1—	No time for real involvement in school and school activities
(1)	Students leave right after school—can't stay for clubs, practices
(1)	Don't have time to attend games, other school functions
	Students sleep in class and skip homework
2—	Stress, extra money contribute to drug and alcohol use
(1)	Teachers frustrated trying to teach tired students
3—	Having extra money makes teens materialistic
(3)	Some get so greedy for money they drop out of school to work full-time
	Students miss the fun of being young, developing talents and social abilities
	Students burn out, even get sick
(2)	Hanging around older co-workers can contribute to drug, alcohol use
(3)	Buying luxuries gives teens unrealistic idea of standard of living

Writing a Thesis Statement
for an Argumentation Essay

Persuading your audience of your viewpoint about a certain controversial subject is the primary objective in the argumentation essay, and never is the direct and clear statement of a viewpoint more important than in the thesis statement of an argumentation essay.

When writing your thesis statement, be direct and unambiguous about your position. Try to avoid the use of conditional verb forms that "soften" your position, as in "Volunteer work *might* help some students to gain experience." You may wish to refer to the main supporting points of your argument in the thesis. This will clearly indicate to readers the direction of your argument.

An example of an argumentation thesis statement follows:

Colleges and universities must set an example, where recycling is concerned.

An example of an argumentation thesis statement that displays its supporting points follows:

Lack of family or peer support, financial pressures, and health problems make students drop out of college and university.

First Draft and Revision

Referring to her list, Anna wrote the following first draft of her essay:

Many people think that working is a valuable experience for young people. However, when teenagers have jobs, they are too likely to neglect their schoolwork, become overly materialistic, and get into trouble with drugs and alcohol.

Schoolwork and the benefits of extracurricular activities tend to go by the wayside when adolescents work long hours. As more and more teens have taken jobs, teachers have faced increasing difficulties. They must keep the attention of tired pupils and give homework to students who simply don't have time to do it. In addition, educators have noticed less involvement in extracurricular activities. School bands and athletic teams are losing players to work, and sports events are poorly attended by working students. Those teens who try to do it all—homework, extracurricular activities, and work—may find themselves exhausted and burned out.

Another drawback of too much work is that it may promote materialism and an unrealistic lifestyle. Most working teens use their earnings to buy luxuries. These young people don't worry about spending wisely; they can just about have it all. They are becoming accustomed to a lifestyle they won't be able to afford several years down the road when they have to support themselves.

Finally, teenagers who work are more likely than others to get involved with alcohol and drugs. Teens who put in long hours may seek a quick release from stress, just like the adults who need to drink a couple of martinis after a hard day at work. Also, teens who have money are more likely to get involved with drugs.

In short, teens and work just don't mix.

Anna's instructor looked over her first draft and suggested these improvements for revision:

Anna—Good beginning. Your thesis may be overstated, but each of your main topics is on the right track. Here are some points to consider:

- *Working a <u>limited</u> number of hours a week might be a good experience.*
- *Acknowledge that there can be good points to students working part-time.*

- *Good support for your first main point ("Schoolwork and the benefits of extracurricular activities tend to go by the wayside when adolescents work long hours"): the effect of too much work on scholastic achievement and extracurricular activities.*
- *Less effective support for points 2 and 3 ("Another drawback of too much work is that it may promote materialism and an unrealistic lifestyle" and "Finally, teenagers who work are more likely than others to get involved with alcohol and drugs").*
- *How do teens become too materialistic?*
- *What evidence is there that working teens use drugs and alcohol more than others?*
- *Can you come up with evidence beyond your own observations to support the idea that too much working is detrimental to teens?*
- *Check magazine indexes in the library and the Internet for support for your thesis.*

I look forward to seeing your final draft.

After considering her instructor's comments, Anna wrote the draft of "Teenagers and Jobs" that appears on pages 245–246.

Writing an Argumentation Essay

Writing Assignment 1

Write an essay in which you argue *for* or *against* any one of the options below. Support and defend your argument by drawing on your reasoning ability and general experience.

Option 1: Because fast food is available in college and university cafeterias, and because it is so familiar and widely advertised, students choose it more often than other options. In fact, other options, if they are available at all, are usually displayed unappealingly. Colleges and universities should drop the fast-food franchises and feed the student body as well as the student mind.

Option 2: By the time many students reach high school, they have learned the basics in most subjects. Some still have much to gain from the courses that high schools offer, but others might be better off spending the next four years in other ways. For their benefit, high school attendance should be voluntary.

Option 3: Many of today's young people are mainly concerned with prestigious careers, making money, and owning things. It seems we no longer teach the benefits of spending time and money to help the community, the country, or the world. Most students, in fact, only pay "lip service" in fulfilling any community service requirements in high schools. Canada can lead the way by requiring young people to spend a year working in some kind of community service.

Prewriting

1 As you write your opening paragraph, acknowledge the opposing point of view. Completing the following exercise will give you practice in acknowledging another way of looking at the issue.

In each item, you will see a statement and then a question related to that statement. Write *two* answers to each question. First, answer "yes" to the question, and briefly explain why. Then, answer "no" to the question, and also state why. The first item is done for you as an example.

a. It has been proven that smoking is bad for one's health. Should it, therefore, be made illegal?

"Yes": Because smoking has been shown to have so many negative effects on one's health, the sale of tobacco should be made illegal.

"No": Although smoking has been linked to various health problems, adults should have the right to make their own decisions about whether or not to smoke. Smoking should not be made illegal.

b. Animals feel pain when they are killed for food. Is eating animals, therefore, immoral?

"Yes": _____

_____

"No": _____

_____

c. Some high school students are sexually active. Should birth control devices and information be given out by high schools to their students?

"Yes": _____

_____

"No": _____

_____

2 Make a list of the thoughts that support your argument. Don't worry about repetition, spelling, or grammar at this point. Just write down everything that occurs to you. Then, identify your strongest points and begin your outline. Are there thoughts in your list that can be used as supporting details for your main supporting points?

3 Plan your three supporting paragraphs. Keep in mind that you are writing for an audience of people who, initially, will not all agree with you. It isn't enough to state your opinion. Show *why* you feel as you do, persuading your audience that your point of view is a valid one.

4 Your concluding paragraph is your final chance to persuade your readers to accept your argument. Consider ending with a prediction of what will happen if your point of view does not prevail. Will an existing situation grow worse? Will a new problem arise?

Revising

After you have completed the first draft of the essay, set it aside for a while. When you review it, try to do so as critically as you would if it were not your own work. Ask yourself these questions:

- Have I provided persuasive details to support my argument?
- Have I acknowledged the opposing point of view, showing that I am a reasonable person, willing to consider other arguments?
- Is my language tactful and courteous, or does it insult anyone who doesn't agree with me?
- Have I used transition words to help readers follow my train of thought?
- Does my final supporting paragraph include a strong argument for my position?
- Does my concluding paragraph summarize my argument or add a final persuasive touch?

Continue to revise your essay until you can answer "yes" to each question. Then, be sure to check the next-to-final draft for the sentence skills listed on the inside front cover.

Writing Assignment 2

In this argument essay, you will write with a **specific purpose** and for a **specific audience**.

Option 1: You would like to live in a big city, but your parent or partner refuses to budge from the suburbs. Write him or her a letter in which you argue for the advantages of city life. Be sure to acknowledge and rebut the other person's objections to city life. Use specific examples wherever possible.

Option 2: Find an editorial in your local newspaper that you either strongly agree or disagree with. Write a letter to the editor in which you state why you agree or disagree with the position taken by the paper in that editorial. Provide several short paragraphs of supporting evidence for your position. Then, send your letter to the newspaper. When you turn in a copy of your letter to your instructor, also turn in the editorial to which you are responding.

Writing Assignment 3

Write an essay in which you use research findings to help support one of the statements in the Argumentation Prewriting Activity on page 249. Be sure to keep the focus on your subject by writing in the third-person point of view. Research the topic in one or both of these ways:

- Look up the topic in the subject section of your library book index or on the Internet. (Review pages 280–289 of "Research Skills.") Think about synonyms and phrases that will be likely keywords and subject headings for some of the statements in the activity. Select the books or websites that seem likely to give you the most appropriate information about your topic. Note your sources in the ways listed in "Writing a Research Paper" (pages 292–322).

- Look up the topic in recent issues of the *Canadian Periodical Index* or on a database or search engine. (Review "Research Skills" first.) Try some of the same keywords and headings. Select articles likely to provide information on your topic.

When you have identified three arguments, or reasons, develop these in an outline. Be sure to note your sources. Note that statistical information, the results of studies, and the advice of experts may all help develop the supporting reasons for your thesis. Do not hesitate to cite such information; it helps make your argument more objective and compelling.

Writing Assignment 4

Read the selection "Black and Blue" by Cecil Foster on pages 513–518. As Foster opens his argument, notice how he nonetheless acknowledges that Clinton Gayle is not a desirable or moral individual. He then uses a mixture of objective and more subjective details to persuade readers to his point about institutional racism

Write a third-person persuasive or argumentation essay in which you argue for or against a concept currently in contention in Canada: separate courses of study, and even different marking systems for different racial and ethnic groups. Is there a justification for offering a different curriculum to African-Canadian students, to Native Canadian students, to Asian Canadian students, or to any other distinct group? Or does doing so further splinter Canadian society? Present your reasons in order of increasing importance, and develop each paragraph's point with plenty of supporting details derived from your own thinking or from some research.

CHECKLIST OF LEARNING OUTCOMES FOR CHAPTER 16

To ensure that you have understood and met the learning outcomes for this chapter, answer the following questions upon completing any of its writing assignments:

✓ Does your opening paragraph provide appropriate background for your thesis? Does the thesis clearly state the point your essay will argue?

✓ Does your essay acknowledge and counter any opposing views?

✓ Does each supporting point and detail clearly support your thesis viewpoint and add to the strength of your argument?

✓ Have you maintained both an objective approach and a courteous tone in presenting your argument?

✓ Does your concluding statement reinforce your argument?

CHAPTER 17

Writing a Summary

LEARNING OUTCOMES

After reading this chapter and working through its activities, you will

- identify essential characteristics of a summary and understand how it differs from an essay;

- analyze a piece of material for its essential content;

- paraphrase another writer's words correctly;

- create an "x-ray" outline and list of the main ideas and support in an original source;

- revise and tighten drafts of a summary by using three methods;

- create an effective summary that presents the main ideas in the same order and proportion as the original.

Summaries are among the most often-used writing formats. You have probably read hundreds of summaries—on search engine pages beneath the titles of sites, on the backs of DVD and video game covers, in the openings of chapters in your textbooks, or perhaps on database indexes of articles. A summary delivers a condensed version of the content of some original work. As such, it is an efficient and useful way to present information and highly valuable in a time when the quantity of information available is expanding so quickly.

You will write academic summaries as separate writing assignments and as components of research papers. In this chapter, you will learn how to create an effective summary, and in Chapter 19 of this part of the book, you will learn how to apply the principles and techniques you learn to the research process.

Writing concise and accurate summaries is also an invaluable career skill. You may be required to summarize technical data, minutes of meetings, reports, media presentations, or interviews. Summaries are integral to business, social and human services, and technical communications.

In a summary (or *précis* or *abstract*), you reduce material in an original work to its main points and key supporting details.

A summary is not . . .	*A summary is . . .*
A summary **is not an essay**. A summary does not present or support your point of view on the original material. It reproduces, in reduced form and in third-person voice, the viewpoint and support of the original text.	A summary **is a concentrated version of the original material**. It presents the main ideas of the original in your own words. A summary does not use the wording of the original source and rarely uses quotations from that source.
A summary **is not an outline**. It is written in sentence and paragraph form so that readers understand the general ideas of the original text, as well as their relationships, in an easy-to-follow form.	A summary **presents the ideas of the original material in the same order** and **preserves the sense and flavour of that material**. Its length depends on the requirements of the situation or medium in which it appears.
A summary **is not a paraphrase.** A paraphrase is a complete restatement of some quantity of text. Paraphrasing focuses on restating, not on concentrating and reducing an original text. But paraphrasing, or rewording an original, is essential to creating a summary.	A summary **is a reduced, reworded version of some original text.** Paraphrasing the original is a necessary step in writing a summary. Reduction and concentration of the original into its main ideas are also necessary steps.
Summarizing **is not note-taking.** Summarizing is a multi-step process that exposes the main ideas in a piece of text, then reduces the word count, and reassembles those main ideas into an original piece of work.	Summarizing **creates a recognized writing format.** Note-taking is simply listing key points from a text, lecture, or presentation. Creating a summary requires drafting the main ideas back into sentences and revising until a concise, clear paragraph (or more) emerges.

Writing a summary brings together reading, study, and writing skills. To condense the original, you must preview, read, evaluate, organize, and outline the assigned material. Summarizing, then, can be a real aid to understanding; you must "get inside" the material and realize fully what is being said before you can reduce its meaning to a few words.

Summarizing is a skill; it does not "come naturally" to most people, but if you learn (1) to read (or watch or listen to) the original carefully, (2) to analyze and outline its main ideas, and (3) to express those main ideas in your own words, you will be prepared to face most summarizing challenges.

HOW TO SUMMARIZE

Summarizing *takes time*. Be prepared to set aside time to read shorter printed pieces several times, to "rescan" a book you have already read, to record and review a TV show, to watch a movie a few times, or to download and print out parts of a website whose content you may be summarizing.

The end product may be brief, but a summary is *concentrated;* every word and phrase you write must restate essential ideas of the original. Therefore, you must know the content of the original thoroughly.

Stage 1: Previewing and Reviewing the Source Material

Summarizing an Article or Shorter Printed Piece

If you are summarizing an article or a shorter printed piece on any subject, begin by photocopying it (or downloading and printing it out) so that you can highlight important points, strike through repetitive phrases or examples, and note the main ideas right on the original.

Take a few minutes to preview the work. You can preview an article in a magazine or journal by taking a quick look at the following:

1 *Title* The title often summarizes what the article is about. Think about the title and how it may condense the meaning of an article. Sometimes, however, a title may be attention-grabbing but so vague that it may not be very helpful (as, for example, the title of the *Saturday Night* magazine article from June 2004 reprinted in this chapter, "The New, Old Jamaica," which could refer to any number of ideas related to Jamaica).

2 *Subtitle* The subtitle (if given), the caption, or any other words in large print under or next to the title often provide a quick insight into the meaning of an article. An example of useful subtitle information appears in an article in *The Kitchener/Waterloo Record* from November 2002. The article's title is "A Good Old-Fashioned Wholesaler." The title alone does not seem informative or even relevant to a business student looking up articles about independent retail on the EBSCOhost database. The article's subtitle, however, "Personal Contacts Help Supplier Sell to Small, Independent Retailers," clearly reveals the gist of the article.

3 *First and last several paragraphs* In the first paragraphs, the author may introduce the subject and state the purpose of the article. In the last several paragraphs, the author may present conclusions or a summary. Opening and closing paragraphs are points of *maximum attention* for readers as they seek information. Journalists, writers for special-interest journals, and many website creators know this and structure their content accordingly. Previews or summaries can give you an overview of what the entire article is about.

4 *Headings, subheadings, special typography, and graphics* Note any headings or subheadings that appear in the article. They often provide clues to the article's main points and give an immediate indication of what each section is about. Look carefully at any pictures, charts, or diagrams that accompany the article. Page space in a magazine or journal is limited, and such visual aids are generally used to illustrate important points in the article. Note any words or phrases set off in *italic type* or **boldface print;** note also bulleted lists or boxed sections of material. Such ideas have probably been emphasized because they are important points in the article.

Read the article once through for a general sense of its meaning. Do not slow down or turn back and reread. Then, *read the article a second time to note its main ideas.* Check or highlight main points and key supporting details. Pay special attention to all the items noted in the preview. Also, look for definitions, examples, and enumerations (lists of items), as these often indicate key ideas. Identify important points by turning any headings into questions and then reading to find the answers to the questions.

Finally, *reread your checked or highlighted sections.* Go back and reread more carefully the areas you have identified as most important. Also, focus on other key points you may have missed in your first reading.

Summarizing a Book, Film, or TV Show

If you are assigned a longer piece of material such as a book or feature film, you must read or watch the material once before beginning the summarizing process. A single episode of a TV series or a "free-standing" one- or two-hour TV program should be recorded as you are watching it so that you can review the material to note its main ideas.

To begin summarizing a book, film, or TV show, first review the aspect of that material that your course touches or focuses on. Try to readjust your own focus on the material so that you "see" course-related ideas, images, dialogue, or characters. Watch, read, or reread with a notepad in hand so that you can jot down ideas as they come to you.

Movies and TV shows (recorded) are easy to replay, frame by frame as needed. If you are summarizing an entire book, you may not have time to reread all of it. To summarize a book, *narrow your focus.* The ideas to look for are either those set out by your instructor or those related to your course material.

When summarizing a book, look at the following for cues to its main ideas:

1 *Title* The title is often the shortest possible expression of what a book is about. Think about how it sums up the whole book.

2 *Table of contents* The contents will tell you the number of chapters in the book and the subject of each chapter. Use the contents to get a general sense of how the book is organized. You should also note the number of pages in each chapter. If thirty pages are devoted to one episode, idea, or area and an average of fifteen pages to other episodes, ideas, or areas, you should probably give more space to the contents of the longer chapter in your summary.

3 *Preface* Here you will probably find out why the author wrote the book. Also, the preface may highlight the main ideas developed in the book and may describe briefly how the book is organized.

4 *First and last chapters* In these chapters, the author may preview or review important ideas and themes developed in the book.

5 *Other items* Note the way the author has used headings and subheadings to organize information in the book. Check the opening and closing paragraphs of each chapter to see if they contain introductions or summaries. Look quickly at charts, diagrams, and pictures in the book since they are probably there to illustrate key points.

Stage 2: Listing, Editing, and Drafting Your Summary

Before you begin to write your summary, you should first list all the main ideas in your source-material. Number these ideas, and leave space after each numbered item to fill in the supporting details. Leave some time, if possible, before reviewing and editing your list. Check your list of ideas and support against your original material. Look for omissions, for possible repetition in either the original or in your list, as well as for duplications of ideas in examples, quotations, or explanations. A piece of supporting information may be repeated for emphasis, or it may be duplicated in dialogue.

With your edited list, you can prepare the first draft of your summary, keeping these points in mind:

1 Identify, at the start of the summary, the title, author, and place of publication of the work. Include, in parentheses, the date of publication. For example, "in 'The New, Old Jamaica' (*Saturday Night*, June 2004), Samra Habib writes . . . ."

2 Write your draft in the third person. You are writing a reduction of the original work, with no commentary or views of your own.

3 Express the main points and key supporting details in your own words. Your task is to *paraphrase* the original concisely; do not imitate the style of the original.

4 Limit the use of quotations. You should quote from the material only to illustrate key points. A one-paragraph summary should not contain more than one quoted sentence.

5 Preserve the balance and proportion of the original work. If the original text devoted 70 per cent of its space to one idea and only 30 per cent to another, your summary should reflect that.

6 Revise the first draft, paying attention to the bases for effective writing—unity, support, coherence, and effective sentence skills—explained in Part 1.

Ideally, first drafts are a bit long. It is better to include a few too many details than to omit necessary information. Prepare your second draft by following these tips:

1 Check again for the required word count or length. Use the word count on your word-processing software to check your document, or simply count each word, including *a* and *the*.

2 Review your summary to reduce *wordy phrases* such as "because of the fact that . . ." (try simply "because"), "in order to . . ." (try simply "to").

3 Note each major idea and its support as it appears on your revised list, and note each in your draft. See if each idea can be rephrased more concisely.

4 Write a final draft of your summary.

Paraphrasing

Paraphrasing—putting another person's ideas into your own words—is a key skill for effective summaries and research papers. When you paraphrase, you must do more than change a word or two. You must express the other writer's material *completely* in your own words.

When summarizing written text, you paraphrase the original source to express its main ideas as concisely as possible. Paraphrasing correctly begins with understanding the exact meaning of the words and phrases you restate. Any time you are not sure of a meaning, look it up in a dictionary. If your original material contains technical or specialized vocabulary, learn what the terms mean so that you paraphrase them accurately. In summaries, it is preferable to put any specialized terms into wording appropriate for a general audience.

Next, keep in mind that paraphrasing *re-expresses* the ideas of another writer. Never simply replace a few words with synonyms while retaining the original author's sentence structure; this is plagiarism (see pages 279–280). Following are examples, based on the summary example in this chapter, of incorrect and correct paraphrasing.

Original Source

"The mento sound is a concoction of calypso beats, Latin American musical influences and hints of American big band, with a three-three-two rhythm."

Incorrect Paraphrasing or Plagiarism

The mento sound mixes calypso beats, Latin American music, and bits of American big band, with an irregular rhythm.

In the example above, the writer has only changed the original's wording in three places: "mixes" for "a concoction of," "bits" for "hints," and "an irregular" for "a three-three-two." These substitutions leave the attempt at paraphrasing too close to the original; this is plagiarism. The sentence structure of the original text is unchanged, indicating that the writer has not fully re-expressed the ideas as his or her own. The examples below show preferable paraphrasings of the original sentence:

Correct Paraphrasing

Traces of calypso, Latin American, swing styles, and an irregular rhythm characterize the mento sound.

Mento sounds like a mix of Jamaican, Latin, and big band music, with a rhythm of its own.

In both examples above, the writer has retained the meaning of the original source while using completely different sentence structure and greater conciseness.

WRITING A SUMMARY

Mark Fernandez, a broadcasting student, was asked to find and summarize a program-related article from a general-interest Canadian magazine. Because he was interested in contemporary music, especially reggae and ska, Mark looked for articles about music genres. He scanned some of the Canadian magazine listings in his college library's databases, then noticed several months' issues of *Saturday Night* in the library's periodicals display. Flipping through a few issues led him to an article about mento, a type of Jamaican music that was new to him.

His assignment required him to choose an article of a length that could be accurately summarized in one paragraph of two to three hundred words. Here is the full text of the article he decided to summarize:

The New, Old Jamaica

Every decade has its musical genre revivals. In the '70s, Sha Na Na brought back the bop; the '80s had a '60s psychedelic flashback; and swing and old-style Cuban ensembles filled dance floors once again in the '90s. Now, North American clubland speakers are throbbing with the sounds of old Jamaica. Mento, a unique Jamaican folk music popular in the 1950s, is finally getting the international attention it deserves.

1

Mento has its roots in music performed with homemade instruments in 19th-century Jamaica; it was extremely popular until the 1960s, when it morphed into ska, reggae and dance hall. The mento sound is a concoction of calypso beats, Latin American musical influences and hints of American big band, with a three-three-two rhythm. As for the name, *mento* may be derived from the Spanish word *mentar*, which means "to mention" (Spain occupied Jamaica from 1494 to 1655). Another theory is that mento is an African word that describes a lewd dance. Lyrical themes, often humorous commentaries on social situations and celebration of sexuality set mento apart from reggae, whose slower rhythms and more political lyrics grew out of the '60s struggle for civil rights. By the time Jamaica began to record and export its culture to the world, mento had already been eclipsed by reggae and ska. So, unlike artists such as Bob Marley and Prince Buster, mento musicians have been largely unknown beyond the island, until recently.

2

The surprising resurgence of mento is a welcome development for DJs and record collectors who have loved it for years. Particularly bedazzled is DJ Rocky, a regular fixture of the Toronto reggae and ska scene who spins records at the Cloak and Dagger pub on College Street. Rocky says he's intrigued by the growing number of downtown Toronto venues that, in the past two years, have started to play vintage Jamaican music. Until recently, this music was heard exclusively in areas where a significant proportion of Jamaican-Canadians reside. Even more surprising, Rocky recounts, is that during recent gigs in Germany and Japan he played to crowds of smitten fans devoted to vintage Jamaican music who, although they didn't speak English, were able to converse in Jamaican patois, which they'd picked up from the music.

3

A measure of the revival of mento is the belated international recognition of seasoned mento artist Stanley Beckford, known in France as *L'Ambassadeur de Mento*. In 2002, Beckford released his first solo album, *Stanley Beckford Plays Mento* (Universal), after years of playing in various Jamaican mento groups. Last year, he played to thousands of fans at festivals around Europe.

4

Internationally, there is renewed interest in mento greats such as the Jolly Boys and ska legend Laurel Aitken. And mento compilation CDs, such as *Boogu Yagga Gal* (Heritage Music) and *Mento Madness* (V2), have recently been released.

5

DJ Iron Will, who spins with Rocky at the Cloak and Dagger, says he's used to people popping into the pub while he's spinning and asking him what kind of

6

music he's playing. "The music really challenges people, because they've never heard it before; it definitely piques their interest."

Samra Habib

Previewing and Reviewing the Article

Mark read through Samra Habib's article quickly, thinking he wanted to listen to some mento tracks. Debating where to begin with summarizing, he looked at the title "The New, Old Jamaica." It seemed too general to suggest much except the idea that something old, related to Jamaica, was being revived, and there was no subtitle to help him out.

He photocopied the article, noting the month and year of the *Saturday Night* issue where it appeared. He then read the article twice more and numbered the article's paragraphs. Mark focused on the opening and closing paragraphs, looking for its most important ideas, and these he highlighted. Here are his point-form notes:

Paragraph 1
- Every decade music genres re-appear
- Examples? 70s Rock & Roll; 80s, 60s music
- Clubs are now reviving mento
- Mento is 1950s Jamaican folk music

Last Paragraph
- Example? Toronto DJ says people are curious about mento
- Mento catches people's attention because they haven't heard it before

Mark then reviewed the article to reassure himself that there were enough interesting ideas for a good one-paragraph summary. The original was just over six hundred words long, and he believed he could reduce it to about one-third of its length. To do so, he highlighted the main points and support in the body of the article. This would help him with the next important stage—listing the main ideas.

Listing the Main Ideas and Writing a First Draft

Having highlighted the article's main points and supporting details, Mark came up with the following list:

Paragraph 1
- Every decade music genres re-appear
- Examples? 70s Rock & Roll; 80s, 60s music
- Clubs are now reviving mento
- Mento is 1950s Jamaican folk music

Paragraph 2
- Mento started in 19th century, with homemade instruments
- Popular pre1960s—developed into ska, reggae, dance hall
- Sound mix of calypso beats, Latin, swing, and 3-3-2 rhythm
- Word "mento"? Spanish mentar = "to mention"
- Jamaica was Spanish—1494–1655

- Mento might be African word for a sexy dance
- Lyrics can be funny—about society and sex
- Not like reggae—slower, more political (60s)
- Ska and reggae popular types of Jamaican music
- Mento artists not known outside Jamaica until now

Paragraph 3
- DJs and record collectors always liked mento
- Toronto DJ Rocky says older Jamaican sounds popular in clubs
- Used to only be played in Jamaican areas
- Germany and Japan—fans of older Jamaican genres
- Non-English speakers and patois—learned it from the music

Paragraph 4
- Evident that mento is revived
- Major mento star—Stanley Beckford, famous in France
- 2002, S.B. released solo album after playing in groups
- S.B. played festivals in 2003 in Europe

Paragraph 5
- New interest in mento artists worldwide
- Jolly Boys and ska artist Laurel Aitken—new CD examples?

Last Paragraph
- Example? Toronto DJ says people are curious about mento
- Mento catches people's attention because they haven't heard it before

The following day, Mark revised his list, comparing it to the original article. He was not sure, especially in the article's second and third paragraphs, which points were main ones and which were support. Here is a section of his revised list in which he has crossed out unnecessary points and indicated main points with an *M* and supporting points with an *S*.

Paragraph 2
- Mento started in 19th century, with homemade instruments *M*
- Popular pre1960s—developed into ska, reggae, dance hall *M*
- Sound mix of calypso beats, Latin, swing, and 3-3-2 rhythm *S*
- Word "mento"? Spanish *mentar* = "to mention" *S*
- ~~Jamaica was Spanish—1494–1655~~ *S*
- ~~Mento might be African word for a sexy dance~~ *S*
- Lyrics can be funny—about society and sex *M*
- Not like reggae—slower, more political (60s) *S*
- Ska and reggae popular types of Jamaican music *S*
- Mento artists not known outside Jamaica until now *S*

Paragraph 3
- DJs and record collectors always liked mento *S*
- Toronto DJ Rocky says older Jamaican sounds popular in clubs *M*
- Used to only be played in Jamaican areas *S*
- Germany and Japan—fans of older Jamaican genres *S*
- ~~Non-English speakers and patois—learned it from the music~~ *S*

After revising his list, Mark was more confident about writing the first draft of his summary, which follows:

> Samra Habib's article "The New, Old Jamaica" (*Saturday Night*, June 2004) discusses the revival of an older Jamaican music genre. Revivals of genres are nothing new; Rock and Roll, for example, made a comeback in the 1970s. But in North American clubs, the mento genre is popular for the first time. Mento began in the 19th century as a kind of folk music, sung and played by musicians who made their own instruments. It was very popular in Jamaica until the 1960s, when ska and reggae took over as the main genres. Mento, whose name may come from Spanish or may be of African origin, sounds like a mix of calypso beats, Latin, and swing, with a rhythm all its own. Unlike reggae, which tends to be slower and politically oriented in its lyrics, mento's lyrics are often funny; they tend to be about society and sex. Until recently, mento was mostly unknown outside Jamaica because when Jamaican music reached world popularity, ska and reggae were what people heard. Only DJs and record collectors were mento fans. Now, though, as Toronto's DJ Rocky says, mento, once popular only among Jamaican-Canadians, is getting some play in clubs. It is also developing a global following, with fans in France, Germany, and Japan. Further signs of mento's revival are long-time mento artist Stanley Beckford's first solo CD, his appearance at European festivals, new appreciation of other mento performers, and new mento compilation CDs. Mento is an old genre that's attracting people's interest just because it's new to them.

Re-examining, or "x-raying," his original article and listing its ideas reassured Mark that he had not eliminated too much of the original in his draft. The word-count tool on his computer showed 255 words, about 20 per cent higher than his goal, so he used three methods to tighten his next draft. He edited wordy phrases, removed repetitions, and condensed related ideas into single phrases or sentences. In the section of his revision work shown below, Mark notes wordy passages with a *W* and repetitions with an *R*.

Note: Write summaries in the present tense. When you restate someone else's material, it is seen as occurring in the "written present" and for the first time for readers of your summary.

> Samra Habib's article "The New, Old Jamaica" (*Saturday Night*, June 2004) ~~discusses the revival of an older~~ *W* Jamaican music genre. Revivals of genres are nothing new; ~~Rock and Roll, for example, made a comeback in the 1970s.~~ *R* But in North American clubs, the mento genre *W* is popular for the first time. Mento began in the 19th century ~~as a kind of~~ *W* folk music, ~~sung and played by~~ *R* musicians who made their own instruments. ~~It was very~~ popular *W* in Jamaica until the 1960s, when ska and reggae took over as the main genres. Mento, ~~whose name may come from~~ *W* Spanish or ~~may be of~~ *W* African origin, sounds like a mix of calypso beats, Latin, and swing, with a rhythm all its own. Unlike reggae, ~~which tends to be~~ *W* slower and politically oriented ~~in its~~ *W* lyrics, mento's lyrics are often funny; ~~they tend to be~~ *W* about society and sex. Until recently, mento was mostly unknown outside Jamaica because when Jamaican music reached world popularity, ~~ska and reggae were what people heard.~~ *R*

Mark now worked on each sentence individually, rephrasing wordy sections, removing repetitions, and joining similar ideas into single phrases and sentences. Here is his final draft:

In "The New, Old Jamaica" (*Saturday Night*, June 2004), Samira Habib covers a newcomer to a familiar media phenomenon—music genre revivals. The newcomer is mento, a Jamaican music genre popular in North American clubs and globally, for the first time. Mento started as a 19th century Jamaican style of folk music, played on homemade instruments. Its popularity continued until the 1960s and the appearance of ska and reggae. Mento's name may be Spanish or African, and its sound is a mix of calypso beats, Latin, and swing. Its rhythm is lively compared to reggae's beat, and its lyrics, less political than reggae's, look humorously at sex and society. Because ska and reggae dominated when Jamaican music hit world popularity, mento endured only among Jamaican fans, DJs, and record collectors. Now, trendy Toronto club people, along with fans in France, Germany, and Japan, have caught onto mento. The worldwide revival of mento has occasioned new interest in notable mento performers, festival appearances by artists, and new mento CDs. Mento is an old genre that catches people's ears because it's a new sound to anyone outside Jamaica.

Mark's final word-count was 186 words. The process of listing his article's main ideas and support ensured the quality of his summary's content, and his revisions produced a tightly worded and effective summary.

Activity

Write a one- or two-paragraph summary of an article from a Canadian magazine. Your summary should be roughly one-third the length of the original. Follow the steps and advice presented in this chapter. The article's content should relate to your main area of study in college. For information on how to find magazine articles and journals about a specific subject, refer to the chapter "Research Skills" in this section.

CHECKLIST OF LEARNING OUTCOMES FOR CHAPTER 17

To ensure that you have understood and met the learning outcomes for this chapter, answer the following questions:

✔ What is a summary, and how does a summary differ from an essay?

✔ What are four parts of an article that you can preview for information about its content?

✔ What is paraphrasing, and what must you do to avoid plagiarism when you paraphrase?

✔ How does listing an original source's main ideas and support help you create a good summary?

✔ What are three methods for revising and tightening drafts of a summary?

✔ What are two requirements for the content of an effective summary?

CHAPTER 18

Research Skills

You have, for most assignments so far, been the main source of information. In most courses, however, you will be required to supplement and extend your own views with material from other sources. To assist you, this chapter presents the process, purposes, and methods of conducting college- or university-level research. The next chapter, "Writing a Research Paper," follows directly from this chapter as it takes you on to assembling an effective research paper.

THE RESEARCH PROCESS: AN OVERVIEW

Conducting effective research may be *the* essential skill you can acquire as part of your college or university education. Research can be among the most enjoyable aspects of education. Advancement in all areas of knowledge relies on the acquisition and intelligent use of research. In learning to participate in the research process, you join experts and scholars in exploring and expanding the knowledge base of all subjects. You are also, as you polish and widen your research skills, learning techniques for handling and crediting information that you will use and modify throughout your career.

Research: Misconceptions, Risks, and Facts About the Process

Students often believe that each time they are asked to do some research, they are doing a single, isolated activity unrelated to any other research assignment in any other subject. Each research task feels like a completely new challenge; each assignment takes them to unmapped territory: where will they find the information this time, and how will they use it?

Saddled with this misconception, students scramble to locate facts from online searches or a book or two, scratch together a patchwork of borrowed ideas, and maybe attempt haphazardly to list some sources. The risk here? A poor, if not failing grade. This scenario carries a far greater risk, though. Students who have not yet learned, or are unwilling to learn research skills are often so relieved to find useful information that they incorporate it straight into their work. The ideas, images, or data created by others appear as the students' own. Whether done knowingly or unknowingly, this is plagiarism. Plagiarism does not mean simply a zero grade; it may result in failing the subject and possible expulsion.

No one is born knowing how to conduct or use research; everyone can learn the process and the skills. Every student can begin with some important facts right away.

Facts About the Research Process

1. Conducting research means following a set of steps; it is a process. The research process begins with understanding the task involved and concludes with an assignment that meets the requirements of that task.

2. The research process can be learned, just like any other set of skills and techniques.

3. The research process, once learned, is a basic pattern that can be adapted to all subjects and situations.

4. Successfully pursuing the steps of the research process *takes time* and requires dedication and care; there are no shortcuts.

Goals for Academic Research

Generally, the first goal of academic research is to explore a topic, a limited subject, to a degree of depth appropriate to the assigned task. Doing so brings students to the next goal: learning the conventions, technical or special terminology, and areas of information related to a subject-area. Ultimately, as is the case with research essays, students will add to the current knowledge base in their topic-area by presenting their own thesis and supporting ideas integrated with the ideas from reliable resources.

These are significant goals, and to reach them, all researchers must "begin at the beginning," by clearly understanding what is needed for each task and assignment.

Preparing for Research

What are the Specifics of Your Research Assignment?

Academic subjects offer various types of research assignments. There will be very notable differences in assignment goals, handling of source material, and overall format. For example, some subjects (psychology, media studies, and scientific/technical disciplines) assign research surveys. These are *not* research essays. Instead, student survey-writers examine resources available for a given topic and, impartially note their quality and depth. Research essays, on the other hand, follow essay structure, present a thesis, and integrate research findings with the author's own views. While the research process for the survey and the essay may be similar, the techniques for completing each are very different. A student who does not take the time to understand the differences between a research survey and a research essay cannot do a good job with either one. Because the research essay is common to nearly every subject, this chapter and the next cover its creation in detail.

Make it your first task to be absolutely certain you understand the nature and requirements of any assignment involving research. Find out what format is expected, and how you are to manage your resources. This point is so important that it reappears as the first step in the research process.

The Two Main Goals for Research Essays

Traditionally, research essays or papers have been longer, printed works that demonstrated a writer's insight into, and responses to, material compiled on a specialized topic. Today, the research assignment may appear in online form, as a multimedia creation, as a presentation with text support, or as the familiar print essay. Whichever form the final research assignment takes, it follows a specific pattern of construction that imposes two main goals on the writer:

1. **Discover** your own thoughts about your subject and appropriate secondary support for your ideas.

2. **Blend** your own points with support from research sources to create a clear and correctly documented paper.

Notice that *you* are the key to, and the creator of your research essay. You will begin by **discovering** your own responses to your subject; you, as you did with other essays, will create a thesis statement and supporting points.

Your new challenges here will be to pursue the research process in a focused way, to select solid and appropriate resource material, and to **blend** your research with your own ideas clearly and correctly. Think of your research paper as a "prepared conversation" or dialogue between yourself and authorities in your topic-area. You set the structure and drive the conversation, and you decide which "outside" voices and ideas best serve the point of your thesis.

Discovery (investigation) and **blending** (synthesis) are your two overall goals during the creation of your research essay. They represent the key stages that all writers work through. In this chapter, you will learn steps to follow during the *dis-*

covery stage of the research process; the following chapter addresses the *blending* of your own ideas with your research findings for an effective research paper.

Below are the steps that will guide you through the discovery stage of the research process. First, though, be sure to allow yourself enough time: research assignments often have three-week to one-month deadlines. These do not represent a lot of time: you will need to take the list below and make a rough time plan that you can update and modify* as you go along. Be aware that you will need to allot time for the construction and drafting of your essay as well.

These steps comprise a complete and proven strategy for tackling any research task; they are a clear map to follow. Work one step at a time and allow yourself the time to complete each one. Each time you work through the research process, you will find your investigations less demanding and more rewarding.

The Discovery Stage: Eight Steps for Effective Research

1. Understand all aspects of your assignment.
   Once past this step, the discovery stage, like the writing process, may be iterative or wayward, meaning it may turn back on itself. For example, as you are examining articles from an academic database, you may wish to revise supporting points in your trial outline.
2. Explore your subject to develop ideas and a viewpoint on it.
3. Establish your topic focus.
4. Create a trial outline.
5. Discover what you need from your research.
6. Find information using the library and the Internet.
7. Evaluate and select appropriate information.
8. Take time to absorb findings. Begin research notes.

Step 1: Understand All Aspects of Your Assignment

If you make errors due to overlooking or not requesting information when you receive an assignment, you may go farther and farther in the wrong direction, wasting time and marks.

1 Ask Questions

Each time you receive a research assignment in any subject, do two things. First, begin a list of questions for your instructor. Use a notebook small enough to carry every day, but large enough to allow you to write the details of your professor's answers and to add more questions as you go along. Speak to your instructor any time you are uncertain.

In the box that follows, you will find questions asked by researchers, students, and professionals alike. These may help to prompt discussions with your instructor.

Typical General Research Questions

1. What forms of information will be suitable for this task? (i.e., general background information, news/journalism, statistics)
2. How much of which types of information will be needed?
3. Where will I find appropriate resources?
4. How soon will I need main research to be completed?
5. Is current or up-to-date information needed here?
6. What is the required format or structure for the assignment? Is this an essay, a report, a research summary, an annotated bibliography, or some other format?
7. Based on the above, how is research to be used in the assignment?
8. How is the research assignment evaluated?
9. Which citation method is required?
10. Where should I go for help with citation?

In this chapter and the next, answers to many of these questions will be covered. Please keep in mind, though, your instructor's specific requirements for any given assignment.

2   Manage and Plan Your Time

Your second task is to set up your rough time plan. Allow for your research (*discovering*) and essay creation (*blending*) and drafting. You may, like the student whose schedule is below, set up one time plan for research and another for drafting the essay. Just establish the habit, set aside enough time, and then follow your plan each time you receive such an assignment. If you are unsure about how much time to allow for research or assignment completion, ask your professor and your library technicians.

If, for example, your research essay is due in four to five weeks, you could set up a schedule as follows. Naturally, you will be working around classes, other assignments, and other obligations, so try to be realistic. Sonya Phillips' plan below indicates "days missing" between items—days when her class-load makes research difficult. Keep adjusting your time plan as needed, whenever you make changes.

DISCOVERY RESEARCH PLAN

ESSAY DUE: May 5

DATE TODAY: March 28

1. Explore subject—3 days [Mar. 29–31]
2. Establish topic focus—2 days [Apr. 2–3]
3. Create trial outline—2 days [Apr. 5–6]
4. Discover what I need from research—2–3 days [Apr. 8–10]
5. Find information in library and on Internet—4 days? [Apr. 11–14]
6. Evaluate and select appropriate information—3 days [Apr. 16–18]
7. Take time to absorb findings. Begin research notes—3 days [Apr. 20–22]

An Introduction

During high school, Sonya found research work confusing. Now that she is considering a career in social work and further post-secondary education, she is determined to get all the help she can in this area. In this chapter and the next, you will shadow Sonya's progress as she works through the research process and writes her essay.

In the previous section, a typical research question appears: *how soon will you need your research information?* Creating a time plan can give you at least an approximate idea. As shown above, Sonya will need to have her resources chosen by April 18th. Later, she will probably adjust this schedule as she goes along, and will add her plans for drafting her essay due on May 5th, but she now has a general idea of how to space out her tasks.

Step 2: Explore Your Subject

Research essays are usually based on multifaceted, controversial, or topical subjects in order to expand students' knowledge of important areas of course content. Depending on your instructor's preference, you may be assigned a tidy, pre-narrowed topic, or a list of general subjects. Research papers are longer than standard essays, and the subjects involved are more complex, so an additional step precedes narrowing or defining your topic within the subject-area. You must first choose and then explore your subject.

As you would do for an essay, choose a subject that interests you. You will be spending a lot of time with aspects of this subject, and enthusiasm will help to fuel your research.

- **If your subject is new or unknown to you . . .**
  If you know almost nothing about your subject, or if it is an extremely broad one, you will find it difficult to proceed to the next step of narrowing a topic. Brainstorming for an outline of your own thoughts on that subject will be equally difficult. Therefore, budget more, rather than less time to investigate your subject. Begin by reading some *secondary sources* (books, articles, sites about the subject): you will gain introductory knowledge, an awareness of any specialized terminologies in that subject-area, and understanding of some subtopics or divisions within the subject. Now you are ready to define your topic and develop your own viewpoint or thesis.

- **If your subject is a familiar one . . .**
  If, on the other hand, your subject is a topic you know something about, or is a *primary source* (a story, article, or text you know from class), it is better to proceed to the next step. Work out your own topic, ideas, thesis, and rough outline before examining secondary sources. Your preliminary thinking will be clearer when uncluttered by ideas derived from external sources. Moreover, until you have worked out a thesis and support, you will not know which of your ideas will benefit from secondary-source-derived information.

An Illustration

Sonya Phillips' English 101 instructor distributed a list of general subjects for the spring semester research paper. Because Sonya was leaning toward either social work or early childhood education as a career, she was most interested in a one-word subject: *Parenting*. But the subject was vast, and Sonya had no sense of even a general direction in which to proceed.

She was doing her research time plan at this point, and she felt confused, so she allowed herself three sessions in a row to find resources. Her only ideas about parenting seemed to come from talk shows and supermarket magazines. It was time to *learn how to learn* about a subject, she thought, so she asked a library technician for help. The librarian asked where Sonya was in her research, and suggested that she begin at a general level with some wide-ranging background information: an encyclopedia article, the introduction to a book on parenting, or a good non-commercial website. These offered an overview of aspects of parenting, stimulated her thinking, and showed her some general directions in which to proceed.

After only two sessions, Sonya's confusion had lessened, she learned how to use the *subject index* on the library site, and best of all, she had notes of numerous ideas and topics related to parenting. She was less leery of using the library and ready to begin working on a topic focus.

Step 3: Establish Your Topic Focus

Once you have selected, and perhaps explored a subject, it is time to work out a focus area within that subject. College and university research papers explore limited topics; they examine a single aspect of a subject in depth. The general background information you read while exploring your subject is therefore not suitable for a research essay. The information you will seek, once you have narrowed your topic and made a rough outline, will be specific and clearly tied to your essay's points and support.

The length of the essay required by your instructor will be one determiner of how narrow your topic and thesis should be: the briefer the essay, the narrower the topic. For example, if the subject is *the halo effect,* a short seven-hundred-word essay could likely cover in five or six paragraphs the topic of its effect in one situation (classrooms) with one type of people (popular students). On the other hand, if the required essay length is two to three thousand words, that essay could examine the positive and negative values of the effect as it applies to a range of media and sports figures.

Your task is to discover a topic, then to establish a viewpoint of your own on that topic. Your research paper presents *your viewpoint* on one single aspect (a topic) of some subject. Your support for your viewpoint derives from your own thoughts as well. What you create with a research essay is a dialogue—you propose your thesis and support, then present others' ideas to agree with, oppose, extend, and augment your own voice.

Your goal in narrowing your topic is to discover one aspect that interests you and provides a potentially rewarding area for research. One way to narrow your topic, which will ultimately help you create a trial thesis, is to ask yourself a series of *research questions.*

Typical Research Questions

- *What* do I want to discover about _____ ?
- *Who* are the relevant people (or characters) I should find out about?

- *When* do things occur in _____?
- *Where* does/do _____ happen ?
- *Why* or *how* does/do _____ occur, or *why* is/are _____ so _____?

Having answered one or more of these questions, you may be prepared to state the focus of your research. Your trial thesis may be as simple as, "Five events led to _____." It is a guide to help you move on to a trial outline. Moreover, you may, as with any prewriting, change your trial thesis as you go on.

An interesting way to explore a range of aspects connected to your topic is to try a directory search with a good search engine such as Google (www.google.ca). Type in a keyword or phrase related to your topic. Depending on your keyword(s), Google offers you several avenues for finding various facets and subcategories of your subject. If you input some very popular keywords or abstract terms such as "wisdom," the search engine automatically returns a "searches related to . . ." section at the bottom of the screen. Generally, though, just select the "more" option at the top of the screen where Google presents its search options, including "Images," "Groups," and "News." On the "more" screen, you will see a variety of icons with links such as *Catalogs, Answers, Special Searches.* Choose *Directory*, and put in your keyword or phrase. You will then see a *Directory* screen dedicated to your keyword. By examining some of the sites in the directory area, you will find numerous specific aspects of your topic.

Another excellent way to explore varied aspects of your topic is to use your college or public library's online catalogue. Search for books and magazines by subject. (For more information about library catalogues, see page 282.) Subject headings will give you helpful ideas about how to limit your topic. Titles of books and magazine articles can also suggest different directions to pursue in narrowing your topic.

Prepare to spend some time limiting your topic and working out a trial thesis. Read some of the webpages, which you find in your directory search, or book-summaries in the online catalogue to help you narrow a topic that you wish to explore.

An Illustration

After spending a couple of sessions exploring background information on the subject of *Parenting*, Sonya Phillips knew she had taken in a lot of varied ideas and possibilities. She decided to try listing whatever words she associated with *Parenting*, and came up with "parenting and responsibility," "parenting challenges," "parenting and teenagers," and even "parenting—why?" to try to discover a focus. The idea of "challenges" kept coming up, but Sonya wanted a clearer focus, so she tried something different.

Using the *Subject* heading in her college's online library catalogue, she found headings under *Parenting*, including "moral and ethical considerations of parenting," "step parenting," and "parenting and discipline." She also found eighty books listed, with titles suggesting other focuses: "parents and media influences," "parenting and adolescent girls," and "parents' questions about teenage development." On the same screen were also magazine and journal articles with titles and summaries suggesting more limited topic possibilities.

"I thought I'd try Google," Sonya said. (For more information about using search engines, read pages 286–287.) "I typed the word *parenting*, and I got fifty million hits! Next I noticed that the first page of results listed a set of links called 'Searches related to parenting.' There were eight possibilities, such as 'parenting teenagers,' 'Christian parenting,' and so on. I tried a couple of the links and they showed me pages and pages of more focused results. In turn, that prompted me to start making up my own keyword combinations; I tried 'parenting and teenagers,' 'parenting and television,' 'parenting and adolescents.' Combining search terms really refined my results. I decided I'd work the ideas of *media and TV* into my paper. My topic was starting to come into focus: the challenges of today's culture and parenting." Sonya then wrote a trial thesis of her focused topic: "Parents face many challenges raising children and teenagers in today's culture." She now knew research could help her try to answer the question, "What are the challenges?"

Step 4: Create a Trial Outline

With a trial thesis, you can begin a trial outline to shape your research. Do not expect to work out a final thesis of your limited topic quickly. The time you spend discovering a single line of argument that interests you helps you discover what to look for during your research and what your ultimate thesis statement should be.

Below is a diagram of a trial outline. Create a word-processed version of this diagram, and save it as a blank outline that you can copy and paste into new outline documents. Continue to revise your outline, saving different versions with appropriate names. As you work out your first trial outline, you will have blanks in your support. You may even have more blanks than supporting points or details; those are ideal places to do some research. Do not be too critical of yourself; your day-dreaming and intuitive sense of why you think your trial thesis is valid will provide some surprisingly strong ideas.

Trial Outline Diagram

Paragraph I: Thesis Statement

Plan of Development: Supporting Points

A. _____

B. _____

C. _____

Paragraph II: Supporting Point A

Details:

1. _____

2. _____

3. _____

Paragraph III: Supporting Point B

Details:

1. _____

2. _____

3. _____

Paragraph IV: Supporting Point C

                Details:

                      1. _____

                      2. _____

                      3. _____

Paragraph V: Conclusion

A Note about Research Essay Length

As you see, both the trial outline diagram and Sonya's outline below show a five-paragraph essay outline pattern. If you turn to the model research paper on pages 314–321, you will notice that it, like nearly all research papers, is significantly longer than five paragraphs.

The five-paragraph essay is a convenient one for routine assignments, and importantly, its structure is the model for many longer pieces of writing such as research papers and some reports. As you will see in the next chapter, the five-paragraph format can be expanded at any point in its structure: if background introductory material is needed to set up or explain the thesis, then a first paragraph appears before the second, or thesis paragraph. As well, each supporting point for the thesis will have its own body paragraph, and these will not normally be limited to three.

Here, the trial outlines show five paragraphs as a starting point because of the familiarity of this form of outline. Both the blank template diagram and Sonya's trial outline can and will be expanded to reflect changes in essay content development.

Sonya's trial thesis allowed her to work out three positive supporting points for her thesis question, "What can parents do to overcome negative influences hurting their families?" She wrote the trial outline below, complete with plenty of blanks:

Thesis: There are things parents can do to overcome the negative influences hurting their families.

    Supporting Point A: Create quality time with families
    1. single-parent families—how?
    2. both parents work—?
- _____
- working less?
- _____

    Supporting Point B: "Extended families"/Communities
- people don't have community groups much
- _____
- what kinds of communities can there be?
- _____

    Supporting Point C: ???? something about media?
- Internet?
- too much TV—not many good shows
- _____
- _____

Note: Writing a research paper always begins with your own ideas and trial outline to guide you. It does *not* entail simply finding information and piecing it together as a patchwork of others' ideas.

Step 5: Discover What You Need from Your Research

Your instructor may specify the types of research material required for your assignment. Even so, discovering precisely what information you will need from resources can be a challenge. Examine your outline with the following questions in mind:

- What, in general, do I need to know more about to add supporting details?
- Where do I need more facts to expand my support and fill in my blanks?
- What kinds of information—facts, statistics, details, quotations, technical data—are relevant to this course or subject-area and will make parts of my research paper stronger?
- Where can I find some reliable information in the areas I've noted above?

Now is the time to begin a notebook or document called "Research Notes," in which you record the answers you give to the questions above. Maintaining your notes as a computer document allows you to insert ideas exactly where they should go and update or expand your notes cleanly. Using a notebook has the advantage of portability—as does a notebook computer. Many researchers use file or index cards; in whatever form you keep your notes, remember to date each entry. Keep a copy of your trial outline with the notes, so you can refer to it when you are in the library or online.

Begin and maintain your research notes correctly. Doing so will help you avoid having to re-find sources later, and importantly, will help you avoid plagiarism. Creating good and correct research notes means (1) recording the information in an appropriate form, and (2) noting all necessary citation material.

Record your source material as:

- **Quotations:** the exact words of another writer, enclosed by double quotation marks; *or*
- **Paraphrases:** complete restatements of another writer's words in your own words; *or*
- **Summaries:** condensed versions of another writer's ideas in your own words.

Then add all required citation information for each research note (page 295).

For each item of research you record, you will note specific citation and location information: the author, title of the work, and other essential items. As you do so, you are also preparing the material for your Works Cited or Sources list. To find the complete list of required citation information required, please turn to page 299 in Chapter 19.

Plagiarism

Plagiarism is presenting someone else's ideas, words, technical data, or images as your own. Plagiarism does not depend on the *quantity of borrowed material*; it is *not* a matter of degree. Any uncredited borrowing, even a few words, without credit information is as much plagiarism as is an entire paper not of your own creation: theft is theft.

- **Avoid "unconscious plagiarism."**
  As you start college or university, you may not be aware of how easy it is to "unconsciously plagiarize" material. Learn how to quote, paraphrase, and cite correctly. Know that your writing style is as personal as your fingerprint. To any instructor who has seen a paragraph of yours even once or twice, phrases in another person's style are immediately detectable. There are many "giveaways" in basic aspects of your sentence structure and word choices that will be readily evident to your professors.

  If, because of earlier educational or cultural training, a student unconsciously and unknowingly copies words or phrases, then explaining the situation immediately to the instructor is the best course of action. If, on the other hand, a student knowingly decides to use someone else's work, then he or she has made a conscious decision to defraud the instructor. This dishonesty is outright plagiarism; the student risks failure and expulsion.

- **Plagiarism is not simply copying another person's words.**
  Plagiarism is not confined to stealing text and misrepresenting sources of ideas in research papers. Every day students buy essays, photograph tests with cell phones, have friends do assignments, and copy and paste text and images from online sources. Growing use of the Internet and file-sharing have given rise to a more lenient view of ownership of intellectual or artistic property. Whatever the cause, students sometimes feel that if no one gets caught, then there is no crime.

  Artists, musicians, designers, writers, and research scientists work extremely hard. Why is it acceptable to steal their work simply because you can? The educational community is the model for your future workplace; neither tolerates theft or fraud—these are taken seriously, and result in disgrace and heavy penalties. Colleges, universities, and businesses operate within legal frameworks in which the theft of ideas is illegal.

- **Plagiarism is easier to catch every year.**
  Students who plagiarize seem blissfully unaware that methods for its detection grow more sophisticated each year. Technology is a double-edged weapon— more research information is available online, but tracing the sources of such information is easier and faster than ever. Purchased essays are traceable, no matter what claims essay vendors make. Colleges and universities use such applications as *turnitin.com*, but even without these applications, unusual-sounding phrases are easily sourced online. Dealing with plagiarism costs you, in the long run, because time spent tracing sources is time instructors could better spend on course development or careful marking.

Mastering research skills and techniques speaks for your ethics and values as a person. When you document your research correctly, you set up a trust, a contract among you, your readers, and the sources of your information, a guarantee that all parties respect each other and give due credit when needed.

Paraphrasing and Plagiarism

One aspect of incorporating research findings in particular causes problems for many students: paraphrasing. Correct paraphrasing means putting another writer's words completely into your own words, then giving credit to the original source.

The following examples show how to paraphrase correctly and avoid plagiarism. Here, a student wishes to use the ideas in a passage from page 36 of *A History of Reading* by Alberto Manguel.

Original Source

By the time the first scribe scratched and uttered the first letters, the human body was already capable of the acts of writing and reading that still lay in the future; that is to say, the body was able to store, recall, and decipher all manner of sensations, including the arbitrary signs of written language yet to be invented.

Example of Plagiarism

As soon as people had figured out alphabets, the human body was already capable of writing and reading letters. The body could store, recall, and decipher feelings and letters that had yet to be invented.

If the student writes the sentences immediately above without crediting the source, he or she is plagiarizing. The student has borrowed Manguel's wording without acknowledging him as the author. Even though the student has shortened and changed the general form of the passage, sections of the phrasing belong to the original.

Example of Acceptable Use of Paraphrasing

Alberto Manguel suggests in *A History of Reading* that once people had figured out alphabets, the human body was ready to read and write letters. He contends that the body could store, recall, and decipher feelings and letters that had yet to be invented (36).

Here the student has indicated the source of the ideas (Alberto Manguel) and used correct MLA style by inserting the page reference in parentheses at the end of the sentence. A better method of writing a paraphrase that uses some of the exact wording of an original source is to put that wording in quotation marks.

Example of Good Use of Paraphrasing

Alberto Manguel suggests in *A History of Reading* that once people had figured out alphabets, the human body was ready to read and write letters. He contends that the body could "store, recall, and decipher" feelings and letters that had "yet to be invented" (36).

Beginning to Evaluate Research Information

In the box below are some general guidelines to help you with the fifth and sixth steps in your research process.

<u>What kind</u> of information are you searching for?
Information that
(a) is clearly relevant to points and details in your trial outline;
(b) is clearly understandable to you;
(c) you can paraphrase or reasonably incorporate;
(d) comes from reputable, reliable sources.

<u>Why</u> are you performing this research?
To find information that
(a) supports the views that you hold;
(b) expands on and strengthens points you make;
(c) lends authority to your viewpoints.

At this stage, you are starting to focus your research. Background or general information resources such as encyclopedias are not appropriate from this point on. What you seek now are resources whose content is closely tied to your topic and to the supporting points in your trial outline.

You are, however, not yet at the stage of trying to find precise sources for your essay; you are setting up a list of "things to look for." You are scanning areas of information to find and list possible, good quality material. By doing this preparation, you will greatly simplify the next step.

An Illustration

As Sonya looked over her trial outline, she felt anxious for several reasons. First, she knew the essay would have to be several thousand words long, and five paragraphs weren't going to do the job. Telling herself she was weeks away from actually writing it, she wondered how she would even figure out where to start. Would she have enough time to read large sections of books and whole articles? How long would it take to get through all those websites she saw on Google?

Rather than succumbing to panic, she decided to follow her instructor's advice and stay with the plan she had made. She started her Research Notes document, typed in the date, and pasted in her outline to give her a starting point. "My first question mark was after "single-parent families," and I knew I had seen a whole list of sites and book listings on that subject, so . . . 'single-parent families' was the first item on my list of things to look for information on." Here is Sonya's first research note:

April 8, 2008

First point in my support

<u>Single-parent families</u>
- my thesis is about what families can do to stop negative influences
- how do single-parent families make time for each other?
- I should find out how they do & what happens if they don't

- Are there statistics on this?
- Try single-parent families and time management as key words
- Use magazine/periodicals, too—ask librarian
- Write down names of books and articles—bookmark sites

Sonya now has a "map," for her first point at least, to direct her. Once she has completed her notes based on her outline and any new ideas that have come to mind, she will be ready to move on to step 6, to conduct a focused search in the library and online.

Step 6: Find Information Using the Library and the Internet

Library Resources

Your campus or local library contains many resources for your research in the forms of printed and computerized material. This material is stored systematically.

Discover how your library's storage systems work; this is essential to finding useful information. Learn what is available from your library's cataloguing system and technological resources; it makes starting your research much easier.

Also, do not forget librarians and helpdesk staff. They are information experts and are there to help you.

Research Tip: Primary and Secondary Sources

There are, as mentioned, two broad categories of information available to you: primary and secondary sources.

- **Primary sources are original**, first-hand sources that are the subject itself or inform you directly about the subject. Primary sources *do not* comment on, explain, or analyze the subject. A primary source could be a story or article you are writing about for a research paper, a fact-finding interview with a person on the subject of your research, or an event or experiment you are observing as the basis of your paper. These are direct sources of information.
- **Secondary sources are works** in any medium that refer to, comment on, or analyze your subject-area. They are second-hand information—material that has been published on the subject of your research; in other words, secondary sources are the viewpoints of others. Included among secondary sources are encyclopedia articles; reference books; journal, newspaper, magazine, and even blog articles; TV programs; and websites.

Library Catalogues

The library catalogue is your first key to available information. The catalogue is usually an online listing of two types of holdings: those in your library and those available on loan from affiliated library collections.

- **Library collections** consist of information in a variety of media: books, periodicals, encyclopedias, films, CDs, and so on.
- **Campus libraries' online resources** are usually part of the college or university website and use a system like BIBCAT, which allows you to look up all kinds of reference materials in different media.
- **Electronic book access** means that your library has electronic publication services that gather and provide the full texts of books, journals, and the latest publications from sources in business and technology. E-books are great up-to-date resources in subject-areas where timeliness is important.
- **Library databases** are special tools containing carefully selected information related to programs offered by your college or university. The catalogue and databases will be accessible to you on any of the terminals in your library.

Research Tip: Learn the Value of *Author, Title,* and *Subject Searches*

Most library catalogues allow you to search by *author, title,* or *subject,* or by keywords. Author and title screens display useful information, including call numbers to help you locate items, and current availability status. For these searches, you will need to know the authors and/or titles of items you seek.

Most often, searching initially by *subject* will be most productive.

The *subject* section of the catalogue performs three valuable functions:

1. It will give you a list of books, articles, and other publications on a given topic.
2. It will often provide related topics that may yield information on your subject.
3. It will suggest more limited topics, helping you to further narrow your topic.

As you look at *subject* section screens, you see books, the traditional source of information, listed. You also see listings for other sources, such as articles from special-interest and professional journals, and periodicals. Libraries and resource centres have bound volumes and computerized versions of journals and periodicals. Do not forget that, as a student, you have access to a wide range of material on these databases—much of this information is specialized and not available from search engines and ordinary online sites.

Books

Books have traditionally been the most trusted starting point for research, and in some subject-areas, this is still the case. Books are time-consuming to write and publish, and therefore are good resources when you seek reputable information that is not necessarily time sensitive. Books often cover a topic more deeply and from more viewpoints than could periodical articles or websites. Books and periodical articles usually offer comparable levels of expertise and knowledge on the parts of their authors. However, it takes time to locate the right books and to read them. To locate books you find in the library catalogue, ask a librarian to explain the call-number system by which your library arranges books on the shelves. Once you find the book you seek, try the following tips to help you judge the usefulness of a particular book:

- Look at the front and back pages and cover text on the book. Check the date of publication, and look for information on the author's credentials.
- Check the table of contents for material related to your topic. If many chapters relate to your topic, the book may be a good resource.
- Look through the back index of the book for words and phrases related to your topic. If there are many pages pertaining to those words and phrases, consider using the book.
- Scan the introduction or preface for the author's statement of intentions, viewpoint, and a summary of the book's content.
- Look for a bibliography to find related books on the same subject.

Examine at least two books on your topic so that you can practise thinking critically; weigh one author's views against another's and against your own ideas.

Periodicals

Periodicals (magazines, journals, and newspapers), as research tools, may be new to you, but they are essential sources of specific, focused, current information that is up to date with professional standards in your program. To use periodical articles, you must learn to locate them and then judge their content for quality and currency.

Periodical Indexes

If this is your first experience with using periodicals for research, ask a librarian to help you find out which periodicals your library carries, how these are indexed, and how to access the articles contained in the indexes. There are both printed and online indexes of every kind of periodical, from daily newspapers to highly specialized professional and scientific journals.

Librarians can direct you to the large bound indexes of various periodicals and help you to use them. The *Readers' Guide to Periodical Literature* and the *Canadian Periodical Index* are good places to begin; these are printed each year as new books and articles are listed by author and subject with cross-references to related articles. The *Canadian Periodical Index* or *CPI* lists articles from Canadian specialized and academic publications as well as popular magazines. Other bound volumes of more specialized periodical indexes will be shelved near these volumes, so check for any related to your topic or subject-area.

The *CPI* and other periodical indexes are also available on library online databases and on CDs in most libraries. You may find these versions easier to use. Search by subject or author, as you would with the library catalogue.

Once you have found articles whose titles sound promising, or whose listings offer summaries relevant to your topic, you must locate the full text of the article itself. If your library stocks a periodical, simply ask the librarian to help you locate the issue you need. If you are using an online index, you may also be able to access the full-text version of the article onscreen. Alternatively, your library may offer database help with finding such articles, and the following section of this chapter covers research databases, which can be real assets for college research.

An Illustration

On an early visit to the college library, Sonya Phillips decided to ask a librarian about locating periodicals. She was shown the library website and its *Find Articles and More* link, which included a page called "Article Database by Subject." On that page were Canadian content databases and online databases restricted to students and faculty. She chose the *CPI.Q* link, typed "single-parent families" into the subject guide search box, and *Infotrac* retrieved three hundred articles related to her keywords. She read the summaries of some articles, noted her keywords and that she had been using *CPI.Q*'s index, and then printed the full text of one article.

Research Databases and Online Search Services

It is essential to learn how to use the electronic research databases and online search services available through your school's library site. Academic research tasks require specialized or scholarly information you will not find online at general access sites or through search engines. In fact, over 70 percent of this high-quality information exists only on what is called the "invisible web"—pages protected by firewalls and inaccessible to search engines. Colleges and universities purchase library portals and databases to give you entry to these essential online resources, which are available in three forms:

- Controlled websites to which your college or university has purchased access rights
- Online databases to which your college or university provides access
- CD ROM databases owned by your school's library

Databases include *Lexis Nexis Proquest*, and *ERIC* (Educational Resources Information Centre). EBSCOhost and PowerWeb house online computer search services. *Dialog* and *CPI.Q* (the *Canadian Periodical Index* search service) give you access to thousands of magazine articles listed by subject. Listings have summaries or abstracts and sometimes whole articles. Using the EBSCOhost service, you can perform keyword searches through hundreds of periodicals for articles on your topic. You can then e-mail the results of your searches, including summaries or full texts of articles, to yourself at home or print them in the library. Additionally, some databases allow you to open a folder wherein you can collect articles that you find; if this is possible, you will see a "folder" icon on the screen. Finally, your user ID and password or other student code gives you access to database publications ranging from trade and technological publications to encyclopedias and online collections.

An Illustration

After using the *CPI.Q* index, Sonya decided to take an initial look at EBSCOhost. From the "Electronic Research Databases" screen, she chose *Academic Search Premier* and was taken to an EBSCOhost search page. Using the same keywords, "single-parent families," she found 587 articles. "The screen can even filter the articles by categories like Scholarly Journals, Magazines, Newspapers, and Monographs. I could never have found all these articles on my own!" Sonya registered herself with EBSCOhost and maintained a folder of articles.

Activity

Look up a recent article about video games, using the *Canadian Periodical Index* on your campus library's site. Fill in the following information:

a. Article title _____

b. Author (if given) _____

c. Name of publication _____

d. Pages _____ Date of publication _____

Now, narrow your search by choosing one of the subdivisions offered under the keywords "video games." Choose a new article from one of the subdivisions, and fill in its information below:

a. Topic subdivision name _____

b. Article title _____

c. Author (if given) _____

d. Name of publication _____

e. Pages _____ Date of publication _____

Internet Resources

Doing research on the Internet allows you to work almost anywhere, but requires special skills because of its limitless nature. Your campus library's contents are selected to be of interest and use to the student body, but the Internet's vast contents have no such limits. If you learn some basic guidelines for sorting through its mix of commercial and non-commercial material, you will work online more effectively. Following is a general introduction to online research.

Search Engines

A search engine performs like a computerized "card catalogue" for the Internet. Search engines use automated software called bots, spiders, or crawlers that "crawl" through the Internet seeking content when you type in keywords. Directory engines are specialized; they contain information assembled and categorized by people who collect that material from various databases. About.com and LookSmart are directory engines that display categories for your topic and Google can perform directory searches as well. If you are still working on your focus, or wish to confine your search to a specific area, you will find a directory search useful. To use various engines more effectively, go to http://www.lib.berkeley.edu/TeachingLib/Guides/Internet/SearchEngines.html. Several engines today combine robot and directory functions. Metasearch engines like Google search other engines as well as their own databases, then compile the results. Google (and some other engines) can also search for results in newsgroups and different media, returning findings as text files, image files, and sound files.

There are three important reasons to allow yourself some time to work with search engines. First, even if you have narrowed your research topic, you will need time for trials with your search words. Next, you need time to sift through and scan the sites and links your searches bring up. Finally, you need time to read screens and decide which sites and which passages will be most useful. Outlining and discovering directions for your paper before going online pays off here because you will spot relevant material more quickly.

Finally, online research, for all its apparent ease, involves several pitfalls; the main one being the unreliability of many sites and webpages. Learning to evaluate online information takes time and practice. Later in this chapter you will find guidelines for judging online resources, but if your campus library offers an online research tutorial, take it as soon as possible.

 ## Research Tip: Increase Your Keyword Power

Entering keywords tells a search engine's database what to look for. Use words from your subject area or discipline, try synonyms, and try placing your words in order of importance. Allow time for some trial and error; no one is an expert at choosing exactly "the right keywords."

Learning to increase the power of your search words and phrases by using search engines' help pages; combining words with Boolean operators such as "and," and "not,"; using plus and minus symbols; and trying subsearches are skills that maximize the effectiveness of your online research time. Here are some general guidelines to help you search effectively:

- Search engines are generally *case insensitive*; it does not matter if you capitalize a name. On occasion, though, you may wish to check a search engine's "search help" page for information about using capitals.
- Check your search engine's instructions for information for adding "operators" or "codes" such as + or *and* to link or alter the meanings of groups of keywords.
- Check your search engine's instructions for defining word groups to be taken together or *strings,* such as *liquid crystal display.*
- If you are researching only aspects of a topic that relate to Canada, choose the "Canadian sites only" option on Google and add the word *Canada* or *Canadian* to limit your search.

Try placing your keywords in order of their importance, with the most important idea first. Some engines "weight" a search by the order of the words.

Step 7: Evaluate and Select Appropriate Information

Each time you identify suitable information from library and online sources, list the names and locations of books, articles, and database information you find useful.

For each reference listing, write down the author's name; the title of the book, article, or website; the page number; and some point-form notes of the most important information you found. You should have more items than you will need because you will eliminate some during the step of evaluating each source of information for its quality and relevance.

With your list at hand, review your assignment's requirements for clues as to how many sources will be appropriate. Reference specialists recommend a variety of secondary sources. As mentioned, books tend to offer careful scholarship and a range of viewpoints; periodical articles offer specific explorations of single viewpoints and timeliness; and websites vary widely in quality of information. If your paper should be fairly brief, select only the best pieces of information from your list; if a minimum or specified number of sources is stipulated, then use that as a guideline. In any case, research should support and extend your own ideas; it is *not* the backbone of your paper.

Deciding how useful your sources are and how much of each to use are skills you will refine throughout your academic program, but the following specific guidelines, which build on the "tips" on page 289, will help you evaluate sources. Three criteria will be of particular importance as you examine any source of information: *relevance* to your topic, *reliability* of content, and *timeliness* of its information.

Relevance

- Use sources that are more, rather than less, devoted to your topic. If a source's main focus is your topic area, its information will be less superficial and more specialized.
- Check that a source's treatment of topic-related information is suited to your understanding and needs. Is it too technical or too general?
- Consider, with a periodical source, the type of publication. Is it a general-interest magazine or specialized journal? Journals offer superior research and content quality compared to general-interest magazines and newspapers.
- Rank the source in terms of its importance to your paper's focus in order to make your final selection easier.

Reliability

- If possible, use sources whose authors are recognized in the field. Look for the author's biography, or ask your instructor or a librarian for help.
- Check for authors who have published other material in your topic area and whose books and articles contain bibliographies and reference lists.
- Learn all you can about the author's overall view of or bias on your topic. Check biographical material, the introduction or preface to the work, or other writers' views of the author.
- Check for references within the source to other material and authors on the subject. If these are not named, the information may be one-sided or biased.
- Look for well-supported arguments, clear logic, and solid proof for points made in your source.
- Always verify important pieces of information in at least three sources. If some information reappears frequently, then it is probably reliable.

Timeliness

- Check for recent publication dates of books and periodical articles.

- On websites, look for the most recent updating. This information often appears on the homepage or final page of a site.

Evaluating Internet Sources

Choosing information sources online is a special challenge because the Internet is unregulated by design. The additional criteria listed below for judging online resources will help you evaluate your own choices.

- **Author's Reliability**: Always check for any possible information about the author of a site. Does he or she list any credentials? Has the author published other material on the topic? Website authors should include e-mail contact information.
- **Affiliations and Sponsors**: Is the site affiliated with any known organization? If so, is the organization likely to provide unbiased information? Does the site have affiliations with commercial groups? If so, does this affect the quality of the information on the site? Is the site sponsored by a corporation or special-interest group? If so, will its content reflect this?
- **Objectivity and Completeness**: Read the entire site carefully before deciding to use pieces of information from it. Ask yourself if the author presents all content objectively. Are all sides of any topic stated before the author argues his or her own views? Does the author produce solid support for his or her views?
- **Nature of Links Provided**: What kinds of links are provided on the site? Do they demonstrate serious research or interests? Are they wide-ranging in content? Are they commercial or non-commercial?
- **Organization of Information**: How well is the site's information organized? Is there a site map or index to help you locate information on your topic?
- **Date**: Is the information up to date? Check near the opening or on the last page of the site for copyright, publication, or revision dates. If the site contains articles by a number of writers, check for the dates of these. Knowing such dates will help you decide whether the material is current enough for your needs. Check that the links on a website are active and reliable.

Tips for Evaluating College Research Findings

When you are trying to decide how valuable some source of information is, consider the following questions:

- **Focus**: How focused is this material on my subject-area and topic? Is the information I need a small part of the material or its main content?
- **Depth of Information**: How deeply does this material treat my area of interest? Does it offer a good quantity of information that is new to me?
- **Currency of Information**: How recently was this material published? For this course and for my topic, how important is recent information?
- **Quality of Information**: Is this material at a level of expertise that my instructor expects for this assignment? Is the author a reputable source or a specialist in this field?

● ● ● ● ● **Activity**

Part A

Go to Google's homepage (www.google.ca), and perform a search for the word "education." Use "the web" option for your search; do not restrict your search to pages from Canada. Then, answer the questions that follow.

1. a) How many items did your search yield?

   b) In the first three pages of listings, you will probably find each of the following domain-name extensions: *edu*, *gov*, *org*, and *com*. Pick one site with each extension, and write the site's title and its full URL.

2. Choose one of the sites you identified, and use it to complete the following evaluation:

   a) What is the name of the site's author or authoring institution?

   b) Is the site's information current (within two years)?

   c) Does the site serve obvious business or commercial purposes? (Check for advertising, banners, or pop-ups.)

   d) Does the site have an obvious connection to a governmental, special-interest, or religious organization? If so, which one?

   e) Does the site's information seem fair and objective? Why or why not?

   f) Based on the information above, would you say the site appears reliable?

Part B

Now, restrict your search to the "pages from Canada" option, and perform the same search for the word "education." Answer the questions above for your new search of Canadian sites. Instead of 1(b) above, respond to the following:

In the first three pages of Canadian listings, you will probably find these domain-name extensions: *gov*. plus the provincial abbreviation *.ca*; *u* plus the name of the university *.ca*; *.net* and *.com*. Pick one site with each extension, and write the site's title and its full URL.

Step 8: Absorb Your Research Findings and Take Notes

Set some time aside to consider the sources you have selected. Read carefully each book section, article, and webpage on your reference list. Look for similarities and differences among them. You are digesting and absorbing ideas while you read.

Do not try to review your reference choices in one sitting. Your understanding of material deepens as you take time to read, make connections, and find new ideas of your own.

Keep your trial outline nearby and extra paper for notes of ideas and connections as well as their sources. Continue to refer to your outline to maintain your focus and to help you make decisions on what to record for which part of your outline.

Purposes for Recording Information from Research Sources

As you make your notes, think about *why* you are doing so. Information from other sources has three functions:

1. To expand on facts with examples, statistics, or data that clarify and strengthen your points and ideas

2. To present another explanation or view of some point that strengthens your points and ideas

3. To support with some recognized authority a point or claim you make

Taking notes should, therefore, extend and support your own ideas rather than replace them. In the next chapter, you will learn how to blend your notes with your own ideas and to give credit for the information you incorporate—both critical aspects of writing an effective research paper.

CHECKLIST OF LEARNING OUTCOMES FOR CHAPTER 18

To ensure that you have understood and met the learning outcomes for this chapter, answer the following questions:

✓ Describe why research may accurately be called a process.

✓ What are the general goals for academic-level research?

✓ What specifically are the goals for an academic research paper? Explain the key words for each goal in your own words.

✓ What are the steps to follow for conducting effective research?

✓ Why is it essential to prepare a time plan for research assignments?

✓ Under what circumstances would you do some research *before* narrowing a topic for a research essay?

✓ How would you go about limiting a research topic?

✓ What are the main sources of information available to you for research assignments?

✓ What are the three criteria for evaluating the quality of a source?

✓ Explain the three functions of secondary sources in a research paper.

CHAPTER 19

Writing a Research Paper

The first goal for a research paper, as discussed in the previous chapter, is the *discovery* of your own ideas about your topic and of research material to strengthen, support, or lend authority to those ideas. This chapter addresses the second key goal: *blending* your ideas with support from outside sources. It guides you through assembling and writing an effective research paper and provides a model research paper.

The blending of your own ideas with your research findings requires you

- to have a firm enough sense of the quality of your own points and support so that you do not substitute ideas from other sources simply because they seem preferable or impressive;

- to be familiar enough with the content of your research sources to select material of relevance and appropriate length;

- to combine your words with those of others into smooth sentences, introducing your quotations correctly into your text;

- to give credit to your sources each time you use them as quotations, paraphrases, or summaries, using an appropriate style of citation. Assemble your paper one step at a time, following the steps in the box below, and you will acquire a solid working strategy for all research assignments.

Six Steps for Preparing a Research Paper

1. Revise your trial outline.
2. Review and refine your research notes.
3. Write your first draft.
4. Revise your first draft to insert and cite your reference materials.
5. Document your research and prepare a Works Cited or References list.
6. Write your final draft.

Step 1: Revise Your Trial Outline

Now that you have read and made rough notes on different sources relating to your topic and support, revise your outline to create a clear, detailed guide as you mesh your own ideas with appropriate research. First, though, consider your trial thesis statement and the purpose of your paper.

The requirements for your assignment may present a purpose, but, if not, there are two main purposes for all research papers—to inform or to persuade.

Recall the research questions (pages 274–275) that were part of the research process. Do you wish to answer a *what* or *who* question? In that case, your purpose may be to inform—to supply a well-detailed, logical answer to your research question. Was a *why* or *how* question most useful to you? You may then want to persuade your reader. Use the question you found most relevant, along with your assignment's requirements, to help you decide on your purpose. Making this decision helps you reformulate your trial thesis into a stronger thesis statement that guides your choices of supporting details.

An Illustration

Sonya Phillips rewrote her thesis several times during a week of research. She started with a focused version of her topic: "Parents face many challenges raising children and teenagers in today's culture." She then wrote a more positive version: "There are things parents can do to overcome the negative influences hurting their families." She knew that she really wanted her research paper to emphasize the "things parents can do." While acknowledging external negative influences, she wanted to persuade her audience that there are functioning, successful families who raise teenagers equipped to cope with life. Sonya believed she could best balance these two concepts by expanding her introduction. Her first paragraph presents the media's portrayal of teenagers; this serves as background and contrast to the second paragraph. This paragraph introduces parents and families and leads up to the thesis, a statement that makes her purpose clear: "Although these are difficult times to be raising teenagers, successful families are finding ways to cope with the challenges." She opened with some opposing facts and then presented her thesis to show how families raise teenagers successfully. (The final version of Sonya's thesis statement appears near the end of paragraph 2 in the model research paper on pages 314–315.)

Once you have revised your thesis to your satisfaction, review your supporting points. Be sure that each one is truly distinct from the others and that each one clearly proves, supports, and clarifies one aspect of your thesis.

Set up your revised outline document by copying and pasting your trial outline into a new document. Add your revised thesis and your supporting points, leaving blank spaces under each supporting-point heading so that you can later note supporting details as well as the quotations and paraphrases from your research. Instructors may require an outline to be handed in along with a research paper, so revising your outline in this manner will be well worth the effort.

The diagram below shows how to modify a research paper outline so that you can add quotations and paraphrases from your research sources in the appropriate places.

Revised Outline Diagram

Paragraph I: Thesis Statement

Plan of Development: Supporting Points
A. _____
B. _____
C. _____

Paragraph II: Supporting Point A

My details:
1. _____
2. _____
3. _____ Add quotation from _____ (page #)

Paragraph III: Supporting Point B

My details:
1. _____
2. _____ Add paraphrase from _____ (page #)
3. _____

Paragraph IV: Supporting Point C

My details:
1. _____ Add quotation from _____ (page #)
2. _____
3. _____

Paragraph V: Conclusion

As noted in the previous chapter, research papers, even shorter ones, will rarely be five paragraphs in length. As in the model at the end of this chapter, research papers may have two introductory paragraphs, depending on the quantity of background information an audience may need. The number of body paragraphs will be determined by the number of supporting points. Additionally, some of your supporting points may require division into subtopics, each with its own paragraph, as is the case in the model research paper. The boxed outline also includes the page numbers for the quotations and paraphrases to be included. Transfer the author's name and the page-number information from your research notes each time you incorporate material from a research source. The next section of this chapter will show you how to prepare your research notes correctly, using accurate and properly credited quotations, paraphrases, and summaries.

Note: Research papers are nearly always written in the third-person point of view. The emphasis in a research paper is on your ideas, proof, and the quality of your research rather than on personal response. Therefore, using "I" could distract readers from the content and argument in your paper and should be avoided. Let your facts speak for themselves.

Step 2: Review and Refine Your Research Notes

Preparing your research notes means that you have already recorded the words and ideas of others correctly as noted on page 278 of the previous chapter.

Refining and completing your notes from other sources of information also means correctly and fully recording all the necessary information from those sources.

Choose one method for setting up your revised research notes, and use it consistently. For example, use 3" × 5" cards, a small notebook, or a computer document. Begin each research note with a phrase or keyword that refers to the point or idea that the note applies to. For each research note, you will then need to record

- the name(s) of the author(s) of the work;
- the title of the work;
- the page numbers you have referred to or quoted from or paraphrased from;
- the publisher of the work;
- the city of publication;
- the year the work was published (and the edition, if applicable);
- locating information.

For **journal articles**, you will also need

- the volume, number, and date of the journal in which the article appears;
- the page numbers on which the article appears.

For **a website**, you will also need

- the date listed for the website or name and section of the site you refer to;
- locating information: the URL of the website;
- the date or dates on which you accessed the website.

Be sure that your final research notes are complete, with indications of when you are paraphrasing or incorporating another author's ideas into your own writing. In a research paper, you must document all information that is not common knowledge or a matter of historical record. For example, Stephen Harper's birth date is an established fact and does not need documenting. As you read several sources on a subject, you will develop a sense of what authors regard as generally shared or common information about a subject and what is more specialized informa-tion that must be documented. If you do not document and show the source of specialized information about a subject, you are plagiarizing, or, in effect, stealing someone else's work.

By keeping complete and correct research notes, you will find that inserting your source-material into drafts of your paper will be much easier, as will creating the Works Cited or References section that appears at the end of your research paper.

Quotations

What is a quotation?

Each time you use the exact words of another writer, you must identify these words as a *direct quotation*—with double quotation marks. Quoting means using phrases or sentences word for word, with punctuation exactly as it appears in the original. Here is a sample of a direct quotation:

> "Conversely, the category of boredom implies a set of expectations of the external world that apparently did not afflict our remote predecessors" (11).

The parentheses and number at the end of the quotation indicate the page number of the source in which the words quoted appear. You may omit words from a quo-tation as long as you do not change its meaning by doing so. To signal omission, you must use an *ellipsis*, or three dots. Here is an example of a direct quotation with missing words replaced by an ellipsis:

> "[T]he larger the landed estate then the more scope there was for introducing change . . . and the more complex, professional, and efficient was the estate organisation that conceived, nurtured, and developed that change" (87).

Note that the capital letter *T* in brackets above shows that the word has been capi-talized by the student. It has been changed from a lower case *t* in the original source where the statement was part of a longer sentence.

When should you use a quotation?

Use quotations sparingly and only when they truly extend, explain, or lend author-ity to your own points. Quotations are accepted and expected in formal research and academic writing, but they are only supplementary material in research assign-ments; they do not make up most of the body of the work.

In a short (i.e., one-thousand-word) research paper, five brief quotations (i.e., fewer than four lines each) would be sufficient. Papers created out of chunks of quo-tations strung together are annoying and confusing to read; the effect is like overhear-ing a babble of voices. The writer's intention is lost under all those other voices.

If you must use a quotation of more than forty words or four lines of text, do so cautiously and correctly. In short papers, such long quotations give the impres-sion of "filling space" to replace your own thoughts. To insert a long quotation, set it up as follows:

> It has been customary to describe the seasonal festivals of so-called native peoples as efforts to control nature. This is a misrepresentation. There is much of the will to control in every act of man, and particularly in those magical

> ceremonies that are thought to bring rain clouds, cure sickness, or stay the flood; nevertheless, the dominant motive in all truly religious . . . ceremonial is that of submission to the inevitables of destiny . . . (384).

Long quotations are set off from the body of your text on a new line. They are not enclosed by quotation marks and are indented for their full length from the left margin. A long quotation concludes with the page number (in parentheses) of the source where it appears. Notice that the quotation above contains two ellipses; the first indicates that words are omitted (without changing the meaning or altering the grammatical flow of the quotation) and the second shows that the sentence in the original does not end there. MLA style uses the final ellipses; APA does not.

Note as well the longer quotation used on page 2 of the model paper at the end of this chapter (page 315). Sonya's reason for quoting this long passage is that its content includes factual and numerically exact support for her point, which is best stated directly. Paraphrasing is inadvisable where exactness is essential (i.e., for statistics, technical data, or complex numerical information).

Paraphrases

What is a paraphrase?

As discussed in Chapter 17, paraphrasing involves putting the words of another writer *completely* into your *own* words. Paraphrasing requires care and some skill for three reasons. First, you must understand the meaning of the words you paraphrase so clearly that you can restate that meaning in different words. Second, you must not simply change a few words in the original; you must use synonyms, modify the grammatical structure, and present the original source's idea as you understand it. Third, you must not borrow even two- or three-word phrases from your original source; if you include these in a paraphrase, put quotation marks around them. To avoid plagiarism, you must always credit a paraphrase just as you would a quotation.

When should you paraphrase?

Paraphrasing is essential to the process of *blending*—of synthesizing your research with your own ideas on your topic. Paraphrases make reading your paper a smooth process for readers because paraphrases do not interrupt the flow of your words as much as quotations. Paraphrases demonstrate your understanding of your research sources and your ability to use these intelligently. Good paraphrases (1) shorten lengthy passages, (2) eliminate or explain unnecessary technical language, and (3) make the ideas in the source-material clear in the context of your paper. For examples that show how to paraphrase correctly and avoid plagiarism, see Chapter 18. Methods of integrating paraphrases appropriately are covered in step 4.

Summaries

Should you wish to summarize material for a research paper, follow the guidelines in Chapter 17. A summary in a research essay might logically consist of only a few sentences. As with quoting and paraphrasing, it is essential to properly acknowledge your original source when summarizing.

Step 3: Write Your First Draft

Once you have reviewed your research notes, use your revised outline as a guide, and write the first draft of your research paper. Concentrate on writing clear sentences that get your ideas across. At points where you wish to insert support from your research, make a note to yourself of what you would like to add. Do not worry about documenting items now; simply write in reminders of where quotations and paraphrases should go.

Put your draft away for a day at least. Then, read it aloud to yourself or someone else, noting any weak spots, repetitions, or logic problems.

Step 4: Revise Your First Draft to Insert and Cite Your Reference Materials

Revise your draft in two stages. First, focus only on inserting quotations and paraphrases from your sources. To prepare, arrange your research notes in the order in which you will use them. Concentrate on working quotations and paraphrases into the flow of your sentences and on placing your citations correctly. Remember to use quotation marks and to insert citations according to the style your instructor prefers. Citing your sources correctly signals to your readers that you have taken the time to do your research and incorporate it carefully into your work; it tells them you recognize that they need to see certain signals to know when you are borrowing ideas. Trust between reader and writer, between instructor and student, is maintained, and you as the writer are seen as trustworthy and careful.

In the second stage of revising, focus on editing and proofreading for clear expression of your meaning. Follow the same methods you learned in Chapter 5. Revise your sentences for clarity and variety of structure. Then, proofread your paper for sentence-skills and mechanical errors, referring to Part 4 of this book and to your dictionary for help.

Integrating Material from Another Source

To integrate a piece of research material into the overall flow of your paper, write the idea that you wish to support with a quotation or paraphrase in clear sentences. Your quoted or paraphrased source-material must be understandable in the context of your paper. Create a background for the ideas you are supporting so that your quoted or paraphrased material makes sense to readers and adds to the quality of your own thoughts. Integrate your quoted or paraphrased material by identifying the author either before or immediately after that material. Finally, complete the context for your quotation or paraphrase by explaining it further, adding your own ideas to it, or arguing against it.

To integrate a direct quotation, according to MLA style, follow one of the methods shown in the examples below.

Identify your source before your quotation.

E.A. Thompson, in *The Huns*, argues that Rome did not fall because of the force of one powerful leader: "there is not much evidence to show that Attila was a genius. It is only in terms of the development of their society that we can explain why the Huns attacked Rome at all . . ." (46).

This student will then go on to explain why he or she agrees or disagrees with Thompson's point, thus completing the context for the quotation with his or her own ideas. Notice that the page number in parentheses appears before the period that ends the student's sentence. Note also the use of the colon after the independent clause that precedes the quotation.

Identify your source following your quotation.

"[T]here is not much evidence to show that Attila was a genius. It is only in terms of the development of their society that we can explain why the Huns attacked Rome at all . . . ," writes E.A. Thompson in *The Huns* (46).

Notice, in this example, that the quotation flows grammatically into the end of the sentence, following the comma after the ellipsis.

To integrate a paraphrase, follow the same methods.

Identify your source before your paraphrase.

In *The Prospect Before Her*, Olwen Huften gives examples of early forms of daycare used by working mothers in the 1700s in England and France whose jobs prevented them from raising children at home (197).

This student would then explain the relationship of this paraphrase to the point he or she is making in his paper to ensure that the purpose of the paraphrase is clear to readers.

Identify your source after your paraphrase.

Working mothers' use of daycare for infants and children is not a recent development. In fact, there are recorded examples of women in the silk industry and in mills in France and England in the 1700s whose jobs required them to arrange daycare for their children, as Olwen Huften writes in *The Prospect Before Her* (197).

Integrate short summaries of passages in the same ways as you would paraphrases.

Step 5: Document Your Research and Prepare a "Works Cited" or "References" List

Citation Styles: MLA and APA

Two of the most often used styles of documentation and citation are MLA, or Modern Language Association style, used for English and Humanities subjects, and APA, or American Psychological Association style, used for Social Sciences subjects. Always ask your instructor which style he or she would like you to follow. This book uses MLA style (the documentation style of the *MLA Handbook for Writers of Research Papers*) and presents information about MLA citation first, but brief coverage of some aspects of APA style is offered in this section as well.

MLA-Style Documentation

You have already seen MLA-style documentation in the preceding examples. MLA citation appears in two locations in your research paper: in the identification of author and page number within the text of your paper and in the Works Cited list at the end of your paper.

In-text Citation

In-text citations are the signals you place directly in the text of your paper to acknowledge information from any source you quote or paraphrase. They are the author's name and page numbers placed in parentheses either at the end of a sentence containing a quotation or paraphrase or at the end of a quotation or paraphrase itself.

There are several points to note about citations within the text of your paper:

1. When the author's name and title of the book or article are given in the introduction to the material cited, only the page number (or numbers) is given in parentheses.

2. If the author's name is not given before or after the cited material, then the author's last name only is placed within the parentheses before the page number, with no punctuation between the name and page number: (Atkins 328).

3. If you are using more than one work by the same author, include a shortened version of the title of that work within the parenthetical citation. If you are using two books by Freda Marshall and you included a quotation from her book *Marketing Trends in Canadian Retail Development*, your citation within the text would be (Marshall, *Marketing Trends* 122). A comma separates the author's last name from the abbreviated title and page number.

4. If an organization or committee is the author, then the organization's name is given as the author. Abbreviate the name if it is long.

5. If your source is a website, follow the guidelines for print sources. If there is no author available, identify the online source by title, either in the essay's text or in the parenthetical citation. Because online sources do not generally have numbered pages, the entire site is cited.

6. If you are citing a passage from a novel or literary work, and have already noted the author and work in your essay, place the page number(s) in the parentheses, followed by a semicolon, a space, and the chapter number.

7. The parenthetical citation is placed after the borrowed material but before the period at the end of the sentence containing it.

Works Cited List

In order for readers to trace your in-text citations, you create a Works Cited section at the end of your paper. This is a list of all the sources you actually used in the paper.

To set up your Works Cited list, refer to the model entries on page 301, and follow the steps below. Keep in mind that the model entries do not show all possible sources. Your college library will have a copy of the MLA style guide, but if you are uncertain of how to document some source, ask a reference librarian to help you, or check your campus library's website under "MLA citation" for more information.

1. Place your page number (as for your other pages) in the upper-right corner of a new page within the "header" area.

2. Centre the title "Works Cited" in regular typeface (without underlining, italics, or quotations marks) at the top of your page. Double space before the first entry.

3. Begin each entry at the left margin. When the entry runs more than one line of text, indent each additional line by five spaces, or use the indent tab on your keyboard.

4. Organize your list alphabetically by the authors' last names. If no author is given, the entry is alphabetized by title, ignoring *A, An,* and *The.*

5. Do not number entries.

6. Double space between and within each entry.

7. In publication information, use abbreviations for publishers' names and months of the year: i.e., *Farrar* instead of *Farrar Straus and Giroux; Oct.* instead of *October.*

8. When listing numbers of pages used at the end of a book entry, use only numbers. Do not use *p., pp.,* or *page(s).*

Model Entries for a List of "Works Cited"

Use these entries as guides as you prepare your list of reference sources. Capitalize words in titles exactly as they appear in the works themselves, and use the exact punctuation marks you see between items for each type of entry you list. You will now use the information you listed for each source when you revised your reference notes.

Books

Book by One Author

Author's Last name, First name.
↓

 Hoffert, Paul. <u>All Together Now</u>. Toronto: Stoddart, 2000.
 ↑ ↑
 <u>Title</u>.   City of publication: Publisher, year of publication.

Notice that author's names are reversed, with the last name first, and separated from the first name or initials by a comma. After the title (underlined), record the publication information—the city, name of the publisher, and the year of publication. These appear at the front of any book, often on the reverse side of the title page.

If a book's full title (as on the title page inside the book) includes a subtitle, include it by placing a colon after the main title and then copying the subtitle, word for word, as in the example below:

 Nuland, Sherwin B. <u>How We Die: Reflections on Life's Final Chapter</u>. New York: Vintage, 1995.

Notice that the second line of the entry is indented by five spaces.

Two or More Entries by the Same Author

> ---. The Mysteries Within: A Surgeon Reflects on Medical Myths. New York:
> Simon & Schuster, 2000.

Here, a second book by Sherwin B. Nuland is cited. With two or more books by the same author, do not repeat the author's name. Instead, begin with a line of three hyphens followed by a period. Arrange works by the same author in alphabetical order.

Book by Two or More Authors

> Kalman, Harold, Ron Phillips, and Robin Ward. Exploring Vancouver: The
> Essential Architectural Guide. Vancouver: UBC Press, 1993.

Give all the authors' names, but reverse only the first name. For a book with more than three authors, cite only the first author's name, followed by a comma and the phrase *et al.*

Second or Later Edition of a Book

> Myers, David G. Social Psychology. 6th ed. New York: McGraw-Hill, 1999.

Organization or Group as Author

> Council for Ecumenical Study. High-Church Influence in Victorian London.
> London: Faber, 2003.

Book by an Editor

> Nolan, Tom. Ed. Strangers in Town: Three Newly Discovered Mysteries by Ross
> Macdonald. New York: Crippen & Landru, 2001.

Book with an Author and an Editor

> Schweitzer, Albert. Albert Schweitzer: A Biography. Ed. James Brabazon.
> Syracuse: Syracuse UP, 2000.

Book by Unknown or Anonymous Author

> The Canadian Encyclopedia. 2nd ed. Toronto: McLelland & Stewart, 1988.

If you use one volume of a multivolume work, such as an encyclopedia, then you should indicate the volume used as below:

> Martin, Brendt. Encyclopedia of Music. Vol. 2. New York: Greenwood, 1998.

Selection from an Edited Book or Anthology

> Lear, Edward. "The Owl and the Pussy-Cat." Classics of Children's Literature.
> Eds. John W. Griffith and Charles H. Frey. 3rd ed. New York: Macmillan
> Publishing Company, 1992. 190–91.

This entry ends with the inclusive page numbers for the item used in the anthology. Citations should list the pages actually used in your essay as the final item, followed by a period.

The editor of the collection or anthology's name appears after the title of the work, preceded by *Ed.*, the abbreviation of the word *Editor*.

Chapter or Section in a Book by One Author

> Secunda, Victoria. "A New Sense of Family." <u>Losing Your Parents, Finding Yourself: The Defining Turning Point of Adult Life</u>. New York: Hyperion, 2000. 242–56.

In the entry above, the numbers after the year of publication are the consecutive page numbers of the chapter of the book cited.

Periodicals

Article in a Magazine Published Monthly

After the title of the magazine, the month and year of the issue is listed, followed by a colon, then the pages on which the article appears.

Article in a Magazine Published Weekly

> Chin, Paula. "You Were a Good Man, Charlie Brown." <u>People</u> 28 Feb. 2000: 52–59.

For an article from a magazine published every week or every two weeks, put in the complete date (starting with the day and abbreviating the month, except for May, June, and July) and the page numbers on which the article appears.

Article in a Scholarly Journal with Volume Paging

> Maynard, Charles. "Coding Correlations." <u>Computers and the Humanities</u> 33 (1999): 675–690.

This example shows an entry from a bound version of a scholarly journal. The *33* after the title of the journal is the annual volume number for the year 1999. The pages in this volume run consecutively for an entire year's worth of this journal. Notice also that the year of publication is placed within parentheses for such journal articles.

Article in a Scholarly Journal with Paging by Issue

> Lisander, Mary. "ROI in a Declining Economy," <u>Journal of Canadian Marketing</u>. 15.4 (2001): 81–89.

Some scholarly journals maintain the paging of the original issues. In such cases, you record the volume number, then the issue number, separated by a period.

Newspaper Article

> Goddard, Peter. "The New Crime Photography." <u>Toronto Star</u> 17 Jan. 2004: J1+.

When citing newspaper articles, omit *The*, if it is part of the newspaper's name. To show continuation pages, add a + sign to the first page of an article (6+, 23+), because newspaper articles are often not printed on consecutive pages, and be sure to include any letter designation used to indicate the section of the newspaper that the article appears in, such as "B4+."

Editorial

"Trade Wars Laughable." Editorial. <u>The Winnipeg Free Press</u> 15 Mar. 1995: A10.

Editorials are often unsigned, so no author's name appears in this entry. Indicate the nature of the article by adding the word *Editorial* in regular type after the article's title.

Government Publication

Canada. National Student Load Service Centre. <u>Budget 2004: The Importance of Learning</u>. Ottawa: Social Development Canada, 2002.

With government publications, place either the name of the government or agency first, or the author's name. If the name of the government is placed first, then after the title of the document, place the writer's name preceded with *By*, or the editor's name preceded with *Ed.*, or a compiler's name preceded by *Comp*.

Published Interview

Frum, Linda. "Peter Bergen Talks to Linda Frum." <u>Maclean's</u> 30 Jan. 2006: 10–11.

Sources in Other Media

Article from a Website

One section of this website is cited, the article, "Texas Blues." Its title is placed in quotation marks, and because the author is not listed on the site, the listing begins with the title.

When you cite a complete website, include the title of the site underlined, the name of the editor [if any], the electronic publishing information [version, if available], the date of publication or last update of site, and the name of the sponsoring institution.

Online Book

McFarlane, Celia. <u>Library Workplace Design</u>. East Lansing: Mitchell Publishing, 2005. <u>Questia.com</u>. Apr. 2006. 14 Oct. 2007 <http://www.questia.com/DM.qu?a=a455>.

An online book is cited like a print book, adding the title of the database or project, date of electronic publication, sponsoring organization, date accessed, and the URL.

Online Article

Ehrenreich, Barbara. "Will Women Still Need Men? Time Online 21 Feb. 2000.
    15 April 2004 <http://www.time.com/time/reports/v21/live/men_mag.html>.

Online Source in a Reference Database

"Heredity." Britannica Online. Sept. 1999. Encyclopaedia Britannica. 2 Mar.
    2000 <http://www.britannica.com/bcom/eb/article/4/0,5716,120934,00.
    html#Article>.

Article from a Database

Lavallee, David. "The Digest." Journal of Sport and Exercise Psychology 27.4
    (2005): 521–7. Academic Search Premier. EBSCO. Weldon Library, U of
    Western Ontario. 8 Jan. 2007.

With articles accessed through library databases such as *EBSCO, InfoTrac,* or *Lexis-Nexis,* follow article citation with the name of the online service used, the library's name, date accessed, and, if available, the URL of the site's search page.

E-mail Message

Baer, Max. "Re: Submitting Design Proposal." E-mail to Harold Ziegler.
    11 May 2008.

Listserv or Discussion Group Posting

Burke, Ella. "Concerns with Romeo and Juliet." Listserv post. 15 Oct. 2006.
    NCTE-Talk. 22 May 2007 <http://www.ncte.org/lists/notetalk/oct2006/
    msg01154.html>.

Television Program

"Salmon Farming." The Nature of Things. Narr. David Suzuki. CBC. 21 Nov.
    1993.

Notice here that the episode of the TV show is cited in quotation marks, and the title of the series to which the episode belongs is underlined. Items such as narrator or director are optional, but the name of the network presenting the program and the date of broadcast must be included.

Film

Titanic. Dir. James Cameron. Paramount Pictures, 1997.

Not a Love Story: A Film about Pornography. Dir. Bonnie Sher Klein. National
    Film Board of Canada, 1986.

DVD or Videocassette

Kurosawa, Akira. Rashomon. 1950. DVD. Criterion, 2003.

Cite the DVD or videotape version of a film just as you would a film, but add the original year of release, and the medium (not underlined or in quotation marks) just before the name of the distributor.

CD or Sound Recording

Gray, Macy. <u>The Trouble with Being Myself</u>. Epic, 2003.

If you are citing one song on a CD, then put its title in quotation marks before the underlined title of the CD.

Activity

On a sheet of paper, convert the information in each of the following reference-list items into the correct MLA form for a "Works Cited" page. Use the appropriate model from the preceding section as a guide.

- An article by Alex Yannis titled "In New League, Women Get Payoff and Payday" on page D5 of the April 13, 2001 issue of the <u>New York Times</u>.
- An article by Marni Jackson titled "Our Bodies, Our Suits" on pages 71–72 of the March 2003 issue of <u>Saturday Night</u> magazine.
- A book by Francis McInerney and Sean White called <u>Futurewealth: Investing in the Second Great Wave of Technology</u> and published in New York by St. Martin's in 2000.
- A book by Ellen N. Junn and Chris Boyatzis titled <u>Child Growth and Development</u> and published in a seventh edition by McGraw-Hill in New York in 2000.
- An article called "Evolution of Alphabets" on a University of Maryland website called <u>Workstations at Maryland</u> dated February 10, 2000 at the URL http://www.wam.umd.edu/%7Erfradkin/alphapage.html. The site was accessed on March 16th, 2005.

APA-Style Documentation

Like MLA style, APA style (the documentation style of the *Publication Manual of the American Psychological Association*) requires in-text citation of sources each time one is used as well as a list of sources at the end of the research paper. Basic coverage of some aspects of APA style follows; for more information, check your campus's library website, or consult your instructor.

MLA and APA styles also differ in a number of specific areas. One significant difference concerns the importance of dates of publication in the social sciences. Therefore, in APA style, the date is always included in in-text citations.

In-text Citation

Whether you are introducing a paraphrase or quotation, or placing the documentation within parentheses at the end of borrowed material, APA style requires you to include both the author's name and the date of publication.

Integrating a Paraphrase into a Sentence

Developments in satellite carrier digital transmission have sped up the progress of convergence among different media, according to Miller's 2003 article.

If you do not mention the author's name or date at the beginning or end of a sentence containing a paraphrase, then these items must be included in parentheses at an appropriate place in the sentence, as in the following example:

As noted in a recent article (Miller, 2003), developments in satellite carrier digital transmission have sped up the progress of convergence among different media.

Both citations above refer to a listing of Miller's article in the References list at the end of a paper that uses APA style.

Integrating a Quotation into a Sentence

More students than ever are "suffering financially through years, even decades of their careers because of enormous loans incurred to pay tuition fees" (LaRose, 2002, p. 310).

In the example above, the student is quoting a specific sentence from the source. In APA style, the number of the page on which the quoted material appears is placed after the complete work's publication date and is preceded by the abbreviation *p.* for *page.* Other abbreviations used in such APA parenthetical citations include *pp.* for *pages, chap.* for *chapter,* and *sec.* for *section.*

Citing a Work with Two or More Authors

In APA style, every author of a given work (up to five authors) is mentioned in a citation in the body of a paper:

Changes in patient behaviour are rapid and long lasting during intensive therapies (Annis, McLellan, Stuart, & Main, 2001, chap. 6).

References List

The APA-style References list is the equivalent of an MLA Works Cited list.

To set up your References list, refer to the model entries on page 308, and follow the steps below.

Keep in mind that the model entries do not show all possible sources. Style sheets for APA documentation will also be available from your campus library or its website. Your library will have a copy of the *APA Publication Manual,* but if you are uncertain of any aspect of APA style, ask a librarian for assistance.

1. Place your page number (as for your other pages) in the upper-right corner of the page within the "header" area.
2. Centre the title "References" in regular typeface (without underlining, italics, or quotations marks) at the top of your page. Double space before the first entry.
3. Begin each entry at the left margin. Second and further lines of an entry are indented from the left margin.
4. Organize your list alphabetically by the last name of the authors or, if no author is given, by the first main word in the title, ignoring *A, An,* and *The.*
5. Do not number entries.
6. Double space between and within each entry.

In addition to the importance of dates in APA, another notable difference between MLA and APA styles of documentation lies in the formatting of titles. In an MLA-style Works Cited list, a book's title is capitalized, as it appears in the source, and underlined (i.e., The Common Writer). However, within printed material, such as this textbook, titles are most often italicized. In an APA-style References list, only the first word of a book's title is capitalized (i.e., *The common writer*). In APA style, titles of books, journals, magazines, websites, films, and so on are italicized rather than underlined.

Model Entries for an APA References List

Use these entries as guides as you prepare your APA-style list of reference sources. Be very careful to use capitals and lower-case letters in titles exactly as the models below present them. Use the exact punctuation marks you see between items for each type of entry you list. You will now use the information you listed for each source when you revised your reference notes.

Books

Book by One Author

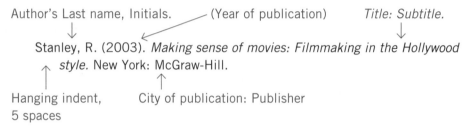

Author's Last name, Initials.   (Year of publication)   *Title: Subtitle.*

Stanley, R. (2003). *Making sense of movies: Filmmaking in the Hollywood style.* New York: McGraw-Hill.

Hanging indent,   City of publication: Publisher
5 spaces

Book by Two or More Authors

Marriott, L., & Lennard, P. (1997). *Heralding the new age.* Vancouver: Raincoast Press.

Second or Later Edition of a Book

Garofalo, R. (2003). *Rockin' out: Popular music in American culture* (2nd ed.). New York: Pearson.

Organization or Group as Author

Canadian Diabetes Association. (2005). *Living with diabetes.* Toronto: Dorling Kindersley.

Book by Unknown Author

Study of waste retrieval. (2005). Windsor: Urban Press.

One Volume from a Multivolume Series

Fredrickson, B. (1997). *Jungian studies* (Vol. 3). Chicago: Northeastern Press.

Chapter from a Book

Wellinski, J. (2000). Variable audience demographics. In *Media patterns* (pp. 134–156). Toronto: Sigma.

Periodicals

Article by a Single Author in a Magazine

Author's Last name, Initials.

(Year of publication, Month).
For weekly publication,
(Year of publication, Month and Day).

Silberman, S. (2001, December). The geek syndrome. *Wired, 9*(12), 174–183.

Title of article.   *Title of Magazine,*
Volume(Issue), pages.

After the year of publication, insert the month for magazines published monthly or month and day for magazines published weekly. The volume number is included as well, as it is for scholarly journals.

Article by Two Authors

Thysman, M., & Smythe, L. (1998). Browning's puzzle. *Poetry,* 387–411.

Here, there is no volume number to include.

Article with an Unknown Author

Evolutionary ecology. (2005, April). [Editorial]. *Canadian Science,* 23, 10.

Article in a Scholarly Journal

Zylberberg, M. (2002). Online consumer trends. *Journal of Marketing, 32,* 210–216.

In APA style, the title of the article does not appear in quotation marks and only the first word of the title is capitalized. As well, the title and volume number of the journal are both italicized.

Article in a Newspaper

Gilbert, P. (2004, February 8). Snow removal financing issues. *The Toronto Star,* pp. B1, B6.

Editorial

Marbert, P. (2005, November 8). Social services let-down. [Editorial]. *Saskatoon StarPhoenix,* p. A11+.

Government Documents

Foreign Affairs Canada. (2005). *Foreign policy and EU representation.* Ottawa.

Sources in Other Media

Article from a Website

Author's Last   (Year of
name, Initials.   publication, Month).   Title of article.   *Title of Site.*
    ↓   ↓   ↓   ↓

Ioannou, S. (2004, May). Essay tips for student writers. *Canadian
Student Writing Resources.* Retrieved January 10, 2005, from
http://www3.sympatico.ca/susanio/WWCcomp.html.
                  ↑
                URL   Date retrieved

Notice that the article on this website appears first, with no quotation marks and only the first word of its title capitalized. The date that the student accessed the information is preceded by the word "Retrieved," and the word "from" precedes the URL.

Article from an Online Database

Melino, L. (2003). New treatments for dysgraphia. *Journal of Research Psychology,*
15, 210–228. Retrieved May 12, 2006, from Proquest database.

Article in an Online Scholarly Journal

Simpson, J. (2003). Contested sites: Media today. *Sociological Research
Online,* 7(3). Retrieved October 5, 2006, from http://www.socresonline.
org.uk/7/3/simpson.html.

Article in an Online Newspaper

Pepper, M. (2007, May 19). Main drainage financing issues. *Kamloops Daily
News.* Retrieved December 10, 2007, from http://www.kamloopsnews.ca.

E-mails, Interviews, and Personal Communications

In APA style, no personal communication [e-mails, interviews, conversations] is included in the references list, but writers parenthetically cite them in an essay's main text: (E. Robbins, personal communication, January 4, 2001).

Listserv or Discussion Group Posting

Frook, B. D. (1999, July 23). New inventions in the cyberworld of toylandia
[Msg 25]. Message posted to http://groups.earthlink.com/forum/
messages/00025.html.

Include the title of the message, and the URL of the newsgroup or discussion board.

Television Program

Waldman R. (Writer). (2006). Darkness calls [Television series episode]. In D.
Chase (Producer), *The sopranos.* New York: HBO.

Film

Jackson, P. (Director). (2001). *The lord of the rings: The fellowship of the ring*
[Motion picture]. United States: New Line Productions, Inc.

Music CD

Waits, T. (1980). Ruby's arms. On *Heartattack and vine* [CD]. New York: Elektra.

● ● ● ● ● **Activity**

Convert the information in each of the following references into the correct form for an APA-style References list. Use the appropriate model from the preceding section as a guide.

- A book by Christopher Dewdney called *Acquainted with the Night* and published in Toronto by Harper Collins Canada in 2004.
- An article by Liisa Ladouceur titled "Lords of the New Church" on pages 14–18 of issue number 6 of volume 37, the May/June 2004 issue of *This Magazine.*
- A book by Michael W. Passner and Ronald E. Smith titled *Psychology: The Science of Mind and Behavior* and published in a second edition by McGraw-Hill in New York in 2004.
- An article by Ken Alexander titled "Election Watch: Buddies in Bad Times" found on January 5, 2005, at http://www.walrusmagazine.com in the July/August 2004 issue of *The Walrus* magazine online.
- An article by Ron King titled "We came, We played, We slept on your floor," published January 11, 2004, and found March 2, 2005, on the website *Punk History Canada* at http://punkhistorycanada.ca/home.php.

Step 6: Write Your Final Draft

Having revised your first draft, you can proceed to write the second one. Once again, revise, edit, and then proofread this draft. When revising for content, refer to the revision instructions in Chapter 2 of this book, or use the checklist on the inside front cover to be sure that your paper meets the four bases for effective writing: *unity, support, coherence,* and *effective sentence skills.* Leave yourself enough time to rewrite anything that seems unclear and to check your documentation of quotations, paraphrases, or summarized material.

As you begin revising, create a formal version of an outline, if one is required by your instructor. Generally, either a *topic outline,* as appears on page 294, or a *sentence outline* will be required. A topic outline contains your thesis plus phrases stating your supporting points and subtopics. Roman numerals are used for first-level headings (main supporting points), capital letters for second-level headings (subtopics of supporting points), and numbers for third-level headings (details supporting subtopics). This type of outline differs from a *working outline* diagram as you have seen elsewhere in this book; it is a formalized, hierarchical display of the arrangement of your points and support. A sentence outline may follow the same pattern but will contain complete sentences.

Preparing and revising a second draft of your research paper is essential for two reasons. First, research papers usually have a significant mark-value, and, second, instructors may make significant deductions for documentation, language, usage, and mechanical errors. Be especially careful with proofreading your revision. Correct sentence-skills and mechanical errors; use your dictionary as well as your computer's spell checker to catch spelling errors.

Always leave yourself at least one day between your revising, editing, and proofreading and the writing of your final draft. You will see your content with a clearer eye, and you may spot errors that previously eluded you.

You now have the fundamentals for conducting research, assembling a paper, and documenting your sources. On the pages that follow, you will find a model research paper, in the MLA style, showing how all the steps in the research process come together in the final draft of a paper.

Model Title Page

FOLLOW THE MLA-STYLE SAMPLES BELOW. (WHILE A TITLE PAGE AND OUTLINE ARE NOT SPECIFICALLY REQUIRED, ACCORDING TO THE MLA HANDBOOK, YOUR INSTRUCTOR MAY ASK YOU TO INCLUDE THESE.)

[1]THE TITLE SHOULD BEGIN ABOUT ONE-THIRD OF THE WAY DOWN THE PAGE. CENTRE AND DOUBLE SPACE THE TITLE. LEAVE EXTRA SPACE BETWEEN THE TITLE AND YOUR NAME. ALSO, CENTRE AND DOUBLE SPACE THE INSTRUCTOR'S NAME AND THE DATE.

Successful Families:

Fighting for Their Kids[1]

by

Sonya Phillips

English 101

Professor Lessig

5 May 2008

Model First Page with a Top Heading

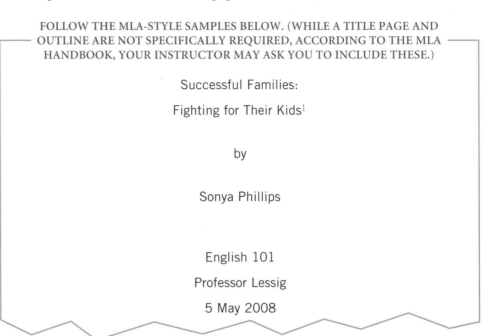

↑ 1 INCH

↑ ½ INCH

Phillips 1

[2]FOR A PAPER WITHOUT A TITLE PAGE OR OUTLINE, USE A TOP HEADING ON THE FIRST PAGE.

Sonya Phillips

Professor Lessig

English 101

5 May 2008[2]

Successful Families: Fighting for Their Kids

It is a terrible time to be a teenager, or even a teenager's parent.

[3]DOUBLE SPACE BETWEEN LINES. LEAVE A ONE-INCH MARGIN ON ALL SIDES.

[3]That message is everywhere. The TV, the magazines, and the newspapers are all full of frightening stories about teenagers and families. They say that North American families are falling apart, that kids do not care about anything, and that parents have trouble doing anything. . . .

Model Outline Page

Outline[5]

Thesis: Although these are difficult times to be raising teenagers, successful families are finding ways to cope with the challenges.

I. Meeting the challenge of spending quality time together

    A. Barriers to spending quality time

        1. Increased working hours

        2. Rising divorce rates

        3. Women in work force

    B. Danger of lack of quality time

    C. Ways found to spend time together

        1. Working less and scaling back lifestyle

        2. Home schooling allows some families to spend more time together

II. Meeting the challenge of creating sense of community

    A. Lack of traditional community ties

    B. Ways found to create sense of community

        1. Intentional communities

        2. Religious ties

III. Meeting the challenge of limiting the negative impact of media and technology

    A. Negative impact of media and technology

        1. Creation of environment without protection

        2. Flood of uncontrolled, inappropriate information

    B. Ways of controlling media and technology

        1. Banning TV

        2. Using technology in beneficial ways

[4]AFTER THE TITLE PAGE, NUMBER ALL PAGES IN UPPER-RIGHT CORNER A HALF-INCH FROM THE TOP. PLACE YOUR NAME BEFORE THE PAGE NUMBER. USE SMALL ROMAN NUMERALS ON OUTLINE PAGES. USE ARABIC NUMBERS ON PAGES FOLLOWING THE OUTLINE.

[5]THE WORD *OUTLINE* (WITHOUT UNDERLINING OR QUOTATION MARKS) IS CENTRED ONE INCH FROM THE TOP. DOUBLE SPACE BETWEEN LINES. LEAVE A ONE-INCH MARGIN ON ALL SIDES.

Model Research Paper

NOTE TITLE ONLY
IF A SEPARATE
TITLE PAGE IS
INCLUDED.

⁶DOUBLE SPACE
BETWEEN LINES
OF THE TEXT.
LEAVE A ONE-INCH
MARGIN ALL THE
WAY AROUND THE
PAGE. YOUR NAME
AND THE PAGE
NUMBER APPEAR
AS A HEADER HALF
AN INCH FROM
THE TOP OF THE
PAGE.

⁷COMMON
KNOWLEDGE
IS NOT
DOCUMENTED.

⁸A TYPICAL
CITATION
CONSISTS OF
THE AUTHOR'S
LAST NAME OR
(IF NO AUTHOR IS
PROVIDED) THE
TITLE OF THE
SOURCE (AND IF
RELEVANT, A PAGE
NUMBER). THE
"WORKS CITED"
PROVIDES FULL
INFORMATION
ABOUT THE
SOURCE.

Phillips 1

Successful Families: Fighting for Their Kids[6]

It is a terrible time to be a teenager, or even a teenager's parent. That message is everywhere. The TV, the magazines, and the newspapers are all full of frightening stories about teenagers and families. They say that North American families are falling apart, that kids do not care about anything, and that parents have trouble doing anything about it.[7] Bookstores are full of scary-sounding titles like these: <u>Teenage Wasteland</u>, <u>Cold New World</u>, <u>A Tribe Apart</u>, and <u>Teen Torment</u>. These books describe teenage problems that include apathy, violence, suicide, sexual abuse, depression, loss of values, poor mental health, teen crime, gang involvement, and drug and alcohol addiction.

Naturally, caring parents are worried by all this. According to a 2004 Ipsos-Reid poll sponsored by <u>The Globe and Mail</u>, less than half of Canadian parents feel they are doing a better job of raising their teenagers than their parents did ("Parents").[8] But leaving aside globally popular Canadian shows like <u>DeGrassi: The Next Generation</u>, most popular TV shows do not give a realistic view of North American teens, so these frightening books and depressing statistics do not provide a complete picture of what is going on in families today. The fact is that *not* all teens and families are lost and without values. While they struggle with problems in our culture like everyone else, successful families, especially families from Canada's diverse newer cultures, are doing what they have always done: finding ways to protect and nurture their children. They are fighting the battle for their families in three ways: by fighting against the loss of quality family time, by fighting against

Phillips 2

the loss of community, and by fighting against the influence of the

media and technology.[9]

It is true that these days, parents face more challenges than

ever before when it comes to finding quality time to spend with

their children. Economist Edward Wolff[10] explains the loss of time:

> [11]Over a thirty-year time span, parental time has declined
> 13 percent. The time parents have available for their
> children has been squeezed by the rapid shift of mothers
> into the paid labour force, by escalating divorce rates and
> the subsequent abandonment of children by their fathers,
> and by an increase in the number of hours required on the
> job. The average worker is now at work 163 hours a year
> more than in 1969, which adds up to an extra month of
> work annually (qtd.[12] in Hewlett and West 48).

As a result, more children are at home alone than ever before. And

this situation does leave children vulnerable to getting in trouble.

Numerous studies show that children who are home alone after

school are twice as likely to experiment with drugs and alcohol

than children who have a parent (or another adult) home in the

after-school hours.

Yet, creative parents still come up with ways to be there for

their kids. For some, it has been a matter of cutting back on

working hours and living more simply. For example, in her book

<u>The Shelter of Each Other</u>, Mary Pipher[13] tells the story of a

couple with three-year-old twin boys. Edwardo worked sixty-hour

weeks at a factory. Sabrina supervised checkers at a K-Mart, cared

for the boys, and tried to watch over her mother, who had cancer.

Money was tight, especially since daycare was expensive, and

the parents felt they had to keep the twins stylishly dressed and

supplied with new toys. The parents were stressed over money

problems, their lack of time together, and especially having so

[9]THESIS, FOLLOWED BY PLAN OF DEVELOPMENT.

[10]SOURCE IS IDENTIFIED BY NAME AND AREA OF EXPERTISE.

[11]DIRECT QUOTATIONS OF FOUR TYPED LINES OR MORE ARE SINGLE-SPACED AND INDENTED TEN SPACES FROM THE LEFT MARGIN. QUOTATION MARKS ARE NOT USED.

[12]THE ABBREVIATION *QTD.* MEANS *QUOTED.* NO COMMA IS USED BETWEEN THE AUTHORS' NAMES AND THE PAGE NUMBER.

[13]WHEN CITING A WORK IN GENERAL, NOT A PART OF THE WORK, IT IS BEST TO INCLUDE THE AUTHOR'S NAME IN THE TEXT INSTEAD OF USING A PARENTHETICAL CITATION. NO PAGE NUMBER IS NEEDED AS THE CITATION REFERS TO THE FINDINGS OF THE STUDY OVERALL.

Phillips 3

[14]ONLY THE PAGE NUMBER IS NEEDED AS THE AUTHOR HAS ALREADY BEEN NAMED IN THE TEXT.

[15]QUOTATION MARKS ACKNOWLEDGE THE PHRASE IS COPIED FROM PREVIOUS CITATION.

[16]THE CAPITAL LETTER IN BRACKETS SHOWS THE WORD WAS CAPITALIZED BY THE STUDENT BUT DID NOT BEGIN THE SENTENCE IN THE ORIGINAL SOURCE.

[17]THE SPACED PERIODS (ELLIPSES) SHOW THAT MATERIAL FROM THE ORIGINAL SOURCE HAS BEEN OMITTED.

[18]AUTHOR AND PAGE NUMBER, WITH NO COMMA.

little time with their boys. It bothered them that the twins had begun to cry when their parents picked them up at daycare, as if they would rather stay with the daycare workers. Finally, Sabrina and Edwardo made a difficult decision. Sabrina quit her job, and the couple invited her mother (whose illness was in remission) to live with them. With the three adults pooling their resources, Sabrina and Edwardo found that they could manage without Sabrina's salary. The family no longer ate out, and they gave up their cable TV. Their sons loved having their grandmother in the house. Sabrina was able to begin doing relaxed, fun projects with the boys. They planted a garden and built a sandbox together. Sabrina observed, "I learned I could get off the merry-go-round" (195).[14] Other parents have "gotten off the merry-go-round"[15] by working at home, even if it means less money than they had previously. "[H]eading[16] home is a real possibility for those parents who can master the new home-office technology. . . ."[17] If enough people can manage to do this, the neighbourhoods might once again come alive for workers and their children" (Louv 285).[18]

Some parents even home-school their children as a way to be sure they have plenty of time together. Home schooling used to be thought of as a choice made only by very religious people or back-to-nature radicals. In Canada, home schooling is sometimes now called home-based learning, or HBL. HBL, or "deschooling" or "unschooling," is so popular that provincial governments have issued guidelines for parents, and the HBL central organization sponsors an extensive website full of resources including online courses and information for parents (Canadian Home-Based Learning). Home-based learning is seen by its adherents as a superior form of education. Some Canadian universities even have

Phillips 4

admissions officers whose job it is to review applications from home-schooled students. Parents who home-school have different reasons, but, according to a cover story in <u>Newsweek</u>, "Some . . . are looking for a way to reclaim family closeness in an increasingly fast-paced society. . . . Still others worry about unsavoury influences in school—drugs, alcohol, sex, violence" (Kantrowitz and Wingert 66). Home schooling is no guarantee that a child will resist those temptations, but some families do believe it is a great way to promote family closeness. One fifteen-year-old, home-schooled since kindergarten, explained why he liked the way he had been raised and educated. He ended by saying, "Another way I'm different is that I love my family. One guy asked me if I'd been brainwashed. I think it's spooky that liking my family is considered crazy" (Pipher 103).

Quitting their jobs or teaching children at home are things that many parents cannot do. However, other parents find a second way to nurture their children through building community ties. They help their children develop a healthy sense of belonging by creating links with positive, constructive people and activities. In the past, community was not so hard to find. In <u>The Way We Really Are</u>, author Stephanie Coontz writes, "Right up through the 1940s, ties of work, friendship, neighborhood, ethnicity, extended kin, and voluntary organizations were as important a source of identity for most Americans, and sometimes a <u>more</u> important source of obligation, than marriage and the nuclear family" (37). Even when today's parents were teenagers, neighbourhoods were places where children and teens felt a sense of belonging and responsibility. Today, in many parts of Canada, parents miss what one study calls "the centrality of family." This centrality meant that "family time was an extremely important aspect of

Phillips 5

their lives and their leisure . . .[19] that family comes first" (Tirone). Webs of relatives gave children and teens a sense of belonging and provided parents with a sense of security. Today's parents fear their children may grow up isolated and dependent on media products for companionship and guidance.

One way that some families are trying to build old-fashioned community is through "intentional community" or "cohousing." Begun in Denmark in 1972, the cohousing movement is modelled after the traditional village. It brings together a number of families who livein separate houses but share some common space. For instance, families might share central meeting rooms, dining areas, gardens, daycare, workshops, or office space. They might own tools and lawn mowers together rather than each household having its own. The point is that they treat their neighbours as extended family, not as strangers. The Canadian Cohousing Network states on its site that "Cohousing provides personal privacy combined with the benefits of living in a community where people know and interact with their neighbours" ("Cohousing").[20] More than twenty such communities currently exist in Canada.

Other families turn to religion as a source of community. Michael and Diane Medved, authors of Saving Childhood, are raising their family in a religious Jewish home. Their children attend Jewish schools, go to synagogue, and follow religious customs. They frequently visit, eat, play with, and are cared for by neighbouring Jewish families. The Medveds believe their family is stronger because of their belief "in planting roots—in your home, in your family, in your community. That involves making a commitment, making an investment both physically and emotionally, in your surroundings" (Medved and Medved 200). Other religious traditions

[19]ELLIPSES SHOW WHERE THE STUDENT HAS OMITTED MATERIAL FROM THE ORIGINAL SOURCE. THE QUOTED MATERIAL IS NOT CAPITALIZED BECAUSE THE STUDENT HAS BLENDED IT INTO A SENTENCE WITH AN INTRODUCTORY PHRASE.

[20]CITATION FOR AN ONLINE SOURCE. NO PAGE NUMBER IS GIVEN BECAUSE THE ONLINE DOCUMENT DOES NOT PROVIDE IT.

Phillips 6

[21]QUOTED
MATERIAL
EXTENDS FROM
ONE PAGE TO
ANOTHER, SO
BOTII PAGE
NUMBERS ARE
GIVEN.

offer a similar sense of community, purpose, and belonging for a family. Marcus and Tracy Glover are members of the Nation of Islam. They credit the Nation with making their marriage and family strong and breaking a three-generation cycle of single motherhood (Hewlett and West 201–202).[21]

A final way that families are fighting to protect their children is by controlling the impact of the media and technology. Authors Hewlett and West and Pipher use similar words to describe the effect of this impact. As they describe growing up today, Hewlett and West write about children living "without a skin" (xiii), and Pipher writes about "houses without walls" (12). The authors mean that unlike in the old days, when children were protected from the outside world while they were in the home, there is little such protection today. Even in their own living rooms, children only have to turn on a TV, radio, or computer to be hit with a flood of violence and sick humour. Children are growing up watching programs like The Osbournes, a program that celebrates two spoiled, foul-mouthed children and their father, a burnt-out rocker slowed by decades of drug abuse. Sadly, many parents seem to have given up even trying to protect their growing kids against garbage like this. Canadian parents are blessed with children's programming that has been shown all over the world, but Canadian children prefer soaps, music videos, wrestling, and Home Shopping. Canadian parents are like the mother quoted in USA Today as saying, "How can I fight five hundred channels on TV?" (Donahue DI).

Fortunately, other parents are still insisting on control over the information and entertainment that comes into their homes. Some limit their children to public TV stations like Ontario's TVO; others subscribe to "The Television Project," an online educational

Phillips 7

organization that helps parents "understand how television affects their families and community and propose alternatives that foster positive emotional, cognitive, and spiritual development within families and communities." Others ban TV entirely from their homes. More try to find a way to use TV and other electronics as useful tools but not allow them to dominate their homes. One American family, the Millers, who home-school their children, described to Mary Pipher their attitude towards TV. They had not owned a TV for years but purchased one to watch the Olympics. The set is stored in a closet unless a program is on that the family agrees is worthwhile. Some programs the family has enjoyed together include the World Cup soccer games, the TV drama Sarah Plain and Tall, and an educational TV course in sign language. Pipher was impressed by the Miller children, and she thought their limited exposure to TV was one reason why. In her words:

> Calm, happy children and relaxed, confident parents are so rare today. Probably most notable were the long attention spans of the children and their willingness to sit and listen to the grown-ups talk. The family had a manageable amount of information to deal with. They weren't stressed by more information than they could assimilate. The kids weren't overstimulated and edgy. Nor were they sexualized in the way most kids now are (107).

Pipher's words describe children raised by parents who will not give in to the idea that their children are lost. Such parents structure ways to be present in the home, build family ties to a community, and control the impact of the media and technology in their homes. Through their efforts, they succeed in raising nurtured, grounded, successful children. Such parents acknowledge the challenges of raising kids in today's Canada, but they are up to the job.[22]

[22]THE CONCLUSION PROVIDES A SUMMARY AND RESTATES THE THESIS.

"WORKS CITED" LIST SHOULD BE DOUBLE-SPACED. TITLES OF BOOKS, MAGAZINES, AND THE LIKE SHOULD BE UNDERLINED.

Phillips 8

Works Cited

"A Lot Easier Said Than Done: Parents Talk About Raising Children
      in Today's America." <u>Public Agenda</u>. Oct. 2002. 8 Mar. 2008
      <http://www.publicagenda.org/specials/parents/parents1.htm>.

<u>Canadian Home-Based Learning Resource Page</u>. 2001. 12 Mar. 2008[23]
      <http://www.flora.org/homeschool-ca/>.

Coontz, Stephanie. <u>The Way We Really Are</u>. New York: Basic Books, 1997.

Donahue, Deirdre. "Struggling to Raise Good Kids in Toxic Times." <u>USA
      Today</u> 1 Oct. 1998: D1–D2.

Hewlett, Sylvia Ann, and Cornel West. <u>The War Against Parents</u>. Boston,
      New York: Houghton Mifflin, 1998.

<u>The Intentional Communities Home Page</u>. Fellowship of Intentional
      Communities. 8 Mar. 2008 <http://www.ic.org/>.

Kantrowitz, Barbara, and Pat Wingert. "Learning at Home: Does It Pass
      the Test?" <u>Newsweek</u> 5 Oct. 1998: 64–70.

Louv, Richard. <u>Childhood's Future</u>. Boston: Houghton Mifflin, 1990.

Medved, Michael, and Diane Medved. <u>Saving Childhood</u>. New York:
      HarperCollins/Zondervan, 1998.

"Parents on Parenting: Part IV." <u>Ipsos News Center</u>. April 2004. 10
      Mar. 2008 <http://www.ipsos-na.com/news/pressrelease.cfm?id=
      2117&content=full>.

Pipher, Mary. <u>The Shelter of Each Other</u>. New York: Putnam, 1996.

<u>The Television Project Home Page</u>. The Television Project. 8 Mar. 2008
      <http://www.tvp.org>.

Tirone, Susan. "Leisure and Centrality of Family." <u>Journal of
      Leisurability</u> 24.3 (1997). 10 Mar. 2008 <http://adp.lin.ca/
      resource//html/Vol24/v24n3a3.htm>.

"What is Cohousing?" <u>The Canadian Cohousing Network</u>. Winter 2004.
      10 Mar. 2008 <http://www.cohousing.ca/cohousing.htm>.

[23]INCLUDE THE DATE YOU ACCESSED A WEB SOURCE—IN THIS CASE, MARCH 12, 2004.

SEVERAL OF THESE SOURCES ARE ONLINE. BY GOING TO ANY URL NOTED IN THE CITATIONS, YOU CAN ACCESS ANY OF THE SOURCES.

CHECKLIST OF LEARNING OUTCOMES FOR CHAPTER 19

To ensure that you have understood and met the learning outcomes for this chapter, answer the following questions:

✓ What are the six steps for writing an effective research paper?

✓ What is your first task when you revise your trial outline? What are the two general purposes of research papers?

✓ What are three forms that research notes may take? How many items must be recorded for a note on a book used?

✓ When should you use quotations? When should you paraphrase material? What is one essential feature of a good summary?

✓ What are citation styles, and what does correct documentation tell readers?

✓ Why is a second revision essential for research papers?

CHAPTER 20

Subjects and Verbs

The basic building blocks of English sentences are subjects and verbs. Understanding them is an important first step toward mastering a number of sentence skills.

Every sentence has a subject and a verb. Who or what the sentence speaks about is called the *subject;* what the sentence says about the subject is called the *verb.* In the following sentences, the subject is underlined once and the verb twice:

The boy cried.
That fish smells.
Many people applied for the job.
The show is a documentary.

A Simple Way to Find a Subject

To find a subject, ask *whom* or *what* the sentence is about. As shown below, your answer is the subject.

Whom is the first sentence *about*? The boy.
What is the second sentence *about*? That fish.
Whom is the third sentence *about*? Many people.
What is the fourth sentence *about*? The show.

A Simple Way to Find a Verb

To find a verb, ask what the sentence says *about* the subject. As shown below, your answer is the verb.

What does the first sentence *say about* the boy? He cried.
What does the second sentence *say about* the fish? It smells.
What does the third sentence *say about* the people? They applied.
What does the fourth sentence *say about* the show? It is a documentary.

A second way to find the verb is to put *I, you, he, she, it,* or *they* in front of the word you think is a verb. If the result makes sense, you have a verb. For example, you could put *he* in front of *cried* in the first sentence above, with the result, *he cried,* making sense. Therefore, you know that *cried* is a verb. You could use the same test with the other three verbs as well.

Finally, it helps to remember that most verbs show action. In the sentences already considered, the three action verbs are *cried, smells,* and *applied.* Certain other verbs, known as *linking verbs,* do not show action. They do, however, give information about the subject. In "The show is a documentary," the linking verb *(is)* joins the subject *(show)* with a word that identifies or describes it *(documentary).* Other common linking verbs include *feel, appear, look, become,* and *seem.*

● ● ● ● **Activity**

In each of the following sentences, draw one line under the subject and two lines under the verb.

1. The ripening tomatoes glistened on the sunny windowsill.
2. Acupuncture reduces the pain of my headaches.
3. Elena nervously twisted a strand of hair around her fingers.
4. My brother made his bookshelves from bricks and planks of wood.
5. Damon's website confuses me.
6. My roommate Kerry dries her pantyhose with a hair dryer.
7. The band's lead singer's earrings shone in the spotlights.
8. On St. Patrick's Day, our neighbourhood bar serves green beer.
9. My six-year-old brother lives on a diet of tuna casserole.
10. During my parents' divorce, I felt like a rag doll being torn between two people.

More About Subjects and Verbs

1 A sentence may have more than one verb, more than one subject, or several subjects and verbs.

The <u>engine</u> <u>coughed</u> and <u>sputtered</u>.
Broken <u>glass</u> and empty <u>cans</u> <u>littered</u> the parking lot.
<u>Joyce</u>, <u>Brenda</u>, and <u>Robert</u> <u>met</u> after class and <u>headed</u> downtown.

2 The subject of a sentence never appears within a *prepositional phrase.* A prepositional phrase is simply a group of words that begins with a preposition. Following is a list of common prepositions:

about	before	by	inside	over
above	behind	during	into	through
across	below	except	like	to
among	beneath	for	of	toward
around	beside	from	off	under
at	between	in	on(to)	with

Tip: The word *preposition* contains the word *position.* Many prepositions begin a phrase showing the position of something or someone relative to something else or someone else: for example, "The printer is *beside* the computer."

Crossing out prepositional phrases will help you find the subject or subjects of a sentence.

A <u>stream</u> ~~of cold air~~ <u><u>seeps</u></u> in ~~through the space below the door.~~
<u>Specks</u> ~~of dust~~ <u><u>dance</u></u> gently ~~in a ray of sunlight.~~
The <u>people</u> ~~in the apartment above ours~~ <u><u>fight</u></u> loudly.
The murky <u>waters</u> ~~of the polluted lake~~ <u><u>spilled</u></u> ~~over the dam.~~
The amber <u>lights</u> ~~on its sides~~ <u><u>outlined</u></u> the snowplow ~~in the hazy dusk.~~

3 Many verb forms consist of more than one word. Here, for example, are some of the many forms of the verb *work*:

work	worked	should work
works	were working	will be working
does work	have worked	can work
is working	had worked	could be working
are working	had been working	must have worked

4 Words like *not, just, never, only,* and *always* are not part of the verb, although they may appear within the verb.

Ruby has never liked cold weather.
Our manager will not be working out with us this year.
The intersection has not always been this dangerous.

5 No verb preceded by *to* is ever the main verb of a sentence.

At night, my son likes to read under the covers.
Evelyn decided to separate from her husband.

6 No *-ing* word by itself is ever the verb of a sentence. (It may be part of the verb, but it must have a helping verb in front of it.)

They going on a trip this weekend. (not a sentence because the verb is not complete)
They are going on a trip this weekend. (a sentence)

Activity

Draw a single line under subjects and a double line under verbs. Crossing out prepositional phrases may help you to find the subjects.

1. A great heap of dusty pots and pans covers the top of our refrigerator.

2. In June, sagging Christmas decorations were still hanging in the windows of the abandoned house.

3. The people in the all-night coffee shop seemed weary and lost.

4. Every plant in the dim room bent toward the small window.

5. A glaring headline about the conviction of a local city councillor attracted my attention.

6. Two of the biggest stores in the mall are going out of business.

7. The modem's tiny red lights suddenly started to flicker.

8. A neighbour of mine does all her work at home and e-mails it to her office.

9. The jar of peppercorns tumbled from the spice shelf and shattered on the floor.

10. The scar in the hollow of Brian's throat is the result of an emergency operation to clear his windpipe.

Review Test

Draw a single line under subjects and a double line under verbs. Crossing out prepositional phrases may help you to find the subjects.

1. With one graceful motion, the shortstop fielded the grounder and threw to first base.

2. Like human mothers, sheep and goat mothers develop close bonds with their babies.

3. Before class, Jorge and Aaron rushed to the coffee machine in the hall.

4. I punched and prodded my feather pillow before settling down to sleep.

5. Waiting in the long ticket line, Matt shifted his weight from one foot to the other.

6. Ancient Egyptians were branding cattle more than four thousand years ago.

7. Lilacs and honeysuckle perfume our yard on summer nights.

8. The mail carrier abruptly halted her Jeep and backed up toward the mailbox.

9. During the War of 1812, some Upper Canadian families of German background sold their land and moved to Pennsylvania, where Amish and Mennonite communities formed.

10. Frantic with anxiety, the little girl's family called a psychic to help locate the child.

CHAPTER 21

Fragments

Every sentence must have a subject and a verb and must express a complete thought. A word group that lacks a subject or a verb and that does not express a complete thought is a *fragment*. Following are the most common types of fragments that people write:

1 Dependent-word fragments

2 *-ing* and *to* fragments

3 Added-detail fragments

4 Missing-subject fragments

Once you understand the specific kind or kinds of fragments that you may write, you should be able to eliminate them from your writing. The following pages explain all four fragment types.

Dependent-Word Fragments

Some word groups that begin with a dependent word are fragments. Below is a list of common dependent words. Whenever you start a sentence with one of these words, you must be careful that a fragment does not result.

after	if, even if	when, whenever
although, though	in order that	where, wherever
as	since	whether
because	that, so that	which, whichever
before	unless	while
even though	until	who
how	what, whatever	whose

In the example below, the word group beginning with the dependent word *after* is a fragment:

> After I cashed my paycheque. I treated myself to dinner.

A *dependent statement*—one starting with a dependent word like *after*—cannot stand alone. It depends on another statement to complete the thought. *After I cashed my paycheque* is a dependent statement. It leaves us hanging. We expect in the same sentence to find out *what happened after* the writer cashed the cheque. When a writer does not follow through and complete a thought, a fragment results.

To correct the fragment, simply follow through and complete the thought:

> After I cashed my paycheque, I treated myself to dinner.

Remember, then, that *dependent statements by themselves are fragments*. They must be attached to a statement that makes sense standing alone.

Here are two other examples of dependent-word fragments:

> I won't leave the house. Until I hear from you.
> Rick finally picked up the socks. That he had thrown on the floor days ago.

Until I hear from you is a fragment; it does not make sense standing by itself. We want to know in the same statement *what cannot happen* until I hear from you. The writer must complete the thought. Likewise, *That he had thrown on the floor days ago* is not in itself a complete thought. We want to know in the same statement what *that* refers to.

How to Correct Dependent-Word Fragments

In most cases you can correct a dependent-word fragment by attaching it to the sentence that comes after it or the sentence that comes before it:

> After I cashed my paycheque, I treated myself to dinner.
> (The fragment has been attached to the sentence that comes after it.)

> I won't leave the house until I hear from you.
> (The fragment has been attached to the sentence that comes before it.)

> Rick finally picked up the socks that he had thrown on the floor days ago.
> (The fragment has been attached to the sentence that comes before it.)

Another way of correcting a dependent-word fragment is simply to eliminate the dependent word by rewriting the sentence.

> I cashed my paycheque and then treated myself to dinner.
> I will wait to hear from you.
> He had thrown them on the floor days ago.

Notes

1 Use a comma if a dependent-word group comes at the *beginning* of a sentence (see above):

> After I cashed my paycheque, I treated myself to dinner.

However, do not generally use a comma if the dependent word group comes at the end of a sentence:

> I won't leave the house until I hear from you.
> Rick finally picked up the socks that he had thrown on the floor days ago.

2 Sometimes the dependent words *who, that, which,* or *where* appear not at the very start but *near* the start of a word group. A fragment often results:

> I drove slowly past the old brick house. The place where I grew up.

The place where I grew up is not in itself a complete thought. We want to know in the same statement *where the place was* that the writer grew up. The fragment can be corrected by attaching it to the sentence that comes before it:

> I drove slowly past the old brick house, the place where I grew up.

Activity 1

Turn each of the dependent-word groups into a sentence by adding a complete thought. Use a comma after the dependent-word group if a dependent word starts the sentence. Note the examples.

Examples   Although I felt miserable

Although I felt miserable, I tried to smile for the photographer.

The man who found my wallet

The man who found my wallet returned it the next day.

1. If I don't get a raise soon

_____

2. Because it was raining

_____

3. When I heard the news of the power failure downtown

_____

4. Because I couldn't find the car keys that slid under the seat

_____

5. The restaurant that we tried down the street

_____

Activity 2

Underline the dependent-word fragment in each selection. Then, rewrite the selections, correcting each fragment by attaching it to the sentence that comes before or the sentence that comes after—whichever sounds more natural. Use a comma after the dependent-word group if it starts the sentence.

1. Whenever I use a product that sprays. My cat arches her back. She thinks she is hearing a hissing enemy.

_____

_____

2. My father, a sales representative, was on the road all week. We had a great time playing football in the house. Until he came home for the weekend.

_____

_____

3. If Kim takes too long saying goodbye to her boyfriend. Her father will start flicking the porch light. Then, he will come out with a flashlight.

_____

_____

4. Scientists are studying mummified remains. Some of which are thousands of years old. Most of the people were killed by parasites.

_____

_____

5. Before I turn on the microwave to cook something. I have to turn off the overhead light in the kitchen. Otherwise the circuits overload.

_____

_____

-ing and *to* Fragments

When an *-ing* word appears at or near the start of a word group, a fragment may result. Such fragments often lack a subject and part of the verb. *Doing, walking,* and other such verb forms ending in *ing* are *verbals, not complete verbs;* these words alone cannot be the "true verb" in a sentence. *To do, to receive,* and other *to* forms of verbs are *infinitive forms of verbs, not personal finite forms of verbs;* these must be "limited," or "made finite," as in *we do,* or *they received,* or used in combination with "true verbs."

Underline the word groups in the selections below that contain *-ing* words. Each is a fragment.

1. Ellen walked all over the neighbourhood yesterday. Trying to find her dog Bo. Several people claimed they had seen him only hours before.

2. We sat back to watch the movie. Not expecting anything special. To our surprise, we clapped, cheered, and cried for the next two hours.

3. I telephoned the balloon store. It being the day before our wedding anniversary. I knew my wife would be surprised to receive a dozen heart-shaped balloons.

People sometimes write *-ing* fragments because they think the subject in one sentence will work for the next word group as well. Thus, in the first selection, they think the subject *Ellen* in the opening sentence will also serve as the subject for *Trying to find her dog Bo.* But the subject must actually be *in* the sentence.

How to Correct *-ing* Fragments

1 Attach the fragment to the sentence that comes before or the sentence that comes after it, whichever makes sense. Item 1 could read, "Ellen walked all over the neighbourhood yesterday trying to find her dog Bo."

2 Add a subject and change the *-ing* verb to the "true" form of the verb. Selection 2 could read, "We didn't expect anything special."

3 Change *being* to the "true" form of the verb *be (am, are, is, was, were)*. Selection 3 could read, "It was the day before our wedding anniversary."

How to Correct *to* Fragments

When *to* appears at or near the start of a word group, a fragment sometimes results:

> At the Chinese restaurant, Tim used chopsticks. To impress his date. He spent one hour eating a small bowl of rice.

The second word group is a fragment and can be corrected by adding it to the preceding sentence. The *infinitive* verb form *to impress* has been made part of the "true verb" *used:*

> At the Chinese restaurant, Tim used chopsticks to impress his date.

Activity 1

Underline the *-ing* fragment in each of the selections that follow. Then, make it a sentence by rewriting it, using the method described in parentheses.

Example   Stepping hard on the accelerator. Stan tried to beat the truck to the intersection. He lost by a hood.
(Add the fragment to the sentence that comes after it.)

Stepping hard on the accelerator, Stan tried to beat the truck to

the intersection.

1. Flattening the young plants in the cornfield. Marble-sized hailstones fell from the sky. A year's work was lost in an hour.
(Add the fragment to the preceding sentence.)

_____

_____

2. Fire trucks raced wildly through the streets, their sirens blaring. Coming to a stop at my house. I was only burning a pile of leaves.
(Correct the fragment by adding to it a subject and by changing the verbal to a "true verb" form.)

_____

_____

3. My phone doesn't ring. Instead, a light on it blinks. The reason for this added feature being that I am partially deaf.
(Correct the fragment by changing the verbal to a "true verb" form.)

_____

_____

Activity 2

Underline the *-ing* or *to* fragment in each selection. Then, rewrite each selection, correcting the fragment by using one of the methods described above.

1. Looking with horror at the worm on the table. Shelley groaned. She knew she wouldn't like what the biology instructor said next.

_____

_____

2. I put a box of baking soda in the freezer. To try to get rid of the musty smell that greets me whenever I open it. However, my ice cubes still taste like old socks.

_____

_____

3. Staring at the clock on the far wall, perspiring like a long-distance runner, and shifting from foot to foot. I nervously began my speech. I was afraid to look at any of the people in the room.

_____

_____

4. Fantasizing wildly about the upcoming weekend's activities in a kind of hazy daydream. Winston sat quietly at his desk. He might meet the girl of his dreams at Saturday night's party.

_____

_____

5. To find the only available public transportation around here. You have to walk two blocks out of your way. The endless sidewalk construction continuing throughout the season.

_____

_____

Added-Detail Fragments

Added-detail fragments lack a subject and a verb. They often begin with one of the following words:

| also | especially | except | for example | like | including | such as |

Underline the one added-detail fragment in each of the selections that follow:

1. Before a race, I eat starchy food. Such as bread and pasta. The carbohydrates provide quick energy.

2. Bob is taking a night course in auto mechanics. Also, one in plumbing. He wants to save money on household repairs.

3. My son keeps several pets in his room. Including hamsters, mice, and gerbils.

People often write added-detail fragments for much the same reason they write *-ing* fragments. They think the subject and verb in one sentence will serve for the next word group. But the subject and verb must be in *each* word group.

How to Correct Added-Detail Fragments

1 Attach the fragment to the complete thought that precedes it. Item 1 could read, "Before a race, I eat starchy foods such as bread and pasta."

2 Add a subject and a verb to the fragment to make it a complete sentence. Selection 2 could read, "Bob is taking a night course in auto mechanics. Also, he is taking one in plumbing."

3 Insert the fragment within the preceding sentence. Item 3 could read, "My son keeps several pets, including hamsters, mice, and gerbils, in his room."

Activity 1

Underline the added-detail fragment in each of the selections below. Then, make it a sentence by rewriting it, using the method described in parentheses.

Example   My mother likes watching daytime television shows. Especially quiz shows and soap operas. She doesn't mind commercials.
(Add the fragment to the preceding sentence.)

My mother likes watching daytime television shows, especially quiz

shows and soap operas.

1. Luis works evenings in a video store. He enjoys the fringe benefits. For example, seeing the new movies first.
(Correct the fragment by adding a subject and verb to the fragment.)

_____

_____

2. Bob's fingernails are ragged from years of working as a mechanic. And his fingertips are always black. Like ink pads.
(Add the fragment to the preceding sentence.)

_____

_____

3. Electronic devices keep getting smaller. Such as video cameras and cell phones. Some are so tiny they look like toys.
(Correct the fragment by inserting it into the preceding sentence.)

_____

_____

Activity 2

Underline the added-detail fragment in each selection. Then, rewrite to correct the fragment. Use one of the three methods described above.

1. Left-handed students face problems. For example, right-handed desks that make writing almost impossible. Spiral notebooks can also be uncomfortable to use.

_____

_____

2. Mrs. Daly always wears her lucky clothes to bingo. Such as a blouse printed with four-leaf clovers and dancing dollar signs. She also carries a rhinestone horseshoe.

_____

_____

3. Hundreds of moths were fluttering around the stadium lights. Like large flecks of snow in a blizzard. The thirty-degree weather, though, made this form of precipitation unlikely.

_____

_____

4. Luc buys and sells paper collectors' items. For instance, vintage comic books, trading cards, and movie posters. He sets up a display at local flea markets and fall fairs.

_____

_____

5. I wonder now why I had to learn certain subjects. Such as geometry. No one has ever asked me about the hypotenuse of a triangle.

_____

_____

Missing-Subject Fragments

In each item below, underline the word group in which the subject is missing:

1. Alicia loved getting wedding presents. But hated writing the thank-you notes.

2. Mike has orange pop and potato chips for breakfast. Then, eats more junk food, like root beer, chocolate bars, and cookies, for lunch.

How to Correct Missing-Subject Fragments

1 Attach the fragment to the preceding sentence. Item 1 could read, "Alice loved getting her wedding presents but hated writing the thank-you notes."

2 Add a subject (which can often be a pronoun standing for the subject in the preceding sentence). Selection 2 could read, "Then, he eats more junk food, like root beer, chocolate bars, and cookies, for lunch."

Activity

Underline the missing-subject fragment in each selection. Then, rewrite that part of the selection needed to correct the fragment. Use one of the two methods described above.

1. Every other day, Karen runs three kilometres. Then, does fifty sit-ups. She hasn't lost weight, but she is more muscular.

   _____

   _____

2. I like all kinds of fresh pizza. But refuse, under any conditions, to eat frozen pizzas. The sauce on them is always dried out, and the crust tastes like leather.

   _____

   _____

3. Many people are allergic to seafood. Their mouths swell up and they choke when they eat it by mistake. And can even have trouble breathing or need to go to the emergency ward.

   _____

   _____

4. To distract me, the dentist tugged at the corner of my mouth. Then, jabbed a needle and very speedily injected a pain killer. I hardly felt it.

   _____

   _____

5. Last semester, I took six courses. And worked part-time in a discount drug store, snoozing during some of the late shifts. Now that the term is all over, I don't know how I did it.

   _____

   _____

A Review: How to Check for Sentence Fragments

1   Read your paper aloud from the *last* sentence to the *first*. You will be better able to see and hear whether each word group you read is a complete thought.

2   Ask yourself of any word group you think is a fragment: Does this contain a subject and a verb and express a complete thought?

3   More specifically, be on the lookout for the most common fragments:
   • Dependent-word fragments (starting with words like *after, because, since, when,* and *before*)
   • *-ing* and *to* fragments (*-ing* or *to* at or near the start of a word group)
   • Added-detail fragments (starting with words like *for example, such as, also,* and *especially*)
   • Missing-subject fragments (a verb is present but not the subject)

■   Review Test 1

Each word group in the following student paragraph is numbered. In the space provided, write *C* if a word group is a complete sentence; write *F* if it is a fragment. You will find eight fragments in the paragraph.

_____ 1.
_____ 2.
_____ 3.
_____ 4.
_____ 5.
_____ 6.
_____ 7.
_____ 8.
_____ 9.
_____ 10.
_____ 11.
_____ 12.
_____ 13.
_____ 14.
_____ 15.
_____ 16.
_____ 17.
_____ 18.
_____ 19.
_____ 20.

¹I'm starting to think that there is no safe place left. ²To ride a bicycle. ³When I try to ride on the highway, in order to go to school. ⁴I feel like a rabbit being pursued by predators. ⁵Drivers whip past me at high speeds. ⁶And try to see how close they can get to my bike without actually killing me. ⁷When they pull onto the shoulder of the road or make a right turn. ⁸Drivers completely ignore my vehicle. ⁹On city streets, I feel more like a cockroach than a rabbit. ¹⁰Drivers in the city despise bicycles. ¹¹Regardless of an approaching bike rider. ¹²Doors of parked cars will unexpectedly open into the street. ¹³Frustrated drivers who are stuck in traffic will make nasty comments.

¹⁴Or shout out obscene propositions. ¹⁵Even pedestrians in the city show their disregard for me. ¹⁶While jaywalking across the street. ¹⁷The pedestrian will treat me, a law-abiding bicyclist, to a withering look of disdain. ¹⁸Pedestrians may even cross my path deliberately. ¹⁹As if to prove their higher position in the pecking order of the city streets. ²⁰Today, bicycling can be hazardous to the rider's health.

Now (on separate paper) correct the fragments you have found. Attach the fragments to sentences that come before or after them, or make whatever other change is needed to turn each fragment into a sentence.

▪ Review Test 2

Underline the two fragments in each item below. Then, make whatever changes are needed to turn the fragments into sentences.

Example   Sharon was going to charge her new suit. ^*b* ~~But then decided to~~

~~pay cash instead.~~ She remembered her New Year's resolution.

^*t* ~~To cut down on her use of credit cards.~~

1. We both began to tire. As we passed the halfway mark in the race. But whenever I heard Reggie's footsteps behind me. I pumped my legs faster.

2. I have a few phobias. Such as fear of heights and fear of dogs. My nightmare is to be trapped in a hot-air balloon. With three German shepherds.

3. My children joke that we celebrate "Hanumas." With our Jewish neighbours. We share Hanukkah and Christmas activities. Including making potato pancakes at their house and decorating our tree.

4. Punching all the buttons on his radio in sequence. Phil kept looking for a good song. He was in the mood to cruise down the highway. And sing at the top of his voice.

5. I noticed two cartons of cigarettes. Sticking up out of my neighbour's garbage bag. I realized he had made up his mind. To give up smoking for the fifth time this year.

6. I've decided to leave home. And rent an apartment. By being away from home and on my own. I will get along better with my parents.

7. The alley behind our house was flat. Except for a wide groove in the centre. We used to sail paper boats down the groove. Whenever it rained hard enough to create a "river" there.

8. Don passed the computer school's aptitude test. Which qualifies him for nine months of training. Don kidded that anyone could be accepted. If he or she had four thousand dollars.

▪ Review Test 3

Turn each of the following word groups into a complete sentence.

Examples   With trembling hands

With trembling hands, I headed for the front of the classroom.

As the race wore on

Some runners dropped out as the race wore on.

1. After the storm passed

     _____

2. Such as fresh fruits and vegetables

     _____

3. During the mystery movie

     _____

4. But soon grew frustrated

     _____

5. Nico, who works at his uncle's restaurant

     _____

6. To get to class on time

     _____

7. The ants swarming over the lollipop

     _____

8. Hurrying to get dressed

     _____

9. Up in the attic

     _____

10. Losing my temper

     _____

CHAPTER 22

Run-Ons

What are Run-Ons?

A *run-on* is two complete thoughts that are run together with no adequate sign given to mark the break between them.*

Some run-ons have no punctuation at all to mark the break between the thoughts. Such run-ons are known as *fused sentences:* they are fused, or joined together, as if they were only one thought.

Fused Sentences

Mario told everyone in the room to be quiet his favourite show was on.
My blow-dryer overheated and shut off I showed up for work with clown-hair.

In other run-ons, known as *comma splices,* a comma is used to connect, or "splice" together, the two complete thoughts. However, a comma alone is *not enough* to connect two complete thoughts. Some stronger connection than a comma alone is needed.

Comma Splices

Mario told everyone in the room to be quiet, his favourite show was on.
My blow-dryer overheated and shut off, I showed up for work with clown-hair.

Comma splices are the most common kind of run-on. Students sense that some kind of connection is needed between two thoughts, so they often put a comma at the dividing point. Again, however, the comma alone is not sufficient. A comma is simply a punctuation pause-mark, which cannot join ideas. A stronger, clearer mark is needed between the two complete thoughts.

*__Note:__ Some instructors refer to each complete thought in a run-on as an *independent clause.* A *clause* is simply a group of words having a subject and a verb. A clause may be *independent* (expressing a complete thought and able to stand alone) or *dependent* (not expressing a complete thought and not able to stand alone). Using this terminology, we would say that a run-on is two independent clauses run together with no adequate sign given to mark the break between them.

Words that Can Lead to Run-Ons: People often write run-ons when the second complete thought begins with one of the following words:

I	we	there	now
you	they	this	then
he, she, it	that	next	

Remember to be on the alert for run-ons whenever you use one of these words in your writing.

How to Correct Run-Ons

Here are three common methods of correcting a run-on:

1 Use a period and a capital letter to break the two complete thoughts into separate sentences:

> Mario told everyone in the room to be quiet. His favourite show was on.
> My blow-dryer overheated and shut off. I showed up for work with clown-hair.

2 Use a comma plus a joining word (*and, but, for, or, nor, so, yet*) to connect the two complete thoughts:

> Mario told everyone in the room to be quiet, for his favourite show was on.
> My blow-dryer overheated and shut off, and I showed up for work with clown-hair.

3 Use a semicolon to connect the two complete thoughts:

> Mario told everyone in the room to be quiet; his favourite show was on.
> My blow-dryer overheated and shut off; I showed up for work with clown-hair.

A semicolon is a form of "punctuation glue." It can join two independent parts of a sentence without a joining word.

A fourth method of correcting a run-on is to use *subordination*. The following activities will give you practice in the first three methods. Subordination is described on pages 102–103 and on page 346.

Method 1: Period and a Capital Letter

One way of correcting a run-on is to use a period and a capital letter between the two complete thoughts. Use this method especially if the thoughts are not closely related or if another method would make the sentence too long.

Activity

In each of the following run-ons, locate the point at which one complete thought ends and another begins. Each is a *fused sentence*—that is, each consists of two sentences fused, or joined together, with no punctuation at all between them. Reading each sentence aloud will help you "hear" where a major break or split between the thoughts occurs. At such a point, your voice will probably drop and pause.

Correct the run-on by putting a period at the end of the first thought and a capital letter at the start of the next thought.

$$S$$

Example   Rena's clock radio doesn't work anymore. she spilled a glass of pop on it.

1. The men at the door claimed to have paving material left over from another job they wanted to pave our driveway for a "bargain price."

2. Linh, a legal assistant who speaks Vietnamese, helps other people from her country write wills she assists others by going with them when they have to appear in court.

3. Vicky has her own style of dressing she wore a tuxedo with a red bow tie to her cousin's wedding.

4. In the summer, ants are attracted to water they will often enter a house through the dishwasher.

5. Humans have managed to adapt to any environment they can survive in Arctic wastes, tropical jungles, and barren deserts.

6. A five-year-old child knows over six thousand words he or she has also learned more than one thousand rules of grammar.

7. I rummaged around the crowded drawer looking for a pair of scissors they suddenly stabbed me in the finger.

8. Squirrels like to jump from a tree onto our roof their footsteps sound like ghosts running around our attic.

Method 2: Comma and a Joining Word

Another way of correcting a run-on is to use a comma plus a joining word to connect the two complete thoughts. Joining words (also called *conjunctions*) include *and, but, for, or, nor, so,* and *yet.* Here is what the four most common joining words mean:

and   in addition

Teresa works full-time for an accounting firm, and she takes evening classes.

(*and* means "in addition": Teresa works full-time for an accounting firm; *in addition,* she takes evening classes.)

but   however, on the other hand

I turned to the want ads, but I knew my dream job wouldn't be listed.

(*but* means "however": I turned to the want ads; *however,* I knew my dream job wouldn't be listed.)

for   because

Lizards become sluggish at night, for they need the sun's warmth to maintain an active body temperature.

(*for* means "because": Lizards become sluggish at night *because* they need the sun's warmth to maintain an active body temperature.)

so   as a result, therefore

The canoe touched bottom, so Dave pushed it toward deeper water.

(*so* means "as a result": The canoe touched bottom; *as a result,* Dave pushed it toward deeper water.)

Activity 1

Insert the joining word *(and, but, for, so)* that logically connects the two thoughts in each sentence.

1. Napoleon may have been a brave general, _____ he was afraid of cats.

2. The large dog was growling at me, _____ there were white bubbles of foam around his mouth.

3. The library had just closed, _____ I couldn't get any of the reserved books.

4. He checked on the new baby every five minutes, _____ he was afraid something would happen to her.

5. Kate thought the milk was fresh, _____ it broke up into little sour flakes in her coffee.

6. Elephants have no thumbs, _____ baby elephants suck their trunks.

7. Lorne heard a noise and looked out the window, _____ the only thing there was his reflection.

8. Although I like most creatures, I am not fond of snakes, _____ I like spiders even less.

Activity 2

Add a complete and closely related thought to go with each of the following statements. Use a comma plus the joining word in parentheses when you write the second thought.

Example   I decided to leave school an hour early, (for) *for I had a pounding headache.*

1. The corner store is convenient, (but) _____

_____

2. Leo attended night class, (for) _____

_____

3. Aisha studied for an hour before dinner, (and) _____

_____

4. Paul can't retrieve his e-mail, (so) _____

_____

5. I needed a haircut, (but) _____

_____

● ● ● **Activity 3**

Correct each run-on with either (1) a period and a capital letter or (2) a comma and a logical joining word. Do not use the same method of correction for every sentence.

Some of the run-ons are *fused sentences* (there is no punctuation between the two complete thoughts), and some are *comma splices* (there is only a comma between the two complete thoughts).

Example   There was a strange odour in the house, *so* Steve called the gas company immediately. ∧

1. Luis got a can of pop from the refrigerator then he walked outside to sit on the porch steps.

2. Cockroaches adapt to any environment they have even been found living inside nuclear reactors.

3. My dog was panting from the heat I decided to wet him down with the garden hose.

4. Our Environmental Studies class is working on a weather project with students from Russia we communicate by computer almost every day.

5. The best-selling items in the zoo gift shop are the stuffed pandas and the polar bear T-shirts the profits from these items help support the real animals in the zoo.

6. The bristles of the paintbrushes were very stiff, soaking them in turpentine made them soft again.

7. Tri Lee borrows CDs from the library to listen to on the way to work, some are music, and some are recordings of best-selling books.

8. Last week, Rita's two boys chased the babysitter out of the house, now, the girl won't come back.

Method 3: Semicolon

A third method of correcting a run-on is to use a *semicolon* to mark the break between two thoughts. A semicolon (;) looks like a period above a comma. It signals more of a pause than a comma alone but not quite the full pause of a period. When it is used to correct run-ons, the semicolon can be used alone or with a transitional word.

Semicolon Alone: Here are some earlier sentences that were connected with a comma plus a joining word. Now, they are connected by a semicolon alone. Notice that the semicolon alone—unlike the comma alone—can be used to connect the two complete thoughts in each sentence:

> Lorne heard a noise and looked out the window; the only thing there was his reflection.

> He checked on the new baby every five minutes; he was afraid something would happen to her.

> Lizards become sluggish at night; they need the sun's warmth to maintain an active body temperature.

> The large dog was growling at me; there were white bubbles of foam around his mouth.

Using semicolons can also add to sentence variety.

Activity

Insert a semicolon where the break occurs between the two complete thoughts in each of the following sentences.

Example   The plumber gave me an estimate of $150; I decided to repair the tap myself.

1. The children stared at the artichokes on their plates they didn't know how to eat the strange vegetable.

2. The Great Wall of China is immense it's the only architectural structure visible from the moon.

3. Elaine woke up at 3 a.m. to the smell of sizzling bacon her husband was having another insomnia attack.

4. Bissan curled up under the covers she tried to get warm by grasping her icy feet with her chilly hands.

5. Ice had formed on the inside edge of our window Joey scratched a *J* in it with his finger.

6. Charles peered into the microscope he saw only his own eyelashes.

Semicolon with a Transitional Word: A semicolon can be used with a transitional word and a comma to join two complete thoughts. Here are some examples:

Larry believes in being prepared for emergencies; therefore, he stockpiles canned goods in his basement.

I tried to cash my paycheque; however, I had forgotten to bring identification.

Athletic shoes must fit perfectly; otherwise, the wearer may injure his or her feet or ankles.

A short nap at the end of the day relaxes me; in addition, it gives me the energy to spend the evening on my homework.

Some zoo animals have not learned how to be good parents; as a result, baby animals are sometimes brought up in zoo nurseries and even in private homes.

People use seventeen muscles when they smile; on the other hand, they use forty-three muscles when they frown.

Following is a list of common transitional words (also known as *adverbial conjunctions*), with brief meanings.

Transitional Word	*Meaning*
however	but
nevertheless	however
on the other hand	however
instead	as a substitute
meanwhile	in the intervening time
otherwise	under other conditions
indeed	in fact
in addition	also, and
also	in addition
moreover	in addition
furthermore	in addition
as a result	thus, therefore
thus	as a result
consequently	as a result
therefore	as a result

● ● ● Activity

For each sentence, choose a logical transitional word from the box above, and write it in the space provided. Use a semicolon *before* the connector and a comma *after* it.

Example   I dread going to parties; _____*however,*_____ my husband loves meeting new people.

1. Jasmine suffers from migraine headaches _____ her doctor has advised her to avoid caffeine and alcohol.

2. Ray's apartment is always neat and clean _____ the interior of his car looks like the aftermath of a tornado.

3. I try to attend all my math classes _____ I'll get too far behind to pass the weekly quizzes.

4. B.J. was singing Nelly Furtado tunes in the shower _____ his toast was burning in the kitchen.

5. The reporter was tough and experienced _____ even he was stunned by the tragic events.

A Note on Subordination

A fourth method of joining related thoughts is to use *subordination*. Subordination is a way of showing that one thought in a sentence is not as important as another thought. (Review the description of subordination on pages 102–103.) Below are three earlier sentences, recast so that one idea is subordinated to (made less important than) the other idea. In each case, the subordinate (or less important) thought is underlined. Note that each subordinate clause begins with a dependent word.

Because the library had just closed, I couldn't get any of the reserved books.

When the canoe touched bottom, Dave pushed the craft toward deeper water.

I didn't make good time driving to work today because every traffic light was red.

A Review: How to Check for Run-Ons

1 To see if a sentence is a run-on, read it aloud and listen for a break marking two complete thoughts. Your voice will probably drop and pause at the break.

2 To check an entire paper, read it aloud from the last sentence to the first. Doing so will help you hear and see each complete thought.

3 Be on the lookout for words that can lead to run-on sentences:

I	he, she, it	they	this	then	now
you	we	there	that	next	

4 Correct run-ons by using one of the following methods:
- Period and a capital letter
- Comma and a joining word (*and, but, for, or, nor, so, yet*)
- Semicolon alone or with a transitional word
- Subordination

Review Test 1

Correct each run-on with either (1) a period and a capital letter or (2) a comma (if needed) and the joining word *and, but, for,* or *so.* Do not use the same method of correction for every sentence.

Some of the run-ons are fused sentences (no punctuation between the two complete thoughts), and some are comma splices (only a comma between the two complete thoughts). One sentence is correct.

1. Our boss expects us to work four hours without a break, he wanders off to a vending machine at least once an hour.

2. The children in the next car were making faces at other drivers, when I made a face back the youngsters giggled and sank out of sight.

3. Joel bent over and lifted the heavy tray then he heard an ominous crack in his back.

4. The branches of the tree were bare they made a dark feathery pattern against the orange-pink sunset.

5. In the grimy bakery window, cobwebs were in every corner, and a mouse was crawling over a birthday cake.

6. Our class wanted to do something for the tsunami victims, we sent a donation to the Red Cross.

7. Aunt Jeanne wanted to live in a warmer climate for her health she moved to Vancouver.

8. The average Canadian teenager spends thirty-eight hours a week on schoolwork the average Japanese teenager spends about sixty.

Review Test 2

Correct each run-on by using (1) a period and a capital letter, (2) a comma and a joining word, or (3) a semicolon. Do not use one method exclusively.

1. The magazine had lain in the damp mailbox for two days its pages were blurry and swollen.

2. With a groan, Marisa pried off her high heels, then, she plunged her swollen feet into a bucket of baking soda and hot water.

3. Hypnosis has nothing to do with the occult it is merely a state of deep relaxation.

4. Many young adults today live at home with their parents this allows them to save money for the future.

5. I waited for the clanking train to clear the intersection rusty boxcars just kept rolling slowly along the rails.

6. The real Laura Secord had nothing to do with chocolate, she was a brave woman who ran through the forests of southern Ontario, she relied on the help of Native Canadians to warn British troops of an American attack.

7. The words *month, silver, purple,* and *orange* have something in common, no other English words rhyme with them.

8. The broken pop machine dispensed a cup or pop, it would not provide both at the same time.

Review Test 3

Locate and correct the five run-ons in the passage that follows.

My worst experience of the week was going home for lunch, rather than eating at work. My children didn't know I was coming, they had used most of the bread on hand. All I had to make a sandwich with were two thin, crumpled pieces of crust. I sat there eating my tattered sandwich and trying to relax, then the telephone rang. It was for my daughter, who was in the bathroom, she called down to me that I should get the person's name and number. As soon as I sat down again, someone knocked on the door, it was a neatly dressed couple with bright eyes who wanted to talk with me about a higher power in life. I politely got rid of them and went back to finish lunch. I thought I would relax over my coffee I had to break up a fight between my two young sons about which television channel to watch. As a last bit of frustration, my daughter came downstairs and asked me to drive her over to a friend's house before I went back to work.

Review Test 4

Write quickly for five minutes about what you did this past weekend. Don't worry about spelling, punctuation, finding exact words, or organizing your thoughts. Just focus on writing as many words as you can without stopping.

After you have finished, go back and correct any run-ons in your writing.

CHAPTER 23

Regular and Irregular Verbs

Regular Verbs

A Brief Review of Regular Verbs

Every verb has four principal parts: *present, past, past participle,* and *present participle.* These parts can be used to build all the verb tenses (the times shown by a verb).

Most verbs in English are regular. The past and past participles of a regular verb are formed by adding *-d* or *-ed* to the present. The *past participle* is the form of the verb used with the helping verbs *have, has,* or *had* (or some form of *be* with passive verbs). The *present participle* is formed by adding *-ing* to the present.

Here are the principal parts of some regular verbs:

Present	*Past*	*Past Participle*	*Present Participle*
shout	shouted	shouted	shouting
prepare	prepared	prepared	preparing
surprise	surprised	surprised	surprising
tease	teased	teased	teasing
frighten	frightened	frightened	frightening

A Note about Verb Tenses and Other Languages

English verb tenses can be particularly confusing to students of other language backgrounds. Not all languages express time distinctions through their verbs in the same ways that English does. Some language groups may have only three tense-forms; others may have tenses English does not use. Because of the structural differences between Asian languages and English, ESL students from Asian cultures may find English verb tenses confusing. Asian languages do not alter verb forms to indicate changes in time referred to; instead a "time marker" word is used, and the verb's form does not change. For these students, extra patience and practice with English verb tenses are required, but with continued attention to verb tenses, students can master their use.

Present Tense Endings: The verb ending *-s* or *-es* is needed with a regular verb in the present tense when the subject is *he, she, it,* or any *one person* or *thing.* Take care to make the subject *agree* with its verb.

> He read<u>s</u> every night.
> She watch<u>es</u> television every night.
> It appear<u>s</u> they have little in common.

Activity

Verbs in the sentences that follow do not agree with their subjects. Cross out each incorrect verb form, and write the correct present tense of the verb in the space provided.

_____   1. My radio wake me up every morning with soft music.

_____   2. Lynn and Risa always clowns around at the start of the class.

_____   3. My wife watch our baby in the morning, and I take over afternoons.

_____   4. Many more men wants to go to nursing school next year.

_____   5. My brain work much better at night than it does in early morning.

Past Tense Endings: The verb ending *-d* or *-ed* is needed with a regular verb in the past tense.

> This morning I complet<u>ed</u> my research paper.
> The recovering hospital patient walk<u>ed</u> slowly down the corridor.
> Some students hiss<u>ed</u> when the new assignment was given out.

Activity

Verbs in the sentences that follow need *-d* or *-ed* endings. Cross out each incorrect verb form, and write the standard form in the space provided.

_____   1. One of my teeth cave in when I bit on the hard pretzel.

_____   2. The accident victim complains of dizziness right before she passed out.

_____   3. We realize a package was missing when we got back from shopping.

_____   4. I burn a hole in my shirt while I was ironing it.

_____   5. The impatient driver edges her car into the intersection while the light was still red.

Irregular Verbs

Irregular verbs have irregular forms in the past tense and past participle. For example, the past tense of the irregular verb *choose* is *chose;* its past participle is *chosen.*

Almost everyone has some degree of trouble with irregular verbs. When you are unsure about the form of a verb, you can check the list of irregular verbs on the following pages. (The present participle is not shown on this list because it is formed simply by adding *-ing* to the base form of the verb.) You can also check a dictionary, which gives the principal parts of irregular verbs.

A List of Irregular Verbs

Present	Past	Past Participle
arise	arose	arisen
awake	awoke *or* awaked	awoken *or* awaked
be (am, are, is)	was (were)	been
become	became	become
begin	began	begun
bend	bent	bent
bite	bit	bitten
blow	blew	blown
break	broke	broken
bring	brought	brought
build	built	built
burst	burst	burst
buy	bought	bought
catch	caught	caught
choose	chose	chosen
come	came	come
cost	cost	cost
cut	cut	cut
do (does)	did	done
draw	drew	drawn
drink	drank	drunk
drive	drove	driven
eat	ate	eaten
fall	fell	fallen
feed	fed	fed
feel	felt	felt
fight	fought	fought
find	found	found
fly	flew	flown
freeze	froze	frozen
get	got	got *or* gotten
give	gave	given
go (goes)	went	gone
grow	grew	grown
have (has)	had	had
hear	heard	heard
hide	hid	hidden
hold	held	held

Present	Past	Past Participle
hurt	hurt	hurt
keep	kept	kept
know	knew	known
lay	laid	laid
lead	led	led
leave	left	left
lend	lent	lent
let	let	let
lie	lay	lain
light	lit	lit
lose	lost	lost
make	made	made
meet	met	met
pay	paid	paid
ride	rode	ridden
ring	rang	rung
run	ran	run
say	said	said
see	saw	seen
sell	sold	sold
send	sent	sent
shake	shook	shaken
shrink	shrank	shrunk
shut	shut	shut
sing	sang	sung
sit	sat	sat
sleep	slept	slept
speak	spoke	spoken
spend	spent	spent
stand	stood	stood
steal	stole	stolen
stick	stuck	stuck
sting	stung	stung
swear	swore	sworn
swim	swam	swum
take	took	taken
teach	taught	taught
tear	tore	torn
tell	told	told
think	thought	thought
wake	woke *or* waked	woken *or* waked
wear	wore	worn
win	won	won
write	wrote	written

● ● ● ● **Activity**

Cross out the incorrect verb form in each of the following sentences. Then, write the correct form of the verb in the space provided.

flown   ***Example***   After it had ~~flew~~ into the picture window, the dazed bird huddled on the ground.

_____ 1. As graduation neared, Michelle worried about the practicality of the program she'd chose.

_____ 2. Before we could find seats, the theatre darkened and the opening credits begun to roll.

_____ 3. To be polite, I drunk the slightly sour wine that my grandfather poured from his carefully hoarded supply.

_____ 4. The inexperienced nurse shrunk from touching the patient's raw, burned skin.

_____ 5. After a day on the noisy construction site, Sam's ears rung for hours with a steady hum.

_____ 6. Sheila had forget to write her student number on the test form, so the computer rejected her answer sheet.

_____ 7. If I had went to work ten minutes earlier, I would have avoided being caught in the gigantic traffic snarl.

_____ 8. Prehistoric people blowed paint over their outstretched hands to stencil their handprints on cave walls.

Review Test 1

Cross out the incorrect verb form in each sentence. Then, write the correct form in the space provided.

_____ 1. The health inspectors walk into the kitchen as the cook was picking up a hamburger off the floor.

_____ 2. The thieves would have stole my stereo, but I had had it engraved with a special identification number.

_____ 3. He had tore his girlfriend's picture into little pieces and tossed them out the window.

_____ 4. Because I has asthma, I carry an inhaler to use when I lose my breath.

_____ 5. Baked potatoes doesn't have as many calories as I thought.

_____ 6. Yesterday I check my bank balance and saw my money was getting low.

_____ 7. Many childhood diseases has almost vanished in Canada.

_____ 8. Nancy sticked notes on the refrigerator with fruit-shaped magnets.

■ Review Test 2

Write short sentences that use the form requested for the following verbs.

Example   Past of *grow* *I grew my own tomatoes last year.*

1. Past of *know* _____

2. Present of *take* _____

3. Past participle of *give* _____

4. Past participle of *write* _____

5. Past of *do* _____

6. Past of *talk* _____

7. Present of *begin* _____

8. Past of *go* _____

9. Past participle of *see* _____

10. Present of *drive* _____

A Note about Nonstandard Forms of Regular Verbs

Many people have grown up in communities where nonstandard forms of regular verbs are used in everyday speech. Instead of saying, for example, "That girl *looks* tired," a person using a community dialect or patois might say, "That girl *look* tired." Community dialects have richness and power but are generally not accepted in academic and professional writing tasks, where standard English verb forms must be used.

CHAPTER 24

Subject–Verb Agreement

A verb must agree with its subject in number. A *singular subject* (one person or thing) takes a singular verb. A *plural subject* (more than one person or thing) takes a plural verb. Mistakes in subject-verb agreement are sometimes made in the following situations:

1 When words come between the subject and the verb

2 When a verb comes before the subject

3 With compound subjects

4 With indefinite pronouns

Each of these situations is explained on the following pages.

Words Between Subject and Verb

Words that come between the subject and the verb do not change subject–verb agreement. Note the following sentence:

> The crinkly <u>lines</u> *around Joan's eyes* <u>give</u> her a friendly look.

In this sentence, the subject *(lines)* is plural, so the verb *(give)* is plural. The words that come between the subject and the verb are a prepositional phrase: *around Joan's eyes*. They do not affect subject–verb agreement. (A list of prepositions can be found in the box on page 324.)

To find the subject of certain sentences, cross out prepositional phrases.

> The lumpy <u>salt</u> ~~in the shakers~~ <u>needs</u> to be changed.

> An old <u>television</u> ~~with a round screen~~ <u>has sat</u> in our basement for years.

• • • • • **Activity**

Underline the subject and lightly cross out any words that come between the subject and the verb. Then, double underline the verb in parentheses that you believe is correct.

1. Some members of the parents' association (want, wants) to ban certain books from the school library.

2. Chung's trench coat, with its big lapels and shoulder flaps, (make, makes) him feel like a tough private eye.

3. Misconceptions about apes like the gorilla (has, have) turned a relatively peaceful animal into a terrifying monster.

4. The rising costs of necessities like food and shelter (force, forces) some people to live on the streets.

5. In my opinion, a slice of pepperoni pizza and a good video (make, makes) a great evening.

6. Members of the class (design, designs) their own websites as term work.

Verb Before Subject

A verb agrees with its subject even when the verb comes *before* the subject. Words that may precede the subject (when the verb comes before the subject) include *there, here,* and, in questions, *who, which, what,* and *where.*

Here are some examples of sentences in which the verb appears before the subject:

There <u>are</u> wild <u>dogs</u> in our neighbourhood.

In the distance <u>was</u> a <u>billow</u> of black smoke.

Here <u>is</u> the <u>newspaper</u>.

Where <u>are</u> the children's <u>coats</u>?

If you are unsure about the subject, ask *who* or *what* of the verb. With the first example above, you might ask, "*What* are in our neighbourhood?" The answer, *wild dogs,* is the subject.

Activity

Write the correct form of each verb in the space provided.

1. There _____ dozens of frenzied shoppers waiting for the store to open. (is, are)

2. Here _____ the notes from yesterday's computer graphics lecture. (is, are)

3. When _____ we take our break? (do, does)

4. There _____ scraps of yellowing paper stuck between the pages of the cookbook. (was, were)

5. At the very bottom of the grocery list _____ an item that meant a trip all the way back to aisle one. (was, were)

6. Among the students in the class _____ those who can't keep up with the assignments. (is, are)

Compound Subjects

A compound subject is two subjects separated by the joining word *and.* Subjects joined by *and* generally take a plural verb.

A patchwork <u>quilt</u> and a sleeping <u>bag</u> <u>cover</u> my bed in the winter.

<u>Clark</u> and <u>Lois</u> <u>are</u> a contented couple.

When subjects are joined by *either . . . or, neither . . . nor,* or *not only . . . but also,* the verb agrees with the subject closer to the verb.

Neither the <u>negotiator</u> nor the union <u>leaders</u> <u>want</u> the strike to continue.

The nearer subject, *leaders,* is plural, so the verb is plural.

● ● ● **Activity**

Write the correct form of the verb in the space provided.

1. A crusty baking pan and a greasy plate _____ on the countertop. (sit, sits)

2. Spidery cracks and a layer of dust _____ the ivory keys on the old piano. (cover, covers)

3. Not only the assistant manager but also the support staff _____ that the company is folding. (know, knows)

4. In eighteenth-century France, makeup and high heels _____ worn by men. (was, were)

5. Neither Tasha nor the rest of the class _____ to work on that project. (want, wants)

6. Either my dog or the squirrels _____ breadcrusts I put out for the birds. (eat, eats)

Indefinite Pronouns

The following words, known as *indefinite pronouns,* always take singular verbs:

(-one words)	*(-body words)*	*(-thing words)*	
one	nobody	nothing	each
anyone	anybody	anything	either
everyone	everybody	everything	neither
someone	somebody	something	

Note: *Both* always takes a plural verb.

Activity

Write the correct form of the verb in the space provided.

1. Neither of those hairstyles _____ the shape of your face. (suit, suits)

2. Somebody without much sensitivity always _____ my birthmark. (mention, mentions)

3. The people at the local hardware store _____ friendly advice about home fix-it projects. (give, gives)

4. Everyone _____ the college kite-flying contest in the spring. (enter, enters)

5. One of these earrings constantly _____ off my ear. (fall, falls)

6. Each of the students _____ in careful block letters. (print, prints)

7. Anybody in the groups we saw _____ who should belong to the committee. (decide, decides)

Review Test 1

In the space provided, write the correct form of the verb.

1. As a result of a successful experiment, some users of wheelchairs _____ using trained monkeys as helpers. (is, are)

2. Each of their children _____ given a name picked at random from a page of the Bible. (was, were)

3. Many of the headlines in the *National Enquirer* _____ hard to believe. (seem, seems)

4. Envelopes, file folders, and a telephone book _____ jammed into Linda's kitchen drawers. (is, are)

5. Neither of the main dishes at tonight's dinner _____ any meat. (contains, contain)

6. The use of metal chains and studded tires _____ highways by chipping away at the paved surface. (damage, damages)

7. A metal grab bar bolted onto the tiles _____ it easier for elderly people to get in and out of the bathtub. (makes, make)

8. In exchange for a reduced rent, Karla and James _____ the dentist's office beneath their second-floor apartment. (cleans, clean)

Review Test 2

Cross out the incorrect verb form in each sentence. In addition, underline the subject or subjects that go with the verb. Then, write the correct form of the verb.

1. Why is Martha and her mother digging a hole in their garden so late at night?

2. Neither of my children look like me.

3. Three goats, a pot-bellied pig, and a duck was among the entrants in the pet parade.

4. Here is the low-calorie cola and the double-chocolate cake you ordered.

5. The odour of those perfumed ads interfere with my enjoyment of a magazine.

6. One of my roommates are always leaving wet towels on the bathroom floor.

7. A man or woman in his or her forties often begin to think about making a contribution to the world and not just about him- or herself.

8. Each of the child's thirty-four stuffed animals have a name and entire life history.

Review Test 3

Complete each of the following sentences using *is, are, was, were, has,* or *have*. Then, underline the subject.

Example   For me, <u>popcorn</u> at the movies *is* _like coffee at breakfast._

1. Under my roommate's bed _____

2. The car with the purple fenders _____

3. My boss and her secretary _____

4. Neither of the football players _____

5. Here _____

CHAPTER 25

Additional Information about Verbs

The purpose of this special section is to provide additional information about verbs. Some people will find the grammar terms here a helpful reminder of what they learned earlier, in school, about verbs. For them, the terms will increase their understanding of how verbs function in English. Other people may welcome more detailed information about terms used elsewhere in this book. Remember that the most common mistakes with writing verbs have been treated earlier in this section.

Verb Tense

Verbs tell us the time of an action. The time that a verb shows is usually called *tense*. The most common tenses are the simple present, past, and future. In addition, there are nine other tenses that enable us to express more specific ideas about time than we could with the simple tenses alone. Below and on the next page are the twelve verb tenses and examples of each one. Read them over to increase your sense of the many different ways of expressing time in English.

The Twelve English Verb Tenses

Tenses	*Examples*
Simple Tenses	
Present	I *work*.
	Tony *works*.
Past	Ellen *worked* on her car.
Future	You *will work* on a new project next week.
Perfect Tenses	
Present perfect	We *have found* the answer to all your problems.
	The stock market *has suffered* from another major scandal in the world of business.

The present perfect most commonly refers to an action that took place in an indefinite past, at a time that is *not* specified.

> We *have lived* in Moncton for three years.
> He *has studied* at Capilano College since last September.

With certain verbs that suggest a prolonged activity, the present perfect can indicate an action that starts in the past and continues until the present.

Past perfect	When I came home, I noticed that my brother *had eaten* all the cookies.
	By December 31, 1999, programmers *had resolved* most Y2K problems.

The past perfect tense indicates an action that took place *before* a specified time in the past or *before* another action expressed in the simple past.

Future perfect	By the year 2010, engineers *will have developed* an efficient and economical electric car.
	I *will have done* all my homework by the time the party begins.

The future perfect tense refers to an action taking place *before* a specified future time or another future action.

Progressive (or Continuous) Tenses

Present progressive	I *am working* on my speech for the debate.
	You *are working* too hard.
	The printer *is not working* properly.
Past progressive	He *was working* in the basement.
	The contestants *were working* on their talent routines.
Future progressive	My son *will be working* in our store this summer.

Progressive, or *continuous tenses,* as the word *continuous* suggests, refer to ongoing actions in the present, past, or future.

Present perfect progressive	Sarah *has been working* late this week.
	(Sarah began *working* late earlier this week, and *continues to do so.*)
Past perfect progressive	Until yesterday, I *had been working* nights.
	(I *worked* nights for some time in the past, and *continued to do so* until yesterday. The action, while continuous, was *in the past, and is completed.*)
Future perfect progressive	My mother *will have been working* as a nurse for forty-five years by the time she retires.
	(My mother *worked* as a nurse in the past, *continues to do so, and will continue to work as a nurse* in the future, until retirement.)

  • • • • **Activity**

On separate paper, write twelve sentences using the twelve verb tenses.

Helping Verbs

There are three common verbs that can either stand alone or combine with (and "help") other verbs. Here are the verbs and their forms:

> be (am, are, is, was, were, being, been)   do (does, did)
> have (has, having, had)

Here are examples of the verbs:

Used Alone	*Used as Helping Verbs*
I *was* angry.	I *was growing* angry.
Sheila *has* the key.	Sheila *has forgotten* the key.
He *did* well on the test.	He *did fail* the previous test.

Modal Auxiliaries

There are nine other helping verbs (traditionally known as *modals,* or *modal auxiliaries*) that are always used in combination with other verbs. Here are the nine modals and sentence examples of each:

can	I *can see* the rainbow.
could	I *could* not *find* a seat.
may	The game *may be postponed.*
might	Keesha *might resent* your advice.
shall	I *shall see* you tomorrow.
should	He *should get* his car *serviced.*
will	Terry *will want* to see you.
would	They *would* not *understand.*
must	You *must visit* us again.

Note from the examples that these verbs have only one form. They do not, for instance, add an *-s* when used with *he, she, it,* or any one person or thing.

Activity

On separate paper, write nine sentences using the nine helping verbs (modals) listed in the box above.

Verbals

Verbals are words formed from verbs. Verbals, like verbs, often express action. They can add variety to your sentences and vigour to your writing style. (Verbals, as mentioned in Chapter 21, are not "finite," or "true verbs.") The three kinds of verbals are *infinitives, participles,* and *gerunds.*

Infinitive

An infinitive is *to* plus the base form of the verb.

I love *to dance.*
Lina hopes *to write* for a newspaper.
I asked the children *to clean* the kitchen.

Participle

A participle is a verb form used as an adjective (a descriptive word). The present participle ends in *-ing*. The past participle ends in *-ed* or has an irregular ending.

> *Peering* into the cracked mirror, the *crying* woman wiped her eyes.
> The *astounded* man stared at his *winning* lottery ticket.
> *Swinging* a sharp axe, Muhammad split the *cracked* beam.

Gerund

A gerund is the *-ing* form of a verb used as a noun.

> *Swimming* is the perfect exercise.
> *Eating* junk food is my diet downfall.
> Through *doodling,* people express their inner feelings.

● ● ● **Activity**

On separate paper, write three sentences using infinitives, three sentences using participles, and three sentences using gerunds.

Active and Passive Verbs

When the subject of a sentence *performs the action* of a verb, the verb is in the *active voice.* When the subject of a sentence *receives the action* of a verb, the verb is in the *passive voice.*

The passive form of a verb consists of a form of the verb *be* plus the *past participle of the main verb.* Look at the active and passive forms of the verbs below:

Active Voice	*Passive Voice*
Iva *sewed* the curtains. (The subject, *Iva,* is the doer of the action.)	The curtains *were sewn* by Iva. (The subject, *curtains,* does not act. Instead, they receive the action of sewing.)
The tech assistant *fixed* the hard drive. (The subject, *tech assistant,* is the doer of the action.	The hard drive *was fixed* by the tech assistant. (The subject, the *hard drive,* does not act. Instead, it receives the action of fixing.)

In general, active verbs are more effective than passive ones. Active verbs give your writing a simpler and more vigorous style. At times, however, the passive form of verbs is appropriate when the performer of the action is unknown or is less important than the receiver of the action. For example:

> The tests *were graded* yesterday.
> (The performer of the action is unknown.)

> Alan *was hurt* by your thoughtless remark.
> (The receiver of the action, Alan, is being emphasized.)

● ● ● ● **Activity**

Change the following sentences from the passive to the active voice. Note that you may have to add a subject in some cases.

Examples   The dog was found by a police officer.

The police officer found the dog.

The baseball game was called off.

The official called off the baseball game.

(Here a subject had to be added.)

1. Most of our furniture was damaged by the fire.

2. Melissa's new dress was singed by a careless smoker.

3. The problem was solved by the quiet student in the back of the room.

4. The supermarket shelves were restocked after the truckers' strike.

5. The children were mesmerized by the magician's sleight of hand.

CHAPTER 26

Pronoun Agreement and Reference

Pronouns are words that take the place of *nouns* (persons, places, or things). In fact, the word *pronoun* means "for a noun." Pronouns are shortcuts that keep you from unnecessarily repeating words in writing. Here are some examples of pronouns:

> Eddie left *his* camera on the bus. (*His* is a pronoun that takes the place of *Eddie's*.)
> Elena drank the coffee even though *it* was cold. (*It* replaces *coffee*.)
> As I turned the newspaper's damp pages, *they* disintegrated in my hands. (*They* is a pronoun that takes the place of *pages*.)

This section presents rules that will help you avoid two common mistakes people make with pronouns. The rules are:

1 A pronoun must agree in number with the word or words it replaces.
2 A pronoun must refer clearly to the word it replaces.

Pronoun Agreement

A pronoun must agree in number with the word or words it replaces. If the word a pronoun refers to is singular, the pronoun must be singular; if that word is plural, the pronoun must be plural. (Note that the word a pronoun refers to is known as the *antecedent*, or "before-goer." The antecedent is the pronoun's point of reference in the sentence.)

Marie showed me (her) antique wedding band.

Students enrolled in the art class must provide (their) own supplies.

In the first example, the pronoun *her* refers to the singular word *Marie*; in the second example, the pronoun *their* refers to the plural word *Students*.

365

Activity

Write the appropriate pronoun *(their, they, them, it)* in the blank space in each of the following sentences.

Example   I opened the wet umbrella and put _____*it*_____ in the bathtub to dry.

1. Kasey and Bruce left for the movies earlier than usual because _____ knew the theatre would be packed.

2. The clothes were still damp, but I decided to fold _____ anyway.

3. Young adults often face a difficult transition period when _____ leave home for the first time.

4. Paul's grandparents renewed _____ marriage vows at a huge fiftieth wedding anniversary celebration.

5. The car's steering wheel began to pull to one side, and then _____ started to shimmy.

Indefinite Pronouns

The following words are always singular:

(-one words)	*(-body words)*	
one	nobody	each
anyone	anybody	either
everyone	everybody	neither
someone	somebody	

If a pronoun in a sentence refers to one of these singular words (also known as *indefinite pronouns*), the pronoun should be *singular*.

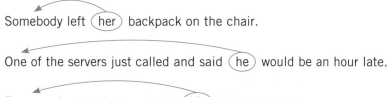

Somebody left (her) backpack on the chair.

One of the servers just called and said (he) would be an hour late.

Everyone in the club must pay (his) dues next week.

Each circled *pronoun* is *singular* because it refers to an *indefinite pronoun*.

Note: There are two important points to remember about indefinite pronouns:

1 In the last example, if everyone in the club was a woman, the pronoun would be *her*. If the club had women and men, the pronouns would be *his or her*:

Everyone in the club must pay his or her dues next week.

Some writers follow the traditional practice of using *his* to refer to both women and men. Most writers now use *his or her* to avoid an implied sexual bias. To avoid using *his* or the somewhat awkward *his or her,* a sentence can often be rewritten in the plural:

Club members must pay their dues next week.

2 In informal spoken English, *plural* pronouns are often used with the indefinite pronouns. We would probably not say:

Everybody has *his or her* own opinion about the election.

Instead, we are likely to say:

Everybody has *their* own opinion about the election.

Here are other examples:

Everyone in the choir must buy *their* robes.
Everybody in the line has *their* ticket ready.
No one in the class remembered to bring *their* books.

In such cases, the indefinite pronouns are clearly plural in meaning. Also, the use of such plurals helps people to avoid the awkward *his or her.* In time, the plural pronoun may be accepted in formal speech or writing. **Until that happens, however, you should use the grammatically correct singular form in your writing.**

Activity

Underline the correct pronoun.

1. Neither of the potential buyers had really made up (her, their) mind.

2. Not one of the new cashiers knows what (he, they) should be doing.

3. Each of these computers has (its, their) drawbacks.

4. Anyone trying to reduce (his or her, their) salt intake should avoid canned and processed foods.

5. If anybody calls when I'm out, tell (him, them) I'll return in an hour.

Pronoun Reference

A sentence may be confusing and unclear if a pronoun appears to refer to more than one word or does not refer to any specific word. *Pronouns must have a clear point of reference, or antecedent.* Look at this sentence:

Miriam was annoyed when they failed her car for a faulty turn signal.

Who failed her car? There is no specific word that *they* refers to. Be clear:

Miriam was annoyed when the safety inspectors failed her car for a faulty turn signal.

Here are sentences with other faulty pronoun references. Read the explanations of why they are faulty and look carefully at how they are corrected.

Faulty	*Clear*
Peter told Vijay that his wife was unhappy. (Whose wife is unhappy: Peter's or Vijay's? Be clear about your *pronoun referent*.)	Peter told Vijay, "My wife is unhappy."
Mia is really a shy person, but she keeps it hidden. (There is no specific word, or *antecedent*, that *it* refers to. The adjective *shy* must be changed to a noun.)	Mia is really a shy person, but she keeps her shyness hidden.
Kizzie attributed her success to her husband's support, which was generous. (Does *which* mean that Kizzie's *action* was generous or that her husband's *support* was generous?)	Generously, Kizzie attributed her success to her husband's support. *Or*: Kizzie attributed her success to her husband's generous support.

Activity

Rewrite each of the following sentences to make clear the vague pronoun reference. Add, change, or omit words as necessary.

Example   Susan and her mother wondered if she had been working out long enough to enter a competition.

Susan's mother wondered if Susan had been working out long enough

to enter a competition.

1. Dad spent all morning birdwatching but didn't see a single one.

   _____

2. At that fast-food restaurant, they give you free glasses with your soft drinks.

   _____

3. Ruth told Annette that her bouts of depression were becoming serious.

   _____

4. Dipping his spoon into the pot of simmering pasta sauce, Kyle felt it slip out of his hand.

   _____

5. Pete visited the tutoring centre because they could help him with his economics course.

   _____

■ Review Test 1

Underline the correct word in parentheses.

1. Each of the little girls may choose one prize for (her, their) own.

2. I asked at the body shop how quickly (they, the shop employees) could fix my car.

3. The coaches told each member of the soccer team that (his or her, their) position was the most important one in the game.

4. Marianna tried to take notes during the class, but she didn't really understand (it, the subject.)

5. When someone has a cold, (they, he or she) should take extra vitamin C and drink a lot of fluids.

■ Review Test 2

Cross out the pronoun error in each sentence below, and write the correction in the space provided at the left. Then, circle the letter that correctly describes the type of error that was made.

Example

his (or her)   Anyone without a ticket will lose ~~their~~ place in the line.
Mistake in: a. pronoun reference   (b.) pronoun agreement

——————   1. Could someone volunteer their services to clean up after the party?
Mistake in: a. pronoun reference   b. pronoun agreement

——————   2. The referee watched the junior hockey game closely to make sure they didn't hurt each other during checking.
Mistake in: a. pronoun reference   b. pronoun agreement

——————   3. If job hunters want to make a good impression at an interview, he should be sure to arrive on time.
Mistake in: a. pronoun reference   b. pronoun agreement

——————   4. Neither of those girls appreciated their parents' sacrifices.
Mistake in: a. pronoun reference   b. pronoun agreement

——————   5. There wasn't much to do on Friday nights after they closed the only movie theatre in the northern Manitoba town.
Mistake in: a. pronoun reference   b. pronoun agreement

CHAPTER 27

Pronoun Types

This section describes some common types of pronouns: *subject* and *object pronouns*, *possessive pronouns*, and *demonstrative pronouns*.

Subject and Object Pronouns

Pronouns change their form depending upon the place they occupy in a sentence. In the following box is a list of subject and object pronouns.

Subject Pronouns	Object Pronouns
I	me
you	you (no change)
he	him
she	her
it	it (no change)
we	us
they	them

Subject Pronouns

Subject pronouns are subjects of verbs.

> *He* is wearing an artificial arm. (*He* is the subject of the verb *is wearing*.)
> *They* are moving into our old apartment. (*They* is the subject of the verb *are moving*.)
> *We* students should have a say in the decision. (*We* is the subject of the verb *should have*.)

Several rules for using subject pronouns—and several kinds of mistakes that people sometimes make with subject pronouns—are explained below.

Rule 1: Use a subject pronoun in spots where you have a compound (more than one) subject.

Incorrect	*Correct*
My brother and *me* are Barenaked Ladies fans.	My brother and *I* are Barenaked Ladies fans.
Him and *me* know the lyrics to all their songs.	*He* and *I* know the lyrics to all their songs.

Hint for Rule 1: If you are not sure what pronoun to use, try each pronoun by itself in the sentence. The correct pronoun will be the one that sounds right. For example, "Him knows the lyrics to all their songs" does not sound right; "He knows the lyrics to all their songs" does.

Rule 2: Use a subject pronoun after forms of the verb *be*. Forms of *be* include *am, are, is, was, were, has been, have been,* and others.

> It was *I* who left the light on.
> It may be *they* in that car.
> It is *he.*

The sentences above may sound strange and stilted to you because they are seldom used in conversation. When we speak with one another, forms such as "It was me," "It may be them," and "It is him" are widely accepted. In formal writing, however, the grammatically correct forms are still required.

Hint for Rule 2: You can avoid having to use the subject pronoun form after *be* by simply rewording a sentence. Here is how the preceding examples could be reworded:

> I was the one who left the light on.
> They may be in that car.
> He is here.

Rule 3: Use subject pronouns after *than* or *as*. The subject pronoun is used because a verb is understood after the pronoun.

> You play better than I (play). (The verb *play* is understood after *I*.)
> Jenny is as bored as I (am). (The verb *am* is understood after *I*.)
> We don't need the money as much as they (do). (The verb *do* is understood after *they*.)

Hint for Rule 3: Avoid mistakes by mentally adding the "missing" verb at the end of the sentence.

Object Pronouns

Object pronouns *(me, him, her, us, them)* are the objects of verbs or prepositions. (*Prepositions* are connecting words like *for, at, about, to, before, by, with,* and *of*. See also page 324.)

> Tamara helped *me*. (*Me* is the object of the verb *helped*.)
> We took *them* to the college. (*Them* is the object of the verb *took*.)

Leave the children with *us*. (*Us* is the object of the preposition *with*.)
I got in line behind *him*. (*Him* is the object of the preposition *behind*.)

People are sometimes uncertain about what pronoun to use when two objects follow the verb.

Incorrect	*Correct*
I gave a gift to Arundhati and *she*.	I gave a gift to Arundhati and *her*.
She came to the movie with Marc and *I*.	She came to the movie with Marc and *me*.

Hint: If you are not sure what pronoun to use, try each pronoun by itself in the sentence. The correct pronoun will be the one that sounds right. For example, "I gave a gift to she" does not sound right; "I gave a gift to her" does.

● ● ● ● **Activity**

Underline the correct subject or object pronoun in each of the following sentences. Then, show whether your answer is a subject or object pronoun by circling the *S* or *O* in the margin. The first one is done for you as an example.

S ⓞ 1. The sweaters Mom knitted for Victor and (I, me) are too small.

S O 2. No one has a quicker temper than (she, her).

S O 3. Your grades prove that you worked harder than (they, them).

S O 4. (We, Us) runners train indoors when the weather turns cold.

S O 5. (She, Her) and Betty never put the cap back on the toothpaste.

S O 6. Chris and (he, him) are the most energetic kids in grade one.

S O 7. Arguing over clothes is a favourite pastime for my sister and (I, me).

S O 8. The head of the ticket committee asked Sam and (I, me) to help with sales.

Possessive Pronouns

Here is a list of possessive pronouns:

my, mine	our, ours
your, yours	your, yours
his	their, theirs
her, hers	
its	

Possessive pronouns show ownership or possession.

> Peter revved up *his* motorcycle and blasted off.
> The keys are *mine.*

Note: A possessive pronoun *never* uses an apostrophe. (See also page 399.)

Incorrect	*Correct*
That coat is *hers'.*	That coat is *hers.*
The card table is *theirs'.*	The card table is *theirs.*

• • • • **Activity**

Cross out the incorrect pronoun form in each of the sentences below. Write the correct form in the space at the left.

Example _____hers_____ Those gloves are ~~hers'~~.

_____ 1. I discovered that my car had somehow lost its' rear licence plate.

_____ 2. Are those seats theirs'?

_____ 3. I knew the sweater was hers' when I saw the monogram.

_____ 4. The dog in that cage is our's.

_____ 5. These butter tarts are yours' if you want them.

Demonstrative Pronouns

Demonstrative pronouns point to or single out a person or thing. There are four demonstrative pronouns:

this	these
that	those

> *This* is my house right in front of us.
> *Those* are your books on the shelf over there.

Generally speaking, *this* and *these* refer to things close at hand; *that* and *those* refer to things farther away. The four pronouns are commonly used in the role of demonstrative adjectives as well.

> Is anyone using *this* spoon?
> I am going to throw away *these* magazines.
> I just bought *that* white Volvo at the curb.
> Pick up *those* toys in the corner.

Note: Do not use *them, this here, that there, these here,* or *those there* to point out. Use only *this, that, these,* or *those.*

Activity

Cross out the incorrect form of the demonstrative pronoun, and write the correct form in the space provided.

Example   _____*Those*_____ ~~Them~~ tires look worn.

_____   1. This here map is out of date.

_____   2. Leave them keys out on the coffee table.

_____   3. I've seen them girls somewhere before.

_____   4. Jack entered that there dog in an obedience contest.

_____   5. Where are them new knives?

Review Test

Underline the correct pronoun in the parentheses.

1. If the contract negotiations are left up to (they, them), we'll have to accept the results.

2. (Them, Those) student crafts have won several awards.

3. Our grandmother told David and (I, me) to leave our muddy shoes outside on the porch.

4. The judge decided that the fault was (theirs', theirs) and ordered them to pay the damages.

5. The black-masked raccoon stared at Rudy and (I, me) for an instant and then ran quickly away.

6. When we saw the smashed window, Lynn and (I, me) didn't know whether to enter the house.

7. (This here, This) is my cousin Ali.

8. This coat can't be (hers, her's); it's too small.

CHAPTER 28

Adjectives and Adverbs

Adjectives

What Are Adjectives?

Adjectives describe nouns (names of persons, places, or things) or pronouns.

> Nicola is a *wise* woman. (The adjective *wise* describes the noun *woman*.)
> She is also *funny*. (The adjective *funny* describes the pronoun *she*.)
> I'll carry the *heavy* bag of groceries. (The adjective *heavy* describes the noun *bag*.)
> It is *torn*. (The adjective *torn* describes the pronoun *it*.)

Adjectives usually come before the word they describe (as in *wise* woman and *heavy* bag). They also come after forms of the verb *be* (*is, are, was, were*, and so on) and verbs such as *look, appear, seem, become, sound, taste*, and *smell*.

> That road is *slippery*. (The adjective *slippery* describes the road.)
> The printers are *noisy*. (The adjective *noisy* describes the printers.)
> Those customers were *impatient*. (The adjective *impatient* describes the customers.)
> Your room looks *neat*. (The adjective *neat* describes the room.)

Using Adjectives to Compare

For all one-syllable adjectives and some two-syllable adjectives, add *-er* when comparing two things and *-est* when comparing three or more things.

> Andrew's beard is *longer* than mine, but Lee's is the *longest*.
> Meg may be the *quieter* of the two sisters; however, that's not saying much since they're the *loudest* girls in school.

For some two-syllable adjectives and all longer adjectives, add *more* when comparing two things and *most* when comparing three or more things.

> Daniel Richler is *more famous* than his brother; however, their late father, Mordecai Richler, is still the *most famous* member of the family.
> The red letters on the sign are *more noticeable* than the black ones, but the Day-Glo letters are the *most noticeable*.

You can usually tell when to use *more* and *most* by the sound of a word. For example, you can probably tell by its sound that "carefuller" would be too awkward to say and that *more careful* is thus correct. In addition, there are many words for which both *-er* or *-est* and *more* or *most* are equally correct. For instance, either "a more fair rule" or "a fairer rule" is correct.

To form negative comparisons, use *less* and *least.*
During my first dance class, I felt *less graceful* than an injured elephant.
When the teacher came to our house to complain to my parents, I offered her the *least comfortable* chair in the house.

Points to Remember about Comparing

Point 1: Use only one form of comparison at a time. In other words, do not use both an *-er* ending and *more* or both an *-est* ending and *most:*

Incorrect	*Correct*
My suitcase is always *more heavier* than my father's.	My suitcase is always *heavier* than my father's.
Blood and Donuts is still the *most frighteningest* movie I've ever seen.	*Blood and Donuts* is still the *most frightening* movie I've ever seen.

Point 2: Learn the irregular forms of the words shown below.

	Comparative *(for comparing things)*	*Superlative* *(for comparing three or more things)*
bad	worse	worst
good, well	better	best
little (in amount)	less	least
much, many	more	most

Do not use both *more* and an irregular comparative or *most* and an irregular superlative.

Incorrect	*Correct*
It is *more better* to give than to receive.	It is *better* to give than to receive.
Last night, I got the *most worst* snack attack I ever had.	Last night, I got the *worst* snack attack I ever had.

Activity

Add to each sentence the correct form of the adjective in parentheses.

Examples   The _____worst_____ job I ever had was babysitting for spoiled four-year-old twins. (bad)

The _most wonderful_ day of my life was when my child was born. (wonderful)

1. The _____ chocolate cake I ever ate had bananas in it. (good)

2. Aunt Sonja is the _____ of the three sisters. (young)

3. A rain that freezes is _____ than a snowstorm. (bad)

4. That's the _____ home I've ever seen—it's shaped like a teapot. (unusual)

5. Being painfully shy has made Leon the _____ friendly person I know. (little)

Adverbs

What Are Adverbs?

Adverbs describe verbs, adjectives, or other adverbs. They usually end in *-ly.*

> The father *gently* hugged the sick child. (The adverb *gently* describes the verb *hugged.*)
> Newborns are *totally* innocent. (The adverb *totally* describes the adjective *innocent.*)
> The lecturer spoke so *terribly* fast that I had trouble taking notes. (The adverb *terribly* describes the adverb *fast.*)

A Common Mistake with Adverbs and Adjectives

People often mistakenly use an adjective instead of an adverb after a verb.

Incorrect	Correct
Sam needs a haircut *bad.*	Sam needs a haircut *badly.*
I laugh too *loud* when I'm embarrassed.	I laugh too *loudly* when I'm embarrassed.
You might have won the race if you hadn't run so *slow* at the beginning.	You might have won the race if you hadn't run so *slowly* at the beginning.

Activity

Underline the adjective or adverb needed. (Remember that adjectives describe nouns, and adverbs describe verbs or other adverbs.)

1. As Mac danced, his earring bounced (rapid, rapidly).

2. A drop of (thick, thickly) pea soup dripped down his chin.

3. I hiccupped (continuous, continuously) for fifteen minutes.

4. The detective opened the door (careful, carefully).

5. All she heard when she answered the phone was (heavy, heavily) breathing.

Well and Good

Two words that are often confused are *good* and *well*. *Good* is an adjective; it describes nouns. *Well* is usually an adverb; it describes verbs.

● ● ● ● ● **Activity**

Write *good* or *well* in each of the sentences that follow.

1. If you girls do a _____ job of cleaning the garage, I'll take you for some ice cream.

2. If I organize the office records too _____, my bosses may not need me any more.

3. When Ernie got AIDS, he discovered who his _____ friends really were.

4. Just because brothers and sisters fight when they're young doesn't mean they won't get along _____ as adults.

■ Review Test 1

Underline the correct word in the parentheses.

1. The server poured (littler, less) coffee into my cup than into yours.

2. Humid air seems to make Sid's asthma (more worse, worse).

3. The movie is so interesting that the three hours pass (quick, quickly).

4. The talented boy sang as (confident, confidently) as a seasoned performer.

5. Our band played so (good, well) that a local firm hired us for its annual dinner.

6. Tri Lee is always (truthful, truthfully), even when it might be better to tell a white lie.

7. The driver stopped the bus (sudden, suddenly) and yelled, "Everybody out!"

8. Pants and shirt in one colour make you look (more thin, thinner) than ones in contrasting colours.

■ Review Test 2

Write a sentence that uses each of the following adjectives and adverbs correctly.

1. careless

2. angrily

3. well

4. most relaxing

5. best

CHAPTER 29

Misplaced Modifiers

Misplaced modifiers are words that, because of awkward placement, do not describe the words the writer intended them to describe. Misplaced modifiers often confuse the meaning of a sentence. To avoid them, place words as close as possible to what they describe.

Misplaced Words	*Correctly Placed Words*
George couldn't drive to work in his small sports car *with a broken leg.* (The sports car had a broken leg?)	With a broken leg, George couldn't drive to work in his small sports car. (The words describing George are now placed next to *George.*)
The toaster was sold to us by a charming salesperson *with a money-back guarantee.* (The salesperson had a money-back guarantee?)	The toaster with a money-back guarantee was sold to us by a charming salesperson. (The words describing the toaster are now placed next to it.)
He *nearly* brushed his teeth for twenty minutes every night. (He came close to brushing his teeth, but in fact did not brush them at all?)	He brushed his teeth for nearly twenty minutes every night. (The meaning—that he brushed his teeth for a long time—is now clear.)

Activity

Underline the misplaced word or words in each sentence. Then, rewrite the sentence, placing related words together to make the meaning clear.

Examples   Frozen shrimp lay in the steel pans <u>that were thawing rapidly</u>.

Frozen shrimp that were thawing rapidly lay in the steel pans.

The speaker discussed the problem of crowded prisons <u>at the college</u>.

At the college, the speaker discussed the problem of crowded prisons.

1. The patient talked about his childhood on the psychiatrist's couch.

_____

2. The crowd watched the tennis players with swivelling heads.

_____

3. Damian put four hamburger patties on the counter which he was cooking for dinner.

_____

4. Steve carefully hung the new suit that he would wear to his first job interview in the bedroom closet.

_____

5. Alexander ripped the shirt on a car door that he made in sewing class.

_____

6. The latest Jet Li movie has almost opened in two hundred theatres across the country.

_____

7. The newscaster spoke softly into a microphone wearing a bullet-proof vest.

_____

8. The tenants left town in a dilapidated old car owing two months' rent.

_____

■ Review Test 1

Write *MM* for *misplaced modifier* or *C* for *correct* in the space provided for each sentence.

_____ 1. I nearly napped for twenty minutes during the biology lecture.

_____ 2. I napped for nearly twenty minutes during the biology lecture.

_____ 3. Ryan paused as the girl he had been following stopped at a shop window.

_____ 4. Ryan paused as the girl stopped at a shop window he had been following.

_____ 5. Marta dropped out of school after taking ten courses on Friday.

_____ 6. On Friday, Marta dropped out of school after taking ten courses.

_____ 7. Under his shirt, the player wore a good luck charm which resembled a tiny elephant.

_____ 8. The player wore a good luck charm under his shirt which resembled a tiny elephant.

■ Review Test 2

Make the changes needed to correct the misplaced modifier in each sentence.

1. Margaret Atwood wrote that someone was as innocent as a bathtub full of bullets in a poem.

_____

2. I almost filled an entire notebook with biology lab drawings.

   _____

3. The apprentice watched the master carpenter expertly fit the door with envious eyes.

   _____

4. The photographer pointed the camera at the shy deer equipped with a special night-vision scope.

   _____

5. The passengers on the bus stared at the ceiling or read newspapers with tired faces.

   _____

CHAPTER 30

Dangling Modifiers

A modifier that opens a sentence must be followed immediately by the word it is meant to describe. Otherwise, the modifier is said to be dangling, and the sentence takes on an unintended meaning. Note, for example, the following sentence:

> While reading the newspaper, my dog sat with me on the front steps.

In this sentence, the unintended meaning is that the *dog* was reading the paper. What the writer meant, of course, was that *he* (or *she*), the writer, was reading the paper. The writer should have said:

> While reading the newspaper, *I* sat with my dog on the front steps.

The dangling modifier could also be corrected by placing the subject within the opening word group:

> While *I* was reading the newspaper, my dog sat with me on the front steps.

Here are other sentences with dangling modifiers. Read the explanations of why they are dangling, and look carefully at the ways they are corrected.

Dangling	*Correct*
Shaving in front of the steamy mirror, the razor nicked Sean's chin. (*Who* was shaving in front of the mirror? The answer is not *razor,* but *Sean.* The subject *Sean* must be added.)	Shaving in front of the steamy mirror, *Sean* nicked his chin with the razor. *Or:* When *Sean* was shaving in front of the steamy mirror, he nicked his chin with the razor.
While stir-frying vegetables, hot oil splashed my arm. (*Who* is stir-frying vegetables? The answer is not *hot oil,* as it unintentionally seems to be, but *I.* The subject *I* must be added.)	While *I* was stir-frying vegetables, hot oil splashed my arm. *Or:* While stir-frying vegetables, *I* was splashed by hot oil.
Taking the exam, the room was so stuffy that Keesha nearly fainted. (*Who* took the exam? The answer is not *the room,* but *Keesha.* The subject *Keesha* must be added.)	Taking the exam, *Keesha* found the room so stuffy that she almost fainted. *Or:* When *Keesha* took the exam, the room was so stuffy that she almost fainted.

Dangling	*Correct*
To impress the interviewer, punctuality is essential.	To impress the interviewer, *you* must be punctual.
(*Who* is to impress the interviewer? The answer is not *punctuality*, but *you*. The subject *you* must be added.)	*Or:* For *you* to impress the interviewer, punctuality is essential.

The preceding examples make clear two ways of correcting a dangling modifier. Decide on a logical subject, and do one of the following:

1 Place the subject *within* the opening word group:

> When *Sean* was shaving in front of the steamy mirror, he nicked his chin.

Note: In some cases an appropriate subordinating word such as *when* must be added, and the verb may have to be changed slightly as well.

2 Place the subject right *after* the opening word group:

> Shaving in front of the steamy mirror, *Sean* nicked his chin.

Activity

Ask *Who?* of the opening words in each sentence. The subject that answers the question should be nearby in the sentence. If it is not, provide the logical subject by using either method of correction described above.

Example   While pitching his tent, a snake bit Tony on the ankle.

> *While Tony was pitching his tent, a snake bit him on the ankle.*

Or: *While pitching his tent, Tony was bitten on the ankle by a snake.*

1. Dancing on their hind legs, the audience cheered wildly as the elephants paraded by.

   _____

   _____

2. Last seen wearing dark glasses and a blond wig, the police spokesperson said the suspect was still being sought.

   _____

   _____

3. Pouring out the cereal, a coupon fell into my bowl of milk.

   _____

   _____

4. Escorted by dozens of police motorcycles, I knew the limousine carried someone important.

   _____

   _____

5. Tired and exasperated, the fight we had was inevitable.

   _____

   _____

6. Packed tightly in a tiny can, Farida had difficulty removing the anchovies.

   _____

   _____

7. Kicked carelessly under the bed, Lisa finally found her sneakers.

   _____

   _____

8. Working at the photocopy machine, the morning dragged on.

   _____

   _____

Review Test 1

Write *DM* for *dangling modifier* or *C* for *correct* in the space provided for each sentence.

_____   1. While riding the bicycle, a vicious-looking Rottweiler snapped at Tim's ankles.

_____   2. While Tim was riding the bicycle, a vicious-looking Rottweiler snapped at his ankles.

_____   3. Afraid to look his father in the eye, Scott kept his head bowed.

_____   4. Afraid to look his father in the eye, Scott's head remained bowed.

_____   5. Boring and silly, I turned the TV show off.

_____   6. I turned off the boring and silly TV show.

_____   7. Munching leaves from a tall tree, the giraffe fascinated the children.

_____   8. Munching leaves from a tall tree, the children were fascinated by the giraffe.

Review Test 2

Make the changes needed to correct the dangling modifier in each sentence.

1. Not having had much sleep, my concentration during class was weak.

   _____

2. Joined at the hip, a team of surgeons successfully separated the Siamese twins.

   _____

3. Wading by the lakeshore, a water snake brushed past my leg.

   _____

4. While being restrained by court officials, the judge sentenced the kidnapper.

_____

5. In a sentimental frame of mind, Céline Dion's song brought tears to Beth's eyes.

_____

Review Test 3

Complete the following sentences. In each case, a logical subject should follow the opening words.

Example Looking through the door's peephole, _I couldn't see who rang the_

doorbell.

1. Noticing the light turn yellow, _____

2. Being fragile, _____

3. While washing the car, _____

4. Although very expensive, _____

5. Driving by the cemetery, _____

CHAPTER 31

Manuscript Form

When you hand in a paper for any course, it will probably be judged first by its format. It is important, then, to make the paper look attractive, neat, and easy to read. Here is a checklist you should use when preparing a paper for an instructor:

1. Is the paper full-sized (8½ × 11 inches)?

2. Are there wide margins all around the paper? In particular, have you been careful not to crowd the right-hand or bottom margin?

3. If the paper is word-processed, have you

   - checked whether your instructor prefers full justification or "ragged right" line format?
   - used an appropriate font, such as Times, Optima, Helvetica, or Arial?
   - chosen a readable point-size such as 12-point?
   - double spaced the text of each paragraph of your essay?
   - used any header information your instructor may require?

4. If the paper is handwritten, have you

   - used a blue or black pen?
   - been careful not to overlap letters or to make decorative loops on letters?
   - made all your letters distinct, with special attention to *a, e, i, o,* and *u*—five letters that people sometimes write illegibly?
   - kept all your capital letters clearly distinct from small letters?

5. Have you centred the title of your paper on the first line of page 1? Have you been careful *not* to put quotation marks around the title or to underline it? Have you capitalized all the words in the title except for short connecting words like *of, for, the, and, in,* and *to?*

6. If your paper is handwritten, have you skipped a line between the title and the first line of your paper?

7. If your paper is word-processed, have you inserted two lines of space between the title and the opening line of your paper?

8. Have you indented the first line of each paragraph about five spaces from the left-hand margin? If you are word-processing your paper, your instructor may prefer that you do not "tab" or indent a first line of a new paragraph but leave two lines of space between each separate paragraph.

_____   9. Have you made commas, periods, and other punctuation marks firm and clear?

_____   10. If you have broken any words at the end of a line, have you been careful to break only between syllables?

_____   11. Have you put your name, the date, and other information on the title page, at the end of the paper, or wherever your instructor has specified?

Also, ask yourself these important questions about the title and the first sentence of your paper:

_____   12. Is your title made up of several words that tell what the paper is about? (The title should be just several words, _not_ a complete sentence.)

_____   13. Does the first sentence of your paper stand independent of the title? (The reader should _not_ have to use the words in the title to make sense of the opening sentence.)

Activity

Use the checklist to locate the seven mistakes in format in the following lines from a student essay. Explain the mistakes in the spaces provided. One mistake is described for you as an example.

	"Being alone"
	This is something that I simply cannot tolera-
	te, and I will go to great lengths to
	prevent it. For example, if I know that I need

1. Hyphenate only between syllables (_toler-ate,_ not _tolera-te_).

2. _____

3. _____

4. _____

5. _____

6. _____

7. _____

CHAPTER 32

Capital Letters

Main Uses of Capital Letters

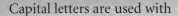

Capital letters are used with

1 first word in a sentence or direct quotation;

2 names of persons and the word *I*;

3 names of particular places;

4 names of days of the week, months, and holidays;

5 names of commercial products;

6 titles of books, magazines, newspapers, articles, stories, poems, films, television shows, songs, papers that you write, and the like;

7 names of companies, associations, unions, clubs, religious and political groups, and other organizations.

Each use is illustrated on the pages that follow.

First Word in a Sentence or Direct Quotation

The corner grocery was robbed last night.
The alien said, "Take me to your leader."
"If you feel lonely," said Teri, "call us. We'll be over in no time."

Note: In the third example above, *If* and *We'll* are capitalized because they start new sentences. But *call* is not capitalized because it is part of the first sentence.

Names of Persons and the Word *I*

Last night, I saw a movie starring Jet Li and Chow Yun-Fat.

Names of Particular Places

Although Bill dropped out of Port Charles High School, he eventually earned his degree and got a job with Atlas Realty Company.

But: Use small letters if the specific name of a place is not given.

Although Bill dropped out of high school, he eventually earned his degree and got a job with a real estate company.

Names of Days of the Week, Months, and Holidays

On the last Friday afternoon in June, the day before Canada Day, my boss is having a barbecue for all the employees.

But: Use small letters for the seasons—summer, fall, winter, spring.

Most people feel more energetic in the spring and fall.

Names of Commercial Products

My little sister knows all the words to the jingles for Maple Leaf hot dogs, Tim Hortons doughnuts, Meow Mix cat food, and Swiss Chalet chicken.

But: Use small letters for the *type* of product (hot dogs, doughnuts, cat food, and so on).

Titles of Books, Magazines, Newspapers, Articles, Stories, Poems, Films, Television Shows, Songs, Papers that You Write, and the Like

We read the book *In the Skin of a Lion* for our cultural studies class.
In the doctor's waiting room, I watched *Canada at Noon*, read an article in *Maclean's*, and leafed through the *Winnipeg Free Press.*

Names of Companies, Associations, Unions, Clubs, Religious and Political Groups, and Other Organizations

Joe Duffy is a Roman Catholic, but his wife is Baptist.
The Hilldale Square Dancers' Club has won many competitions.
Brian, a member of the Canadian Auto Workers union and the Knights of Columbus, works for Ford Canada.

● ● ● ● **Activity**

Underline the words that need capitals in the following sentences. Then, write the capitalized form of each word in the space provided. The number of spaces tells you how many corrections to make in each case.

Example   In our resource management class, each student must write a report on an article in the magazine <u>*canadian geographic*</u>

      <u>*Canadian*</u>   <u>*Geographic*</u>

1. Leon's collection of beatles souvenirs includes a pair of tickets from their last concert at maple leaf gardens.

    _____   _____   _____   _____

2. Yumi read in *chatelaine* magazine that nelly furtado grew up in vancouver.

    _____   _____   _____   _____

3. When i have a cold, I use vicks vapoRub and chew halls cough drops.

    _____   _____

4. Since no man volunteered for the job, the boy scouts in dauphin, manitoba, have a woman pack leader.

   _____   _____   _____   _____

5. A nature trail for the blind in point pelee, ontario, has signs written in braille that encourage visitors to smell and touch the plants.

   _____   _____   _____

6. My father is a confirmed Edmonton oilers fan, though he lives in saskatoon.

   _____   _____

7. Martha bought a pepsi to wash down her vachon flaky.

   _____   _____   _____

8. Vince listened to a Barenaked ladies CD called *Stunt* while Donna read an article in *elm Street* entitled "Where's Your portfolio?"

   _____   _____   _____

Other Uses of Capital Letters

Capital letters are also used with

1 names that show family relationships;

2 titles of persons when used with their names;

3 specific school courses;

4 languages;

5 geographic locations;

6 historical periods and events;

7 races, nations, and nationalities;

8 opening and closing of a letter.

Each use is illustrated on the pages that follow.

Names that Show Family Relationships

All his life, Father has been addicted to gadgets.
I browsed through Grandmother's collection of old photographs.
Aunt Florence and Uncle Bill bought a mobile home.

But: Do not capitalize words like *mother, father, grandmother, grandfather, uncle, aunt,* and so on when they are preceded by a possessive word *(my, your, his, her, our, their).*

All his life, my father has been addicted to gadgets.
I browsed through my grandmother's collection of old photographs.
My aunt and uncle bought a cabin near Tracadie.

Titles of Persons When Used with Their Names

I contributed to Premier Filmon's campaign fund.
Is Dr. Gregory on vacation?
Professor Li announced that there would be no tests in the course.

But: Use small letters when titles appear by themselves, without specific names.

I contributed to my premier's campaign fund.
Is the doctor on vacation?
The professor announced that there would be no tests in the course.

Specific School Courses

The college offers evening sections of Introductory Psychology I, Abnormal Psychology, Psychology and Statistics, and Educational Psychology.

But: Use small letters for general subject areas.

The college offers evening sections of many psychology courses.

Languages

My grandfather's Polish accent makes his English difficult to understand.

Geographic Locations

He grew up in the Maritimes but moved to the West to look for a better job.

But: Use small letters in directions.

Head west for five blocks and then turn east on Queen Street.

Historical Periods and Events

During the Middle Ages, the Black Death killed over one-quarter of Europe's population.

Races, Nations, and Nationalities

The survey asked if the head of our household was Caucasian, Asian, or Native Canadian.
Tanya has lived on armed forces bases in Germany, Italy, and Spain.
Denise's beautiful features reflect her Chinese and Filipino parentage.

Opening and Closing of a Letter

Dear Sir: Sincerely yours,
Dear Ms. Henderson: Truly yours,

Note: Capitalize only the first word in a closing.

⦾ ⦾ ⦾ ⦾ **Activity**

Underline the words that need capitals in the following sentences. Then, write the capitalized forms of the words in the spaces provided. The number of spaces tells you how many corrections to make in each case.

1. During world war II, some canadians were afraid that the japanese would invade British Columbia.

   _____   _____   _____   _____

2. On their job site in korea, the french, swiss, and chinese co-workers used English to communicate.

   _____   _____   _____   _____

3. When uncle harvey got the bill from his doctor, he called the Ontario Medical Association to complain.

   _____   _____

4. Dr. Freeling of the business department is offering a new course called introduction to word processing.

   _____   _____   _____

5. The new restaurant featuring vietnamese cuisine has just opened on the south side of the city.

   _____

Unnecessary Use of Capitals

⦾ ⦾ ⦾ ⦾ **Activity**

Many errors in capitalization are caused by using capitals where they are not needed. Underline the incorrectly capitalized letters in the following sentences, and write the correct forms in the spaces provided. The number of spaces tells you how many corrections to make in each sentence.

1. Kim Campbell—the first female Prime Minister—also had the shortest tenure in Office.

   _____   _____   _____

2. For her fortieth birthday, my Aunt bought herself a red Mini Cooper.

   _____   _____

3. Canadians were delighted when the Toronto Blue Jays were the first Canadian Baseball Team to win the World Series.

   _____   _____

4. In his Book titled *Offbeat Museums,* Saul Rubin tells about various Unusual Museums, such as, Believe it or not, the Barbed Wire Museum.

_____ _____ _____ _____

5. Einstein's theory of relativity, which he developed when he was only twenty-six, led to the invention of the Electron Microscope, Television, and the Atomic bomb.

_____ _____ _____ _____

■ Review Test 1

Add capitals where needed in the following sentences.

Example   In an injured tone, Mary demanded, "~~w~~hy wasn't ~~u~~ncle Lou invited to the party?"

(W above "w", U above "u")

1. To keep warm, a homeless old man sits on a steam vent near the bay store on main street.

2. Silent movie stars of the twenties, like charlie chaplin and mary pickford, earned more than a million tax-free dollars a year.

3. Unique in Canada to the carolinian zone of southwestern ontario are such plants as the green dragon Lily and sassafras trees.

4. When Jean chrétien was first in ottawa, his idols were Wilfrid laurier and Louis st. laurent.

5. In an old movie, an attractive young lady invites groucho marx to join her.

6. "why?" asks groucho. "are you coming apart?"

7. I was halfway to the wash & dry Laundromat on elm street when i realized that my box of sunlight detergent was still at home on the kitchen counter.

8. Although I know that mother loves holidays, even I was surprised when she announced a party in february to celebrate wiarton Willie and groundhog day.

■ Review Test 2

On a separate paper, write

1. seven sentences demonstrating the seven main uses of capital letters;

2. eight sentences demonstrating the eight other uses of capital letters.

CHAPTER 33

Numbers and Abbreviations

Numbers

Here are three helpful rules for using numbers:

Rule 1: Spell out numbers that take no more than two words. Otherwise, use the numbers themselves.

> In Jody's kitchen is her collection of seventy-two cookbooks.
> Jody has a file of 350 recipes.

> It will take about two weeks to fix the computer database.
> Since a number of people use the database, the company will lose over 150 work days.

> Only twelve students have signed up for the field trip.
> Nearly 250 students came to the lecture.

Rule 2: Be consistent when you use a series of numbers. If some numbers in a sentence or paragraph require more than two words, then use numbers in every case involving the same category of items.

> After the storm, maintenance workers unclogged 46 drains, removed 123 broken tree limbs, and rescued 3 kittens that were stuck in a drain pipe.

Rule 3: Use numbers to show dates, times, addresses, percentages, and parts of a book.

> The burglary was committed on October 30, 2001, but not discovered until January 2, 2002.
> Before I went to bed, I set my alarm for 6:45 a.m.

But: Spell out numbers before *o'clock*. For example: I didn't get out of bed until seven o'clock.

> The library is located at 45 West 52d Street.
> When you take the skin off a piece of chicken, you remove about 40 per cent of the fat.
> The name of the murderer is revealed in Chapter 8 on page 236.

● ● ● ● **Activity**

Cross out the mistakes in numbers, and write the corrections in the spaces provided.

1. The Labour Day Parade will begin at three-thirty in front of the newspaper building at one-oh-six Main Street.

   _____   _____

2. It took 4 hours to proofread all 75 pages of the manuscript.

   _____   _____

3. We expect to have fifty per cent of the work completed by March tenth.

   _____   _____

Abbreviations

Using abbreviations can save you time when you take notes. In formal writing, however, you should avoid most abbreviations. Listed below are some of the few abbreviations that are considered acceptable in compositions. Note that a period is used after most abbreviations.

1 Mr., Mrs., Ms., Jr., Sr., Dr. when used with proper names:

   Mrs. Levesque   Dr. DaSilva   Howard Kelley, Jr.

2 Time references:

   A.M. or a.m.   P.M. or p.m.   B.C., A.D.

3 Initials in a person's name:

   Pierre E. Trudeau   John F. Kennedy   Michael J. Fox

4 Organizations, technical words, and company names known primarily by their initials:

   IBM   UNICEF   CBC   NHL   NDP   AIDS   CAT scan

● ● ● ● **Activity**

Cross out the words that should not be abbreviated, and correct them in the spaces provided.

1. Between mid-Oct. and the beginning of Jan., I typically gain about three kgs.

   _____   _____   _____

2. I had such a bad headache this aftern. that I called my doc. for an appt.

   _____   _____   _____

3. I stopped at the p.o. at about twenty min. past ten and bought five dol. worth of stamps.

   _____   _____   _____   _____

■ Review Test

Cross out the mistakes in numbers and abbreviations, and correct them in the spaces provided.

1. Sanjay was shocked when he transferred from a small h.s. to one with over 5000 students.

   _____   _____   _____   _____

2. Grandpa lived to be ninety-nine despite smoking 2 doz. cheap cigars per mo.

   _____   _____   _____

3. Although the 2 girls are twins, they have different birthdays: one was born just before midnight on Feb. twenty-fifth, and the other a few minutes later after midnight.

   _____   _____   _____

4. In their first week of Fr. class, students learned to count from 1 to twenty-one and studied Chapter One in their textbook.

   _____   _____   _____

5. When I cleaned out the junk drawer in the kitch., I found twelve rubber bands, thirty-seven paper clips, and 3 used-up batteries.

   _____   _____

CHAPTER 34

Apostrophe

The two main uses of the apostrophe are

1 to show the omission of one or more letters in a contraction;

2 to show ownership or possession.

Each use is explained on the pages that follow.

Apostrophe in Contractions

A *contraction* is formed when *two words* are combined *into one* to make one word. An apostrophe is used to show where letters are omitted in forming the contraction. Here are two contractions:

> have + not = haven't (the *o* in *not* has been omitted)
> I + will = I'll (the *wi* in *will* has been omitted)

Following are some other common contractions:

I + am = I'm	it + is = it's
I + have = I've	it + has = it's
I + had = I'd	is + not = isn't
who + is = who's	could + not = couldn't
do + not = don't	I + would = I'd
did + not = didn't	they + are = they're

Note: *Will + not* has an unusual contraction: *won't*.

Activity

Write the contractions for the words in parentheses. One is done for you.

1. (Are not) _____*Aren't*_____ the reserve books in the library kept at the circulation desk?

2. If (they are) _____ coming over, (I had) _____ better cook more pasta.

3. (I am) _____ the kind of student (who is) _____ extremely nervous before tests.

4. (We are) _____ hoping to find out (who is) _____ responsible for this error; (it is) _____ important to us to keep our customers happy.

5. I (can not) _____ remember if (there is) _____ gas in the car or not.

Note: Even though contractions are common in everyday speech and in written dialogue, it is often best to avoid them in formal writing.

Apostrophe to Show Ownership or Possession

To show ownership or possession, we can use such words as *belongs to, possessed by, owned by,* or (most commonly) *of.*

the umbrella that *belongs to* Santo
the DVD player *owned by* the school
the gentleness *of* my father

But the apostrophe plus *s* (if the word does not end in *s*) is often the quickest and easiest way to show possession. Thus, we can say:

Santo's umbrella
the school's DVD player
my father's gentleness

Points to Remember

1 The *'s* goes with the owner or possessor (in the examples given, *Santo, the school, my father*). What follows is the person or thing possessed (in the examples given, *the umbrella, the DVD player, gentleness*).

2 When showing possession, the apostrophe should always come before the *s*.

Santo's   not   *Santos'*
Yes   No

Activity 1

Rewrite the *italicized* part of each of the sentences below, using the *'s* to show possession. Remember that the *'s* goes with the owner or possessor.

Example   *The wing of the bluejay* was broken.

The bluejay's wing was broken.

1. *The annoying voice of the comedian* irritated me, so I changed the TV channel.

_____

2. *The performance of the goalie* is inconsistent.

_____

3. *The thin hand belonging to the old lady* felt as dry as parchment.

_____

4. In *the window of the jewellery store* is a sign reading, "Ears Pierced While You Wait."

_____

5. A fly flew into *the mouth of the TV weather person.*

_____

6. *The new denim shirt belonging to Josh* was as scratchy as sandpaper.

_____

7. *The hair belonging to Rachel* is usually not green; she coloured it for Halloween.

_____

8. *The bowl of cereal belonging to Ahmed* refused to snap, crackle, or pop.

_____

Activity 2

Add *'s* to each of the following words to make them the possessors or owners of something. Then, write sentences using the words. The first one is done for you.

1. rock star *rock star's* _____

   The rock star's limousine pulled up to the curb.

2. Javier _____

   _____

3. pilot _____

   _____

4. neighbour _____

   _____

Apostrophe versus Possessive Pronouns

Do not use an apostrophe with possessive pronouns. They already show ownership. Possessive pronouns include *his, hers, its, yours, ours,* and *theirs.*

Incorrect	*Correct*
The sun warped his' vinyl albums.	The sun warped his vinyl albums.
The restored Meteor is theirs'.	The restored Meteor is theirs.
The decision is yours'.	The decision is yours.
The plaid suitcase is ours'.	The plaid suitcase is ours.
The lion charged its' prey.	The lion charged its prey.

Apostrophe versus Simple Plurals

When you want to make a word plural, just add an *s* at the end of the word. Do *not* add an apostrophe. For example, the plural of the word *movie* is *movies,* not *movie's* or *movies'*. Look at this sentence:

Tim coveted his roommate's collection of vinyl albums and compact discs.

The words *albums* and *discs* are simple plurals, meaning more than one album, more than one disc. The plural is shown by adding *s* only. On the other hand, the *'s* after *roommate* shows possession—that the roommate owns the albums and discs.

⦁ ⦁ ⦁ ⦁   **Activity**

Insert an apostrophe where needed to show possession in the following sentences. Write *plural* above words where the *s* ending simply means more than one thing.

plural   plural

Example   Arlene's tinted contact lenses protect her eyes from glare.

1. Harry grasped his wifes arm as she stood up on in-line skates for the first time.

2. Vivians decision to study computer science is based on predictions of good opportunities for women in that field.

3. The fires extreme heat had melted the telephones in the office and welded the metal chairs into a twisted heap.

4. At the doctors request, Troy pulled up his shirt and revealed the zipper-like scars from his operation.

5. Of all the peoples names in all the worlds countries, the most common is Mohammed.

6. At the end of the day, Cams shirt and pants smelled like gasoline, and his fingernails were rimmed with grease.

7. The childrens shouts of delight grew louder as the clown added eggs, light-bulbs, and a bowling ball to items he was juggling.

8. Tinas camping handbook suggests that we bring water purification tablets and nylon ropes.

Apostrophe with Words Ending in *-s*

Plurals that end in *-s* show possession simply by adding the apostrophe rather than an apostrophe plus *s.*

the Thompsons' porch
the players' victory
her parents' motor home
the Barenaked Ladies' last album
the soldiers' hats

· · · ·   **Activity**

Add an apostrophe where needed.

1. Several campers tents collapsed during the storm.

2. The Murrays phone bills are often over $100 a month.

3. Users of wheelchairs cannot get up the steep steps at the entrances to many buildings.

4. The twins habit of dressing alike was started by their parents when the twins were children.

5. At the crowded intersection, several young men rushed out to wash the cars windshields.

◾   **Review Test**

In each sentence, underline the two words that need apostrophes. Then, write the words correctly in the spaces provided.

_____   1. The sagging sofas stuffing was coming out in places, and one of the chairs legs was broken.

_____   2. A shaky rope ladder led from the barns wooden floor to the haylofts dusty shadows.

_____   3. The paperback books glaring purple and orange cover was designed to attract a hurrying customers eye.

_____   4. Alicias essay was due in a matter of hours, but she suffered a writers block that emptied her brain.

_____   5. While she waited in her bosss office, Marlas nervous fingers shredded a Styrofoam coffee cup into a pile of jagged white flakes.

_____   6. Ivan could not remember whether he had left his wallet in his cars glove compartment or at his friends house.

_____   7. Members of the parents association constructed a maze made of old tires for the childrens playground.

_____   8. The cats great green eyes grew even wider as the curious dogs sniffing nose came too close to her.

CHAPTER 35

Quotation Marks

The two main uses of quotation marks are

1 to set off the exact words of a speaker or writer;

2 to set off the titles of short works.

Each use is explained on the pages that follow.

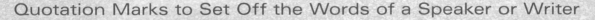

Quotation Marks to Set Off the Words of a Speaker or Writer

Use quotation marks to show the exact words of a speaker or writer.

> "I feel as though I've been here before," Angie murmured to her husband.
> (Quotation marks set off the exact words that Angie spoke to her husband.)

> Margaret Atwood wrote, "Fear has a smell . . ."
> (Quotation marks set off the exact words that Margaret Atwood wrote.)

> "Did you know," said the nutrition expert, "that it's healthier to be a few kilos overweight?"
> (Two pairs of quotation marks are used to enclose the nutrition expert's exact words.)

> The biology professor said, "Ants are a lot like human beings. They farm their own food and raise smaller insects as livestock. And, like humans, ants send armies to war."
> (Note that the end quotation marks do not come until the end of the biology professor's speech. Place quotation marks before the first quoted word and after the last quoted word. As long as no interruption occurs in the speech, do not use quotation marks for each new sentence.)

Punctuation Hint: In the four examples on the preceding page, notice that a comma sets off the quoted part from the rest of the sentence. Also, observe that commas and periods at the end of a quotation always go *inside* quotation marks.

Complete the following statements that explain how capital letters, commas, and periods are used in quotations. Refer to the four examples as guides.

1. Every quotation begins with a _____ letter.

2. When a quotation is split (as in the sentence about the nutrition expert), the second part does not begin with a capital letter unless it is a _____ sentence.

3. _____ are used to separate the quoted part of a sentence from the rest of the sentence.

4. Commas and periods that come at the end of a quotation go _____ the quotation marks.

Activity 1

Place quotation marks around the exact words of a speaker or writer in the sentences that follow.

1. Several people have been credited with saying, The more I see of people, the more I like dogs.

2. Beata asked, Do you give a discount to senior citizens?

3. This hamburger is raw! cried Leo.

4. The bumper sticker on the rear of the battered old car read, Don't laugh—it's paid for.

5. I know why Robin Hood robbed only the rich, said the comedian. The poor don't have any money.

6. These CDs, proclaimed the television announcer, are not sold in any store.

7. When chefs go to great lengths, the woman at the weight-loss centre said, I go to great widths.

8. On a tombstone in a Saskatchewan cemetery are the words, Here lies an atheist, all dressed up and no place to go.

Activity 2

1. Write a sentence in which you quote a favourite expression of someone you know. In the same sentence, identify the person's relationship to you.

   Example   *My grandfather loves to say, "It can't be as bad as all that."*

   _____

   _____

2. Write a quotation that contains the words *Paulo asked Teresa.* Write a second quotation that includes the words *Teresa replied.*

   _____

   _____

   _____

   _____

   _____

   _____

3. Quote an interesting sentence or two from a book or magazine. In the same sentence, identify the title and author of the work.

Example   *In The Dilbert Desk Calendar by Scott Adams, cartoon character*

Dilbert says, "I can please only one person per day. Today isn't your

day, and tomorrow isn't looking good either."

_____

_____

_____

_____

_____

_____

Indirect Quotations

An indirect quotation is a rewording of someone else's comments rather than a word-for-word direct quotation. The word *that* often signals an indirect quotation.

Direct Quotation	*Indirect Quotation*
The nurse said, "Some babies cannot tolerate cows' milk." (The nurse's exact spoken words are given, so quotation marks are used.)	The nurse said that some babies cannot tolerate cows' milk. (We learn the nurse's words indirectly, so no quotation marks are used.)
Vicky's note to Dan read, "I'll be home by 7:30." (The exact words that Vicky wrote in the note are given, so quotation marks are used.)	Vicky left a note for Dan that said she would be home by 7:30. (We learn Vicky's words indirectly, so no quotation marks are used.)

● ● ● **Activity**

Rewrite the following sentences, changing words as necessary to convert the sentences into direct quotations. The first one has been done for you as an example.

1. Ted asked Maria if she wanted to see his spider collection.

   Ted asked Maria, "Do you want to see my spider collection?"

2. Sonya said that her uncle looks just like a large basset hound.

   _____

   _____

3. Angelo said that he wanted a box of the extra-crispy chicken.

   _____

   _____

4. My boss told me that I could make mistakes as long as I didn't repeat them.

_____

_____

5. The instructor announced that Thursday's test had been cancelled.

_____

_____

Quotation Marks to Set Off the Titles of Short Works

Titles of short works are usually set off by quotation marks, while titles of long works are underlined or italicized. Use quotation marks to set off titles of such short works as articles in newspapers or magazines, chapters in a book, short stories, poems, and songs. You should underline or italicize titles of books, newspapers, magazines, plays, movies, record albums, and television shows depending on the citation system you use. Note the following examples:

Quotation Marks	*Underlined or Italicized*
the essay "Bicycles"	in the book <u>Urban Scrawl</u>
the article "New Social Union Deal"	in the newspaper <u>The National Post</u>
the article "Living with Inflation"	in the magazine <u>Maclean's</u>
the chapter "Chinese Religion"	in the book <u>Paths of Faith</u>
the story "The Sin Eater"	in the book <u>Bluebeard's Egg</u>
the poem "When I Have Fears"	in the book <u>Complete Poems of John Keats</u>
the song "Apparitions"	in the album <u>The Dave Matthews Band</u>
the episode "Old Memories"	in the television show <u>Cold Squad</u>
	in the movie <u>Exotica</u>

Note: In printed works, italic type—slanted type that looks *like this*—is used instead of underlining. (See pages 307–308 for more information about the use of italic type and underlining when using either the MLA or APA style in research.)

Activity

Use quotation marks or underlines as needed.

1. In her short story A Sea Worry, Maxine Hong Kingston describes a group of teenage surfers and a mother who tries to understand them.

2. I bought the National Enquirer to read an article entitled Painful Beauty Secrets of the Stars.

3. We studied the chapter The Motive for Metaphor in Northrop Frye's book The Educated Imagination.

4. Jamila used an article titled A Certain Hunger by Maggie Helwig from This Magazine in her research paper about eating disorders.

5. The movie Casablanca, which starred Humphrey Bogart, was originally cast with Ronald Reagan in the leading role.

6. My favourite old TV show on Nick at Nite is Thriller, a horror series hosted by Boris Karloff, the man who starred in the 1931 movie Frankenstein.

7. When the Spice Girls' movie Spice World was first shown, fans screamed so much that no one could hear the songs or the dialogue.

8. On my father's wall is a framed front page of The Vancouver Sun of February 25, 1940—the day he was born.

Other Uses of Quotation Marks

Quotation marks are also used as follows:

1 To set off special words or phrases from the rest of a sentence:

> In elementary school, we were taught a little jingle about the "*i* before *e*" spelling rule.
> What is the difference between "it's" and "its"?
> (In this book, *italics* are often used instead of quotation marks to set off words.)

2 To mark off a quotation within a quotation:

> The physics professor said, "For class on Friday, do the problems at the end of the chapter titled 'Work and Energy.'"
> Brendan remarked, "Did you know that Humphrey Bogart never actually said, 'Play it again, Sam' in the movie *Casablanca*?"

Note: A quotation within a quotation is indicated by *single* quotation marks, as shown above.

Review Test 1

Insert quotation marks where needed in the sentences that follow.

1. The psychology class read a short story called Silent Snow, Secret Snow, about a young boy who creates his own fantasy world.

2. While filming the movie *Vertigo,* actress Kim Novak was agonizing over how to play a particular scene until director Alfred Hitchcock reminded her, Kim, it's only a movie!

3. I'm against elementary school students using calculators, said Fred. I spent three years learning long division, and so should they.

4. Composer George Gershwin wrote many hundreds of hit songs, including classics like Summertime and Somebody Loves Me.

5. When I gagged while taking a foul-tasting medicine, my wife said, Put an ice cube on your tongue first, and then you won't taste it.

6. Gene reported to his business class on an article in *Canadian Business* magazine entitled Cashing In on the Energy Boom.

7. When a guest at the wedding was asked what he was giving the couple, he replied, about six months.

8. Pierre Elliott Trudeau, an occasionally controversial prime minister, once said, Power only tires those who don't exercise it.

Review Test 2

Go through the comics section of a newspaper to find a comic strip that amuses you. Be sure to choose a strip where two or more characters are speaking to each other. Write a full description that will enable people who have not read the comic strip to visualize it clearly and appreciate its humour. Describe the setting and action in each panel, and enclose the words of the speakers in quotation marks.

CHAPTER 36

Comma

Six Main Uses of the Comma

Commas are used mainly

1 to separate items in a series;

2 to set off introductory material;

3 on both sides of words that interrupt the flow of thought in a sentence;

4 between two complete thoughts connected by *and, but, for, or, nor, so, yet*;

5 to set off a direct quotation from the rest of a sentence;

6 for certain everyday material.

You may find it helpful to remember that the comma often marks a slight pause or break in a sentence. Read aloud the sentence examples given for each rule, and listen for the minor pauses or breaks that are signalled by commas.

Comma between Items in a Series

Use commas to separate items in a series.

> The street vendor sold watches, necklaces, and earrings.
> The pitcher adjusted his cap, pawed the ground, and peered over his shoulder.
> The exercise instructor told us to inhale, exhale, and relax.
> Joe peered into the hot, still-smoking engine.

Notes:

1 The final comma in a series is optional, but it is often used. *Be consistent* in your use of commas when you list items.

2 A comma is used between two descriptive words in a series only if *and* inserted between the words sounds natural. You could say:

> Joe peered into the hot *and* still-smoking engine.

Notice, however, in the following sentence that the descriptive words do not sound natural when *and* is inserted between them. In such cases, no comma is used.

> Theo wore a pale green tuxedo. (A pale *and* green tuxedo does not sound right, so no comma is used.)

408

Activity

Place commas between items in a series.

1. The old kitchen cabinets were littered with dead insects crumbs and dust balls.

2. Rudy stretched out on the swaying hammock popped open a frosty can of pop and balanced it carefully on his stomach.

3. The children splashed through the warm deep swirling rainwater that flooded the street.

4. The police officer's warm brown eyes relaxed manner and pleasant smile made him easy to talk to.

5. The musty shadowy cellar with the crumbling cement floor was our favourite playground.

Comma after Introductory Material

Use a comma to set off introductory material.

Just in time, Kami slid a plastic tray under the overwatered philodendron.
Muttering under his breath, Matthias reviewed the terms he had memorized.
In a wolf pack, the dominant male holds his tail higher than the other pack members.
Although he had been first in the checkout line, Devon let an elderly woman go ahead of him.
After the fire, we slogged through the ashes of the burned house.

Note: If the introductory material is brief, the comma is sometimes omitted. In the activities here, you should include the comma.

Activity

Place commas after introductory material.

1. As Chen struggled with the stuck window gusts of cold rain blew in his face.

2. His heart pounding wildly Jesse opened the letter that would tell him whether or not he had been accepted at college.

3. Along the once-pretty Don River people had dumped old tires and loads of household trash.

4. When the band hadn't taken the stage forty-five minutes after the concert was supposed to begin the audience members started shouting and stamping their feet.

5. Setting down a smudged glass of murky water the server tossed Dennis a greasy menu and asked if he'd care to order.

Comma around Words Interrupting the Flow of Thought

Use a comma on both sides of words or phrases that interrupt the flow of thought in a sentence.

> The vinyl car seat, sticky from the heat, clung to my skin.
> Marty's new computer, which his wife got him as a birthday gift, occupies all of his spare time.
> The hallway, dingy and dark, was illuminated by a bare bulb hanging from a wire.

Usually you can "hear" words that interrupt the flow of thought in a sentence by reading it aloud. In cases where you are not sure if certain words are interrupters, remove them from the sentence. If it still makes sense without the words, you know that the words are interrupters and that the information they give is nonessential. *Such nonessential or extra information is set off with commas.*

Note the following sentence:

> Joanna Dodd, who goes to aerobics class with me, was in a serious car accident.

Here, the words *who goes to aerobics class with me* are extra information not needed to identify the subject of the sentence, *Joanna Dodd.* Commas go around such nonessential information. Note, on the other hand, the next sentence:

> The woman who goes to aerobics class with me was in a serious accident.

Here, the words *who goes to aerobics class with me* supply essential information—information needed for us to identify the woman being spoken of. If the words were removed from the sentence, we would no longer know exactly who was in the accident: "The woman was in a serious accident." Here is another example:

> *Watership Down,* a novel by Richard Adams, is the most thrilling adventure story I've ever read.

Here, the words *a novel by Richard Adams* could be left out, and we would still know the basic meaning of the sentence. Commas are placed around such nonessential material. However, note the following sentence:

> Richard Adams' novel *Watership Down* is the most thrilling adventure story I've ever read.

In this case, the title of the novel is essential. Without it, the sentence would read, "Richard Adams' novel is the most thrilling adventure story I've ever read." We would not know which of Richard Adams' novels was so thrilling. Commas are not used around the title because it provides essential information.

Activity

Use commas to set off interrupting words.

1. A slight breeze hot and damp ruffled the bedroom curtains.

2. The defrosting chickens loosely wrapped in plastic left a pool on the counter.

3. Lenny's wallet which he kept in his front pants pocket was linked to his belt with a metal chain.

4. Mr. LaCroix who is an avid Canadiens fan remembers the grand days of Jacques Plante and Bernie Geoffrion.

5. The fleet of tall ships a majestic sight made its way into Halifax Harbour.

Comma between Two Complete Thoughts

Use a comma between two complete thoughts connected by *and, but, for, or, nor, so, yet.*

> Sam closed all the windows, but the predicted thunderstorm never arrived.
> I like wearing comfortable clothing, so I buy oversized shirts and sweaters.
> Peggy doesn't envy the skinny models in magazines, for she is happy with her own healthy-looking body.

Notes:

1 The comma is optional when the complete thoughts are short.

> The ferris wheel started and Wilson closed his eyes.
> Irene left the lecture hall for her head was pounding.
> I made a wrong turn so I doubled back.

2 Be careful not to use a comma to separate two verbs that belong to one subject. The comma is used only in sentences made up of two complete thoughts (two subjects and two verbs). In the sentence below, there is only one subject *(doctor)* and a double verb *(stared* and *lectured)*. No comma is needed.

> The doctor stared over his bifocals and lectured me about smoking.

Likewise, the next sentence has only one subject *(Aaron)* and a double verb *(switched* and *tapped);* therefore, no comma is needed.

> Aaron switched the lamp on and off and then tapped it with his fingers.

Activity

Place a comma before a joining word that connects two complete thoughts (two subjects and two verbs). Remember, do *not* place a comma within a sentence that has only one subject and a double verb. (Some items may be correct as given.)

1. My favourite soap was interrupted for a news bulletin about an ice storm and I poked my head out of the kitchen to listen to the announcement.

2. The puppy was beaten by its former owner and cringes at the sound of a loud voice.

3. The eccentric woman brought all her own clips and rollers to the hairdressers for she was afraid to use the ones there.

4. The tuna sandwich in my lunch is crushed and the cream-filled cupcake is plastered to the bottom of the bag.

5. The property owner promised repeatedly to come and fix the leaking shower but three months later he hasn't done a thing.

6. Bonita was tired of summer reruns so she visited the town library to pick up some interesting books.

7. You can spend hours driving all over town to look for a particular type of camera or you can telephone a few stores to find it quickly.

8. Many people strolled among the exhibits at the comic book collectors' convention and stopped to look at a rare first edition of *Superman*.

Comma with Direct Quotations

Use a comma to set off a direct quotation from the rest of a sentence.

> The carnival barker cried, "Step right up and win a prize!"
> "Now is the time to yield to temptation," my horoscope read.
> "I'm sorry," said the restaurant host. "You'll have to wait."
> "For my first writing assignment," said Scott, "I have to turn in a five-hundred-word description of a stone."

Note: Commas and periods at the end of a quotation go inside quotation marks. (See also page 402.)

● ● ● ● **Activity**

Use commas to set off direct quotations from the rest of the sentence.

1. The coach announced "In order to measure your lung capacity, you're going to attempt to blow up a plastic bag with one breath."

2. "A grapefruit" said the comedian "is a lemon that had a chance and took advantage of it."

3. My father asked "Did you know that the family moving next door has thirteen children?"

4. "Speak louder" a man in the back row said to the guest speaker. "I paid five dollars to hear you talk, not whisper."

5. The zookeeper explained to the visitors "We can't tell the sex of a giant tortoise for almost ten years after its birth."

Comma with Everyday Material

Use a comma with certain everyday material.

Persons Spoken to

> If you're the last to leave, Paul, please switch off the lights.
> Omar, I think we're on the wrong road.
> Did you see the playoff game, Lisa?

Dates

June 30, 2004, is the day I make the last payment on my car.

Addresses

I buy discount children's clothing from Bouncy Baby Wear, Box 900, Vancouver, British Columbia V6H 4Z1.

Note: No comma is used before a postal code.

Openings and Closings of Letters

Dear Santa,	Sincerely yours,
Dear Roberto,	Truly yours,

Note: In formal letters, a colon is used after the opening: Dear Sir: *or* Dear Madam: *or* Dear Allan: *or* Dear Ms. Mohr:.

Numbers

The insurance agent sold me a $50,000 term life insurance policy.

Activity

Place commas where needed.

1. Would you mind Manuel if we borrowed your picnic cooler this weekend?

2. The rotis made at Island Foods 468 Queen Street West are the best in town.

3. On December 29 1989 Vaclav Havel the dissident Czech playwright became president of Czechoslovakia.

4. The mileage chart shows Elaine that we'll have to drive 1231 kilometres to get to Red Deer Alberta.

5. The coupon refund address is 2120 Maritime Highway Halifax Nova Scotia B3J 1V2.

Review Test 1

Insert commas where needed. In the space provided below each sentence, summarize briefly the rule that explains the comma or commas used.

1. "Kleenex tissues" said the history professor "were first used as gas mask filters in World War I."

_____

2. Dee ordered a sundae with three scoops of rocky road ice cream miniature marshmallows and raspberry sauce.

_____

3. While waiting to enter the movie theatre we studied the faces of the people just leaving to see if they had liked the show.

4. I had left my wallet on the store counter but the clerk called me at home to say that it was safe.

5. The demonstrators protesting nuclear arms carried signs reading "Humans have never invented a weapon that they haven't used."

6. Large flowering bushes which now sell for very high prices are being stolen from provincial parks.

7. At the age of 21 Tiger Woods won the 1997 Masters Tournament with the highest margin of victory in the golfing tournament's history.

8. The talk show guest a former child star said that one director threatened to shoot her dog if she didn't cry on cue.

Review Test 2

Insert commas where needed.

1. Before leaving for the gym Nikki added extra socks and a tube of shampoo to the gear in her duffel bag.

2. My father said "Golf isn't for me. I can't afford to buy lots of expensive sticks so that I can lose lots of expensive white balls."

3. Oscar took a time-exposure photo of the busy highway so the cars' tail lights appeared in the developed print as winding red ribbons.

4. The graduating students sweltering in their hot gowns fanned their faces with commencement programs.

5. After her tragic death in Paris France as many as 2.5 billion people worldwide watched the televised funeral of Princess Diana on September 6 1997.

6. In December 2004 hundreds of thousands of people died in Southeast Asia from the effects of the tsunami.

7. "When I was little" said Ernie "my brother told me it was illegal to kill praying mantises. I still don't know if that's true or not."

8. On July 1 1867 Upper and Lower Canada united with two other colonies to form the Dominion of Canada.

■ Review Test 3

In the following passage, there are ten missing commas. Add the commas where needed. The types of mistakes to look for are shown in the box below.

> two commas missing between items in a series
> one comma missing after introductory material
> four commas missing around interrupting words
> two commas missing between complete thoughts
> one comma missing with a direct quotation

When I was about ten years old I developed several schemes to avoid eating liver, a food I despise. My first scheme involved my little brother. Timmy too young to realize what a horrible food liver is always ate every bit of his portion. On liver nights, I used to sit next to Tim and slide my slab of meat onto his plate when my parents weren't paying attention. This strategy worked until older and wiser Tim decided to reject his liver along with the rest of us. Another liver-disposal method I used was hiding the meat right on the plate. I'd cut the liver into tiny squares half the size of postage stamps and then I would carefully hide the pieces. I'd put them inside the skin of my baked potato beneath some mashed peas, or under a crumpled paper napkin. This strategy worked perfectly only if my mother didn't look too closely as she scraped the dishes. Once she said to me "Do you know you left a lot of liver on your plate?" My best liver trick was to hide the disgusting stuff on a three-inch-wide wooden ledge that ran under our dining-room table. I'd put little pieces of liver on the ledge when Mom wasn't looking; I would sneak the dried-up scraps into the garbage early the next day. Our dog would sometimes smell the liver try to get at it, and bang his head noisily against the bottom of the table. These strategies seemed like a lot of work but I never hesitated to take whatever steps I could. Anything was better than eating a piece of meat that tasted like old socks soaked in mud.

■ Review Test 4

On separate paper, write six sentences, one illustrating each of the six main comma rules.

CHAPTER 37

Other Punctuation Marks

Colon (:)

Use the colon at the end of a complete statement to introduce a list or an explanation.

1 A list:

> The store will close at noon on the following dates: October 5, December 24, and December 31.

2 An explanation:

> Here's a temporary solution to a dripping faucet: tie a string to it, and let the drops slide down the string to the sink.

Activity

Place colons where needed in the sentences below.

1. Bring these items to registration a ballpoint pen, your student ID card, and a cheque made out to the college.

2. The road was closed because of an emergency an enormous tree had fallen and blocked both lanes.

Semicolon (;)

The main use of the semicolon is to mark a break between two complete thoughts, as explained on page 344. Another use is to mark off items in a series when the items themselves contain commas. Here are some examples:

> Maya's children are named Melantha, which means "black flower"; Yonina, which means "dove"; and Cynthia, which means "moon goddess."
> My parents' favourite albums are *Rubber Soul,* by the Beatles; *Songs in the Key of Life,* by Stevie Wonder; and *Bridge over Troubled Water,* by Simon and Garfunkel.

• • • • Activity

Place semicolons where needed in the sentences below.

1. Strange things happen at very low temperatures a rose will shatter like glass.

2. My sister had a profitable summer: by mowing lawns, she earned $125 by washing cars, $85 and by walking the neighbour's dogs, $110.

3. The children who starred in the play were Kari Rosoff, nine years old Flora Junco, twelve years old and Ezra Johnson, three years old.

Dash (—)

A dash signals a pause longer than a comma but not as long as a period. Use a dash to set off words for dramatic effect:

I was so exhausted that I fell asleep within seconds—standing up.
He had many good qualities—sincerity, honesty, and thoughtfulness—yet he had few friends.

Notes:

1 A dash is formed on a keyboard by striking the hyphen twice (- -). In handwriting, a dash is as long as two letters would be.

2 Be careful not to overuse dashes.

3 Colons used to begin lists of items are generally more acceptable in formal writing than dashes.

• • • Activity

Place dashes where needed in the following sentences.

1. The victim's leg broken in three places lay twisted at an odd angle on the pavement.

2. The wallet was found in a garbage can minus the cash.

3. After nine days of hiking in the wilderness, sleeping under the stars, and communing with nature, I could think of only one thing a hot shower.

Parentheses ( )

Parentheses are used to set off extra or incidental information from the rest of a sentence:

In 1913, the tax on an annual income of $4000 (a comfortable wage at that time) was one penny.
Arthur C. Clarke, author of science fiction books (including *2001: A Space Odyssey*), was inspired as a young man by the magazine *Astounding Stories*.

Note: Do not use parentheses too often in your writing.

● ● ● ● **Activity**

Add parentheses where needed.

1. Though the first *Star Trek* series originally ran for only three seasons 1965–1968, it can still be seen on many stations around the world.

2. Whenever Jack has too much to drink even one drink is sometimes too much, he gets loud and abusive.

3. When I opened the textbook, I discovered that many pages mostly in the first chapter were completely blank.

Hyphen (-)

1 Use a hyphen with two or more words that act as a single unit describing a noun.

> The light-footed burglar silently slipped open the sliding-glass door.
> While being interviewed on the late-night talk show, the quarterback announced his intention to retire.
> With a needle, Enio punctured the fluid-filled blister on his toe.

2 Use a hyphen to divide a word at the end of a line of writing or typing. When you need to divide a word at the end of a line, divide it between syllables. Use your dictionary to be sure of correct syllable divisions.

> Selena's first year at college was a time filled with numerous new pressures and responsibilities.

Notes:

1 Do not divide words of one syllable.

2 Do not divide a word if you can avoid dividing it.

3 Word processing has eliminated the need to divide words at the end of lines. Unless they contain hyphenation dictionaries, software programs will not split your final word on a line; the word will be fitted into the line you are typing or moved to the beginning of the next line.

● ● ● ● **Activity**

Place hyphens where needed.

1. The blood red moon hanging low on the horizon made a picture perfect atmosphere for Halloween night.

2. My father, who grew up in a poverty stricken household, remembers putting cardboard in his shoes when the soles wore out.

3. The well written article in *The Walrus* magazine described the nerve racking experiences of a journalist who infiltrated the Mob.

■ **Review Test**

At the appropriate spot, place the punctuation mark shown in the margin.

— 1. A bad case of flu, a burglary, the death of an uncle it was not what you would call a pleasant week.

( ) 2. My grandfather who will be ninety in May says that hard work and a glass of wine every day are the secrets of a long life.

- 3. The passengers in the glass bottomed boat stared at the colourful fish in the water below.

( ) 4. Ellen's birthday December 27 falls so close to Christmas that she gets only one set of presents.

; 5. The dog-show winners included Freckles, a springer spaniel King Leo, a German shepherd and Big Guy, a miniature schnauzer.

- 6. Cold hearted stepmothers are a fixture in many famous fairy tales.

; 7. Some people need absolute quiet in order to study they can't concentrate with the soft sounds of a radio, air conditioner, or television in the background.

: 8. A critic reviewing a bad play wrote, "I saw the play under the worst possible circumstances the curtain was up."

CHAPTER 38

Commonly Confused Words

Homonyms

The commonly confused words (also known as *homonyms*) on the following pages have the same sounds but different meanings and spellings. Complete the activity for each set of words, and check off and study the words that give you trouble.

all ready completely prepared
already by then; not earlier than

> It was *already* four o'clock by the time I thought about lunch.
> My report was *all ready,* but the class was cancelled.

Fill in the blanks: Tyrone was _____ to sign up for the course when

he discovered that it had _____ closed.

brake stop
break come apart; pause; fail to observe

> The mechanic advised me to add *brake* fluid to my car.
> During a commercial *break,* Marie lay on the floor and did fifty sit-ups.

Fill in the blanks: Avril, a poor driver, _____ at the last minute and

usually _____ the speed limit as well.

course part of a meal; a school subject; direction
coarse rough

> At the movies, I tried to decide on a *course* of action that would put an end to the *coarse* language of the man behind me.

Fill in the blanks: Over the _____ of time, jagged, _____

rocks will be polished to smoothness by the pounding waves.

hear perceive with the ear
here in this place

> I can *hear* the performers so well from *here* that I don't want to change my seat.

Fill in the blanks: The chairperson explained that the meeting was held

_____ in the auditorium to enable everyone to _____

the debate.

hole   an empty spot
whole   entire

> A *hole* in the crumbling brick mortar made a convenient home for the small
> bird and its *whole* family.

Fill in the blanks: The _____ in Jason's arguments wouldn't exist if

he put his _____ concentration into his thinking.

its   belonging to it
it's   the shortened form for *it is* or *it has*

> The tall giraffe lowered *its* head (the head belonging to the giraffe) to the level
> of the car window and peered in at us.
> *It's* (it is) too late to sign up for the theatre trip to Toronto.

Fill in the blanks: I decided not to take the course because _____ too

easy; _____ content offers no challenge whatever.

knew   past form of *know*
new   not old

> No one *knew* our *new* phone number, but the obscene calls continued.

Fill in the blanks: Even people who _____ Andrew well didn't

recognize him with his _____ beard.

know   to understand
no   a negative

> By the time students complete that course, they *know* two computer languages
> and have *no* trouble writing their own programs.

Fill in the blanks: Dogs and cats usually _____ by the tone of the

speaker's voice when they are being told "_____."

passed   went by; succeeded in; handed to
past   a time before the present; by, as in "I drove past the house"

> As Yvonne *passed* exit six on the highway, she knew she had gone *past* the
> correct turn-off.

Fill in the blanks: Lewis asked for a meeting with his boss to learn why he had

been _____ over for promotion twice in the _____ year.

peace   calm
piece   a part

The best *piece* of advice she ever received was to maintain her own inner *peace.*

Fill in the blanks: Upon hearing that _____ of music, my angry mood was gradually replaced by one of _____ .

plain   simple
plane   aircraft

The *plain* box contained a very expensive model *plane* kit.

Fill in the blanks: After unsuccessfully trying to overcome her fear, Alexandra finally admitted the _____ truth: she was terrified of flying in

_____ .

principal   main; a person in charge of a school
principle   a law or standard

If the *principal* ingredient in this stew is octopus, I'll abandon my *principle* of trying everything at least once.

Fill in the blanks: Our _____ insists that all students adhere to the school's _____ regarding dress, tardiness, and smoking.

right   correct; opposite of *left*
write   to put words on paper

Without the *right* amount of advance planning, it is difficult to *write* a good research paper.

Fill in the blanks: Connie wanted to send for the CDs offered on TV, but she could not _____ fast enough to get all the _____ information down before the commercial ended.

than (thăn)   used in comparisons
then (thĕn)   at that time; next

I made more money *then,* but I've never been happier *than* I am now.

Fill in the blanks: When I was in high school, I wanted a racy two-seater convertible more _____ anything else; but _____ my friends pointed out that only one person would be able to ride with me.

their   belonging to them
there   at that place; a neutral word used with verbs like *is, are, was, were, have,* and *had*
they're   the shortened form of *they are*

> The tenants *there* are complaining because *they're* being cheated by *their* building owner.

Fill in the blanks: The tomatoes I planted _____ in the back of the garden are finally ripening, but _____ bright red colour will attract hungry raccoons, and I fear _____ going to be eaten.

threw   past form of *throw*
through   from one side to the other; finished

> As the inexperienced pizza maker *threw* the pie into the air, he punched a hole *through* its thin crust.

Fill in the blanks: As the prime minister moved slowly _____ the cheering crowd, the RCMP officer suddenly _____ himself at a man waving a small metal object.

to   a verb part, as in *to smile;* toward, as in "I'm going *to* heaven"
too   overly, as in "The pizza was *too* hot"; also, as in "The coffee was hot, *too.*"
two   the number *2*

> I ran *to* the car *to* roll up the windows. (The first *to* means "toward"; the second *to* is a verb part that goes with *roll.*)
> That amusement park is *too* far away; I hear that it's expensive, *too.* (The first *too* means "overly"; the second *too* means "also.")
> The *two* players (2 players) jumped up to tap the basketball away.

Fill in the blanks: The _____ of them have been dating for a year, but lately they seem _____ be arguing _____ often to pretend nothing is wrong.

wear   to have on
where   in what place

> *Where* I will *wear* a purple feather boa is not the point; I just want to buy it.

Fill in the blanks: _____ were we going the night I refused to _____ a tie?

weather   atmospheric conditions
whether   if it happens that; in case; if

Although meteorologists are *weather* specialists, even they can't predict *whether* a hurricane will change course.

Fill in the blanks: The gloomy _____ report in the paper this morning

ended all discussion of _____ to pack a picnic lunch for later.

whose   belonging to whom
who's   the shortened form for *who is* and *who has*

"*Who's* the patient *whose* filling fell out?" the dentist's assistant asked.

Fill in the blanks: _____ the salesperson _____

customers are always complaining about his high-pressure tactics?

your   belonging to you
you're   the shortened form of *you are*

You're making a fool of yourself; *your* Elvis imitation isn't funny.

Fill in the blanks: If _____ having trouble filling out

_____ tax return, why don't you call Canada Revenue Agency's

local line?

Other Words Frequently Confused

Here is a list of other words that people frequently confuse. Complete the activities for each set of words, and check off and study the words that give you trouble.

a   Both *a* and *an* are used before other words to mean "one."
an   Generally, you should use *an* before words starting with a vowel *(a, e, i, o, u)*:

an orange   an umbrella   an indication   an ape   an effort

Generally, you should use *a* before words starting with a consonant (all other letters):

a genius   a movie   a speech   a study   a typewriter

Fill in the blanks: The morning after the party, I had _____ pounding

headache and _____ upset stomach.

accept (ăk sĕpt′)   receive; agree to
except (ĕk sĕpt′)   exclude; but

It was easy to *accept* the book's plot, *except* for one unlikely coincidence at the very end.

Fill in the blanks: Sanka would have _____ the position,

_____ that it would add twenty minutes to his daily commute.

advice (ăd vīs´)   a noun meaning "an opinion"
advise (ăd vīz´)   a verb meaning "to counsel, to give advice"

> I have learned not to take my sister's *advice* on straightening out my life.
> A counsellor can *advise* you about the courses you'll need next year.

Fill in the blanks: Ayesha seems so troubled about losing her job that I

_____ her to seek the _____ of a professional

counsellor.

affect (uh fĕkt´)   a verb meaning "to influence"
effect (ĭ fĕkt´)   a verb meaning "to bring about something"; a noun meaning "result"

> The bad weather will definitely *affect* the outcome of the election.
> If we can *effect* a change in George's attitude, he may do better in his courses.
> One *effect* of the strike will be dwindling supplies in the supermarkets.

Fill in the blanks: Scientists have studied the _____ of large

quantities of saccharine on lab animals but have yet to learn how similar

amounts _____ human beings.

among   implies three or more
between implies only two

> After the team of surgeons consulted *among* themselves, they decided that the
> bullet was lodged *between* two of the patient's ribs.

Fill in the blanks: _____ halves, one enthusiastic fan stood up

_____ his equally fanatic friends and took off his coat and shirt.

beside   along the side of
besides in addition to

> *Besides* doing daily inventories, I have to stand *beside* the cashier whenever
> the store gets crowded.

Fill in the blanks: _____ those books on the table, I plan to use these

magazines stacked _____ me while doing my research paper.

fewer   used with things that can be counted
less   refers to amount, value, or degree

> I've taken *fewer* classes this semester, so I hope to have *less* trouble finding
> time to study.

Fill in the blanks: This beer advertises that it has _____ calories and

is _____ filling.

former   refers to the first of two items named
latter   refers to the second of two items named

> Sue yelled at her sons, Greg and John, when she got home; the *former* had left the refrigerator open and the *latter* had left wet towels all over the bathroom.

Fill in the blanks: Marco collects coupons and parking tickets: the

_____ save him money, and the _____ are going

to cost him a great deal of money some day.

learn   to gain knowledge
teach   to give knowledge

> I can't *learn* a new skill unless someone with lots of patience *teaches* me.

Fill in the blanks: Because she is quick to _____ new things, Mandy

has offered to _____ me how to play the latest video games.

loose (lōōs)   not fastened; not tight-fitting
lose (lōōz)   misplace; fail to win; no longer have

> In this strong wind, the house may *lose* some of its *loose* roof shingles.

Fill in the blanks: A _____ wire in the television set was causing us

to _____ the picture.

quiet (kwī´ĭt)   peaceful
quite (kwĭt)   entirely; really; rather

> Avivah seems *quiet* and demure, but she has *quite* a temper at times.

Fill in the blanks: Most people think the library is _____ a good

place to study, but I find the extreme _____ distracting.

● ● ● ● ● **Activity**

These sentences check your understanding of *its, it's; there, their, they're; to, too, two;* and *your, you're.* Underline the two incorrect spellings in each sentence. Then, spell the words correctly in the spaces provided.

_____   1. "Its not a very good idea," yelled Alexandra's boss, "to tell you're customer that the striped dress she plans to buy makes her look like a pregnant tiger."

_____   2. You're long skirt got stuck in the car door, and now its sweeping the highway.

_____   3. When your young, their is a tendency to confuse a crush with true love.

_____   4. After too hours of writing, Lin was to tired to write any longer.

_____   5. It is unusual for a restaurant to lose it's licence, but this one had more mice in its' kitchen than cooks.

_____   6. The vampires bought a knife sharpener in order too sharpen there teeth.

_____ 7. Your sometimes surprised by who you're friends turn out to be in difficult times.

_____ 8. When the children get to quiet, Clare knows their getting into trouble.

Review Test 1

Underline the correct word in the parentheses. Rather than guessing, look back at the explanations of the words when necessary.

1. I (know, no) that several of the tenants have decided (to, too, two) take (their, there, they're) case to court.

2. (Whose, Who's) the author of that book about the (affects, effects) of eating (to, too, two) much protein?

3. In our supermarket is a counter (where, wear) (your, you're) welcome to sit down and have free coffee and doughnuts.

4. (Its, It's) possible to (loose, lose) friends by constantly giving out unwanted (advice, advise).

5. For a long time, I couldn't (accept, except) the fact that my husband wanted a divorce; (then, than) I decided to stop being angry and get on with my life.

6. I spent the (hole, whole) day browsing (threw, through) the chapters in my business textbook, but I didn't really study them.

7. The newly appointed (principal, principle) is (quite, quiet) familiar with the problems (hear, here) at our school.

8. I found that our cat had (all ready, already) had her kittens (among, between) the weeds (beside, besides) the porch.

Review Test 2

On separate paper, write short sentences using the ten words shown below.

1. accept   6. principal
2. its   7. their
3. you're   8. passed
4. too   9. fewer
5. then   10. who's

CHAPTER 39

Effective Word Choice

Choose your words carefully when you write. Always take the time to think about your word choices rather than simply using the first word that comes to mind. You need to develop the habit of selecting words that are appropriate and exact for your purposes. One way you can show your sensitivity to language is by avoiding slang and clichés.

Slang

We often use *slang* expressions when we talk because they are so vivid and colourful. However, slang is usually out of place in formal writing. Here are some examples of slang expressions:

> Someone *ripped off* Ken's new Nike running shoes from his locker.
> After the game, we *pigged out* at the restaurant.
> I finally told my parents to *get off my case*.
> The movie really *grossed me out*.

Slang expressions have a number of drawbacks. They go out of date quickly, they become tiresome if used excessively in writing, and they may communicate clearly to some readers but not to others. Also, the use of slang can be an evasion of the specific details that are often needed to make one's meaning clear in writing. For example, in "The movie really grossed me out," the writer has not provided the specific details about the movie necessary for us to clearly understand the statement. Was it the acting, the special effects, or the violent scenes in the movie that the writer found so disgusting? In general, then, you should avoid the use of slang in your writing. If you are in doubt about whether an expression is slang, it may help to check a recently published dictionary.

Activity

Rewrite the following sentences, replacing the italicized slang words with more formal ones.

Example   When we told the neighbours to *can the noise*, they *freaked out*.

When we told the neighbours to be quiet, they were upset.

1. I didn't realize how *messed up* Joey was until he stole some money from his parents and *split* for a month.

   _____

   _____

2. After a hard day, I like to *veg out* in front of the *idiot box.*

   _____

   _____

3. Kwame was *so wiped out* after his workout at the gym that he couldn't *get it together* to defrost a frozen dinner.

   _____

   _____

4. When Alex tried to put *the move on* Elaine at the school party, she told him to *shove off.*

   _____

   _____

Clichés

A *cliché* is an expression that has been worn out through constant use. Some typical clichés include the following:

short but sweet	last but not least
drop in the bucket	work like a dog
had a hard time of it	all work and no play
word to the wise	it goes without saying
it dawned on me	at a loss for words
sigh of relief	taking a big chance
too little, too late	took a turn for the worse
singing the blues	easier said than done
in the nick of time	on top of the world
too close for comfort	time and time again
saw the light	make ends meet

Clichés are common in speech but make your writing seem tired and stale. Also, they are often an evasion of the specific details that you must work to provide in your writing. Avoid clichés and try to express your meaning in fresh, original ways.

Activity 1

Underline the cliché in each of the following sentences. Then, substitute specific, fresh words for the trite expression.

Example   My boyfriend has stuck with me <u>through thick and thin</u>, <u>through good times and bad times</u>.

My boyfriend has stuck with me through difficult times and all sorts

of problems.

1. As the only girl in an otherwise all-boy family, I got away with murder.

_____

2. When I realized I'd lost my textbook, I knew I was up the creek without a paddle.

_____

3. My suggestion is just a shot in the dark, but it's better than nothing.

_____

4. Nadine got more than she bargained for when she offered to help Larry with his math homework.

_____

5. Jacques is pushing his luck by driving a car with bald tires.

_____

6. On a hot, sticky, midsummer day, iced tea or any frosty drink really hits the spot.

_____

7. Melissa thanks her lucky stars that she was born with brains, beauty, and humility.

_____

8. Even when we are up to our eyeballs in work, our boss wonders if we have enough to do.

_____

Activity 2

Write a short paragraph, describing the kind of day you had. Try to put as many clichés as possible into your writing. For example, "I got up at the crack of dawn, ready to take on the world. I grabbed a bite to eat. . . ." By making yourself aware of clichés in this way, you will lessen the chance that they will appear in your writing.

■ Review Test

Certain words are italicized in the following sentences. In the space provided, identify the words as slang *(S)* or a cliché *(C)*. Then, replace the words with more effective word choices.

_____ 1. Losing weight is *easier said than done* for someone with a sweet tooth.

_____

_____ 2. Mike wore *truly awesome* pants and a jacket; he was *like way cool.*

_____

_____ 3. Brendan is so stubborn that talking to him is like *talking to a brick wall.*

_____

_____ 4. Michelle spent the summer *watching the tube* and *catching rays.*

_____

_____ 5. The fans, *all fired up* after the game, *peeled out* of the parking lot and honked their horns.

_____

_____ 6. The stew I made contained *everything but the kitchen sink.*

_____

_____ 7. That *dude* isn't really a criminal; he's just gotten a *bum rap.*

_____

_____ 8. I failed the test, and to *add insult to injury,* I got a low grade on my paper.

_____

CHAPTER 40

ESL Pointers

You may have turned to this chapter because English is your second or third language. On the other hand, you may have spoken English all your life but want further information on points of usage and grammar. This chapter offers detailed explanations of points and rules of common usage and English idiomatic structures that most native speakers of English take for granted.

Articles with Count and Non-Count Nouns

Articles are noun markers; they signal that a noun will follow. The indefinite articles are *a* and *an*. (Use *a* before a word that begins with a consonant sound: **a c**ar, **a p**iano, **a u**niform—the *u* in *uniform* sounds like the consonant *y* plus *u*. Use *an* before a word beginning with a vowel sound: **an e**gg, **an o**ffice, **an h**onour—the *h* in *honour* is silent.) The definite article is *the*. An article may immediately precede a noun: **a** smile, **the** reason. It may also be separated from the noun by modifiers: **a** slight smile, **the** very best reason.

To know whether to use an article with a noun and which article to use, you must recognize count and non-count nouns. (A noun is a word used to name something—a person, place, thing, or idea.)

Count nouns name people, places, things, or ideas that can be counted and made into plurals such as *teacher, washroom,* and *joke (one teacher, two washrooms, three jokes)*.

Non-count nouns refer to things or ideas that cannot be counted such as *flour, history,* and *truth*. The box on the following page lists and illustrates common types of non-count nouns.

Note: There are various other noun markers, including quantity words, also called qualifiers *(some, several, a lot of)*; numerals *(one, ten, 120)*; demonstrative pronouns *(this, these)*; possessive pronouns *(my, your, our)*; and possessive nouns *(Jaime's, the school's)*.

In the following two examples, the quantity words (qualifiers) are shown in *italic* type, and the non-count nouns are shown in **boldface** type.

Please have *some* **patience**.
We need to buy *two bags of* **flour** today.

Some words can be either count or non-count nouns, depending on whether they refer to one or more individual items or to something in general.

Certain **cheeses** give some people headaches.

This sentence refers to individual cheeses; *cheese* in this case is a count noun.

Cheese is made in almost every country where milk is produced.

This sentence refers to cheese in general; in this case, *cheese* is a non-count noun.

Common Non-Count Nouns

Abstractions and emotions: anger, bravery, health, pride, truth

Activities: baseball, jogging, reading, teaching, travel

Foods: bread, broccoli, chocolate, cheese, flour

Gases and vapours: air, helium, oxygen, steam

Languages and areas of study: Korean, Spanish, algebra, history, physics

Liquids: blood, gasoline, lemonade, tea, water

Materials that come in bulk form: aluminum, cloth, dust, sand, soap

Natural occurrences: magnetism, moonlight, rain, snow, thunder

Other things that cannot be counted: clothing, furniture, homework, machinery, money, news, transportation, vocabulary, work

---

Using *a* or *an* with Non-specific Singular Count Nouns

Use *a* or *an* with singular nouns that are non-specific. A noun is non-specific when the reader doesn't know its specific identity.

A left-hander faces special challenges with right-handed tools.

The sentence refers to any left-hander, not a specific one.

Today, our cat proudly brought **a** baby bird into the house.

The reader isn't familiar with the bird. This is the first time it is mentioned.

Using *the* with Specific Nouns

In general, use *the* with all specific nouns—specific singular, plural, and non-count nouns.

A noun is specific in the following cases:

• When it has already been mentioned once

Today, our cat proudly brought a baby bird into the house. Luckily, **the** bird was still alive.

The is used with the second mention of *bird*.

- When it is identified by a word or phrase in the sentence

    The pockets in the boy's pants are often filled with sand and dirt.

    Pockets is identified by the words *in the boy's pants.*

- When its identity is suggested by the general context

    At Willy's Diner last night, **the** service was terrible and **the** food was worse.

    The reader can conclude that the service and food being discussed were at Willy's Diner.

- When it is unique

    There will be an eclipse of **the** moon tonight.

    Earth has only one moon.

- When it is preceded by a superlative adjective *(best, biggest, wisest)*

    The best way to store broccoli is to refrigerate it in an open plastic bag.

Omitting Articles

Omit articles with non-specific plurals and non-count nouns. Plurals and non-count nouns are non-specific when they refer to something in general.

> **Pockets** didn't exist until the end of the 1700s.
> **Service** is as important as **food** to a restaurant's success.
> Iris serves her children homemade **lemonade**.

Using *the* with Proper Nouns

Proper nouns name particular people, places, things, or ideas and are always capitalized. Most proper nouns do not require articles; those that do, however, require *the*. Following are general guidelines about when and when not to use *the*.

Do not use *the* for most singular proper nouns, including names of the following:

- *People and animals* (Jean Chrétien, Fido)
- *Continents, provinces or states, cities, streets, and parks* (North America, Alberta, Lethbridge, Portage Street, Banff National Park)
- *Most countries* (France, Mexico, Russia)
- *Individual bodies of water, islands, and mountains* (Lake Erie, Prince Edward Island, Mount Everest)

Use *the* for the following types of proper nouns:

- *Plural proper nouns* (the Turners, the United States, the Great Lakes, the Rocky Mountains)
- *Names of large geographic areas, deserts, oceans, seas, and rivers* (the South, the Gobi Desert, the Atlantic Ocean, the Black Sea, the Mississippi River)
- *Names with the format* the _____ of _____ (the People's Republic of China, the University of Manitoba)

● ● ● ● **Activity**

Underline the correct form of the noun in parentheses.

1. (A library, Library) is a valuable addition to a town.

2. This morning, the mail carrier brought me (a letter, the letter) from my cousin.

3. As I read (a letter, the letter), I began to laugh at what my cousin wrote.

4. We are going to visit our friends in (the British Columbia, British Columbia) next week.

5. Children should treat their parents with (the respect, respect).

6. A famous park in Toronto is (High Park, the High Park).

7. My son would like to eat (the spaghetti, spaghetti) at every meal.

8. It is dangerous to stare directly at (the sun, sun).

Subjects and Verbs

Avoiding Repeated Subjects

In English, a particular subject can be used only once in a clause. Don't repeat a subject in the same clause by following a noun with a pronoun.

Incorrect: The *manager he* asked Dmitri to lock up tonight.
Correct: The **manager** asked Dmitri to lock up tonight.
Correct: **He** asked Dmitri to lock up tonight.

Even when the subject and verb are separated by a long word group, the subject cannot be repeated in the same clause.

Incorrect: The *girl* who danced with you *she is* my cousin.
Correct: The **girl** who danced with you **is** my cousin.

Including Pronoun Subjects and Linking Verbs

Some languages may omit a pronoun as a subject, but in English, every clause other than a command must have a subject. (In a command, the subject *you* is understood: [**You**] Hand in your papers now.)

Incorrect: The Yellowhead Highway is in central Alberta. Runs across the province.
Correct: The Yellowhead Highway is in central Alberta. **It** runs across the province.

Every English clause must also have a verb, even when the meaning of the clause is clear without the verb.

Incorrect: Angelita's piano teacher very patient.
Correct: Angelita's piano teacher **is** very patient.

Including *there* and *here* at the Beginning of Clauses

Some English sentences begin with *there* or *here* plus a linking verb (usually a form of *to be: is, are,* and so on). In such sentences, the verb comes before the subject.

There are masks in every culture on Earth.

The subject is the plural noun *masks,* so the plural verb *are* is used.

Here is your driver's licence.

The subject is the singular noun *licence,* so the singular verb *is* is used.

In sentences like the above, remember not to omit *there* or *here.*

Incorrect: *Are* several chickens in the Bensons' yard.
Correct: **There are** several chickens in the Bensons' yard.

Avoiding the Progressive (or Continuous) Tenses of Certain Verbs

The progressive (or continuous) tenses are made up of forms of *be* plus the *-ing* form of the main verb. They express actions or conditions still in progress at a particular time.

George **will be taking** classes this summer.

However, verbs for mental states, the senses, possession, and inclusion are normally not used in the progressive tense.

Incorrect: During the movie, they *were hearing* whispers behind them.
Correct: During the movie, they **heard** whispers behind them.
Incorrect: That box *is containing* a surprise for Paulo.
Correct: That box **contains** a surprise for Paulo.

Common verbs not generally used in the progressive tense are listed in the box below.

Common Verbs Not Generally Used in the Progressive Tense

Thoughts, attitudes and desires: agree, believe, imagine, know, like, love, prefer, think, understand, want, wish

Sense perceptions: hear, see, smell, taste

Appearances: appear, seem, look

Possession: belong, have, own, possess

Inclusion: contain, include

Using Only Transitive Verbs for the Passive Voice

Only *transitive* verbs—verbs that need direct objects to complete their meaning—can have a passive form (one in which the subject receives the action instead of performing it). Intransitive verbs cannot be used in the passive voice.

Incorrect: If you don't fix those brakes, an accident *may be happened.*

Happen is an intransitive verb—no object is needed to complete its meaning.

Correct: If you don't fix those brakes, an accident **may happen**.

If you aren't sure whether a verb is transitive or intransitive, check your dictionary. Transitive verbs are indicated with an abbreviation such as *tr. v.* or *v. t.* Intransitive verbs are indicated with an abbreviation such as *intr. v.* or *v. i.*

Using Gerunds and Infinitives after Verbs (Idiomatic Verb Structures)

A gerund is the *-ing* form of a verb that is used as a noun: "For Walter, **eating** is a day-long activity." An infinitive is *to* plus the basic form of the verb (the form in which the verb is listed in the dictionary): "He likes **to eat** fast food most of the time." Some verbs can be followed by only a gerund or only an infinitive; other verbs can be followed by either. Examples are given in the following lists. There are many others; watch for them in your reading.

Verb + gerund   *(admit + stealing)*
Verb + preposition + gerund   *(apologize + for + yelling)*

Some verbs can be followed by a gerund but not by an infinitive. In many cases, there is a preposition (such as *for, in,* or *of*) between the verb and the gerund. Following are some verbs and verb/preposition combinations that can be followed by gerunds but not by infinitives:

admit (to)	deny	look forward to
apologize for	discuss	postpone
appreciate	dislike	practise
approve of	enjoy	recommend
avoid	feel like	talk about
be used to	finish	thank for
believe in	insist on	think about

Incorrect: He must *avoid to jog* until his knee heals.
Correct: He must **avoid jogging** until his knee heals.
Incorrect: The instructor *apologized for to be* late to class.
Correct: The instructor **apologized for being** late to class.

Verb + infinitive   *(agree + to leave)*

Following are common verbs that can be followed by an infinitive but not by a gerund:

agree	decide	plan
arrange	have	refuse
claim	manage	want

Incorrect: The children *want going* to the beach.
Correct: The children **want to go** to the beach.

Verb + noun or pronoun + infinitive   *(cause + them + to flee)*

Below are common verbs that are first followed by a noun or pronoun and then by an infinitive (not a gerund):

cause	force	remind
command	persuade	warn

> Incorrect: The coach *persuaded Carmelo studying* harder.
> Correct: The coach **persuaded Carmelo to study** harder.

Following are common verbs that can be followed by either an infinitive alone or a noun or pronoun and an infinitive:

ask	need	want
expect	promise	would like

> Dena **asked to have** a day off next week.
> Her boss **asked her to work** on Saturday.

Verb + gerund or infinitive   *(begin + packing or begin + to pack)*

Following are some verbs that can be followed by either a gerund or an infinitive:

begin	hate	prefer
continue	love	start

The meaning of each of the above verbs remains the same or almost the same whether a gerund or an infinitive is used.

> Faith **hates being** late.
> Faith **hates to be** late.

With the verbs below, the gerunds and the infinitives have very different meanings.

forget	remember	stop

> Esta **stopped to call** home.
> (She interrupted something to call home.)

> Esta **stopped calling** home.
> (She discontinued calling home.)

Activity

Underline the correct form in parentheses.

1. The doctor (asked me, she asked me) if I smoked.

2. The coffee is very fresh. (Is, It is) strong and delicious.

3. (Are mice, There are mice) living in our kitchen.

4. The box (is containing, contains) a beautiful necklace.

5. Unless you take your foot off the brake, the car will not (be gone, go).

6. Most basketball players (very tall, are very tall).

7. Many people (enjoy to spend, enjoy spending) a day in the city.

8. The teacher (plans taking, plans to take) us on a field trip tomorrow.

Adjectives

Following the Order of Adjectives in English

Adjectives modify nouns and pronouns. In English, an adjective usually comes directly before the word it describes or after a linking verb (a form of *be* or a "sense" verb such as *look, seem* and *taste*), in which case it modifies the subject. In each of the following two sentences, the adjective is **boldfaced** and the noun it describes is *italicized*.

That is a **false** *story*.
The *story* is **false**.

When more than one adjective modifies the same noun, the adjectives are usually stated in a certain order, though there are often exceptions. Following is the typical order of English adjectives:

Typical Order of Adjectives in a Series

1 **An article or other noun marker:** a, an, the, Lee's, this, three, your

2 **Opinion adjective:** dull, handsome, unfair, useful

3 **Size:** big, huge, little, tiny

4 **Shape:** long, short, round, square

5 **Age:** ancient, medieval, old, new, young

6 **Colour:** blue, green, scarlet, white

7 **Nationality:** Italian, Korean, Mexican, Vietnamese

8 **Religion:** Buddhist, Catholic, Jewish, Muslim

9 **Material:** cardboard, gold, marble, silk

10 **Noun used as an adjective:** house (as in *house call*), tea (as in *tea bag*), wall (as in *wall hanging*)

Here are some examples of the above order:

a long cotton scarf
the beautiful little silver cup
your new lavender evening gown
Anna's sweet Italian grandmother

In general, use no more than *two or three* adjectives after the article or other noun marker. Numerous adjectives in a series can be awkward: **the beautiful big new blue cotton** sweater.

Using the Present and Past Participles as Adjectives

The present participle ends in *-ing*. Past participles of regular verbs end in *-ed* or *-d*; a list of the past participles of many common irregular verbs appears on pages 351–352. Both types of participles may be used as adjectives. A participle used as an adjective may precede the word it describes: "It was an **exciting** *ballgame*." It may also follow a linking verb and describe the subject of the sentence: "The *ballgame* was **exciting**."

While both present and past participles of a particular verb may be used as adjectives, their meanings differ. Use the present participle to describe whoever or whatever causes a feeling: an **embarrassing** *incident* (the incident is what causes the embarrassment). Use the past participle to describe whoever or whatever experiences the feeling: the **embarrassed** *parents* (the parents are the ones who are embarrassed).

> The long day of holiday shopping was **tiring**.
> The shoppers were **tired**.

Following are pairs of present and past participles with similar distinctions:

annoying / annoyed	exhausting / exhausted
boring / bored	fascinating / fascinated
confusing / confused	frightening / frightened
depressing / depressed	surprising / surprised
exciting / excited	interesting / interested

● ● ● ● ● **Activity**

Underline the correct form in parentheses.

1. The Johnsons live in a (stone big, big stone) house.

2. Mr. Kim runs a (popular Korean, Korean popular) restaurant.

3. For her party, the little girl asked if her mother would buy her a (beautiful long velvet, beautiful velvet long) dress.

4. When their son didn't come home by bedtime, Mr. and Mrs. Singh became (worried, worrying).

5. In the centre of the city is a church with (three enormous, colourful, stained-glass; three stained-glass, colourful, enormous) windows.

Prepositions of Time and Place

The use of prepositions in English is often idiomatic, and exceptions to general rules are common. Therefore, correct preposition use must be learned gradually through experience. Following is a chart showing how three of the most common prepositions are used in some customary references to time and place:

The Use of On, In, *and* At *to Refer to Time and Place*

Time

> **On** *a specific day:* on Monday, on January 1, on your anniversary
> **In** *a part of a day:* in the morning, in the daytime (but at night)
> **In** *a month or a year:* in December, in 1867
> **In** *a period of time:* in an hour, in a few days, in a while
> **At** *a specific time:* at 10:00 a.m., at midnight, at sunset, at dinnertime

Place

> **On** *a surface:* on the desk, on the counter, on a ceiling
> **In** *a place that is enclosed:* in my room, in the office, in the box
> **At** *a specific location:* at the mall, at his house, at the ballpark

---

Activity

Underline the correct preposition in parentheses.

1. Can you babysit my children (on, at) Thursday?

2. Please come to my office (on, at) 3:00 p.m.

3. You will find some computer discs (in, on) the desk drawer.

4. Miguel will begin his new job (in, at) two weeks.

5. A fight broke out between two groups of friends (on, at) the park.

Review Test

Underline the correct form in parentheses.

1. During the storm, I was startled by the loud (thunder, thunders).

2. (Is, Here is) your new textbook.

3. The ending of the movie was very (surprised, surprising).

4. Many animals that sleep all day are active (at, in) night.

5. (The people, People) in the photograph are my mother's relatives.

6. The city streets were full of (big yellow, yellow big) taxis.

7. My friend and I (are usually agreeing, usually agree) with each other.

8. In the West, New Year's Day is celebrated (in, on) January 1.

CHAPTER 41

Editing Tests

The twelve editing tests in this chapter will give you practice in revising for sentence-skills mistakes. Remember that if you don't edit carefully, you run the risk of sabotaging much of the work you have put into a paper. If readers see too many surface flaws, they may assume you don't place much value on what you have to say, and they may not give proper attention to your ideas. Revising to eliminate sentence-skills errors is a basic part of clear, effective writing.

In half of the tests, the spots where errors occur have been underlined; your job is to identify and correct each error. In the rest of the tests, you must locate as well as identify and correct the errors. (For a review of parallel structure and pronoun point of view, specified in some of those tests, see pages 93–94 and 95–96 respectively.)

Editing Hints

Here are some hints that can help you edit the next-to-final draft of a paper for sentence skills mistakes:

1 Have at hand two essential tools: a good dictionary and a handbook (you can use Part 4 of this book).

2 Use a sheet of paper to cover your work so that you will expose only one sentence at a time. Look for errors in grammar, spelling, and typing. It may help to read each sentence out loud. If it does not read clearly and smoothly, chances are something is wrong.

3 Pay special attention to the kinds of errors you tend to make. For example, if you tend to write run-ons or fragments, be especially on the lookout for those errors.

4 Proofreading symbols that may be of particular help are the following:

⌒ ℮	omit	draw two ~~two~~ conclusions
i ∧	insert missing letter or word	acheve (i) ∧
cap, lc	Add a capital (or a lowercase) letter	My english Class

◼ Editing Test 1

In the spaces at the bottom, write the numbers of the ten word groups that contain fragments or run-ons. Then, in the spaces between the lines, edit by making the necessary corrections.

¹I remember my childhood as being generally happy and can recall experiencing some of the most carefree times of my life. ²But I can also remember, even more vividly, other moments. ³When I was deeply frightened. ⁴As a child, I was truly terrified of the dark and of getting lost. ⁵These fears were very real, they caused me some extremely uncomfortable moments.

⁶Maybe it was the strange way things looked and sounded in my familiar room at night. ⁷That scared me so much. ⁸The streetlight outside or passing car lights would create shadows in my room. ⁹As a result, clothes hung over a chair taking on the shape of an unknown beast. ¹⁰Out of the corner of my eye, I saw curtains move when there was no breeze. ¹¹A faint creak in the floor would sound a hundred times louder than in daylight, my imagination would take over. ¹²Creating burglars and monsters on the prowl. ¹³Because darkness always made me feel so helpless. ¹⁴I would lie there motionless so that the "enemy" would not discover me.

¹⁵Another of my childhood fears was that I would get lost. ¹⁶Especially on the way home from school. ¹⁷After school, all the buses lined up along the curb I was terrified that I'd get on the wrong one. ¹⁸Scanning the bus windows for the faces of my friends. ¹⁹I'd also look to make sure that the bus driver was the same one I had in the morning.

1. _____   3. _____   5. _____   7. _____   9. _____

2. _____   4. _____   6. _____   8. _____   10. _____

■ Editing Test 2

Identify the five sentence fragments and five run-on sentences in the student composition that follows. From the box below, choose the letter that describes the mistakes, and write that letter in the space provided. Then, correct each mistake.

a. fragment	b. run-on

A Unique Object

¹A unique object in my family's living room is an ashtray. ²Which I made in second grade. ³I can still remember the pride I felt. ⁴When I presented it to my mother. ⁵To my second-grade eyes, it was a thing of beauty. ⁶Now, I'm amazed that my parents didn't hide it away at the back of a shelf it is a remarkable ugly object. ⁷The ashtray is made out of brown clay. ⁸I had tried to mould it into a perfect circle, unfortunately my class was only forty-five minutes long. ⁹The best I could do was to shape it into a lopsided oval. ¹⁰Its most distinctive feature, though, was the grooves sculpted into its rim. ¹¹I had theorized that each groove could hold a cigarette or cigar, I made at least fifty of them. ¹²I somehow failed to consider that the only person who smoked in my family was my father. ¹³Who smoked about five cigars a year. ¹⁴Further, although our living room is decorated in sedate tans and blue, my ashtray is bright purple. ¹⁵My favourite colour at the time. ¹⁶Just for variety, it also has stripes around its rim they are coloured neon green. ¹⁷For all its shortcomings, my parents have proudly displayed my little masterpiece on their coffee table for the past ten years. ¹⁸If I ever wonder if my parents love me. ¹⁹I look at that ugly ashtray, the answer is plain to see.

1. _____   3. _____   5. _____   7. _____   9. _____

2. _____   4. _____   6. _____   8. _____   10. _____

■ Editing Test 3

Identify the ten sentence-skills mistakes at the underlined spots in the student composition that follows. From the box below, choose the letter that describes each mistake, and write that letter in the space provided. (The same kind of mistake may appear more than once.) Then, in the spaces between the lines, edit and correct each mistake.

a. fragment	d. dangling modifier
b. run-on	e. missing comma
c. inconsistent verb tense	f. spelling mistake

I had a strange experience last <u>winter, I</u> was shopping for Christmas
                               1
presents when I came to a small clothing shop. I was going to pass it by.

<u>Until I saw a beautiful purple robe on a mannequin in the window.</u> <u>Stopping to</u>
                               2   3
<u>look at it,</u> the mannequin seemed to wink at me. I was really <u>startled, I</u> looked
                                                                  4
around to see if anyone else was watching. Shaking my <u>head</u> I stepped closer
                                                        5
to the window. Then, I really began to question my <u>sanity,</u> it looked as if the
                                                    6
mannequin moved <u>it's</u> legs. My face must have shown alarm because the
                  7
mannequin then <u>smiles.</u> <u>And even waved her arm.</u> I sighed with <u>relief, it</u> was a
                 8   9   10
human model after all.

1. _____   3. _____   5. _____   7. _____   9. _____

2. _____   4. _____   6. _____   8. _____   10. _____

■ Editing Test 4

Identify the ten sentence-skills mistakes at the underlined spots in the student composition that follows. From the box below, choose the letter that describes each mistake, and write that letter in the space provided. (The same kind of mistake may appear more than once.) Then, in the spaces between the lines, edit and correct each mistake.

a. run-on	d. missing quotation marks
b. mistake in subject-verb agreement	e. wordiness
	f. slang
c. faulty parallel structure	g. missing comma

It is this writer's opinion that smokers should quit smoking for the sake of
1

those who are around them. Perhaps the most helpless creatures that suffer

from being near a smoker is unborn babies, one study suggests that the risk of
2   3

having an undersized baby is doubled if pregnant women are exposed to

cigarette smoke for about two hours a day. Pregnant women both should refrain

from smoking and to avoid smoke-filled rooms. Spouses of smokers are also
4

in big trouble. They are more likely than spouses of non-smokers to die of heart
5

disease and the development of fatal cancers. Office workers are a final group
6

that can be harmed by a smoke-filled environment. The Minister of Health and

Welfare has said "Workers who smoke are a health risk to their co-workers.
7   8

While it is undoubtedly true that one can argue that smokers have the right to
9

hurt themselves they do not have the right to hurt others. Smokers should
10

abandon their deadly habits for the health of others at home and at work.

1. _____   3. _____   5. _____   7. _____   9. _____

2. _____   4. _____   6. _____   8. _____   10. _____

Editing Test 5

Identify the ten sentence-skills mistakes at the underlined spots in the student composition that follows. From the box below, choose the letter that describes each mistake, and write that letter in the space provided. (The same kind of mistake may appear more than once.) Then, in the spaces between the lines, edit and correct each mistake.

a. fragment	e. dangling modifier
b. run-on	f. missing comma
c. mistake in subject-verb agreement	g. wordiness
d. misplaced modifier	h. slang

North America will never be a drug-free <u>society but</u> we could eliminate
                                              1
many of our drug-related problems by legalizing drugs. Drugs would be sold by

companies and not criminals <u>if they were legal</u>. The drug trade would then take
                                     2
place like any other <u>business freeing</u> the police and courts to devote their time
                            3
to other problems. Lawful drugs would be sold at a fair <u>price, no</u> one would
                                                               4
need to steal in order to buy them. <u>By legalizing drugs,</u> organized crime would
                                           5
lose one of its major sources of revenue. <u>It goes without saying that</u> we would,
                                                   6
instead, create important tax revenues for the government. Finally, if drugs

<u>was</u> sold through legal outlets, we could reduce the drug problem among our
 7
young people. It would be illegal to sell drugs to people under a certain age.

<u>Just as is the case now with alcohol</u>. And because the profits on drugs would
                          8
no longer <u>be out of sight</u>, there would be little incentive for drug pushers to
                    9
sell to young people. Decriminalizing drugs, in short, could be a solution.

<u>To many of the problems that result from the illegal drug trade</u>.
                                        10

1. _____   3. _____   5. _____   7. _____   9. _____

2. _____   4. _____   6. _____   8. _____   10. _____

■ Editing Test 6

Identify the ten sentence-skills mistakes at the underlined spots in the student composition that follows. From the box below, choose the letter that describes each mistake, and write that letter in the space provided. (The same kind of mistake may appear more than once.) Then, in the spaces between the lines, edit and correct each mistake.

a. fragment	e. mistake with quotation marks
b. run-on	f. mistake in pronoun point of view
c. mistake in subject-verb agreement	g. spelling error
d. mistake in verb tense	h. missing comma

One reason that I enjoy the commute to school is that the drive gives me

<u>uninterupted</u> time to myself. The classes and socializing at college <u>is</u> great,
　　　1　　　　　　　　　　　　　　　　　　　　　　　　　　　　　　2

and so is the time I spend with my family, but sometimes all this togetherness

keeps <u>you</u> from being able to think. In fact, I look forward to the time I have
　　　3

<u>alone</u>, it gives me a chance to plan what I'll accomplish in the day ahead. For
　4

example, one Tuesday afternoon my Marketing professor <u>announces</u> that a
　　　　　　　　　　　　　　　　　　　　　　　　　　　　　　5

rough outline for our semester report was due that Friday. <u>Fortunatly,</u> I had
　　　　　　　　　　　　　　　　　　　　　　　　　　　　　6

already done some <u>reading and I</u> had checked my proposed topic with her the
　　　　　　　　　　　7

week before. <u>Therefore, on the way home in the car that evening.</u> I planned the
　　　　　　　8

entire history report in my mind. Then, all I had to do when I got home was

quickly jot it down before I forgot it. <u>When I handed the professor the outline at
　　　　　　　　　　　　　　　　　　　　　　　　　　9

8:30 Wednesday morning.</u> She asked me <u>"if I had stayed up all night working
　　　　　　　　　　　　　　　　　　　　　　　　　　10

on it."</u> She was amazed when I told her that I owed it all to commuting.

1. _____   3. _____   5. _____   7. _____   9. _____

2. _____   4. _____   6. _____   8. _____   10. _____

■ Editing Test 7

Identify the ten sentence-skills mistakes at the underlined spots in the student composition that follows. From the box below, choose the letter that describes each mistake, and write that letter in the space provided. (The same kind of mistake may appear more than once.) Then, in the spaces between the lines, edit and correct each mistake.

a. fragment	f. dangling modifier
b. run-on	g. homonym mistake
c. mistake in subject-verb agreement	h. missing apostrophe
d. missing comma	i. cliché
e. missing capital letter	j. spelling mistake

Cars can destroy your ego. First of <u>all the</u> kind of car you drive can make
₁
you feel like a second-class citizen. <u>If you can't afford a new, expensive car,</u>
₂
<u>and are forced to drive an old clunker.</u> You'll be the object of pitying stares and

nasty sneers. Drivers of newer-model cars just <u>doesn't</u> appreciate it when a
₃
<u>'78 buick</u> with terminal body rust lurches into the next parking space.
₄
You may even find that drivers go out of <u>there</u> way not to park near you.
₅
Breakdowns, too, can damage your self-respect. You may be an assistant bank

manager or a job <u>foreman, you'll</u> still feel <u>like two cents</u> when <u>you'r</u> sitting on
₆   ₇   ₈
the side of the road. As the other cars whiz past, you'll stare helplessly at your

<u>cars</u> open hood or steaming radiator. In cases like this, you may even be turned
₉
into that lowest of creatures, the pedestrian. <u>Shuffling humbly along the</u>
₁₀
<u>highway to the nearest gas station</u>, your car has delivered another staggering

blow to your self-esteem.

1. _____   3. _____   5. _____   7. _____   9. _____

2. _____   4. _____   6. _____   8. _____   10. _____

Editing Test 8

Try to locate the ten sentence-skills mistakes in the following passage. The mistakes are listed in the box below. As you locate each mistake, write the number of the word group in the space provided. Then, in the spaces between the lines, edit and correct each mistake.

one fragment _____	one mistake in pronoun point of view _____
one run-on _____	
one mistake in verb tense _____	one missing comma after introductory material _____
one non-parallel structure _____	
one dangling modifier _____	two missing quotation marks
one missing apostrophe _____	_____ _____

¹The greatest of my everyday fears is technology. ²Beginning when I couldn't master bike riding and extending to the present day. ³Fear kept me from learning to operate a jigsaw, start an outboard motor, or even using a simple tape recorder. ⁴I almost didn't learn to drive a car. ⁵At age sixteen, Dad lifted the hood of our Chevy and said, All right, you're going to start learning to drive. ⁶Now, this is the distributor . . . When my eyes glazed over he shouted, "Well, I'm not going to bother if youre not interested!" ⁷Fortunately, the friend who later taught me to drive skipped what goes on under the hood. ⁸My most recent frustration is the digital camera, I would love to take professional-quality pictures. ⁹But the little screen and digital readouts confuse me. ¹⁰As a result, my unused camera is hidden away on a shelf in my closet. ¹¹Just last week, my sister gives me a beautiful sports watch for my birthday. ¹²I may have to put it on the shelf with the camera—the alarm keeps going off, and you can't figure out how to stop it.

Editing Test 9

Try to locate the ten sentence-skills mistakes in the following passage. The mistakes are listed in the box below. As you locate each mistake, write the number of the word group in the space provided. Then, in the spaces between the lines, edit and correct each mistake.

one fragment _____	one mistake in subject-verb agreement _____
one run-on _____	
one missing comma around an interrupter _____	two missing quotation marks _____ _____
two apostrophe mistakes _____ _____	one misplaced modifier _____
	one non-parallel structure _____

¹I was six years old when, one day, my dog was struck by a car while getting ready for school. ²My mother and I heard the terrifying sound of squealing brake's. ³In a low voice, she said, Oh, my God—Dusty. ⁴I remember trailing her out the door and seeing a car filled with teenagers and a spreading pool of bright blood on our cobblestoned street. ⁵To me, it seemed only a matter of seconds until a car pulled up. ⁶The driver glanced at the crumpled dog under the car. ⁷And said something about "putting Dusty down." ⁸My mother shouted, "No!" ⁹She crawled halfway under the car and took the dog, like a sack of flour, out from under the wheels. ¹⁰Her clothes were splashed with blood, she cradled the limp dog in her arms and ordered the officers to drive her to the vets office. ¹¹It was only then that she remembered me, I think. ¹²She patted my head, was telling me to walk up to school, and reassured me that Dusty would be all right. ¹³The rest of the story including Dusty's slow recovery and few more years of life, are fuzzy and vague now. ¹⁴But the sights and sounds of those few moments are as vivid to me now as they were twenty-five years ago.

■ Editing Test 10

Try to locate the ten sentence-skills mistakes in the following passage. The mistakes are listed in the box below. As you locate each mistake, write the number of the word group in the space provided. Then, in the spaces between the lines, edit and correct each mistake.

two fragments _____ _____	one non-parallel structure _____
one run-on _____	two apostrophe mistakes _____
one mistake in subject-verb	_____
agreement _____	three missing commas _____
	_____ _____

¹Most products have little or nothing to do with sex a person would never know that by looking at ads'. ²A television ad for a headache remedy, for example shows the product being useful because it ends a womans throbbing head pain just in time for sex. ³Now she will not say "Not tonight, Honey." ⁴Another ad features a detergent that helps a single woman meet a man in a laundry room. ⁵When it comes to products that do relate to sex appeal advertisers often present more obvious sexuality. ⁶A recent magazine ad for women's clothing, for instance, make no reference to the quality of or how comfortable the company's clothes are. ⁷Instead, the ad features a picture of a woman wearing a low-cut sleeveless T-shirt and a very short skirt. ⁸Her eyes are partially covered by semi-wild hair. ⁹And stare seductively at the reader. ¹⁰A recent television ad for perfume goes even further. ¹¹In this ad, a boy not older than twelve reaches out to a beautiful woman. ¹²Sexily dressed in a dark room filled with sensuous music. ¹³With such ads, it is no wonder that young people seem preoccupied with sex.

■ Editing Test 11

Try to locate the ten sentence-skills mistakes in the following passage. The mistakes are listed in the box below. As you locate each mistake, write the number of the word group in the space provided. Then, in the spaces between the lines, edit and correct each mistake.

---

one fragment _____

one run-on _____

one mistake in subject-verb
   agreement _____

two missing commas after
   introductory material
   _____ _____

two missing apostrophes _____
   _____

one non-parallel structure _____

one dangling modifier _____

one mistake in pronoun point of
   view _____

---

¹Being a server is an often under-rated job. ²A server needs the tact of a diplomat, she must be as organized as a business executive, and the ability of an acrobat. ³Working as the link between customers and kitchen, the most demanding diners must be satisfied and the often-temperamental kitchen help must be kept tamed. ⁴Both groups tend to blame the server whenever anything goes wrong. ⁵Somehow, she is held responsible by the customer for any delay (even if it's the kitchens fault), for an overcooked steak, or for an unavailable dessert. ⁶While the kitchen automatically blames her for the diners who change their orders or return those burned steaks. ⁷In addition she must simultaneously keep straight who ordered what at each table, who is yelling for the bill, and whether the new arrivals want cocktails or not. ⁸She must be sure empty tables are cleared, everyone has refills of coffee, and no one is scowling because a request for more rolls are going unheard. ⁹Finally the server must travel a hazardous route between the busy kitchen and the crowded dining room, she has to dodge a diners leg in the aisle or a swinging kitchen door. ¹⁰And you must do this while balancing a tray heaped with steaming platters. ¹¹The hardest task of the server, though, is trying to maintain a decent imitation of a smile on her face—most of the time.

■ Editing Test 12

Try to locate the ten sentence-skills mistakes in the following passage. The mistakes are listed in the box below. As you locate each mistake, write the number of the word group in the space provided. Then, in the spaces between the lines, edit and correct each mistake.

---

two fragments _____ _____   two missing capital letters _____

one run-on _____   _____

two irregular verbs _____   one mistake in pronoun point of
                                                              view _____
_____

one misplaced modifier _____   one subject pronoun mistake

                                                              _____

---

¹The thirtieth anniversary party of my uncle and aunt was the worst family gathering I've ever attended. ²On a hot saturday morning in july, Mom and I drived out into the country to Uncle Ted's house. ³It had already rained heavily, and the only place left to park was in a muddy field. ⁴Then, you would not believe the crowd. ⁵There must have been two hundred people in Uncle Ted's small yard, including his five daughters with their husbands and children, all the other relatives, all the neighbours, and the entire congregation of their church. ⁶Since the ground was soaked and light rain was falling. ⁷Mom and me went under the big rented canopy with everybody else. ⁸We couldn't move between the tables, and the humidity fogged my glasses. ⁹After wiping my glasses, I seen that there was a lot of food. ¹⁰It was mainly cold chicken and potato and macaroni salads, I ate a lot just because there was nothing else to do. ¹¹We were surprised that Uncle Ted and his wife were doing all the work themselves. ¹²They ran back and forth with trays of food and gathered trash into plastic bags, staggering with exhaustion. ¹³It didn't seem like much of a way to celebrate. ¹⁴Mom was upset that she didn't get to speak with them. ¹⁵When we left, I was hot, sticky, and sick to my stomach from overeating. ¹⁶But quickly pushed our car out of the mud and got us on the road. ¹⁷I have never been happier to leave a party.

CHAPTER 42

Introduction to the Readings

The reading selections in Part 5 will help you find topics for writing. Each selection deals in some way with interesting, often thought-provoking concerns or experiences of contemporary life. One selection, for example, forces readers to consider poverty at close range, and another imagines the changes Canada may have experienced by its 153rd birthday. The varied subjects should inspire lively class discussions as well as serious individual thought. The selections should also provide a continuing source of high-interest material for a wide range of writing assignments.

The selections serve another purpose as well. They will help develop reading skills, which are of direct benefit to you as a writer. Through close reading, you will learn how to recognize the thesis in a selection and to identify and evaluate the supporting material that develops the thesis. In your own writing, you will aim to achieve the same essential structure: an overall thesis with detailed and valid support for that thesis. Close reading will also help you to thoroughly explore a selection and its content. The more you understand about what is said in a piece, the more ideas and feelings you may have about writing on an assigned topic or a related topic of your own. A third benefit of close reading is that you will become more aware of authors' stylistic devices—for example, their introductions and conclusions, their ways of presenting and developing a point, their use of transitions, and their choice of language to achieve a particular tone. Recognizing these devices in other people's writing will help you enlarge your own range of writing techniques.

The Format of Each Selection

Each selection begins with a short overview that gives helpful background information and stimulates interest in the piece. The selection is followed by two sets of questions.

- First, there are reading comprehension questions to help you measure your understanding of the material. These questions involve several important reading skills: understanding vocabulary in context, recognizing a subject or topic, determining the thesis or main idea, identifying key supporting points, and making inferences. Answering the questions will enable you and your instructor to check your basic understanding of a selection quickly. More significantly, as you move from one selection to the next, you will sharpen your reading skills as well as your thinking skills—two key factors in making you a better writer.

- Following the comprehension questions are at least seven discussion questions. In addition to dealing with issues of content, these questions focus on matters of structure, style, and tone.

Finally, several writing assignments accompany each selection. The assignments range from narratives to expository and persuasive essays about issues in the world at large. Many assignments provide detailed guidelines on how to proceed, including suggestions for prewriting and appropriate methods of development. When writing your essay responses to the readings, you will have opportunities to apply all the methods of development presented in Part 2 of this book.

How to Read Well: Four General Steps

Skillful reading is an important part of becoming a skillful writer. Following is a series of steps that will make you a better reader—of the selections here and in all your own reading.

1   Concentrate as You Read

To improve your concentration, follow these tips:

- First, read in a place where you can be quiet and alone. Don't choose a spot where there is a TV or stereo on or where friends or family are talking nearby. Turn off your MP3 player and take out your earplugs.
- Next, sit in an upright position when you read. If your body is in a completely relaxed position, sprawled across a bed or nestled in an easy chair, your mind is also going to be completely relaxed. The light muscular tension that comes from sitting in an upright chair promotes concentration and keeps your mind ready to work.
- Third, consider using your index finger (or a pen) as a pacer while you read. Lightly underline each line of print with your index finger as you read down a page. Hold your hand slightly above the page, and move your finger at a speed that is a little too fast for comfort. This pacing with your index finger, like sitting upright on a chair, creates a slight physical tension that will keep your body and mind focused and alert.

2   Skim Material before You Read It

In skimming, you spend about two minutes rapidly surveying a selection, looking for important points, and skipping secondary material. Follow this sequence when skimming:

- Begin by reading the overview that precedes the selection.
- Then, study the title of the selection for a few moments. A good title is the shortest possible summary of a selection; it often tells you in a few words—or even a single word—just what a selection is about. For example, the title "Shame" suggests that you're going to read about a deeply embarrassing condition or incident in a person's life.

- Next, form a basic question (or questions) out of the title. For instance, for the selection titled "Shame," you might ask, "What exactly is the shame?" "What caused the shame?" "What is the result of the shame?" Forming questions out of a title is often a key to locating a writer's thesis, your next concern in skimming.
- Read the first and last couple of paragraphs in the selection. Very often a writer's thesis, *if* it is directly stated, will appear in one of these places and will relate to the title.
- Finally, look quickly at the rest of the selection for other clues to important points. Are there any subheadings you can relate in some way to the title? Are there any words the author has decided to emphasize by setting them off in *italic* or **boldface** type? Are there any major lists of items signalled by words such as *first, second, also,* and *another*?

3   Read the Selection Straight through with a Pen in Hand

Read the selection without slowing down or turning back; just aim to understand as much as you can the first time through. Place a check or star beside answers to basic questions you formed from the title and beside other ideas that seem important. Number as *1, 2, 3 . . .* lists of important points. Circle words you don't understand. Put question marks in the margin next to passages that are unclear and that you will want to reread.

4   Work with the Material

Go back and reread passages that were not clear the first time through. Look up words that block your understanding of ideas, and write their meanings in the margin. Also, reread carefully the areas you identified as most important; doing so will enlarge your understanding of the material. Once you have a sense of the whole, prepare a short written outline of the selection by answering the following questions:

- What is the thesis?
- What key points support the thesis?
- What seem to be other important ideas in the selection?

By working with the material in this way, you will significantly increase your understanding of a selection. Effective reading, just like effective writing, does not happen all at once; it must be worked on. Often, you begin with a general impression of what something means, and then, by working at it, you move to a deeper level of understanding of the material.

How to Answer the Comprehension Questions: Specific Hints

Several important reading skills are involved in the reading comprehension questions that follow each selection. These skills include the following:

- Understanding vocabulary in context
- Summarizing the selection in a title
- Determining the main idea

- Recognizing key supporting details
- Making inferences

The hints below will help you apply each of these reading skills:

- *Vocabulary in context* To decide on the meaning of an unfamiliar word, consider its context. Ask yourself whether there are any clues in the sentence that suggest what the word means.
- *Subject or title* Remember that the title should accurately describe the entire selection. It should be neither too broad nor too narrow. It should answer the question, "What is this about?" as specifically as possible. Note that you may, at times, find it easier to answer the title question *after* the main-idea question.
- *Main idea* Choose the statement that you think best expresses the main idea—also known as the *main point* or *thesis*—of the entire selection. Remember that the title will often help you focus on the main idea. Then, ask yourself the question, "Does most of the material in the selection support this statement?" If you can answer yes to this question, you have found the thesis.
- *Key details* If you were asked to give a two-minute summary of a selection, the key details are the ones you would include in that summary. To determine the key details, ask yourself the question, "What are the major supporting points for the thesis?"
- *Inferences* Answer these questions by drawing upon the evidence presented in the selection and your own common sense. Ask yourself, "What reasonable judgments can I make on the basis of the information in the selection?"

See the Online Learning Centre for a chart on which you can keep track of your performance as you answer the questions for each selection. The chart will help you identify reading skills you may need to strengthen.

Looking Inward

SHAME

Dick Gregory

In this selection, Dick Gregory—the comedian and social critic—narrates two painful experiences from his boyhood. Although the incidents show graphically what it can be like to grow up black and poor, the essay also deals with universal emotions: shame, embarrassment, and the burning desire to hold onto one's self-respect.

I never learned hate at home, or shame. I had to go to school for that. I was about seven years old when I got my first big lesson. I was in love with a little girl named Helene Tucker, a light-complected little girl with pigtails and nice manners. She was always clean and she was smart in school. I think I went to school then mostly to look at her. I brushed my hair and even got me a little old handkerchief. It was a lady's handkerchief, but I didn't want Helene to see me wipe my nose on my hand. The pipes were frozen again, there was no water in the house, but I washed my socks and shirt every night. I'd get a pot, and go over to Mister Ben's grocery store, and stick my pot down into his soda machine. Scoop out some chopped ice. By evening the ice melted to water for washing. I got sick a lot that winter because the fire would go out at night before the clothes were dry. In the morning I'd put them on, wet or dry, because they were the only clothes I had.

Everybody's got a Helene Tucker, a symbol of everything you want. I loved her for her goodness, her cleanness, her popularity. She'd walk down my street and my brothers and sisters would yell, "Here comes Helene," and I'd rub my tennis sneakers on the back of my pants and wish my hair wasn't so nappy and the white folks' shirt fit me better. I'd run out on the street. If I knew my place and didn't come too close, she'd wink at me and say hello. That was a good feeling. Sometimes

1

2

I'd follow her all the way home, and shovel the snow off her walk and try to make friends with her Momma and her aunts. I'd drop money on her stoop late at night on my way back from shining shoes in the taverns. And she had a Daddy, and he had a good job. He was a paper hanger.

I guess I would have gotten over Helene by summertime, but something happened in that classroom that made her face hang in front of me for the next twenty-two years. When I played the drums in high school it was for Helene and when I broke track records in college it was for Helene and when I started standing behind microphones and heard applause I wished Helene could hear it, too. It wasn't until I was twenty-nine years old and married and making money that I finally got her out of my system. Helene was sitting in that classroom when I learned to be ashamed of myself.   3

It was on a Thursday. I was sitting in the back of the room, in a seat with a chalk circle drawn around it. The idiot's seat, the troublemaker's seat.   4

The teacher thought I was stupid. Couldn't spell, couldn't read, couldn't do arithmetic. Just stupid. Teachers were never interested in finding out that you couldn't concentrate because you were so hungry, because you hadn't had any breakfast. All you could think about was noontime, would it ever come? Maybe you could sneak into the cloakroom and steal a bite of some kid's lunch out of a coat pocket. A bite of something. Paste. You can't really make a meal of paste, or put it on bread for a sandwich, but sometimes I'd scoop a few spoonfuls out of the big paste jar in the back of the room. Pregnant people get strange tastes. I was pregnant with poverty. Pregnant with dirt and pregnant with smells that made people turn away, pregnant with cold and pregnant with shoes that were never bought for me, pregnant with five other people in my bed and no Daddy in the next room, and pregnant with hunger. Paste doesn't taste too bad when you're hungry.   5

The teacher thought I was a troublemaker. All she saw from the front of the room was a little black boy who squirmed in his idiot's seat and made noises and poked the kids around him. I guess she couldn't see a kid who made noises because he wanted someone to know he was there.   6

It was on a Thursday, the day before the Negro payday. The eagle always flew on Friday. The teacher was asking each student how much his father would give to the Community Chest. On Friday night, each kid would get the money from his father, and on Monday he would bring it to the school. I decided I was going to buy a Daddy right then. I had money in my pocket from shining shoes and selling papers, and whatever Helene Tucker pledged for her Daddy I was going to top it. And I'd hand the money right in. I wasn't going to wait until Monday to buy me a Daddy.   7

I was shaking, scared to death. The teacher opened her book and started calling out names alphabetically.   8

"Helene Tucker?"   9

"My Daddy said he'd give two dollars and fifty cents."   10

"That's very nice, Helene. Very, very nice indeed."   11

That made me feel pretty good. It wouldn't take too much to top that. I had almost three dollars in dimes and quarters in my pocket. I stuck my hand in my pocket and held onto the money, waiting for her to call my name. But the teacher closed her book after she called everybody else in the class.   12

I stood up and raised my hand.   13

"What is it now?"   14

"You forgot me?"   15

She turned toward the blackboard. "I don't have time to be playing with you,   16
Richard."

"My Daddy said he'd . . ."   17

"Sit down, Richard, you're disturbing the class."   18

"My Daddy said he'd give . . . fifteen dollars."   19

She turned around and looked mad. "We are collecting this money for you   20
and your kind, Richard Gregory. If your Daddy can give fifteen dollars you have
no business being on relief."

"I got it right now, I got it right now, my Daddy gave it to me to turn in today,   21
my Daddy said . . ."

"And furthermore," she said, looking right at me, her nostrils getting big and her   22
lips getting thin and her eyes opening wide, "we know you don't have a Daddy."

Helene Tucker turned around, her eyes full of tears. She felt sorry for me. Then   23
I couldn't see her too well because I was crying, too.

"Sit down, Richard."   24

And I always thought the teacher kind of liked me. She always picked me to   25
wash the blackboard on Friday, after school. That was a big thrill, it made me feel
important. If I didn't wash it, come Monday the school might not function right.

"Where are you going, Richard!"   26

I walked out of school that day, and for a long time I didn't go back very often.   27
There was shame there.

Now there was shame everywhere. It seemed like the whole world had been   28
inside that classroom, everyone had heard what the teacher had said, everyone had
turned around and felt sorry for me. There was shame in going to the Worthy Boys
Annual Christmas Dinner for you and your kind, because everybody knew what a
worthy boy was. Why couldn't they just call it the Boys Annual Dinner, why'd they
have to give it a name? There was shame in wearing the brown and orange and white
plaid mackinaw the welfare gave to three thousand boys. Why'd it have to be the
same for everybody so when you walked down the street the people could see you
were on relief? It was a nice warm mackinaw and it had a hood, and my Momma
beat me and called me a little rat when she found out I stuffed it in the bottom of a
pail full of garbage way over on Cottage Street. There was shame in running over to
Mister Ben's at the end of the day and asking for his rotten peaches, there was shame
in asking Mrs. Simmons for a spoonful of sugar, there was shame in running out to
meet the relief truck. I hated that truck, full of food for you and your kind. I ran into
the house and hid when it came. And then I started to sneak through alleys, to take
the long way home so the people going into White's Eat Shop wouldn't see me. Yeah,
the whole world heard the teacher that day, we all know you don't have a Daddy.

It lasted for a while, this kind of numbness. I spent a lot of time feeling sorry for   29
myself. And then one day I met this wino in a restaurant. I'd been out hustling all
day, shining shoes, selling newspapers, and I had googobs of money in my pocket.
Bought me a bowl of chili for fifteen cents, and a cheeseburger for fifteen cents, and
a Pepsi for five cents, and a piece of chocolate cake for ten cents. That was a good
meal. I was eating when this old wino came in. I love winos because they never hurt
anyone but themselves.

The old wino sat down at the counter and ordered twenty-six cents worth of **30**
food. He ate it like he really enjoyed it. When the owner, Mister Williams, asked
him to pay the check, the old wino didn't lie or go through his pocket like he suddenly found a hole.

He just said: "Don't have no money." **31**

The owner yelled: "Why in hell you come in here and eat my food if you don't **32**
have no money? That food cost me money."

Mister Williams jumped over the counter and knocked the wino off his stool **33**
and beat him over the head with a pop bottle. Then he stepped back and watched
the wino bleed. Then he kicked him. And he kicked him again.

I looked at the wino with blood all over his face and I went over. "Leave him **34**
alone, Mister Williams. I'll pay the twenty-six cents."

The wino got up, slowly, pulling himself up to the stool, then up to the counter, **35**
holding on for a minute until his legs stopped shaking so bad. He looked at me
with pure hate. "Keep your twenty-six cents. You don't have to pay, not now. I just
finished paying for it."

He started to walk out, and as he passed me, he reached down and touched my **36**
shoulder. "Thanks, sonny, but it's too late now. Why didn't you pay it before?"

I was pretty sick about that. I waited too long to help another man. **37**

● ● ● ● ● **READING COMPREHENSION QUESTIONS**

1. The word *pregnant* in "pregnant with poverty" (paragraph 5) means
   a. full of.
   b. empty of.
   c. sick.
   d. satisfied.

2. The word *hustling* in "I'd been out hustling all day" (paragraph 29) means
   a. learning.
   b. stealing.
   c. making friends.
   d. working hard.

3. Which of the following would be a good alternative title for this selection?
   a. Helene Tucker
   b. The Pain of Being Poor
   c. Losing a Father
   d. Mr. Williams and the Wino

4. Which sentence best expresses the main idea of the selection?
   a. Richard felt that being poor was humiliating.
   b. Richard liked Helene Tucker very much.
   c. Richard had to work hard as a child.
   d. The wino refused Richard's money.

5. The teacher disliked Richard because he
   a. was dirty.
   b. liked Helene.

    c. was a troublemaker.
    d. ate paste.

6. *True or false?* Helene Tucker felt sorry for Richard when the teacher embarrassed him.

7. Richard's problems in school were due to his being
    a. hungry.
    b. distracted by Helene.
    c. lonely.
    d. unable to read.

8. The author implies that Richard
    a. was not intelligent.
    b. was proud.
    c. had many friends.
    d. and Helene became friends.

9. The author implies that
    a. Mr. Williams felt sorry for the wino.
    b. Richard's teacher was insensitive.
    c. Richard liked people to feel sorry for him.
    d. Richard's father was dead.

10. The author implies that
    a. the mackinaws were poorly made.
    b. Helene was a sensitive girl.
    c. Helene disliked Richard.
    d. the wino was ashamed of his poverty.

DISCUSSION QUESTIONS

About Content

1. How might Dick Gregory's teacher have handled the Community Chest incident without making him feel ashamed?

2. What are some of the lessons Gregory learns from the incident involving the wino at the restaurant?

3. Where in "Shame" do we find evidence that Dick Gregory finally does escape from poverty?

About Structure

4. Since Dick Gregory is actually writing about an embarrassing incident in school, why does he devote his first three paragraphs to his feelings about Helene Tucker?

5. What is the connection between the incident involving the wino at the restaurant and the rest of the story?

About Style and Tone

6. In the paragraph beginning, "Now there was shame everywhere," Gregory uses a device called *repetition* when he begins several sentences with the words "There was shame . . . ." What is the effect of this repetition?

7. Why does Gregory use dialogue when he narrates the incidents in the classroom and in the restaurant?

• • • • WRITING ASSIGNMENTS

Assignment 1

Dick Gregory tells us in "Shame" that he was ashamed of his poverty and of being on welfare—to the point that he threw away the warm-hooded mackinaw he had been given simply because it was obvious proof that he and his family were on welfare. Do you think Gregory was justified in feeling so ashamed of his situation? Are other people who are on welfare justified if they feel ashamed? Choose either of the following thesis statements, and develop it in an essay of several paragraphs.

People on welfare are justified in feeling ashamed.
People on welfare should not feel ashamed.

Begin by thinking of several reasons to support the statement you have chosen. You might consider any of the following:

- Availability of jobs
- Education or lack of education
- Number of young children at home requiring care
- Illness, physical disability
- Psychological factors (depression, work habits, expectations, mental illness)
- Society's attitude toward people on welfare

Assignment 2

Many people have endured a hurtful or demeaning experience like Dick Gregory's in "Shame," whether it was an event in a classroom, with a group of friends or peers, or in a family situation. Whatever that experience, it is usually embarrassing but educational—it stings, but it teaches.

Write an essay that turns shame or hurt inside out: this essay could be called "The Power of Pain," or something similar. This is an effects essay written in the third-person point of view, for a self-help group, which explains the positive effects or growth that resulted from a shameful or hurtful instance.

Assignment 3

Write an essay about three basic things that people must have in order to feel self-respect. In your thesis statement, name these three necessities, and state that a person must possess them in order to feel self-respect. You could consider any of the following ideas:

- A certain number of material possessions
- A job

- A loving family or a special person
- A clear conscience
- A feeling of belonging
- Freedom from addictions

In your supporting paragraphs, discuss the factors you have chosen, showing specifically why each is so important. In order to avoid falling into the trap of writing generalities, you may want to give examples of people who lack these necessities and show how such people lose self-respect. Your examples may be drawn from personal experience, or they may be hypothetical examples.

MY BODY IS MY OWN BUSINESS

Naheed Mustafa

On many streets in Canada today, women and girls from African and Near or Far Eastern nations wear the traditional long robes of Muslim female dress and the *hijab*, or head covering, as well. Those accustomed to feminist thought of the last thirty years see such dress as symbolic of male oppression in Islamic cultures, but Naheed Mustafa presents an opposing argument. Mustafa, educated at the University of Toronto and Ryerson University, is a journalist in her native Pakistan, who *chooses* to wear the *hijab* for reasons that are at odds with stereotypes of Muslim belief and behaviour.

I often wonder whether people see me as a radical, fundamentalist Muslim terrorist packing an AK-47 assault rifle inside my jean jacket. Or maybe they see me as the poster girl for oppressed womanhood everywhere. I'm not sure which it is.   1

I get the whole gamut of strange looks, stares and covert glances. You see, I wear the *hijab*, a scarf that covers my head, neck and throat. I do this because I am a Muslim woman who believes her body is her own private concern.   2

Young Muslim women are reclaiming the *hijab*, reinterpreting it in light of its original purpose—to give back to women ultimate control of their own bodies.   3

The Koran teaches us that men and women are equal, that individuals should not be judged according to gender, beauty, wealth or privilege. The only thing that makes one person better than another is her or his character.   4

Nonetheless, people have a difficult time relating to me. After all, I'm young, Canadian born and raised, university-educated—why would I do this to myself, they ask.   5

Strangers speak to me in loud, slow English and often appear to be playing charades. They politely inquire how I like living in Canada and whether or not the cold bothers me. If I'm in the right mood, it can be very amusing.   6

But why would I, a woman with all the advantages of a North American upbringing, suddenly, at 21, want to cover myself so that with the *hijab* and the other clothes I choose to wear, only my face and hands show?   7

Because it gives me freedom.   8

Women are taught from early childhood that their worth is proportional to their   9
attractiveness. We feel compelled to pursue abstract notions of beauty, half realizing that such a pursuit is futile.

When women reject this form of oppression, they face ridicule and contempt.   10
Whether it's women who refuse to wear makeup or to shave their legs or to expose
their bodies, society, both men and women, have trouble dealing with them.

In the Western world, the *hijab* has come to symbolize either forced silence   11
or radical, unconscionable militancy. Actually, it's neither. It is simply a woman's
assertion that judgment of her physical person is to play no role whatsoever in
social interaction.

Wearing the *hijab* has given me freedom from constant attention to my physi-   12
cal self. Because my appearance is not subjected to public scrutiny, my beauty, or
perhaps lack of it, has been removed from the realm of what can legitimately be
discussed.

No one knows whether my hair looks as if I just stepped out of a salon, whether   13
or not I can pinch an inch, or even if I have unsightly stretch marks. And because
no one knows, no one cares.

Feeling that one has to meet the impossible male standards of beauty is tiring   14
and often humiliating. I should know, I spent my entire teenage years trying to do
it. I was a borderline bulimic and spent a lot of money I didn't have on potions and
lotions in hopes of becoming the next Cindy Crawford.

The definition of beauty is ever-changing; waifish is good, waifish is bad, ath-   15
letic is good—sorry, athletic is bad. Narrow hips? Great. Narrow hips? Too bad.

Women are not going to achieve equality with the right to bare breasts in pub-   16
lic, as some people would like to have you believe. That would only make us party
to our own objectification. True equality will be had only when women don't need
to display themselves to get attention and won't need to defend their decision to
keep their bodies to themselves.

● ● ● ● ● READING COMPREHENSION QUESTIONS

1. The word *unconscionable* in "radical, unconscionable militancy"
   (paragraph 11) means
   a. unbelievable.
   b. unsuitable.
   c. unmanageable.
   d. unthinkable.

2. The word *waifish* in "waifish is good, waifish is bad, athletic is good"
   (paragraph 15) means
   a. womanly, robust in appearance.
   b. curvaceous, shapely.
   c. sickly.
   d. skinny, neglected-looking.

3. Which of the following would be a good alternative title for this selection?
   a. The Mysterious Eastern Woman
   b. Eastern Privacy and Western Prejudice

c. Habits and Headgear
d. My Culture and My Choice of Clothing

4. Which sentence best expresses the main idea of the selection?
   a. Muslim women have the right to dress as they wish.
   b. Women should wear clothing that disguises their bodies to avoid harassment.
   c. Women will be truly free when their appearance is no longer of primary importance.
   d. Every woman has the right to privacy of her person.

5. People don't know what to make of Naheed Mustafa because
   a. she chooses to dress in an outlandish Eastern way.
   b. the *hijab* symbolizes stereotypes of women as victims or Islamic terrorists.
   c. her clothing disguises her true identity.
   d. she is hiding her identity as an educated Canadian under an ethnic costume.

6. *True or false?* Only men have trouble dealing with women who no longer pursue media-dictated ideals of grooming and beauty.

7. The Koran's teaching about the sexes states
   a. that women unintentionally represent temptation to men.
   b. that men and women are judged by their actions.
   c. that no one should be judged by external factors.
   d. that both sexes have the right to privacy.

8. The author implies that
   a. people see her as a militant feminist.
   b. people find stereotyping easier than looking beyond appearances.
   c. people don't want to know her.
   d. her Canadian upbringing and education are disadvantages.

9. The author implies that
   a. women can achieve a degree of personal freedom by clothing choices.
   b. Western women are slow to catch up with Muslim wisdom about dress.
   c. women will never understand what beauty is all about.
   d. women everywhere are totally obsessed by impossible ideas of beauty.

10. Wearing the *hijab* has given the author
    a. a decent anti-fashion statement appropriate to her religion.
    b. a sense of being able to be whoever she truly is by her own standards.
    c. a place to hide from men's expectations of her.
    d. an exotic refuge from the everyday world of Canadian society.

DISCUSSION QUESTIONS

About Content

1. How does the author feel that people on the street see her? Why does the author feel that way?

2. What are the practical advantages of wearing the *hijab?* What are the ideological reasons for Mustafa's adoption of the garments?

3. What does the author suggest is the basic problem with beauty?

About Structure

4. The clearest statement of the author's thesis is in the last third of the essay. Find the statement and write it down.

5. What is the "change of direction" word in paragraph 11?

About Style and Tone

6. What is your perception of Naheed Mustafa when you read such statements as, "I was a borderline bulimic" who "spent a lot of money I didn't have . . . in hopes of becoming the next Cindy Crawford" and "waifish is good, waifish is bad . . ."?

7. We describe subjects by saying what they are not as well as by saying what they are. In what terms does the author set up her reasons for believing the *hijab* is an ideal form of clothing for her?

8. The author begins her essay with an exaggerated description of one stereotyped image and confesses her defeat at trying to become another stereotyped ideal. Do the examples in the essay give you a clear picture of the "real" person?

● ● ● ● WRITING ASSIGNMENTS

Assignment 1

Naheed Mustafa writes about a personal decision to wear certain clothing, which defines her in one way to observers but means something very different to her as wearer. Our clothing choices *do*, in some ways, define us and communicate information about us to others. The message sent out may not always be the one we intend to communicate. Think about the clothes and accessories you wear to class every day. What is the result of your choice(s) among those who observe you? What do certain garments and jewellery "say" about you, to yourself and to others? Do these messages occasionally conflict?

Write an article for your campus newspaper, defending some choice of personal attire or decoration that may be misinterpreted by others. You could discuss something like a baseball cap, a pierced nostril, a garment representing your ethnic background, or even a certain type of makeup. Use the third-person voice and the cause-effect method of organization to develop your article.

Assignment 2

The image of beauty in any society is constantly changing and subject to the whims of advertising. Nearly our entire consumer economy is based on selling various products to us that will make us more like someone else's ideal of what a beautiful, strong, healthy, or even "good" person is. Should any of us, men or women, model ourselves on TV and magazine concepts of what is attractive?

Write an essay involving one of the following sentences as the basis for your thesis statement, and argue for its validity from your own experience and knowledge.

People are losing their ability to decide what they should look like because of ads showing mostly famished female and six-packed male models.

Ideals of male and female beauty have always evolved from people's dreams and wishes, and portray people's desires to be the best they can be.

Fitness and beauty are not sins.

Assignment 3

What stereotypes, based on aspects of appearance or behaviour, do we carry around with us of various national and cultural groups? Are there any points of truth in these stereotypes? Do such preconceived notions blind us to the characters of people inside the clothing or behind the counter at the store? Think about a specific stereotype based on appearance or on behaviour patterns.

Discuss, in an examples essay, your own reaction to this stereotype. Has your reaction changed as a result of knowing individuals who broke down this stereotype, or is your attitude unchanged?

SMASH THY NEIGHBOR

John McMurtry

We think of football as one of those great North American sports, like hockey or basketball. Children play football from grade school through university. Hours of network TV are devoted to football coverage of Grey Cup games and *Monday Night Football*. In this selection, however, a former Canadian football player says that football games are cruel contests that injure players and bring out the worst in fans.

A few months ago my neck got a hard crick in it. I couldn't turn my head; to look   1
left or right I had to turn my whole body. But I'd had cricks in my neck since I
started playing grade-school football and hockey, so I just ignored it. Then I began
to notice that when I reached for any sort of large book (which I do pretty often as
a philosophy teacher at the University of Guelph), I had trouble lifting it with one
hand. I was losing the strength in my left arm, and I had such a steady pain in my
back that I often had to stretch out on the floor to relieve the pressure.

Several weeks after my problems with book-lifting, I mentioned to my brother,   2
an orthopedic surgeon, that I'd lost the power in my arm since my neck began to
hurt. Twenty-four hours later I was in a Toronto hospital, not sure whether I might
end up with a wasted upper limb. Apparently the steady pounding I had received
playing college and professional football in the late fifties and early sixties had
driven my head into my backbone so that the disks had crumpled together at the
neck—"acute herniation"—and had cut the nerves to my left arm like a pinched
telephone wire (without nerve stimulation, of course, the muscles atrophy, leaving the arm crippled). So I spent my Christmas holidays in the hospital in heavy
traction, and much of the next three months with my neck in a brace. Today most

of the pain has gone, and I've recovered most of the strength in my arm. But from time to time I still have to don the brace, and surgery remains a possibility.

Not much of this will surprise anyone who knows football. It is a sport in which body wreckage is one of the leading conventions. A few days after I went into the hospital for that crick in my neck, another brother, an outstanding football player in college, was undergoing spinal surgery in the same hospital two floors above me. In his case it was a lower, more massive herniation, which every now and again buckled him so that he was unable to lift himself off his back for days. By the time he entered the hospital for surgery he had already spent several months in bed. The operation was successful, but, as in all such cases, it will take him a year to recover fully.   3

These aren't isolated experiences. Just about anybody who has ever played football for any length of time, in high school, college, or one of the professional leagues, has suffered for it later.   4

Indeed, it is arguable that body shattering is the very *point* of football, as killing and maiming are of war. (In the United States, for example, the game results in fifteen to twenty deaths a year and about fifty thousand major operations on knees alone.) To grasp some of the more conspicuous similarities between football and war, it is instructive to listen to the imperatives most frequently issued to the players by their coaches, teammates, and fans. "Hurt 'em!" "Level 'em!" "Kill 'em!" "Take 'em apart!" Or watch for the plays that are most enthusiastically applauded by the fans, where someone is "smeared," "knocked silly," "creamed," "nailed," "broken in two," or even "crucified." (One of my coaches when I played corner linebacker with the Calgary Stampeders in 1961 elaborated, often very inventively, on this language of destruction: admonishing us to "unjoin" the opponent, "make 'im remember you," and "stomp 'im like a bug.") Just as in hockey, where a fight will bring fans to their feet more often than a skillful play, so in football the mouth waters most of all for the really crippling block or tackle. For the kill. Thus the good teams are "hungry," the best players are "mean," and "casualties" are as much a part of the game as they are of a war.   5

The family resemblance between football and war is, indeed, striking. Their languages are similar: "field general," "long bomb," "blitz," "take a shot," "front line," "pursuit," "good hit," "the draft," and so on. Their principles and practices are alike: mass hysteria, the art of intimidation, absolute command and total obedience, territorial aggression, censorship, inflated insignia and propaganda, blackboard maneuvers and strategies, drills, uniforms, formations, marching bands, and training camps. And the virtues they celebrate are almost identical: hyperaggressiveness, coolness under fire, and suicidal bravery.   6

One difference between war and football, though, is that there is little or no protest against football. Perhaps the most extraordinary thing about the game is that the systematic infliction of injuries excites in people not concern, as would be the case if they were sustained at, say, a rock festival, but a collective rejoicing and euphoria. Players and fans alike revel in the spectacle of a combatant felled into semiconsciousness, "blindsided," "clotheslined," or "decapitated." I can remember, in fact, being chided by a coach in pro ball for not "getting my hat" injuriously into a player who was lying helpless on the ground.   7

After every game, of course, the papers are full of reports on the day's injuries, a sort of post-battle "body count," and the respective teams go to work with doctors   8 and trainers, tape, whirlpool baths, cortisone, and morphine to patch and deaden the wounds before the next game. Then the whole drama is reenacted—athletes held together by adhesive, braces, and drugs—and the days following it are filled with even more feverish activity to put on the show yet again at the end of the week. (I remember being so taped up in college that I earned the nickname "Mummy.") The team that survives this merry-go-round spectacle of skilled masochism with the fewest incapacitating injuries usually wins. It is a sort of victory by ordeal: "We hurt them more than they hurt us."

My own initiation into this brutal circus was typical. I loved the game from the   9
moment I could run with a ball. Played shoeless on a green, open field with no one keeping score and in a spirit of reckless abandon and laughter, it's a very different sport. Almost no one gets hurt, and it's rugged, open, and exciting (it still is for me). But, like everything else, it starts to be regulated and institutionalized by adult authorities. And the fun is over.

So it was as I began the long march through organized football. Now there were   10
a coach and elders to make it clear by their behavior that beating other people was the only thing to celebrate and that trying to shake someone up every play was the only thing to be really proud of. Now there were severe rule enforcers, audiences, formally recorded victors and losers, and heavy equipment to permit crippling bodily moves and collisions (according to one survey, more than 80 percent of all football injuries occur to fully equipped players). And now there was the official "given" that the only way to keep playing was to wear suffocating armor, to play to defeat, to follow orders silently, and to renounce spontaneity in favor of joyless drill. The game has been, in short, ruined. But because I loved to play, and play skillfully, I stayed. And progressively and inexorably, as I moved through high school, college, and pro leagues, my body was dismantled. Piece by piece.

I started off with torn ligaments in my knee at thirteen. Then, as the organiza-   11
tion and the competition increased, the injuries came faster and harder. Broken nose (three times), broken jaw (fractured in the first half and dismissed as a "bad wisdom tooth," so I played with it for the rest of the game), ripped knee ligaments again. Torn ligaments in one ankle and a fracture in the other (which I remember feeling relieved about because it meant I could honorably stop drill-blocking a 270-pound defensive end). Repeated rib fractures and cartilage tears (usually carried, again, through the remainder of the game). More dislocations of the left shoulder than I can remember (the last one I played with because, as the Calgary Stampeders' doctor said, it "couldn't be damaged any more"). Occasional broken or dislocated fingers and toes. Chronically hurt lower back (I still can't lift with it or change a tire without worrying about folding). Separated right shoulder (as with many other injuries, like badly bruised hips and legs, needled with morphine for the games). And so on. The last pro game I played—against the Winnipeg Blue Bombers in the Western finals in 1961—I had a recently dislocated left shoulder, a more recently wrenched right shoulder, and a chronic pain center in one leg. I was so tied up with soreness that I couldn't drive to the airport. But it never occurred to me that I should miss a play as a corner linebacker.

By the end of my football career, I had learned that physical injury—giving it   12
and taking it—is the real currency of the sport. And that in the final analysis, the "winner" is the man who can hit to kill even if only half his limbs are working. In

brief, a warrior game with a warrior ethos into which (like almost everyone I played with) my original boyish enthusiasm had been relentlessly conditioned.

In thinking back on how all this happened, though, I can pick out no villains. 13 As with the social system as a whole, the game has a life of its own. Everyone grows up inside it, accepts it, and fulfills its dictates as obediently as Helots. Far from questioning the principles of the activity, most men simply concentrate on executing these principles more aggressively than anybody else. The result is a group of people who, as the leagues become of a higher and higher class, are progressively insensitive to the possibility that things could be otherwise. Thus, in football, anyone who might question the wisdom or enjoyment of putting on heavy equipment on a hot day and running full speed at someone else with the intention of knocking him senseless would be regarded as not really a devoted athlete and probably "chicken." The choice is made straightforward. Either you, too, do your very utmost to smash efficiently and be smashed, or you admit incompetence or cowardice and quit. Since neither of these admissions is very pleasant, people generally keep any doubts they have to themselves, and carry on.

Of course, it would be a mistake to suppose that there is more blind acceptance 14 of brutal practices in organized football than elsewhere. On the contrary, a recent Harvard study argues that football's characteristics of "impersonal acceptance of inflicted injury," an overriding "organization goal," the "ability to turn oneself on and off," and being, above all, "out to win" are prized by ambitious executives in many large corporations. Clearly, football is no sicker than the rest of our society. Even its organized destruction of physical well-being is not anomalous. A very large part of our wealth, work, and time is, after all, spent in systematically destroying and harming human life; manufacturing, selling, and using weapons that tear opponents to pieces; making ever bigger and faster predator-named cars with which to kill and injure one another by the million every year; and devoting our very lives to outgunning one another for power in an ever-more-destructive rat race. Yet all these practices are accepted without question by most people, even zealously defended and honored. Competitive, organized injuring is integral to our way of life, and football is one of the more intelligible mirrors of the whole process: a sort of colorful morality play showing us how exciting and rewarding it is to Smash Thy Neighbor.

Now, it is fashionable to rationalize our collaboration in all this by arguing that, 15 well, men *like* to fight and injure their fellows, and such games as football should be encouraged to discharge this original-sin urge into less harmful channels than, say, war. Public-show football, this line goes, plays the same sort of cathartic role as Aristotle said stage tragedy does: without real blood (or not much), it releases players and audience from unhealthy feelings stored up inside them.

As an ex-player in this seasonal coast-to-coast drama, I see little to recommend 16 such a view. What organized football did to me was make me *suppress* my natural urges and reexpress them in alienating, vicious form. Spontaneous desires for free bodily exuberance and fraternization with competitors were shamed and forced under ("If it ain't hurtin', it ain't helpin'"), and in their place were demanded armored, mechanical moves, and cool hatred of all opposition. Endless authoritarian drill and dressing-room harangues (ever wonder why competing teams can't prepare for a game in the same dressing room?) were the kinds of mechanisms employed to reconstruct joyful energies into mean and alien shapes. I am quite certain that everyone else around me was being similarly forced into this heavily equipped military precision and angry antagonism, because there was always a mutinous attitude about full-dress practices, and everybody (the pros included) had to concentrate incredibly hard for days to whip himself into just one hour's hostility a week against another club. The players never speak of these things, of course, because everyone is anxious to appear tough.

The claim that men like seriously to battle one another to some sort of finish is   17
a myth. It endures only because it wears one of the oldest and most propagandized of masks—the romantic combatant. I sometimes wonder whether the violence all around us doesn't depend for its survival on the existence and preservation of this tough-guy disguise.

As for the effect of organized football on the spectator, the fans are not so   18
much released from supposed feelings of violent aggression by watching their athletic heroes perform it as they are encouraged in the view that people-smashing is an admirable mode of self-expression. The most savage attackers, after all, are, by general agreement, the most efficient and worthy players of all (the biggest applause I ever received as a football player occurred when I ran over people or slammed them so hard that they couldn't get up). . . . Watching well-advertised strong men knock other people around, make them hurt, is in the end like other tastes. It does not weaken with feeding and variation in form. It grows.

I got out of football in 1962. In a preseason intersquad game, I ripped the car-   19
tilage in my ribs on the hardest block I'd ever thrown. I had trouble breathing, and I had to shuffle-walk with my torso on a tilt. The doctor in the local hospital said three weeks rest; the coach said scrimmage in two days. Three days later I was back home reading philosophy.

• • • • • READING COMPREHENSION QUESTIONS

1. The word *atrophy* in "without nerve stimulation, of course, the muscles atrophy, leaving the arm crippled" (paragraph 2) means
   a. get stronger.
   b. flex.
   c. weaken.
   d. be unaffected.

2. The word *imperatives* in "It is instructive to listen to the imperatives most frequently issued to the players. . . . 'Hurt 'em!' 'Level 'em!' 'Kill 'em!'" (paragraph 5) means
   a. insults.
   b. commands.
   c. compliments.
   d. questions.

3. Which of the following would be a good alternative title for this selection?
   a. The Violence of Football
   b. Football in North America
   c. A Man Who Played Football
   d. Football and Corporate Competition

4. Which sentence best expresses the main idea of the selection?
   a. Playing football has caused the author much physical pain.
   b. Most football coaches try to make the game less violent.
   c. Football's popularity is a reflection of some negative aspects of society.
   d. Violence is a central part of organized football both for the teams and for the fans.

5. The author says that organized football is like
   a. all other sports.
   b. philosophy.
   c. war.
   d. football played without coaches and rules.

6. For the author, football was ruined by
   a. people who play without equipment.
   b. the regulation of adult authorities.
   c. people who dislike its violence.
   d. ambitious executives.

7. According to the author, watching football makes people
   a. believe that "smashing thy neighbor" is good.
   b. realize that football is too violent.
   c. feel a great release from their own violent feelings.
   d. escape from the anxieties of their jobs.

8. The author implies that
   a. society is much less brutally competitive than football.
   b. football players never have doubts about the brutality of the game.
   c. the brutal values of football exist in other parts of society.
   d. many people question the violence in football.

9. The author implies that fans
   a. get rid of unhealthy feelings when watching football.
   b. encourage the violence in football.
   c. are unaware of the violence in football.
   d. discourage the really savage attacks in football.

10. In the last paragraph of the selection, the author implies that
    a. his injuries were mild.
    b. the doctor exaggerated the extent of his injuries.
    c. the coach thought that his injuries were mild.
    d. the coach cared more about winning than about his players' injuries.

DISCUSSION QUESTIONS

About Content

1. According to McMurtry, what qualities of our society are reflected in football?

2. The author makes an analogy between war and football. In what ways are the two activities alike?

3. Do you agree with McMurtry that the violence of football encourages people's taste for "people-smashing [as] an admirable mode of self-expression" (paragraph 18)?

About Structure

4. What method of introduction does the author use?
   a. Anecdote
   b. An opposite
   c. Quotation

5. What method of development is used in paragraphs 5 and 6?
   a. Reasons
   b. Comparison
   c. Examples

About Style and Tone

6. Why does the author call his essay "Smash Thy Neighbor"? To answer, think about how the title may be a play on the words in a familiar biblical command.

7. McMurtry uses terms such as *body wreckage, body shattering*, and *skilled masochism* to describe organized football. What effect does he hope this language will have on the reader? Find three other phrases the author uses to describe football (beginning with paragraph 9).

• • • • WRITING ASSIGNMENTS

Assignment 1

You are a college or university football coach, and you have just read "Smash Thy Neighbor." Instead of ranting at your student players or colleagues, you decide to write a response to the magazine that published the article.

You wish to portray yourself as a calm, rational individual, so you choose to write in the third-person viewpoint and offer as many facts as possible. Study McMurtry's article carefully so that you choose three points for which you can supply enough opposing-side support.

Assignment 2

Write an examples essay about the bad experiences young people may have with sports. Consider the following topics:

- An injury
- Not being chosen for a team
- Missing an important point or goal
- Being pressured by a parent or coach
- Being the clumsiest person in gym class
- Being embarrassed while trying to learn a sport

Your thesis should state one specific experience and, of course, tell or suggest to readers that the experience was bad, humiliating, disillusioning, or whatever seems appropriate. Your essay, written in third-person voice to emphasize your content, will show with vividly detailed examples just why the experience was so dreadful.

Assignment 3

Write an essay about a sport you feel is a good one. In each of your supporting paragraphs, give one reason this sport is good for either players or spectators.

THREE PASSIONS

Bertrand Russell

Bertrand Russell (1872–1970), a philosopher and mathematician, was a controversial figure on the world stage. He was imprisoned twice, first in 1918 for his outspoken criticism of British involvement in World War I, and again in 1961 for "inciting civil disobedience" while campaigning for nuclear disarmament. His writings on social, political, and educational issues led to his winning the Nobel Prize for Literature in 1950. "Three Passions" is taken from the prologue to his autobiography.

Three passions, simple but overwhelmingly strong, have governed my life: the   1
longing for love, the search for knowledge, and unbearable pity for the suffering of mankind. These passions, like great winds, have blown me hither and thither, in a wayward course, over a deep ocean of anguish, reaching to the very verge of despair.

I have sought love, first, because it brings ecstasy—ecstasy so great that I would   2
often have sacrificed all the rest of life for a few hours of this joy. I have sought it, next, because it relieves loneliness—that terrible loneliness in which one shivering consciousness looks over the rim of the world into the cold unfathomable lifeless abyss. I have sought it, finally, because in the union of love I have seen, in a mystic miniature, the prefiguring vision of the heaven that saints and poets have imagined. This is what I sought, and though it might seem too good for human life, this is what—at last—I have found.

With equal passion I have sought knowledge. I have wished to understand   3
the hearts of men. I have wished to know why the stars shine. And I have tried to apprehend the Pythagorean power by which number holds sway above the flux. A little of this, but not much, I have achieved.

Love and knowledge, so far as they were possible, led upward toward the heav-   4
ens. But always pity brought me back to earth. Echoes of cries of pain reverberate in my heart. Children in famine, victims tortured by oppressors, helpless old people a hated burden to their sons, and the whole world of loneliness, poverty, and pain make a mockery of what human life should be. I long to alleviate the evil, but I cannot, and I too suffer.

This has been my life. I have found it worth living, and would gladly live it again   5
if the chance were offered me.

● ● ● ● ● READING COMPREHENSION QUESTIONS

1. The word *alleviate* in "I long to alleviate the evil, but I cannot, and I too suffer" means
   a. increase.
   b. tolerate.
   c. enjoy.
   d. relieve.

2. Which of the following would be a good alternative title for this selection?
   a. The Forces Driving Me
   b. The Truth about Love
   c. The Anguish of Life
   d. The Power of Knowledge

3. What sentence best expresses the main idea of the selection?
   a. People's inhumanity to other humans has been a source of great pain in the author's life.
   b. The author wishes he had his life to live over again.
   c. The author sees his life driven by three passions.
   d. The author has found life's struggle to be painful but ultimately rewarding.

4. Russell compares his life's passions to
   a. great winds.
   b. the stars.
   c. a bottomless abyss.
   d. a boundless ocean.

5. Which of the following is *not* a reason that Russell sought love?
   a. It relieves loneliness.
   b. It leads to marriage.
   c. It brings ecstasy.
   d. It provides a glimpse of heaven.

6. *True or false?* Russell believes that he has gained considerable knowledge in life.

7. When Russell uses the metaphor of a "deep ocean" to describe his anguish, he implies that it is
   a. cold.
   b. without life.
   c. almost bottomless.
   d. lacking in colour.

8. Russell implies that loneliness, at its core, is
   a. a self-defeating impulse.
   b. impossible to avoid.
   c. a sign of selfishness.
   d. a fear of death.

9. Russell implies that life for him has been
   a. passionately complex.
   b. simpler than he would have imagined.
   c. so troubled that it has increased his faith in God.
   d. more materialistic than he would have wished.

10. We can conclude that the author would agree with which statement?
    a. It is difficult to free oneself of pity.
    b. Human love is ultimately disappointing.
    c. Heaven is merely a poetic invention.
    d. A loving person naturally wants to relieve the suffering of others.

DISCUSSION QUESTIONS

About Content

1. What three reasons does Russell give for seeking love in his life? How do his reasons compare to or contrast with your own reasons for seeking love?

2. What are the two aspects of knowledge that Russell has pursued?

3. How did Russell's passion for pity differ from his desire for knowledge?

4. Do you find Russell's statement an uplifting or a saddening one? What elements of each do you find within it? What makes one element outweigh another in your mind?

About Structure

5. Does this essay follow the traditional one-three-one essay model of introduction, support, and conclusion? How would you outline the essay?

6. This essay is organized primarily in terms of three causes and their overall effect. What is the effect and what are the causes? The essay can also be seen as an examples essay. What examples does the author provide to help the reader understand each of his lifelong passions?

7. What kind of traditional signals—time, space, or addition—does Russell employ in the second paragraph? List the transitions you find there.

About Style and Tone

8. This selection is a mixture of simplicity and complexity in terms of style. Where do you find examples of simple, direct statements? Do you find these effective, and why? Where, in contrast, do you find complex statements? Choose one that you find meaningful, and explain why.

9. Russell is a master of the use of metaphorical language. For instance, as has already been seen, he compares his anguish to an "ocean." What other examples of metaphorical language can you find? Why do you think Russell chose to use such imaginative language rather than plain, direct language?

• • • • **WRITING ASSIGNMENTS**

Assignment 1

Write an essay in which you identify three passions that have strongly influenced your life. As it is with Russell's essay, first-person viewpoint is appropriate here; you are explaining *connections to you*, explaining why each passion has been so important to you.

Alternatively, select one particular passion, and write about three areas of your life in which this passion has influenced you.

If you choose the first alternative, your thesis statement might be something like this:

> The love of family, a rebellious streak, and affection for the outdoors are three passions that have governed my life.

If you choose the second alternative, this is how your thesis might look:

> My rebellious streak has strongly influenced my family life, my performance in school, and my choice of career.

Assignment 2

Write a descriptive essay that vividly portrays for readers three earthly things you've observed or experienced that have given you something like Russell's "prefiguring vision of heaven." In other words, they have given you a sense of something ideal, pure, perfect, and beautiful. Describe your observations or experiences in rich detail so that your reader will understand why you found them so special, and explain what effect they have had on you.

Assignment 3

Clearly, love is a multi-faceted emotion. People might say they love their spouse, love their children, love their friends, and love humanity in general, but they mean quite different things in each case.

Write an essay in which you divide and classify love into three different types. Give detailed examples that illustrate how each type of love is demonstrated.

WHAT IS POVERTY?

Jo Goodwin Parker

"What is Poverty?" is shocking in its directness—the writer glares back, speaks angrily to the reader, demanding "listen to me." About its author, Jo Goodwin Parker, virtually nothing is known, except that she first presented this selection as a speech. Imagine yourself in her audience—how would you react to her words, her tone? Is poverty nothing more than an abstract noun to you, a word with no specific meanings? If so, Goodwin Parker offers a wealth of specific and bitterly plain details to help you not just see, but feel.

You ask me what is poverty? Listen to me. Here I am, dirty, smelly, and with no "proper" underwear on and with the stench of my rotting teeth near you. I will tell you. Listen to me. Listen without pity. I cannot use your pity. Listen with understanding. Put yourself in my dirty, worn out, ill-fitting shoes, and hear me.

Poverty is getting up every morning from a dirt- and illness-stained mattress. The sheets have long since been used for diapers. Poverty is living in a smell that never leaves. This is a smell of urine, sour milk, and spoiling food sometimes joined with the strong smell of long-cooked onions. Onions are cheap. If you have smelled this smell, you did not know how it came. It is the smell of the outdoor privy. It is the smell of young children who cannot walk the long dark way in the night. It is the smell of the mattresses where years of "accidents" have happened. It is the smell of the milk which has gone sour because the refrigerator long has not worked, and it costs money to get it fixed. It is the smell of rotting garbage. I could bury it, but where is the shovel? Shovels cost money.

Poverty is being tired. I have always been tired. They told me at the hospital when the last baby came that I had chronic anemia caused from poor diet, a bad case of worms, and that I needed a corrective operation. I listened politely—the poor are always polite. The poor always listen. They don't say that there is no money for iron pills, or better food, or worm medicine. The idea of an operation is frightening and costs so much that, if I had dared, I would have laughed. Who takes care of my children? Recovery from an operation takes a long time. I have three children. When I left them with "Granny" the last time I had a job, I came home to find the baby covered with fly specks, and a diaper that had not been changed since I left. When the dried diaper came off, bits of my baby's flesh came with it. My other child was playing with a sharp bit of broken glass, and my oldest was playing alone at the edge of a lake. I made twenty-two dollars a week, and a good nursery school costs twenty dollars a week for three children. I quit my job.

Poverty is dirt. You can say in your clean clothes coming from your clean house, "Anybody can be clean." Let me explain about housekeeping with no money For breakfast I give my children grits with no oleo or cornbread without eggs and oleo. This does not use up many dishes. What dishes there are, I wash in cold water and with no soap. Even the cheapest soap has to be saved for the baby's diapers. Look at my hands, so cracked and red. Once I saved for two months to buy a jar of Vaseline for my hands and the baby's diaper rash. When I had saved enough, I went to buy it and the price had gone up two cents. The baby and I suffered on. I have to decide every day if I can bear to put my cracked sore hands into the cold water and strong soap. But you ask, why not hot water? Fuel costs money. If you have a wood fire it costs money. If you burn electricity, it costs money Hot water is a luxury. I do not have luxuries. I know you will be surprised when I tell you how young I am, I look so much older. My back has been bent over the wash tubs every day for so long, I cannot remember when I ever did anything else. Every night I wash every stitch my school age child has on and just hope her clothes will be dry by morning.

Poverty is staying up all night on cold nights to watch the fire knowing one spark on the newspaper covering the walls means your sleeping child dies in flames. In summer, poverty is watching gnats and flies devour your baby's tears when he cries. The screens are torn and you pay so little rent you know they will never be

1
2
3
4
5

fixed. Poverty means insects in your food, in your nose, in your eyes, and crawling over you when you sleep. Poverty is hoping it never rains because diapers won't dry when it rains and soon you are using newspapers. Poverty is seeing your children forever with runny noses. Paper handkerchiefs cost money and all your rags you need for other things. Even more costly are antihistamines. Poverty is cooking without food and cleaning without soap.

Poverty is asking for help. Have you ever had to ask for help, knowing your children will suffer unless you get it? Think about asking for a loan from a relative, if this is the only way you can imagine asking for help. I will tell you how it feels. You find out where the office is that you are supposed to visit. You circle that block four or five times. Thinking of your children, you go in. Everyone is very busy. Finally, someone comes out and you tell her that you need help. That never is the person you need to see. You go see another person, and after spilling the whole shame of your poverty all over the desk between you, you find that this isn't the right office after all—you must repeat the whole process, and it never is any easier at the next place.   **6**

You have asked for help, and after all it has a cost. You are again told to wait. You are told why, but you don't really hear because of the red cloud of shame and the rising cloud of despair.   **7**

Poverty is remembering. It is remembering quitting school in junior high because "nice" children had been so cruel about my clothes and my smell. The attendance officer came. My mother told him I was pregnant. I wasn't, but she thought that I could get a job and help out. I had jobs off and on, but never long enough to learn anything. Mostly I remember being married. I was so young then. I am still young. For a time, we had all the things you have. There was a little house in another town, with hot water and everything. Then my husband lost his job. There was unemployment insurance for a while and what few jobs I could get. Soon, all our nice things were repossessed and we moved back here. I was pregnant then. This house didn't look so bad when we first moved in. Every week it gets worse. Nothing is ever fixed. We now had no money. There were a few odd jobs for my husband, but everything went for food then, as it does now. I don't know how we lived through three years and three babies, but we did. I'll tell you something, after the last baby I destroyed my marriage. It had been a good one, but could you keep on bringing children in this dirt? Did you ever think how much it costs for any kind of birth control? I knew my husband was leaving the day he left, but there were no goodbys between us. I hope he has been able to climb out of this mess somewhere. He never could hope with us to drag him down.   **8**

That's when I asked for help. When I got it, you know how much it was? It was, and is, seventy-eight dollars a month for the four of us; that is all I ever can get. Now you know why there is no soap, no needles and thread, no hot water, no aspirin, no worm medicine, no hand cream, no shampoo. None of these things forever and ever and ever. So that you can see clearly, I pay twenty dollars a month rent, and most of the rest goes for food. For grits and cornmeal, and rice and milk and beans. I try my best to use only the minimum electricity. If I use more, there is that much less for food.   **9**

Poverty is looking into a black future. Your children won't play with my boys. They will turn to other boys who steal to get what they want. I can already see them   **10** behind the bars of their prison instead of behind the bars of my poverty. Or they will turn to the freedom of alcohol or drugs, and find themselves enslaved. And my daughter? At best, there is for her a life like mine.

But you say to me, there are schools. Yes, there are schools. My children have no extra books, no magazines, no extra pencils, or crayons, or paper and most important of all, they do not have health. They have worms, they have infections, they have pinkeye all summer. They do not sleep well on the floor, or with me in my one bed. They do not suffer from hunger, my seventy-eight dollars keeps us alive, but they do suffer from malnutrition. Oh yes, I do remember what I was taught about health in school. It doesn't do much good. In some places there is a surplus commodities program. Not here. The county said it cost too much. There is a school lunch program. But I have two children who will already be damaged by the time they get to school.

But, you say to me, there are health clinics. Yes, there are health clinics and they are in the towns. I live out here eight miles from town. I can walk that far (even if it is sixteen miles both ways), but can my little children? My neighbor will take me when he goes; but he expects to get paid, *one way or another.* I bet you know my neighbor. He is that large man who spends his time at the gas station, the barber-shop, and the comer store complaining about the government spending money on the immoral mothers of illegitimate children.

Poverty is an acid that drips on pride until all pride is worn away. Poverty is a chisel that chips on honor until honor is worn away. Some of you say that you would do *something* in my situation, and maybe you would, for the first week or the first month, but for year after year after year?

Even the poor can dream. A dream of a time when there is money. Money for the right kinds of food, for worm medicine, for iron pills, for toothbrushes, for hand cream, for a hammer and nails and a bit of screening, for a shovel, for a bit of paint, for some sheeting, for needles and thread. Money to pay *in money* for a trip to town. And, oh, money for hot water and money or soap. A dream of when asking for help does not eat away the last bit of pride. When the office you visit is as nice as the offices of other governmental agencies, when there are enough workers to help you quickly, when workers do not quit in defeat and despair. When you have to tell your story to only one person, and that person can send you for other help and you don't have to prove your poverty over and over and over again.

I have come out of my despair to tell you this. Remember I did not come from another place or another time. Others like me are all around you. Look at us with an angry heart, anger that will help you help me. Anger that will let you tell of me. The poor are always silent. Can you be silent too?

● ● ● ● ● **READING COMPREHENSION QUESTIONS**

1. The word *oleo* in "I give my children grits with no oleo or cornbread without eggs and oleo" (paragraph 4) means
   a. syrup.
   b. margarine.
   c. butter.
   d. oil.

2. The word *commodities* in "there is a surplus commodities program"
   (paragraph 11) means
   a. services.
   b. school supplies.
   c. groceries.
   d. goods.

3. Which of the following would be a good alternative title for this selection?
   a. The Poor Cry Out; Do You Hear?
   b. Listen, Learn, and Do Something
   c. The Poor are the Same Everywhere
   d. The Silence of the Poor

4. Which sentence best expresses the main idea of the selection?
   a. Poverty is so overwhelming that it is impossible to understand.
   b. There is no escape from the sour, grinding world of poverty.
   c. Being poor means losing hope.
   d. Helping the poor means understanding their damaged souls and deadened
      wills.

5. What were the author's problems after having her last child? What are the
   reasons she was unable to do anything about each of these problems?

6. The author says "poverty is dirt" because
   a. she has given up on trying to clean her house.
   b. keeping herself, the children, and the house clean is just too much.
   c. every household action must be calculated to cost as little as possible.
   d. hot water and soap cost money she does not have.

7. *True or false?* The author's husband left her because they had too many
   children too quickly.

8. The author implies that the babysitter she hired
   a. was the only person she tried.
   b. was irresponsible.
   c. was her mother.
   d. was trying to hurt the children.

9. When Goodwin Parker describes her neighbour as "that large man who
   spends his time . . . complaining about the government spending money on
   the immoral mothers of illegitimate children," she implies
   a. she is ashamed of having to comply with his method of payment.
   b. that he is an evil hypocrite.
   c. he is a typical church-going, moral person with more opinions than
      common sense.
   d. he has nothing better to do than complain about government spending.

10. The author implies that poverty
    a. is a cycle that can be broken with help.
    b. destroys its victims.
    c. traps people for generations.
    d. makes education and escape impossible.

DISCUSSION QUESTIONS

About Content

1. What are the different odours in paragraph 2? What is the cause of each smell and how is each related to poverty?

2. What is the author recalling when she says "poverty is remembering"? What connects these memories?

3. What does the author see as her sons' futures? Why do you think she feels as she does?

About Structure

4. As well as definition as an overall means, Goodwin Parker uses the cause-and-effect method of development within some of her paragraphs. Choose one such paragraph and identify, then explain its series of causes or events.

5. How often is the "poverty is . . ." paragraph opening used, compared to the total number of paragraphs in the selection? How many paragraphs appear before she first changes her paragraph opening? In the second half of the essay, is there a discernable pattern in the paragraph openings? If so, explain it.

6. In which paragraph does the author repeat this pattern within the paragraph itself? What is the effect of this repetition?

About Style and Tone

7. Who is the audience that Goodwin Parker is addressing? Describe who they might be, and why, based on specifics in the text, you believe as you do.

8. Choose one body paragraph and note the sentence variety within it. How many longer and how many short sentences do you find in the paragraph you choose? Is there a pattern or alternating rhythm of short-to-long sentences? What is the effect of the short sentences? Of the longer sentences?

9. Although the author's style seems plain-spoken, she does use figurative language, such as "red cloud of shame" (paragraph 8). Choose two examples of such figures of speech and discuss their effectiveness related to the selection.

WRITING ASSIGNMENTS

Assignment 1

Write an essay in the form of a letter to Jo Goodwin Parker. Respond to three points of hers that affect you most (negatively or positively), giving plenty of supporting examples and details; be sure to quote correctly as you write to her.

In this case, because Goodwin Parker's essay is less than formal in style, and because you are writing a letter, you may choose to use first-person viewpoint if doing so will make your responses more vivid to your reader.

Assignment 2

"What is Anxiety?" "What is Shyness?" Write a definition essay about some challenge or difficulty you face or endure. Support the aspects of your definition with the most specific details possible, as does Goodwin Parker. If appropriate, consider using some cause or effect method of development within a body paragraph or two.

Assignment 3

"I have come out of my despair to tell you this. Remember I did not come from another place or another time." So opens Goodwin Parker's final paragraph, carrying much the same message as media campaigns for various social service organizations. One television awareness campaign shows "the invisible people," the street people and the poor that one group helps.

Consider the concept of "invisible people": the elderly, night-shift workers, anyone whom other groups do not "see." In a division and classification essay, come up with your own three categories of "invisible people." Why are they invisible, and to whom? Why should we be aware of them?

Observing Others

WHY ARE STUDENTS TURNED OFF?

Casey Banas

A teacher pretends to be a student and sits in on several classes. What does she find in the typical class? Boredom. Routine. Apathy. Manipulation. Discouragement. If this depressing list sounds familiar, you will be interested in the following analysis of why classes often seem to be more about killing time than about learning.

Ellen Glanz lied to her teacher about why she hadn't done her homework; but, of course, many students have lied to their teachers. The difference is that Ellen Glanz was a twenty-eight-year-old high school social studies teacher who was a student for six months to improve her teaching by gaining a fresh perspective of her school. 1

She found many classes boring, students doing as little as necessary to pass tests and get good grades, students using ruses to avoid assignments, and students manipulating teachers to do the work for them. She concluded that many students are turned off because they have little power and responsibility for their own education. 2

Ellen Glanz found herself doing the same things as the students. There was the day when Ellen wanted to join her husband in helping friends celebrate the purchase of a house, but she had homework for a math class. For the first time, she knew how teenagers feel when they think something is more important than homework. 3

She found a way out and confided: "I considered my options: Confess openly to the teacher, copy someone else's sheet, or make up an excuse." Glanz chose the third—the one most widely used—and told the teacher that the pages needed to 4 complete the assignment had been ripped from the book. The teacher accepted the story, never checking the book. In class, nobody else did the homework; and student after student mumbled responses when called on.

"Finally," Glanz said, "the teacher, thinking that the assignment must have been difficult, went over each question at the board while students copied the problems at their seats. The teacher had 'covered' the material and the students had listened to the explanation. But had anything been learned? I don't think so." 5

Glanz found this kind of thing common. "In many cases," she said, "people simply didn't do the work assignment, but copied from someone else or manipulated the teacher into doing the work for them." 6

"The system encourages incredible passivity," Glanz said. "In most classes one sits and listens. A teacher, whose role is activity, simply cannot understand the passivity of the student's role," she said. "When I taught," Glanz recalled, "my mind was going constantly—figuring out how best to present an idea, thinking about whom to call on, whom to draw out, whom to shut up; how to get students involved, how to make my point clearer, how to respond; when to be funny, when serious. As a student, I experienced little of this. Everything was done to me." 7

Class methods promote the feeling that students have little control over or responsibility for their own education because the agenda is the teacher's, Glanz said. The teacher is convinced the subject matter is worth knowing, but the student may not agree. Many students, Glanz said, are not convinced they need to know what teachers teach; but they believe good grades are needed to get into college. 8

Students, obsessed with getting good grades to help qualify for the college of their choice, believe the primary responsibility for their achievement rests with the teacher, Glanz said. "It was his responsibility to teach well rather than their responsibility to learn carefully." 9

Teachers were regarded by students, Glanz said, not as "people," but as "role-players" who dispensed information needed to pass a test. "I often heard students describing teachers as drips, bores, and numerous varieties of idiots," she said. "Yet I knew that many of the same people had traveled the world over, conducted fascinating experiments or learned three languages, or were accomplished musicians, artists, or athletes." 10

But the sad reality, Glanz said, is the failure of teachers to recognize their tremendous communications gap with students. Some students, she explained, believe that effort has little value. After seeing political corruption they conclude that honesty takes a back seat to getting ahead any way one can, she said. "I sometimes estimated that half to two-thirds of a class cheated on a given test," Glanz said. "Worse, I've encountered students who feel no remorse about cheating but are annoyed that a teacher has confronted them on their actions." 11

Glanz has since returned to teaching at Lincoln-Sudbury. Before her stint as a student, she would worry that perhaps she was demanding too much. "Now I know I should have demanded more," she said. Before, she was quick to accept the excuses of students who came to class unprepared. Now she says, "You are responsible for learning it." But a crackdown is only a small part of the solution. 12

The larger issue, Glanz said, is that educators must recognize that teachers and students, though physically in the same school, are in separate worlds and have an ongoing power struggle. "A first step toward ending this battle is to convince 13 students that what we attempt to teach them is genuinely worth knowing," Glanz said. "We must be sure, ourselves, that what we are teaching is worth knowing." No longer, she emphasized, do students assume that "teacher knows best."

• • • • **READING COMPREHENSION QUESTIONS**

1. The word *ruses* in "students using ruses to avoid assignments" (paragraph 2) means
   a. questions.
   b. sicknesses.
   c. parents.
   d. tricks.

2. The word *agenda* in "the agenda is the teacher's" (paragraph 8) means
   a. program.
   b. boredom.
   c. happiness.
   d. book.

3. Which of the following would be a good alternative title for this selection?
   a. How to Get Good Grades
   b. Why Students Dislike School
   c. Cheating in Our School System
   d. Students Who Manipulate Teachers

4. Which sentence best expresses the main idea of the selection?
   a. Ellen Glanz is a burnt-out teacher.
   b. Ellen Glanz lied to her math teacher.
   c. Students need good grades to get into college.
   d. Teachers and students feel differently about schooling.

5. How much of a class, according to Glanz, would often cheat on a test?
   a. One-quarter or less
   b. One-half
   c. One-half to two-thirds
   d. Almost everyone

6. *True or false?* As a result of her experience, Glanz now accepts more of her students' excuses.

7. Glanz found that the school system encourages an incredible amount of
   a. enthusiasm.
   b. passivity.
   c. violence.
   d. creativity.

8. The author implies that
   a. few students cheat on tests.
   b. most students enjoy schoolwork.
   c. classroom teaching methods should be changed.
   d. Glanz had a lazy math teacher.

9. The author implies that
    a. Glanz should not have become a student again.
    b. Glanz is a better teacher than she was before.
    c. Glanz later told her math teacher that she lied.
    d. social studies is an unimportant subject.

10. The author implies that
    a. most students who cheat on tests are caught by their teachers.
    b. most teachers demand too little of their students.
    c. students who get good grades in high school also do so in college.
    d. students never question what teachers say.

• • • • DISCUSSION QUESTIONS

About Content

1. What were Ellen Glanz's main discoveries when she first re-entered high school classes as a student? What did she conclude as a result of these observations?

2. Why, in paragraph 5, did the teacher believe that an assignment must have been too challenging?

3. Why, according to Glanz, is it so difficult for teachers to understand students' passivity? Why, in turn, do students tend to be passive?

4. What could cause a student caught cheating to respond with anger?

About Structure

5. Which method of introduction does Banas use in her essay?
    a. Movement from general to specific
    b. Anecdote
    c. Background information
    d. Questions

    Why do you think she chose this approach?

6. List the time transitions that Banas uses in paragraph 12. How do they help the author make her point?

About Style and Tone

7. Throughout "Why Are Students Turned Off?" Banas shifts between summarizing Ellen Glanz's words and quoting Glanz directly. Find an instance in the essay in which both direct and indirect quotations are used in the same paragraph. What does the author gain or lose from using this technique? (Refer to page 404 for definitions and examples of direct and indirect quotations.)

8. Parallel structures are often used to emphasize similar information. They can create a smooth, readable style. For example, note the series of participles, or *-ing* verb forms, in the following sentence from paragraph 2: "students *doing* as little as necessary to pass tests and get good grades, students *using* ruses

to avoid assignments, and students *manipulating* teachers to do the work for them." Find two other uses of parallel structure, one in paragraph 4 and one in paragraph 7.

● ● ● ● WRITING ASSIGNMENTS

Assignment 1

Play the role of student observer in one of your classes. Then, write an essay with *either* of the following thesis statements:

- In _____ class, students are turned off because . . .

- In _____ class, students are active and interested because . . .

In each supporting paragraph, state and explain one reason why that particular class is either boring or interesting. You might want to consider areas such as these:

Instructor: presentation, tone of voice, level of interest and enthusiasm, teaching aids used, ability to handle questions, sense of humour
Students: level of enthusiasm, participation in class, attitude (as shown by body language and other actions)
Other factors: conditions of classroom, length of class period, noise level in classroom

Assignment 2

Glanz says that students like to describe their teachers as "drips, bores, and numerous varieties of idiots." Write a description of one of your instructors, past or present, who either *does* or *does not* fit that description. *Show* in your essay that your instructor was weak, boring, and idiotic *or* dynamic, creative, and bright. In either case, your focus should be on providing specific details that enable your readers to see for themselves that your thesis is valid.

Assignment 3

How does the classroom situation Ellen Glanz describes compare with a classroom situation with which you are familiar—either one from your earlier educational experience or one from the school you presently attend? Write an essay in the third-person voice in which you compare or contrast a class of your experience with those Ellen Glanz describes. Here are some points for comparison or contrast you might wish to include in your essay:

- How interesting the class was/is
- How many of the students did/do their assignments
- What the teaching methods were/are
- How much was/is actually learned
- How active the instructor was/is
- How passive or engaged the students were/are
- What the students thought/think of the instructor

Choose any three of these points for comparison or contrast, or any other three that come to mind. Then, decide which specific method of development you will use: *one side at a time* or *point by point*.

THE GREATEST STORY NEVER TOLD

Bob McKeown

The word "survivor" is often misused these days to mean people who outwit, outplay, or outlast each other on a reality show. Bob McKeown, host of CBC's *the fifth estate*, discovered the story of a real, extraordinary survivor—a four-year-old girl. "The Greatest Story Never Told" takes us back to the year 1913 and Robert Bartlett's Canadian Arctic Expedition. McKeown recounts the story of an incredible, yet overlooked, expedition and of a small Inuit girl's extraordinary resilience. She not only survived; she lived on to tell the author her story at the age of ninety-two. Enjoy this fascinating adventure, the story of a genuine survivor.

1 She is a cheerful woman, not five feet tall, with a joyous grin and a house full of great-grandchildren. She is simply called Mugpi. And in tiny Barrow, Alaska, at the edge of the Arctic Ocean, where she's spent all but one of her 92 years, everyone knows her name.

2 None of this is remarkable. What's remarkable is that the woman known as Mugpi is not a living legend in the Great White North that borders Alaska on the east. Because Mugpi is the last survivor of what is probably the greatest Canadian adventure story ever lived or told. It is the tale of the incredible year Mugpi spent not next to the Arctic ice, but trapped on it—marooned along with two dozen other people, adrift in one of the most desolate and unforgiving places on earth.

3 Today, from her home on the northernmost tip of North America, she can look out over the vast expanse of ice that stretches to the North Pole and beyond, to the other side of the world. And when she takes her afternoon stroll along that frigid shore and gazes toward the horizon, where it all happened so long ago, an onlooker can't help but wonder, "How did she make it back alive? How did any of them?"

4 The years leading up to the First World War were a golden age of exploration, when expedition leaders were international celebrities, their exploits funded by the rich and powerful, reported by the press and followed by an adoring public. Their names still form a pantheon of human daring and adventure: American Admiral Robert Peary, first to claim the North Pole; Robert Falcon Scott and Ernest Shackleton of Britain, who raced to the South Pole; and Norway's Roald Amundsen, who beat them to it.

5 Almost nine decades later, the world has rediscovered Shackleton, whose attempt to cross the Antarctic was such an extraordinary saga of leadership and survival that NASA made it required reading for prospective astronauts, the ultimate example of the right stuff. In the past year or so, there have been Shackleton books and documentaries, an IMAX film and a TV miniseries starring Kenneth Branagh.

6 It may be news to many—not to say most—Canadians, but months before Ernest Shackleton even departed on his legendary journey, a boatload of explorers from Canada faced an eerily similar battle between life and death: not in the Antarctic, but a world away, in the Far North. The explorers were members of the Canadian Arctic Expedition, under the command of their own indomitable—if to date largely unheralded—polar explorer, Newfoundlander Robert Bartlett.

On January 11, 1914, in the same year that the First World War began, Robert   7
Bartlett and his expedition found themselves stranded on the ice-covered Arctic
Ocean, in a place so cold that exposed human flesh froze in seconds; so dark they
wouldn't see sunlight for weeks; so isolated no one else had any idea where they
were. Like Shackleton's ship, Bartlett's would be frozen in place, then crushed by
the polar ice. Like Shackleton and his crew, Bartlett and his party were left stranded
without a vessel on the ice pack, cut off from the outside world. And like Ernest
Shackleton himself, Robert Bartlett knew that if they were ever to be rescued, they'd
have to do it themselves.

But there was one striking difference between the two expeditions: Shackleton's   8
crew included no four-year-old girls.

The Canadian Arctic Expedition had sailed from Victoria, B.C., seven months   9
before that ominous January day, with glorious hopes and dreams. Conceived by
a Manitoba-born anthropologist named Vilhjalmur Stefansson and funded by the
federal government, the expedition was expected to take up to four years, mapping
uncharted territory in the high Arctic and searching for undiscovered land.

Stefansson wanted to be the first to find the lost continent that many believed to   10
be hidden beneath the polar ice cap. If Antarctica could be a land mass covered by ice,
why not the Arctic, too? Stefansson convinced Ottawa that if there *were* land under
all that ice and snow, it would simplify the sovereignty issue if Canadians found it.
Before long he had $80,000, and the Canadian Arctic Expedition was born.

Stefansson hurriedly purchased equipment and supplies and hired scientists   11
and crew. And he made two decisions—one bad, one good—that would ultimately
determine whether some of his men lived or died. For the expedition's lead ship,
Stefansson chose not an icebreaker but an old wooden whaler called the *Karluk*;
and as its captain he selected a 37-year-old seafarer from the outport of Brigus,
Newfoundland, Robert Bartlett.

In the world of exploration at the time, Bartlett was no unknown. In fact, he   12
was considered the best in the business at navigating the treacherous Arctic waters,
a skill that had earned him the nickname the "Ice Master." But Bartlett's greatest
accomplishment had also been his biggest disappointment. Four years earlier, in
1909, he'd captained the ship and blazed the dogsled trail for Admiral Peary's successful assault on the North Pole, only to be denied a place on the historic final leg
of that journey.

It had been a bitter blow for Bartlett, and Stefansson's invitation to take the   13
helm of the *Karluk* seemed a golden opportunity to get back in the game. At least it
did until Bartlett first stepped onto his new ship and realized just how inadequate
it was. Decades old, the *Karluk* had the bare minimum of survival equipment and
not even enough winter clothing for everyone on board.

And then there was the crew. Rushing to depart before winter set in, Stefansson   14
had hired almost no one with prior polar experience. Though most crewmen were
Canadian, many of the scientists were from abroad, such as Scottish schoolteacher
turned meteorologist William McKinlay. The closest McKinlay had ever been to
the Arctic was visiting a polar bear at the Edinburgh Zoo. "I was flabbergasted,"
McKinlay wrote in his diary. "Me! William Laird McKinlay invited to be an explorer
in the frozen wastes of the Arctic Circle! Me! Only 5 feet 4, being asked to join the
ranks of boyhood heroes like Peary, Amundsen, Captain Scott!"

But William McKinlay was far from the least likely—or even the shortest— **15**
member of the expedition. That distinction belonged to a cheerful little girl with
a joyous grin, named Mugpi. After steaming through the Bering Strait, the *Karluk*
stopped at Barrow, at the very top of Alaska, to take on Inuit hunters who would
supply the expedition with food. One hunter brought his family along—Mugpi's
father, Kuraluk.

Mugpi remembers her father as a strong, quiet man, who couldn't bear the **16**
thought of spending years away from his wife and children. "He loved us, and we
loved him, and it was only natural we went, too," she says. "Hunters are like that.
They don't leave their families. They take them along."

Kuraluk's wife, Kiruk (whom everyone knew as "Auntie"), began sewing skins **17**
into boots and winter clothing for the crew; his daughters, five-year-old Helen and
little Mugpi, soon became the ship's mascots. But as they set out into the Arctic
Ocean on August 6, 1913, neither they nor anyone else on the *Karluk* imagined that
before the next year was up, almost half their party would be dead.

Though it was the better part of a century ago, there is, amazingly, film footage **18**
of the beginning of the voyage, as the *Karluk*'s wooden prow nudged its way north
and east through the menacing icefield—jagged bergs on all sides as far as the lens
could see. But there is no footage of what happened barely a week after Mugpi and
her family came aboard. With the expedition still hundreds of miles from its initial
destination—Herschel Island in the Canadian Arctic—the pack ice slammed shut
around the *Karluk*.

Eighty-eight years later, in a world eased by technology, it's difficult to fathom **19**
the peril in which that creaky wooden ship and those aboard it found themselves.
Paul Schurke, an internationally renowned modern-day explorer who has travelled
to the North Pole five times by dogsled, simply shakes his head when trying to
describe the pressure of the ice pack. "The polar ice is an entity unto itself, almost
a dynamic living thing. Those blocks of ice out there are the size of islands, moving along with millions of tons of force, and nothing in their path is going to stop
their progress."

"Nothing" included the *Karluk*, which, according to Schurke, stood the same **20**
chance of surviving the ice as "a pile of matchsticks." Robert Bartlett was more
than stunned, then, when a month after they were trapped Vilhjalmur Stefansson
announced he'd be leaving the ship to go hunting. He said he'd be gone about 10
days, though he took dogs and supplies for much longer than that. Bartlett clearly
suspected Stefansson had simply abandoned the expedition to find another ship to
continue his explorations. But two days later, it was a moot point. A raging blizzard
arrived, cracking the ice pack, separating a huge chunk surrounding the *Karluk* and
blowing it farther away from the Alaskan coast. The ship was still helpless, stuck in
the middle of an enormous ice island, drifting out into the Arctic Ocean.

September passed, then October, with the *Karluk* drifting up to 60 miles a day **21**
out into the frozen ocean. By now hundreds of miles from land, the expedition's
situation grew even worse as the sun disappeared and the long polar night engulfed
the ship. For the next two months—November and December—they would drift
in total darkness.

Bartlett tried to keep everyone busy and well fed, while resisting mounting **22**
entreaties from the expedition's physician, Alister Mackay, an experienced cold-

weather explorer who demanded that the party evacuate the ship immediately and try to reach Alaska on foot. But then, one January evening, it happened. With a loud grating sound and a powerful shudder, the ice ripped through the hull of the *Karluk*. After five months frozen in the drift, the ship was finally sinking. Shortly before the *Karluk* disappeared forever, Bartlett stepped, last, off its deck, Chopin's "Funeral March" still playing on the ship's gramophone.

"Had we been on a desert island things might have been brighter," Bartlett   23
wrote. "But to be out there on the ever-shifting ice pack, far from land, and faced with the coldest months of the winter night, I could not look ahead without some uneasiness." It was a dramatic understatement, composed by a man who fully understood the cosmic shift in his world. Vilhjalmur Stefansson was gone; the expedition's lofty aims were irrelevant. Their only mission now was to survive.

For two weeks after the *Karluk*'s sinking, Bartlett and his party—23 adults and   24
two little girls—huddled in rough snow huts they named Shipwreck Camp, while outside the temperature plummeted to minus 50 degrees Fahrenheit. But in late January, a glimmer of hope arrived. As the sun began to return after the long winter night, the group could just make out in the distance the peaks of what they believed to be the only habitable land within reach. It was a place called Wrangel Island, about a hundred miles away. But Bartlett knew that for an inexperienced crew like his, seeing that island and getting to it were two very different things.

His misgivings weren't unfounded. According to Paul Schurke, one of the   25
greatest dangers of shifting pack ice occurs when channels of open water, known as "leads," appear. To the accompaniment of an unholy screeching, they open as suddenly as trap doors and are so cold that anyone falling into them will freeze in less than a minute. It was something Mugpi's family experienced first-hand the night a lead opened up right under their snow house, sending their sleeping four-year-old daughter sliding toward the water below.

"I don't remember that," Mugpi admits, "but my mother told me the story. She   26
said she grabbed me just before I went into the ocean. The water was right there. She says if I went in, I never would have come out."

According to Mugpi, after that close call her father became even more quiet   27
than usual. She knew that the man known as such a great Arctic hunter wasn't worried about himself, but about his wife and little girls. It was in those anxious moments that Kuraluk the hunter would turn to his youngest child and ask, "Are we going to live?"

And Mugpi would smile at him and say, "We're living now, aren't we? We're   28
still living."

And then her father would smile, too.   29

With the ice about to break up around them, Robert Bartlett made a crucial   30
decision. He sent six of his most dependable men ahead with a dog team to locate the best route to Wrangel Island. But before long, the scouting party encountered an enormous lead that they couldn't cross or find a way around. Two of the scouts took the dogs back to camp to report to the captain; the other four continued on foot—dragging almost a ton of supplies—trying to circumnavigate the lead and reach the island.

They were never seen alive again.   31

For Bartlett, one crisis followed another. Once again, the expedition's doctor, **32**
Alister Mackay, challenged the captain's judgment, charging that the decision to
send a scouting party had cost four lives and announcing that he was heading to
land right away and that anyone else could come with him. Three crew members
volunteered. Declining Bartlett's offer of a dog team, they set off pulling their sled
and supplies on foot. A week later, another crew member on a scouting mission
encountered the doctor and his party, frostbitten and disoriented, wandering aim-
lessly a scant 40 miles from where they'd started. Still, they refused to return to
Shipwreck Camp. It was the last time they were ever seen alive as well.

To this point, everyone who'd left Shipwreck Camp trying to reach land was **33**
dead.[1] Of the 25 original members of the party, only 17 remained. But now, with
the ice threatening to deteriorate around them, they had no choice. They had to
head for Wrangel Island, too.

Bartlett had tried to train his crew about the unpredictable ice, but nothing **34**
could have prepared them for what they saw two days into their trip. Looming
ahead was a mountain of ice up to 10 storeys high, stretching beyond their sight-
lines in either direction, miles from one end to the other. And beyond the first
mountain there appeared to be dozens more, a mountain range of ice separating
them from land.

Turning back or going around would have been a deadly waste of time. So **35**
Bartlett chose the route that seemed most impossible—ordering his crew to begin
gouging their way with ice picks up, over and across each towering ice ridge.

For six days and nights they hacked away at the ice, then hauled their sleds from **36**
peak to peak. Bartlett later wrote, "Building a road across them was like making
the overland trail through the Rockies. Time and again we smashed our sledges
and bruised our bodies. The temperature was always between 45 degrees and 55
degrees below zero."

"Remember," says Paul Schurke. "this whole thing is moving and changing as **37**
you're traversing it. At any given time a plate of ice the size of a car or building can
slide out from under you or onto you. This chapter of the story goes down in my
book as the most amazing epic in all Arctic travels on the polar sea."

No one was as eager to reach Wrangel Island as Kuraluk. As experienced in **38**
Arctic survival as he was, the thought of his wife and daughters struggling to stay
alive terrified him. So day after day, Kuraluk was the first to climb each ice ridge
and start carving a path across it.

Today, nine decades later, Mugpi says she didn't understand the urgency driv- **39**
ing her father at the time. But she remembers smiling when she saw him jumping
up and down one day, shouting, "*Nuna! Nuna!*" because Mugpi understood that
nuna meant "land."

It was March 12, 1914. After seven months marooned on the Arctic Ocean, the **40**
surviving members of the Canadian Arctic Expedition were back on terra firma:
Wrangel Island. But they were far from safe.

---

[1]Stefansson, who left the ship before it sank, actually survived and went on to glory in further Arctic
Circle explorations.

"We were on land, but we were a long way from civilization," Bartlett recalled.   41
"We need not drown but we might starve or freeze to death. There was no chance
that any ship would come so far out from the mainland, so that the only way to
expect help to reach the party was to go after it."

In the "Ice Master's" repertoire of improbably calm statements, this may have   42
been the zenith. Bartlett was about to attempt the unfathomable. By dogsled, he
and Kataktovik, the youngest of the Inuit hunters, would try to cross another 100
miles of dangerous, deteriorating ice to the Siberian mainland. Once there, they
would have to travel 600 miles *more* to find a ship to get back to Alaska—where
Bartlett could finally start organizing a rescue.

It wasn't just an ambitious plan; it was virtually hopeless. But Bartlett, being   43
Bartlett, put the best face on it, predicting that if all went well he might get back
with a rescue ship by June.

But by May on Wrangel Island, two months after Bartlett left, rescue seemed   44
like a cruel dream. With the provisions the party had brought with them all but
gone, the crew were so desperate they'd eat almost anything—blood soup, seal
hairs, rotting blubber. Perversely, though, they were almost all too sick to keep
anything down, the result, it would turn out, of kidney damage caused by too much
protein in their emergency supply of pemmican, a foul-tasting mixture of dried fat
and meat. The last-ditch food supply that was meant to keep them alive was in fact
poisoning them. Soon, two more crew members died, the ninth and tenth victims
of the Canadian Arctic Expedition—but not the last.

By June—the month Bartlett had hoped he'd be back—the camp on Wrangel   45
Island was consumed by hunger, suspicion and tension. One morning the party
awoke to the sound of a gunshot and the sight of one more lifeless crew member.
His tentmates called it suicide, but no one could be sure. "It's nothing but murder,"
one crew member later wrote.

Mugpi says that from that morning on, her father refused to leave any of his   46
family alone. To keep them safe from the arguments and guns at the camp, he took
them hunting with him. And when it seemed there was no wildlife left to hunt,
Kuraluk would turn to his four-year-old girl. She was the one person who had
seemed oblivious to the tension that enveloped the crew, who smiled at everyone,
perhaps because everyone smiled at her. All these years later, Mugpi still has no
doubt what her father said.

"He would ask again, 'Are we going to live?' And I would tell him, 'Yes, we're   47
going to live. We're living now, aren't we?'"

Her father would keep hunting. And what little game Kuraluk could kill or   48
catch somehow kept those starving on Wrangel Island barely alive.

July arrived, then August. Bartlett was now overdue by two months. Winter   49
was just weeks away. "When will she come? *Will* she come?" William McKinlay
wrote. "That is our only thought in our waking moments."

"She" was a ship.   50

Meanwhile, though his crew had almost certainly given up hope of ever seeing   51
Robert Bartlett again, Bartlett hadn't given up on them.

Time and again, for a hundred harrowing miles from Wrangel Island to Siberia,   52
Bartlett and Kataktovik's sled broke through the ice, sending them and their dogs
into the freezing water. Polar bears lurked nearby. Blinding blizzards threw them

off course. Each night there was a desperate search for a piece of ice big enough to hold a tent.

But against all odds, on the 17th day after they departed to save 15 lives, Bartlett **53** and his companion made out human figures on the horizon: Siberian Inuit, as amazed to see Bartlett emerge from the ice as Bartlett was himself. He stepped onto land, stuck out his hand and said, "How do you do?"

The niceties couldn't last long. After a good night's sleep, the two would-be res- **54** cuers left their hosts, their journey still far from over. For another month, they kept driving on at an inhuman pace—up to 20 hours every day on foot or dogsled—in the coldest temperatures the captain had ever known, up to 70 below zero.

Finally, they reached a Siberian outpost called Emma Harbour, 240 miles **55** across the Bering Strait from Alaska, where Bartlett found a ship to make the crossing. When he arrived in North America at the end of May, it was headline news. The world had believed the *Karluk* was lost with all aboard. Now newspapers carried the incredible details of the captain's courageous journey to save his crew.

But Bartlett had no time to bask in the accolades. With winter coming on, the **56** ice was once again closing in on Wrangel Island. Desperately, he drafted a veritable fleet of vessels to try to penetrate the pack and reach his crew. Over the next two months, several of the vessels he chartered tried to breach the ice without success. Finally, on August 27, the ship carrying Robert Bartlett himself lost its fight with the ice and had to turn back, too. It was a devastating blow—after all he'd survived to get there, a final, terrible irony.

But in the misery of Wrangel Island, where the expedition was now facing the **57** reality of another Arctic winter, Bartlett's dashed hope was irrelevant. For them, hope had been extinguished long ago. Which is why no one was prepared for what happened on September 7. By now the survivors had divided themselves into two separate camps, with the Inuit and the diarist William McKinlay on one side of the island, and the rest of the crew members on the other. Mugpi was out with some of the adults on her side of the island that day, helping to skin a walrus carcass, when she looked up and saw something on the horizon. She tried to get the grown-ups' attention, but they were too hungry and busy to notice. Finally her father looked up, too. In his tent William McKinlay heard Kuraluk's yell. He strained to understand what it was: "Maybe a ship!"

There, about three miles offshore, was an unbelievable sight—a ship indeed, the **58** *King and Winge*, the last of the vessels Bartlett had drafted for his rescue mission.

"We started shouting," McKinlay recorded, "so loud we must have scared every **59** seal in the Arctic. Then we saw her lower her sail, and as we watched, hardly able to believe our eyes, a party of men disembarked and began to walk toward the beach. We were saved."

Mugpi says she will never forget the feeling. "Just the excitement. The joy. The **60** boat came in, and they were hollering, and we were hollering. It was so exciting."

There is actual film footage of the rescue, too. On that film the grainy grey **61** and white figures shake hands. They hug. They dance. More than a year after the *Karluk* had been trapped by the ice pack, eight months after it sank, leaving them stranded in an Arctic wilderness that would claim 11 of their lives, the ordeal of the Canadian Arctic Expedition was finally over. A day later—September 8, 1914, almost six months after they'd last seen Captain Bartlett—the 13 surviving crew members were reunited with the man who had risked his own life to save theirs.

That night, on board the rescue ship, William McKinlay, the schoolteacher 62 turned explorer, wrote his first letter home in over a year. "None of you know what life is, nor will you ever know until you are as near losing it as we were," he told his family back in Scotland. "Just think of it, all of you. I am alive."

While the survivors of the *Karluk* steamed toward home, safe for the first time 63 in over a year, Ernest Shackleton and the crew of his ship, the *Endurance*, were on their way south, bound for Antarctica—and legend. Over the years, as the Shackleton legend was destined to grow, the saga of the Canadian Arctic Expedition would fade gradually but inexorably, first into history, then obscurity, until, a century later, few of his compatriots would recognize the name of the man responsible for perhaps the most miraculous rescue ever to touch their national soul: Captain Robert Bartlett of Newfoundland.

But in Barrow, Alaska, there is an old woman who remembers. That cheerful 64 little girl who made everyone else smile, too, and who inspired her father the hunter to keep finding food that helped the rest of them survive, is now 92 years old, still living where it all began.

And when a visitor asks Mugpi how she's doing today, she breaks into the same 65 joyous grin and says, "I'm living now, aren't I? I'm still living."

● ● ● ● ● **READING COMPREHENSION QUESTIONS**

1. The word *indomitable* in "under the command of their own indomitable—if to date largely unheralded—polar explorer" (paragraph 6) means
   a. unknown.
   b. unfortunate.
   c. incredible.
   d. unconquerable.

2. The word *niceties* in "The niceties couldn't last long" (paragraph 54) means
   a. comforts.
   b. civilities.
   c. social contacts.
   d. surprises.

3. Which of the following would be a good alternative title for the selection?
   a. Only the Strong Survive
   b. Robert Bartlett's Story
   c. An Expedition Bound for Obscurity
   d. The Nearly Lost Voyage

4. Which sentence best expresses the selection's main point?
   a. The Canadian Arctic Expedition deserves to be remembered for its leader's steadfastness and its survivors' endurance.
   b. The Canadian Arctic Expedition should be remembered for Vilhjalmur Stefansson's remarkable contributions.
   c. The Canadian Arctic Expedition is mainly notable because of the desperate, even savage behaviour of its crew marooned on Wrangel Island.

    d. Robert Bartlett's Canadian Arctic Expedition made no particular
      contributions to scientific or geographic knowledge.

5. The Canadian Arctic Expedition's original goal was to
    a. locate and claim the North Pole for Canada.
    b. find a lost continent thought to lie under polar ice.
    c. find a water route through polar ice fields.
    d. discover unknown land masses and chart unmapped territory.

6. *True or false?* Robert Bartlett had successfully reached the North Pole prior to the 1913 expedition.

7. In September 1913, Vilhjalmur Stefansson
    a. left the *Karluk* to go hunting for ten days.
    b. left the expedition completely.
    c. was lost in an Arctic blizzard.
    d. left to continue exploring alone.

8. *True or false?* For the ship's crew, the most dangerous aspect of crossing the ice pack was the sudden appearance of "leads" in the ice surface.

9. We can infer from this selection that the author feels
    a. Bartlett's five-month effort to return to his crew was truly heroic.
    b. Bartlett was foolhardy to attempt to find his crew.
    c. Bartlett had, in fact, given up on returning to his crew.
    d. Bartlett enjoyed the media attention he received.

10. We might conclude from this selection that
    a. Ernest Shackleton's Antarctic expedition did not deserve its historical fame.
    b. the media of the time were too fickle to pay attention to Bartlett's feat.
    c. sometimes fame or recognition does not come to those who deserve it.
    d. simply surviving, as Mugpi and twelve others did, is not seen as heroic.

• • • • DISCUSSION QUESTIONS

About Content

1. Who was Vilhjalmur Stefansson, and what argument did he use to persuade the Canadian government to fund the expedition?

2. What was the good decision made by Stefansson? What was his bad decision? What were the outcomes of each of these decisions?

3. Who was Mugpi, and why was she a part of the expedition?

4. How did Bartlett and his crew get to Wrangel Island from Shipwreck Camp?

5. What was ironic about the crew's diet on Wrangel Island?

About Structure

6. How do the first three paragraphs and the final two paragraphs unify the selection? Which other paragraphs in the selection continue the "thread" begun in the first three paragraphs?

7. McKeown mainly uses the chronological method to organize his narrative. How many paragraphs begin with transitional words or phrases to indicate the order of events? List five such transitional words or phrases and the paragraph numbers to which they belong. How many "change of direction" transitions open paragraphs in this selection?

8. In which paragraphs do you find the comparison-contrast method of development used? Who or what is being compared or contrasted, and why?

About Style and Tone

9. What is the effect of the simple style of the opening paragraph, considered in relation to the style of the rest of the selection?

10. McKeown quotes from the diary of William McKinlay and also quotes the spoken words of two other people in "The Greatest Story Never Told." Who are the two individuals who "speak" in this selection? What do each person's words add to your understanding of the piece, and why?

11. In which paragraphs do you find especially effective descriptions of various locations and situations? Choose two such paragraphs, and explain why the descriptions are so effective.

WRITING ASSIGNMENTS

Assignment 1

Mugpi is a survivor. The repetition of her words, "We're living now, aren't we? We're still living," reveal a kind of grounded optimism that may well have helped her through many ordeals in life aside from the year she spent marooned with the Canadian Arctic Expedition. Write a third-person viewpoint essay that defines someone you know as a survivor. Which personal qualities made this person a survivor? What has he or she survived?

Assignment 2

Explorers were celebrities before World War I. Astronauts were famous during the 1960s and 1970s. What explorers do we have today? What unknown places remain to be discovered, with manned space exploration in abeyance for the time being?

Write an essay in which you argue why one "explorer" in some field (scientific, spiritual, or other) is worthy of being recognized for his or her courage and/or discoveries. Defend the person you choose with specific facts about his or her achievement, and explain why these deserve more attention. Do some research on the Internet, if necessary, to discover any information you may require. Refer to Chapter 18 for help with using search engines or databases.

Assignment 3

In this assignment, you have the opportunity to learn more about the story that was "never told." Go to "The Story of the Canadian Arctic Expedition" pages of *Civilization.ca* at http://www.civilization.ca/hist/cae/int02e.html. Read the section or sections that interest you most.

Write a third-person examples essay about some aspect of the expedition that was not covered in McKeown's article. In your essay, explain, with examples, what you discovered that added to your knowledge of the expedition and why this interested you. If you use quotations or paraphrases, be sure to do so correctly. Read pages 298–310 of Chapter 19 for help with integrating and citing quotations and paraphrases.

PATTERNS OF EATING

Peter Farb and George Armelagos

Have you ever been told to "mind your manners"? Do you know what table manners consisted of in the Middle Ages? When and why do people's dining habits change? What do "good manners" mean? Peter Farb and George Armelagos are anthropologists who, in this selection, train their scientific gazes on what can be learned from the seemingly mundane matters of eating and manners. Their findings are interesting and often surprising.

Among the important societal rules that represent one component of cuisine are   1
table manners. As a socially instilled form of conduct, they reveal the attitudes typical of a society. Changes in table manners through time, as they have been documented for western Europe, likewise reflect fundamental changes in human relationships. Medieval courtiers saw their table manners as distinguishing them from crude peasants; but by modern standards, the manners were not exactly refined. Feudal lords used their unwashed hands to scoop food from a common bowl and they passed around a single goblet from which all drank. A finger or two would be extended while eating, so as to be kept free of grease and thus available for the next course, or for dipping into spices and condiments—possibly accounting for today's "polite" custom of extending the finger while holding a spoon or small fork. Soups and sauces were commonly drunk by lifting the bowl to the mouth; several diners frequently ate from the same bread trencher. Even lords and nobles would toss gnawed bones back into the common dish, wolf down their food, spit onto the table (preferred conduct called for spitting under it), and blew their noses into the tablecloth.

By about the beginning of the sixteenth century, table manners began to move   2
in the direction of today's standards. The importance attached to them is indicated by the phenomenal success of a treatise, *On Civility in Children*, by the philosopher Erasmus, which appeared in 1530; reprinted more than thirty times in the next six years, it also appeared in numerous translations. Erasmus' idea of good table manners was far from modern, but it did represent an advance. He believed, for example, that an upper class diner was distinguished by putting only three fingers of one hand into the bowl, instead of the entire hand in the manner of the lower class. Wait a few moments after being seated before you dip into it, he advises. Do not poke around in your dish, but take the first piece you touch. Do not put chewed food from the mouth back on your plate; instead, throw it under the table or behind your chair.

By the time of Erasmus, the changing table manners reveal a fundamental   3
shift in society. People no longer ate from the same dish or drank from the same
goblet, but were divided from one another by a new wall of constraint. Once the
spontaneous, direct, and informal manners of the Middle Ages had been repressed,
people began to feel shame. Defecation and urination were now regarded as private
activities; handkerchiefs came into use for blowing the nose; nightclothes were now
worn, and bedrooms were set apart as private areas. Before the sixteenth century,
even nobles ate in their vast kitchens; only then did a special room designated for
eating come into use away from the bloody sides of meat, the animals about to be
slaughtered, and the bustling servants. These new inhibitions became the essence of
"civilized" behavior, distinguishing adults from children, the upper classes from the
lower, and Europeans from the "savages" then being discovered around the world.
Restraint in eating habits became more marked in the centuries that followed. By
about 1800, napkins were in common use, and before long they were placed on the
thighs rather than wrapped around the neck; coffee and tea were no longer slurped
out of the saucer; bread was genteelly broken into small pieces with the fingers
rather than cut into large chunks with a knife.

Numerous paintings that depict meals—with subjects such as the Last Supper,   4
the wedding at Cana, or Herod's feast—show what dining tables looked like before
the seventeenth century. Forks were not depicted until about 1600 (when Jacopo
Bassano painted one in a Last Supper), and very few spoons were shown. At least
one knife is always depicted—an especially large one when it is the only one available for all the guests—but small individual knives were often at each place. Tin
disks or oval pieces of wood had already replaced the bread trenchers. This change
in eating utensils typified the new table manners in Europe. (In many other parts
of the world, no utensils at all were used. In the Near East, for example, it was
traditional to bring food to the mouth with the fingers of the right hand, the left
being unacceptable because it was reserved for wiping the buttocks.) Utensils were
employed in part because of a change in the attitude toward meat. During the
Middle Ages, whole sides of meat, or even an entire dead animal, had been brought
to the table and then carved in view of the diners. Beginning in the seventeenth
century, at first in France but later elsewhere, the practice began to go out of fashion. One reason was that the family was ceasing to be a production unit that did its
own slaughtering; as that function was transferred to specialists outside the home,
the family became essentially a consumption unit. In addition, the size of the family was decreasing, and consequently whole animals, or even large parts of them,
were uneconomical. The cuisines of Europe reflected these social and economic
changes. The animal origin of meat dishes was concealed by the arts of preparation.
Meat itself became distasteful to look upon, and carving was moved out of sight to
the kitchen. Comparable changes had already taken place in Chinese cuisine, with
meat being cut up beforehand, unobserved by the diners. England was an exception
to the change in Europe, and in its former colonies—the United States, Canada,
Australia, and South Africa—the custom has persisted of bringing a joint of meat
to the table to be carved.

Once carving was no longer considered a necessary skill among the well-bred,   5
changes inevitably took place in the use of the knife, unquestionably the earliest
utensil used for manipulating food. (In fact, the earliest English cookbooks were

not so much guides to recipes as guides to carving meat.) The attitude of diners toward the knife, going back to the Middle Ages and the Renaissance, had always been ambivalent. The knife served as a utensil, but it offered a potential threat because it was also a weapon. Thus taboos were increasingly placed upon its use: It was to be held by the point with the blunt handle presented; it was not to be placed anywhere near the face; and most important, the uses to which it was put were sharply restricted. It was not to be used for cutting soft foods such as boiled eggs or fish, or round ones such as potatoes, or to be lifted from the table for courses that did not need it. In short, good table manners in Europe gradually removed the threatening aspect of the knife from social occasions. A similar change had taken place much earlier in China when the warrior was supplanted by the scholar as a cultural model. The knife was banished completely from the table in favor of chopsticks, which is why the Chinese came to regard Europeans as barbarians at their table who "eat with swords."

The fork in particular enabled Europeans to separate themselves from the 6 eating process, even avoiding manual contact with their food. When the fork first appeared in Europe, toward the end of the Middle Ages, it was used solely as an instrument for lifting chunks from the common bowl. Beginning in the sixteenth century, the fork was increasingly used by members of the upper classes—first in Italy, then in France, and finally in Germany and England. By then, social relations in western Europe had so changed that a utensil was needed to spare diners from the "uncivilized" and distasteful necessity of picking up food and putting it into the mouth with the fingers. The addition of the fork to the table was once said to be for reasons of hygiene, but this cannot be true. By the sixteenth century people were no longer eating from a common bowl but from their own plates, and since they also washed their hands before meals, their fingers were now every bit as hygienic as a fork would have been. Nor can the reason for the adoption of the fork be connected with the wish not to soil the long ruff that was worn on the sleeve at the time, since the fork was also adopted in various countries where ruffs were not then in fashion.

Along with the appearance of the fork, all table utensils began to change and 7 proliferate from the sixteenth century onward. Soup was no longer eaten directly from the dish, but each diner used an individual spoon for that purpose. When a diner wanted a second helping from the serving dish, a ladle or a fresh spoon was used. More and more special utensils were developed for each kind of food: Soup spoons, oyster forks, salad forks, two-tined fondue forks, blunt butter knives, special utensils for various desserts and kinds of fruit, each one differently shaped, of a different size, with differently numbered prongs and with blunt or serrated edges. The present European pattern eventually emerged, in which each person is provided with a table setting of as many as a dozen utensils at a full-course meal. With that, the separation of the human body from the taking of food became virtually complete. Good table manners dictated that even the cobs of maize were to be held by prongs inserted in each end, and the bones of lamb chops covered by ruffled paper pantalettes. Only under special conditions—as when Western people consciously imitate an earlier stage in culture at a picnic, fish fry, cookout, or campfire—do they still tear food apart with their fingers and their teeth, in a nostalgic reenactment of eating behaviors long vanished.

Today's neighborhood barbecue recreates a world of sharing and hospitality   8
that becomes rarer each year. We regard as a curiosity the behavior of hunters in
exotic regions. But every year millions of North Americans take to the woods and
lakes to kill a wide variety of animals—with a difference, of course: What hunters
do for survival we do for sport (and also for proof of masculinity, for male bond-
ing, and for various psychological rewards). Like hunters, too, we stuff ourselves
almost whenever food is available. Nibbling on a roasted ear of maize gives us, in
addition to nutrients, the satisfaction of participating in culturally simpler ways.
A festive meal, however, is still thought of in Victorian terms, with the dominant
male officiating over the roast, the dominant female apportioning vegetables, the
extended family gathered around the table, with everything in its proper place—a
revered picture, as indeed it was so painted by Norman Rockwell, yet one that
becomes less accurate with each year that passes.

● ● ● ● ● **READING COMPREHENSION QUESTIONS**

1. The word *genteelly* in "bread was genteelly broken into small pieces with the
   fingers. . ." (paragraph 3) means
   a. graciously.
   b. roughly.
   c. hastily.
   d. manually.

2. The word *proliferate* in "all table utensils began to change and proliferate
   from the sixteenth century onward" (paragraph 7) means
   a. emerge.
   b. disappear.
   c. multiply.
   d. specialize.

3. Which of the following would be a good alternative title for this selection?
   a. Disgusting Dining Habits Through the Ages
   b. A Tale of Table Manners
   c. Cutlery Past and Present
   d. Manners Mirror Society

4. What sentence best expresses the main idea of the selection?
   a. The story of table manners is the story of the development of cutlery.
   b. Manners and eating patterns reflect societies' attitudes through the ages.
   c. European cooking is an indicator of social change through the centuries.
   d. Table manners form an important element in human history.

5. Which specific details support the authors' point that medieval nobility's
   manners were coarse by today's standards?

6. Changing attitudes toward meat meant that
   a. meat recipes disguised the animal nature of the product.
   b. meat was seen as a disgusting type of food.
   c. families went out of the butchery business.
   d. roast beef was no longer carved at the table.

7. *True or false?* People began using forks to avoid germs.

8. The authors imply that
   a. attention to cleanliness distinguished one class from another.
   b. the relaxed, lively nature of medieval life was preferable to renaissance inhibitions.
   c. crowded, dirty kitchens did not allow the upper classes to develop good table manners.
   d. the idea of gentility emerged from a growing self-awareness and restraint.

9. The authors imply that
   a. the emergence of so many forms of cutlery eventually led to confusion.
   b. there is no need for a specific item of cutlery for each separate type of food served.
   c. the evolution of cutlery and individual place settings isolate people further from communal experience.
   d. an artificial barrier has developed between people and the natural world.

10. The authors imply that
    a. class distinctions and manners are basically nonsense because they are so changeable.
    b. our current manners, though reflecting other times, are still evolving.
    c. people are basically still savages, as their manners on special occasions indicate.
    d. people long for the crude, basic medieval lifestyle and manners.

DISCUSSION QUESTIONS

About Content

1. What did Erasmus note as actions at the dinner table that would set the upper classes apart from the less well-bred?

2. What changes occurred to table manners around 1800?

3. What restrictions were placed on the use of a knife as a utensil? Why?

About Structure

4. Where do you find the clearest statement of the authors' thesis?

5. What overall organizing method do the authors use in this selection, chronological or emphatic? List any transitional words or phrases from the openings of paragraphs that support your answer.

6. In which paragraph do you find cause and effect method of development used in its second half?

About Style and Tone

7. The authors, although academics and scientists, sometimes use a lively, plain style. Which word choices and phrases in paragraph 1 demonstrate this style? Is the style suited to the content here?

8. Where in the selection do you find a more sophisticated style of writing? Which word choices and phrases support your view?

9. This selection is distinguished by its richness of detailing. Supporting points within paragraphs are carefully developed with specific details, lists of facts, explanations, and examples. Choose one such point whose supporting specifics you find especially effective and explain why you make this choice.

• • • • WRITING ASSIGNMENTS

Assignment 1

Self-help and how-to articles and books are popular, and new self-help websites appear every day. People of all ages can be self-conscious about their table manners, and could be interested in some how-to information.

For this assignment, you will write a process piece for a lifestyle website or blog. The audience is your peers. Your topic is "How to Eat Like a _____."

Assignment 2

Write an essay with the title "Patterns of Eaters," that divides people's eating styles into three different groups. You may choose the classifying principles for your groups of eaters; for example, eating styles based on speed, or messiness, or energy, or any other quality. Your thesis, as in the selection, should indicate what your classification of eaters shows about people.

Assignment 3

How many people still sit down at a dinner table each evening, or eat any meal with others with any regularity? Write an essay that speculates on how three aspects of dining (i.e., manners, utensils, meal habits, food) could change in the next twenty years, based on changes in society.

As "Patterns of Eating" does, support your points with clear and appropriate examples. Pay particular attention, as the authors do, to the number, quality, and vividness of your details.

DIOGENES AND ALEXANDER

Gilbert Highet

Although Alexander the Great may be familiar to some readers from the recent Oliver Stone movie, Gilbert Highet's essay will probably be most people's introduction to the eccentric Greek philosopher Diogenes. These characters may be centuries old, but Highet brings them to vibrant life in this selection; they are as strange and compellingly alive as figures in any street-corner crowd, and their ideas perhaps more important today than ever.

Lying on the bare earth, shoeless, bearded, half-naked, he looked like a beggar or   1
a lunatic. He was one, but not the other. He had opened his eyes with the sun at dawn, scratched, done his business like a dog at the roadside, washed at the public

fountain, begged a piece of breakfast bread and a few olives, eaten them squatting on the ground, and washed them down with a few handfuls of water scooped from the spring. (Long ago he had owned a rough wooden cup, but he threw it away when he saw a boy drinking out of his hollowed hands.) Having no work to go to and no family to provide for, he was free. As the market place filled up with shoppers and merchants and gossipers and sharpers and slaves and foreigners, he had strolled through it for an hour or two. Everybody knew him, or knew of him. They would throw sharp questions at him and get sharper answers. Sometimes they threw jeers, and got jibes; sometimes bits of food, and got scant thanks, sometimes a mischievous pebble, and got a shower of stones and abuse. They were not quite sure whether he was mad or not. He knew they were mad, all mad, each in a different way; they amused him. Now he was back at his home.

It was not a house, not even a squatter's hut. He thought everybody lived far too 2 elaborately, expensively, anxiously. What good is a house? No one needs privacy; natural acts are not shameful; we all do the same things, and need not hide them. No one needs beds and chairs and such furniture; the animals live healthy lives and sleep on the ground. All we require, since nature did not dress us properly, is one garment to keep us warm, and some shelter from rain and wind. So he had one blanket—to dress him in the daytime and cover him at night—and he slept in a cask. His name was Diogenes. He was the founder of the creed called Cynicism (the word means "doggishness"); he spent much of his life in the rich, lazy, corrupt Greek city of Corinth, mocking and satirizing its people, and occasionally converting one of them.

His home was not a barrel made of wood: too expensive. It was a storage jar 3 made of earthenware, something like a modern fuel tank—no doubt discarded because a break had made it useless. He was not the first to inhabit such a thing: the refugees driven into Athens by the Spartan invasion had been forced to sleep in casks. But he was the first who ever did so by choice, out of principle.

Diogenes was not a degenerate or a maniac. He was a philosopher who wrote 4 plays and poems and essays expounding his doctrine; he talked to those who cared to listen; he had pupils who admired him. But he taught chiefly by example. All should live naturally, he said, for what is natural is normal and cannot possibly be evil or shameful. Live without conventions, which are artificial and false; escape complexities and superfluities and extravagances; only so can you live a free life. The rich man believes he possesses his big house with its many rooms and its elaborate furniture, his pictures and expensive clothes, his horses and his servants and his bank accounts. He does not. He depends on them, he worries about them, he spends most of his life's energy looking after them, the thought of losing them makes him sick with anxiety. They possess him. He is their slave. In order to procure a quantity of false, perishable goods he has sold the only true lasting good, his own independence.

There have been many men who grew tired of human society with its com- 5 plications, and went away to live simply—on a small farm, in a quiet village, in a hermit's cave, or in the darkness of anonymity. Not so Diogenes. He was not a recluse, or a stylite, or a beatnik. He was a missionary. His life's aim was clear to him; it was "to restamp the currency." (He and his father had once been convicted for counterfeiting, long before he turned to philosophy, and this phrase was

Diogenes' bold, unembarrassed joke on the subject.) To restamp the currency; to take the clean metal of human life, to erase the old false conventional markings, and to imprint it with its true values.

The other great philosophers of the fourth century before Christ taught mainly their own private pupils. In the shady groves and cool sanctuaries of the Academy, Plato discoursed to a chosen few on the unreality of this contingent existence. Aristotle, among the books and instruments and specimens and archives and research-workers of his Lyceum, pursued investigations and gave lectures that were rightly named *esoteric* "for those within the walls." But for Diogenes, laboratory and specimens and lecture halls and pupils were all to be found in a crowd of ordinary people. Therefore he chose to live in Athens or in the rich city of Corinth, where travelers from all over the Mediterranean world constantly came and went. And, by design, he publicly behaved in such ways as to show people what real life was. He would constantly take up their spiritual coin, ring it on a stone, and laugh at its false superscription. 6

He thought most people were only half-alive, most men only half-men. At bright noonday he walked through the market place carrying a lighted lamp and inspecting the face of everyone he met. They asked him why. Diogenes answered, "I am trying to find a *man*." 7

To a gentleman whose servant was putting on his shoes for him, Diogenes said, "You won`t be really happy until he wipes your nose for you: that will come after you lose the use of your hands." 8

Once there was a war scare so serious that it stirred even the lazy, profit-happy Corinthians. They began to drill, clean their weapons, and rebuild their neglected fortifications. Diogenes took his old cask and began to roll it up and down, back and forward. "When you are all so busy," he said, "I felt I ought to do *something*." 9

And so he lived—like a dog, some said, because he cared nothing for privacy and other human conventions, and because he showed his teeth and barked at those whom he disliked. Now he was lying in the sunlight, as contented as a dog on the warm ground, happier (he himself used to boast) than the Shah of Persia. Although he knew he was going to have an important visitor, he would not move. 10

The little square began to fill with people. Page boys elegantly dressed, spearmen speaking a rough foreign dialect, discreet secretaries, hard-browed officers, suave diplomats, they all gradually formed a circle centered on Diogenes. He looked them over, as a sober man looks at a crowd of tottering drunks, and shook his head. He knew who they were. They were the attendants of the conqueror of Greece, the servants of Alexander, the Macedonian king, who was visiting his newly subdued realm. 11

Only twenty, Alexander was far older and wiser than his years. Like all Macedonians he loved drinking, but he could usually handle it; and toward women he was nobly restrained and chivalrous. Like all Macedonians he loved fighting; he was a magnificent commander, but he was not merely a military automaton. He could think. At thirteen he had become a pupil of the greatest mind in Greece, Aristotle. No exact record of the schooling survives. It is clear, though, that Aristotle 12 took the passionate, half-barbarous boy and gave him the best of Greek culture. He taught Alexander poetry; the young prince slept with the *Iliad* under his pillow and longed to emulate Achilles , who brought the mighty power to Asia to ruin. He taught him philosophy, in particular the shapes and uses of political power: a few years later Alexander was to create a supranational empire that was not merely a power system but a vehicle for the exchange of Greek and Middle Eastern cultures.

Aristotle taught him the principles of scientific research: during his invasion   **13** of the Persian domains Alexander took with him a large corps of scientists, and shipped hundreds of zoological specimens back to Greece for study. Indeed, it was from Aristotle that Alexander learned to seek out everything strange which might be instructive—Jugglers and stunt artists and virtuosos of the absurd he dismissed with a shrug; but on reaching India he was to spend hours discussing the problems of life and death with naked Hindu mystics, and later to see one demonstrate Yoga self-command by burning himself impassively to death.

Now, Alexander was in Corinth to take command of the League of Greek States   **14** which, after conquering them, his father Philip had created as a disguise for the New Macedonian Order. He was welcomed and honored and flattered. He was the man of the hour, of the century: he was unanimously appointed commander-in-chief of a new expedition against old, rich, corrupt Asia. Nearly everyone crowded to Corinth in order to congratulate him, to seek employment with him, even simply to see him: soldiers and statesmen, artists and merchants, poets and philosophers. He received their compliments graciously. Only Diogenes, although he lived in Corinth, did not visit the new monarch. With that generosity which Aristotle had taught him was a quality of the truly magnanimous man, Alexander determined to call upon Diogenes. Sure Dio-genes, the God-born, would acknowledge the conqueror's power by some gift of hoarded wisdom.

With his handsome face, his fiery glance, his strong supple body, his purple and   **15** gold cloak, and his air of destiny, he moved through the parting crowd, toward the Dog's kennel. When a king approaches, all rise in respect. Diogenes did not rise, he merely sat up on one elbow. When a monarch enters a precinct, all greet him with a bow or an acclamation. Diogenes said nothing.

There was silence. Some years later Alexander speared his best friend to the   **16** wall, for objecting to the exaggerated honors paid to His Majesty; but now he was still young and civil. He spoke first, with a kindly greeting. Looking at the poor broken cask, the single ragged garment, and the rough figure lying on the ground, he said, "Is there anything I can do for you, Diogenes?"

"Yes," said the Dog. "Stand to one side. You're blocking the sunlight."   **17**

There was silence, not the ominous silence preceding a burst of fury, but a hush   **18** of amazement. Slowly, Alexander turned away. A titter broke out from the elegant Greeks, who were already beginning to make jokes about the Cur that looked at the King. The Macedonian officers, after deciding that Diogenes was not worth the trouble of kicking, were starting to guffaw and nudge one another. Alexander was still silent. To those nearest him he said quietly, "If I were not Alexander, I should be Diogenes." They took it as a paradox, designed to close the awkward little scene with a polite curtain line. But Alexander meant it. He understood Cynicism as the others could not. Later he took one of Diogenes' pupils with him to India as a philosophical interpreter (it was he who spoke to the naked *saddhus*). He was what Diogenes called himself, a *cosmopolites*, "citizen of the world." Like Diogenes, he admired the heroic figure of Hercules, the mighty conqueror who labors to help mankind while others toil and sweat only for themselves. He knew that of all men then alive in the world only Alexander the conqueror and Diogenes the beggar were truly free.

• • • • READING COMPREHENSION QUESTIONS

1. The word *jibes* in "Sometimes they threw jeers, and got jibes" (paragraph 1) means
   a. coins.
   b. jokes.
   c. dirt.
   d. insults.

2. The word *contingent* in "Plato discoursed to a chosen few on the unreality of this contingent existence" (paragraph 6) means
   a. everyday.
   b. conditional.
   c. unhappy.
   d. superstitious.

3. Which of the following would be a good alternative title for this selection?
   a. The Ruler and His Dog
   b. The Wisdom of Alexander
   c. Two Kings
   d. Ancient Philosophy

4. Which sentence best expresses the main idea of the selection?
   a. Being free means learning one's values and living by them.
   b. Diogenes' self-denial made him a celebrity in ancient Greek society.
   c. Teaching by example is the most effective form of instruction.
   d. Philosophy teaches the most powerful lessons.

5. Diogenes scoops water from the spring with his hands because
   a. he felt sorry for the young boy drinking from his hands.
   b. he realized he could drink without a cup.
   c. he could no longer afford to buy a cup.
   d. he did not want to carry a cup around with him.

6. *True or false?* Diogenes preferred a solitary, contemplative life.

7. The most significant lesson Alexander learned from Aristotle was
   a. the story of Achilles in the *Iliad*.
   b. how to conduct scientific research.

  c. to learn from, and not dismiss anything out of the ordinary.
  d. the philosophy of political power.

8. The author implies that
   a. marketplace crowds were uncertain of Diogenes' sanity because he was different from them.
   b. the crowds rejected Diogenes because he was an unkempt homeless person.
   c. people were fascinated and repulsed by Diogenes because he was so rude.
   d. Diogenes' idleness annoyed people.

9. The author implies that
   a. Diogenes was a humourless crank.
   b. Diogenes thought of insults as instructive.
   c. Diogenes despaired of people's ability to learn.
   d. Diogenes saw the absurdity in human behaviour.

10. Readers can infer from Alexander's statement, "If I were not Alexander, I should be Diogenes" that
    a. Alexander envied Diogenes his carefree life.
    b. Alexander recognized Diogenes' self-knowledge and power.
    c. Alexander was too polite to insult Diogenes.
    d. Alexander pitied Diogenes' situation.

● ● ● ● DISCUSSION QUESTIONS

About Content

1. What details in paragraph 1 show readers why an observer would see Diogenes as "a beggar or a lunatic"? What might your own reaction to him have been?

2. Why, according to Diogenes, did no one need a house?

3. Of what crime had Diogenes been found guilty? What were his feelings about being thus convicted?

4. How did Diogenes' teaching methods differ from those of Plato and Aristotle?

5. Based on the selection, what does Alexander's question to Diogenes say about the young king?

About Structure

6. Which of the two methods of development for comparison and contrast does Highet use for comparing and contrasting Diogenes and Alexander? Is this method effective for this selection? Why?

7. Identify two paragraphs in which you find other sets of contrasts. Who or what is being contrasted in each paragraph and which method of development is used in each?

8. In which paragraph is there the first shift to another character? What change of direction word indicates this shift?

About Style and Tone

9. In which paragraphs do you find vividly detailed descriptions? Which do you find most effective and why?

10. What analogy is used in paragraph 10? Where else is this analogy first introduced? What is the pun related to Diogenes based on this analogy and in which paragraph is it explained? Where else do references to the analogy appear in the selection?

11. In which paragraph does Highet return readers to the square and why? How does he echo his almost cinematic introduction of Diogenes in paragraph 1 in this paragraph?

• • • • WRITING ASSIGNMENTS

Assignment 1

Live without conventions, complexities, and extravagances, was Diogenes' creed. How many of us would have enough courage to do so? Without which conventions, behaviours, and possessions would people live better lives? Why?

Write an essay that argues that people would be better off without three items or conventional behaviours. Support your points with specific examples that justify your choices.

Assignment 2

Imagine you, like Diogenes, carry a kind of lantern in search of a truly vital person. What qualities would you search for?

In an essay intended for publication in your college or university's newspaper, define the elements that make up a truly "alive" individual. What attitudes, actions, and beliefs constitute living a fulfilled, or fully realized life? Describe vividly and explain three aspects of your definition.

Assignment 3

Compare or contrast two people whom you find to be remarkable or inspirational. Are these people similar in some ways or very different? Using the "point by point" method of development, and using the third-person point of view, write an essay that vividly portrays exactly why you admire or find inspiration in these people.

For this essay, unless you write about people whom you know well, doing some research may provide you with the specific details that will show readers your subjects in a lively and interesting way, as Highet does in his essay. Be sure to quote, paraphrase, and cite your sources correctly; refer to Chapter 19 for help.

BLACK AND BLUE

Cecil Foster

**(M)ulticulturalism in Canada is an idealist celebration of hope," writes Cecil Foster, the author of "Black and Blue," in an excerpt from his book *A Place Called Heaven: The Meaning of Being Black in Canada.* In this selection, Foster depicts a situation where idealism disappeared, and with it, hope for many Canadian citizens. Do the prejudices and slanderous ideas portrayed here still narrow Canadian vision today?

1   At its heart, the colour of Canadian justice is blue. At least that is the case in Etobicoke Courtroom 208, Metropolitan Toronto on December 7, 1994. This is the day the state begins bringing to justice one Clinton Junior Gayle for the murder of a Toronto policeman, Todd Baylis, and the attempted murder of his partner, P.C. Michael Leone. This is the trial that would be the catharsis for an entire nation, especially for those who feel this country is too soft when it comes to questions of law and order, when it comes to dealing firmly with perennial whiners and misfits, such as members of the black community.

2   In this case, colour means everything. Gayle is a black man accused of killing a white policeman. After the shooting, the media and talk shows did not try to disguise the racism in their commentary. Neither did anyone appear to pretend that Gayle would, at the very least, be considered innocent until proven guilty in the court. From the moment the story of the killing broke, media reports and talk-show hosts dispensed with the routine use of the word "alleged" when describing a murderer named Gayle. Such a formality might have been misconstrued as a weakness, a sop to the black community, an encouragement to others harbouring such bad intentions. In this case, the general population doesn't worry too much about a miscarriage of justice or about ensuring that Gayle gets a fair trial. Rather, it's about retribution. In this case, in the eyes of many, Clinton Junior Gayle represents all black men in this country, and dealing with him appropriately is the right way to send a stern message to all those whiners, to all those who do not respect Canadian institutions, to all those living outside the Canadian mainstream who should be brought to heel.

3   Gayle's case had ramifications for many, including a nondescript immigration adjudicator, Ivan Rashid, who ordered Gayle released from jail while waiting for deportation. Rashid, his identity made public before an almost incensed Canadian citizenry, had to atone publicly for a "bad" decision.

4   Gayle was held up as this brutal and brutish thug who gunned down an officer of the law, robbing the community of a fine young man, and Baylis' girl-friend of a future husband and father of her children. All of which was true. But the condemnation went further than just a battle of good and evil: race and skin colour made a difference. Soon broad swipes were being taken at any breathing black person.

**From http://www.penguin.ca/nf/shared/SharedDisplay/0,,214132,00.html

That Gayle is black and from the Caribbean, specifically Jamaica, gave added   5
colour to the incident and eventually made it an international issue. But the harsh-
est effects were felt on the streets of Toronto, especially in neighbourhoods with
a strong black presence. In one fell swoop, Blacks were painted as gangsters, irresponsible louts who had little respect for life. Furthermore, here was an example
of what happens when Canada throws open its doors to the dredges of the world,
people with no respect for institutions, for law and order, the result of an immigration policy too lax and ill-suited for this country.

There were some factors that gave legitimacy for these virulent attacks on   6
Gayle—but not on all other Blacks. Gayle had been in trouble many times with the
law, running up 13 convictions, including possession of firearms, and had been
ordered deported to Jamaica. At the time he fired the bullets that killed Baylis and
wounded Leone, Gayle was under a 10-year ban prohibiting him from possessing
firearms. Along the way, his deportation papers got lost. Some critics jumped on
this as an example of how the immigration process and the justice system had
broken down, how the two federal departments were conspiring to let loose on
society heinous criminals, most of them black, and notably, Jamaican or West
Indian. The Metro Toronto Police Association, supposedly also representing the
black members of the force, took the argument one step further. It followed up its
virulent anti-Black rhetoric with action: a lawsuit for $100 million, in the names
of the slain, against the federal government. Somebody has to pay for the killing of
one of its members, and the police association was not willing to settle only for the
price that society would demand of Gayle in a criminal trial.

For months preceding the shooting of Todd Baylis, there was much talk about   7
justice and Blacks in Canada. Several months earlier, the mainstream media had
a special story to tell. It was about young black man in Nova Scotia who set up a
white prostitution ring across the country. As the story was told, innocent young
girls from Halifax were finding themselves in Montreal, Toronto, Vancouver and
any big city or town in between, in the inescapable clutches of black pimps. This
was not just another prostitute and pimp story. Nobody in the media worked to
find out if any of these supposedly innocent white women were runaways, attracted
to the big city, and finding themselves having to get by the same way many others
have always had to survive in the streets of Los Angeles, New York or Toronto.
Also noticeable was that nobody seemed too concerned about whether any of these
innocent young women on the hustle were black. But the colour of the pimps was
of the utmost importance. Here is how the issue was reported in *The Globe and
Mail* on April 24th, 1993:

> When Joan is out on the baseball mound, the ball spinning toward her, she
> likes to imagine she's about to swing her bat at the head of a black pimp. She
> knows she shouldn't harbour such anger towards other people, but she just
> can't help it, Joan is mad as hell at the men she blames for destroying her
> daughter's life.
>
> Hillary, her eldest child, is one of hundreds of hookers who got their start
> in the Halifax area in recent years. Today many of these girls, most of them over
> 13 but some as young as 10, populate big-city "strolls," the streets and byways

walked by prostitutes across Canada and as far afield as New York, California and Europe.

Most of these young prostitutes, virtually all of them white, work for a loosely organized community of Nova Scotia Black men.

The writing could hardly be more graphic or coloured. With so much talk of this **8** white slave ring, life became a lot tougher for young black men in the Preston area of Halifax. The police came frequently knocking, often with the national media in tow. Some of the youths saw the inside of jails. Others just had to put up with police harassment. Some men from the Preston area were arrested across the country, charged and convicted. Of course, the convictions were duly recorded as if to ease the fears of the wider community that the black menace was finally under control.

The concern about Blacks and justice took on an even greater dimension across **9** the country in the summer of 1994. In Toronto, three black men entered an eating establishment named Just Desserts in a trendy part of the city. While robbing the restaurant and its patrons, a patron was killed by a shotgun blast. The city, and indeed parts of the country, reacted viscerally. The murdered woman, Georgina "Vivi" Leimonis, became a representative of all the ills black men can inflict on white women. Just as with the hype over the so-called white prostitution ring, the colour of the perpetrators seemed to be the most important aspect of this robbery and murder. The police also acted as though colour were the only thing that mattered; they issued out-of-focus photographs to the media with instructions that citizens call the police if they saw any of the men. The pictures were splashed on the television screens and on the front pages of newspapers, along with instructions for people to clip them out and keep the pictures handy in their car for easy reference. But the pictures were so murky, the only thing clear about the suspects was the colour of their skin. Immediately, every black man became a suspect. As was the case in Halifax, the mainstream dismissed this concern. Much emphasis was placed on the loss of innocence in the city. Who would not shed a tear for a young woman cut down in her prime, a woman who wore her intended wedding gown as a burial shroud?

Similar claims about the city being robbed of its innocence had been made only **10** two years earlier when a crowd of primarily black youth "rioted" on Yonge Street. This so-called riot coincided with the destruction and pillage in Los Angeles that came to be known as the Rodney King riots, the spark occurring when an all-white jury acquitted some Los Angeles police officers for brutally beating a black man. The fact that Rodney King's beating was captured on video was dismissed by the jury. Blacks across North America rose up against this affront, and the hard feelings boiled over in Toronto, too, where there had been many recent flashpoints over police shootings of Blacks. This would not be the first or last time that parallels would be drawn between the treatment of Blacks in Canada and the United States. As the Yonge Street disturbances proved—as did smaller but similar incidents in Halifax and other Canadian centres—few people in the black community see any differences in the way the police and justice systems treat Blacks on either side of the border.

Eventually, the ranting quietened down. Many people, in sombre reflection, **11** examined why society felt so threatened over this one killing at Just Desserts. It was pointed out that the only difference in this case was that three black men were accused of killing a white woman. After all, murders and heists at restaurants are quite routine in major Canadian cities. Most people argued that it was the "randomness" of the shooting that frightened them. "You mean to say that you can't even go into a restaurant to eat a piece of cake without getting shot?" some asked. But two points were undefeatable in this argument. For a long time, these types of killings had been happening in the black community. Many young men and women had been slaughtered at illegal house parties and after-hours clubs. Some of the killings hardly merited mention in the newspapers and certainly not an outpouring of sympathy. The national media paid no attention when anyone was brought to trial, or when the murdered persons were buried. It seemed that as long as Blacks were killing Blacks, the city was still safe. Also, there was no doubt the security of feeling that as long as Blacks killed Blacks in black areas, then the wider community didn't have to worry. If a white person walked through a predominantly black area of Toronto like Jane and Finch, Lawrence Heights or the Peanut in North York, then they deserved what they got.

People reacted to the Just Desserts killing as though it were anything but random. They made it appear as though the entire city had become lawless—black youths with ski masks were running rampant throughout the city, and anyone, especially Whites, could be slaughtered. What they were, in fact, arguing is that because the killing had spilled over into a middle-class and largely white area, the mainstream was sitting up and taking notice. And they wanted this supposedly random violence stamped out,   12

Gayle's shooting of Constable Todd Baylis in the garage of an apartment building in a mixed neighbourhood was another example of this violence, spilling over into other areas, affecting the wrong people. It would become the lightning rod for feelings in the mainstream.   13

The morning the news came that someone had shot a cop I was in the newsroom of the CBC writing news scripts for *World Report,* the first major newscast heard right across the country every morning. As I read the news flashes on the wires, I knew this shooting was serious, and I hoped that I would not have to write that a *black* man had killed a policeman. (Many black people have admitted feeling the same way when they hear the first reports of a shooting, murder or robbery. How they hope a black person is not involved and how they release a collective sigh of relief when they find out the criminal is white. Talk about collective guilt; or is it collective responsibility? Either one, many Blacks respond this way to news because they know that if the criminal is black, innocent Blacks can expect to be scrutinized on the subway and on buses, in convenience stores, and at work and at play.)   14

At the time we began to write the scripts, we knew only that two cops and the alleged gunman were in hospital. One of the policemen was in critical condition. A short while later, CBC police reporter Raj Ahluwalia arrived in the newsroom to prepare a report. He confirmed that the worst had happened, although the news was not official. "Looks like the cop is dead. They are holding off making the announcement until they have informed his family." The first edition of the newscast to the Maritimes told of the shooting and critical wounding of a cop in Toronto. Shortly thereafter, I would read the confirmation of the death on my computer screen, and would amend the newscast. Listeners in Manitoba, Alberta and British Columbia   15 and in U.S. border states were to hear on their first major newscast about the murder of a cop on the beat. Eventually, the news of the shooting would be broadcast around the world on the various CBC national and international programs.

In the following week, listeners, many in the Caribbean, would hear similar **16** reports on the discussion about the violence and lawlessness, of the failure of the judicial and immigration systems. And they would hear the explanation that all of these things were responsible for the death of one of Metro's finest at the hands of one of Canada's most undesirable. Most of the media unquestioningly bought into the statements of the Metro police, and their reports resorted to caricature, depicting Gayle as lawless, a drug dealer, fatherless, a street hustler and someone who should have been kicked out of the country long ago. *The Toronto Sun* took to running billboards across the city under the caption, "We'll be there." Underneath the statement was a picture of three men with the word DEPORTED stamped across their faces. Many in the black community felt that these billboards had a direct connection with the death of Toronto policeman Baylis. And it was hard not to make this connection after a series of articles and columns linked the crime with deportation.

"Almost every day now, we could present another case of someone who should **17** have been deported, and wasn't; or was deported, but came back; or was ordered deported, but was then released to disappear into the streets," wrote *Sun* columnist Christie Blatchford.

"This is how dreadfully routine such cases have become, this in the 20 days **18** since Clinton Junior Gayle, a Jamaican immigrant whose deportation order was never executed, was arrested in the slaying of Metro Toronto Police Const. Todd Baylis and the wounding of his partner, Const. Mike Leone."

"Today's poster boy fits all three categories, with the added little fillips that a) **19** he apparently enjoys posing with a gun in his hand and b) that on one of the last occasions his presence was officially noted, he was driving Clinton Gayle's car."

And to bring home her point she later added: "If it is safe to say that the Gayle **20** case has opened eyes and lips both . . . and provided Canadians with a window into the shambles that is their federal immigration department, it is also a sure thing that this is just the tip of the proverbial iceberg."[1]

Who says hysteria doesn't sell?   **21**

The general outcry in reaction to this death would come from across the coun- **22** try and would be heard across the nation. Police officers poured into Toronto from all corners of the world, including Jamaica, to form the largest contingent of foreign police officers to attend a funeral in Canada. (That some of the policemen came from Jamaica was important to the media because Gayle is Jamaican. But more important, Gayle's biological father is a superintendent in the Jamaica Police Force and on hearing of the shooting is reported to have roundly condemned his son. Apparently, that was the first time Gayle's father had heard of his whereabouts in years.) And the funeral was huge. Local television stations carried it live. The streets of north Metro Toronto were closed off for hours as police officers paraded and paid their last respects. Photojournalists snapped pictures as members of 12

[1] *The Toronto Sun*, July 6, 1994.

Division of the Metro Toronto Police Force, colleagues of the slain officer, served as pallbearers. The coffin was draped in the Canadian flag. And once again, every Black in the city felt those eyes on us. We were all Clinton Gayles, cop killers and murderers.

Now, in this courtroom, society was seeking to start the long process of hand- **23** ing out justice for someone cut down in the line of duty, by someone who ought not to have been in the country. But does the fact that the man who shot Baylis grew up in Canada, learned to become a criminal in Canada and knew nobody in the country of his birth matter to this discussion? It certainly did enter the debate in the Caribbean, where the argument was intense and became an international issue. But Gayle was Jamaican and was being rejected physically and psychologically from the country in which he had lived almost continuously for 20 years.

This case of *Regina v. Clinton Junior Gayle* was to be a test of the will of this **24** country. Can a black person ever fully become a Canadian citizen? At what point do you stop being a Jamaican, Barbadian, Trinidadian, Ghanaian or Nigerian and become a full-fledged citizen of this country, to be accepted, faults and all, as a product of this society? This preliminary hearing was the start of the process of sending a clear, unmistakable message. Someone was going to sing the blues for this killing. Real Canadians were going to take back their country. And they were going to impose some common sense on how real Canadians run this country's judiciary, police and immigration systems.

● ● ● ● ● **READING COMPREHENSION QUESTIONS**

1. The word *sop* in "Such a formality might have been misconstrued as a weakness, a sop to the black community . . ." (paragraph 2) means
   a. insult.
   b. compliment.
   c. apology.
   d. concession.

2. The word *fillips* in "with the added little fillips that (a) he apparently enjoys posing with a gun in his hand, and (b) that on one of the last occasions his presence was officially noted, he was driving Clinton Gayle's car." (paragraph 19) means
   a. treats.
   b. incitements.
   c. embarrassments.
   d. distractions.

3. Which of the following would be a good alternative title for this selection?
   a. Canadian Justice is Colour Blind.
   b. Racism in Canadian Courts.
   c. Tarring With the Same Brush
   d. The Harder They Come, The Harder They Fall

4. Which sentence best expresses the main idea of the selection?
   a. The Canadian population does not care about justice.
   b. Mass hysteria can be as deadly as murder.

    c. Black Canadians lack the full benefits of citizenship.
    d. There is no fair media coverage in Canada.

5. When Foster writes that this trial "would be the catharsis for an entire nation," he means
    a. that the trial would air and cleanse repressed feelings.
    b. that the trial would bring out the worst in hardline racists.
    c. that the trial give fair voice to all sides.
    d. that the trial would be an example of Canadian justice.

6. At the time that Gayle shot Baylis,
    a. he was ready to leave for Jamaica.
    b. he was avoiding deportation.
    c. he was forbidden to own guns.
    d. the government was ignoring his convictions.

7. *True or false?* Gayle's father did not attend his funeral because of embarrassment.

8. The author implies that
    a. the immigration department was at fault in the Gayle case.
    b. there were direct parallels with the Rodney King case.
    c. people in many Canadian cities felt frightened at that time.
    d. the press and other media are selective in their coverage.

9. *True or false?* Foster implies that Gayle could be innocent.

10. The author implies that
    a. Canada does not assume responsibility for its citizens.
    b. it is impossible for any immigrant to become a full-fledged Canadian.
    c. Canadians are a nation of vigilantes.
    d. Clinton Gayle was just a scapegoat, a victim.

DISCUSSION QUESTIONS

About Content

1. What does Foster mean by his opening sentence, "At its heart, the colour of Canadian justice is blue"?

2. How does the author define the meaning of the word "retribution" for some Canadians, in Gayle's case?

3. What facts gave some credence to media's attacks on Gayle?

4. What does Foster mean by the phrases "collective guilt" and "collective responsibility" in paragraph 14?

About Structure

5. What method or combination of methods does Foster use to open his article?
    a. Ask questions
    b. Supply background information or context

    c. Use a brief story

    d. Explain importance of topic to reader

6. Where do you find the clearest statement of the author's thesis?

7. Foster uses various quoted passages from newspaper articles. Why has he done so? Choose two of these and explain their significance.

About Style and Tone

8. Foster repeatedly uses the word *colour* throughout this selection. Find two examples where *colour* is not used in its simple sense as a noun. Why do you think the author chose to emphasize the word?

9. Where in "Black and Blue" does Foster shift pronoun voice to first-person singular, and why? In which paragraphs does he shift to first-person plural viewpoint, and why?

10. References to opening paragraphs in concluding paragraphs offer a sense of unity or closure. Where is the sentence in the closing paragraph of this selection that refers to its opening paragraph? How does the meaning of the repeated word change in the conclusion?

• • • • WRITING ASSIGNMENTS

Assignment 1

Cecil Foster uses the phrase "real Canadians" in his final paragraph. Just who are "real Canadians," anyway? In the strictest sense probably only Native Canadians; but there are as many answers to this question as there are citizens.

In a definition essay, explain to readers of your parents' age group who "real Canadians" are, and why you define them as you do.

Assignment 2

The gangsta rap stance and visual cliché of the gun-toting black male has been prevalent since the early 1990s. Unquestionably it is a posture and image that lends itself to misuse by many groups. Write an essay of argumentation in which you defend one of the following rough thesis statements:

> Media stereotypes such as the gangsta or the . . . do not influence young people's behaviour.

> Media stereotypes have a way of seeping into the public's subconscious, and can do real harm.

Assignment 3

Racism, conscious or not, is too often part of Canadian society. Write an essay that will be the basis of an article in your college or university's handbook for next year. The topic of your article is "Eliminating Every Kind of Racism."

You many wish to write a process-style article, or use classification and division as your method of development (dividing racism into various forms).

THE DOCTOR IS TOTALLY IN

Norman Doidge

Dr. Norman Doidge started out in classics and philosophy at the University of Toronto, but it was his poetry that won him prizes. After graduating, he studied medicine and then trained in psychiatry and psychoanalysis. Evidently, he is a person of immense abilities and wide interests. In the following selection, he reminds readers of just how impressive contemporary science has shown another great psychoanalyst, Sigmund Freud, to be.

It's Freud's 150th birthday on May 6 and I'm in Vienna, standing in the now empty consulting room in Freud's home office at Berggasse 19, where the psychoanalytic couch was, and where all those now famous patients—the Wolf Man, the Rat Man, and Dora—unburdened themselves. Here Freud learned, by listening to Dora, about our tendency to unconsciously transfer scenes and wishes from the past onto the present. In his bedroom down the hall, he dreamed his dreams and began to analyze them. A few steps away, in his library, he wrote *The Interpretation of Dreams*, the book that argued the scientists of his day were wrong: dreams were not merely the flotsam and jetsam of tired brains, but decodable visual images of unconscious wishes, feelings and conflicts that drive so much human behaviour.   1

This year is Sigmund Freud Year in Vienna, which is honouring Freud as its great intellectual. Austrian President Dr. Heinz Fischer is patron and will visit this place, now a museum, on May 6. But these rooms are mostly empty because Austria did little to save Freud, a Jew, when the Nazi Gestapo knocked on the door in 1938, arrested his daughter, Anna, and took her for interrogation. That was Freud's worst day. Ultimately, Freud, Anna and the immediate family were rescued by a French princess, Marie Bonaparte, Napoleon's descendant, who asked to be arrested along with Anna; Bonaparte whisked them, Freud's library and furniture, off to London, but neither Bonaparte, nor Freud's stature, could save his two sisters from being murdered in concentration camps. (Freud's brother, Alexander, escaped via Switzerland and died in Toronto in 1943.) Forced by the Gestapo to sign a statement saying he had not been ill-treated, the cancer-stricken 82-year-old ironist wrote, "I can most highly recommend the Gestapo to everyone."   2

Yet this year the mood is festive, and Freud's scientific stature is having a revival. When Freud died in 1939, poet W.H. Auden summed up his influence in his elegy: *To us he is no more a person now / but a whole climate of opinion / under whom we conduct our different lives.* Toward the end of the 20th century, Freud became the most cited intellectual in the Western world. But now that he was at the top of the intellectual heap, the Freud-bashing began. *Time* and other magazine covers declared "Freud is Dead." Some psychopharmacologists, behaviourists and feminists declared Freud passé, or wrong. Practitioners of briefer therapies, often lasting 10 sessions, asserted they could accomplish as much as analysts who saw patients four times a week for several years, while managed-care insurance companies, anxious to substitute cheaper drug treatments for therapy, asserted analysis didn't work—though not on the basis of any scientific studies, which in fact showed it did. They often got away with it because "talk therapy" did not seem as exciting   3 as the new neuroscience, and scientists weren't sure how to prove the brain had "unconscious" thoughts. Psychiatry became increasingly interested in the brain and behaviour, and inclined to leave out the mind and subjective experience.

So—how are things looking today, scientifically speaking?   4

Psychoanalysis is having a very good day today. In 2005, a new study from the   5
University of Gottingen, Germany, showed that 80 per cent of patients in analysis showed significant improvement: their symptoms decreased and they improved their interpersonal problems and general sense of well-being—and continued to improve a year after their analyses ended. These patients did better than those in shorter-term treatments. This supplements a series of recent German studies that show patients in psychoanalysis and related therapies end up using less medication, have fewer visits to doctors, days off work, or days in hospital than others. Another study, by Rolf Sandell of Linköping University, Sweden, showed that patients in psychoanalysis—compared to those who have less intensive therapy— continue to make more gains, even three years after therapy, and to hold on to the gains they have made. Those who have had analysis are also far less likely to require more treatment later in life.

But the most exciting story is the way neuroscience, with its new generation   6
of brain scans, is supporting Freud's assertion that the majority of our think-ing, and much of our motivation, goes on beyond our conscious awareness, or is unconscious.

Freud was originally neither a psychiatrist nor psychologist, but a neuroscien-   7
tist, who worked in a lab and made important discoveries about the brain's nerve cells, or neurons. Freud argued, in the 1890s, that neurons connect between small junctions, now called synapses, and that when we learn, two neurons fire at the same time and they connect more closely. When he began seeing patients, he wrote a manuscript called "The Project." His goal was to unite the science of the brain with a science of the mind and meaning. But he eventually concluded that brain science was not yet up to the task. So he turned to understanding the mental trig-gers for, and meaning of, emotional and psychiatric symptoms. Psychoanalysis was born. Still, he made sure it was consistent with what was known about the brain. He soon discovered we are often not conscious of the triggers of our symptoms or emotional reactions.

Now, brain-scanning techniques can show us our brain while it does mental   8
processing, and study of the mind and brain can be bridged. A new discipline called neuropsychoanalysis is completing Freud's project, made up of many of the world's most impressive neuroscientists, such as Nobel Prizewinner Eric Kandel, Antonio Damasio, Jaak Panksepp, Oliver Sacks, Joseph LeDoux, V.S. Ramachandran, and like-minded psychoanalysts. They are drawn to Freud because they see him as hav-ing a far more adequate picture of mind and brain integration than those who see the brain as nothing more than a sophisticated chemistry set, into which you add medi-cations to make it work better. Medication has a role, but it is not everything.

Kandel is one of the driving forces behind these developments. Kandel says he   9
himself "benefited greatly" from being psychoanalyzed, and wanted to become a psychoanalyst. He reasoned that psychoanalysis and other therapies work by learn-ing, and he set out to understand learning and memory in the brain. He won his

Nobel Prize in 2000 for showing that when animals learn and remember, the actual structure between the nerves changes, and the synaptic connections strengthen—as Freud imagined, sitting in Berggasse 19. Kandel's was one of the most compelling proofs that the brain is "plastic," and that thinking changes the brain structure. Indeed, a number of recent studies show that psychotherapy actually rewires the brain, and its changes are no less structural than those seen with medication.

10   Brain scans now show that thought processing goes on beyond awareness, and desires, emotions and emotional conflicts can actually be unconscious. This means we can, for example, have guilt without being aware of it, or anger or attraction toward others that we dare not face. A 2004 study by Kandel and his colleagues at Columbia University, New York, published in *Neuron*, demonstrated that when people are shown photos of frightened faces too fast for them to register consciously, the almond-shaped amygdyla, a part of the brain that processes anxiety and emotions, lights up on functional magnetic resonance imaging—fMRI scans. The study also showed that the amygdyla uses one set of neurons when we "perceive" an emotional experience unconsciously, and another set when we perceive it consciously.

11   Scientists studying brainwaves—the electrical fields given off when thousands of our neuron cells fire—have learned to detect "recognition waves," forms of brain activity manifested when the brain recognizes something. Dr. Howard Shevrin at the University of Michigan has used these techniques to examine Freud's theories. After subjects received extensive psychological testing by clinicians to determine their core unconscious emotional conflicts—e.g. hidden guilt, anxiety, or love and hate for someone—words summarizing those conflicts were flashed at them in two ways. First they were flashed subliminally, too fast for the subjects to consciously register them. Next they were flashed "supraliminally," or just fast enough for them to register. When words connected to a patient's unconscious conflicts were flashed subliminally, their brains had a quick recognition wave. When they were flashed supraliminally, or consciously, the patients were very slow to recognize them. In other words, their brains recognized their conflicts unconsciously, but had inhibited conscious recognition of them. When words having nothing to do with their conflicts were flashed, the pattern was reversed—i.e. we don't repress unconflicted ideas.

12   Freud's theory that dreams are "the royal road" to understanding unconscious thought has also received support from brain imaging. Allen Braun, a researcher at the National Institutes of Health in Washington, has used positron emission tomography (PET) scans to measure brain activity in dreaming subjects. He has shown that the region known as the limbic system, which processes emotion, sexual, survival and aggressive instincts, and interpersonal attachments, shows high activity in dreaming. But the prefrontal cortex, an area responsible for achieving goals, discipline, postponing gratification and controlling our impulses, shows lower activity.

13   With the emotional-instinctual processing areas of the brain turned on, and the part that controls our impulses relatively inhibited, it is no wonder wishes and impulses we normally restrain, or are unaware of, are more likely to be expressed in dreams.

14   Another Freudian idea that is being vindicated by brain scans is how formative early childhood experience is. Before Freud, it was assumed that since most adults

couldn't recall very early childhood, all that occurred then—good or bad—was forgotten. Now, brain scans and other techniques show that when infants undergo great stress (such as extended separation) or depression, a part of the brain called the hippocampus, required for laying down verbal or "explicit" memories, shrinks and stops functioning normally. A study in the *American Journal of Psychiatry* in 2002 showed the hippocampus of depressed adults who suffered childhood trauma is 18 per cent smaller than that of depressed adults without childhood trauma. This contributes to sketchy memories of traumatic events. But that doesn't mean that events don't affect us. Another memory system, called the implicit memory system, which encodes our emotional patterns for relating, does register the trauma. So traumas can be encoded without us being able to remember them.

Freud divided the mind into the ego (the aspect of ourselves, part conscious, **15** part unconscious, that regulates the rest of us, and is the seat of rational thought and our sense of who we are), and the id (which includes our repressed unconscious wishes). The goal of the analytic cure was "Where id was, there shall ego be," i.e. to learn to consciously reclaim and regulate those unconscious parts of ourselves that seemed like alien, driven urges. Scans show that the prefrontal lobes are the part of the brain that performs ego functions of regulation. (During post-traumatic states, when people have flashbacks and emotional control is lost, blood flow to the prefrontal lobes decreases.) A 2001 brain scan study from UCLA of depressed patients treated with interpersonal psychotherapy—a treatment Kandel's Columbia colleague Myrna Weissman developed by taking some key features from psychoanalytic approaches—showed that prefrontal brain activity normalizes with treatment. Kandel is now on the board of the Ellison Medical Foundation, which is looking into developing routine ways of using MRI scans to evaluate psychotherapy outcomes, and his institution, Columbia University, just received the largest-ever grant to a single university faculty, $200 million, for a neuroscience research program called "Mind, Brain and Behavior," which Kandel will co-direct. This will help realize Freud's "project" of developing a picture of humanity in which mind and brain are not kept separate, but are seen as two sides of the same coin.

We all should be so dead.   **16**

• • • • READING COMPREHENSION QUESTIONS

1. The word *discipline* in "A new discipline called neuropsychoanalysis is completing Freud's project," (paragraph 8) means
   a. science.
   b. treatment.
   c. process.
   d. subject.

2. The word *vindicated* in "Another Freudian idea that is being vindicated by brain scans . . ." (paragraph 14) means
   a. contradicted.
   b. justified.
   c. demonstrated.
   d. explored.

3. Which of the following would be a good alternative title for this selection?
   a. The Brain Scientist's 150th Birthday
   b. Freud Knows Best
   c. Freud's Foresight: the Integrated Mind and Brain
   d. The Future of Psychiatry

4. Which sentence best expresses the main idea of the selection?
   a. Freud was the greatest mind of the twentieth century.
   b. Brain scans now demonstrate the correctness of Freud's main theories.
   c. Freud's "talk therapy," psychoanalysis, has proved the most effective treatment for psychiatric and emotional problems.
   d. Freudian analysis is much less effective than drug treatment or short-term therapies.

5. When Freud wrote "The Project," he wanted to
   a. integrate understanding of the brain with that of the mind.
   b. explain his theories about neuron activity.
   c. explore the meanings of emotional and psychiatric symptoms.
   d. publicize his theory of the unconscious.

6. The concept that the brain is "plastic" means that
   a. it is not made of ordinary human tissue.
   b. it is similar to "a sophisticated chemistry set."
   c. medication softens it, allowing it to change shape.
   d. thoughts change the brain's structure.

7. Brain scans now show
   a. that adults forget childhood experiences, so these do not affect them.
   b. babies and children often experience great stress.
   c. that childhood trauma shrinks a part of a depressed person's brain.
   d. the implicit memory system as part of the hippocampus.

8. The author implies that
   a. intellectuals and ideas are as subject to trends as anything else.
   b. Freud's theories were outdated and ineffectual in the 1990s.
   c. insurance companies were involved with pharmaceutical manufacturers.
   d. Psychoanalysis lacks an objective, scientific basis.

9. The author implies that
   a. contemporary neuroscientists are still uncertain about Freud's ideas.
   b. Freud's intuitive connections between brain, mind, and emotions were remarkably correct.
   c. despite research, the unconscious mind remains fundamentally unknowable.
   d. Freud anticipated the electrical theory behind the study of brain waves.

10. After reading the selection, readers can assume that
    a. Freud was unfortunate to have lived when he did.
    b. Freud would not be so fashionable without the emergence of brain scans.
    c. Freud's current elevated status is likely to fall again, as all trends and fads do.
    d. Freud's revived renown, based on scientific revelations, is likely to endure.

● ● ● ● **DISCUSSION QUESTIONS**

About Content

1. What details support the author's point about "Freud-bashing"? Who levelled charges against Freud and what were they?

2. Why, according to Doidge, is psychoanalysis "having a very good day today"?

3. What was Freud's profession? How does it relate to the content of the second part of the selection? (paragraphs 8 through 15)

4. What have PET scans shown about brain activity during dreams? How do findings relate to Freud's theory of dreams?

About Structure

5. What method, or combination of methods of introduction does Doidge use in this selection?
   a. Questions
   b. Anecdote
   c. Starting with an Opposite
   d. Background Information

   Why, related to the article's content, do you think the author chose the method(s)?

6. Beginning with paragraph 3, identify and list any transitional words or phrases used in the opening sentences of the remaining paragraphs. Which paragraph-openings do not contain transitional material? Why not, in your opinion?

7. Where in the selection do you find the clearest statement of the author's thesis? Identify the paragraphs that provide support for the thesis.

About Style and Tone

8. Explain specifically how the first three paragraphs of this article prepare readers for the thesis and body of the essay.

9. Do you find that all scientific and medical terms are explained clearly enough? List one or two that you find clearly defined; then, note any terms whose meaning you find unclear. Who do you think are the main audiences for this selection? How understandable will the scientific and medical terms used be to these readers?

10. What does the one-sentence concluding paragraph mean? How does it relate to the article's content?

● ● ● ● **WRITING ASSIGNMENTS**

Assignment 1

In life, an individual's or a group's opinions of people may change radically over time. First impressions or opinions may prove to be very wrong, or long-held views may give way to completely different feelings about a person.

Such is the case with Sigmund Freud. In a third-person viewpoint essay, explain with vivid and specific supporting examples, the situation of one such person about whom people changed their minds. Your thesis may present the initial viewpoint, as in "Uncle Spiro was one of the most disagreeable people on earth," or may state the revised opinion, as in "Professor Kaminsky turned out to be a very soft-hearted woman."

Assignment 2

Freud stressed "how formative early childhood experience is" (14). What are three aspects (good or bad) of childhood that adults may appear to have forgotten? What is the significance of each?

Write a third-person causes or effects essay that explains any three aspects of childhood you believe that adults seem to forget; i.e., a child's (lack of) sense of time, or the intensity of a child's emotions. Explain each aspect with lots of specific details, so as to make your points come alive for readers.

Assignment 3

After reading this article, you have a brief introduction to Sigmund Freud and his theories concerning dreams.

Write an essay that could be the basis of a presentation to an audience of post-secondary counsellors. Your paper will argue for or against the importance of dreams in people's everyday lives. Do some online research to add to your support for your thesis. When doing so, refer to Chapters 18 and 19 on the use of online resources, and be sure to quote, paraphrase, and cite your research correctly. Write your essay in the third person viewpoint.

Considering Concepts

HERE'S TO YOUR HEALTH

Joan Dunayer

Dunayer contrasts the glamorous "myth" about alcohol, as presented in advertising and popular culture, with the reality—which is often far less appealing. After reading her essay, you will be more aware of how we are encouraged to think of alcohol as being tied to happiness and success. You may also become a more critical observer of images presented by advertisers.

As the only freshman on his high school's varsity wrestling team, Tod was anxious to fit in with his older teammates. One night after a match, he was offered a tequila bottle on the ride home. Tod felt he had to accept, or he would seem like a sissy. He took a swallow, and every time the bottle was passed back to him, he took another swallow. After seven swallows, he passed out. His terrified teammates carried him into his home, and his mother then rushed him to the hospital. After his stomach was pumped, Tod learned that his blood alcohol level had been so high that he was lucky not to be in a coma or dead.

Although alcohol sometimes causes rapid poisoning, frequently leads to long-term addiction, and always threatens self-control, our society encourages drinking. Many parents, by their example, give children the impression that alcohol is an essential ingredient of social gatherings. Peer pressure turns bachelor parties, fraternity initiations, and spring-semester beach vacations into competitions in "getting trashed." In soap operas, glamorous characters pour Scotch whiskey from crystal decanters as readily as most people turn on the faucet for tap water. In films and rock videos, trend-setters party in nightclubs and bars. And who can recall a televised baseball or basketball game without a beer commercial? By the age of 21, the average American has seen drinking on TV about 75,000 times. Alcohol ads appear with pounding frequency—in magazines, on billboards, in college newspapers—contributing to a harmful myth about drinking.

Part of the myth is that liquor signals professional success. In a slick men's magazine, one full-page ad for Scotch whiskey shows two men seated in an elegant restaurant. Both are in their thirties, perfectly groomed, and wearing expensive-looking gray suits. The windows are draped with velvet, the table with spotless white linen. Each place-setting consists of a long-stemmed water goblet, silver utensils, and thick silver plates. On each plate is a half-empty cocktail glass. The two men are grinning and shaking hands, as if they've just concluded a business deal. The caption reads, "The taste of success."

Contrary to what the liquor company would have us believe, drinking is more closely related to lack of success than to achievement. Among students, the heaviest drinkers have the lowest grades. In the work force, alcoholics are frequently late or absent, tend to perform poorly, and often get fired. Although alcohol abuse occurs in all economic classes, it remains most severe among the poor.

Another part of the alcohol myth is that drinking makes you more attractive to the opposite sex. "Hot, hot, hot," one commercial's soundtrack begins, as the camera scans a crowd of college-age beachgoers. Next it follows the curve of a woman's leg up to her bare hip and lingers there. She is young, beautiful, wearing a bikini. A young guy, carrying an ice chest, positions himself near to where she sits. He is tan, muscular. She doesn't show much interest—until he opens the chest and takes out a beer. Now she smiles over at him. He raises his eyebrows and, invitingly, holds up another can. She joins him. This beer, the song concludes, "attracts like no other."

Beer doesn't make anyone sexier. Like all alcohol, it lowers the levels of male hormones in men and of female hormones in women—even when taken in small amounts. In substantial amounts, alcohol can cause infertility in women and impotence in men. Some alcoholic men even develop enlarged breasts, from their increased female hormones.

The alcohol myth also creates the illusion that beer and athletics are a perfect combination. One billboard features three high-action images: a baseball player running at top speed, a surfer riding a wave, and a basketball player leaping to make a dunk shot. A particular light beer, the billboard promises, "won't slow you down."

"Slow you down" is exactly what alcohol does. Drinking plays a role in over six million injuries each year—not counting automobile accidents. Even in small amounts, alcohol dulls the brain, reducing muscle coordination and slowing reaction time. It also interferes with the ability to focus the eyes and adjust to a sudden change in brightness—such as the flash of a car's headlights. Drinking and driving, responsible for over half of all automobile deaths, is the leading cause of death among teenagers. Continued alcohol abuse can physically alter the brain, permanently impairing learning and memory. Long-term drinking is related to malnutrition, weakening of the bones, and ulcers. It increases the risk of liver failure, heart disease, and stomach cancer.

Finally, according to the myth fostered by the media in our culture, alcohol generates a warm glow of happiness that unifies the family. In one popular film, the only food visible at a wedding reception is an untouched wedding cake, but beer, whiskey, and vodka flow freely. Most of the guests are drunk. After shouting into the microphone to get everyone's attention, the band leader asks the bride and groom to come forward. They are presented with two wine-filled silver drinking cups branching out from a single stem. "If you can drink your cups without spilling any wine," the band leader tells them, "you will have good luck for the rest of your lives." The couple drain their cups without taking a breath, and the crowd cheers.

A marriage, however, is unlikely to be "lucky" if alcohol plays a major role in it. **10** Nearly two-thirds of domestic violence involves drinking. Alcohol abuse by parents is strongly tied to child neglect and juvenile delinquency. Drinking during pregnancy can lead to miscarriage and is a major cause of such birth defects as deformed limbs and mental retardation. Those who depend on alcohol are far from happy: over a fourth of the patients in state and county mental institutions have alcohol problems; more than half of all violent crimes are alcohol-related; the rate of suicide among alcoholics is fifteen times higher than among the general population.

Alcohol, some would have us believe, is part of being successful, sexy, healthy, **11** and happy. But those who have suffered from it—directly or indirectly—know otherwise. For alcohol's victims, "Here's to your health" rings with a terrible irony when it is accompanied by the clink of liquor glasses.

● ● ● ● **READING COMPREHENSION QUESTIONS**

1. The word *caption* in "The caption reads, 'The taste of success'" (paragraph 3) means
   a. menu.
   b. man.
   c. words accompanying the picture.
   d. contract that seals the business deal.

2. The word *impairing* in "Continued alcohol abuse can physically alter the brain, permanently impairing learning and memory" (paragraph 8) means
   a. postponing.
   b. doubling.
   c. damaging.
   d. teaching.

3. Which one of the following would be a good alternative title for this selection?
   a. The Taste of Success
   b. Alcohol and Your Social Life
   c. Too Much Tequila
   d. Alcohol: Image and Reality

4. Which sentence best expresses the main idea of the selection?
   a. Sports and alcohol don't mix.
   b. The media and our culture promote false images about success and happiness.
   c. The media and our culture promote false beliefs about alcohol.
   d. Liquor companies should not be allowed to use misleading ads about alcohol.

5. According to the selection, drinking can
   a. actually unify a family.
   b. lower hormone levels.
   c. temporarily improve performance in sports.
   d. increase the likelihood of pregnancy.

6. *True or false?* Alcohol abuse is most severe among the middle class.

7. *True or false?* The leading cause of death among teenagers is drinking and driving.

8. From the first paragraph of the essay, we can conclude that
   a. even one encounter with alcohol can actually lead to death.
   b. tequila is the worst type of alcohol to drink.
   c. wrestlers tend to drink more than other athletes.
   d. by the time students reach high school, peer pressure doesn't influence them.

9. *True or false?* The author implies that one or two drinks a day are probably harmless.

10. The author implies that heavy drinking can lead to
    a. poor grades.
    b. getting fired.
    c. heart disease.
    d. all of the above.

DISCUSSION QUESTIONS

About Content

1. According to Dunayer, how many parts are there to the myth about alcohol? Which part do you consider the most dangerous?

2. Drawing on your own experience, provide examples of ways in which our culture encourages drinking.

About Structure

3. What method does Dunayer use to begin her essay?
   a. Movement from general to specific
   b. An opposite
   c. An incident

4. The body of Dunayer's essay is made up of four pairs of paragraphs (paragraphs 3 and 4, 5 and 6, 7 and 8, 9 and 10) that serve to introduce and develop each of her four main supporting points. What is the pattern by which she divides each point into two paragraphs?

5. Dunayer introduces the first part of the myth about alcohol with the words, "Part of the myth is . . ." (paragraph 3). She then goes on to use an addition transition to introduce each of the three other parts of the myth—in the first sentences of paragraphs 5, 7, and 9. What are those transitions?

6. What method does Dunayer use to conclude her essay?
   a. Prediction or recommendation
   b. Summary and final thought
   c. Thought-provoking question

About Style and Tone

7. Why is the title of the essay appropriate?

• • • • WRITING ASSIGNMENTS

Assignment 1

Describe and analyze several recent advertisements for wine, beer, or liquor on television or radio, in newspapers or magazines, or on billboards. Argue whether the ads are socially responsible or irresponsible in the way that they portray drinking. Your thesis might be something like one of the following examples:

> In three recent ads, ad agencies and liquor companies have acted irresponsibly in their portrayal of alcohol.

> In three recent ads, ad agencies and liquor companies have acted with a measure of responsibility in their portrayal of alcohol.

Alternatively, write about what you consider responsible or irresponsible advertising for some other product or service. Clothing, weight loss, and cosmetics are possibilities to consider.

Assignment 2

Imagine you have a friend, relative, or classmate who drinks a lot. Write a letter to that person, warning him or her about the dangers of alcohol. If appropriate, use information from Dunayer's essay. Since your purpose is to get someone you care about to control or break a dangerous habit, you should make your writing very personal. Don't bother explaining how alcoholism affects people in general. Instead, focus directly on what you see it doing to your reader.

Divide your argument into at least three supporting paragraphs. You might, for instance, talk about how your reader is jeopardizing his or her relationship with three of the following: family, friends, boss and co-workers, teachers and classmates.

Assignment 3

Dunayer describes how alcohol advertisements promote false beliefs such as the idea that alcohol will make you successful. Imagine that you work for a public service ad agency given the job of presenting the negative side of alcohol. What images would you choose to include in your ads?

Write an informal report to your boss in which you propose, in detail, three anti-alcohol ads. Choose from among the following:

- An ad countering the idea that alcohol leads to success
- An ad countering the idea that alcohol is sexy
- An ad countering the idea that alcohol goes well with athletics
- An ad countering the idea that alcohol makes for happy families

IMAGINING CANADA'S 153rd BIRTHDAY

Andrew Cohen

If you imagine Canada little more than a decade from now, what will you see? Will what you see be anything like Andrew Cohen's imaginings in this selection? Cohen is a professor of journalism and international affairs at Carleton University in Ottawa, and he initially contributed the essay below to the "Canada in 2020" online writing challenge.

Ottawa, July 1, 2020—On the 153rd anniversary of Confederation, Canada goes through the motions yet again. On Parliament Hill, the bells toll mournfully and the Maple Leaf hangs listlessly. Soldiers fire a 21-gun salute and Snowbirds fly overhead. Under sweltering skies, the Prime Minister still insists that Canada is "a young country," as he and his untutored predecessors have done since it really was a young country. 1

Thousands gather on the grass. They hear breathless politicians declare that Canada is the best country in the world, a boast once thought terribly unCanadian, but lately as predictable as the National Time Signal. In the shadow of the Peace Tower, they watch entertainers of every ethnicity reflecting this extraordinarily diverse society. The show is as inclusive as Canada itself. Everyone must be represented—there was a minor scandal last year when Karen dancers from Burma were overlooked in the festivities—because peoples from around the globe are reserving rooms in Hotel Canada. All want a role in this spectacle, as if to confirm their arrival. 2

Troupe after troupe of new Canadians in traditional national costume march across the stage. Recalling national birthdays long past, there are some high-stepping Ukrainians, fiddlers from Quebec and throat-singers from Nunavut. But these are passé today. Now the headliners are drummers from Senegal and acrobats from Brunei. After a half-generation of open immigration, Canada is home to millions who have fled the drought and desertification that have turned parts of Africa and Asia into a netherworld and made the environment humanity's ruin. The land that God gave to Cain and Voltaire called "a few acres of snow" now looks like Shangri-la in a beleaguered world. No wonder Canada's birthday party goes on for three days, as if it were a Hindu wedding. 3

This is the new complexion of Canada: black, tan and yellow. Canadians are proud to call themselves the most moderate of people. Tolerance has become their vocation, a kind of raison d'être, and that seems to be the breadth of their ambition. In a fragmenting world spawning new countries as casually as Arctic glaciers crack and calve, they are happy to have survived as a nation for a century and a half—even if they're not sure what that means anymore. 4

No, this isn't your father's Canada. Nor is it the Canada of Sir John A. MacDonald, Mackenzie King, John Diefenbaker, Lester Pearson, Pierre Berton, Margaret Atwood, Michael Bliss, Douglas Coupland or Avril Lavigne. They would not recognize it, and few in this new country would recognize them. The nation roams around under a cloud of amnesia, as if nothing happened before yesterday. This summer holiday—what do they call it? This capital—what does it represent? 5

This Parliament—what does it do? July 1 was once Canada Day (in prehistoric times, it was Dominion Day) and this was a national celebration. Ottawa was a national capital and Parliament was a national legislature.

There is no "national" anymore because there is no nation, at least not as we **6** knew it. In 2020, Canada is a country in little more than name. It has taken the 19th century idea of the nation-state and turned it on its head; Canada is now a collection of many nations (its ethnic minorities) who know only their own past, and many states (its provinces) that [k]now only their own interests. For many who have come here, Canada is a country of convenience. It offers security and anonymity and asks for conformity and equanimity. People take rooms in this grand hotel, as the novelist Yann Martel once put it, with little knowledge of—or attachment to—the place itself. In a rootless world of shifting loyalty and no fixed address, Canada is just another comfort station on the road to somewhere else.

The federal government is an antique notion in the era of sub-governments **7** and supra-governments. Canada's provinces have turned into princely states like those of British India, governed by pashas who have the powers of minor monarchs. Within these kingdoms are city-states. "National," an anachronistic term, now competes with "provincial" and "municipal" at home and "international" abroad.

So, Canada Day is now called People's Day, a celebration of our great mingling **8** of races from the corners of the earth. The Parliament of Canada is no longer a supreme body of lawmakers but a jumped-up town council of superannuated time-servers taking up space in that grand Gothic pile on the Ottawa River. The House of Commons has had little to do since the federal government transferred its remaining powers to the provinces some ten years ago. No wonder Ottawa is only a symbol these days. It is overshadowed by the real centres of power in post-confederation Canada—Vancouver, Edmonton, Toronto and Montreal—which drew the country's best minds from Ottawa [years] ago, as Pierre Elliott Trudeau had warned long ago. In happier times, a travel writer compared Ottawa to Cetinje, the capital of Montenegro up to 1918. Now, with cruel irony, it is Cetinje that has reclaimed its imperial glory as the seat of a renewed Montenegro, while Ottawa has become backwater in a diminished Canada.

What we have here is a virtual country. In the 500-nation universe, Canada **9** is an area code and an e-mail address. Yes, it is still fantastically rich, awash in petrodollars, endowed with mountains, forests, minerals and unfathomable space between three great oceans. Its biggest export is water and it is more expensive than oil. But today, 153 years after it was created, a visitor from the past might wonder what the country is celebrating. After all, what is Canada, anyway?

Physically, it may be hard to tell the difference between the country in 2006 **10** and 2020. It will surprise many to learn that Canada still includes Quebec, despite all those bond-traders and currency speculators who thought otherwise and lost money. With all of Quebec's new powers, the sovereigntists shrewdly concluded that independence would be unnecessary, even redundant. After all, with federalism like this, who needs sovereignty?

But there is indeed a new Canada, and it is the product of twin forces that had **11** been at work for some time. Contemporary historians have come to call them "the great migration" and "the quiet devolution."

The "great migration" was a byword for the greatest influx of immigrants **12** Canada had ever known. By 2010, the country's political parties were treating immigration as an auction, bidding against each other for ethnic voters in urban Canada to raise the quotas of immigrants from 250,000 to 500,000 a year. There was a sound economic reason (a shortage of unskilled labour) and a moral reason (boatloads of refugees were washing up on our shores, just as they were in Spain, Malta and Sicily). As global warming began to wreak havoc around 2012, a suddenly popular Green Party formed the government in Ottawa. The United Nations began to pressure empty, enormous Canada to ease the refugee crisis. By opening the country's borders, politicians could feel that they'd helped the world, as well as themselves.

Of course, immigration has benefited Canada. Even with a low birth rate the **13** population grew from 33 million in 2007 to 38 million in 2012 and to 45 million in 2018. Within two years, Statistics Canada predicts there will be 50 million Canadians. Fifty million! Finally, in size, Canada is the nation that Sir Wilfrid Laurier imagined a century ago.

While the influx has made the country's big cities even bigger (Toronto's **14** population is now 11 million, served by high-speed rail service and three airports), it has developed regions like northern Ontario, where Sudbury, Sault St. Marie, Thunder Bay and North Bay are flourishing. Down East, immigrants have re-made Saint John, Moncton, and Halifax. They have also made things interesting. Oh, how things have changed in old, Anglo-Saxon Canada. You can now eat pad thai in Red Deer and chapattis in Estevan.

For the most part, Canada has taken a laissez-faire view of its new arrivals. **15** Multiculturalism is a kind of narcissism for Canadians. We are in love with it and the image it gives us around the world. We look down at old Europe for its difficulty in integrating immigrants of different cultures, spawning ghettos in lily-white Stockholm, Amsterdam and Oslo.

Still, as immigration has brought Canada prosperity, it has also brought it **16** ambiguity. No one has taught these new Canadians much about their new country, its past, its triumphs, its myths. In Canada, where the provinces are responsible for education, no one teaches Canadian history anymore. Captured by the canons of political correctness, schools celebrate multiculturalism as an end in itself, failing to teach the superiority of civic nationalism over ethnic nationalism. In the voiceless country, no one speaks for Canada anymore. East Indians, Pakistanis and Chinese come here and live their lives happily in Hindi, Urdu and Mandarin. Sadly, they import their prejudices and struggles, too, which often find violent expression in grim urban corridors.

But as the country changed you couldn't talk about this. The public campaign **17** to persuade immigrants to adopt our mores and accept our rules was attacked as chauvinistic, even racist. Over time we diminished our citizenship, offering it freely and asking little in return. We became more interested in rights than responsibilities. The truth was that few Canadians of the last generation shared very much with each other, and even fewer have known what it means to be Canadian. No one has told them. It begged a variation of the biblical question: What hath a country if it gaineth the world but loseth its soul? If Canada was becoming more cosmopolitan, it was also becoming less cohesive.

While the wave of immigrants was flooding across our borders, the provinces **18** were re-asserting themselves. They demanded more powers—and they got them. This is the other part of the re-making of Canada. There was a time Confederation represented a division of powers between governments. Once the province of the province was the province; now the province of the province is the nation, for that is how they see themselves. The quiet devolution has created swaggering potentates presiding over wealthy fiefdoms, especially Alberta, which continually threatened to leave. This happened subtly, through administrative agreements, when no one was looking. It was the natural outcome of decades of whining and petitioning. True, it had been going on since the 1960s, but the system always assumed an intergovernmental negotiation, not unilateral disarmament.

In 2014, the centre collapsed. The provinces already had spending power, tax- **19** ing power, and their own pensions and social programs. They were choosing their immigrants and even running their own foreign policies. Indeed, for more than a decade they had embassies—no one bothered with the fiction of calling them "tourist offices" or "cultural legations" anymore—in international capitals. When the government allowed Quebec to send a representative to UNESCO, the province soon asked the same for the World Health Organization, the Human Rights Council and the International Labour Organization. As usual, what Quebec got, all provinces got. Now a once-influential country speaks to the world not with a single, eloquent voice, but in a contradictory and confusing cacophony.

When the provinces started raising their own armies—the last great federal **20** preserve—the game was over. Ottawa handed the provinces monetary policy and divided up its military assets. The centre had nothing but the post office and the Parliament Buildings, now a Victorian architectural curiosity for Chinese tourists.

All along, of course, the accommodationists said this was the price of unity. **21** Quebec was still in, wasn't it? Alberta and Newfoundland, with their oil wealth, had not left us, had they? We had chanted the hymn of unity for so long that it had become a mantra, blinding us from seeing our purpose as a nation. In the name of unity, we abandoned the symbols of our nationhood, allowed the provinces a free hand in the world, stopped teaching history, shared no collective ideas and promoted no great project beyond diversity itself. Oh, we were a good country, but not a great one.

Now in 2020 we look around in despair. In the voiceless country, there is no **22** one left to recall its past, no one left to celebrate its principles, and no one left to speak its name.

● ● ● ● ● **READING COMPREHENSION QUESTIONS**

1. The word *netherworld* in "turned parts of Africa and Asia into a netherworld and made the environment humanity's ruin" (paragraph 3) means
   a. barren place.
   b. paradise.
   c. hell.
   d. disaster.

2. The word *narcissism* in "Multiculturalism is a kind of narcissism for Canadians" (paragraph 15) means
    a. vanity.
    b. disease.
    c. arrogance.
    d. charity.

3. Which of the following would be a good alternative title for this selection?
    a. Canada: A Survival Story
    b. Oh Canada, We Stand on Guard for What?
    c. Canada: The World's Refuge
    d. The Rich New Canada

4. Which sentence best expresses the main idea of the selection?
    a. Canada in 2020 will be much the same as Canada in 2008.
    b. Multiculturalism has been Canada's undoing as a nation.
    c. Canada has always been a good, not great country.
    d. The future Canada will be diverse, but bland, and internally divided.

5. Which groups formerly performed at Canada Day celebrations? Who now performs on People's Day?

6. *True or false?* Canadian provinces in 2020 will be governed by foreign rulers.

7. Why will future citizens not be taught Canadian history?

8. The author implies that
    a. Canada is ahead of its time with multicultural policies.
    b. multiculturalism will ruin national celebrations.
    c. multiculturalism is risky to a country with little sense of identity.
    d. Canada's survival will be attributed to multiculturalism.

9. The author implies that
    a. open immigration policies were based on moral choices.
    b. Canadians do not have a strong enough sense of themselves.
    c. massive immigration has been the key to Canada's prosperity.
    d. immigration policies require national planning.

10. The author implies that
    a. increasing provincial governments' powers is potentially dangerous.
    b. increasing provincial powers will hold Canada together.
    c. the House of Commons did little, anyway.
    d. provinces crave more power, even today.

● ● ● ● **DISCUSSION QUESTIONS**

About Content

1. Why, according to this selection, is the phrase "Canada is the best country in the world" now predictable?

2. What are the reasons why Sir John A. MacDonald and even Avril Lavigne would no longer recognize their native country?

3. What has become of Ottawa and the federal government in 2020?

About Structure

4. In which paragraph of this selection do you find an example of the "causes" method of development? Which paragraph demonstrates use of the "definition" method of development?

5. Which paragraphs directly compare or contrast the Canada of today with the Canada of 2020?

6. Which method of conclusion does Cohen use in this selection?
   a. Summary and a final thought
   b. Thought-provoking question(s)
   c. Prediction or recommendation to act

About Style and Tone

7. Which phrases and descriptive words in the opening paragraph contradict the idea of a national celebration?

8. Which words and phrases in the closing paragraph recall the feeling of those unusual words and phrases in the first paragraph? How does this unify the selection?

9. Cohen uses a number of arresting figures of speech, comparisons, similes ("as predictable as the National Time Signal"), and metaphors ("Hotel Canada"). Find an example of an intriguing comparison or simile, metaphor, and of personification, and explain your choices.

● ● ● ● **WRITING ASSIGNMENTS**

Assignment 1

What does Cohen mean by referring to the Canada of 2020 as "a virtual country"? In an essay that uses examples drawn from this selection, explain your understanding of the author's meaning.

Your thesis could be something like the following:

Andrew Cohen's vision of Canada as "a virtual country" denies the nation genuine existence, a sense of itself, or any possible heritage.

Be sure, in your essay, to paraphrase and quote correctly, and to use in-text MLA citation to identify paragraphs to which you refer. See Chapter 19 for help with doing so.

Assignment 2

Write an essay that defines for an audience of your peers the concept of "political correctness." Using third-person voice, begin with your own understanding of the term and then support your definition thesis with three distinct illustrations that show readers exactly why you define the phrase as you do.

Assignment 3

How do you see the Canada of 2020? Will it be a country ignorant of its past, a country that has lost its identity? Or could Canada become an example of tolerance and ecologically sound action to the world?

Compare or contrast your view of a near-future Canada with that of Andrew Cohen (pages 533–536), based on three clear and valid criteria. Your thesis will express agreement or disagreement with Cohen. Your essay will compare or contrast specific points in "Imagining Canada's 153rd Birthday" with specific points of your own. Remember to paraphrase, quote, and cite correctly.

COFFEE

Alan Durning

Is there a mug of coffee in your hand as you read this page? Have you ever stopped to think about what went into that mug before it reached your hands? You may have gone as far as to grind the beans, measure the coffee, pour the water into the tank of the coffee maker, place a filter in the machine's basket, and then turn on the power, but where did the ingredients themselves come from? How did they reach you? In his essay, Alan Durning "deconstructs" a simple cup of coffee into its basic elements and traces them back to their origins. In this "reverse process essay," we see the complex nature of an everyday substance.

Beans

I brewed a cup of coffee. It took 100 beans—about one fortieth of the beans that grew on the coffee tree that year. The tree was on a small mountain farm in the region of Colombia called Antioquia. The region was cleared of its native forests in the first coffee boom three generations ago. These "cloud forests" are among the world's most endangered ecosystems. **1**

The beans ripened in the shade of taller trees. Growing them did not require plowing the soil, but it did take several doses of insecticides, which were synthesized in factories in the Rhine River Valley of Europe. Some of the chemicals entered the respiratory systems of farm workers. Others washed downstream and were absorbed by plants and animals. **2**

The beans were picked by hand. In a diesel powered crusher they were removed from the fruit that encased them. They were dried under the sun and shipped to New Orleans in a 132 pound bag. The freighter was fueled by Venezuelan oil and made in Japan. The shipyard built the freighter out of Korean steel. The Korean steel mill used iron mined on tribal lands in Papua New Guinea. **3**

At New Orleans the beans were roasted for 13 minutes at temperatures above 400 degrees F. The roaster burned natural gas pumped from the ground in Oklahoma. The beans were packaged in four-layer bags constructed of polyethylene, nylon, aluminum foil and polyester. They were trucked to a Seattle warehouse and later to a retail store. **4**

Bag

I carried the beans out of the grocery in a brown paper bag made at an unbleached 5
kraft paper mill in Oregon. I transported them home in an automobile that burned
one sixth of a gallon of gasoline during the five mile round-trip to the market.

Grinder

In the kitchen, I measured the beans in a disposable plastic scoop molded in New 6
Jersey and spooned them into the grinder. The grinder was assembled in China
from imported steel, aluminum, copper, and plastic parts. It was powered by electricity generated at the Ross Dam on the Skagit River.

I dumped the coffee into a gold-plated mesh filter made in Switzerland of 7
Russian ore. I put the filter into a plastic-and-steel drip coffee maker.

I poured eight ounces of tap water into the appliance. The water came by pipe 8
from the Cedar River on the west slope of the Cascade Mountains. An element
heated the water to more than 200 degrees F. The hot water seeped through the
ground coffee and dissolved some of its oils and solids. The brew trickled into a
glass carafe.

Paper Cup

The coffee mugs were all dirty so I poured the coffee into a paper cup. The cup 9
was made from bleached wood pulp in Arkansas. A fraction of the chlorine in the
bleach was discharged from the pulp mill into the Arkansas River. In the river, the
chlorine ended up as TCDD, which is often simply called dioxin. It is the most
carcinogenic substance known.

Cream

I stirred in one ounce of cream. The cream came from a grain-fed dairy cow in the 10
lowlands north of Seattle. The cow liked to graze on a stream bank and walk in the
stream. This muddied the water and made life difficult for native trout.

The cow's manure was rich in nitrogen and phosphorus. The soils of the pas- 11
ture where the cow grazed were unable to absorb these quickly enough, so they
washed into the stream when it rained. The infusion of nutrients fertilized algae,
which absorbed a larger share of the oxygen dissolved in the water. The shortage of
oxygen made life more difficult for native trout.

Sugar

I measured out two tablespoons of sugar. It came from the canefields south of Lake 12
Okeechobee in Florida. These plantations have deprived the Everglades of water,
endangering waterfowl and reptile populations.

• • • • **READING COMPREHENSION QUESTIONS**

1. The word *synthesized* in "several doses of insecticides, which were synthesized
   in factories in the Rhine River Valley of Europe" (paragraph 2) means
   a. processed.
   b. manufactured.

    c. combined.

    d. packaged.

2. The word *infusion* in "The infusion of nutrients fertilized algae, which absorbed a larger share of the oxygen dissolved in the water" (paragraph 11) means

    a. pollution.

    b. instilling.

    c. formula.

    d. combination.

3. Which one of the following would make a good alternative title for this selection?

    a. Eco-Disaster in the a.m.

    b. Fair Trade, Good Coffee

    c. The Whole World in Your Pot

    d. Your Daily Cup of Toxins

4. Which statement best expresses the main idea of the selection?

    a. No single item in our world is detachable from other aspects of existence.

    b. The production of coffee entails many polluting and harmful processes.

    c. Everything is more complex than it first seems.

    d. All foods are ecologically disastrous to manufacture.

5. According to the selection,

    a. destruction of Colombian rainforests is the most disastrous effect of coffee-growing and production.

    b. coffee production is a completely automated process.

    c. producing coffee is a combination of agriculture, human labour, and technical expertise.

    d. world resources are being depleted to produce coffee.

6. *True or false?* All the paper products mentioned by the author create toxic substances in their manufacture.

7. *True or false?* The normal habits of a dairy cow affect the balance of the ecology.

8. From the first three paragraphs of the article, we can conclude that the author

    a. feels nothing but environmentally based guilt about making his cup of coffee.

    b. worries too much about problems caused by coffee production.

    c. feels sorry for the farm labourers involved in coffee growing.

    d. understands both the industrial problems and the global trade interconnections in coffee production.

9. *True or false?* All instances of water pollution in the essay arise from industrial waste.

10. We might infer that the author

    a. believes we often don't know when we are harming the environment.

    b. believes we don't care about pollution or Third World industrial oppression.

    c. is careful to use only ecologically safe, nonexploitive products.

    d. puts all the blame for ecological imbalances on human beings.

DISCUSSION QUESTIONS

About Content

1. In the opening paragraphs of his essay, the author points out two major industrially based ecological problems. What are they? Which would seem the more harmful to you, and why?

2. How many countries does it take to produce Alan Durning's cup of coffee? How many American states are needed to assist in the process? What do these numbers tell you about products we use every day?

About Structure

3. This essay "deconstructs" a cup of coffee. If this is a "reverse process essay," which method of introduction has the author used "in reverse"?
   a. Explanation of the importance of the topic
   b. An opposite
   c. Movement from general to specific

4. Durning divides his essay into sections with sparse headings. Does each section cover only the subject named by its title? If not, which sections cover more than one subject? Why do they cover more than one subject?

5. This is a rare example of a process essay almost devoid of simple or obvious transitions. If there are no ordinary transitions, what rhetorical device has the author used in their place? What method of ordering ideas, common to all process writing, has the author used? How does this method help you to follow the sequence of ideas?

About Style and Tone

6. Durning's style in "Coffee" is as plain and severe as his title. How many sentences are simple statements starting with *I*? What is the effect of this style on you as a reader? Is the information conveyed by the essay as uncomplicated as the style?

7. Writers with strong biases or social concerns are often accused of being unfair or overbearing because of the vehement tone of their work. Alan Durning is a prominent environmentalist. Does his tone allow readers room to consider their own point of view? If so, how is this goal achieved?

WRITING ASSIGNMENTS

Assignment 1

Coffee is an ordinary product with a fascinating story behind it. How much does any of us know about everyday foods and beverages? Choose one fairly simple item, preferably one whose package does not have thousands of untraceable chemicals, and do some research into the origins of its ingredients. Phone the manufacturer, visit some websites, or consult your library to find out where its ingredients originate.

Write a process essay about the history and the geographical origins of the raw materials in your chosen product. Place the ingredients in three groups for ease of paragraphing. You should organize your essay as Durning has done, starting "from the end" and taking your product apart piece by piece. You may choose to start with either the largest or the smallest of its ingredients, depending on the order you feel your reader will find most interesting.

Assignment 2

If our world is shrinking and we are all interdependent, why do we still drink coffee and drive cars powered by fossil fuels? Many manufacturers and retailers would like the public to believe that they are doing their best to preserve the world's ecological balance. Are their claims sincere or just more sophisticated marketing tactics? Will concern for the world's biological condition ever change business? Will damage to the world's ecosystems force business to change its methods?

Write an argumentation essay in the third-person voice in which you either defend the efforts of one "world-conscious" company or argue that such efforts are merely a way of "jumping on the bandwagon." Justify your argument logically, and make use of some objective information from your own knowledge or from outside reading.

Assignment 3

You have chosen to write an article for the "World Watch" column in your campus newspaper. Your article describes three specific ways in which college students could be active in improving their school and local environment. Your article may extend and relate each example to a relevant global concern.

HOW TO MAKE IT IN COLLEGE, NOW THAT YOU'RE HERE

Brian O'Keeney

The author of this selection presents a compact guide to being a successful student. He will show you how to pass tests, how to avoid becoming a student zombie, how to find time to fit in everything you want to do, and how to deal with personal problems while keeping up with your studies. The tips that O'Keeney presents have been culled from his own experience and his candid interviews with fellow students.

Today is your first day on campus. You were a high school senior three months ago.   1
Or maybe you've been at home with your children for the last ten years. Or maybe you work full time and you're coming to school to start the process that leads to a better job. Whatever your background is, you're probably not too concerned today with staying in college. After all, you just got over the hurdle (and the paperwork) of applying to this place and organizing your life so that you could attend. And today, you're confused and tired. Everything is a hassle, from finding the classrooms to

standing in line at the bookstore. But read my advice anyway. And if you don't read it today, clip and save this article. You might want to look at it a little further down the road.

By the way, if this isn't your very first day, don't skip this article. Maybe you haven't been doing as well in your studies as you'd hoped. Or perhaps you've had problems juggling your work schedule, your class schedule, and your social life. If so, read on. You're about to get the inside story on making it in college. On the basis of my own experience as a final-year student, and of dozens of interviews with successful students, I've worked out a no-fail system for coping with college. These are the inside tips every student needs to do well in school. I've put myself in your place, and I'm going to answer the questions that will cross (or have already crossed) your mind during your stay here.

What's the Secret of Getting Good Grades?

It all comes down to getting those grades, doesn't it? After all, you came here for some reason, and you're going to need passing grades to get the credits or degree you want. Many of us never did much studying in high school; most of the learning we did took place in the classroom. College, however, is a lot different. You're really on your own when it comes to passing courses. In fact, sometimes you'll feel as if nobody cares if you make it or not. Therefore, you've got to figure out a study system that gets results. Sooner or later, you'll be alone with those books. After that, you'll be sitting in a classroom with an exam sheet on your desk. Whether you stare at that exam with a queasy stomach or whip through it fairly confidently depends on your study techniques. Most of the successful students I talked to agreed that the following eight study tips deliver solid results.

1   **Set Up a Study Place.** Those students you see "studying" in the cafeteria or game room aren't learning much. You just can't learn when you're distracted by people and noise. Even the library can be a bad place to study if you constantly find yourself watching the clouds outside or the students walking through the stacks. It takes guts to sit, alone, in a quiet place in order to study. But you have to do it. Find a room at home or a spot in the library that's relatively quiet—and boring. When you sit there, you won't have much to do except study.

2   **Get into a Study Frame of Mind.** When you sit down, do it with the attitude that you're going to get this studying done. You're not going to doodle in your notebook or make a list for the supermarket. Decide that you're going to study and learn *now*, so that you can move on to more interesting things as soon as possible.

3   **Give Yourself Rewards.** If you sweat out a block of study time, and do a good job on it, treat yourself. You deserve it. You can "psych" yourself up for studying by promising to reward yourself afterwards. A present for yourself can be anything from a favorite TV show to a relaxing bath to a dish of double chocolate ice cream.

4   **Skim the Textbook First.** Lots of students sit down with an assignment like "read chapter five, pages 125–150" and do just that. They turn to page 125 and

start to read. After a while, they find that they have no idea what they just read. For the last ten minutes, they've been thinking about their five-year-old or what they're going to eat for dinner. Eventually, they plod through all the pages but don't remember much afterwards.

In order to prevent this problem, skim the textbook chapter first. This means: **8** look at the title, the subtitles, the headings, the pictures, the first and last paragraphs. Try to find out what the person who wrote the book had in mind when he or she organized the chapter. What was important enough to set off as a title or in bold type? After skimming, you should be able to explain to yourself what the main points of the chapter are. Unless you're the kind of person who would step into an empty elevator shaft without looking first, you'll soon discover the value of skimming.

5   Take Notes on What You're Studying. This sounds like a hassle, but it **9** works. Go back over the material after you've read it, and jot down key words and phrases in the margins. When you review the chapter for a test, you'll have handy little things like "definition of rationalization" or "example of assimilation" in the margins. If the material is especially tough, organize a separate sheet of notes. Write down definitions, examples, lists, and main ideas. The idea is to have a single sheet that boils the entire chapter down to a digestible lump.

6   Review after You've Read and Taken Notes. Some people swear that talk- **10** ing to yourself works. Tell yourself about the most important points in the chapter. Once you've said them out loud, they seem to stick better in your mind. If you can't talk to yourself about the material after reading it, that's a sure sign you don't really know it.

7   Give Up. This may sound contradictory, but give up when you've had **11** enough. You should try to make it through at least an hour, though. Ten minutes here and there are useless. When your head starts to pound and your eyes develop spidery red lines, quit. You won't do much learning when you're exhausted.

8   Take a College Skills Course If You Need It. Don't hesitate or feel embar- **12** rassed about enrolling in a study skills course. Many students say they wouldn't have made it without one.

How Can I Keep Up with All My Responsibilities without Going Crazy?

You've got a class schedule. You're supposed to study. You've got a family. You've **13** got a husband, wife, boyfriend, girlfriend, child. You've got a job. How are you possibly going to cover all the bases in your life and maintain your sanity? This is one of the toughest problems students face. Even if they start the semester with the best of intentions, they eventually find themselves tearing their hair out trying to do everything they're supposed to do. Believe it or not, though, it is possible to meet all your responsibilities. And you don't have to turn into a hermit or give up your loved ones to do it.

The secret here is to organize your time. But don't just sit around half the **14** semester planning to get everything together soon. Before you know it, you'll be confronted with midterms, papers, family, and work all at once. Don't let yourself reach that breaking point. Instead, try these three tactics.

1   Monthly Calendar. Get one of those calendars with big blocks around the   15
dates. Give yourself an overview of the whole term by marking down the due dates
for papers and projects. Circle test and exam days. This way those days don't sneak
up on you unexpectedly.

2   Study Schedule. Sit down during the first few days of this semester and   16
make up a sheet listing the days and hours of the week. Fill in your work and class
hours first. Then try to block out some study hours. It's better to study a little
every day than to create a huge once-or-twice-a-week marathon session. Schedule
study hours for your hardest classes for the times when you feel most energetic. For
example, I battled my tax law textbook in the mornings; when I looked at it after
7:00 P.M., I may as well have been reading Chinese. The usual proportion, by the
way, is one hour of study time for every class hour.

In case you're one of those people who get carried away, remember to leave   17
blocks of free time, too. You won't be any good to yourself or anyone else if you
don't relax and pack in the studying once in a while.

3   A "To Do" List. This is the secret that single-handedly got me through col-   18
lege. Once a week (or every day if you want to), write a list of what you have to do.
Write down everything from "write English paper" to "buy cold cuts for lunches."
The best thing about a "to do" list is that it seems to tame all those stray "I have
to" thoughts that nag at your mind. Just making the list seems to make the tasks
"doable." After you finish something on the list, cross it off. Don't be compulsive
about finishing everything; you're not Superman or Wonder Woman. Get the
important things done first. The secondary things you don't finish can simply be
moved to your next "to do" list.

What Can I Do If Personal Problems Get in the Way of My Studies?

One student, Roger, told me this story: 19

> *Everything was going OK for me until the middle of the spring semester. I went
> through a terrible time when I broke up with my girlfriend and started seeing her
> best friend. I was trying to deal with my ex-girlfriend's hurt and anger, my new
> girlfriend's guilt, and my own worries and anxieties at the same time. In addition
> to this, my mother was sick and on a medication that made her really irritable. I
> hated to go home because the atmosphere was so uncomfortable. Soon, I started
> missing classes because I couldn't deal with the academic pressures as well as my
> own personal problems. It seemed easier to hang around my girlfriend's apartment
> than to face all my problems at home and at school.*

Another student, Marian, told me: 20

> *I'd been married for eight years and the relationship wasn't going too well. I saw
> the handwriting on the wall, and I decided to prepare for the future. I enrolled
> in college, because I knew I'd need a decent job to support myself. Well, my hus-
> band had a fit because I was going to school. We were arguing a lot anyway, and
> he made it almost impossible for me to study at home. I think he was angry and*

almost jealous because I was drawing away from him. It got so bad that I thought about quitting college for a while. I wasn't getting any support at home and it was just too hard to go on.

Personal troubles like these are overwhelming when you're going through **21** them. School seems like the least important thing in your life. The two students above are perfect examples of this. But if you think about it, quitting or failing school would be the worst thing for these two students. Roger's problems, at least with his girlfriends, would simmer down eventually, and then he'd regret having left school. Marian had to finish college if she wanted to be able to live independently. Sometimes, you've just got to hang tough.

But what do you do while you're trying to live through a lousy time? First **22** of all, do something difficult. Ask yourself, honestly, if you're exaggerating small problems as an excuse to avoid classes and studying. It takes strength to admit this, but there's no sense in kidding yourself. If your problems are serious, and real, try to make some human contacts at school. Lots of students hide inside a miserable shell made of their own troubles and feel isolated and lonely. Believe me, there are plenty of students with problems. Not everyone is getting A's and having a fabulous social and home life at the same time. As you go through the term, you'll pick up some vibrations about the students in your classes. Perhaps someone strikes you as a compatible person. Why not speak to that person after class? Share a cup of coffee in the cafeteria or walk to the parking lot together. You're not looking for a best friend or the love of your life. You just want to build a little network of support for yourself. Sharing your difficulties, questions, and complaints with a friendly person on campus can make a world of difference in how you feel.

Finally, if your problems are overwhelming, get some professional help. Why **23** do you think colleges spend countless dollars on counseling departments and campus psychiatric services? More than ever, students all over the country are taking advantage of the help offered by support groups and therapy sessions. There's no shame attached to asking for help, either; in fact, almost 40 percent of college students (according to one survey) will use counseling services during their time in school. Just walk into a student center or counseling office and ask for an appointment. You wouldn't think twice about asking a dentist to help you get rid of your toothache. Counselors are paid—and want—to help you with your problems.

Why Do Some People Make It and Some Drop Out?

Anyone who spends at least one semester in college notices that some students give **24** up on their classes. The person who sits behind you in accounting, for example, begins to miss a lot of class meetings and eventually vanishes. Or another student comes to class without the assignment, doodles in his notebook during the lecture, and leaves during the break. What's the difference between students like this and the ones who succeed in school? My survey may be nonscientific, but everyone I asked said the same thing: attitude. A positive attitude is the key to everything else—good study habits, smart time scheduling, and coping with personal difficulties.

What does "a positive attitude" mean? Well, for one thing, it means avoiding **25** the zombie syndrome. It means not only showing up for your classes, but also doing something while you're there. Really listen. Take notes. Ask a question if you want to. Don't just walk into a class, put your mind in neutral, and drift away to never-never land.

Having a positive attitude goes deeper than this, though. It means being mature   26 about college as an institution. Too many students approach college classes like six-year-olds who expect first grade to be as much fun as *Sesame Street*. First grade, as we all know, isn't as much fun as *Sesame Street*. And college classes can sometimes be downright dull and boring. If you let a boring class discourage you so much that you want to leave school, you'll lose in the long run. Look at your priorities. You want a degree, or a certificate, or a career. If you have to, you can make it through a less-than-interesting class in order to achieve what you want. Get whatever you can out of every class. But if you simply can't stand a certain class, be determined to fulfill its requirements and be done with it once and for all.

After the initial high of starting school, you have to settle in for the long haul.   27 If you follow the advice here, you'll be prepared to face the academic crunch. You'll also live through the semester without giving up your family, your job, or *Monday Night Football*. Finally, going to college can be an exciting time. You do learn. And when you learn things, the world becomes a more interesting place.

● ● ● ●   **READING COMPREHENSION QUESTIONS**

1. The word *queasy* in "with a queasy stomach" (paragraph 3) means
   a. intelligent.
   b. healthy.
   c. full.
   d. nervous.

2. The word *tactics* in "try these three tactics" (paragraph 14) means
   a. proofs.
   b. problems.
   c. methods.
   d. questions.

3. Which of the following would be a good alternative title for this selection?
   a. Your First Day on Campus
   b. Coping with College
   c. How to Budget Your Time
   d. The Benefits of College Skills Courses

4. Which sentence best expresses the main idea of the selection?
   a. In high school, most of us did little homework.
   b. You should give yourself rewards for studying well.
   c. Sometimes personal problems interfere with studying.
   d. You can succeed in college by following certain guidelines.

5. According to the author, "making it" in college means
   a. studying whenever you have any free time.
   b. getting a degree by barely passing your courses.
   c. quitting school until you solve your personal problems.
   d. getting good grades without making your life miserable.

6. If your personal problems seem overwhelming, you should
   a. drop out for a while.
   b. try to ignore them.
   c. tell another student.
   d. seek professional help.

7. Which of the following is *not* described by the author as a means of time control?
   a. Monthly calendar
   b. To-do list
   c. Study schedule
   d. Flexible job hours

8. We might infer that the author
   a. is a writer for the school newspaper.
   b. is president of his or her class.
   c. has taken a study-skills course.
   d. was not a successful student in his or her first year of college.

9. From the selection we can conclude that
   a. college textbooks are very expensive.
   b. it is a good practice to write notes in your textbook.
   c. taking notes on your reading takes too much time.
   d. a student should never mark up an expensive textbook.

10. The author implies that
    a. fewer people than before are attending college
    b. most students think that college is easy.
    c. most students dislike college.
    d. coping with college is difficult.

• • • • DISCUSSION QUESTIONS

About Content

1. What pitfalls does O'Keeney think are waiting for students just starting college? Are there other pitfalls not mentioned in the article?

2. What is the secret that the author says got him through college? What do you think is the most helpful or important suggestion the author makes in the selection?

3. Do you agree with the author that Roger and Marian should stay in school? Are there any situations in which it would be better for students to quit school or leave temporarily?

About Structure

4. What is the thesis of the selection? In which paragraph is it stated?

5. Why does the article begin with the first day on campus?

6. What method of introduction does the author use in the section on personal problems (starting on page 545)? What is the value of using this method?

About Style and Tone

7. This essay is obviously written for college students. Can you guess where an essay like this one would appear? (**Hint:** Reread the first paragraph.)

• • • • WRITING ASSIGNMENTS

Assignment 1

Write a process essay that explains how to succeed in some other situation—for example, a job, a sport, marriage, child rearing. First, brainstorm the three or four problem areas a newcomer to this experience might encounter. Then, under each area you have listed, jot down some helpful hints and techniques for overcoming these problems. For example, a process essay on "How to Succeed as a Server" might describe the following problem areas in this kind of job:

- Developing a good memory
- Learning to do tasks quickly
- Coping with troublesome customers

Each supporting paragraph in this essay would discuss specific techniques for dealing with these problems. Be sure that the advice you give is detailed and specific enough to really help a person in such a situation.

Assignment 2

Write a letter to Roger or Marian, giving advice on how to deal with his or her personal problem. You could recommend any or all of the following:

- Face the problem realistically. (By doing what?)
- Make other contacts at school. (How? Where?)
- See a counsellor. (Where? What should this person be told?)
- Realize that the problem is not so serious. (Why not?)
- Ignore the problem. (How? By doing what instead?)

In your introductory paragraph, explain why you are writing the letter. Include a thesis statement that says what plan of action you are recommending. Then, in the rest of the letter, explain that plan of action in detail.

Assignment 3

Write a third-person essay contrasting college or university *as students imagine it will be* with college or university *as it is*.

For instance, you may decide to contrast expectations of (1) a residence or rented room, (2) roommates, and (3) night-life, with reality. Alternatively, you could contrast your expectations of (1) fellow students, (2) professors, and (3) post-secondary courses, with reality.

Before making an outline, decide whether you will use the *one-side-at-a-time* or *point-by-point* method of development.

THE PLOT AGAINST PEOPLE

Russell Baker

Our relationships with our belongings can be rocky. We love and value them when they work, but when they misbehave, break down, or get lost, our feelings change—we may be ready to break up with our possessions, or worse. . . .

The creator of this selection's world of antagonistic objects, Russell Baker, has been a journalist for over sixty years. He enjoys using stylish techniques like personification and irony, but describes working these into 800-word articles as being like "trying to do a ballet in a telephone booth."

1 Inanimate objects are classified scientifically into three major categories—those that break down, those that get lost, and those that don't work.

2 The goal of all inanimate objects is to resist man and ultimately to defeat him, and the three major classifications are based on the method each object uses to achieve its purpose. As a general rule, any object capable of breaking down at the moment when it is most needed will do so. The automobile is typical of the category.

3 With the cunning peculiar to its breed, the automobile never breaks down while entering a filling station which has a large staff of idle mechanics. It waits until it reaches a downtown intersection in the middle of the rush hour, or until it is fully loaded with family and luggage on the Ohio Turnpike. Thus it creates maximum inconvenience, frustration, and irritability, thereby reducing its owner's lifespan.

4 Washing machines, garbage disposals, lawn mowers, furnaces, TV sets, tape recorders, slide projectors—all are in league with the automobile to take their turn at breaking down whenever life threatens to flow smoothly for their enemies.

5 Many inanimate objects, of course, find it extremely difficult to break down. Pliers, for example, and gloves and keys are almost totally incapable of breaking down. Therefore, they have had to evolve a different technique for resisting man.

6 They get lost. Science has still not solved the mystery of how they do it, and no man has ever caught one of them in the act. The most plausible theory is that they have developed a secret method of locomotion which they are able to conceal from human eyes.

7 It is not uncommon for a pair of pliers to climb all the way from the cellar to the attic in its single-minded determination to raise its owner's blood pressure. Keys have been known to burrow three feet under mattresses. Women's purses, despite their great weight, frequently travel through six or seven rooms to find hiding space under a couch.

8 Scientists have been struck by the fact that things that break down virtually never get lost, while things that get lost hardly ever break down. A furnace, for example, will invariably break down at the depth of the first winter cold wave, but it will never get lost. A woman's purse hardly ever breaks down; it almost invariably chooses to get lost.

9 Some persons believe this constitutes evidence that inanimate objects are not entirely hostile to man. After all, they point out, a furnace could infuriate a man

even more thoroughly by getting lost than by breaking down, just as a glove could upset him far more by breaking down than by getting lost.

Not everyone agrees, however, that this indicates a conciliatory attitude. Many 10 say it merely proves that furnaces, gloves and pliers are incredibly stupid.

The third class of objects—those that don't work—is the most curious of all. 11 These include such objects as barometers, car clocks, cigarette lighters, flashlights and toy-train locomotives. It is inaccurate, of course, to say that they *never* work. They work once, usually for the first few hours after being brought home, and then quit. Thereafter, they never work again.

In fact, it is widely assumed that they are built for the purpose of not work- 12 ing. Some people have reached advanced ages without ever seeing some of these objects—barometers, for example—in working order.

Science is utterly baffled by the entire category. There are many theories about 13 it. The most interesting holds that the things that don't work have attained the highest state possible for an inanimate object, the state to which things that break down and things that get lost can still only aspire.

They have truly defeated man by conditioning him never to expect anything of 14 them. When his cigarette lighter won't light or his flashlight fails to illuminate, it does not raise his blood pressure. Objects that don't work have given man the only peace he receives from inanimate society.

• • • • READING COMPREHENSION QUESTIONS

1. The word *plausible* in "The most plausible theory is that they have developed a secret method of locomotion" (paragraph 6) means
   a. ridiculous.
   b. well known.
   c. believable.
   d. common.

2. The word *conciliatory* in ". . . that this indicates a conciliatory attitude" (paragraph 10) means
   a. contrary.
   b. pacifying.
   c. provocative.
   d. good-natured.

3. Which of the following would be a good alternative title for the selection?
   a. Our Spiteful Stuff
   b. The Malice of Machines
   c. Revenge Against the Things
   d. Everything is Against Us

4. Which sentence best expresses the main idea of the selection?
   a. The idea of objects having wills of their own is a product of our imaginations.
   b. Inanimate objects that break down at the wrong time seem spiteful.
   c. Inanimate things seem alive as they influence everyone's lives.
   d. The world of inanimate objects is very mysterious.

5. "The automobile is typical of the category" because
   a. it is a sneaky, smart machine.
   b. it belongs to the same group as garbage disposals and lawn mowers.
   c. its behaviour puzzles most people.
   d. it breaks down at the most inconvenient times.

6. *True or false?* In Baker's world, purses can get lost and break down.

7. Baker's third class of objects
   a. usually works only once.
   b. does not work at all.
   c. is designed not to work.
   d. is composed of the most complex objects.

8. What is Baker saying with the clause "The goal of all inanimate objects is to resist man and ultimately to defeat him"?
   a. Our inventions have turned against us.
   b. Objects can be so frustrating as to seem malicious.
   c. We are so attached to material things that we give them personalities.
   d. Modern life and its technology are just too difficult.

9. The author implies that
   a. people's homes are messy.
   b. women lose their purses frequently.
   c. we lose things too often.
   d. most of us are a bit careless about our belongings.

10. *True or false?* The author confesses at the end of the selection that inanimate objects have won the battle against humans.

DISCUSSION QUESTIONS

About Content

1. Which "actions" display the "cunning" of automobiles?

2. How have pliers, gloves, and keys "evolved," according to the author, and why?

3. Why is it assumed that some objects "are built for the purpose of not working" (paragraph 12)? Can you think of other things that fit this description?

About Structure

4. What is the point of Baker's one-sentence opening paragraph? In what respects does this paragraph differ from most opening paragraphs?

5. On what does the author base his classification of objects?

6. How does the author introduce his second category of objects? In which paragraph? Do you find this transition effective? Why or why not?

7. Is there any evidence of the use of time order or emphatic order as an organizing principle in this selection? If so, where do you find it?

About Style and Tone

8. How would you describe the overall tone of "The Plot Against People"? What in the selection supports your description?

9. Baker uses a rhetorical device called personification—he attributes human characteristics to objects. Where does he begin to personify things? With which words? Identify and describe two effective instances of personification in this selection.

10. This selection is written in third-person voice. Does this distance readers too much from the author's sense of frustration? Why or why not?

• • • • WRITING ASSIGNMENTS

Assignment 1

If inanimate objects do have lives of their own, what would a typical day be like in the life of a shoe, or a laptop, or a backpack? If they are sentient, what are they thinking and trying to do?

Write a narrative case-study essay that is an observer's report on one day's activities in the life of an object you own. You are an observer recording events and perhaps drawing conclusions; you write in the third-person voice. Remember that narrative essays "teach a lesson" with their thesis statements, supporting points, and structure; they do not simply follow an "and then this happened . . " wandering structure.

Assignment 2

Write a classification and division essay in which you divide one of the following: (a) useful objects, (b) annoying objects, or (c) stylish objects, into three different categories. Remember, as Baker does, to state your categories and perhaps your reason for choosing them in your thesis statement. In your body paragraphs, explain with clear details and examples why each object within a category deserves to be there, and balance your body paragraphs so that they are roughly equal in length.

Assignment 3

Despite Baker's humorous treatment of humanity's relationship with its possessions, there may be an element of seriousness in the frustration we feel when deprived of our *things* for any reason. Do we, in fact, have too many *things*? Are we trapped by them? Do they make our lives more difficult, rather than easier and more pleasant?

Write an essay that argues one of the following viewpoints:

People are so dominated by their desire to own things that they have lost track of non-materialistic values.

People in first-world countries definitely benefit from owning items that help them to be healthier, more informed, and more productive.

People will not "drown" in a sea of material possessions, nor damage the environment further with their castoffs.

IMAGES OF CANADA: CANADIAN BANK NOTES

Laura Millard

Laura Millard is a visual artist who works with mixed media pieces, blending painting with photography. In this selection, her artist's eye has drawn her to the design of Canadian paper money; not just its design, but its cyclic redesigns.

What does the look of currency say about a country? What if the use of cash continues to decline? Will we have visions of Canada on our bank cards?

1   *"The nature of our government, our bilingual heritage and the diversity of Canada's geography and wildlife are emphasized by the portraits, legends, landscapes, birds and national symbols which appear on every bank note."*

2   This quotation from the display text in the "Paper Puzzles" exhibition at the Currency Museum in Ottawa states that aspects of our "nature" as Canadians are emphasized through the appearance of our bank notes and suggests that every note provides a cryptic combination of elements which signify "Canada." The text goes on to say, "Bank notes are worth getting to know better—not only because of their value but because of the fascinating secrets they have to tell." The key for unlocking these secrets, however, is not provided by official texts.

3   Just as our nature as Canadians apparently "appears" to us on our bank notes, the bank note imagery itself seems to "appear" through a conjuring act which is unfettered by accompanying explanations. The routes taken which lead to the specific images selected are not marked. The official literature does not discuss the process through which it is decided how Canada is portrayed, but states simply that Canada is portrayed. Clues to the nature of this portrayal, to the identity of this Canada, spring from the hope that a picture is indeed worth a thousand words and that an analysis of the Bank of Canada's bank note imagery from its first issue to the present will provide these clues.

4   The history of the Bank of Canada's control over note design begins in 1935 when it struggled for the sole right to issue notes. Provincial governments and chartered banks had previously issued their own. The issue then, as now, was security and control and the newly founded Bank claimed to be better able to control counterfeiting. It set out to improve printing technology so that increasingly intricate designs could be issued to ensure its claim. The Bank of Canada pursues this endeavour to this day. Unlike the tradition of American paper currency which has not deviated from its "green-back," Canadian bank notes have undergone numerous design and imagery changes.

5   Through a self-propelled flurry of continuing improvement, set in motion by the initial rush to prove itself to angry provincial governments and banks, the Bank of Canada now claims to have arrived at the forefront of currency design. A line is devoted in each press release to the fact that counterfeiting is not a problem in Canada, nor has it been for years. Regardless, the Bank of Canada maintains a program of deterring counterfeiting.

6   The pursuit of the technologically more advanced note is the rationale behind the almost constant changes and plans to change our bank note design. An example of this can be seen in the creation of the new optical security device (OSD).

According to a Bank of Canada press release of 1989, "Canadians can be justly proud of this technological breakthrough, which puts Canadian notes a good step ahead of advanced copying and printing techniques. Canada does not have a counterfeiting problem and the OSD will help to make sure it stays that way."

What "fascinating secret" might this aspect of bank note design tell us? The preoccupation it suggests with security, control and the law, is met with the relentless pursuit of a technology that will ensure the maintenance of that preoccupation, in spite of the fact that there are no real threats or enemies to protect against. Compare this with the situation in the United States which have, according to the Currency Museum's employee, the most counterfeited currency in the world, and yet employ design technology equivalent to what ours was in 1935. Perhaps the American government is just less inclined to interrupt the cash flow of its spirited entrepreneurs, but more certainly it shows that country's own preoccupation with its history and the tradition of its "greenback."   7

Beginning with its first issue in 1935, which was issued in separate French and English versions, the images presented on both versions were as follows: 8

$1.00 bill: "Agriculture allegory: Seated female with agricultural products."

$2.00 bill: "Harvest allegory: Seated female with fruits of harvest."

$5.00 bill: "Electric Power allegory: Seated male with symbols of electricity."

$10.00 bill: "Transportation allegory: Mercury with ships, trains and planes."

$20.00 bill: "Toiler allegory: Kneeling male exhibiting the produce of the field to the Spirit of Agriculture."

$50.00 bill: "Modem Inventions allegory: Seated female with symbols of radio broadcasting."

$100.00 bill: "Commerce and Industry allegory: Seated male showing ship to child, harbour scene and blast furnace in background."

The same images were used on the following 1937 bilingual issue. When I first saw these images I was taken aback by how foreign they appear, slightly European but predominantly American. The promise, the optimism and the reassurance offered by the supernatural beings portrayed are not aspects of the nature of Canada as I understand it. Portrayed in these bank notes is what Gaile McGregor, in *The Wacousta Syndrome, Explorations in Canadian Landscape*, describes as the American colonist's experience of the New World environment: "Under the influence of the millennial expectations of the 17th century, the early American colonist, borrowing concepts from scriptural explication, tended to interpret the empirical environment predominantly in terms of signs or types of supernatural events." Through this association, "the entire world became charged with cosmic significance and every human life was seen as part of a cosmic conflict between the forces of Good and Evil."   9

The landscapes in these images have been won over by Good. The landscape is set in the distance and poses no threat, only the promise of space fully inhabitable and hospitable. It is almost completely obscured by the archetypal and supernatural figures which foreground and fill the frame. As allegories for the human domination and domestication of the New World, these images clearly present the wilderness as tamed.   10

In 1954, when the Bank of Canada, issued its next series, it did so with the stated aim of creating "a Canadian dimension" through a complete change of   11 these note images. Concerning the selection of the new images, the Bank of Canada stated only that a prominent Canadian dimension was created by replacing the earlier allegorical figures with Canadian landscapes." They are described simply as a series of "realistic landscapes and seascapes."

Clearly the Bank of Canada felt that the previous imagery was not Canadian **12** enough. The difference between the 1935 images and the 1954 images is startling. The 1954 images are as follows:

$1.00 bill: "Prairie View Saskatchewan."
$2.00 bill: "View of Upper Melbourne, Richmond, Quebec."
$5.00 bill: "Otter Falls at Mile 996 of the Alaska Highway."
$10.00 bill: "Mount Burgess, Alberta."
$20.00 bill: "Laurentian Winter."
$50.00 bill: "Atlantic Seashore."
$100.00 bill: "Okanagan Lake, British Columbia."
$1000.00 bill: "Anse St. Jean, Saguenay River, Quebec."

It is assumed, or hoped, that the Canadian dimension that these images create **13** is self-apparent. How does this created dimension imagine itself and how do these images locate it? The allegory of garden paradise in the previous images is gone, replaced by realism. This realism is attained by beginning the image production process with a photograph of the landscape. The photograph is then used as the source for a painted image, a procedure also employed by many Canadian landscape painters from Tom Thomson to Jack Chambers. The painted step in the procedure, which brings in a "human" touch, is almost apologized for in the Currency Museum's display text: "Because of some of the technical and esthetic considerations of Bank note design, the illustrations may vary slightly from the actual locations depicted." The engraving made from the painting renders it mechanically reproducible but so intricately detailed that it is as difficult to copy as possible. The resulting landscape has a technological esthetic, a realism devoid of subjective interpretation or of the mythicized encounter with the landscape in the 1935 series. This process of demythicizing the landscape is also commented on by McGregor: "Too extensively demythicized the environment tends simply to become a kind of void that resists all human connection. This is what happens in Canada."

What evidence of this void can be found in the Canadian dimension series? **14** Whereas all the previous issue images celebrated the inhabitable and benevolent landscape, only half of the 1934 series show any sign of a human presence at all and it is revealing to look at how this human presence is portrayed.

For example, the $1 bill presents the landscape as a vast expanse under a stormy **15** sky. Cutting through it are telephone poles, a dirt road and a barbed wire fence that recedes in one-point perspective to a distant grain elevator poised on the horizon. A large thunderhead hangs just above the tiny structure. It is a far and rather lonely cry from the Agriculture allegory seated on her throne surrounded by heaps of produce. The thin threads of transportation (road) and communication (poles) provide little reassurance against the distant storm and vast space.

The $2 bill shows three or four small farm houses and a church clustered in **16** the center of the mid-ground. The distant houses are alone and unreachable. The $1000 image is like the $2 one, showing a few structures in the mid-ground, but here the foreground is greatly reduced and mountains loom on the horizon which almost obscures the sky. The vast landscape again engulfs a few buildings. This image is also in stark contrast to its previous image of the Security allegory.

The remaining images of the 1954 series depict landscapes devoid of human presence, and of these only the $100 one has a foreground which it seems possible to enter. The other images do not suggest possible passage through them, their foregrounds blocked by rapids, trees or snow. The images on the $5, $10 and $20 bills specifically appear utterly wild and alien. McGregor suggests that, "The real relevance of the wilderness mythos to Canada can be seen only if we pay attention to what its proponents show us unconsciously, rather than giving too much weight to what they say they are doing." 17

What do the 1954 images show us, given that they are to create a dimension that is Canadian? With regard to the portrayal of Canadians within the Canadian landscape, they unquestionably show a great deal of It and a little of Us. We huddle together while the landscape surrounds us and look out at a wilderness that prohibits our entry. Northrop Frye has termed this response to the Canadian landscape the "garrison mentality" and McGregor has termed it the "Wacousta syndrome." 18

Between 1969 and 1975 a new set of images replaces the 1954 issue. They are as follows: 19

$1.00 bill: "Parliament Hill across Ottawa River."
$2.00 bill: "Inuit hunting scene on Baffin Island."
$5.00 bill: "Salmon seine, Johnson Strait, Vancouver Island."
$10.00 bill: "Polymer Corporation, Sarnia, Ontario."
$20.00 bill: "Morraine Lake, Alberta."
$50.00 bill: "Dome Formation, Royal Canadian Mounted Police, Musical Ride."
$100.00 bill: "Waterfront scene at Lunenburg."

These images again provide an interesting set of comparisons. In this series the landscape becomes inhabitable again, but without the assistance of supernatural beings. Technology, government and the law are now features and, with the exception of the image on the $20 bill (found within the confines of a National Park), all these new images show clear signs of human presence. In the new $10 bill this presence overwhelms the landscape: it presents a techno-scape where not a trace of Nature remains. This complete reversal is all the more remarkable because of the extremes it represents. 20

Into this new configuration of It and Us, a third term is introduced by the first appearance of Them in Bank of Canada notes. "They" are the Inuit pictures on the $2 bill, appearing in the harshest of the series landscapes. With minimal (low-tech) means, they interact with the icy environment in a nostalgic hunting scene. Nostalgia plays a part as well in the ship-building industry pictures on the $100 bill with its sailing ships of a bygone era. 21

The government is presented on the $1 bill back and center, crowning Parliament Hill and overlooking the river. The threatening storm and the vast distances portrayed on the previous $1 bill are replaced by an image of a log-choked river (prosperity through natural resources), overseen by government's central body. It is worth mentioning here that the industrial scene on the $10 bill of this series depicts Polymer Corp., which was at the time of issue a crown-owned company. 22

While, the government is portrayed on the $1 bill centrally placed and look- **23** ing outward from its vantage on the hilltop, the law is portrayed as a ring look- ing inward. The R.C.M.P. Dome Formation on the $50 bill gives the unfortunate impression of a law force poised to attack itself, its weapons pointed in. The threat of the sea presented in the previous $50 bill is replaced by an image which shows the national police ceremonially closed in on itself in a circle with nothing at the center save the threat of its own spear.

The idea of generalized landscapes reemerges with the current series issue. The **24** current series began in 1986 and the Bank of Canada's decision to make the change is described as follows: "There were three principal reasons for its introduction: technological advances in printing and photocopying of coloured graphic material that made the earlier series more vulnerable to counterfeiting; the need to facili- tate the operation of high-speed, note-sorting machines by means of a bar code; and the development of features to assist the visually impaired." These new notes, which come to be through "advanced Canadian technology" and make "le Canada à l'avant-garde de la conception des billets de banque" picture the Canadian land- scape utterly devoid of any human presence. The word "CANADA" now fills the sky of a landscape solely inhabited by birds.

Buried under assurances that these new notes are even more secure and are **25** more helpful than before, the question that lurks is "Where did We go?" Optical security devices, electronic readers and high-speed note-sorting machines do not provide an answer. Perhaps the question is not a relevant one, the "predominantly Canadian dimension" being technology itself and not the imagistic concern of locating Us, Here.

The 1986 issue images are as follows: **26**

$2.00 bill: "Robin."
$5.00 bill: "Belted Kingfisher."
$10.00 bill: "Osprey."
$20.00 bill: "Common Loon."
$50.00 bill: "Snowy Owl."
$100.00 bill: "Canada Goose."

The bird images are constructed so that they best accommodate the advanced **27** security printing technology. The design criteria state, however, that specific birds were selected because they have wide nesting ranges and would therefore be most familiar to Canadians. There is a concern, then, for recognizability.

While the birds are specifically named, the landscapes are general; the wetlands, **28** the grasslands, the northern wilderness. The specific locations of "here" in most of the previous images (Otter Falls at mile 996 on the Alaska Highway, Upper Melbourne, Richmond, etc.) is now replaced by a general image of "there." The placement of birds, large in the immediate foreground, right of center and fac- ing left, is done for reasons concerning printing and verifiability. The landscapes are minimal, primarily to contrast the detail in the birds, and for reasons of cost. Because of this, the birds seem separate from the landscape—momentarily halted, ready to fly off again.

The Canadian landscape here is seen as utterly uninhabitable and unenterable, **29** the possibility of moving through it blocked by the apparition of its own name in huge block letters. The unconscious treatment of this landscape may be more familiar and more recognizable to Canadians than are the birds that fly in front of it. Looking out across a sparse and unlocatable land we see only the ghostly name of ourselves, a mirage which names our country but prohibits passage over its horizon.

• • • • READING COMPREHENSION QUESTIONS

1. The word *unfettered* in "the bank note imagery itself seems to "appear" through a conjuring act which is unfettered by accompanying explanations" (paragraph 3) means
   a. marred.
   b. disturbed.
   c. restricted.
   d. unhampered.

2. The word *empirical* in "tended to interpret the empirical environment predominantly in terms of signs or types of supernatural events" (paragraph 10) means
   a. observed.
   b. hostile.
   c. spiritual.
   d. surrounding.

3. Which of the following would be a good alternative title for this selection?
   a. Banking on Canada
   b. How the Bank Sees Us
   c. Our Changing Monetary Landscape
   d. Canadian Dollars, Canadian Dreams

4. Which sentence best expresses the main idea of the selection?
   a. Canadian bank notes reveal just how empty and intimidating our country is.
   b. Images on Canada's changing currency reveal varying perceptions of our country.
   c. Canadian bank note designs have generally been changed to more effectively prevent counterfeiting.
   d. The history of Canadian currency design is the history of the Canadian people.

5. Frequent redesigning of Canadian bank notes is due to
   a. the impetus to create bills that cannot be counterfeited.
   b. changing ideas about the appearance of the country.
   c. the desire to stay one step ahead of provincial governments and chartered banks.
   d. advancements in printing technology.

6. The 1954-issue bank notes
   a. offer an image of the American north.
   b. show images from each of the prairie provinces.

    c. show many images of wintry landscapes.

    d. present no images of Ontario.

7. *True or false?* With the 1986 issue, the birds and background landscapes are balanced in detail.

8. The author implies that

    a. security is a major concern with bank note production.

    b. the Bank of Canada's obsession with counterfeiting is confusing.

    c. the Bank of Canada is obsessed with technology.

    d. provinces did a better job of issuing bank notes.

9. The author implies that

    a. Canadians just accept the distorted images of themselves and their country that appears on their money.

    b. Canadians find their country too empty and intimidating to want it to be accurately portrayed on bank notes.

    c. Canadians are not that concerned with how they appear, relative to their country, on their money.

    d. the money-redesigning cycles of the Bank of Canada are a sham.

10. *True or false?* We can infer that Millard believes that, for citizens of a vast, open country, Canadians relate less to nature than to constructed images.

● ● ● ● DISCUSSION QUESTIONS

About Content

1. What led to the Bank of Canada taking over bank note design in 1935?

2. What does the word *allegory* mean as it is used in the descriptions of the 1935–1937 issue of bank notes? Explain your definition of the word as it applies to two of the bill designs.

3. Describe in detail each stage in the portrayal of Canada's landscape on our bank notes.

4. What does the author find strange about the 1969–1975 $50 bill?

About Structure

5. Where do you find the clearest statement of the author's thesis?

6. What title would you give to each of Millard's categories of bank notes? Why would you choose each title?

7. For "Images of Canada: Canadian Bank Notes," the overall main rhetorical mode is classification and division. However, as with most writers, Millard uses other secondary methods of development within the selection. In which paragraphs do you find other methods and what are they?

About Style and Tone

8. This selection presents quotations from several sources. What are those sources, and why has Millard chosen to include each?

9. In which paragraphs does the author change pronoun point of view, and why? Is these shifts necessary or effective?

10. What do you believe to be the tone of this selection? Support your view with specifics.

WRITING ASSIGNMENTS

Assignment 1

What images do you feel would best portray the Canada of today? Think of a set of (or category of) three images that would suit a $20, a $50, and a $100. In a cause or effect essay, justify your choice of images that would represent Canada of the early 21st century.

Assignment 2

What, for you and your peer group, is the relationship between you and "It"? The word "It" here is used as Millard has in her article, to represent the Canadian landscape. What aspects of the landscape are meaningful to you and why?

Write an essay that would serve as the text for a presentation to a Canadian ecology group in your area.

Assignment 3

Why *does* the Bank of Canada spend all that money every twenty years or so to redesign our bank notes? If the aim is to make counterfeiting more difficult, then why commission artists and expend so much time and energy on the design and aesthetics of our bills?

In an essay, argue for or against the cyclic redesign of Canadian money. Here, for reference purposes, is the Bank of Canada site: http://www.bank-banque-canada.ca/en/banknotes/general/character/index.html. You may wish to do some additional research online to buttress your arguments. Do not forget to paraphrase, quote, and cite correctly; refer to Chapter 19 for help.

Index